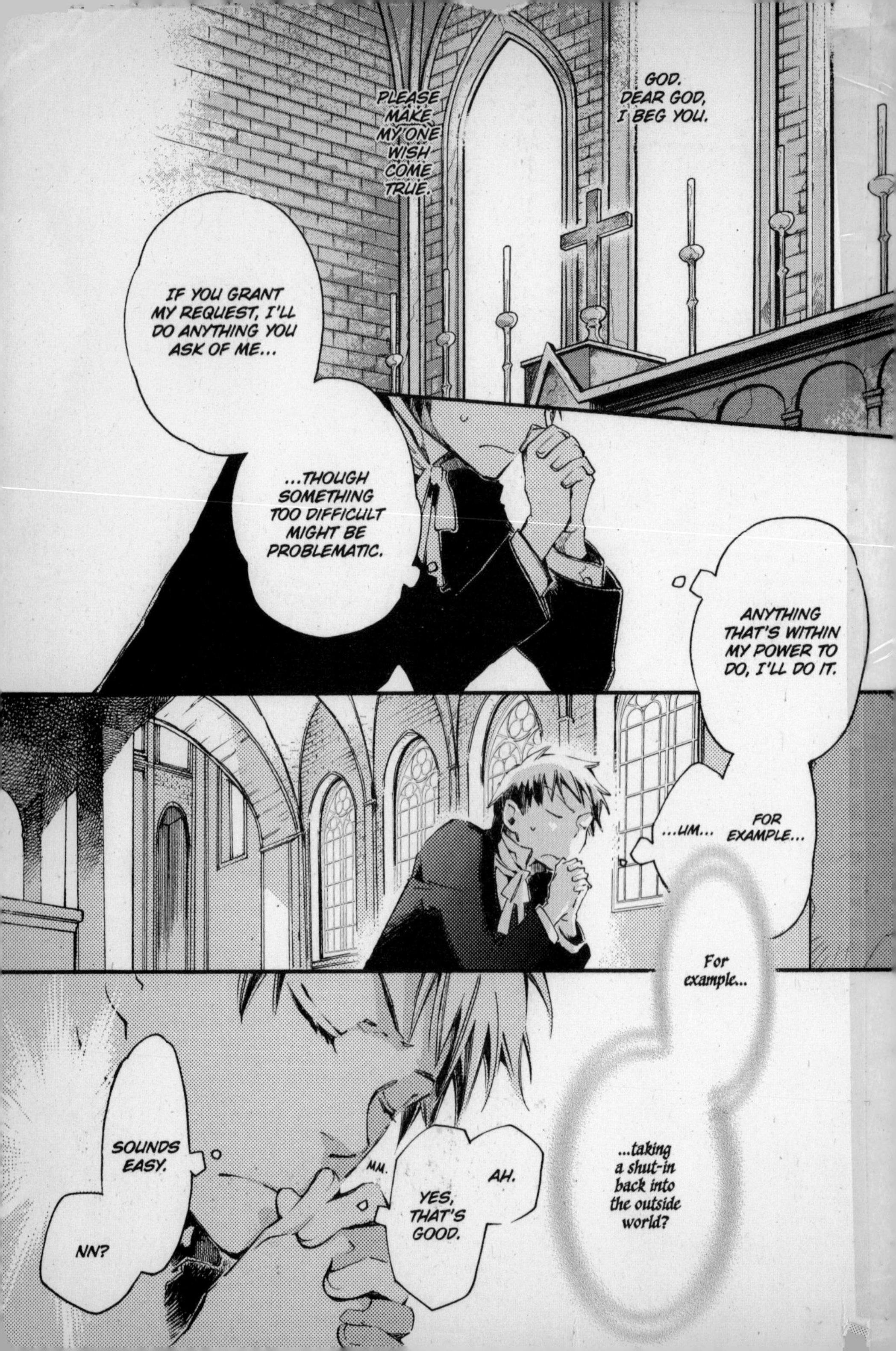
GOD. DEAR GOD, I BEG YOU.
PLEASE MAKE MY ONE WISH COME TRUE.
IF YOU GRANT MY REQUEST, I'LL DO ANYTHING YOU ASK OF ME...
...THOUGH SOMETHING TOO DIFFICULT MIGHT BE PROBLEMATIC.
ANYTHING THAT'S WITHIN MY POWER TO DO, I'LL DO IT.
FOR EXAMPLE...
...UM...
For example...
...taking a shut-in back into the outside world?
AH.
YES, THAT'S GOOD.
MM.
SOUNDS EASY.
NN?

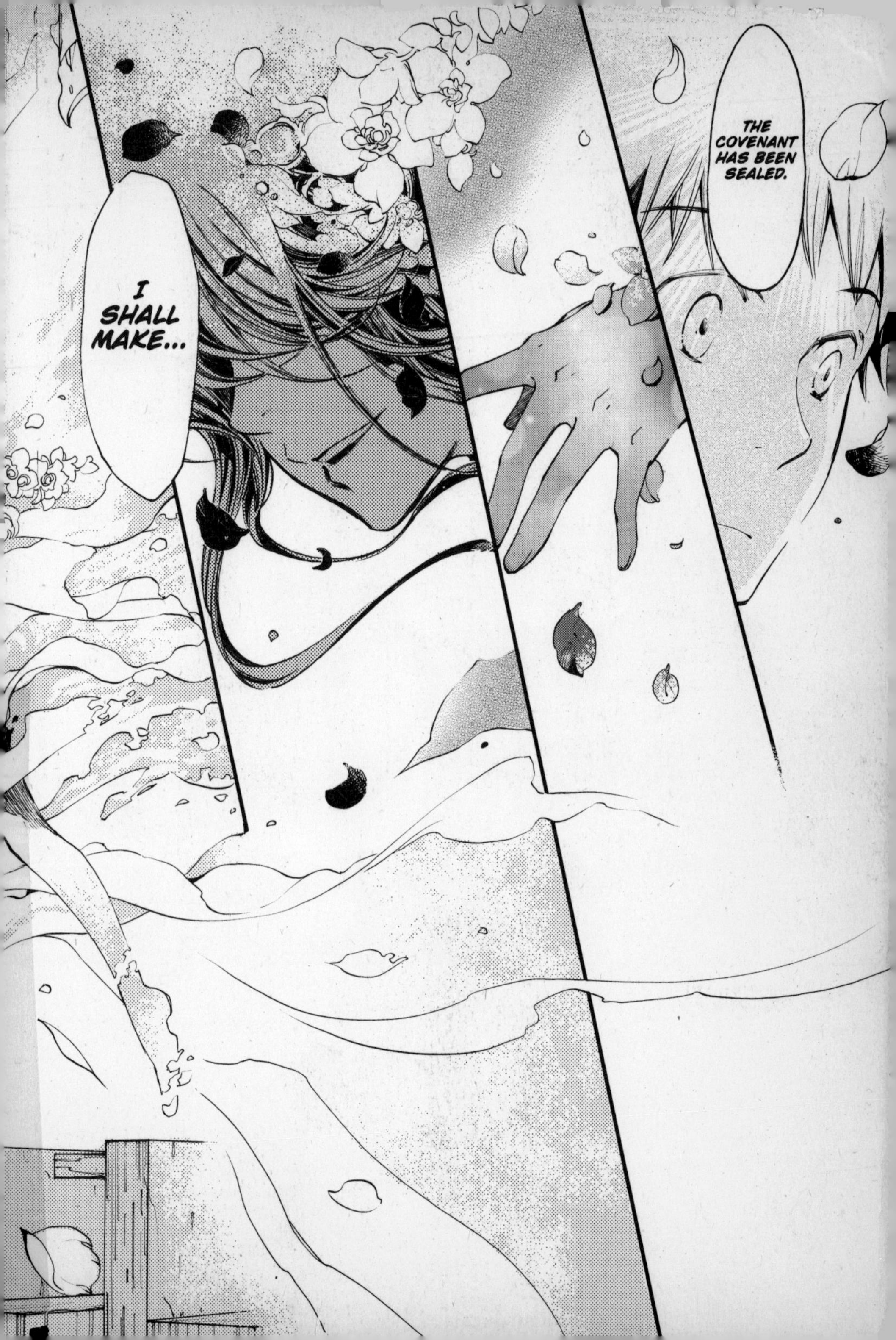
THE COVENANT HAS BEEN SEALED.
I SHALL MAKE...

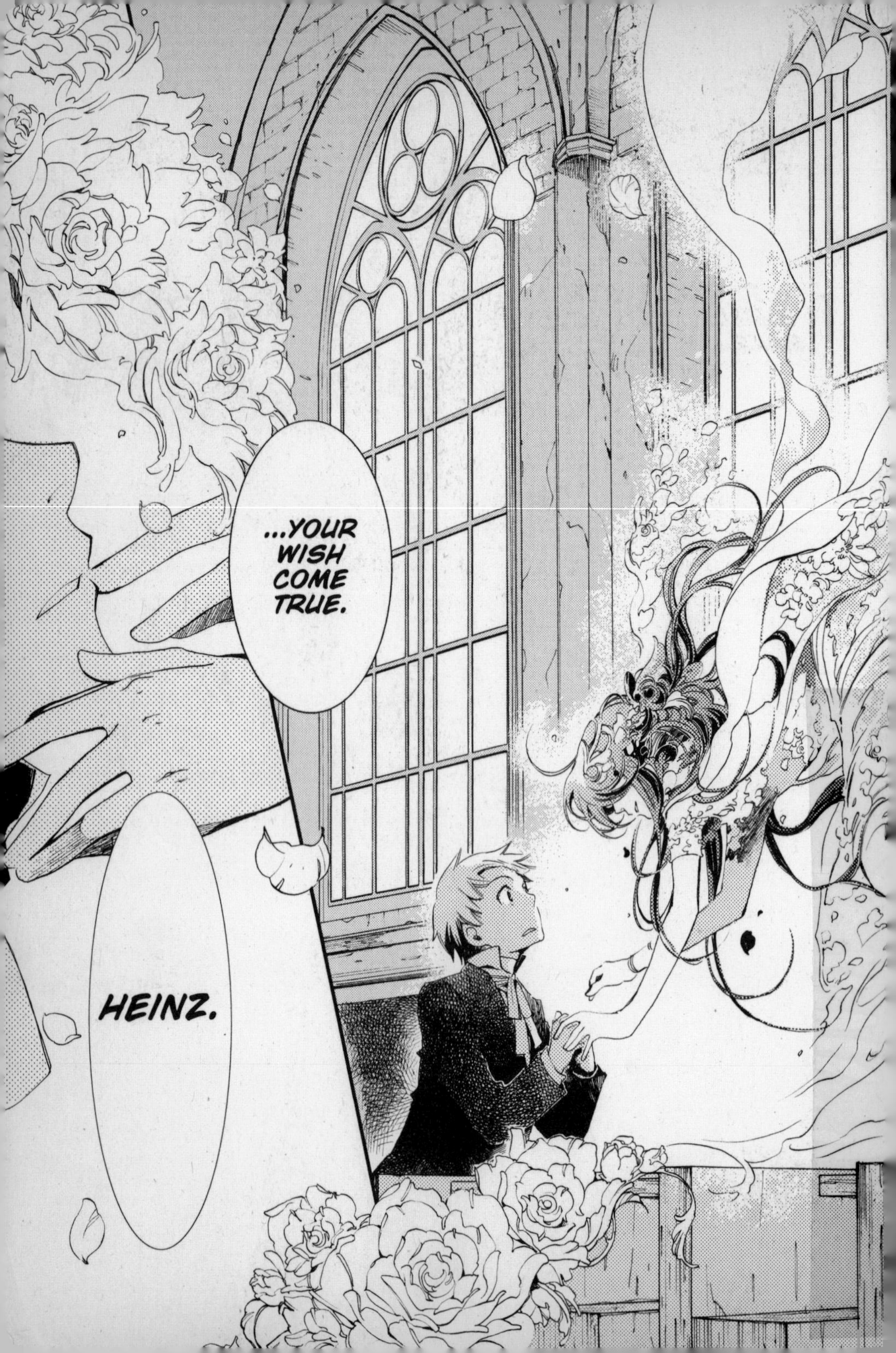
...YOUR WISH COME TRUE.
HEINZ.

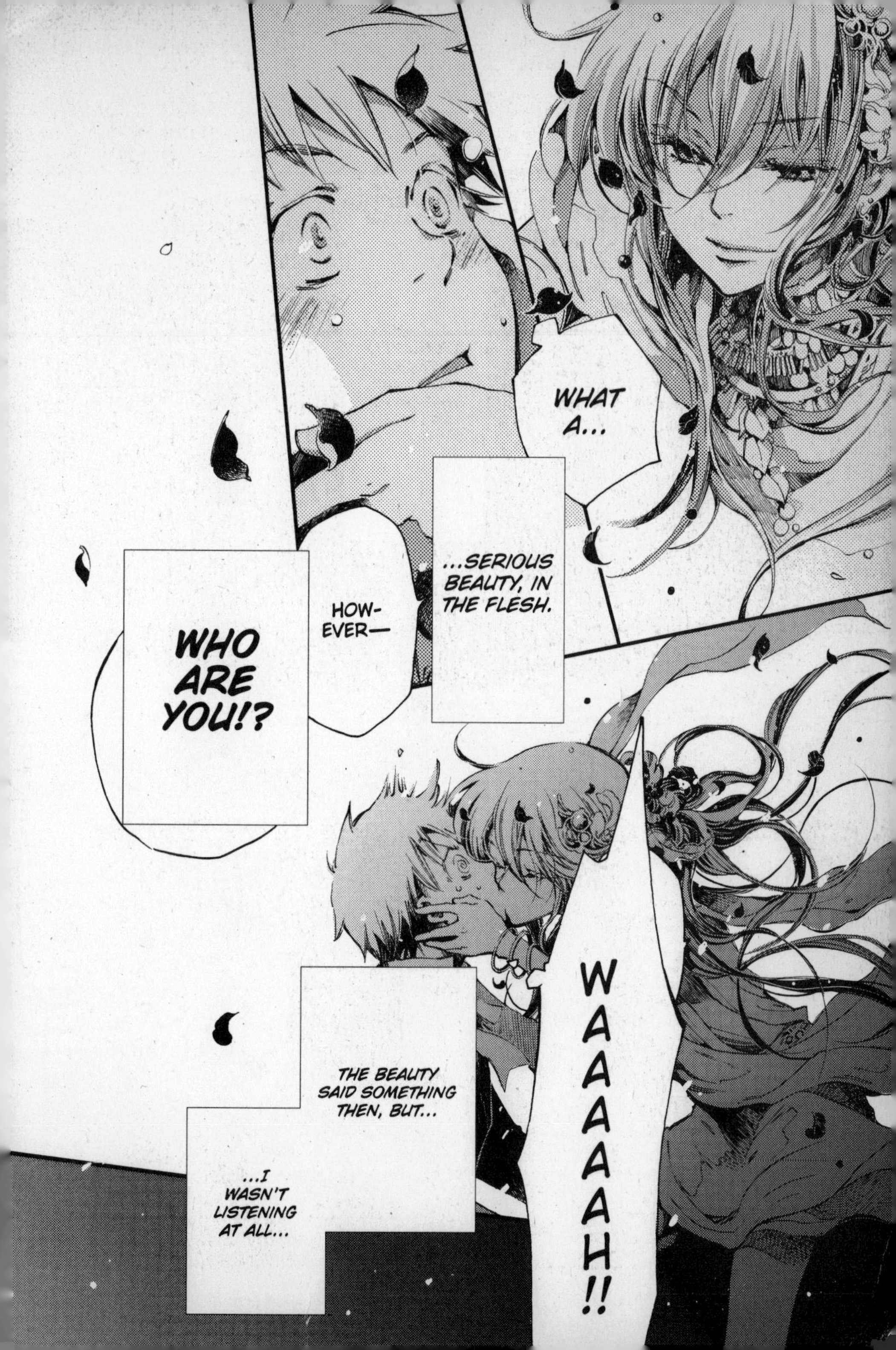
WHAT A...
...SERIOUS BEAUTY, IN THE FLESH.
HOW-EVER—
WHO ARE YOU!?
WAAAAAH!!
THE BEAUTY SAID SOMETHING THEN, BUT...
...I WASN'T LISTENING AT ALL...

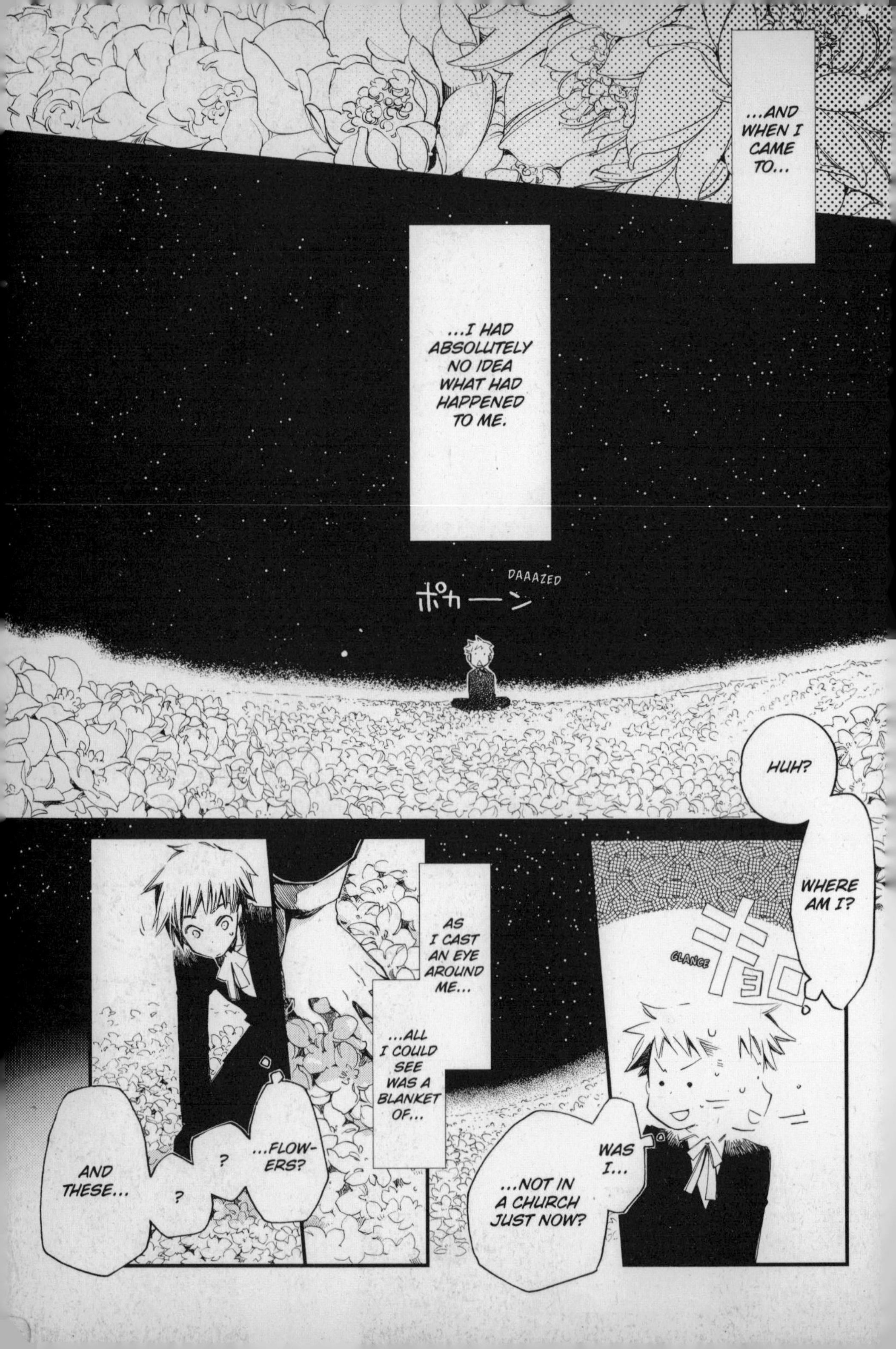
...AND WHEN I CAME TO...
...I HAD ABSOLUTELY NO IDEA WHAT HAD HAPPENED TO ME.
ポカーン
DAAAZED
HUH?
WHERE AM I?
キョロ
GLANCE
WAS I...
...NOT IN A CHURCH JUST NOW?
AS I CAST AN EYE AROUND ME...
...ALL I COULD SEE WAS A BLANKET OF...
...FLOWERS?
?
AND THESE...
?

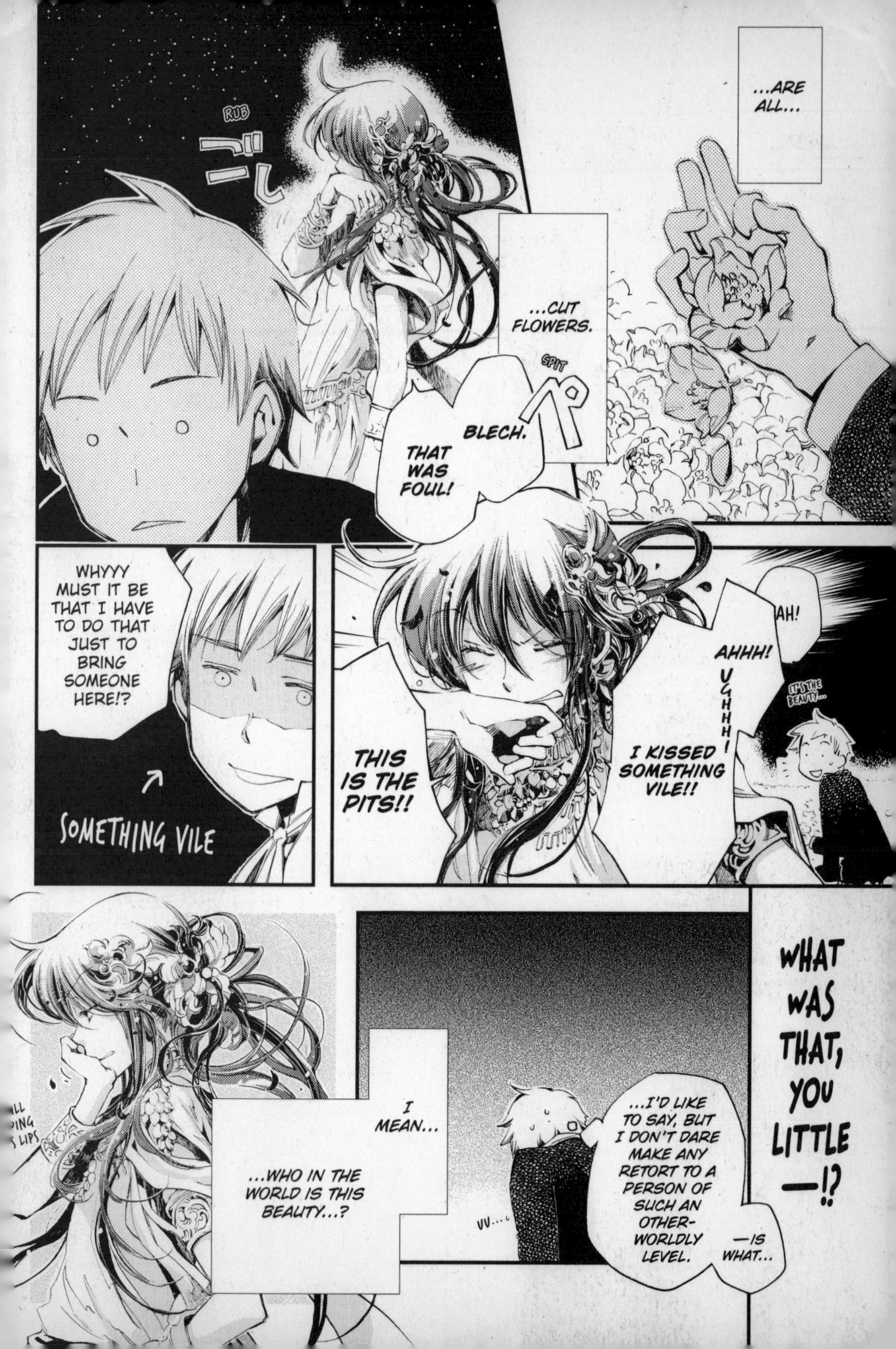
...ARE ALL...
...CUT FLOWERS.
SPIT
BLECH.
THAT WAS FOUL!
RUB
AH!
AHHH!
UGHHH!
I KISSED SOMETHING VILE!!
IT'S THE BEAUTY...
THIS IS THE PITS!!
WHYYY MUST IT BE THAT I HAVE TO DO THAT JUST TO BRING SOMEONE HERE!?
SOMETHING VILE
WHAT WAS THAT, YOU LITTLE—!?
—IS WHAT...
...I'D LIKE TO SAY, BUT I DON'T DARE MAKE ANY RETORT TO A PERSON OF SUCH AN OTHER-WORLDLY LEVEL.
VU...
I MEAN...
...WHO IN THE WORLD IS THIS BEAUTY...?

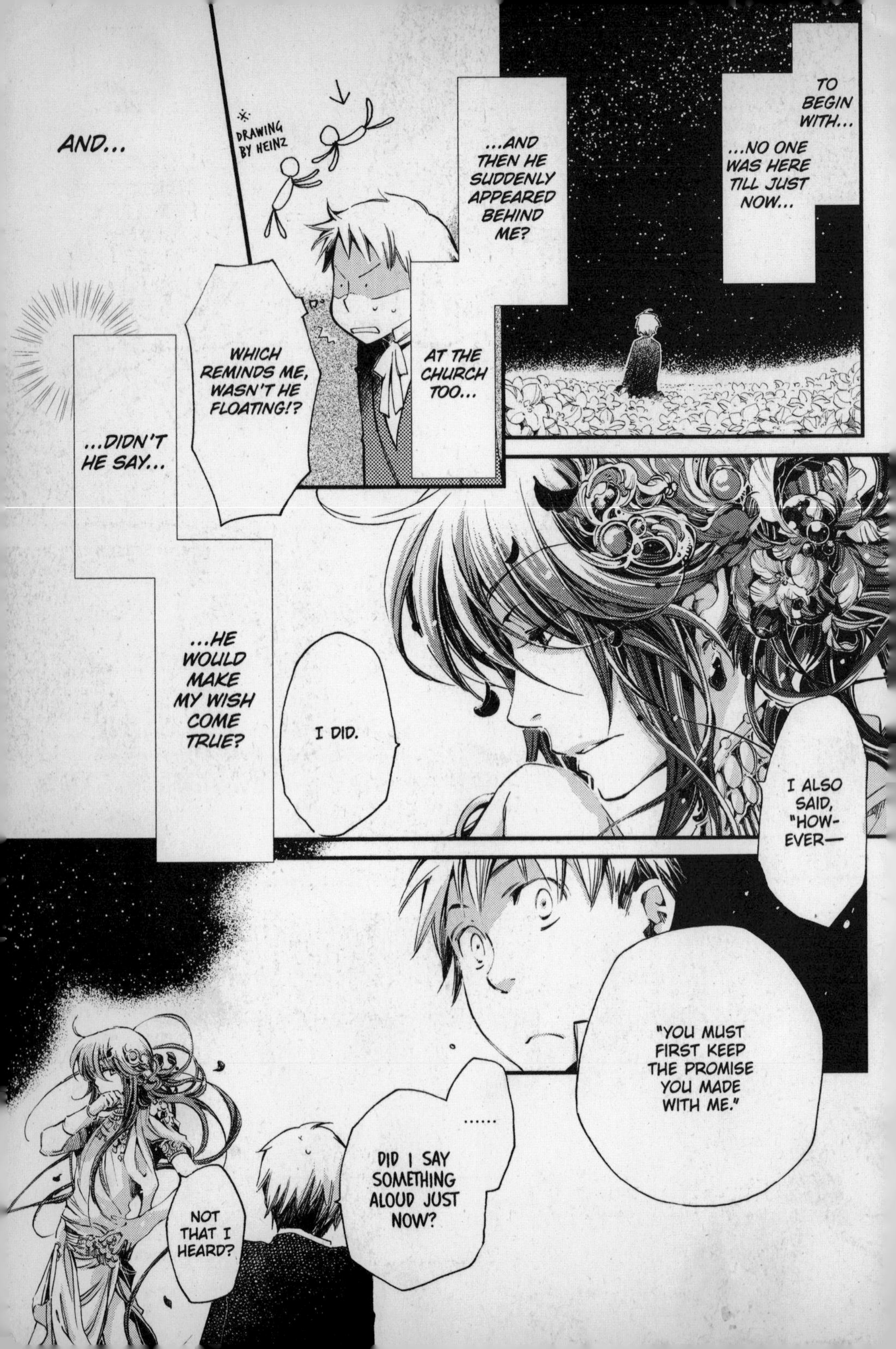
TO BEGIN WITH...
...NO ONE WAS HERE TILL JUST NOW...
...AND THEN HE SUDDENLY APPEARED BEHIND ME?
AT THE CHURCH TOO...
WHICH REMINDS ME, WASN'T HE FLOATING!?
※DRAWING BY HEINZ
AND...
...DIDN'T HE SAY...
...HE WOULD MAKE MY WISH COME TRUE?
I DID.
I ALSO SAID, "HOW-EVER—
"YOU MUST FIRST KEEP THE PROMISE YOU MADE WITH ME."
......
DID I SAY SOMETHING ALOUD JUST NOW?
NOT THAT I HEARD?

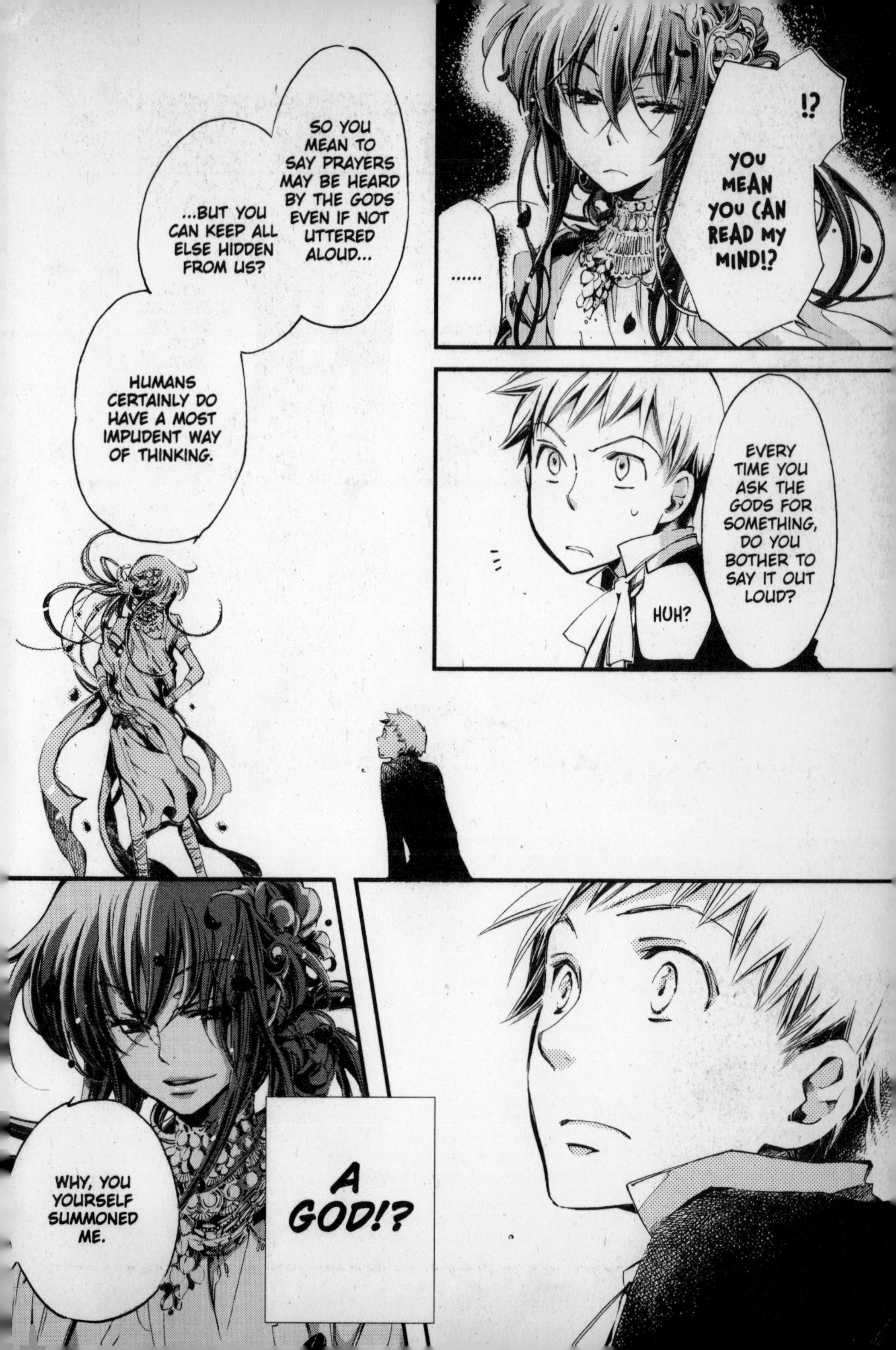
!?
YOU MEAN YOU CAN READ MY MIND!?
......
EVERY TIME YOU ASK THE GODS FOR SOMETHING, DO YOU BOTHER TO SAY IT OUT LOUD?
HUH?
SO YOU MEAN TO SAY PRAYERS MAY BE HEARD BY THE GODS EVEN IF NOT UTTERED ALOUD...
...BUT YOU CAN KEEP ALL ELSE HIDDEN FROM US?
HUMANS CERTAINLY DO HAVE A MOST IMPUDENT WAY OF THINKING.
WHY, YOU YOURSELF SUMMONED ME.
A GOD!?

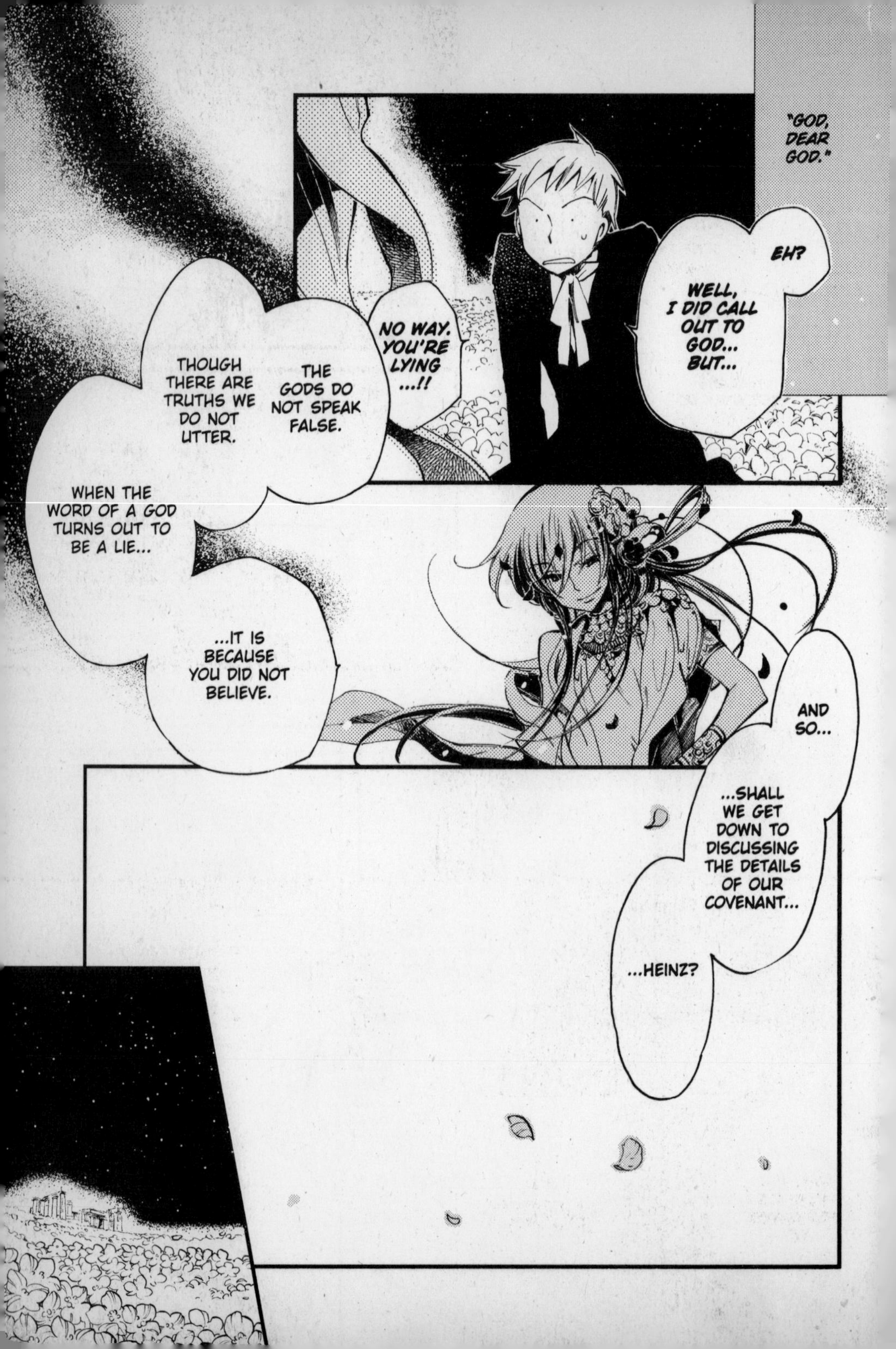
"GOD, DEAR GOD."
EH?
WELL, I DID CALL OUT TO GOD... BUT...
NO WAY. YOU'RE LYING...!!
THE GODS DO NOT SPEAK FALSE.
THOUGH THERE ARE TRUTHS WE DO NOT UTTER.
WHEN THE WORD OF A GOD TURNS OUT TO BE A LIE...
...IT IS BECAUSE YOU DID NOT BELIEVE.
AND SO...
...SHALL WE GET DOWN TO DISCUSSING THE DETAILS OF OUR COVENANT...
...HEINZ?

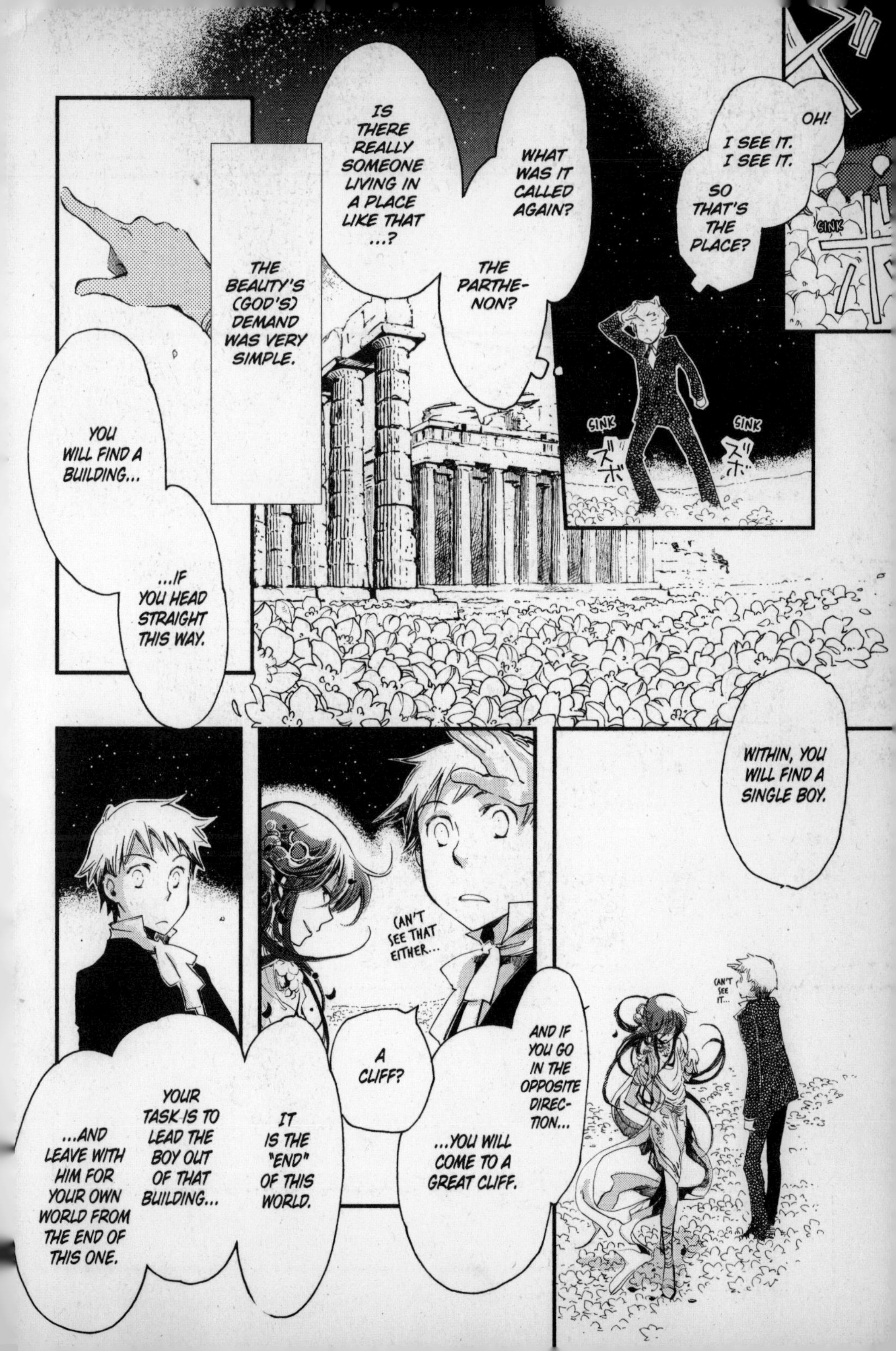
OH!
I SEE IT. I SEE IT.
SO THAT'S THE PLACE?
SINK
SINK
ズボ
SINK
ズボ
WHAT WAS IT CALLED AGAIN?
IS THERE REALLY SOMEONE LIVING IN A PLACE LIKE THAT...?
THE PARTHENON?
THE BEAUTY'S (GOD'S) DEMAND WAS VERY SIMPLE.
YOU WILL FIND A BUILDING...
...IF YOU HEAD STRAIGHT THIS WAY.
WITHIN, YOU WILL FIND A SINGLE BOY.
CAN'T SEE IT...
AND IF YOU GO IN THE OPPOSITE DIRECTION...
...YOU WILL COME TO A GREAT CLIFF.
CAN'T SEE THAT EITHER...
A CLIFF?
IT IS THE "END" OF THIS WORLD.
YOUR TASK IS TO LEAD THE BOY OUT OF THAT BUILDING...
...AND LEAVE WITH HIM FOR YOUR OWN WORLD FROM THE END OF THIS ONE.

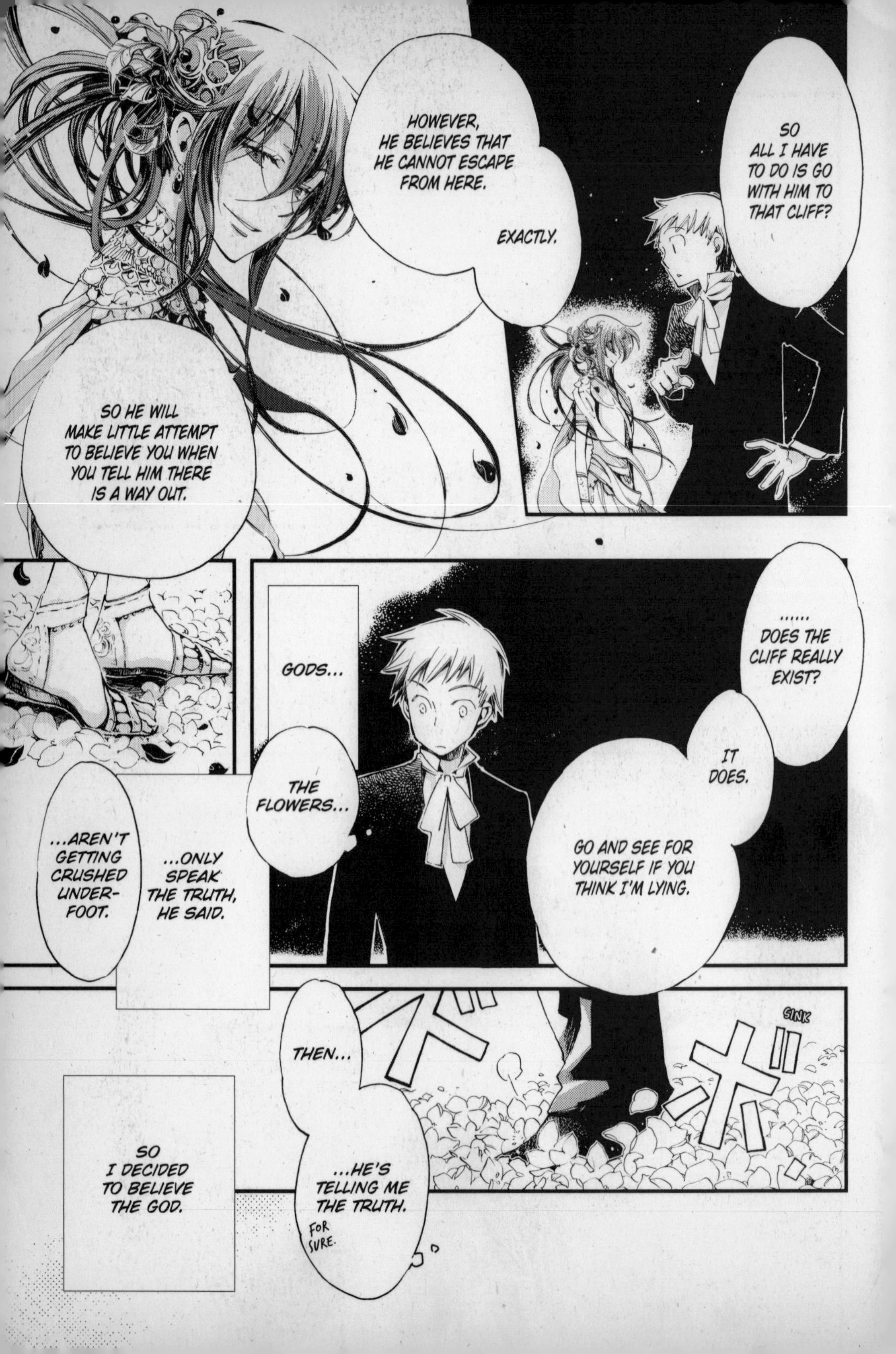
SO ALL I HAVE TO DO IS GO WITH HIM TO THAT CLIFF?
EXACTLY.
HOWEVER, HE BELIEVES THAT HE CANNOT ESCAPE FROM HERE.
SO HE WILL MAKE LITTLE ATTEMPT TO BELIEVE YOU WHEN YOU TELL HIM THERE IS A WAY OUT.
...... DOES THE CLIFF REALLY EXIST?
IT DOES.
GO AND SEE FOR YOURSELF IF YOU THINK I'M LYING.
GODS...
...ONLY SPEAK THE TRUTH, HE SAID.
THE FLOWERS...
...AREN'T GETTING CRUSHED UNDER-FOOT.
SINK
THEN...
...HE'S TELLING ME THE TRUTH.
FOR SURE.
SO I DECIDED TO BELIEVE THE GOD.

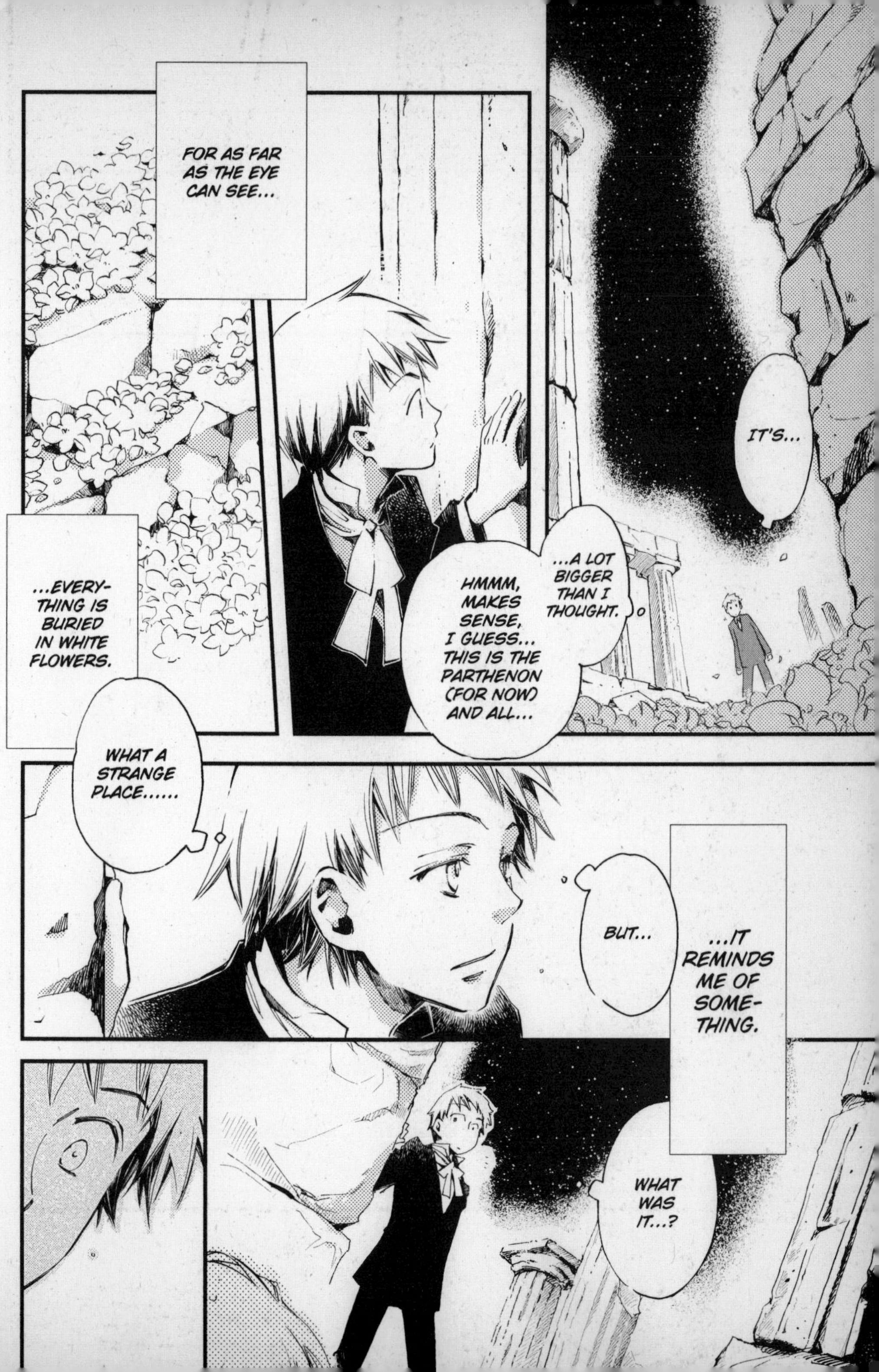
IT'S...
...A LOT BIGGER THAN I THOUGHT.
HMMM, MAKES SENSE, I GUESS... THIS IS THE PARTHENON (FOR NOW) AND ALL...
FOR AS FAR AS THE EYE CAN SEE...
...EVERY-THING IS BURIED IN WHITE FLOWERS.
WHAT A STRANGE PLACE......
BUT...
...IT REMINDS ME OF SOME-THING.
WHAT WAS IT...?

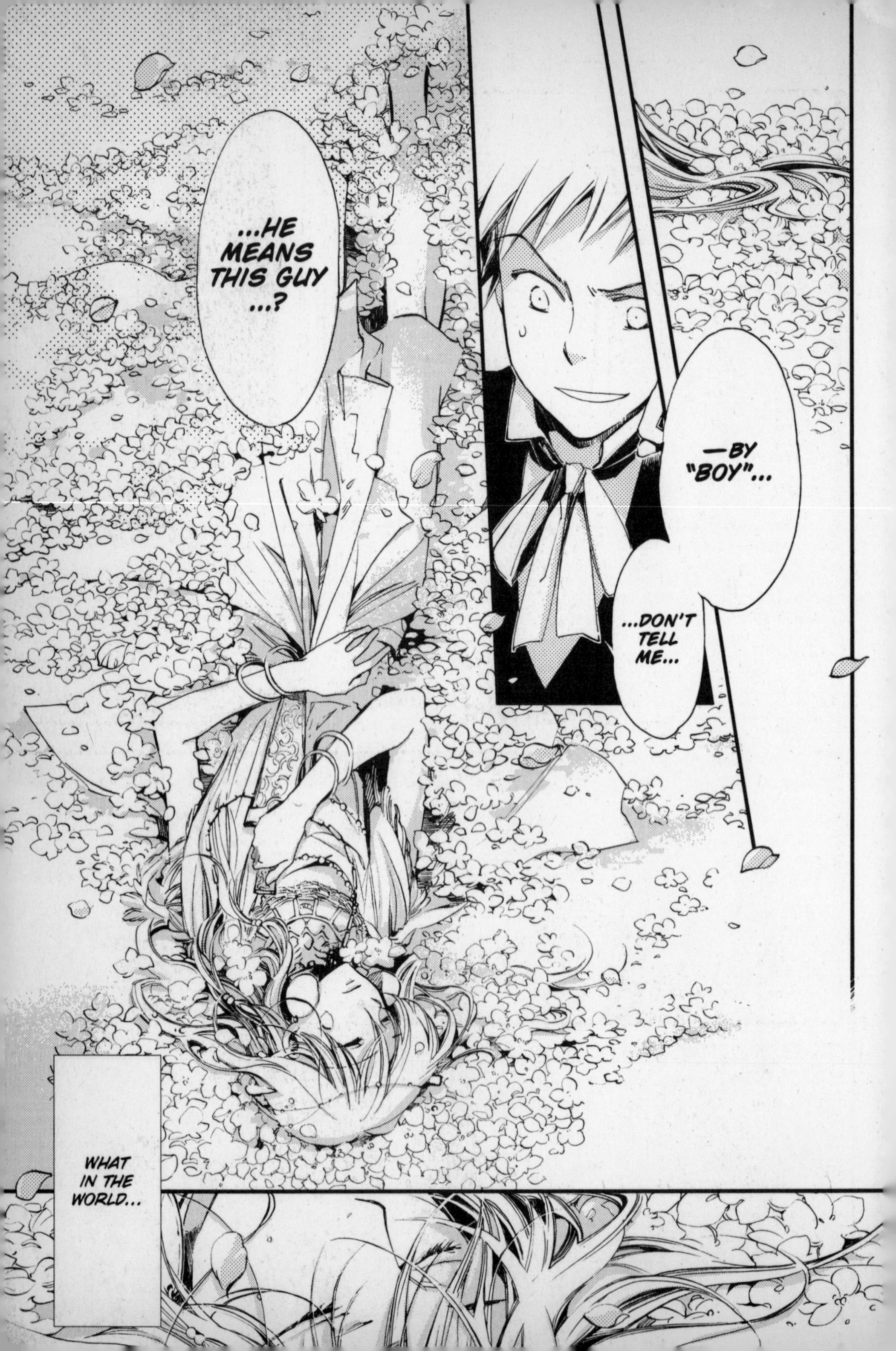
—BY "BOY"...
...DON'T TELL ME...
...HE MEANS THIS GUY ...?
WHAT IN THE WORLD...

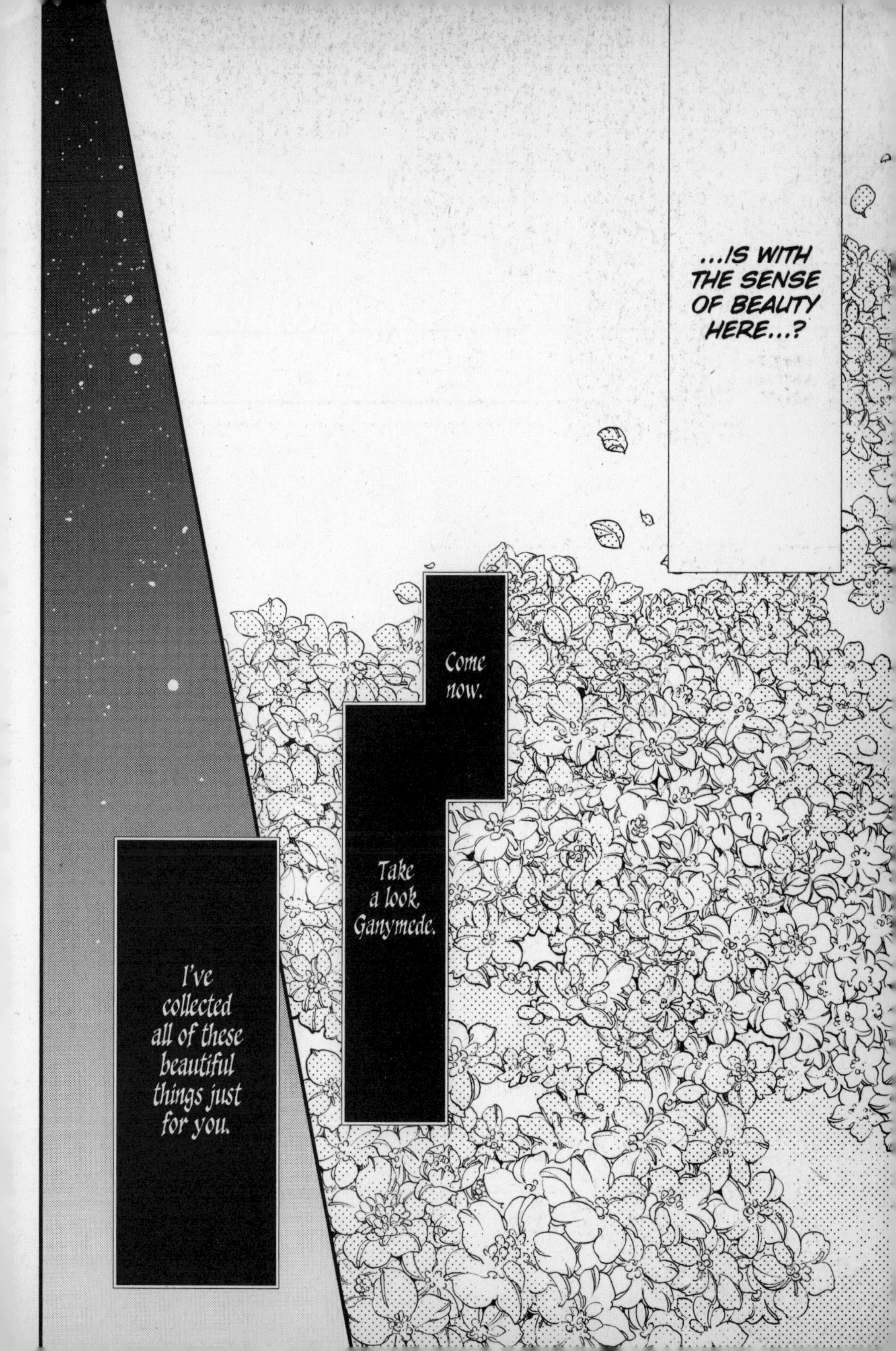
...IS WITH THE SENSE OF BEAUTY HERE...?
Come now.
Take a look Ganymede.
I've collected all of these beautiful things just for you.

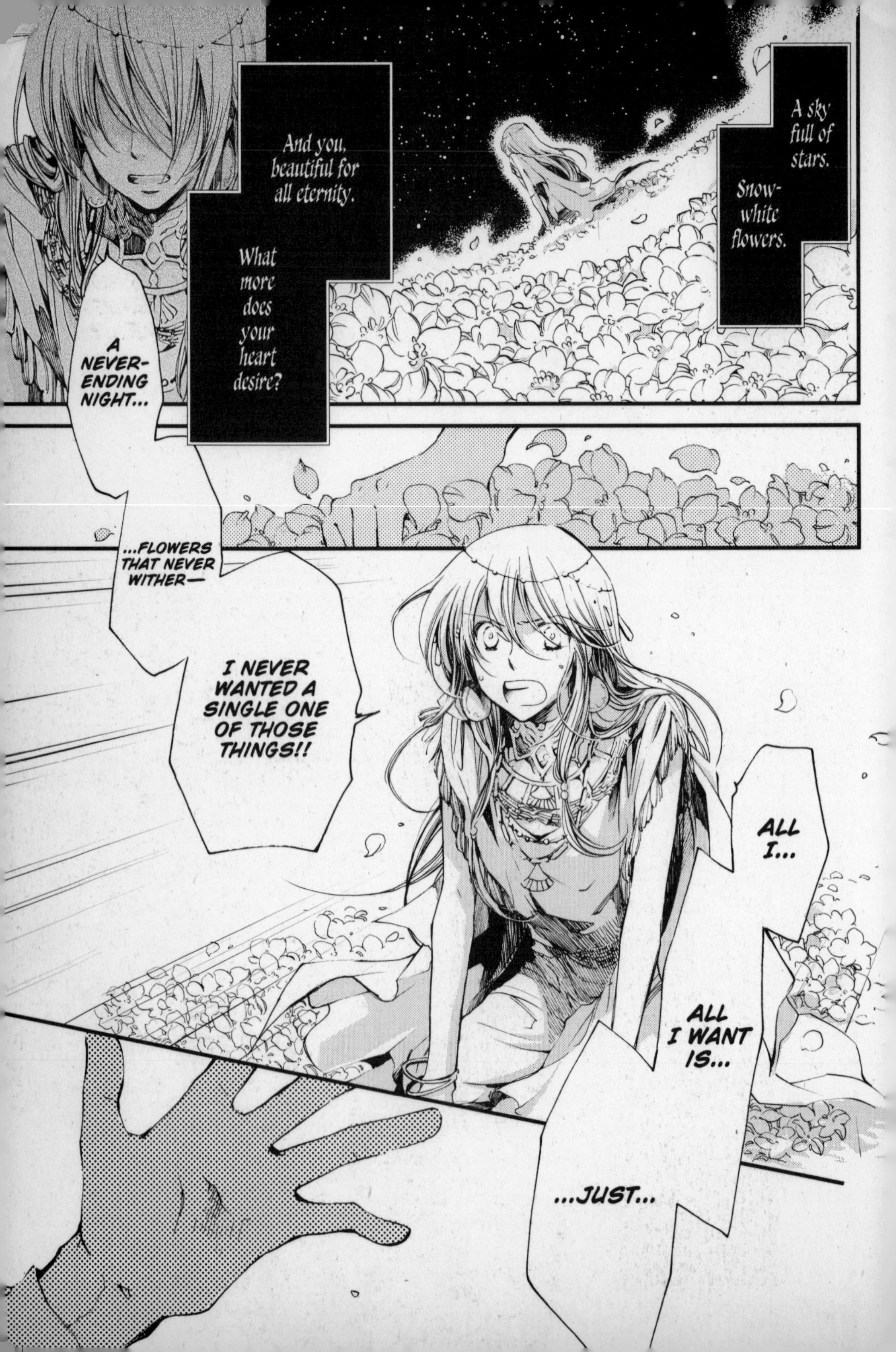
A sky full of stars.
Snow-white flowers.
And you, beautiful for all eternity.
What more does your heart desire?
A NEVER-ENDING NIGHT...
...FLOWERS THAT NEVER WITHER—
I NEVER WANTED A SINGLE ONE OF THOSE THINGS!!
ALL I...
ALL I WANT IS...
...JUST...

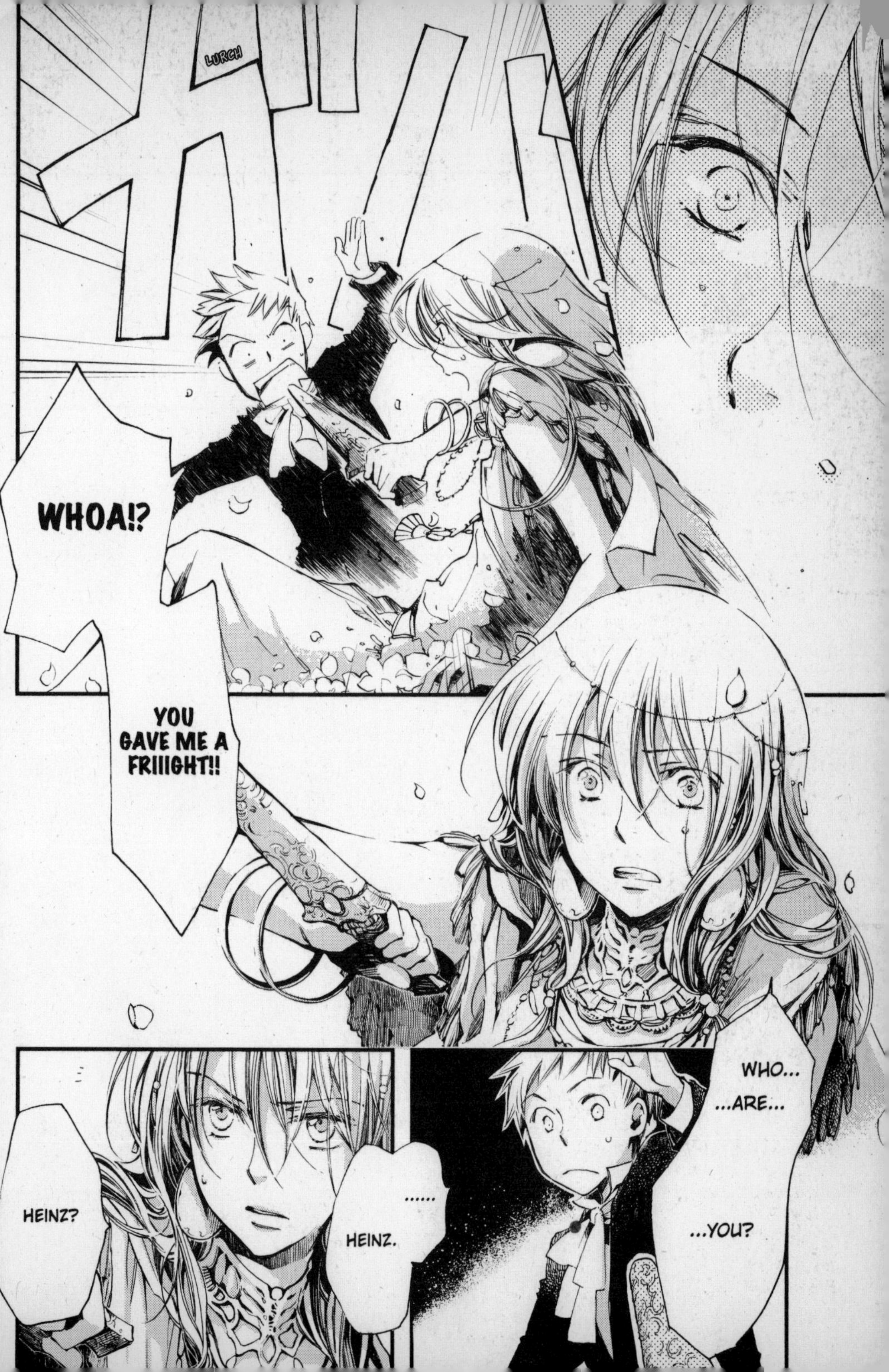
LURCH
WHOA!?
YOU GAVE ME A FRIIIGHT!!
WHO...
...ARE...
...YOU?
......
HEINZ.
HEINZ?

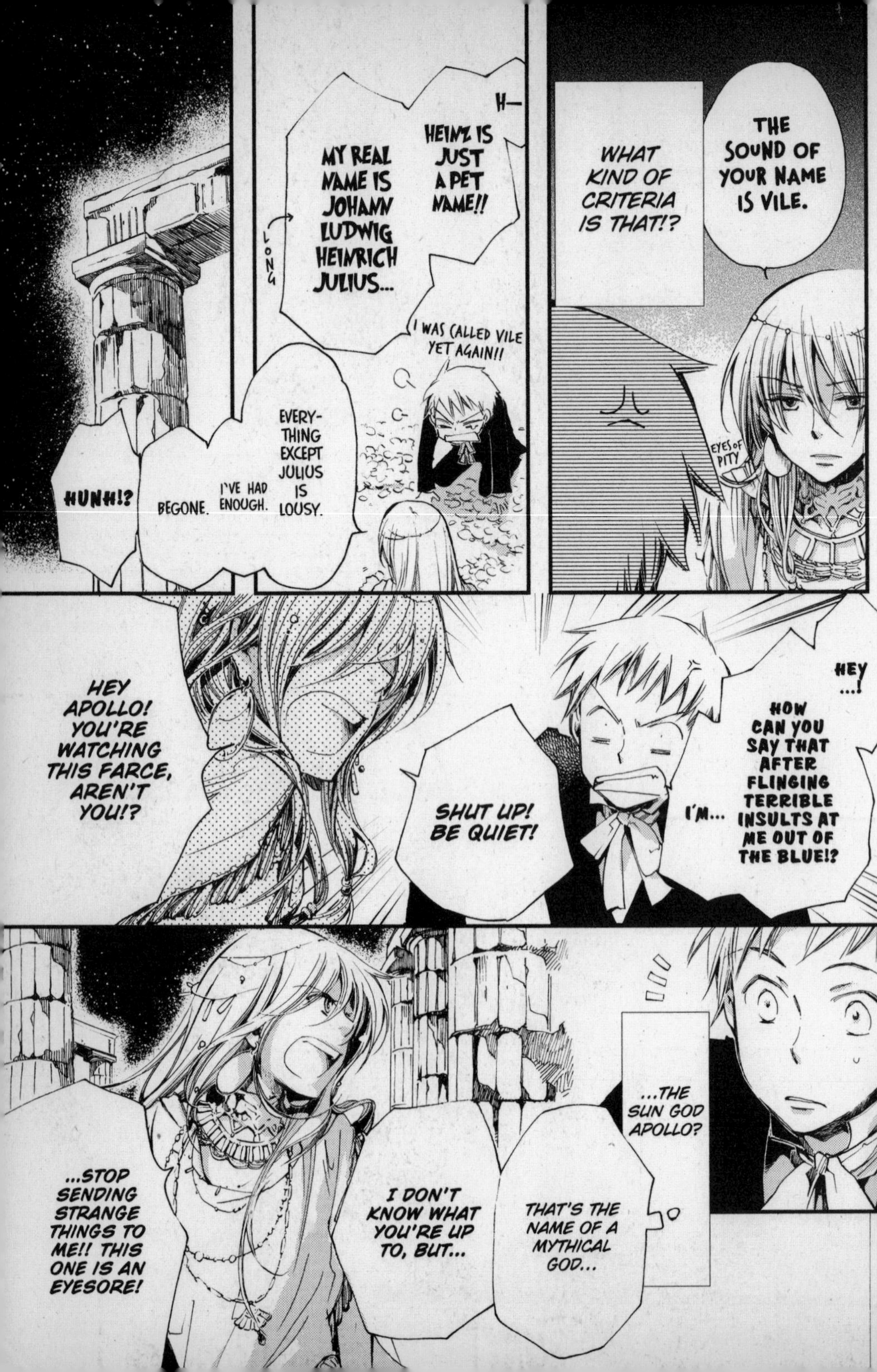
THE SOUND OF YOUR NAME IS VILE.
WHAT KIND OF CRITERIA IS THAT!?
EYES OF PITY
H—
HEINZ IS JUST A PET NAME!!
MY REAL NAME IS JOHANN LUDWIG HEINRICH JULIUS...
LONG
I WAS CALLED VILE YET AGAIN!!
EVERYTHING EXCEPT JULIUS IS LOUSY.
I'VE HAD ENOUGH.
BEGONE.
HUNH!?
HEY ...!
HOW CAN YOU SAY THAT AFTER FLINGING TERRIBLE INSULTS AT ME OUT OF THE BLUE!?
I'M...
SHUT UP! BE QUIET!
HEY APOLLO! YOU'RE WATCHING THIS FARCE, AREN'T YOU!?
...THE SUN GOD APOLLO?
THAT'S THE NAME OF A MYTHICAL GOD...
I DON'T KNOW WHAT YOU'RE UP TO, BUT...
...STOP SENDING STRANGE THINGS TO ME!! THIS ONE IS AN EYESORE!

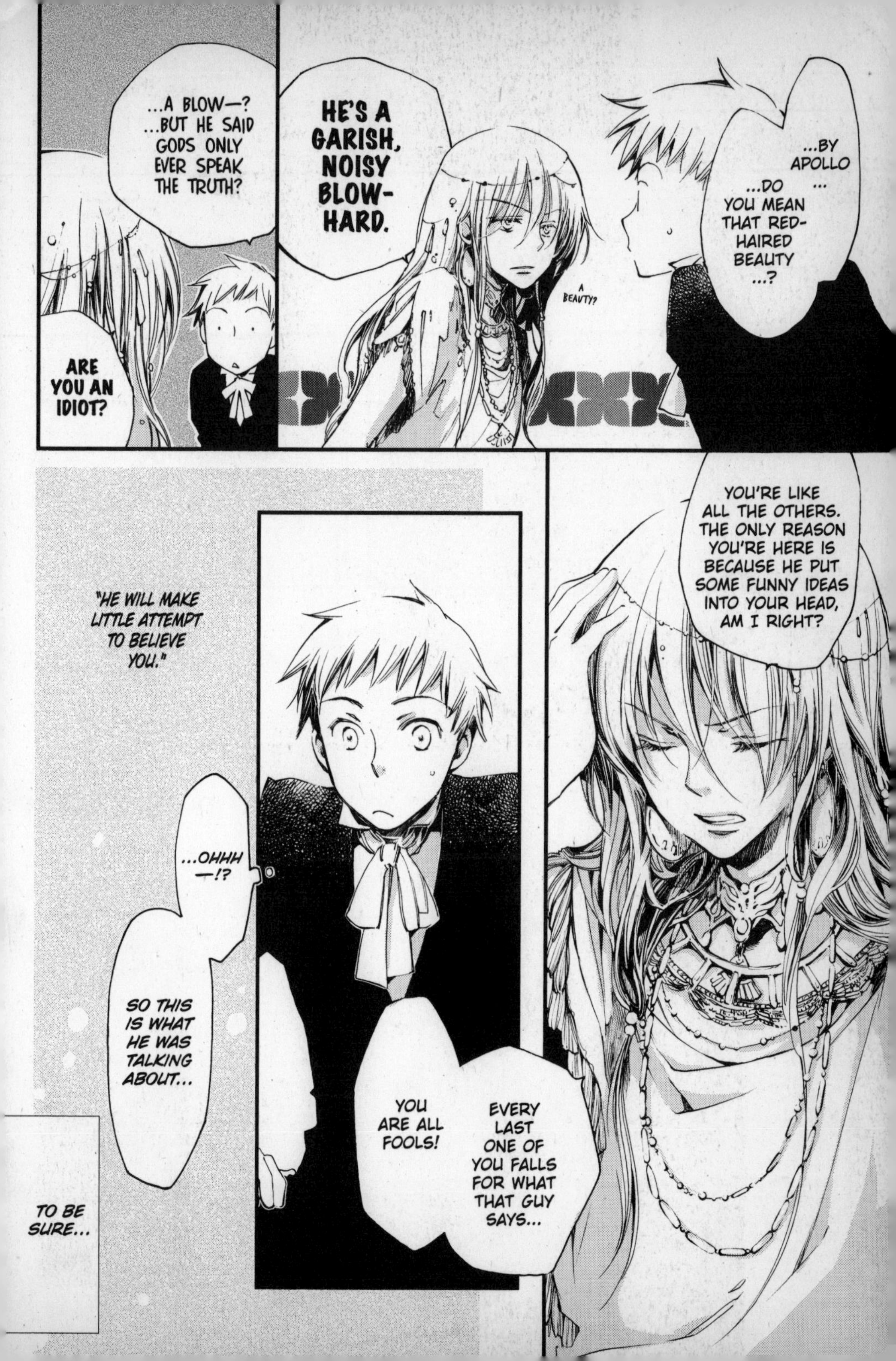
...BY APOLLO ... ...DO YOU MEAN THAT RED-HAIRED BEAUTY ...?
A BEAUTY?
HE'S A GARISH, NOISY BLOW-HARD.
...A BLOW—? ...BUT HE SAID GODS ONLY EVER SPEAK THE TRUTH?
ARE YOU AN IDIOT?
YOU'RE LIKE ALL THE OTHERS. THE ONLY REASON YOU'RE HERE IS BECAUSE HE PUT SOME FUNNY IDEAS INTO YOUR HEAD, AM I RIGHT?
EVERY LAST ONE OF YOU FALLS FOR WHAT THAT GUY SAYS...
YOU ARE ALL FOOLS!
"HE WILL MAKE LITTLE ATTEMPT TO BELIEVE YOU."
...OHHH—!?
SO THIS IS WHAT HE WAS TALKING ABOUT...
TO BE SURE...

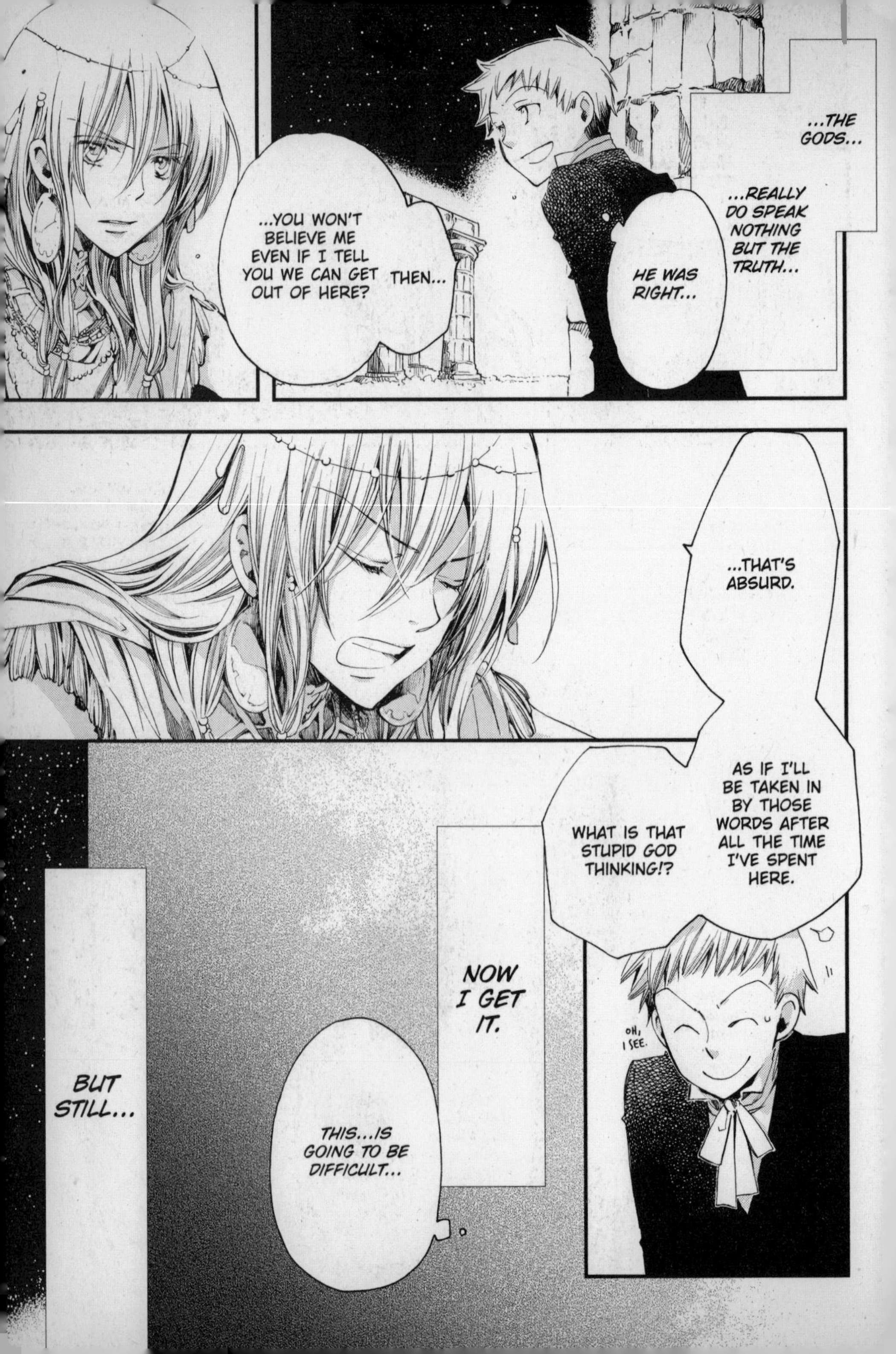
...THE GODS...
...REALLY DO SPEAK NOTHING BUT THE TRUTH...
HE WAS RIGHT...
THEN...
...YOU WON'T BELIEVE ME EVEN IF I TELL YOU WE CAN GET OUT OF HERE?
...THAT'S ABSURD.
AS IF I'LL BE TAKEN IN BY THOSE WORDS AFTER ALL THE TIME I'VE SPENT HERE.
WHAT IS THAT STUPID GOD THINKING!?
OH, I SEE.
NOW I GET IT.
THIS...IS GOING TO BE DIFFICULT...
BUT STILL...

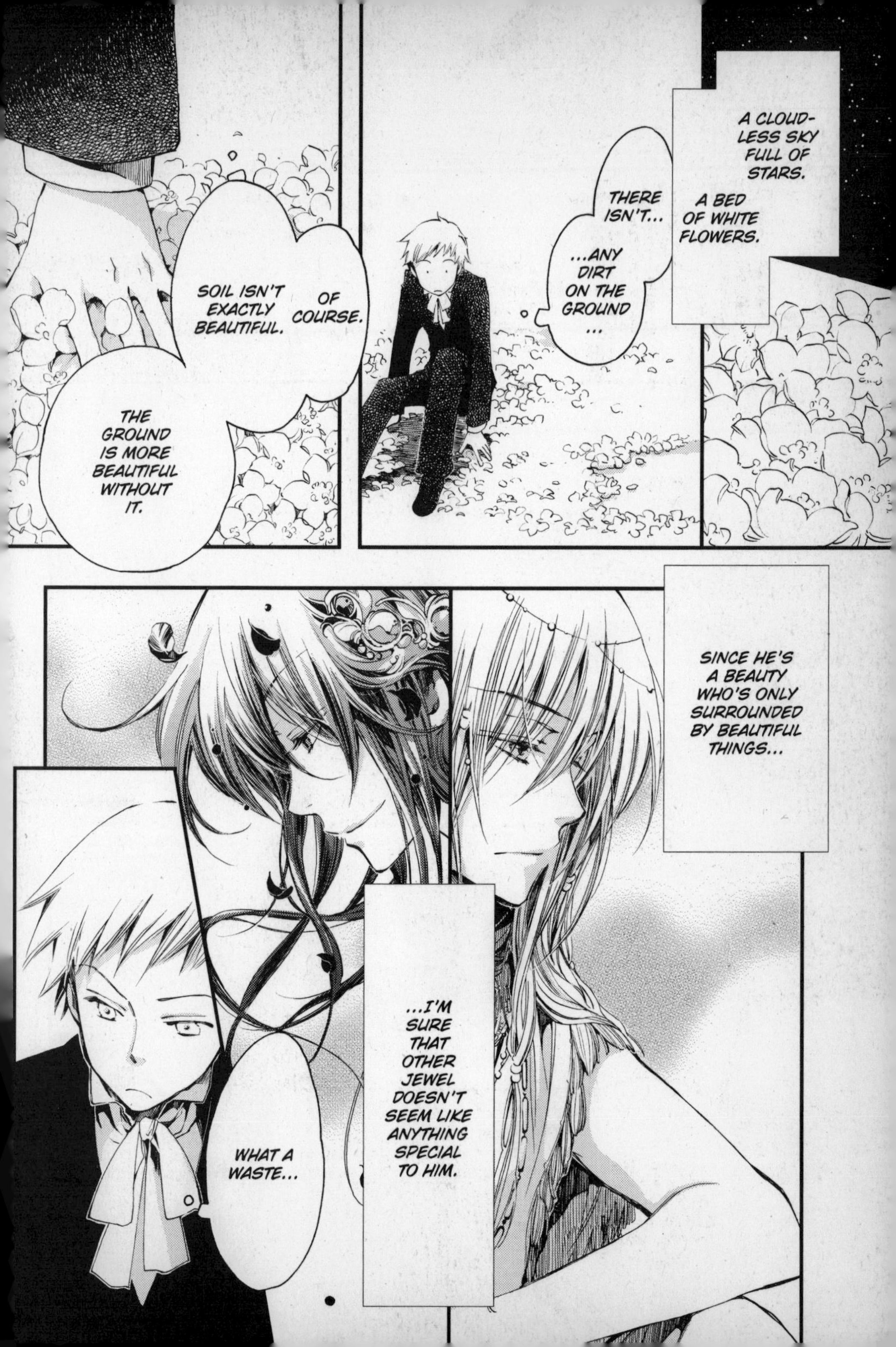
A CLOUDLESS SKY FULL OF STARS.
A BED OF WHITE FLOWERS.
THERE ISN'T...
...ANY DIRT ON THE GROUND...
OF COURSE.
SOIL ISN'T EXACTLY BEAUTIFUL.
THE GROUND IS MORE BEAUTIFUL WITHOUT IT.
SINCE HE'S A BEAUTY WHO'S ONLY SURROUNDED BY BEAUTIFUL THINGS...
...I'M SURE THAT OTHER JEWEL DOESN'T SEEM LIKE ANYTHING SPECIAL TO HIM.
WHAT A WASTE...

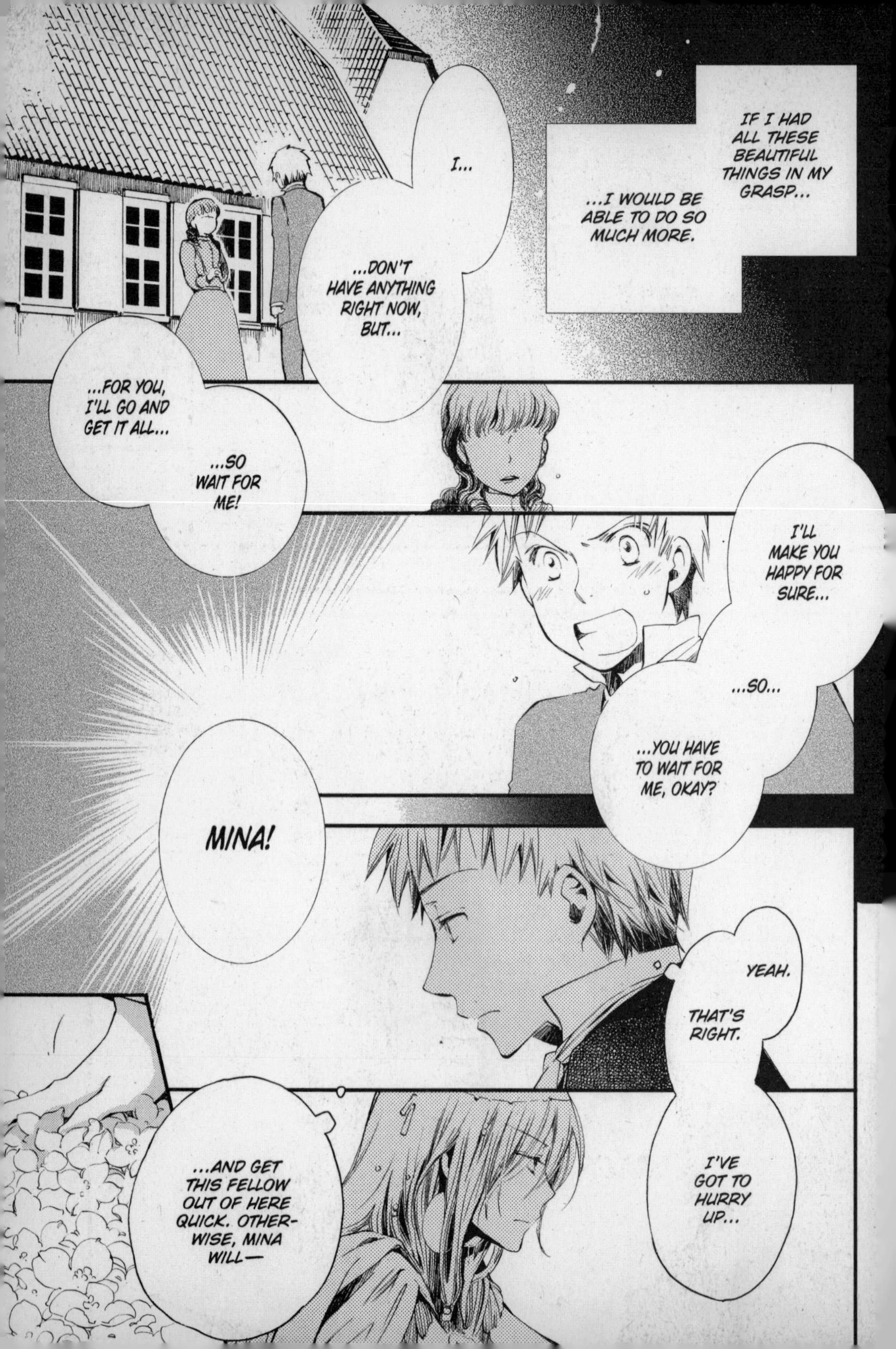
IF I HAD ALL THESE BEAUTIFUL THINGS IN MY GRASP...
...I WOULD BE ABLE TO DO SO MUCH MORE.
I...
...DON'T HAVE ANYTHING RIGHT NOW, BUT...
...FOR YOU, I'LL GO AND GET IT ALL...
...SO WAIT FOR ME!
I'LL MAKE YOU HAPPY FOR SURE...
...SO...
...YOU HAVE TO WAIT FOR ME, OKAY?
MINA!
YEAH.
THAT'S RIGHT.
I'VE GOT TO HURRY UP...
...AND GET THIS FELLOW OUT OF HERE QUICK. OTHER-WISE, MINA WILL—

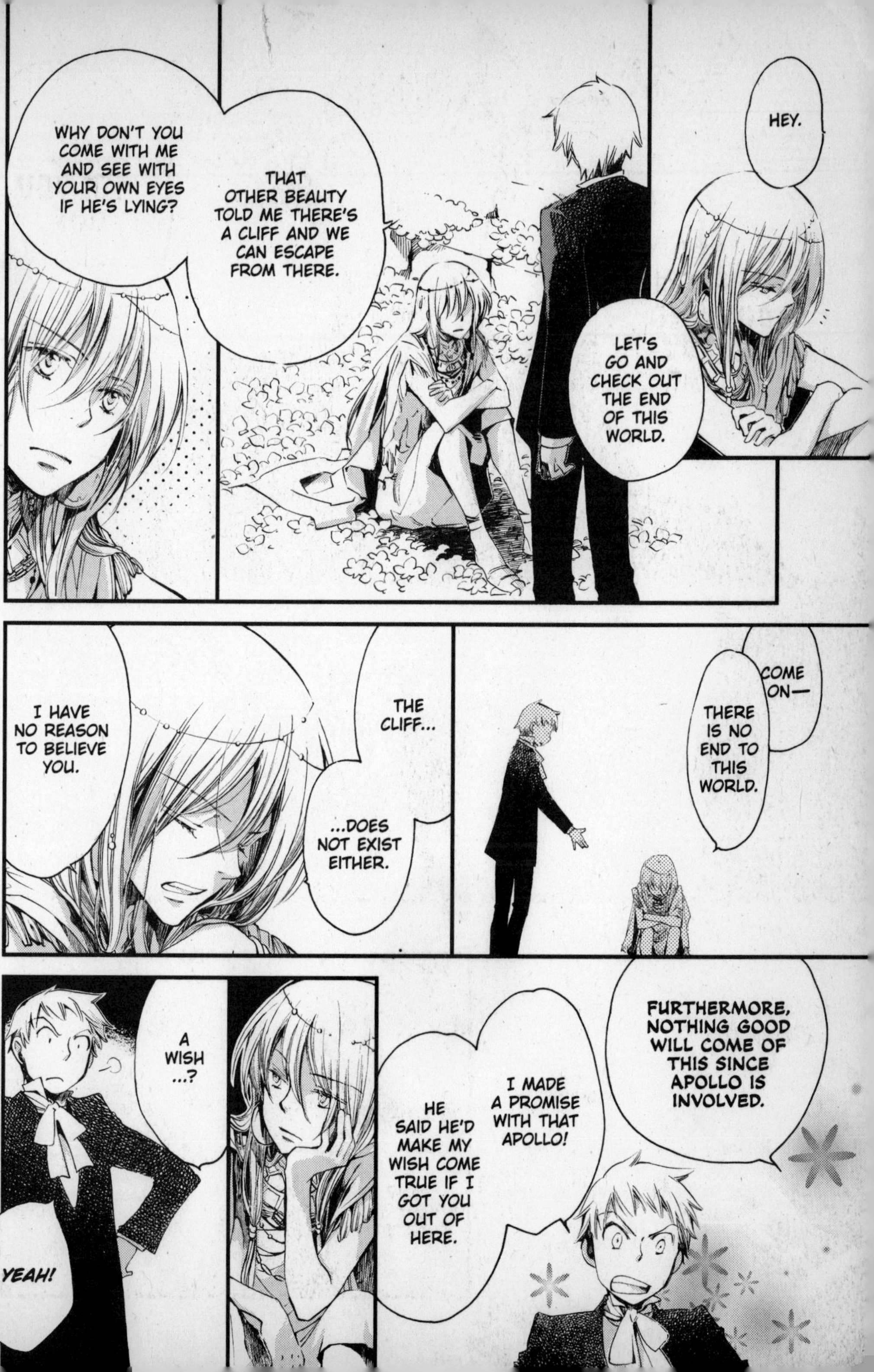
HEY.
LET'S GO AND CHECK OUT THE END OF THIS WORLD.
THAT OTHER BEAUTY TOLD ME THERE'S A CLIFF AND WE CAN ESCAPE FROM THERE.
WHY DON'T YOU COME WITH ME AND SEE WITH YOUR OWN EYES IF HE'S LYING?
COME ON—
THERE IS NO END TO THIS WORLD.
THE CLIFF...
...DOES NOT EXIST EITHER.
I HAVE NO REASON TO BELIEVE YOU.
FURTHERMORE, NOTHING GOOD WILL COME OF THIS SINCE APOLLO IS INVOLVED.
I MADE A PROMISE WITH THAT APOLLO!
HE SAID HE'D MAKE MY WISH COME TRUE IF I GOT YOU OUT OF HERE.
A WISH ...?
YEAH!

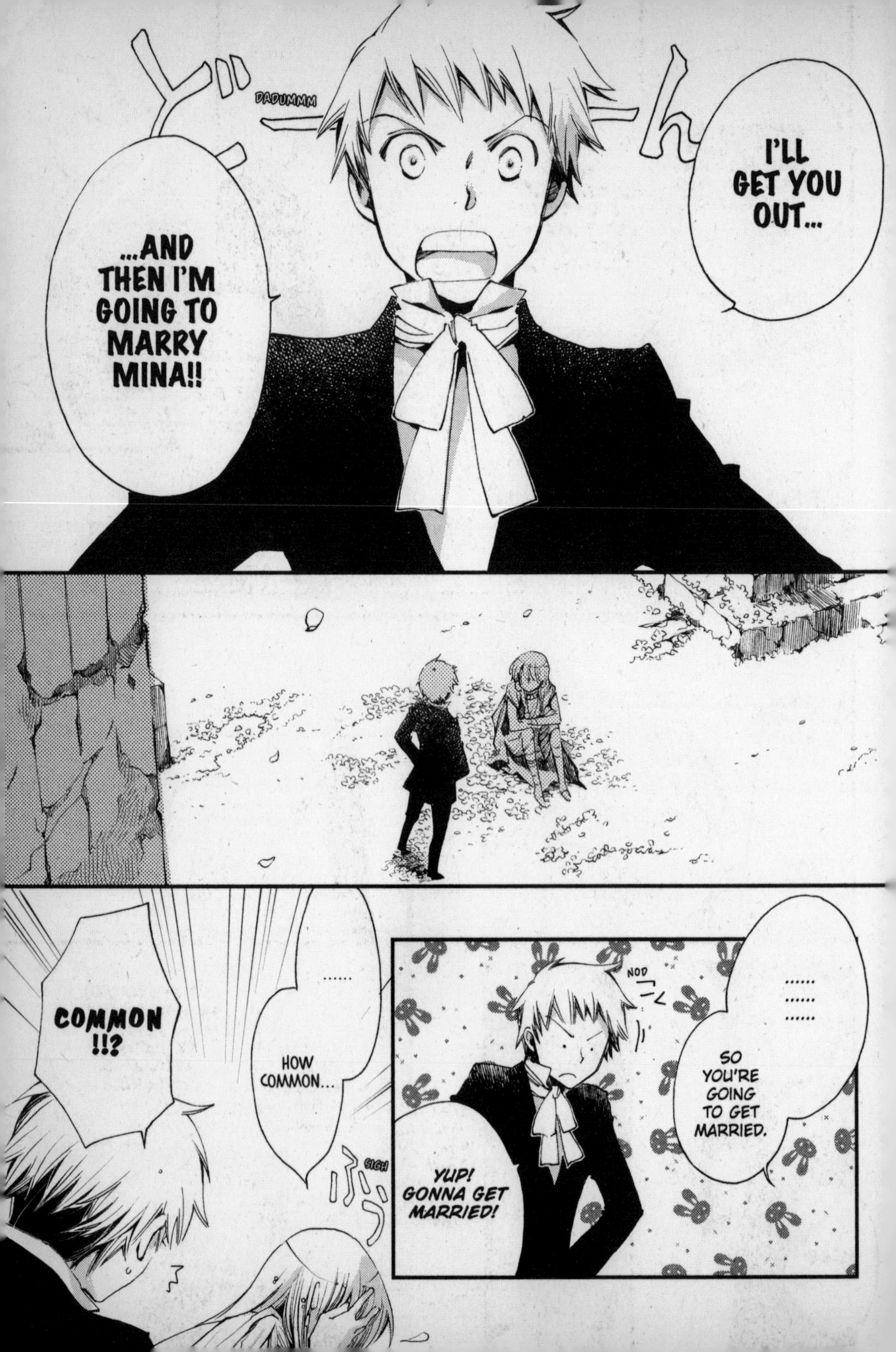
I'LL GET YOU OUT...
DADUMMM
...AND THEN I'M GOING TO MARRY MINA!!
NOD
....
SO YOU'RE GOING TO GET MARRIED.
YUP! GONNA GET MARRIED!
......
HOW COMMON...
SIGH
COMMON!!?

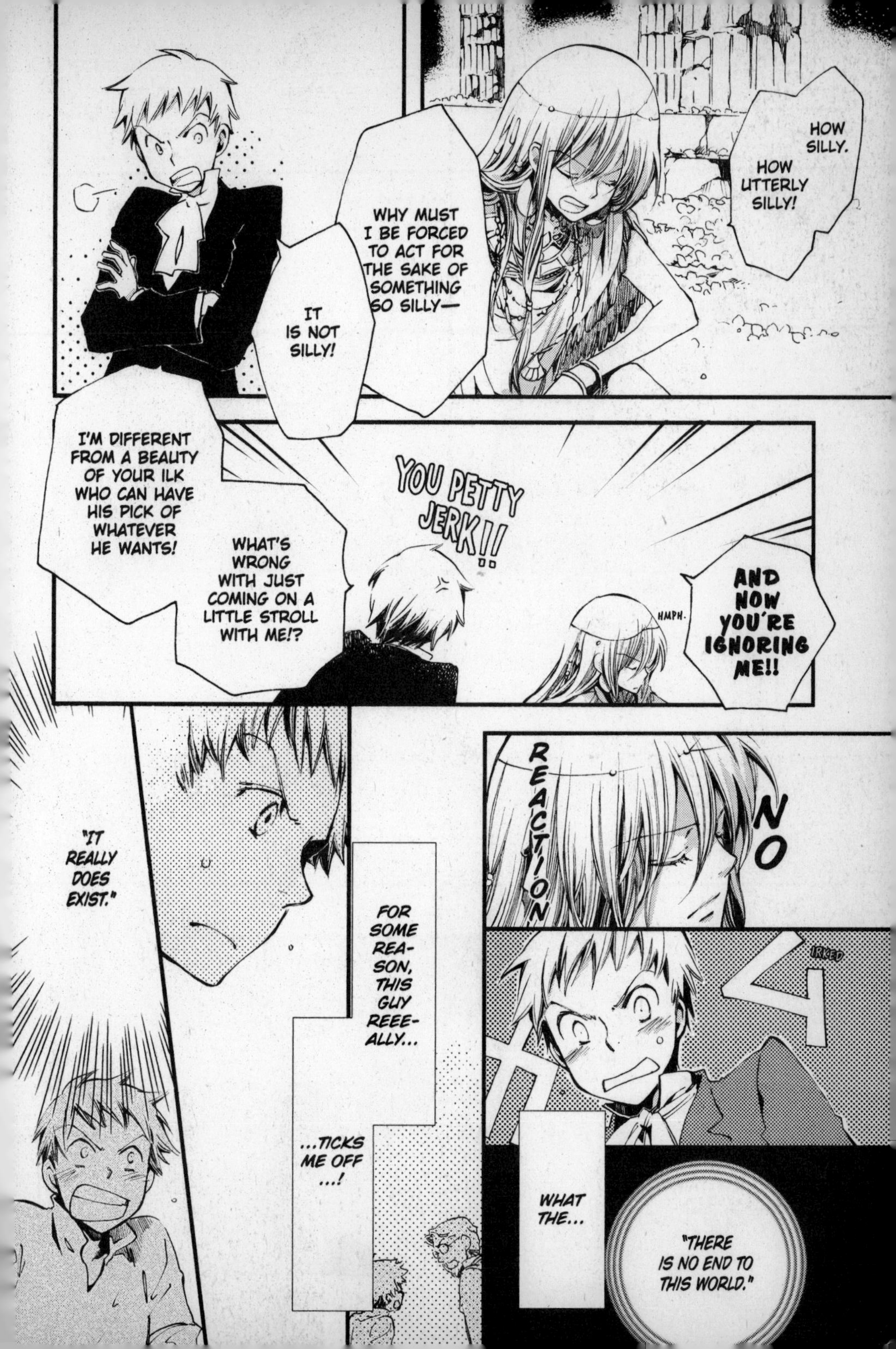
HOW SILLY. HOW UTTERLY SILLY!
WHY MUST I BE FORCED TO ACT FOR THE SAKE OF SOMETHING SO SILLY—
IT IS NOT SILLY!
I'M DIFFERENT FROM A BEAUTY OF YOUR ILK WHO CAN HAVE HIS PICK OF WHATEVER HE WANTS!
WHAT'S WRONG WITH JUST COMING ON A LITTLE STROLL WITH ME!?
HMPH.
AND NOW YOU'RE IGNORING ME!!
YOU PETTY JERK!!
NO REACTION
IRKED
WHAT THE...
"THERE IS NO END TO THIS WORLD."
FOR SOME REA-SON, THIS GUY REEE-ALLY...
...TICKS ME OFF ...!
"IT REALLY DOES EXIST."

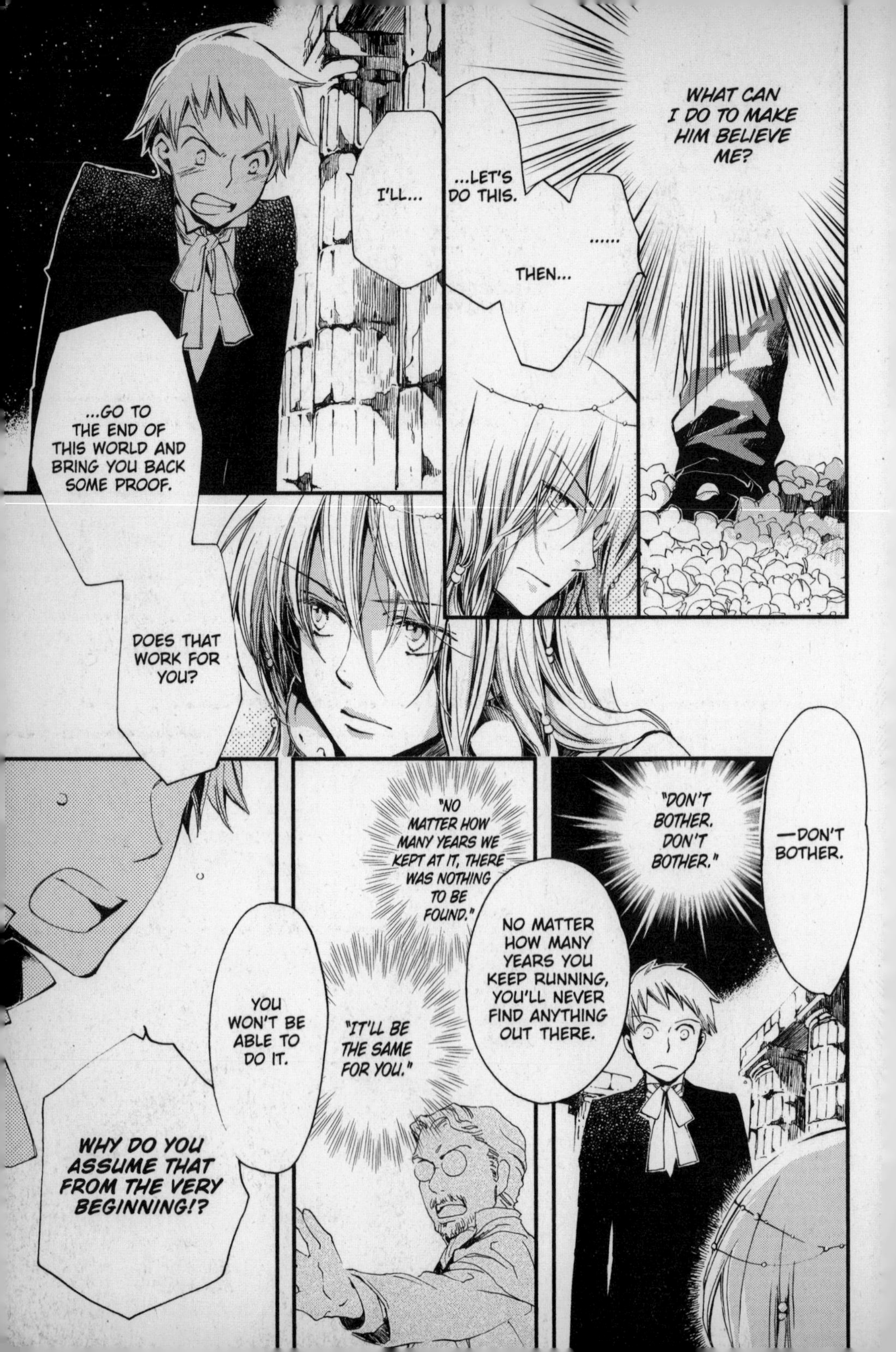

WHAT CAN I DO TO MAKE HIM BELIEVE ME?
......
THEN...
...LET'S DO THIS.
I'LL...
...GO TO THE END OF THIS WORLD AND BRING YOU BACK SOME PROOF.
DOES THAT WORK FOR YOU?
—DON'T BOTHER.
"DON'T BOTHER. DON'T BOTHER."
NO MATTER HOW MANY YEARS YOU KEEP RUNNING, YOU'LL NEVER FIND ANYTHING OUT THERE.
"NO MATTER HOW MANY YEARS WE KEPT AT IT, THERE WAS NOTHING TO BE FOUND."
"IT'LL BE THE SAME FOR YOU."
YOU WON'T BE ABLE TO DO IT.
WHY DO YOU ASSUME THAT FROM THE VERY BEGINNING!?

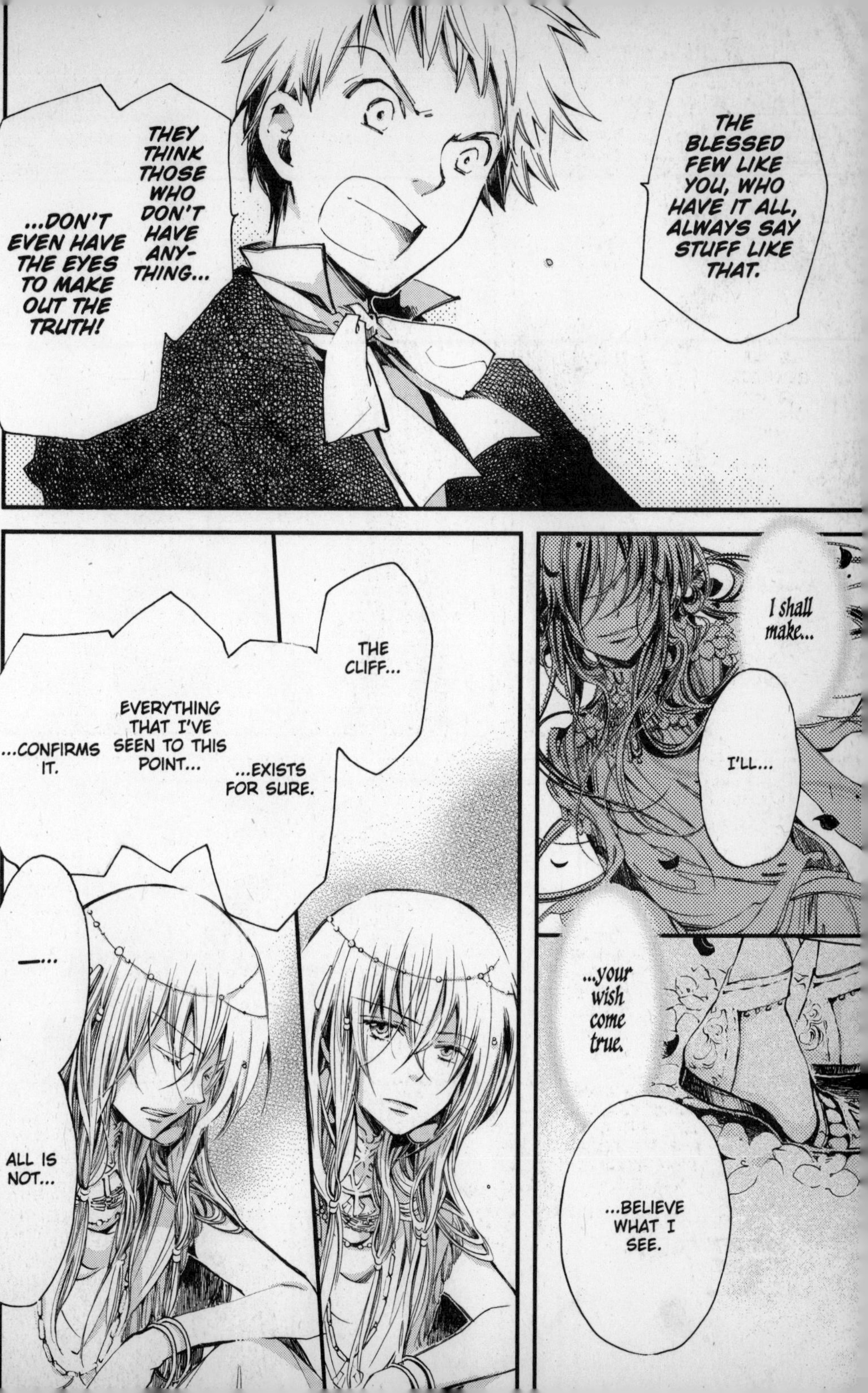
THE BLESSED FEW LIKE YOU, WHO HAVE IT ALL, ALWAYS SAY STUFF LIKE THAT.
THEY THINK THOSE WHO DON'T HAVE ANYTHING...
...DON'T EVEN HAVE THE EYES TO MAKE OUT THE TRUTH!
I shall make...
I'LL...
...your wish come true.
...BELIEVE WHAT I SEE.
THE CLIFF...
...EXISTS FOR SURE.
EVERYTHING THAT I'VE SEEN TO THIS POINT...
...CONFIRMS IT.
—...
ALL IS NOT...

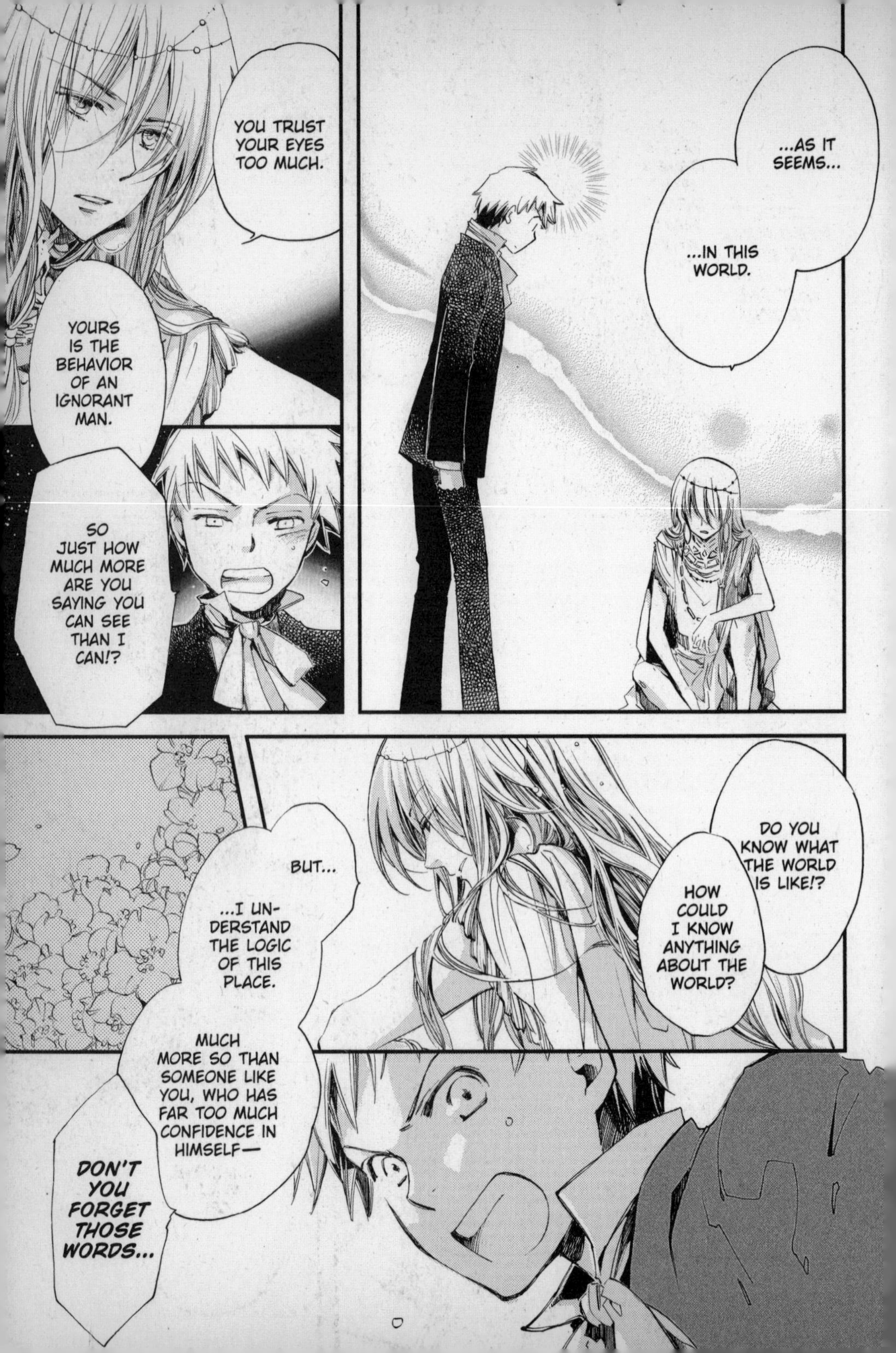
...AS IT SEEMS...
...IN THIS WORLD.
YOU TRUST YOUR EYES TOO MUCH.
YOURS IS THE BEHAVIOR OF AN IGNORANT MAN.
SO JUST HOW MUCH MORE ARE YOU SAYING YOU CAN SEE THAN I CAN!?
DO YOU KNOW WHAT THE WORLD IS LIKE!?
HOW COULD I KNOW ANYTHING ABOUT THE WORLD?
BUT...
...I UNDERSTAND THE LOGIC OF THIS PLACE.
MUCH MORE SO THAN SOMEONE LIKE YOU, WHO HAS FAR TOO MUCH CONFIDENCE IN HIMSELF—
DON'T YOU FORGET THOSE WORDS...

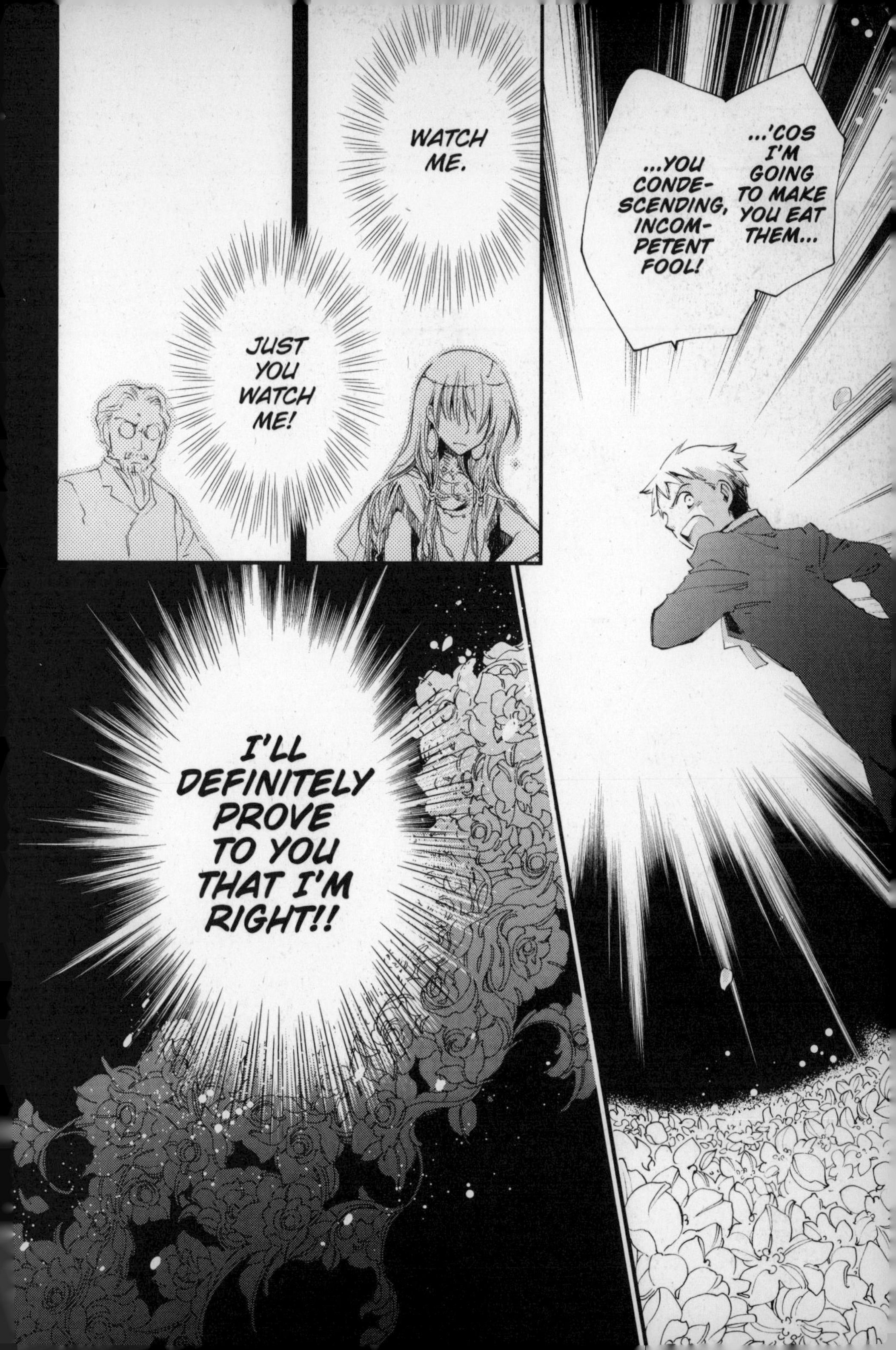
...'COS I'M GOING TO MAKE YOU EAT THEM...
...YOU CONDE-SCENDING, INCOM-PETENT FOOL!
WATCH ME.
JUST YOU WATCH ME!
I'LL DEFINITELY PROVE TO YOU THAT I'M RIGHT!!

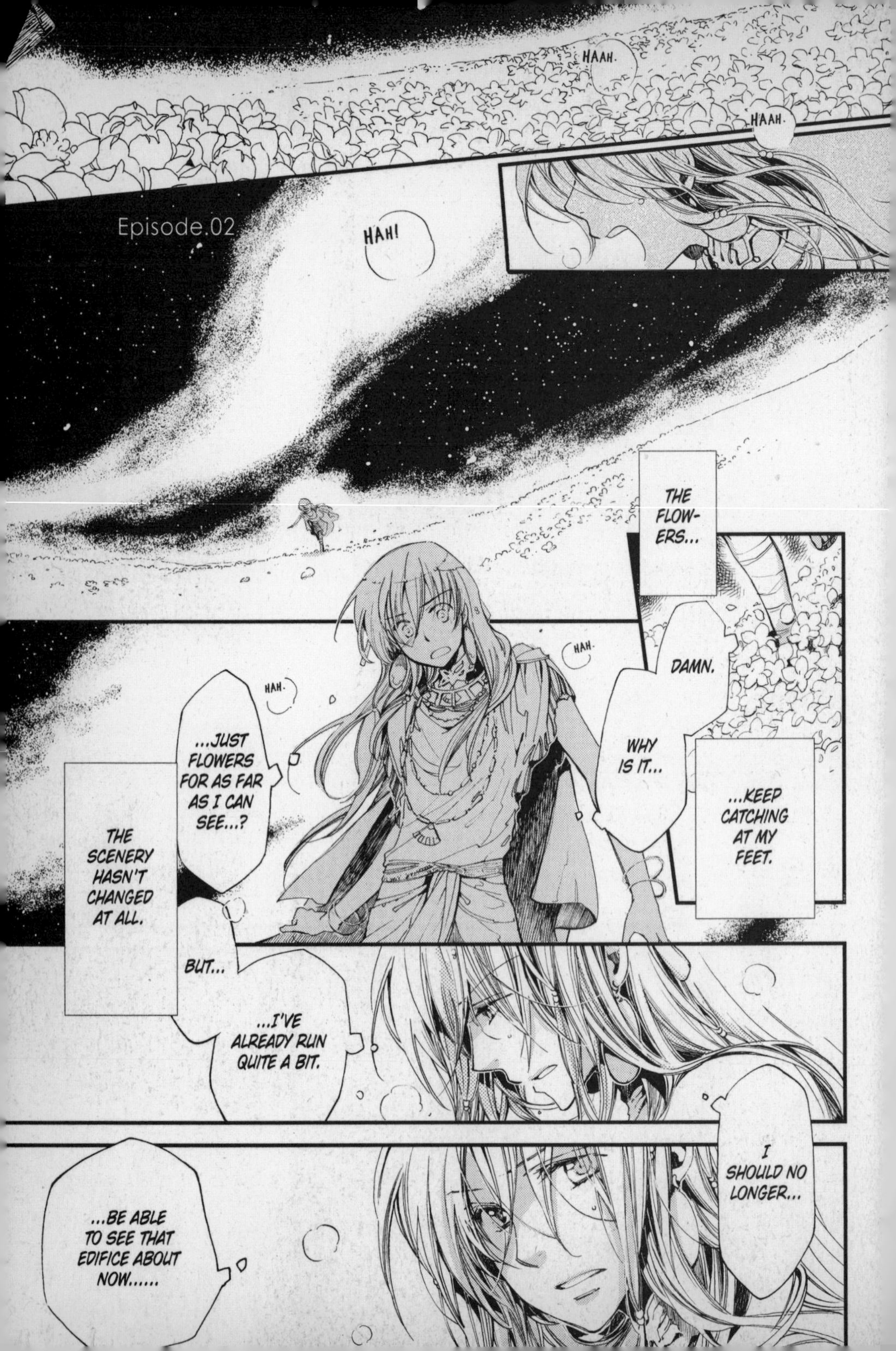
HAAH.
HAAH.
Episode.02
HAH!
THE FLOWERS...
DAMN.
WHY IS IT...
...KEEP CATCHING AT MY FEET.
HAH.
HAH.
...JUST FLOWERS FOR AS FAR AS I CAN SEE...?
THE SCENERY HASN'T CHANGED AT ALL.
BUT...
...I'VE ALREADY RUN QUITE A BIT.
I SHOULD NO LONGER...
...BE ABLE TO SEE THAT EDIFICE ABOUT NOW......

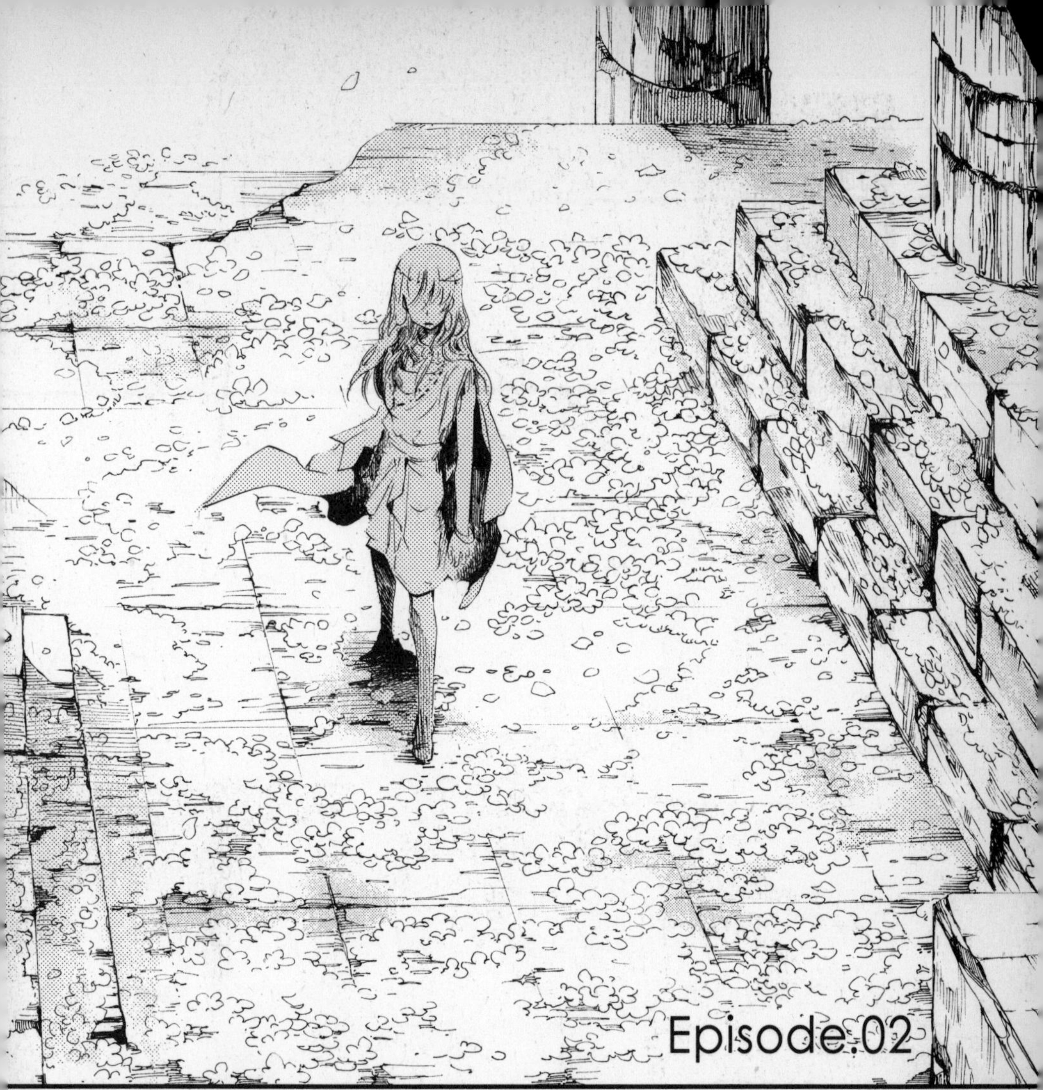
Episode.02

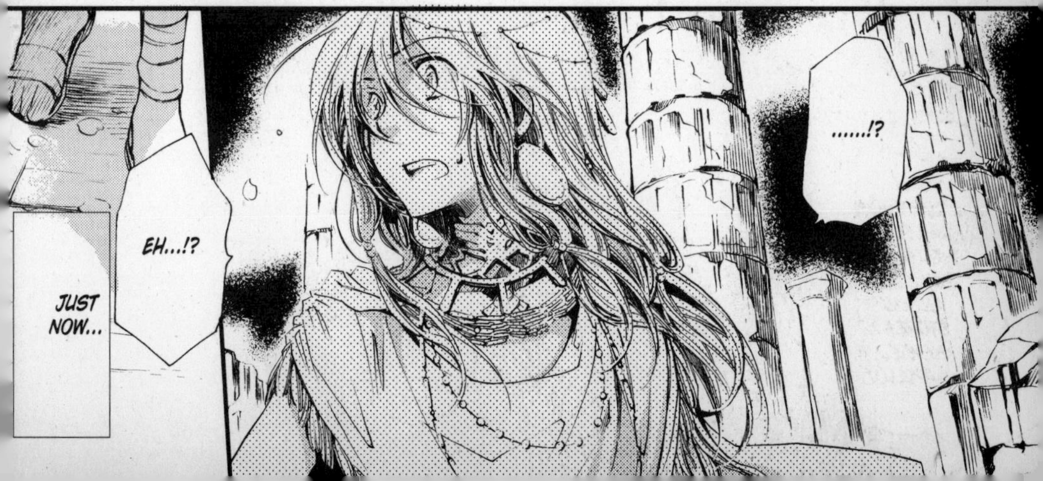
......!?
EH...!?
JUST NOW...

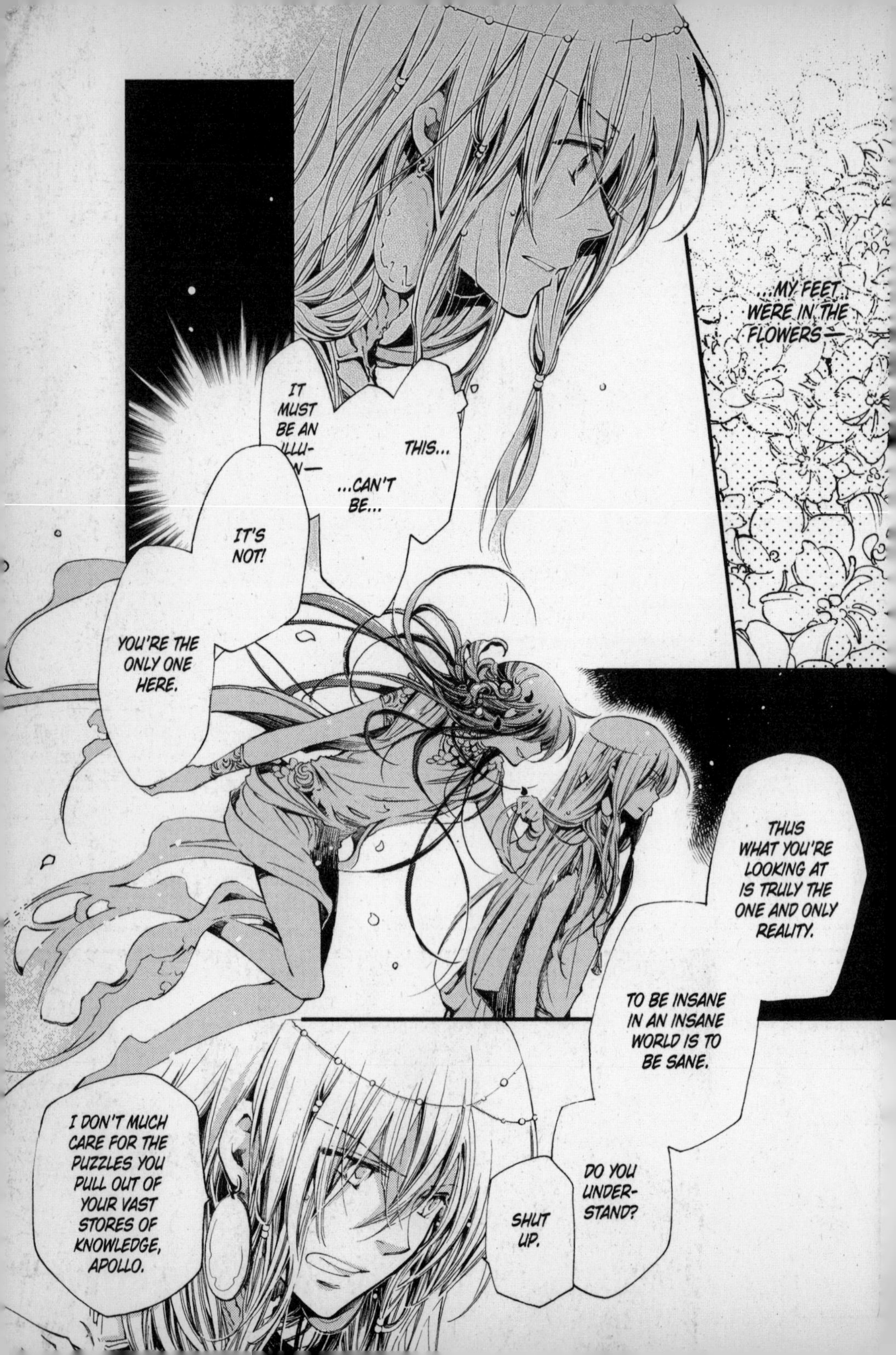
...MY FEET WERE IN THE FLOWERS—
THIS...
...CAN'T BE...
IT MUST BE AN ILLU-
IT'S NOT!
YOU'RE THE ONLY ONE HERE.
THUS WHAT YOU'RE LOOKING AT IS TRULY THE ONE AND ONLY REALITY.
TO BE INSANE IN AN INSANE WORLD IS TO BE SANE.
DO YOU UNDER-STAND?
SHUT UP.
I DON'T MUCH CARE FOR THE PUZZLES YOU PULL OUT OF YOUR VAST STORES OF KNOWLEDGE, APOLLO.

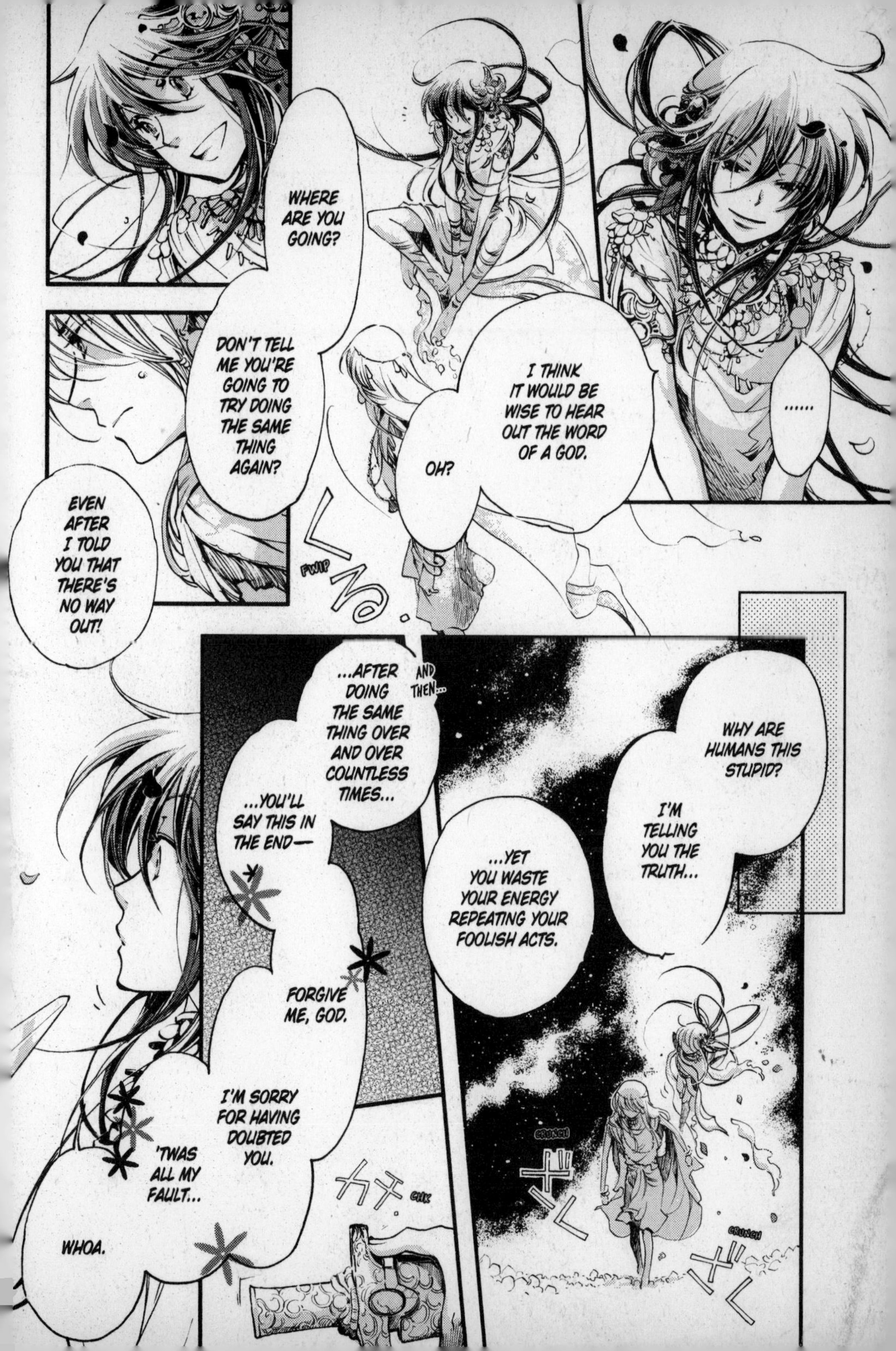
......
I THINK IT WOULD BE WISE TO HEAR OUT THE WORD OF A GOD.
OH?
WHERE ARE YOU GOING?
DON'T TELL ME YOU'RE GOING TO TRY DOING THE SAME THING AGAIN?
FWIP
EVEN AFTER I TOLD YOU THAT THERE'S NO WAY OUT!
WHY ARE HUMANS THIS STUPID?
I'M TELLING YOU THE TRUTH...
...YET YOU WASTE YOUR ENERGY REPEATING YOUR FOOLISH ACTS.
CRUNCH
CRUNCH
AND THEN...
...AFTER DOING THE SAME THING OVER AND OVER COUNTLESS TIMES...
...YOU'LL SAY THIS IN THE END—
FORGIVE ME, GOD.
I'M SORRY FOR HAVING DOUBTED YOU.
'TWAS ALL MY FAULT...
CHK
WHOA.

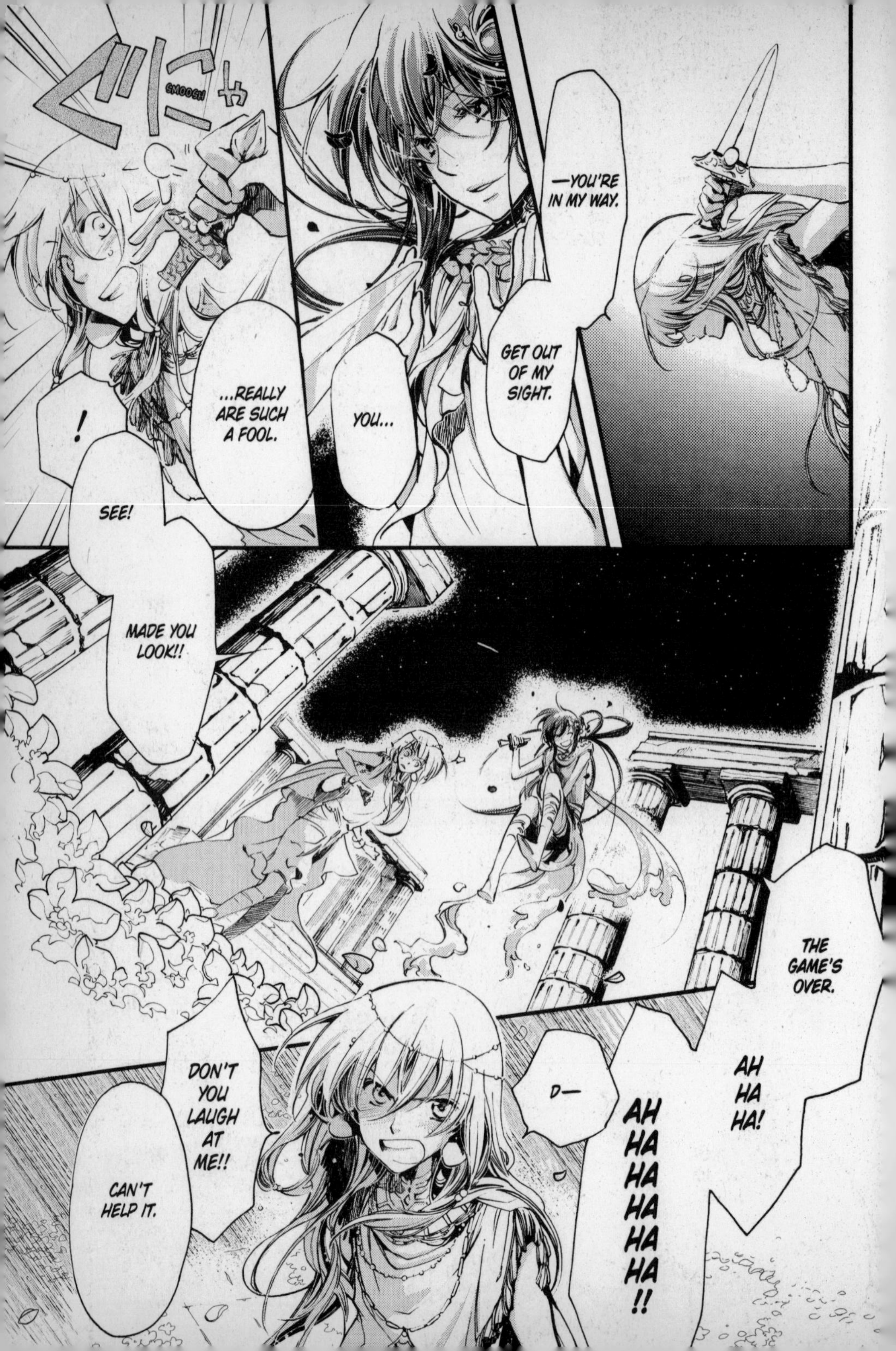
—YOU'RE IN MY WAY.
GET OUT OF MY SIGHT.
YOU...
...REALLY ARE SUCH A FOOL.
SMOOSH
!
SEE!
MADE YOU LOOK!!
THE GAME'S OVER.
AH HA HA!
AH HA HA HA HA HA!!
D—
DON'T YOU LAUGH AT ME!!
CAN'T HELP IT.

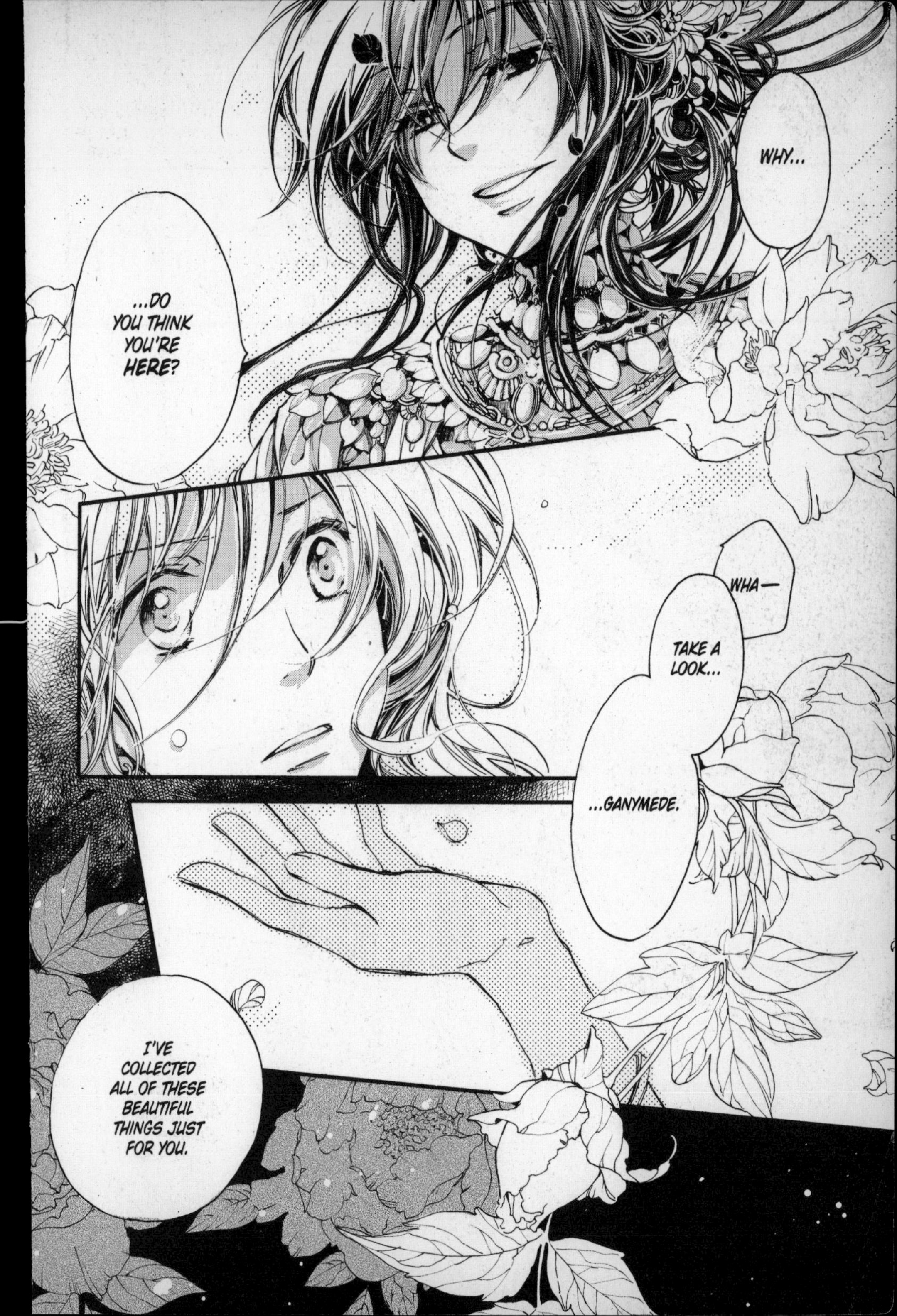
WHY...
...DO YOU THINK YOU'RE HERE?
WHA—
TAKE A LOOK...
...GANYMEDE.
I'VE COLLECTED ALL OF THESE BEAUTIFUL THINGS JUST FOR YOU.

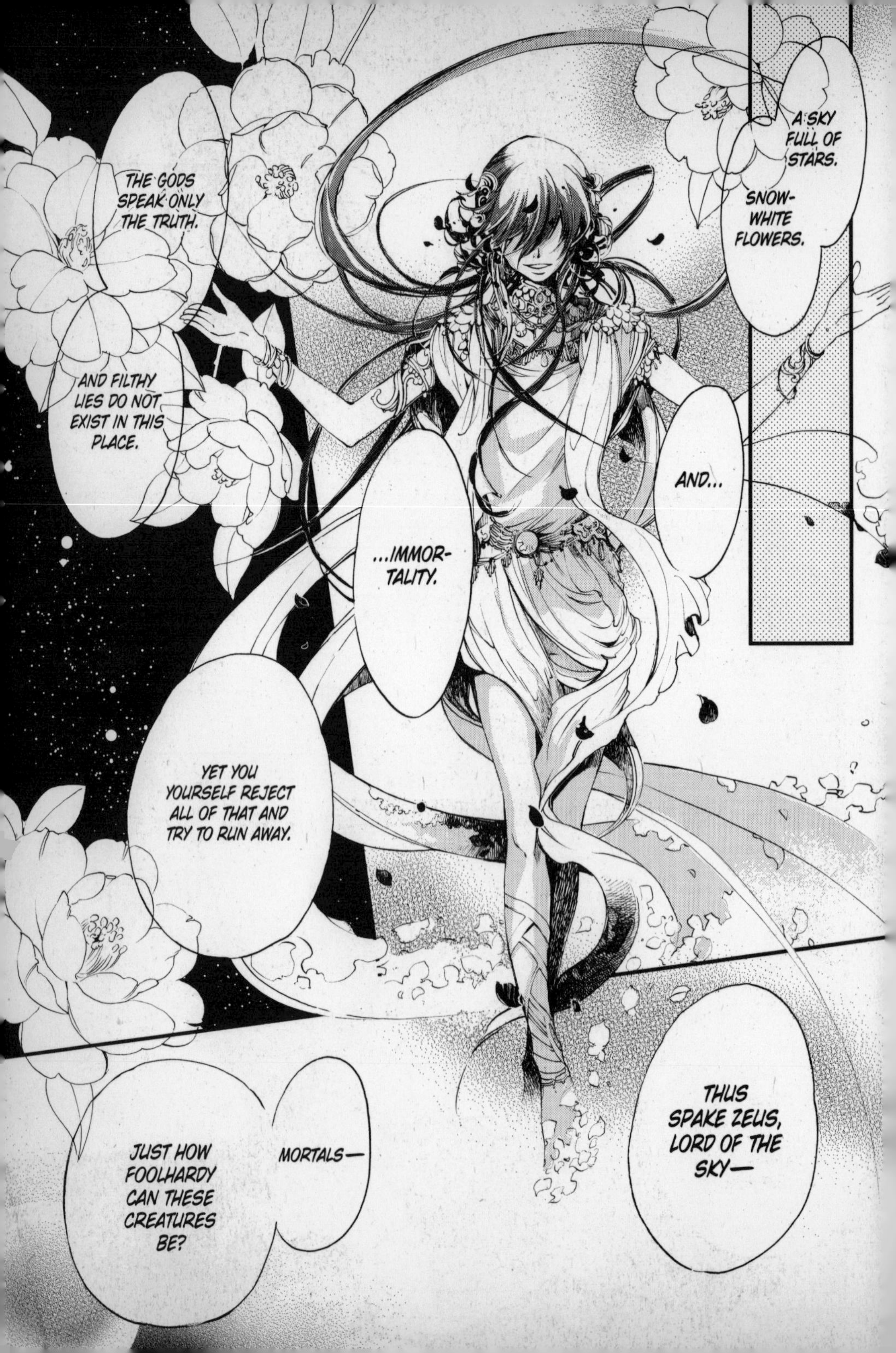
A SKY FULL OF STARS.
SNOW-WHITE FLOWERS.
AND...
...IMMORTALITY.
THE GODS SPEAK ONLY THE TRUTH.
AND FILTHY LIES DO NOT EXIST IN THIS PLACE.
YET YOU YOURSELF REJECT ALL OF THAT AND TRY TO RUN AWAY.
THUS SPAKE ZEUS, LORD OF THE SKY—
MORTALS—
JUST HOW FOOLHARDY CAN THESE CREATURES BE?

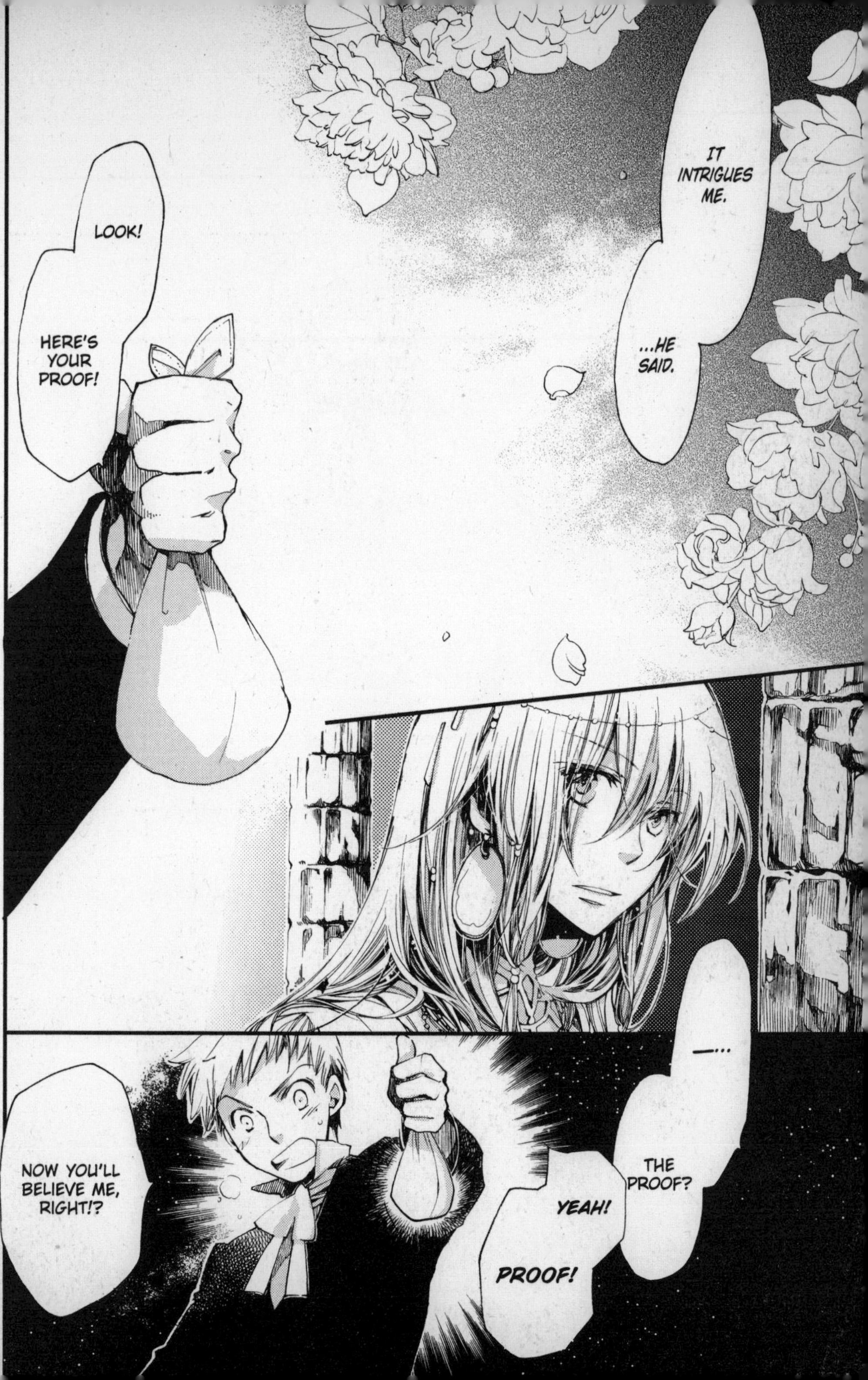
IT INTRIGUES ME.
...HE SAID.
LOOK!
HERE'S YOUR PROOF!
—...
THE PROOF?
YEAH!
PROOF!
NOW YOU'LL BELIEVE ME, RIGHT!?

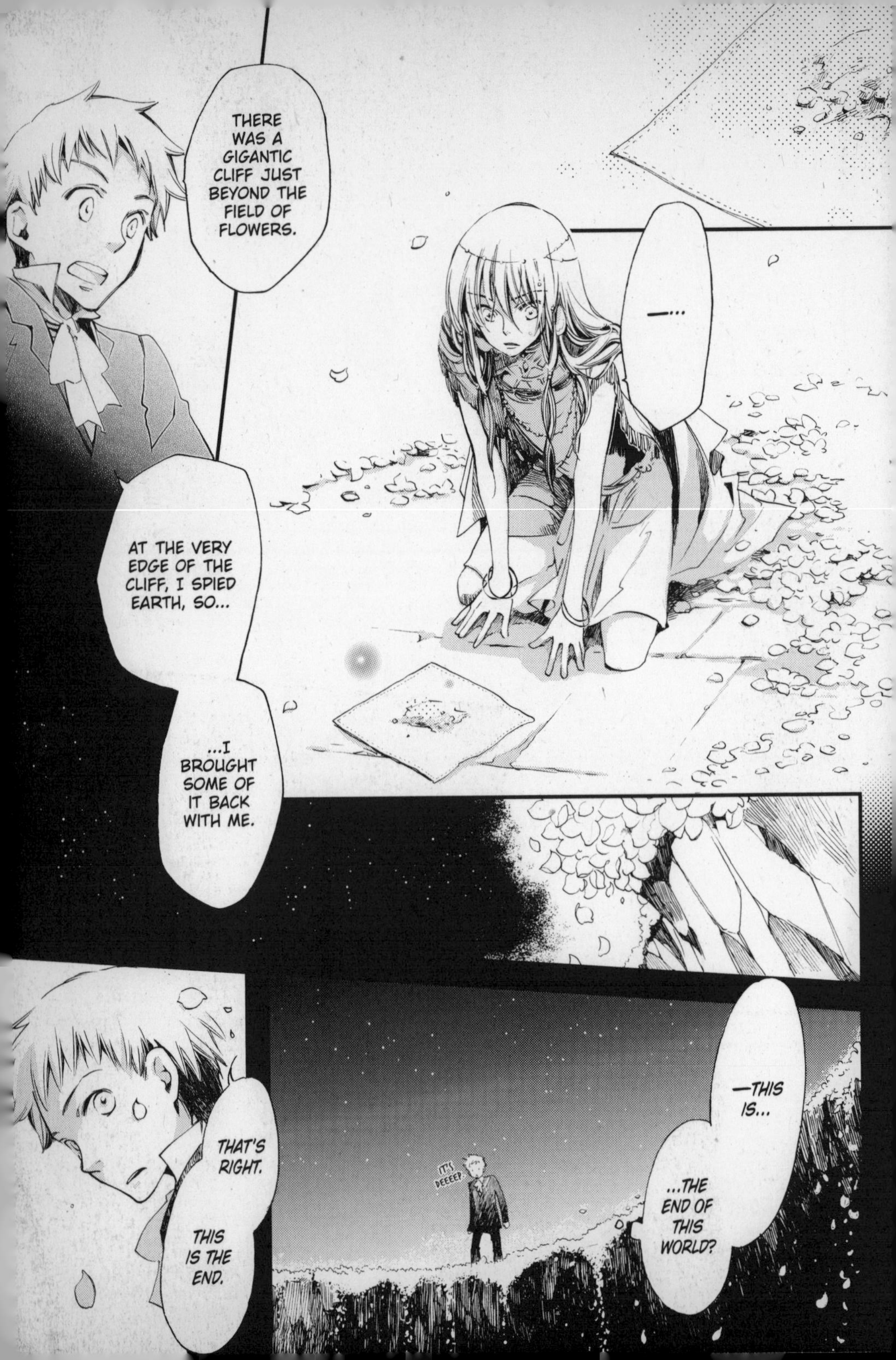
THERE WAS A GIGANTIC CLIFF JUST BEYOND THE FIELD OF FLOWERS.
—...
AT THE VERY EDGE OF THE CLIFF, I SPIED EARTH, SO...
...I BROUGHT SOME OF IT BACK WITH ME.
—THIS IS...
...THE END OF THIS WORLD?
IT'S DEEEEP.
THAT'S RIGHT.
THIS IS THE END.

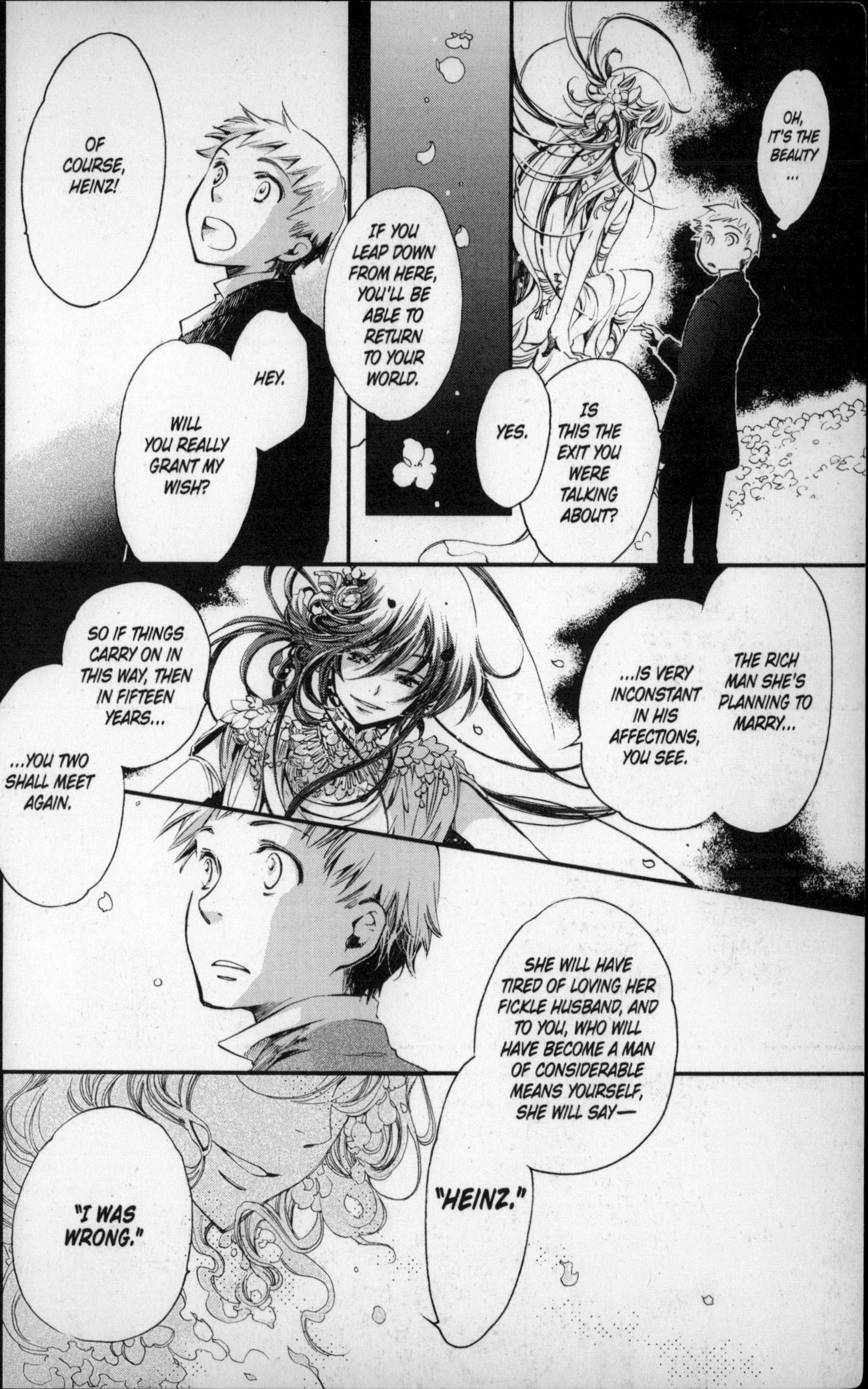
OH, IT'S THE BEAUTY ...
IS THIS THE EXIT YOU WERE TALKING ABOUT?
YES.
IF YOU LEAP DOWN FROM HERE, YOU'LL BE ABLE TO RETURN TO YOUR WORLD.
HEY.
WILL YOU REALLY GRANT MY WISH?
OF COURSE, HEINZ!
THE RICH MAN SHE'S PLANNING TO MARRY...
...IS VERY INCONSTANT IN HIS AFFECTIONS, YOU SEE.
SO IF THINGS CARRY ON IN THIS WAY, THEN IN FIFTEEN YEARS...
...YOU TWO SHALL MEET AGAIN.
SHE WILL HAVE TIRED OF LOVING HER FICKLE HUSBAND, AND TO YOU, WHO WILL HAVE BECOME A MAN OF CONSIDERABLE MEANS YOURSELF, SHE WILL SAY—
"HEINZ."
"I WAS WRONG."

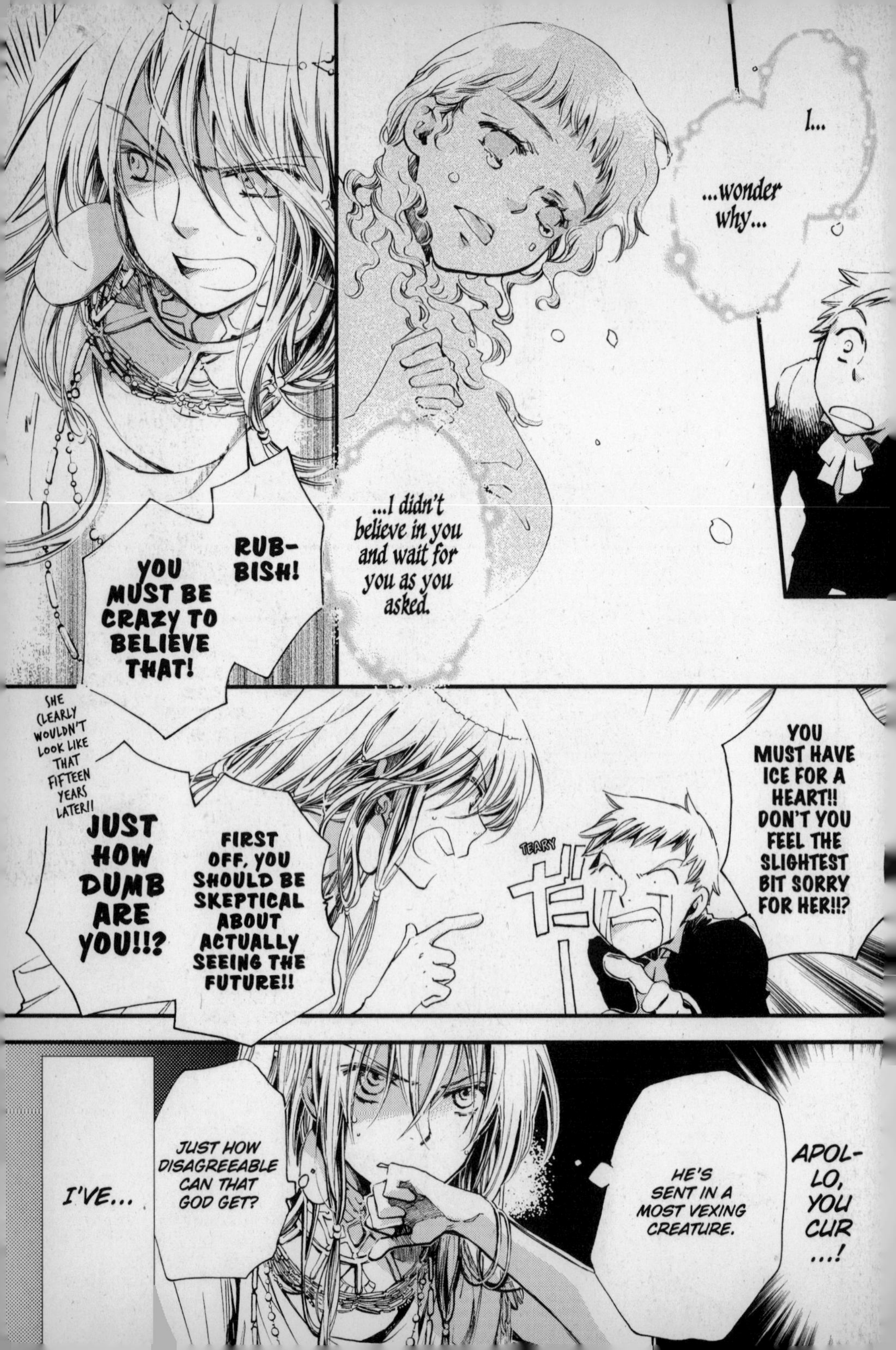
I...
...wonder why...
...I didn't believe in you and wait for you as you asked.
RUB-BISH!
YOU MUST BE CRAZY TO BELIEVE THAT!
YOU MUST HAVE ICE FOR A HEART!! DON'T YOU FEEL THE SLIGHTEST BIT SORRY FOR HER!!?
TEARY
FIRST OFF, YOU SHOULD BE SKEPTICAL ABOUT ACTUALLY SEEING THE FUTURE!!
JUST HOW DUMB ARE YOU!!?
SHE CLEARLY WOULDN'T LOOK LIKE THAT FIFTEEN YEARS LATER!!
APOL-LO, YOU CUR...!
HE'S SENT IN A MOST VEXING CREATURE.
JUST HOW DISAGREEABLE CAN THAT GOD GET?
I'VE...

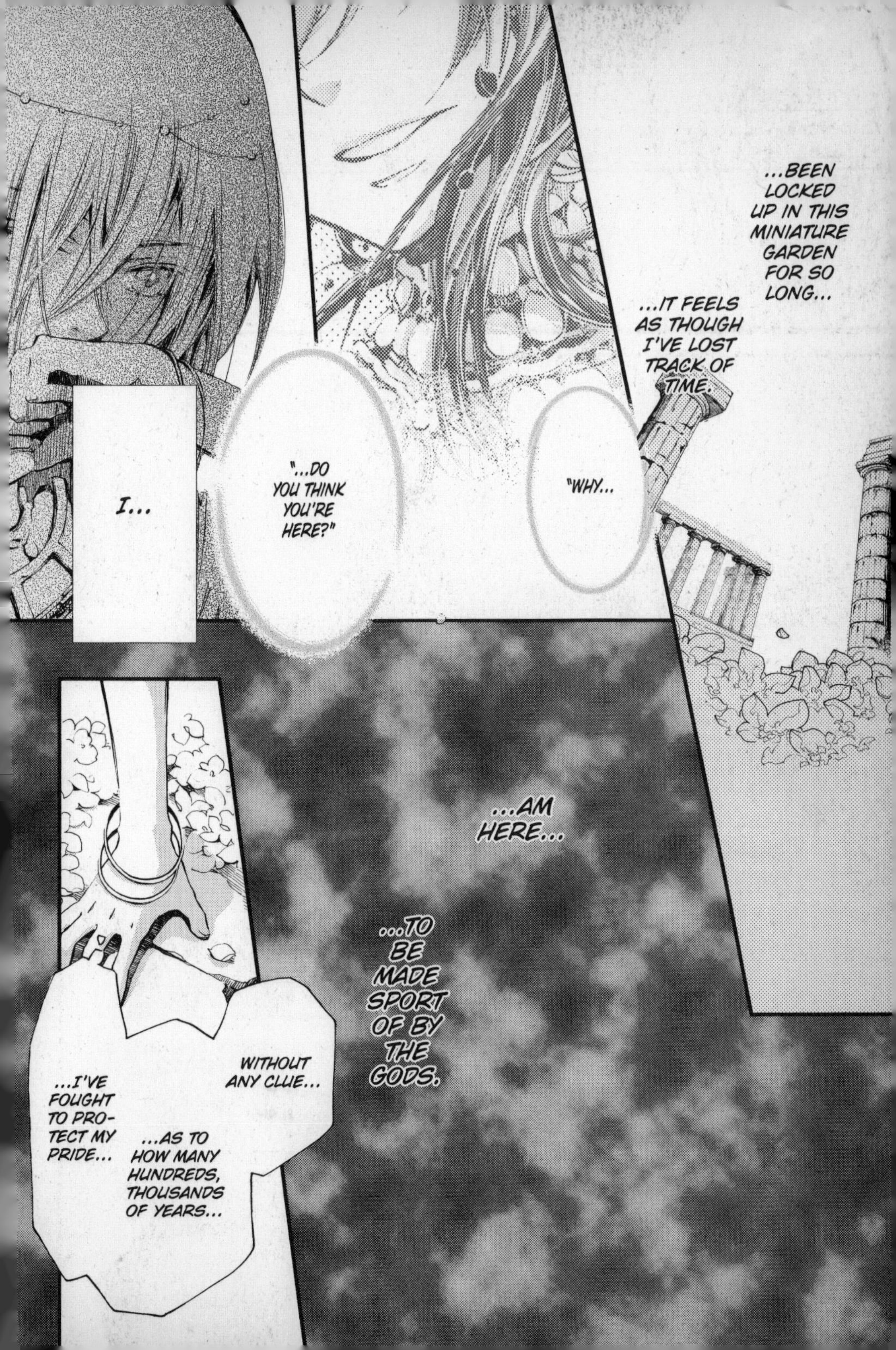

...BEEN LOCKED UP IN THIS MINIATURE GARDEN FOR SO LONG...
...IT FEELS AS THOUGH I'VE LOST TRACK OF TIME.
"WHY...
"...DO YOU THINK YOU'RE HERE?"
I...
...AM HERE...
...TO BE MADE SPORT OF BY THE GODS.
WITHOUT ANY CLUE...
...AS TO HOW MANY HUNDREDS, THOUSANDS OF YEARS...
...I'VE FOUGHT TO PROTECT MY PRIDE...

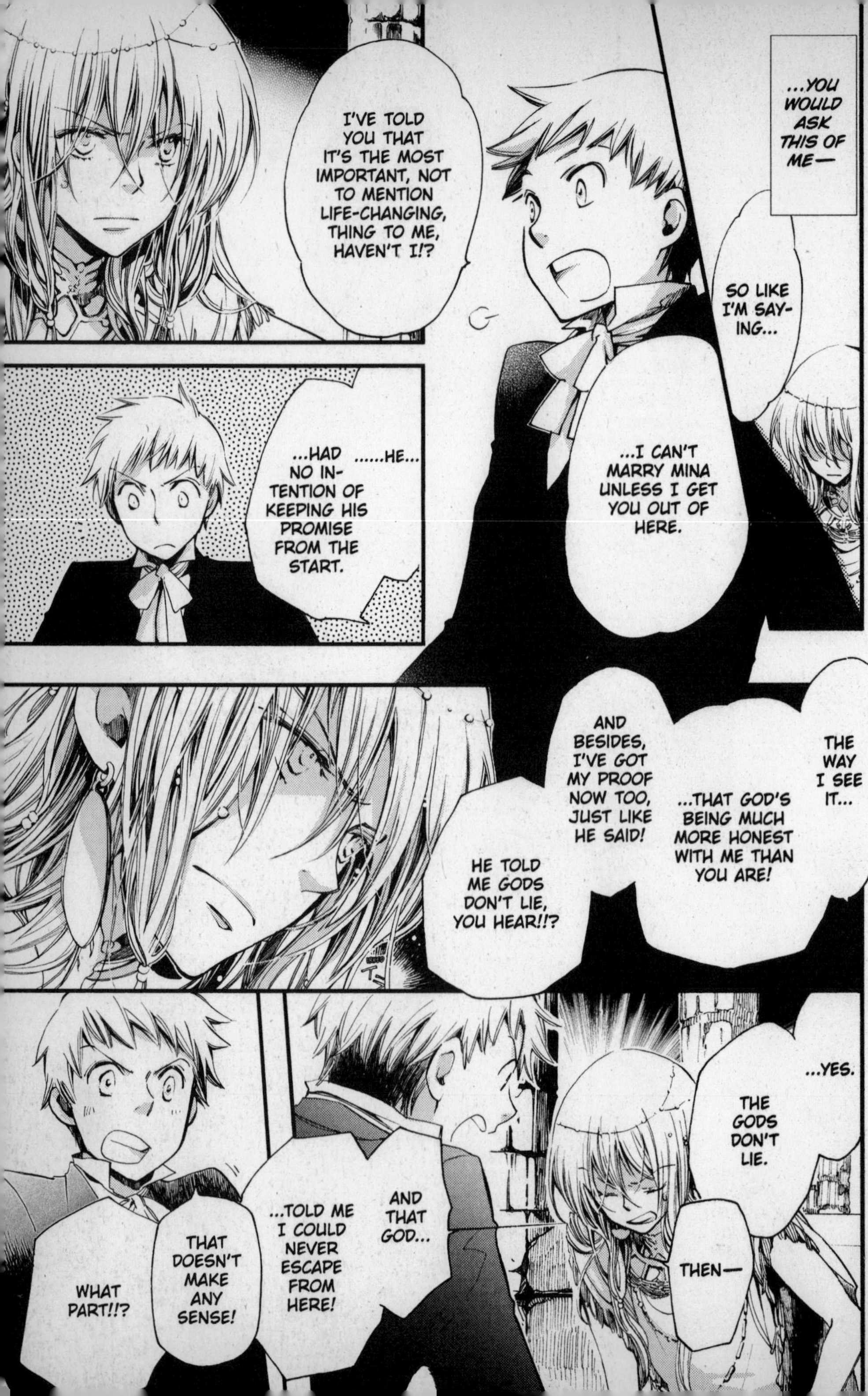
...YOU WOULD ASK THIS OF ME—
I'VE TOLD YOU THAT IT'S THE MOST IMPORTANT, NOT TO MENTION LIFE-CHANGING, THING TO ME, HAVEN'T I!?
SO LIKE I'M SAY-ING...
...I CAN'T MARRY MINA UNLESS I GET YOU OUT OF HERE.
......HE...
...HAD NO IN-TENTION OF KEEPING HIS PROMISE FROM THE START.
THE WAY I SEE IT...
...THAT GOD'S BEING MUCH MORE HONEST WITH ME THAN YOU ARE!
AND BESIDES, I'VE GOT MY PROOF NOW TOO, JUST LIKE HE SAID!
HE TOLD ME GODS DON'T LIE, YOU HEAR!!?
...YES.
THE GODS DON'T LIE.
THEN—
AND THAT GOD...
...TOLD ME I COULD NEVER ESCAPE FROM HERE!
THAT DOESN'T MAKE ANY SENSE!
WHAT PART!!?

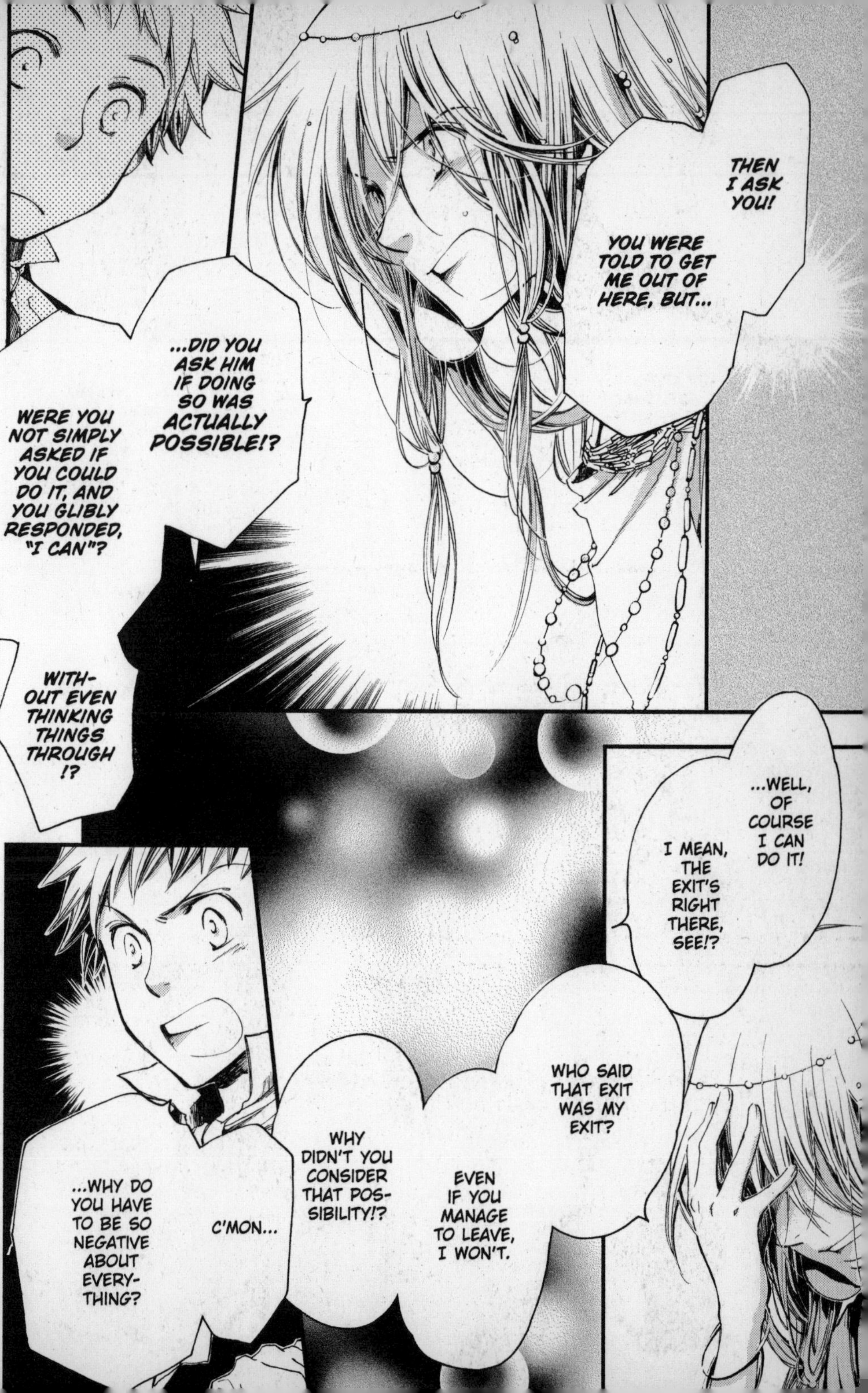
THEN I ASK YOU!
YOU WERE TOLD TO GET ME OUT OF HERE, BUT...
...DID YOU ASK HIM IF DOING SO WAS ACTUALLY POSSIBLE!?
WERE YOU NOT SIMPLY ASKED IF YOU COULD DO IT, AND YOU GLIBLY RESPONDED, "I CAN"?
WITH-OUT EVEN THINKING THINGS THROUGH!?
...WELL, OF COURSE I CAN DO IT!
I MEAN, THE EXIT'S RIGHT THERE, SEE!?
WHO SAID THAT EXIT WAS MY EXIT?
EVEN IF YOU MANAGE TO LEAVE, I WON'T.
WHY DIDN'T YOU CONSIDER THAT POS-SIBILITY!?
C'MON...
...WHY DO YOU HAVE TO BE SO NEGATIVE ABOUT EVERY-THING?

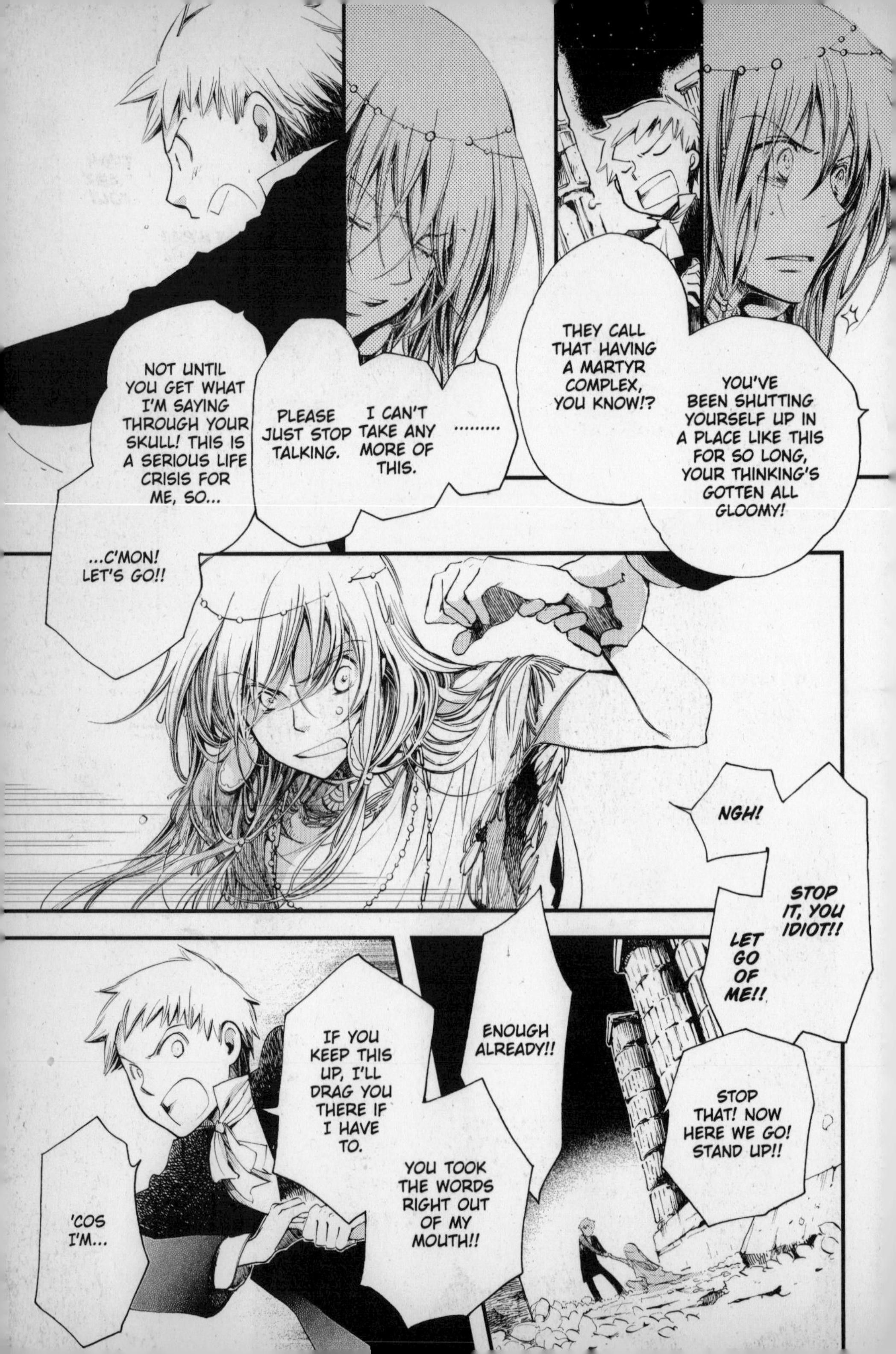
YOU'VE BEEN SHUTTING YOURSELF UP IN A PLACE LIKE THIS FOR SO LONG, YOUR THINKING'S GOTTEN ALL GLOOMY!
THEY CALL THAT HAVING A MARTYR COMPLEX, YOU KNOW!?
....
I CAN'T TAKE ANY MORE OF THIS.
PLEASE JUST STOP TALKING.
NOT UNTIL YOU GET WHAT I'M SAYING THROUGH YOUR SKULL! THIS IS A SERIOUS LIFE CRISIS FOR ME, SO...
...C'MON! LET'S GO!!
NGH!
STOP IT, YOU IDIOT!!
LET GO OF ME!!
STOP THAT! NOW HERE WE GO! STAND UP!!
ENOUGH ALREADY!!
IF YOU KEEP THIS UP, I'LL DRAG YOU THERE IF I HAVE TO.
YOU TOOK THE WORDS RIGHT OUT OF MY MOUTH!!
'COS I'M...

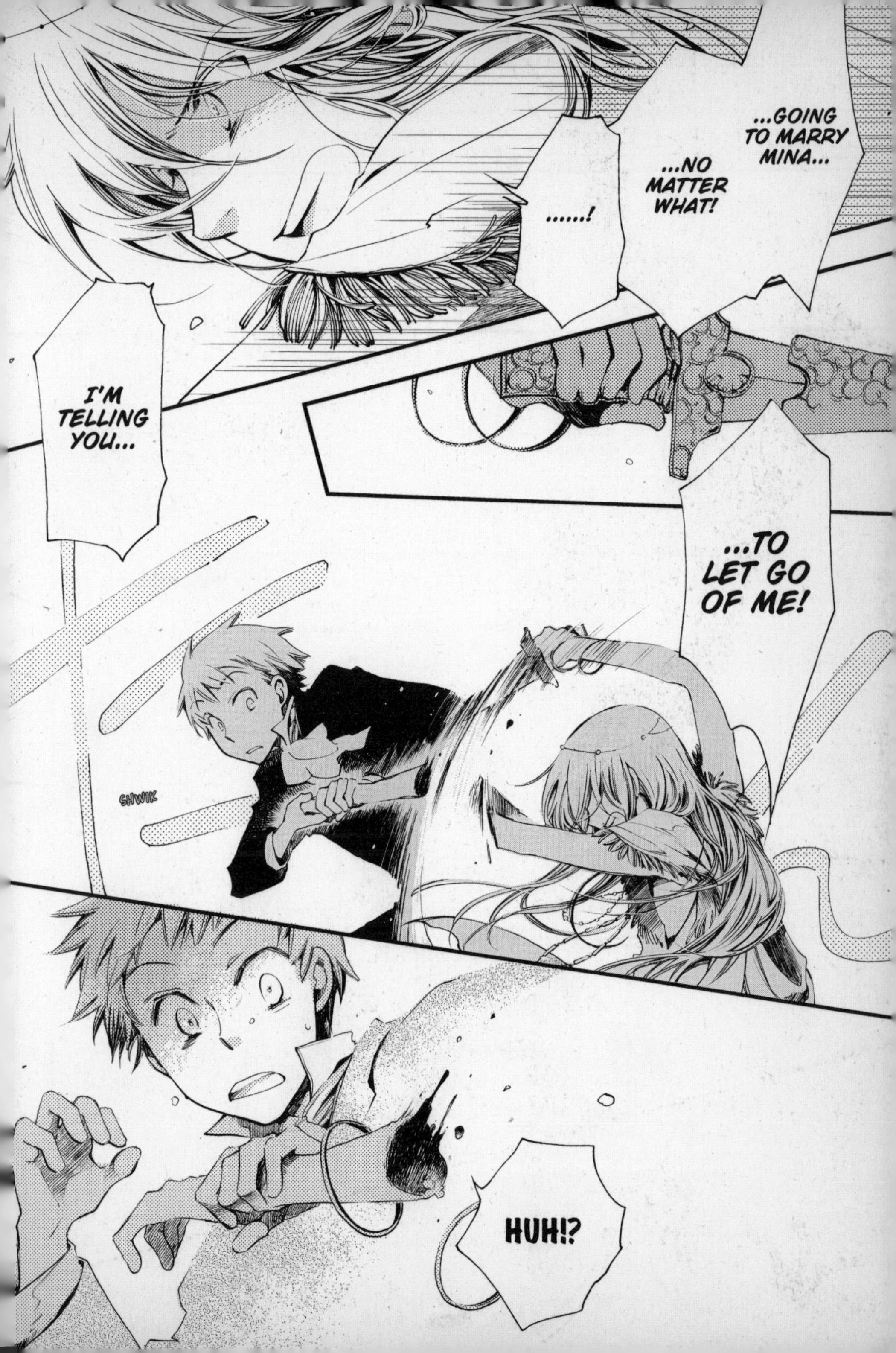
...GOING TO MARRY MINA...
...NO MATTER WHAT!
......!
I'M TELLING YOU...
...TO LET GO OF ME!
SHWIK
HUH!?

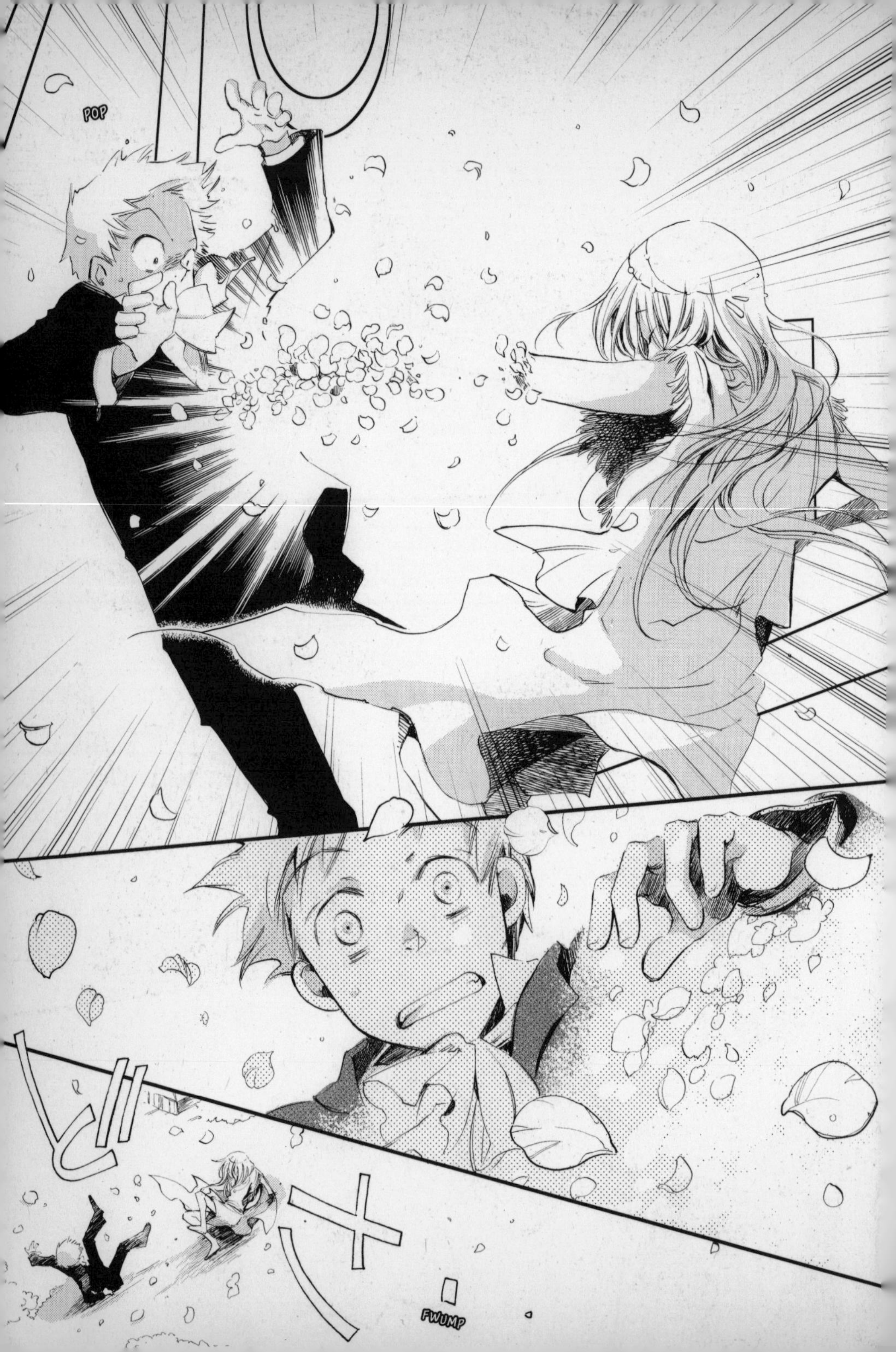
POP
FWUMP

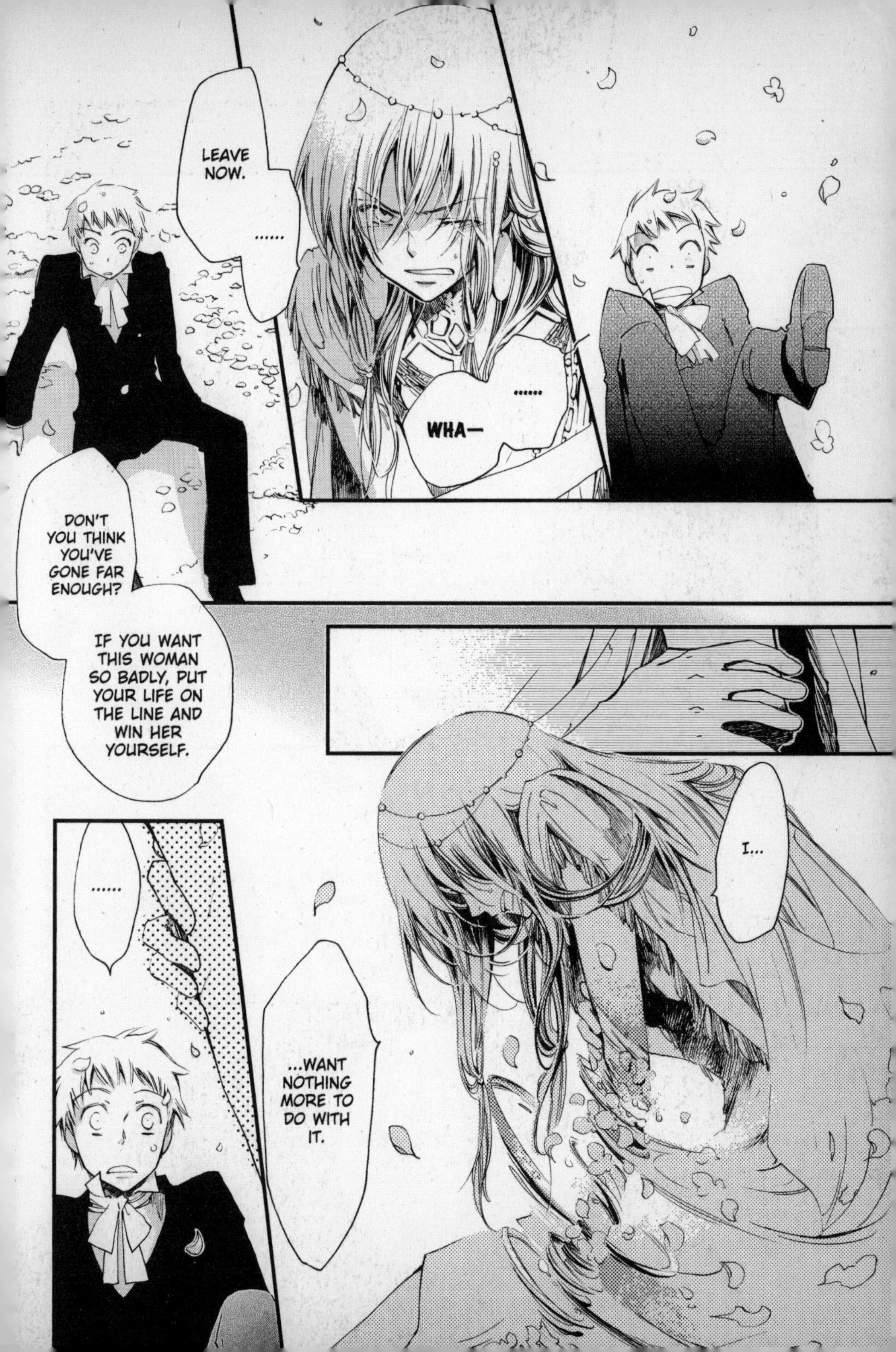
......
WHA—
LEAVE NOW.
......
DON'T YOU THINK YOU'VE GONE FAR ENOUGH?
IF YOU WANT THIS WOMAN SO BADLY, PUT YOUR LIFE ON THE LINE AND WIN HER YOURSELF.
I...
...WANT NOTHING MORE TO DO WITH IT.
......

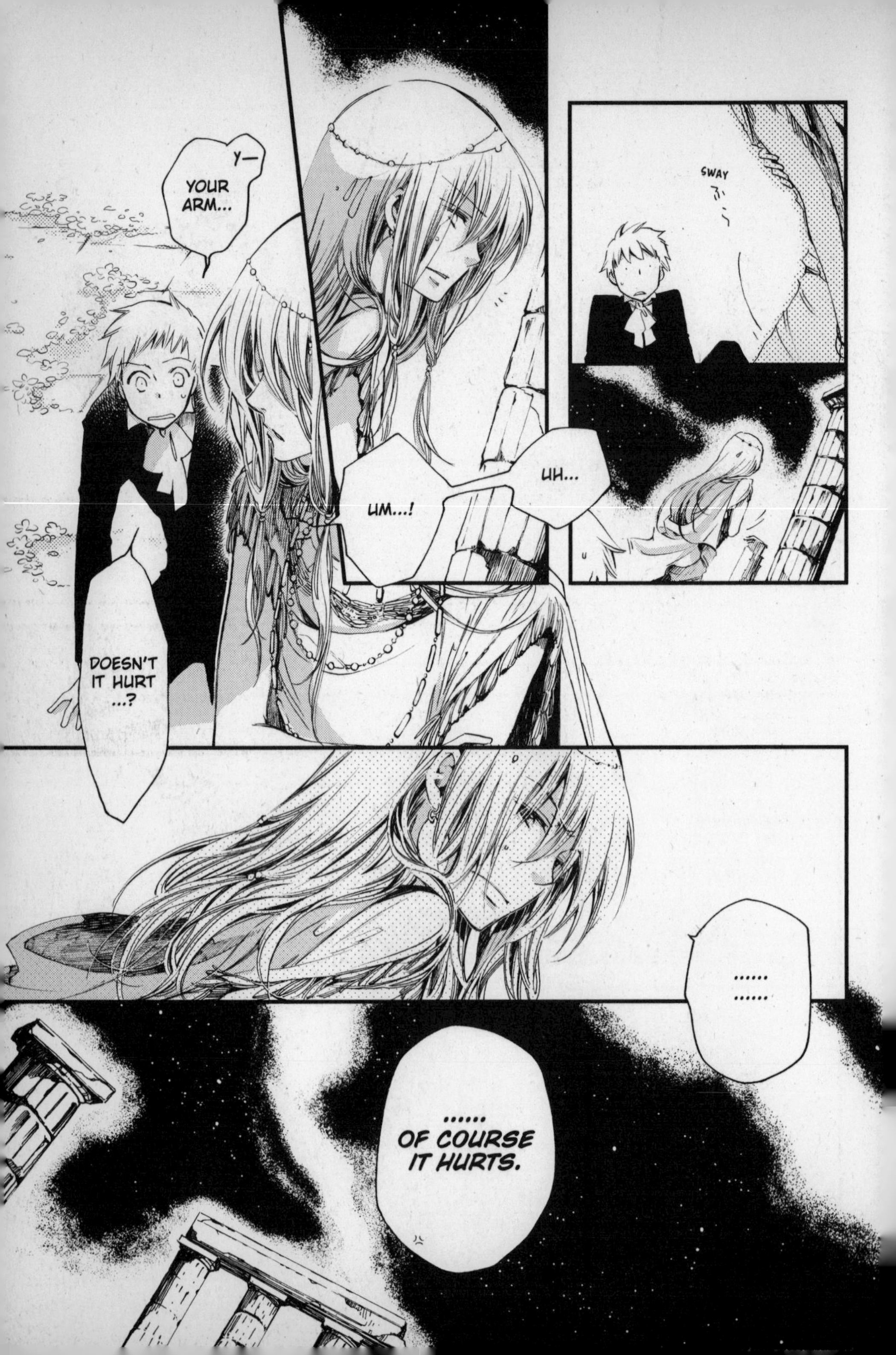
SWAY
UH...
UM...!
Y— YOUR ARM...
DOESN'T IT HURT ...?
....
...... OF COURSE IT HURTS.

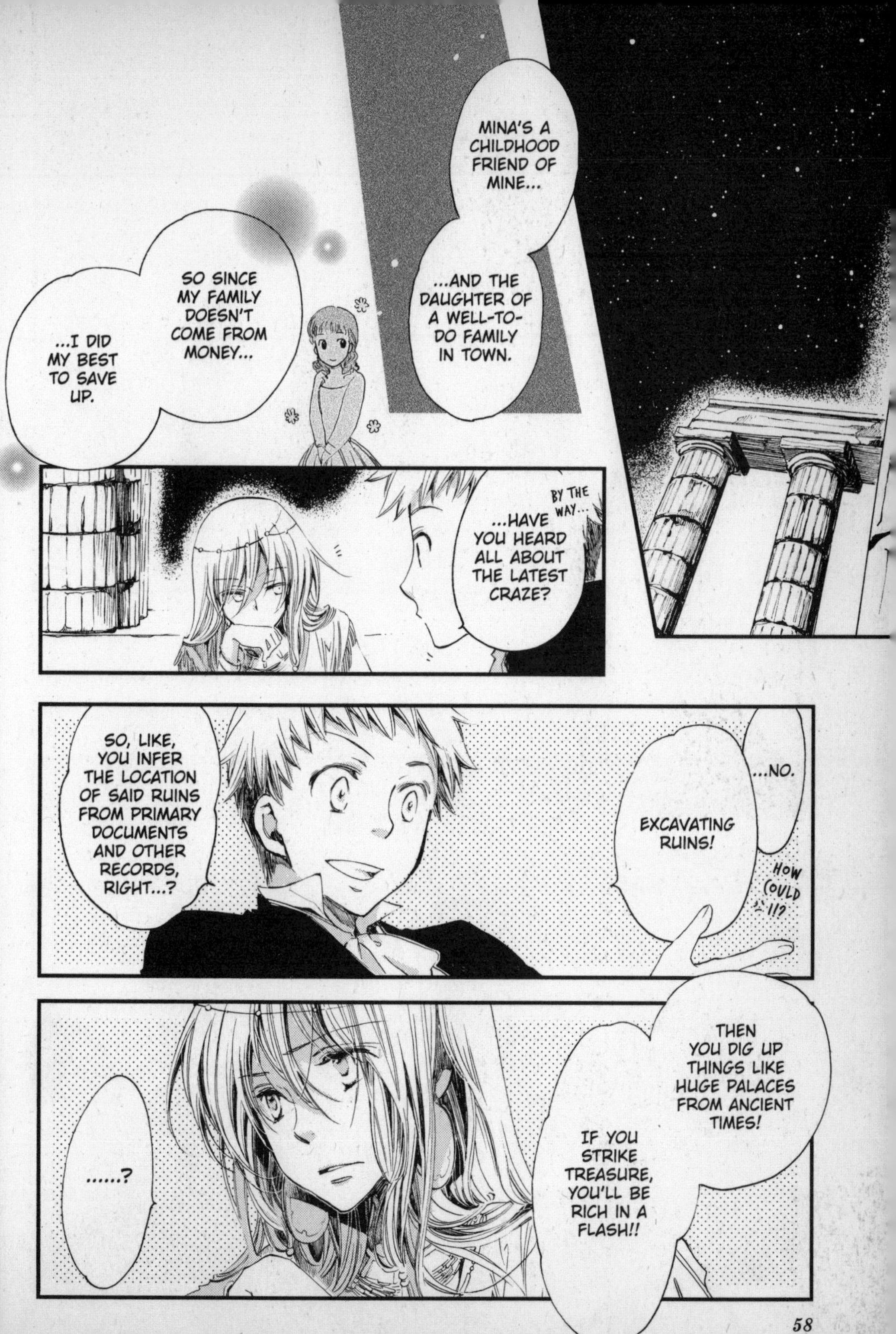
MINA'S A CHILDHOOD FRIEND OF MINE...
...AND THE DAUGHTER OF A WELL-TO-DO FAMILY IN TOWN.
SO SINCE MY FAMILY DOESN'T COME FROM MONEY...
...I DID MY BEST TO SAVE UP.
BY THE WAY...
...HAVE YOU HEARD ALL ABOUT THE LATEST CRAZE?
...NO.
EXCAVATING RUINS!
HOW COULD !!?
SO, LIKE, YOU INFER THE LOCATION OF SAID RUINS FROM PRIMARY DOCUMENTS AND OTHER RECORDS, RIGHT...?
THEN YOU DIG UP THINGS LIKE HUGE PALACES FROM ANCIENT TIMES!
IF YOU STRIKE TREASURE, YOU'LL BE RICH IN A FLASH!!
......?

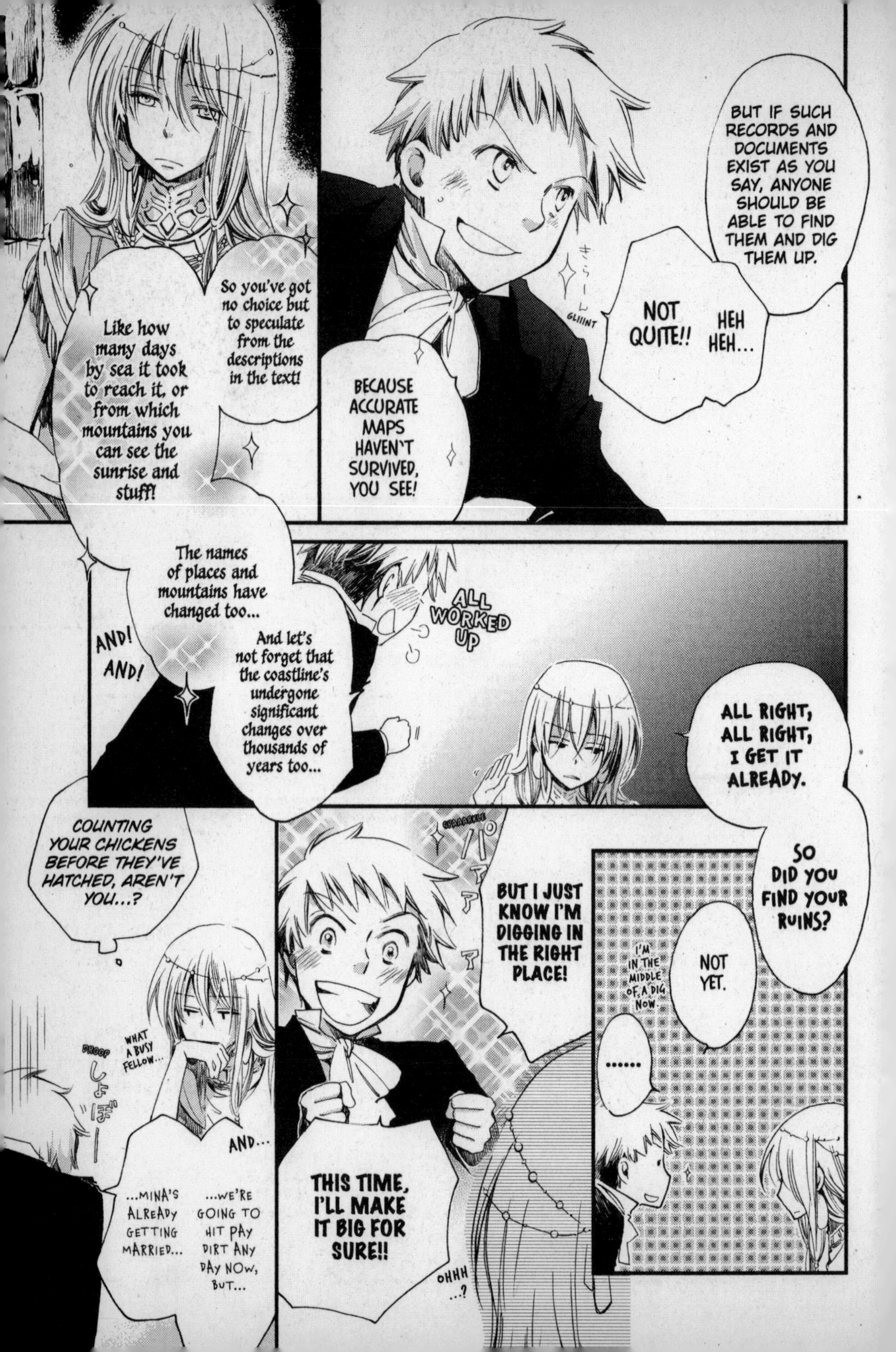
BUT IF SUCH RECORDS AND DOCUMENTS EXIST AS YOU SAY, ANYONE SHOULD BE ABLE TO FIND THEM AND DIG THEM UP.
HEH HEH...
NOT QUITE!!
GLIIINT
BECAUSE ACCURATE MAPS HAVEN'T SURVIVED, YOU SEE!
So you've got no choice but to speculate from the descriptions in the text!
Like how many days by sea it took to reach it, or from which mountains you can see the sunrise and stuff!
The names of places and mountains have changed too...
AND! AND!
And let's not forget that the coastline's undergone significant changes over thousands of years too...
ALL WORKED UP
ALL RIGHT, ALL RIGHT, I GET IT ALREADY.
SO DID YOU FIND YOUR RUINS?
NOT YET.
I'M IN THE MIDDLE OF A DIG NOW.
......
CHAAARKLE
BUT I JUST KNOW I'M DIGGING IN THE RIGHT PLACE!
THIS TIME, I'LL MAKE IT BIG FOR SURE!!
OHHH ...?
COUNTING YOUR CHICKENS BEFORE THEY'VE HATCHED, AREN'T YOU...?
WHAT A BUSY FELLOW...
DROOP
AND...
...WE'RE GOING TO HIT PAY DIRT ANY DAY NOW, BUT...
...MINA'S ALREADY GETTING MARRIED...

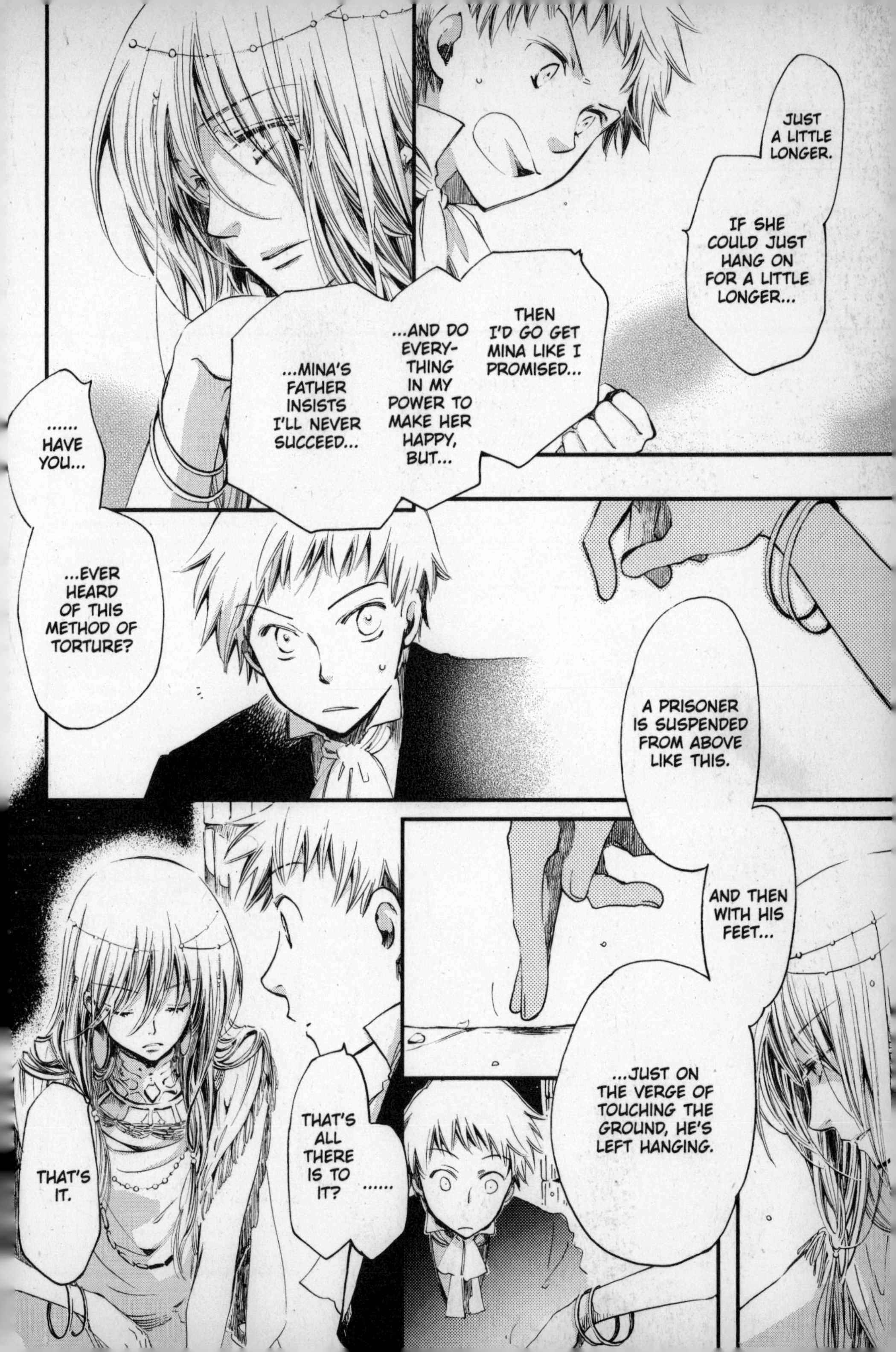
JUST A LITTLE LONGER.
IF SHE COULD JUST HANG ON FOR A LITTLE LONGER...
THEN I'D GO GET MINA LIKE I PROMISED...
...AND DO EVERY-THING IN MY POWER TO MAKE HER HAPPY, BUT...
...MINA'S FATHER INSISTS I'LL NEVER SUCCEED...
...... HAVE YOU...
...EVER HEARD OF THIS METHOD OF TORTURE?
A PRISONER IS SUSPENDED FROM ABOVE LIKE THIS.
AND THEN WITH HIS FEET...
...JUST ON THE VERGE OF TOUCHING THE GROUND, HE'S LEFT HANGING.
......
THAT'S ALL THERE IS TO IT?
THAT'S IT.

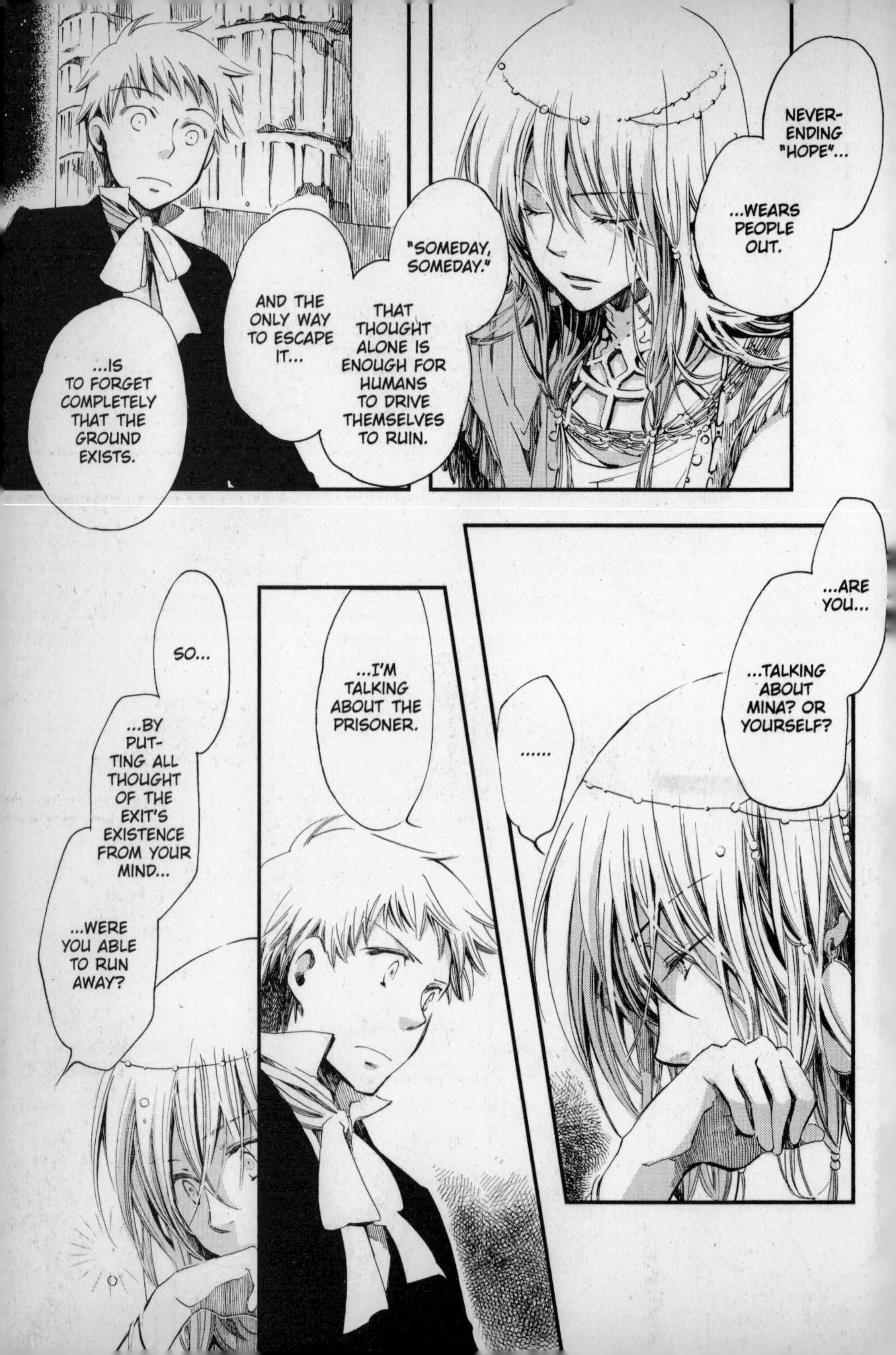
NEVER-ENDING "HOPE"...
...WEARS PEOPLE OUT.
"SOMEDAY, SOMEDAY."
THAT THOUGHT ALONE IS ENOUGH FOR HUMANS TO DRIVE THEMSELVES TO RUIN.
AND THE ONLY WAY TO ESCAPE IT...
...IS TO FORGET COMPLETELY THAT THE GROUND EXISTS.
...ARE YOU...
...TALKING ABOUT MINA? OR YOURSELF?
......
...I'M TALKING ABOUT THE PRISONER.
SO...
...BY PUT-TING ALL THOUGHT OF THE EXIT'S EXISTENCE FROM YOUR MIND...
...WERE YOU ABLE TO RUN AWAY?

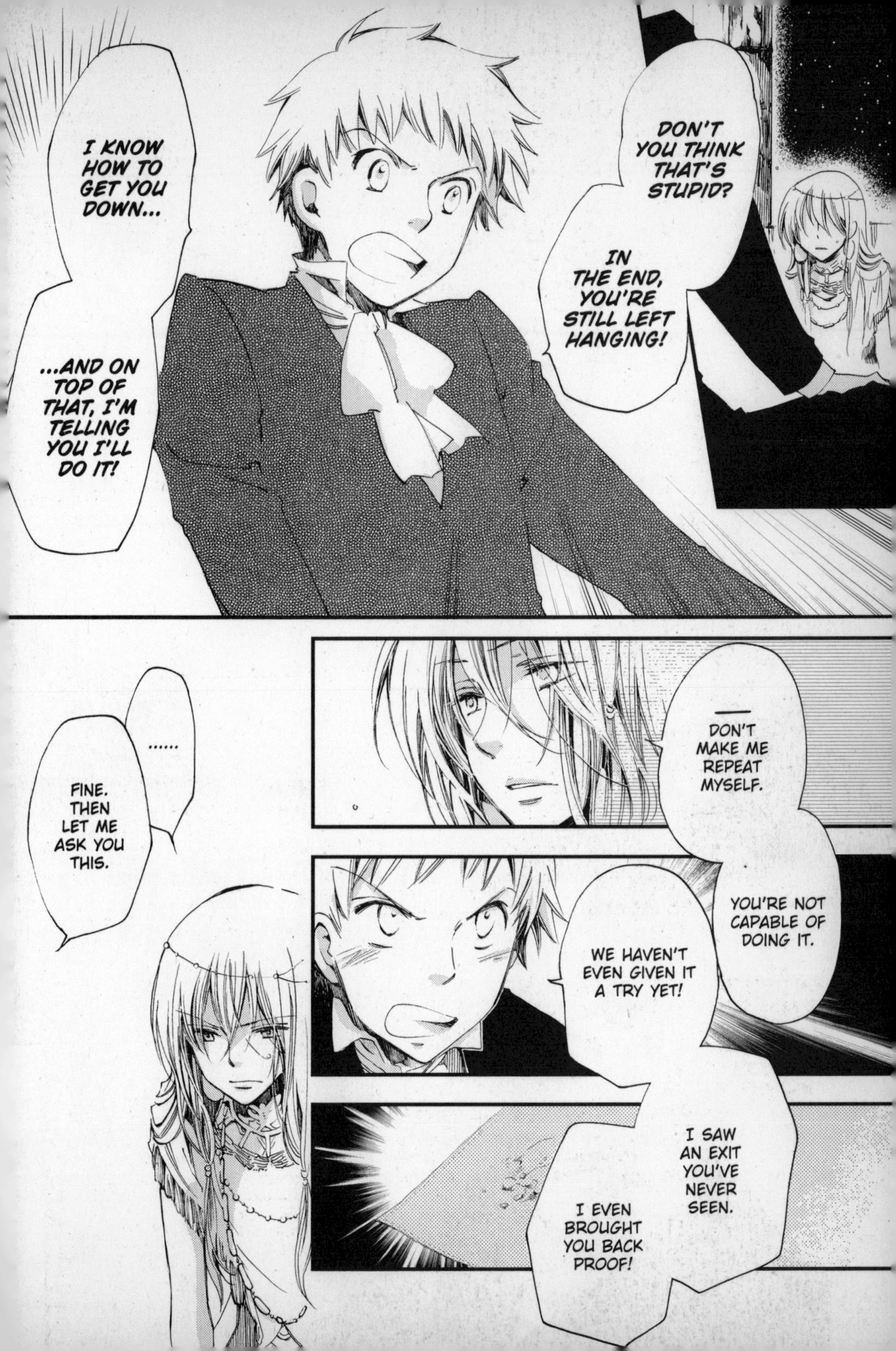
DON'T YOU THINK THAT'S STUPID?
IN THE END, YOU'RE STILL LEFT HANGING!
I KNOW HOW TO GET YOU DOWN...
...AND ON TOP OF THAT, I'M TELLING YOU I'LL DO IT!
— DON'T MAKE ME REPEAT MYSELF.
YOU'RE NOT CAPABLE OF DOING IT.
WE HAVEN'T EVEN GIVEN IT A TRY YET!
I SAW AN EXIT YOU'VE NEVER SEEN.
I EVEN BROUGHT YOU BACK PROOF!
......
FINE. THEN LET ME ASK YOU THIS.

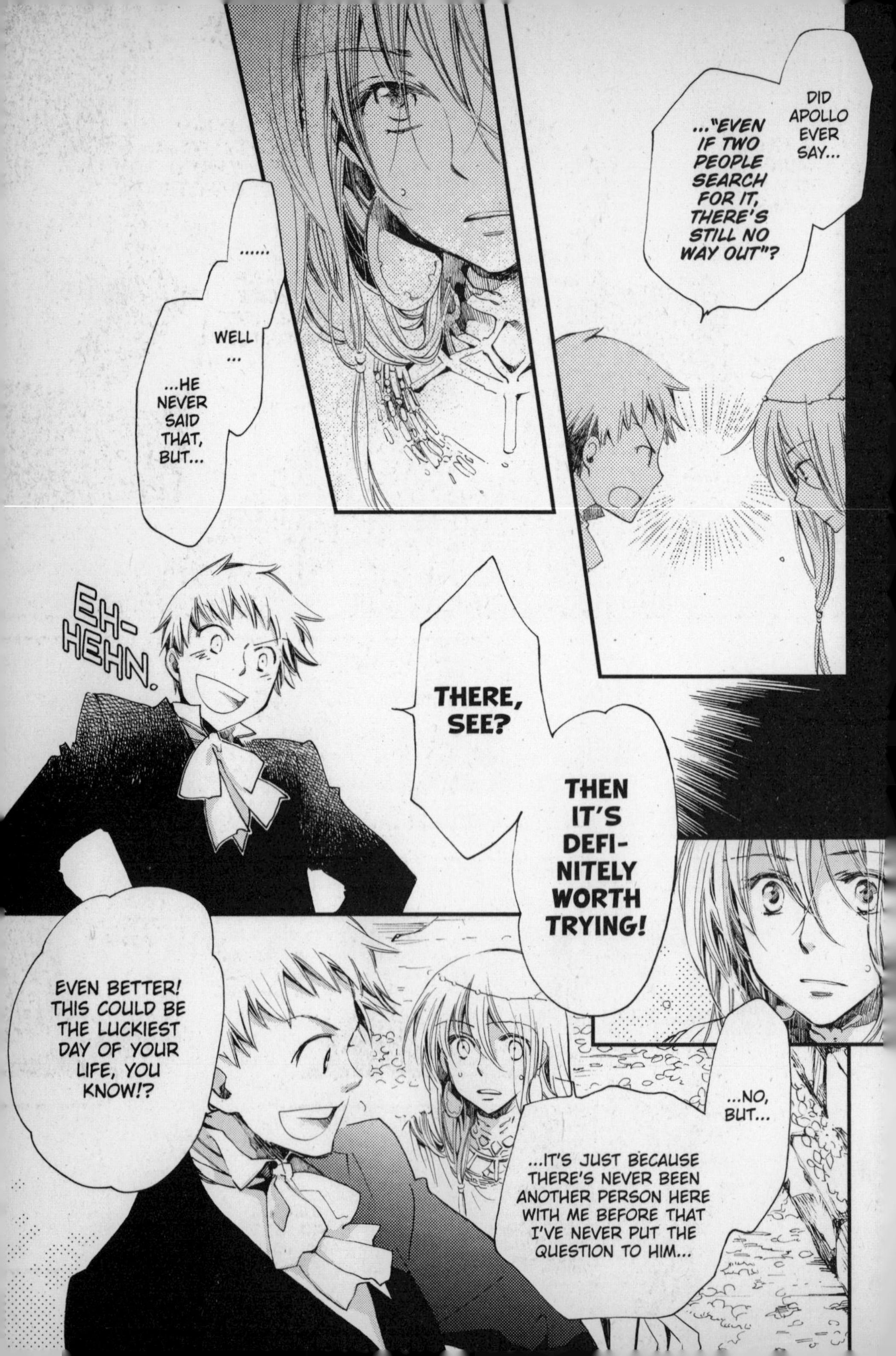
DID APOLLO EVER SAY...
..."EVEN IF TWO PEOPLE SEARCH FOR IT, THERE'S STILL NO WAY OUT"?
......
WELL ...
...HE NEVER SAID THAT, BUT...
THERE, SEE?
EH-HEHN.
THEN IT'S DEFI-NITELY WORTH TRYING!
...NO, BUT...
...IT'S JUST BECAUSE THERE'S NEVER BEEN ANOTHER PERSON HERE WITH ME BEFORE THAT I'VE NEVER PUT THE QUESTION TO HIM...
EVEN BETTER! THIS COULD BE THE LUCKIEST DAY OF YOUR LIFE, YOU KNOW!?

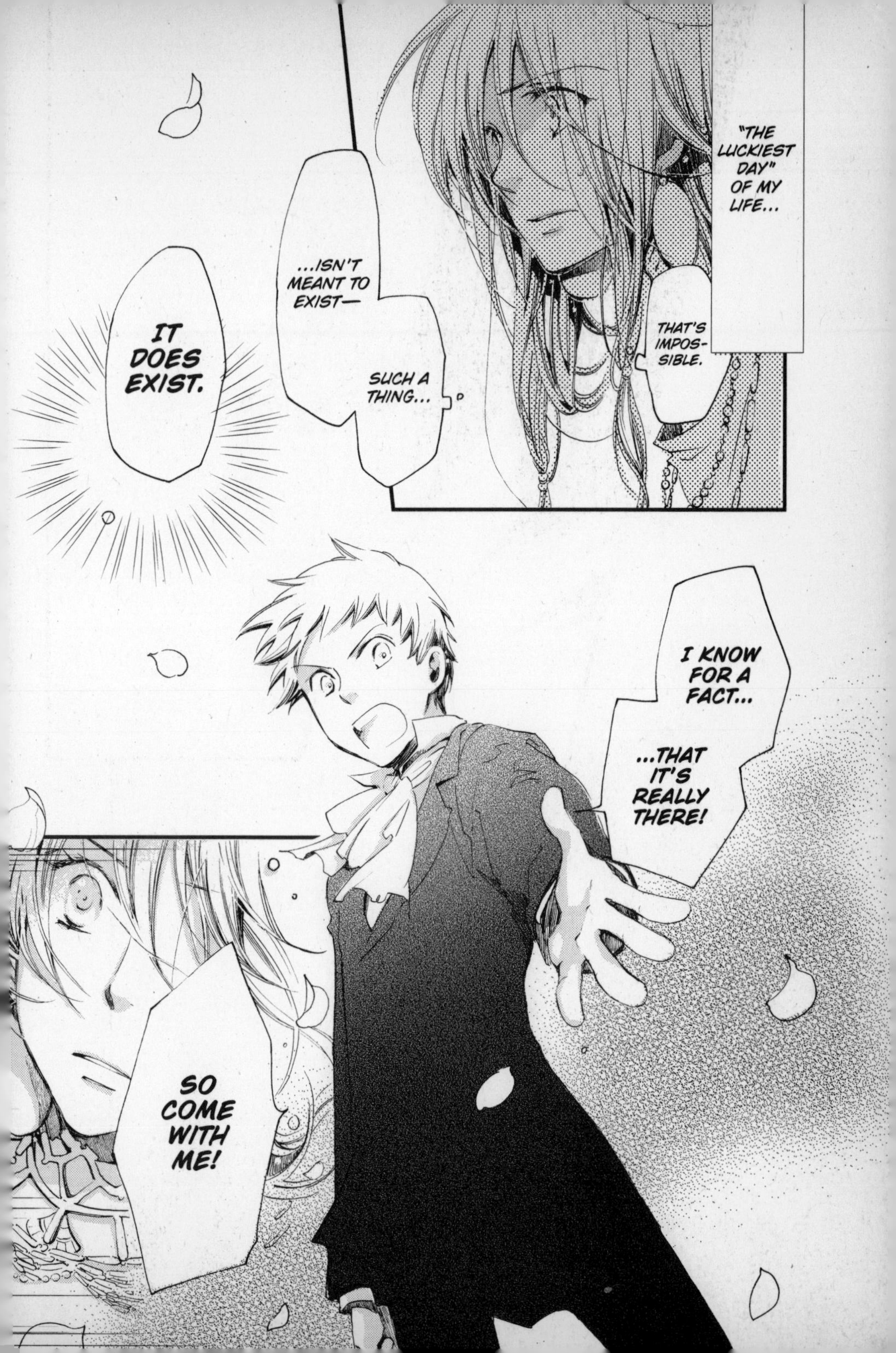
"THE LUCKIEST DAY" OF MY LIFE...
THAT'S IMPOSSIBLE.
SUCH A THING...
...ISN'T MEANT TO EXIST—
IT DOES EXIST.
I KNOW FOR A FACT...
...THAT IT'S REALLY THERE!
SO COME WITH ME!

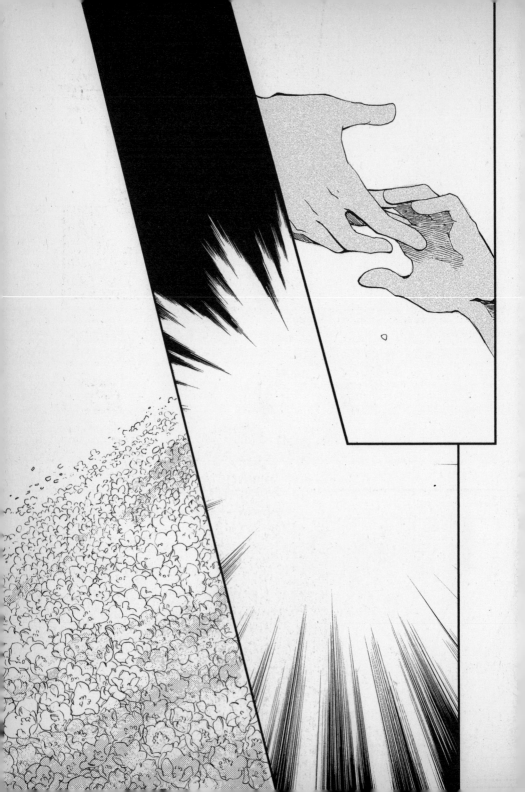

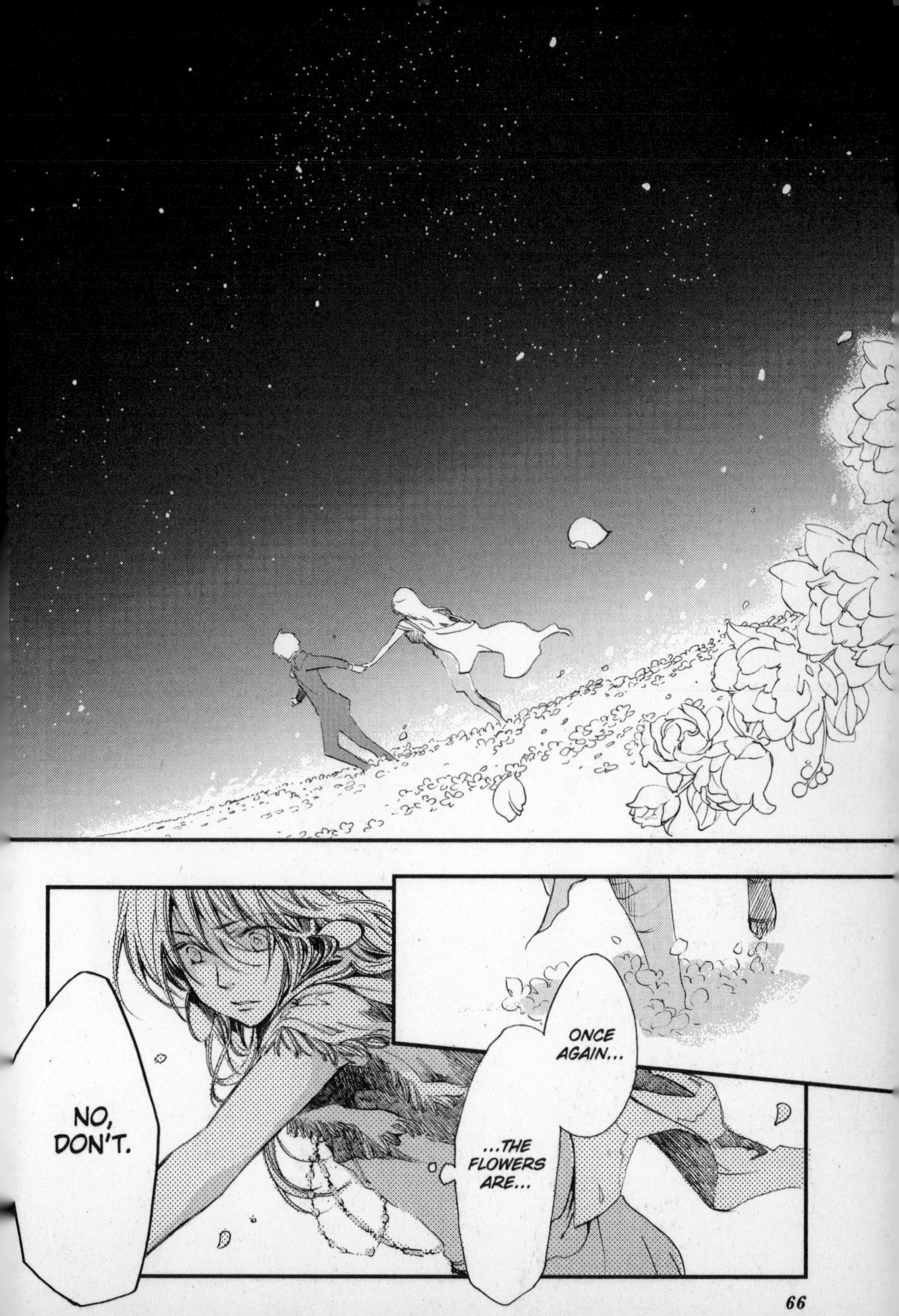
ONCE AGAIN...
...THE FLOWERS ARE...
NO, DON'T.

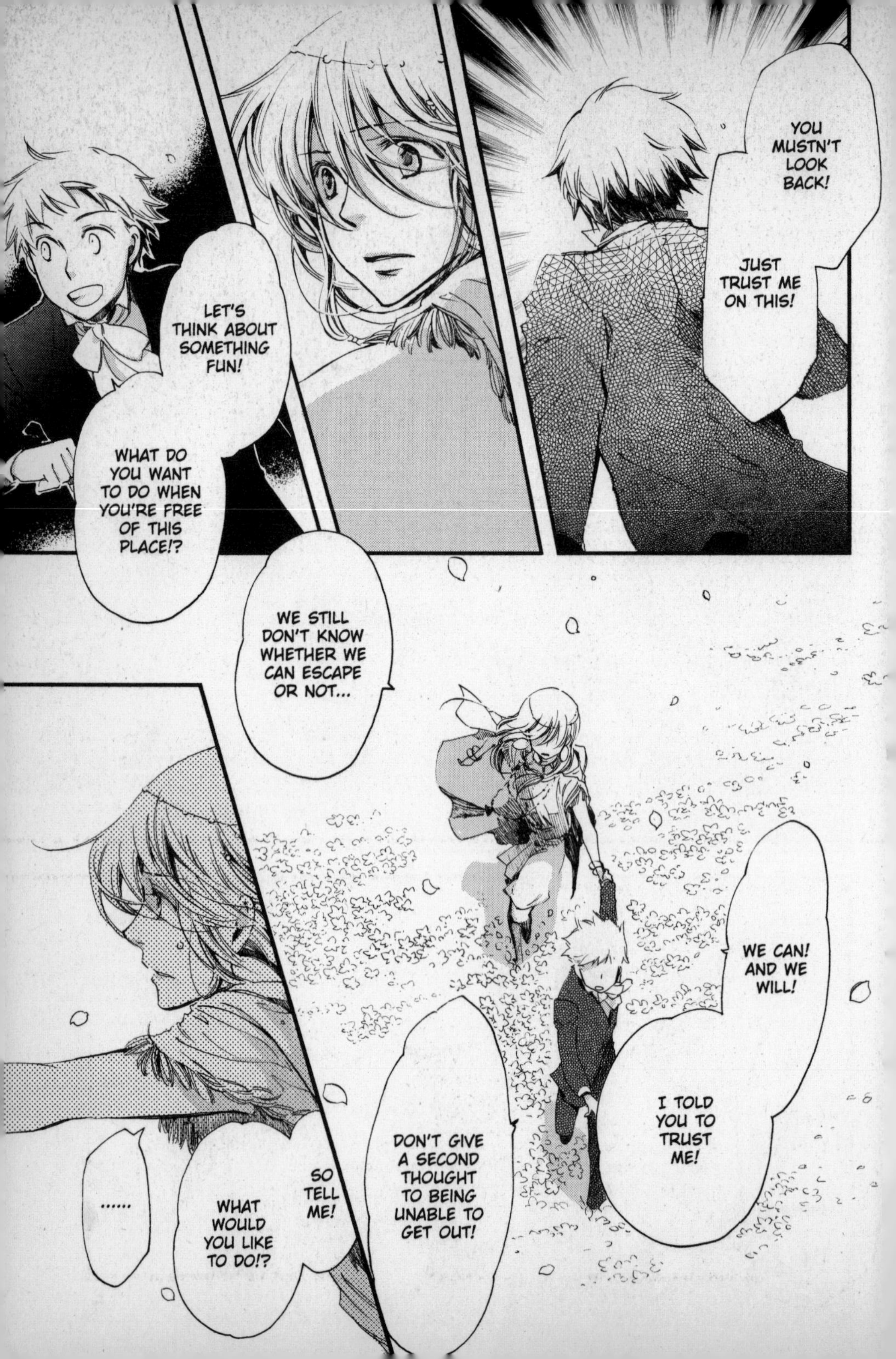
YOU MUSTN'T LOOK BACK!
JUST TRUST ME ON THIS!
LET'S THINK ABOUT SOMETHING FUN!
WHAT DO YOU WANT TO DO WHEN YOU'RE FREE OF THIS PLACE!?
WE STILL DON'T KNOW WHETHER WE CAN ESCAPE OR NOT...
WE CAN! AND WE WILL!
I TOLD YOU TO TRUST ME!
DON'T GIVE A SECOND THOUGHT TO BEING UNABLE TO GET OUT!
SO TELL ME!
WHAT WOULD YOU LIKE TO DO!?
......

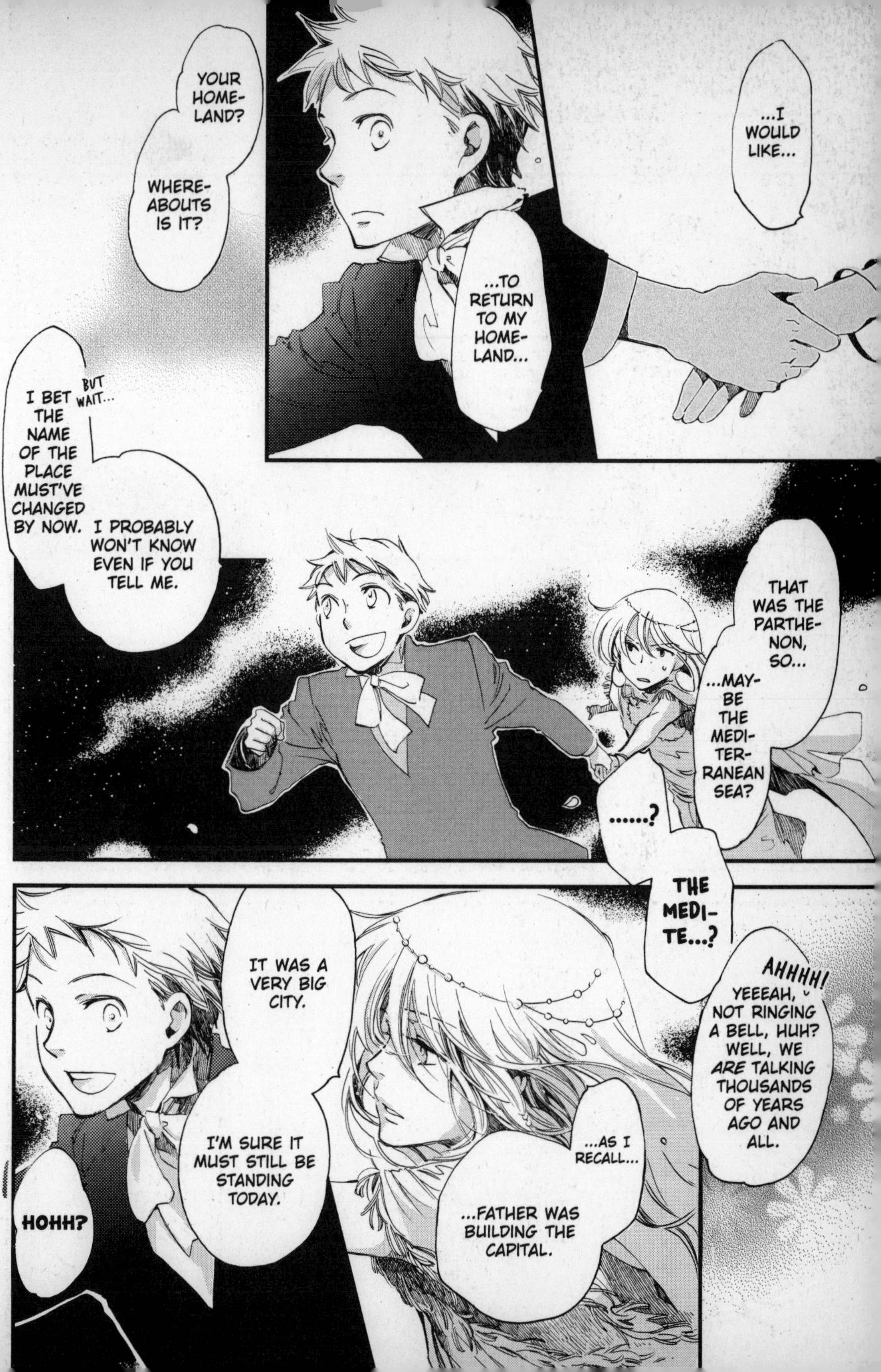
...I WOULD LIKE...
...TO RETURN TO MY HOMELAND...
YOUR HOMELAND?
WHEREABOUTS IS IT?
I BET THE NAME OF THE PLACE MUST'VE CHANGED BY NOW.
BUT WAIT...
I PROBABLY WON'T KNOW EVEN IF YOU TELL ME.
THAT WAS THE PARTHENON, SO...
...MAYBE THE MEDITERRANEAN SEA?
......?
THE MEDITE...?
AHHHH!
YEEEAH, NOT RINGING A BELL, HUH? WELL, WE *ARE* TALKING THOUSANDS OF YEARS AGO AND ALL.
...AS I RECALL...
...FATHER WAS BUILDING THE CAPITAL.
IT WAS A VERY BIG CITY.
I'M SURE IT MUST STILL BE STANDING TODAY.
HOHH?

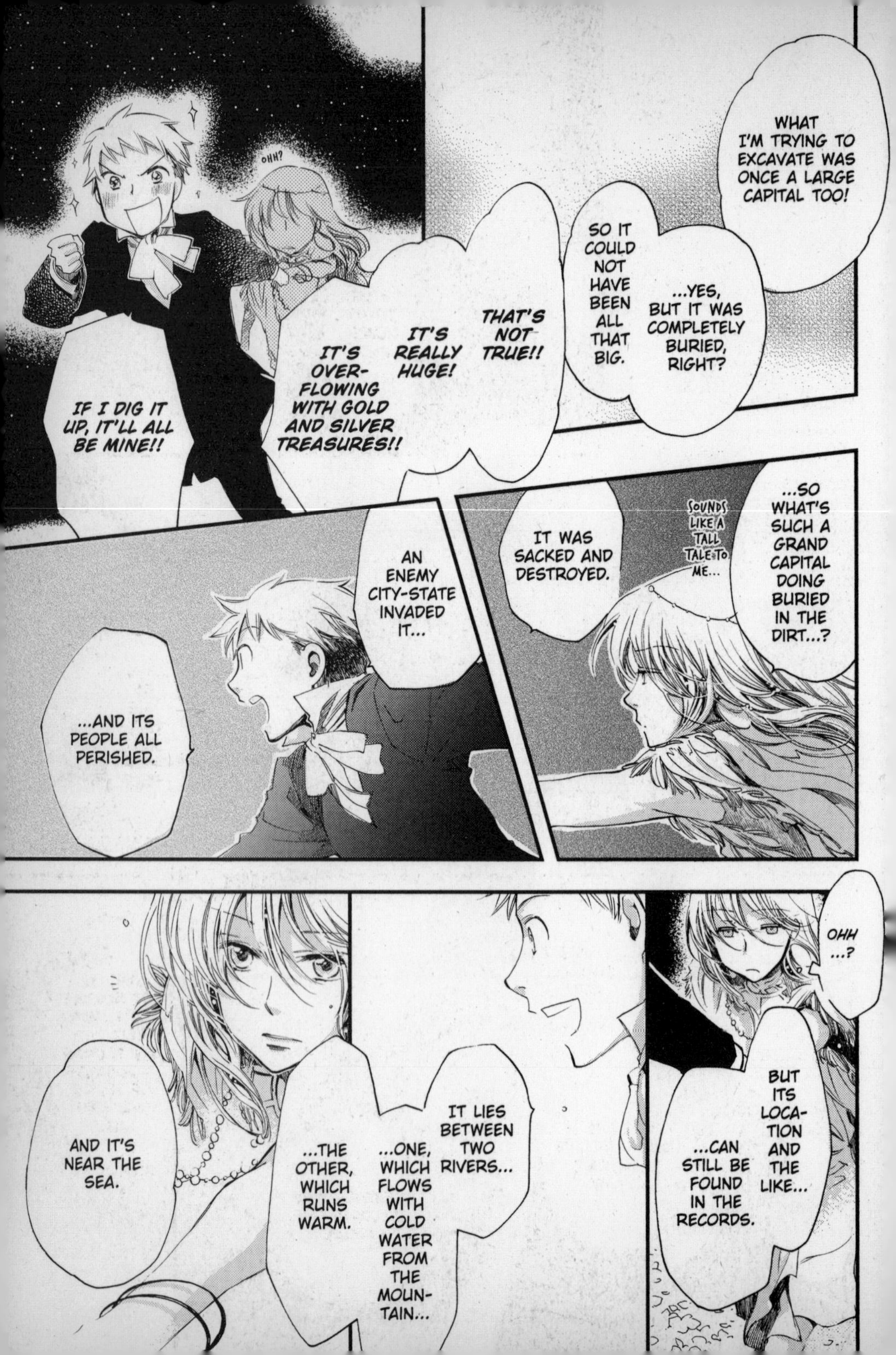

WHAT I'M TRYING TO EXCAVATE WAS ONCE A LARGE CAPITAL TOO!
...YES, BUT IT WAS COMPLETELY BURIED, RIGHT?
SO IT COULD NOT HAVE BEEN ALL THAT BIG.
THAT'S NOT TRUE!!
IT'S REALLY HUGE!
IT'S OVER-FLOWING WITH GOLD AND SILVER TREASURES!!
OHH?
IF I DIG IT UP, IT'LL ALL BE MINE!!
...SO WHAT'S SUCH A GRAND CAPITAL DOING BURIED IN THE DIRT...?
SOUNDS LIKE A TALL TALE TO ME...
IT WAS SACKED AND DESTROYED.
AN ENEMY CITY-STATE INVADED IT...
...AND ITS PEOPLE ALL PERISHED.
OHH ...?
BUT ITS LOCA-TION AND THE LIKE...
...CAN STILL BE FOUND IN THE RECORDS.
IT LIES BETWEEN TWO RIVERS...
...ONE, WHICH FLOWS WITH COLD WATER FROM THE MOUN-TAIN...
...THE OTHER, WHICH RUNS WARM.
AND IT'S NEAR THE SEA.

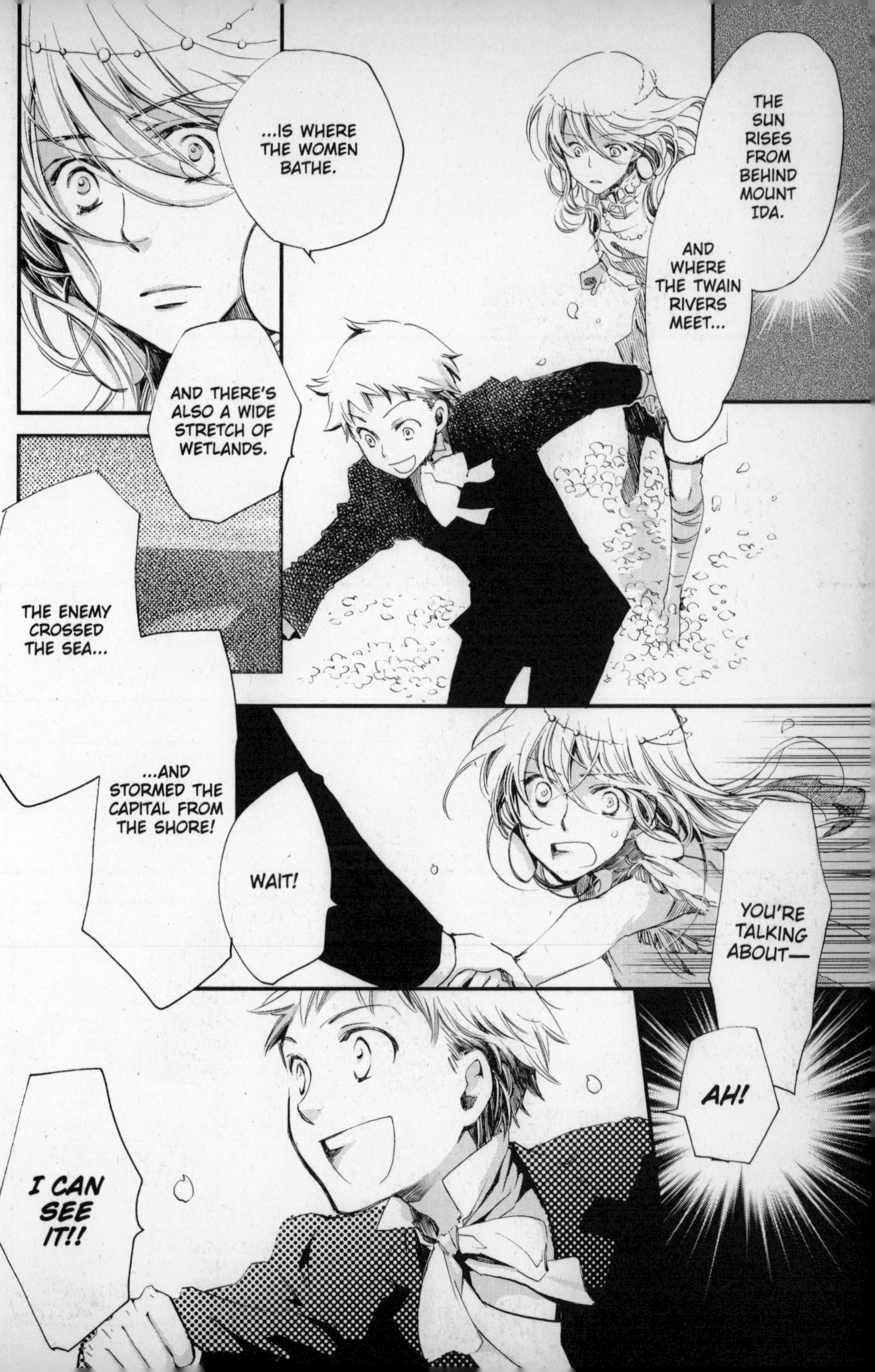
THE SUN RISES FROM BEHIND MOUNT IDA.
AND WHERE THE TWAIN RIVERS MEET...
...IS WHERE THE WOMEN BATHE.
AND THERE'S ALSO A WIDE STRETCH OF WETLANDS.
THE ENEMY CROSSED THE SEA...
...AND STORMED THE CAPITAL FROM THE SHORE!
WAIT!
YOU'RE TALKING ABOUT—
AH!
I CAN SEE IT!!

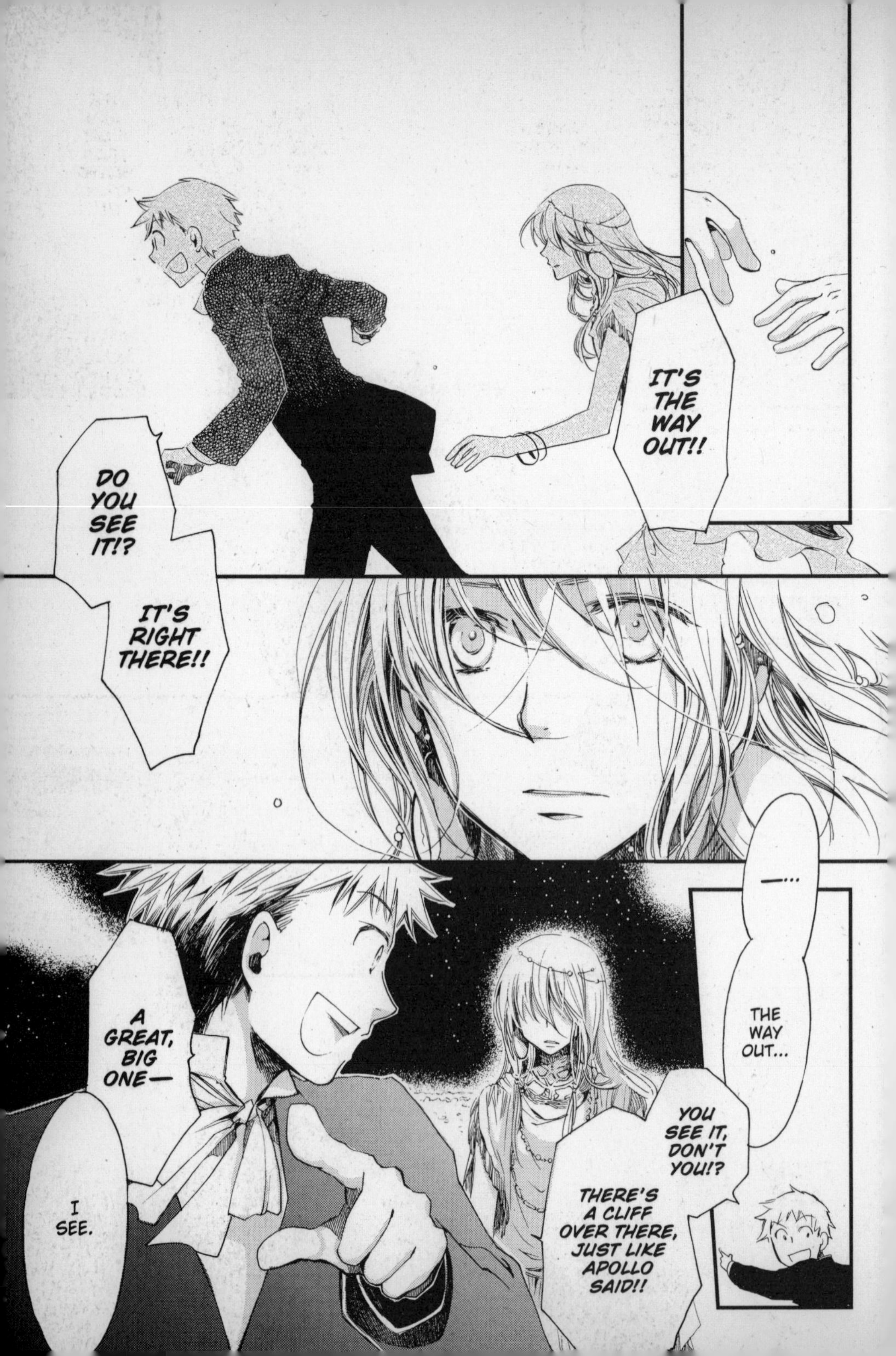
IT'S THE WAY OUT!!
DO YOU SEE IT!?
IT'S RIGHT THERE!!
—...
THE WAY OUT...
YOU SEE IT, DON'T YOU!?
THERE'S A CLIFF OVER THERE, JUST LIKE APOLLO SAID!!
A GREAT, BIG ONE—
I SEE.

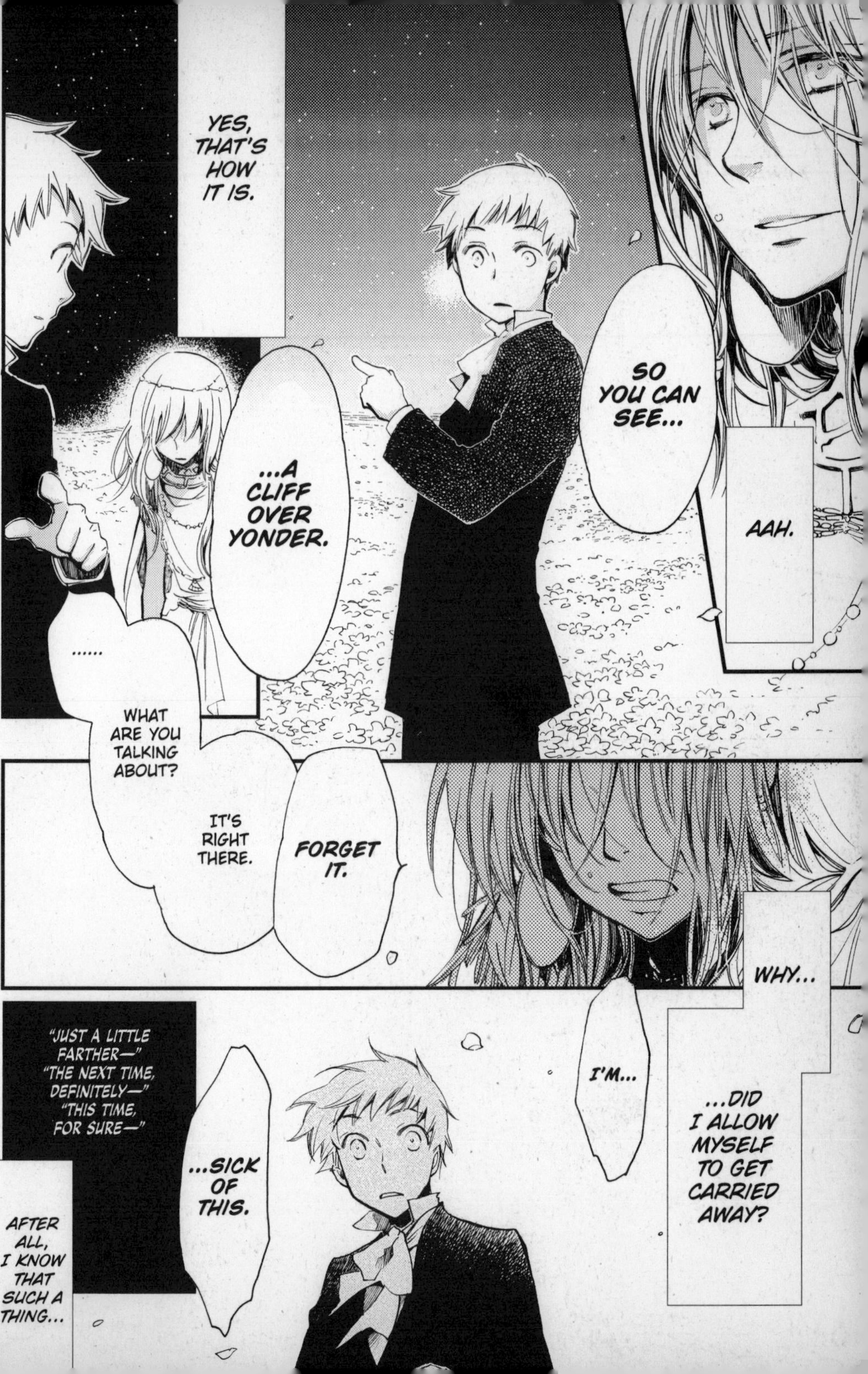
SO YOU CAN SEE...
AAH.
...A CLIFF OVER YONDER.
YES, THAT'S HOW IT IS.
......
WHAT ARE YOU TALKING ABOUT?
IT'S RIGHT THERE.
WHY...
FORGET IT.
...DID I ALLOW MYSELF TO GET CARRIED AWAY?
I'M...
...SICK OF THIS.
"JUST A LITTLE FARTHER—" "THE NEXT TIME, DEFINITELY—" "THIS TIME, FOR SURE—"
AFTER ALL, I KNOW THAT SUCH A THING...

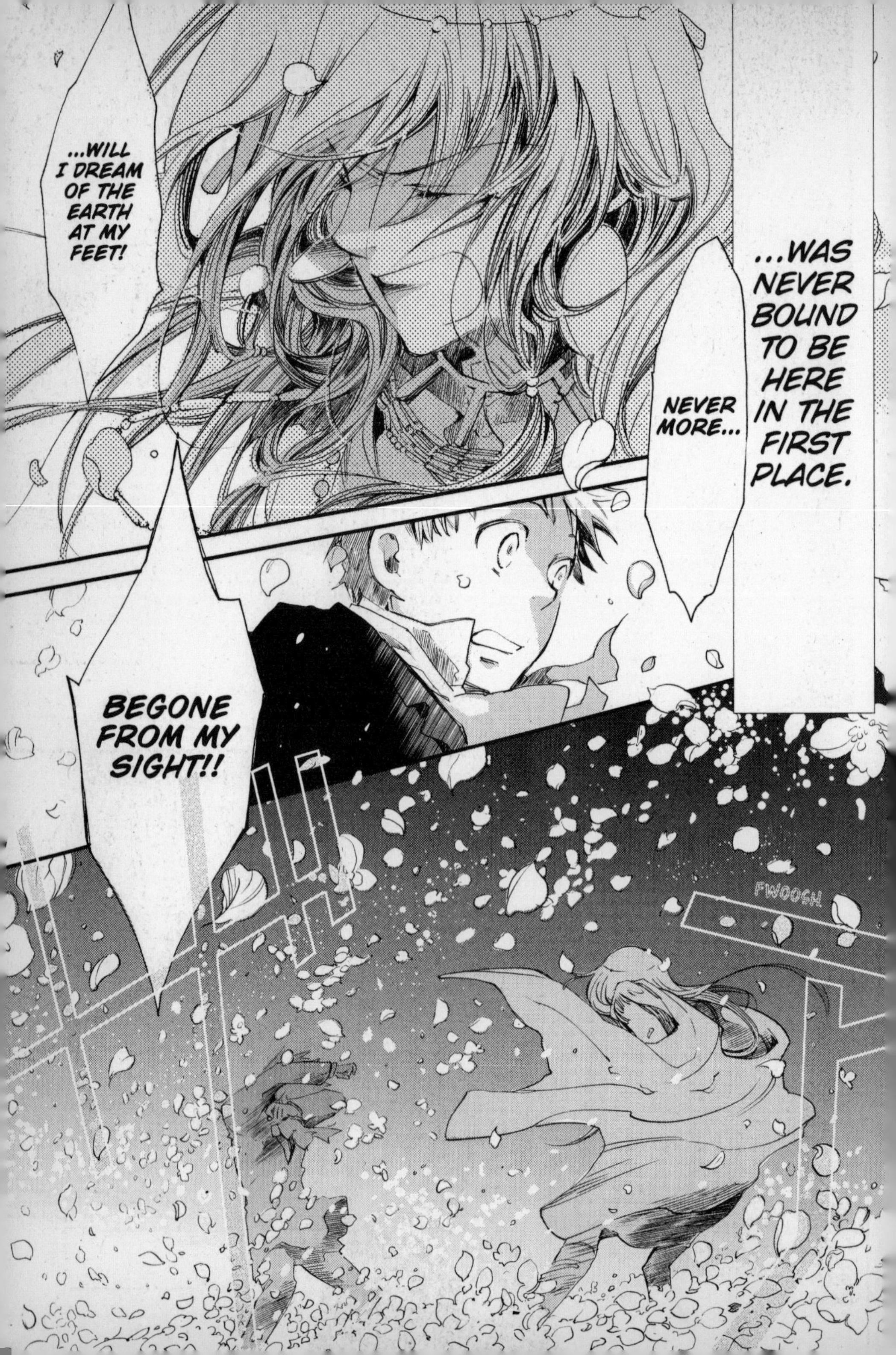
...WAS NEVER BOUND TO BE HERE IN THE FIRST PLACE.
NEVER MORE...
...WILL I DREAM OF THE EARTH AT MY FEET!
BEGONE FROM MY SIGHT!!
FWOOSH

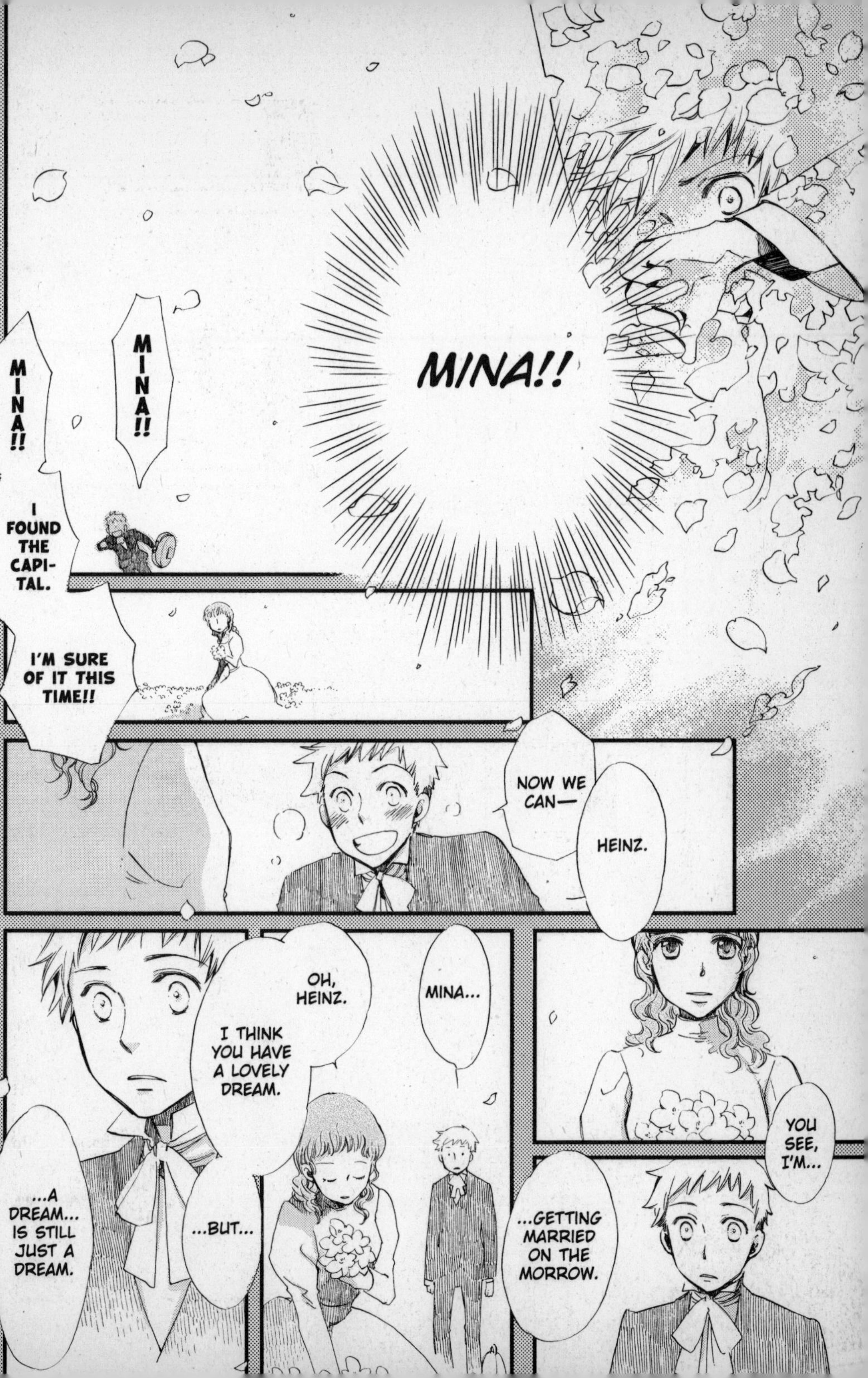
MINA!!
MINA!!
MINA!!
I FOUND THE CAPITAL.
I'M SURE OF IT THIS TIME!!
NOW WE CAN—
HEINZ.
YOU SEE, I'M...
...GETTING MARRIED ON THE MORROW.
MINA...
OH, HEINZ.
I THINK YOU HAVE A LOVELY DREAM.
...BUT...
...A DREAM... IS STILL JUST A DREAM.

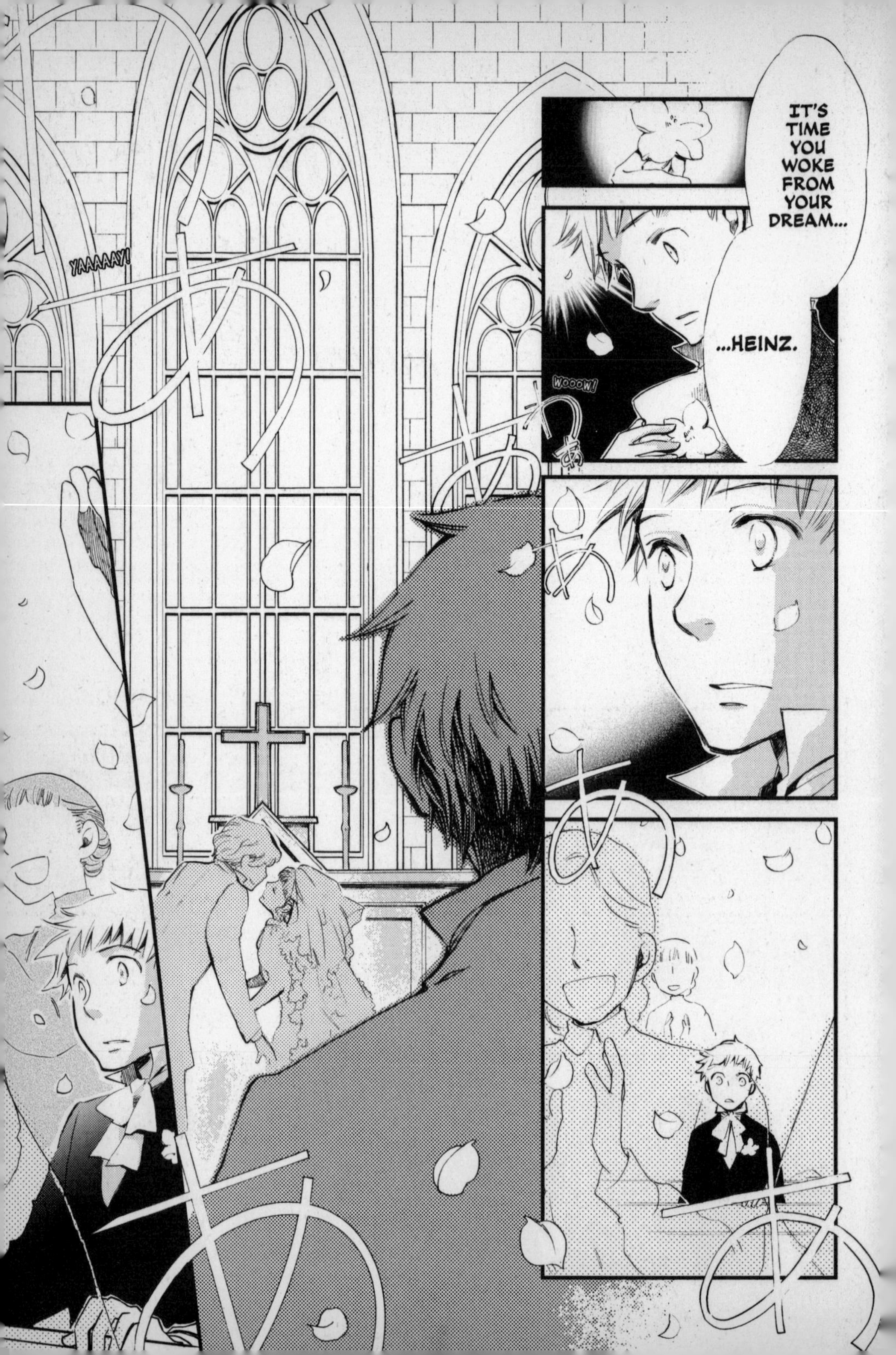
IT'S TIME YOU WOKE FROM YOUR DREAM...
...HEINZ.
WOOOW!
YAAAAAY!

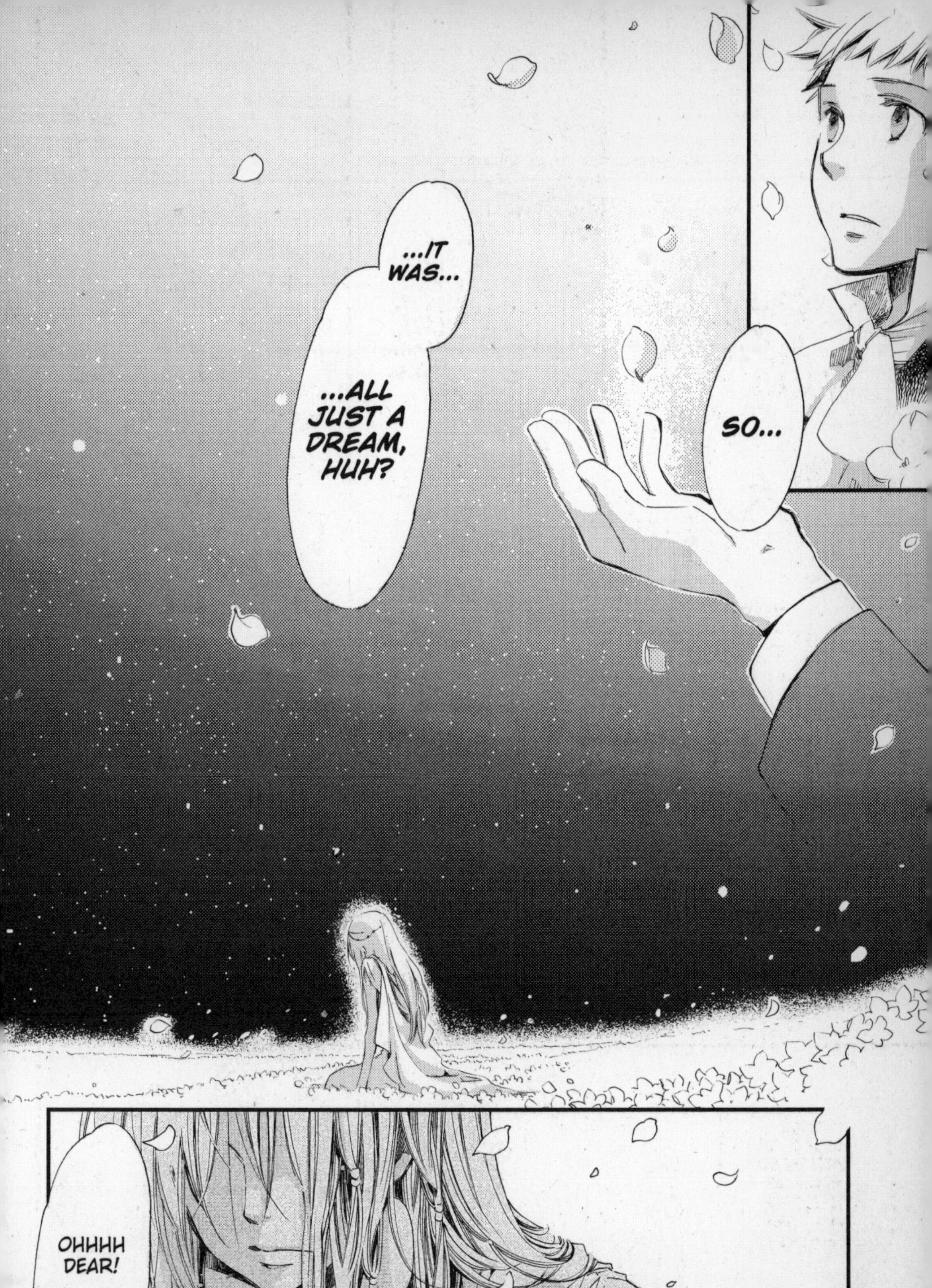
SO...
...IT WAS...
...ALL JUST A DREAM, HUH?
OHHHH DEAR!

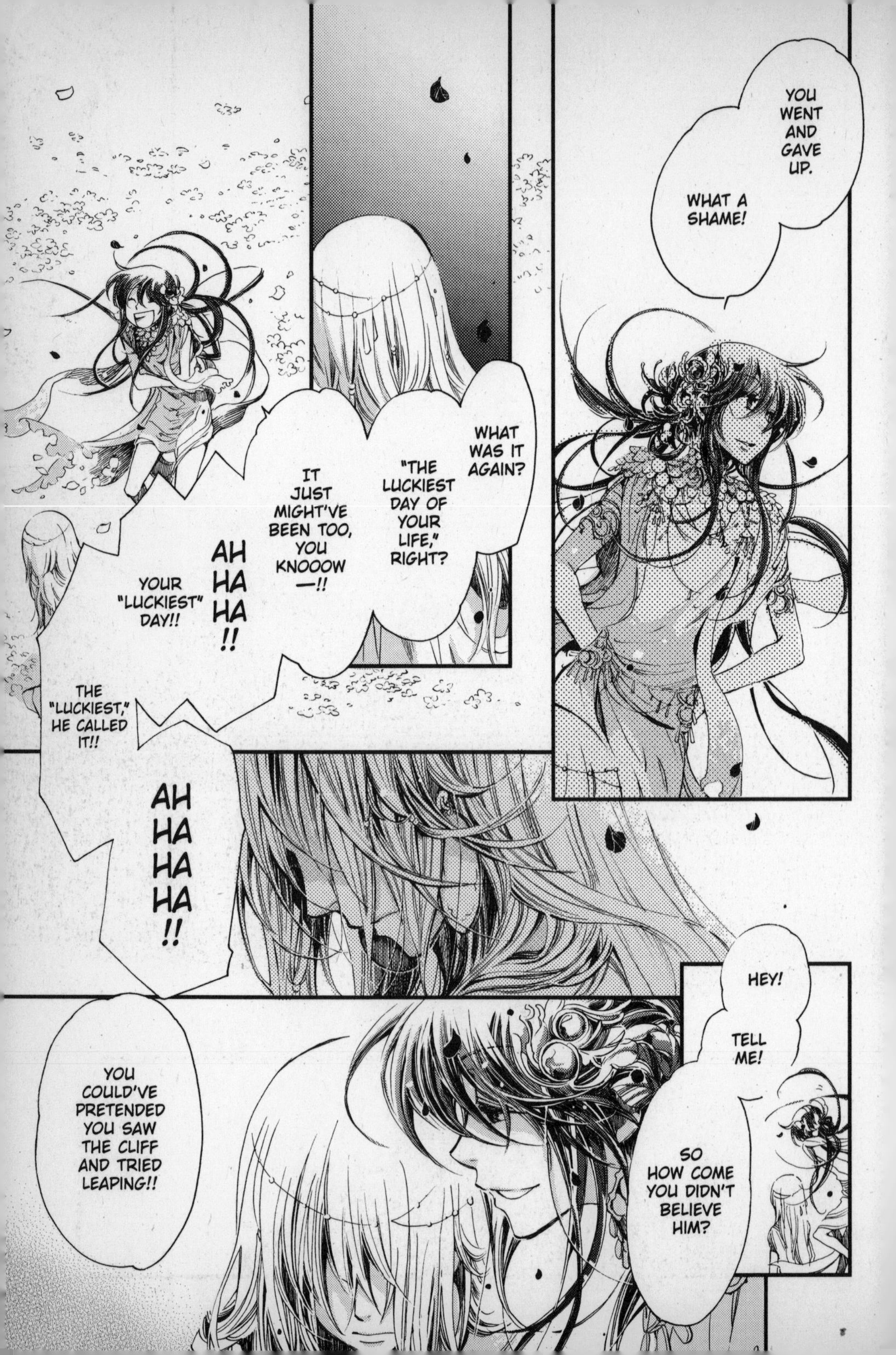
YOU WENT AND GAVE UP.
WHAT A SHAME!
WHAT WAS IT AGAIN?
"THE LUCKIEST DAY OF YOUR LIFE," RIGHT?
IT JUST MIGHT'VE BEEN TOO, YOU KNOOOW—!!
AH HA HA!!
YOUR "LUCKIEST" DAY!!
THE "LUCKIEST," HE CALLED IT!!
AH HA HA HA!!
HEY!
TELL ME!
SO HOW COME YOU DIDN'T BELIEVE HIM?
YOU COULD'VE PRETENDED YOU SAW THE CLIFF AND TRIED LEAPING!!

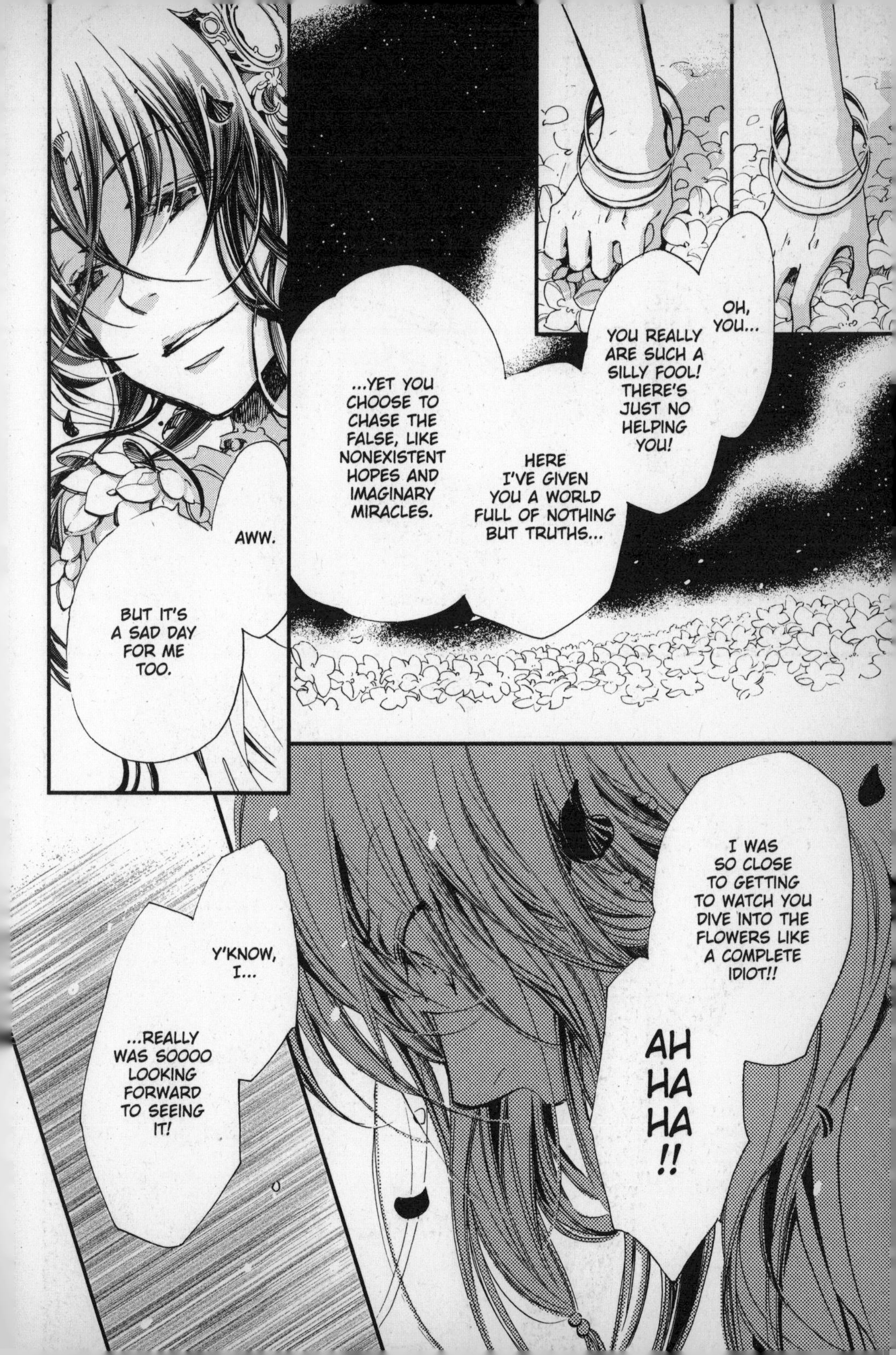
OH, YOU...
YOU REALLY ARE SUCH A SILLY FOOL! THERE'S JUST NO HELPING YOU!
HERE I'VE GIVEN YOU A WORLD FULL OF NOTHING BUT TRUTHS...
...YET YOU CHOOSE TO CHASE THE FALSE, LIKE NONEXISTENT HOPES AND IMAGINARY MIRACLES.
AWW.
BUT IT'S A SAD DAY FOR ME TOO.
I WAS SO CLOSE TO GETTING TO WATCH YOU DIVE INTO THE FLOWERS LIKE A COMPLETE IDIOT!!
Y'KNOW, I...
...REALLY WAS SOOOO LOOKING FORWARD TO SEEING IT!
AH HA HA!!

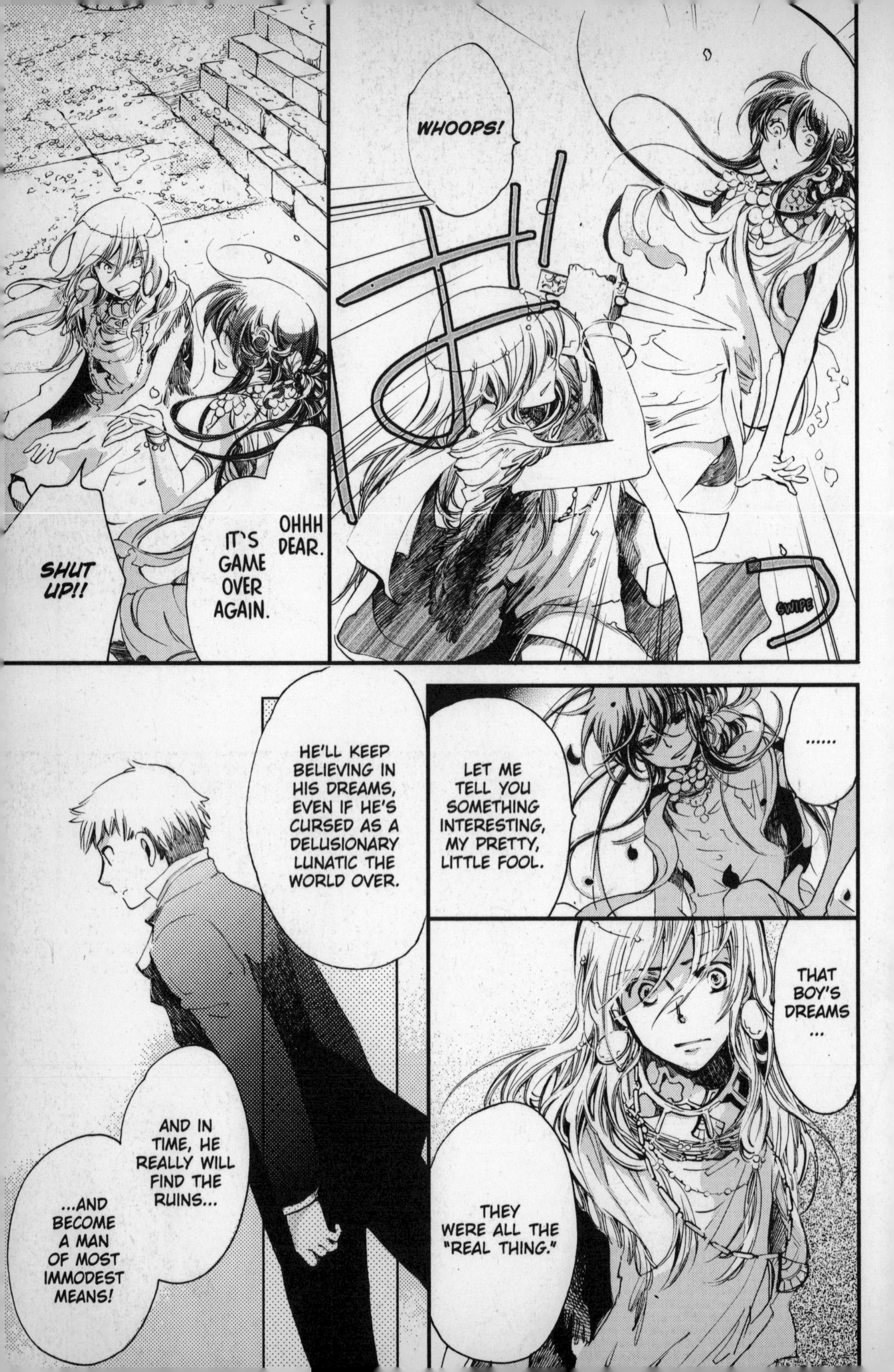
WHOOPS!
SWIPE
OHHH DEAR.
IT'S GAME OVER AGAIN.
SHUT UP!!
......
LET ME TELL YOU SOMETHING INTERESTING, MY PRETTY, LITTLE FOOL.
THAT BOY'S DREAMS ...
THEY WERE ALL THE "REAL THING."
HE'LL KEEP BELIEVING IN HIS DREAMS, EVEN IF HE'S CURSED AS A DELUSIONARY LUNATIC THE WORLD OVER.
AND IN TIME, HE REALLY WILL FIND THE RUINS...
...AND BECOME A MAN OF MOST IMMODEST MEANS!

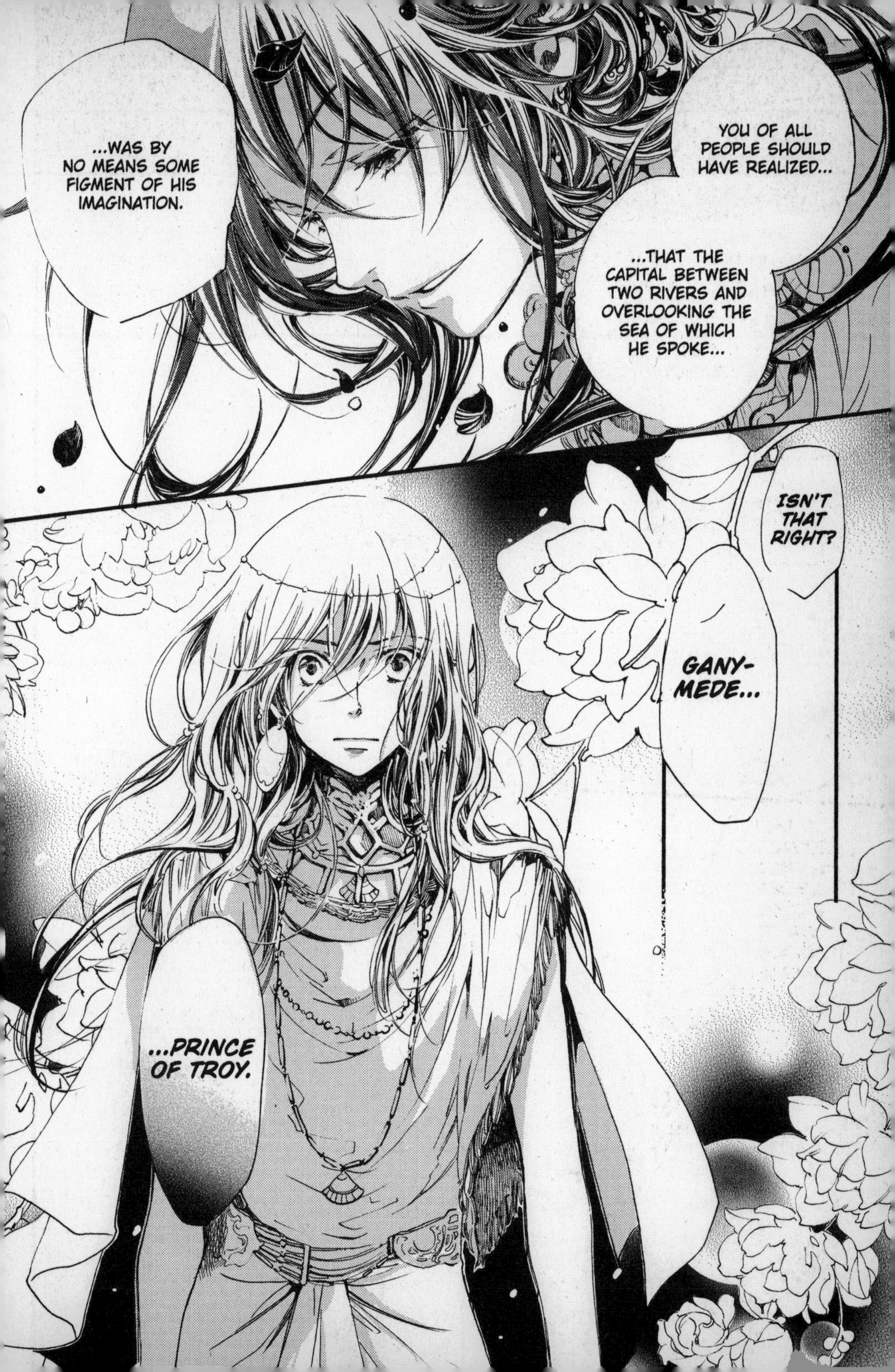
YOU OF ALL PEOPLE SHOULD HAVE REALIZED...
...THAT THE CAPITAL BETWEEN TWO RIVERS AND OVERLOOKING THE SEA OF WHICH HE SPOKE...
...WAS BY NO MEANS SOME FIGMENT OF HIS IMAGINATION.
ISN'T THAT RIGHT?
GANY-MEDE...
...PRINCE OF TROY.

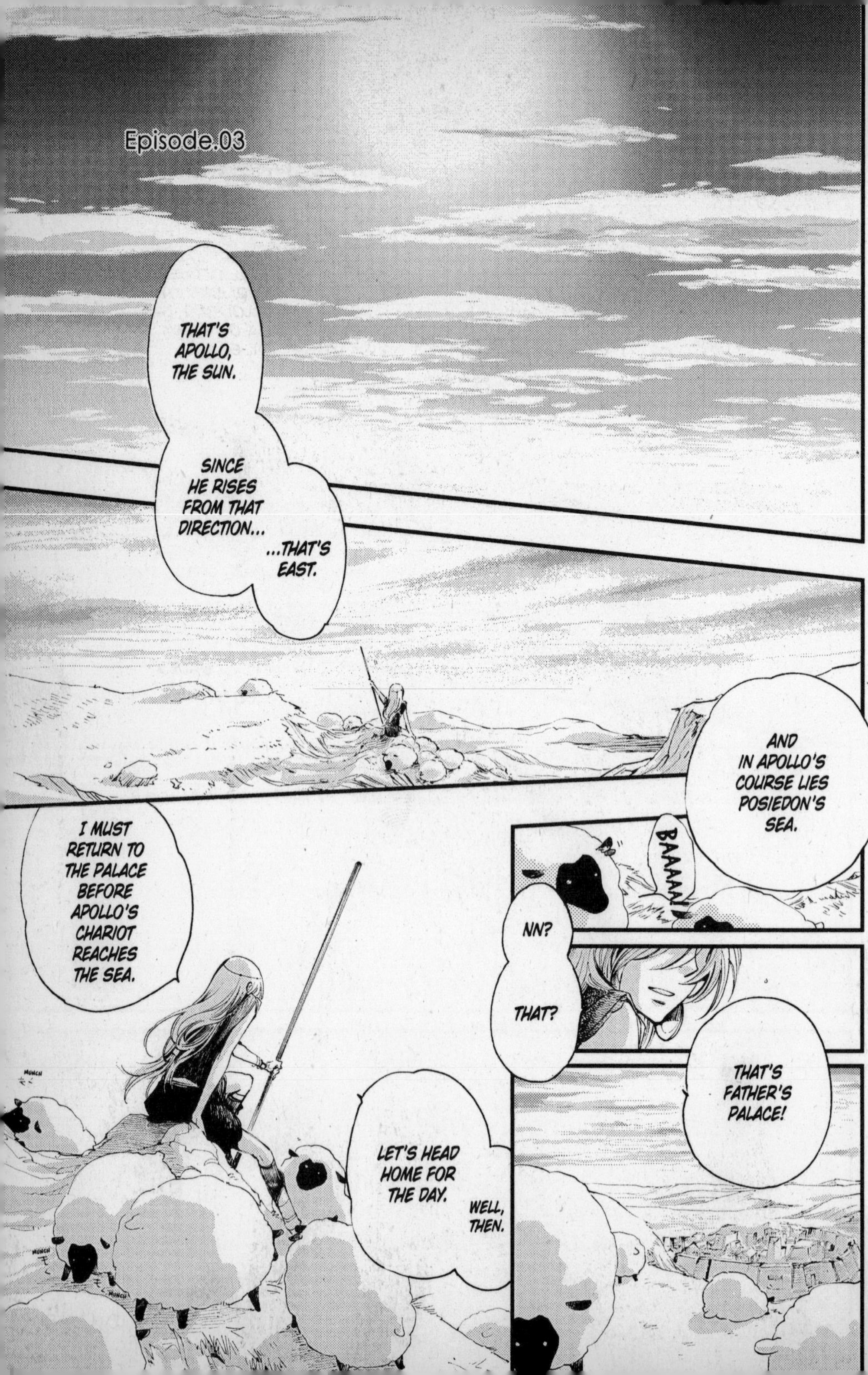
Episode.03
THAT'S APOLLO, THE SUN.
SINCE HE RISES FROM THAT DIRECTION...
...THAT'S EAST.
AND IN APOLLO'S COURSE LIES POSIEDON'S SEA.
BAAAAA!
NN?
THAT?
THAT'S FATHER'S PALACE!
I MUST RETURN TO THE PALACE BEFORE APOLLO'S CHARIOT REACHES THE SEA.
WELL, THEN.
LET'S HEAD HOME FOR THE DAY.
MUNCH
MUNCH
MUNCH

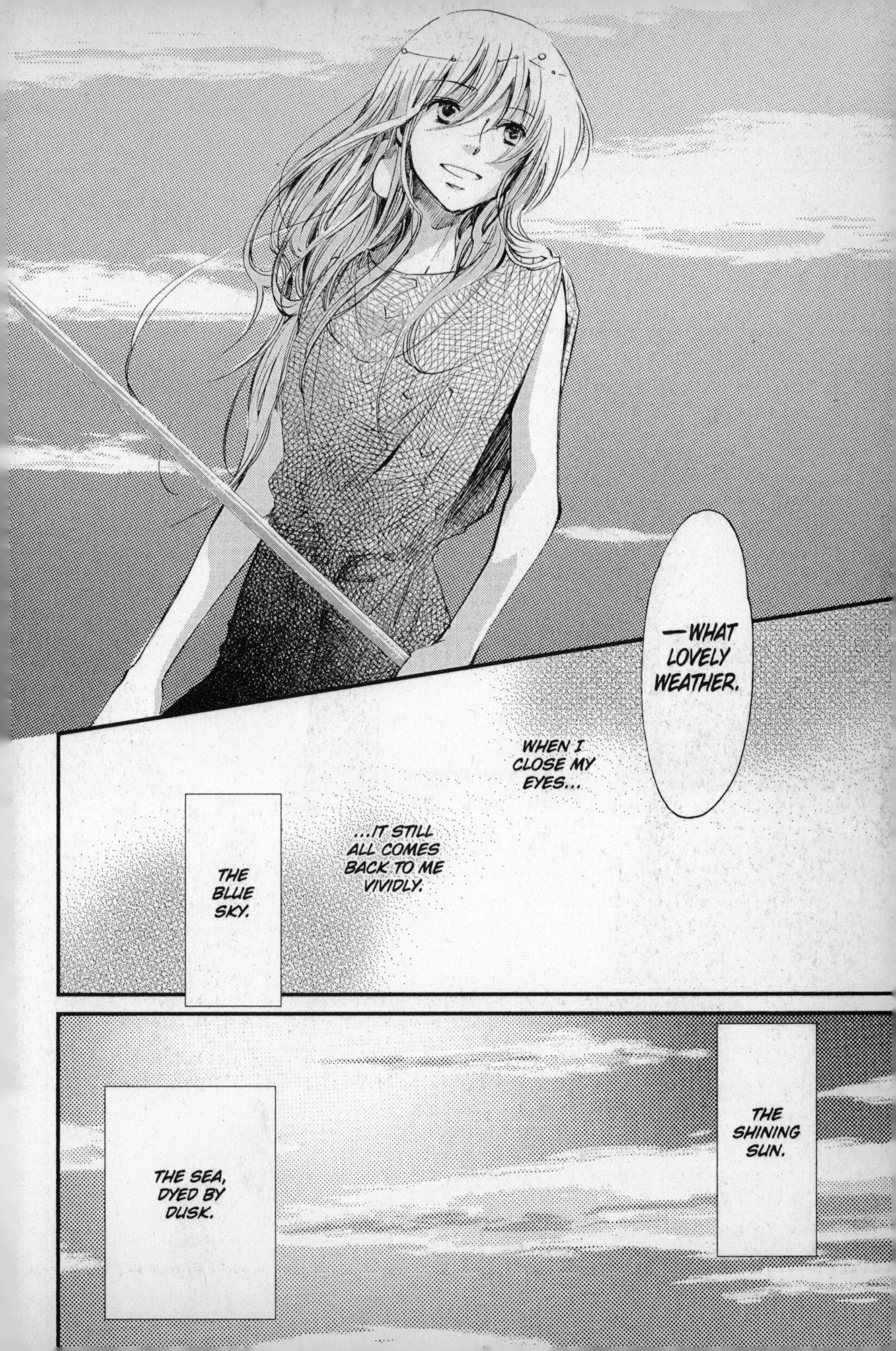
—WHAT LOVELY WEATHER.
WHEN I CLOSE MY EYES...
...IT STILL ALL COMES BACK TO ME VIVIDLY.
THE BLUE SKY.
THE SHINING SUN.
THE SEA, DYED BY DUSK.

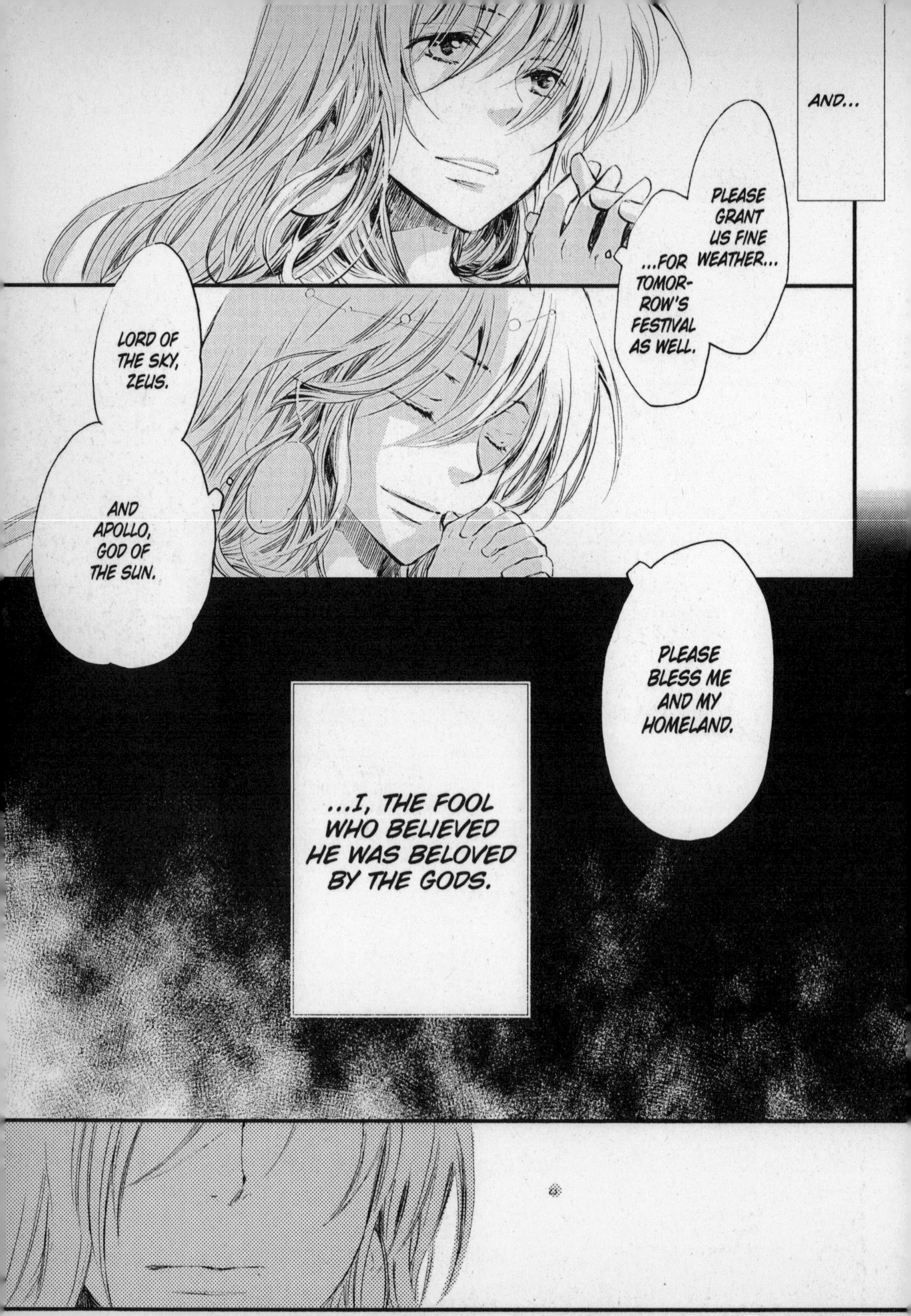
AND...
PLEASE GRANT US FINE WEATHER...
...FOR TOMOR-ROW'S FESTIVAL AS WELL.
LORD OF THE SKY, ZEUS.
AND APOLLO, GOD OF THE SUN.
PLEASE BLESS ME AND MY HOMELAND.
...I, THE FOOL WHO BELIEVED HE WAS BELOVED BY THE GODS.

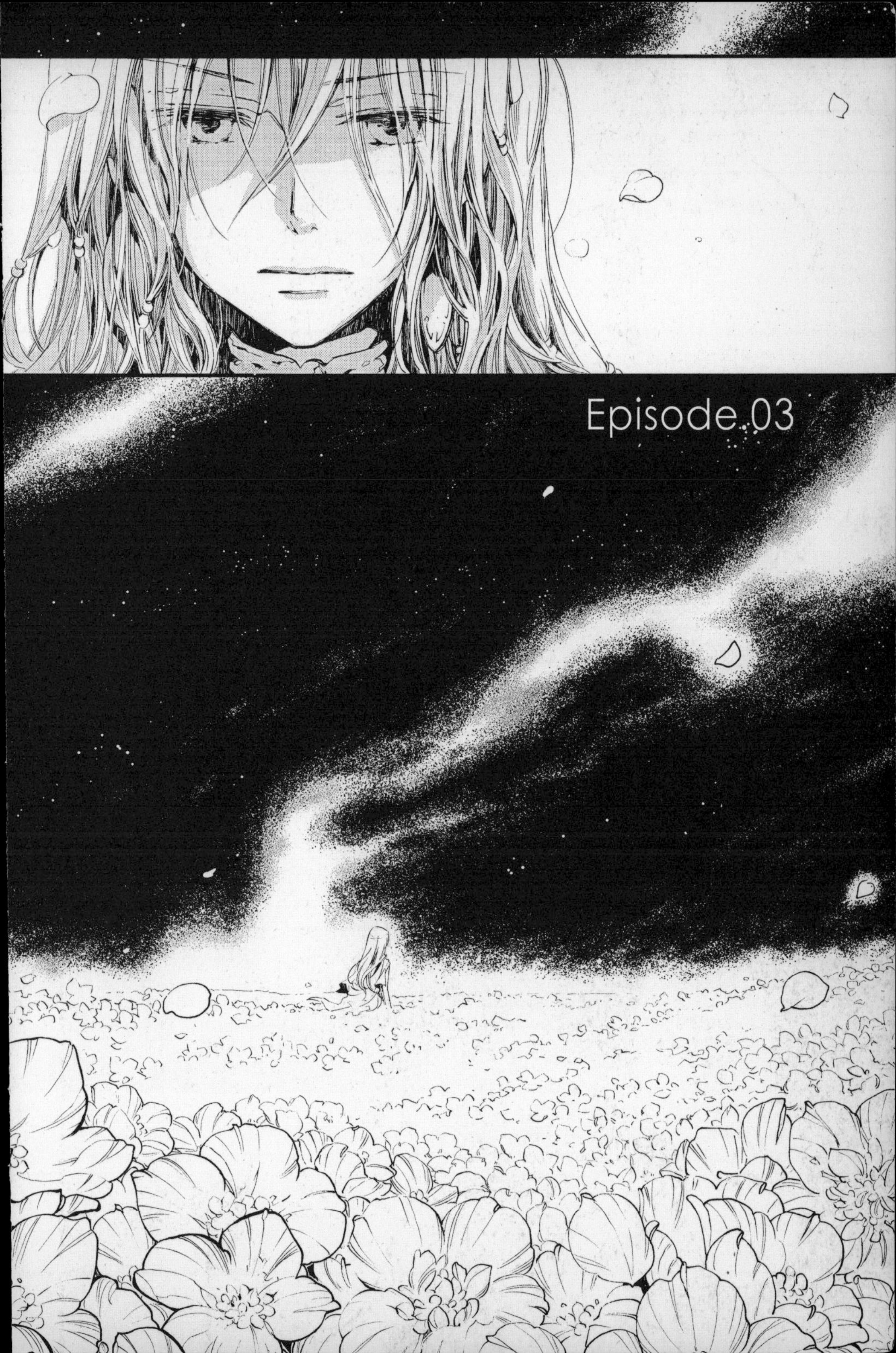
Episode 03

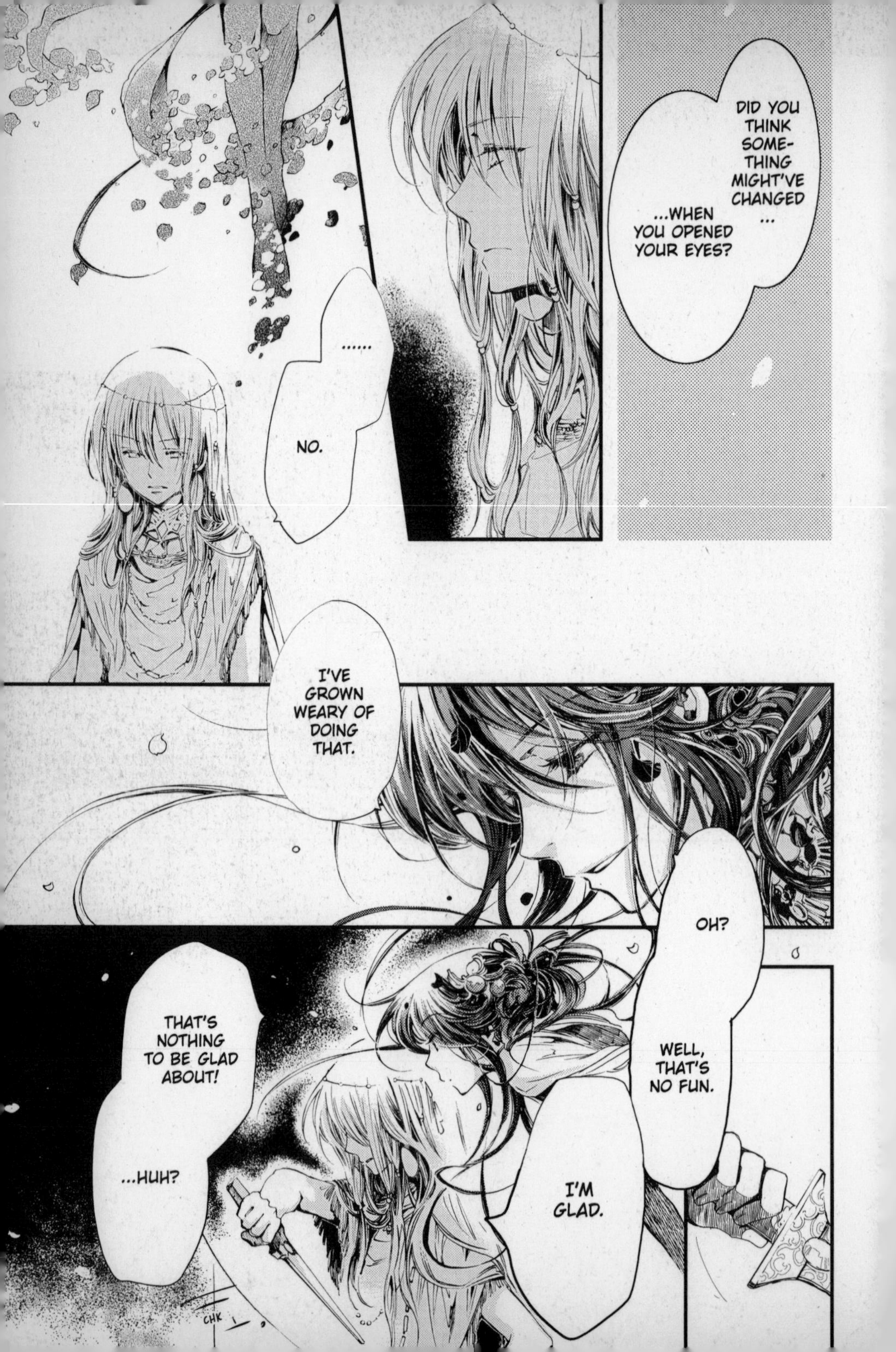
DID YOU THINK SOME-THING MIGHT'VE CHANGED ...
...WHEN YOU OPENED YOUR EYES?
......
NO.
I'VE GROWN WEARY OF DOING THAT.
OH?
WELL, THAT'S NO FUN.
I'M GLAD.
THAT'S NOTHING TO BE GLAD ABOUT!
...HUH?
CHK

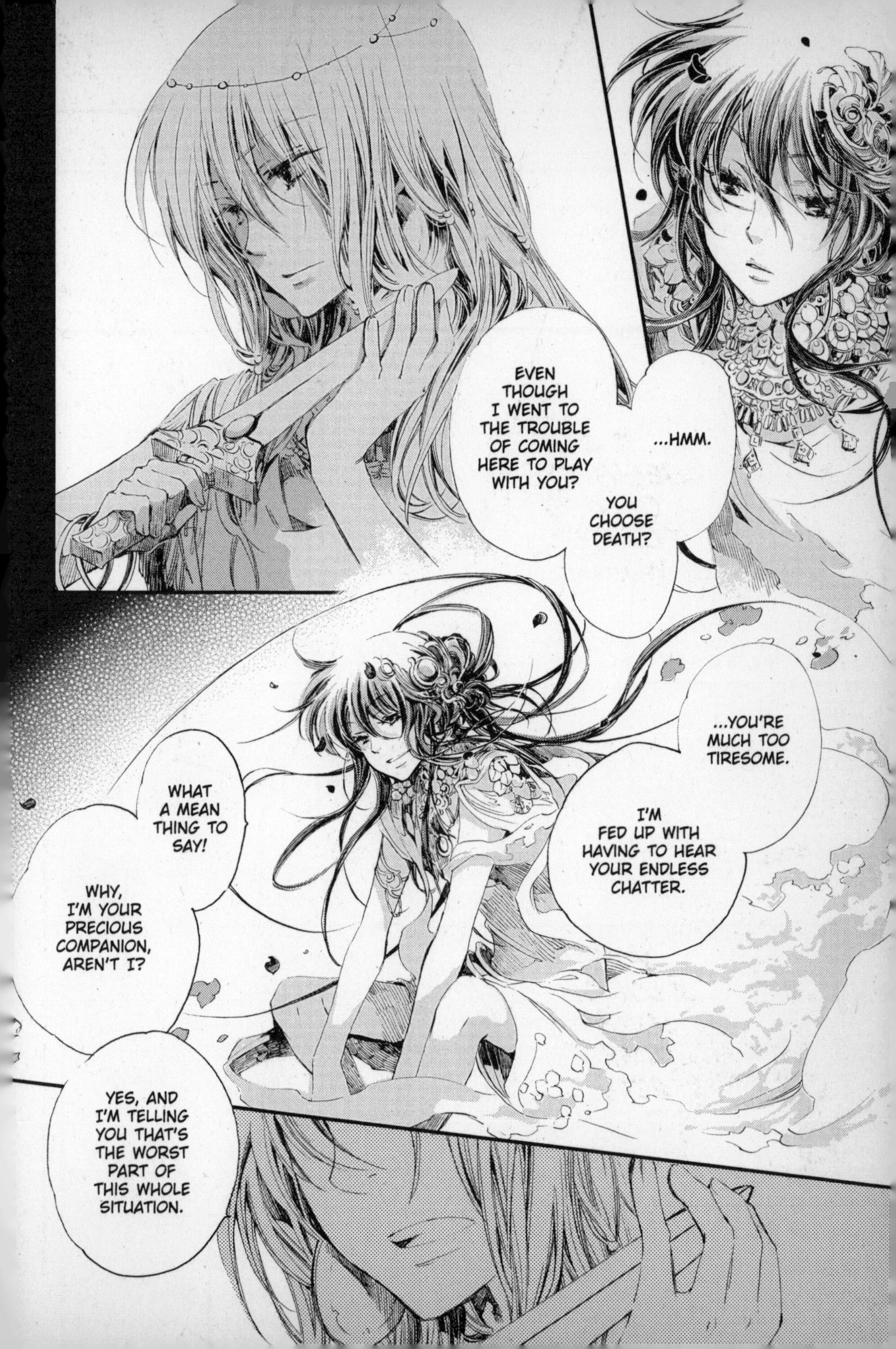
...HMM.
YOU CHOOSE DEATH?
EVEN THOUGH I WENT TO THE TROUBLE OF COMING HERE TO PLAY WITH YOU?
...YOU'RE MUCH TOO TIRESOME.
I'M FED UP WITH HAVING TO HEAR YOUR ENDLESS CHATTER.
WHAT A MEAN THING TO SAY!
WHY, I'M YOUR PRECIOUS COMPANION, AREN'T I?
YES, AND I'M TELLING YOU THAT'S THE WORST PART OF THIS WHOLE SITUATION.

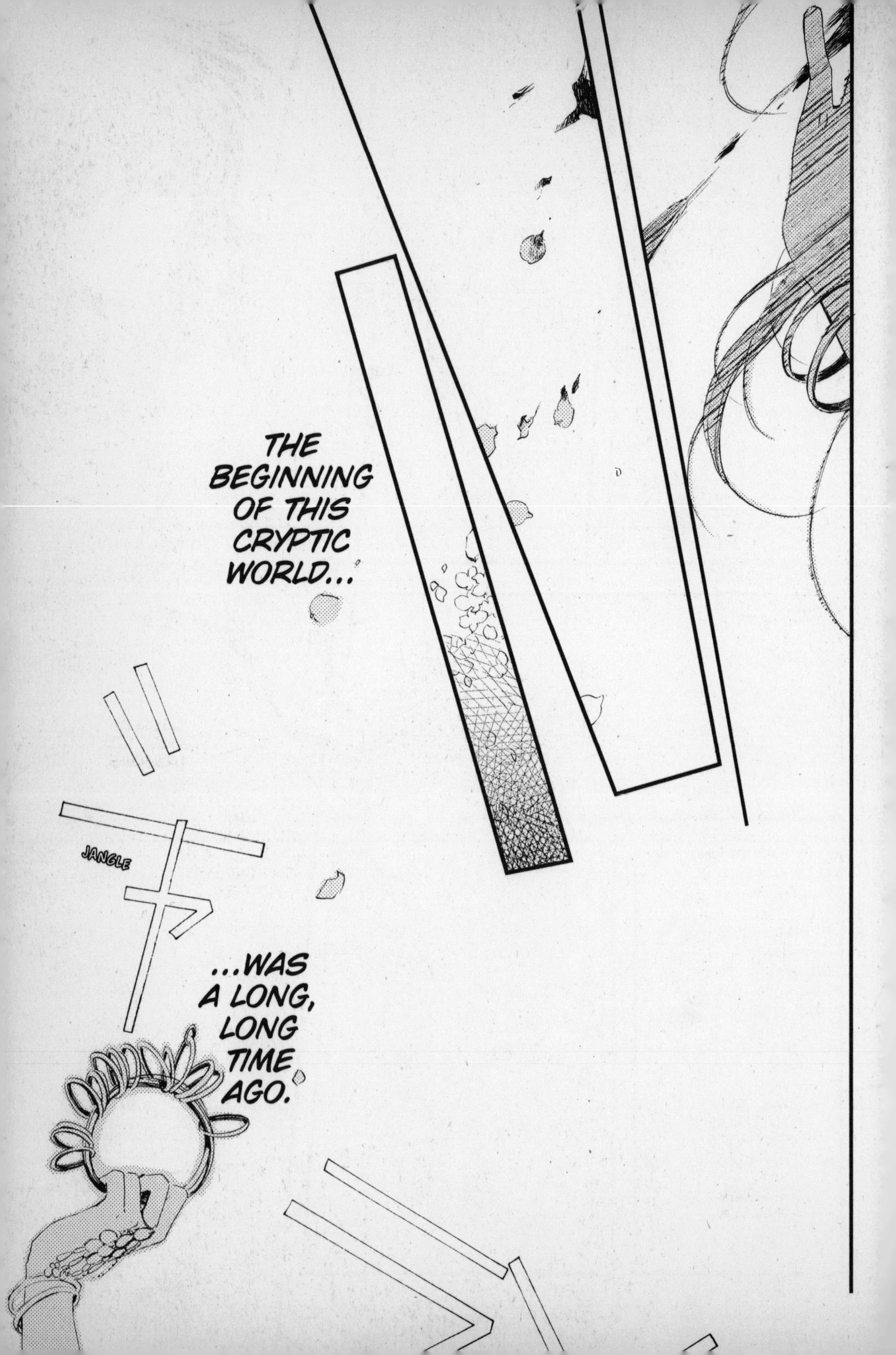
THE BEGINNING OF THIS CRYPTIC WORLD...
JANGLE
...WAS A LONG, LONG TIME AGO.

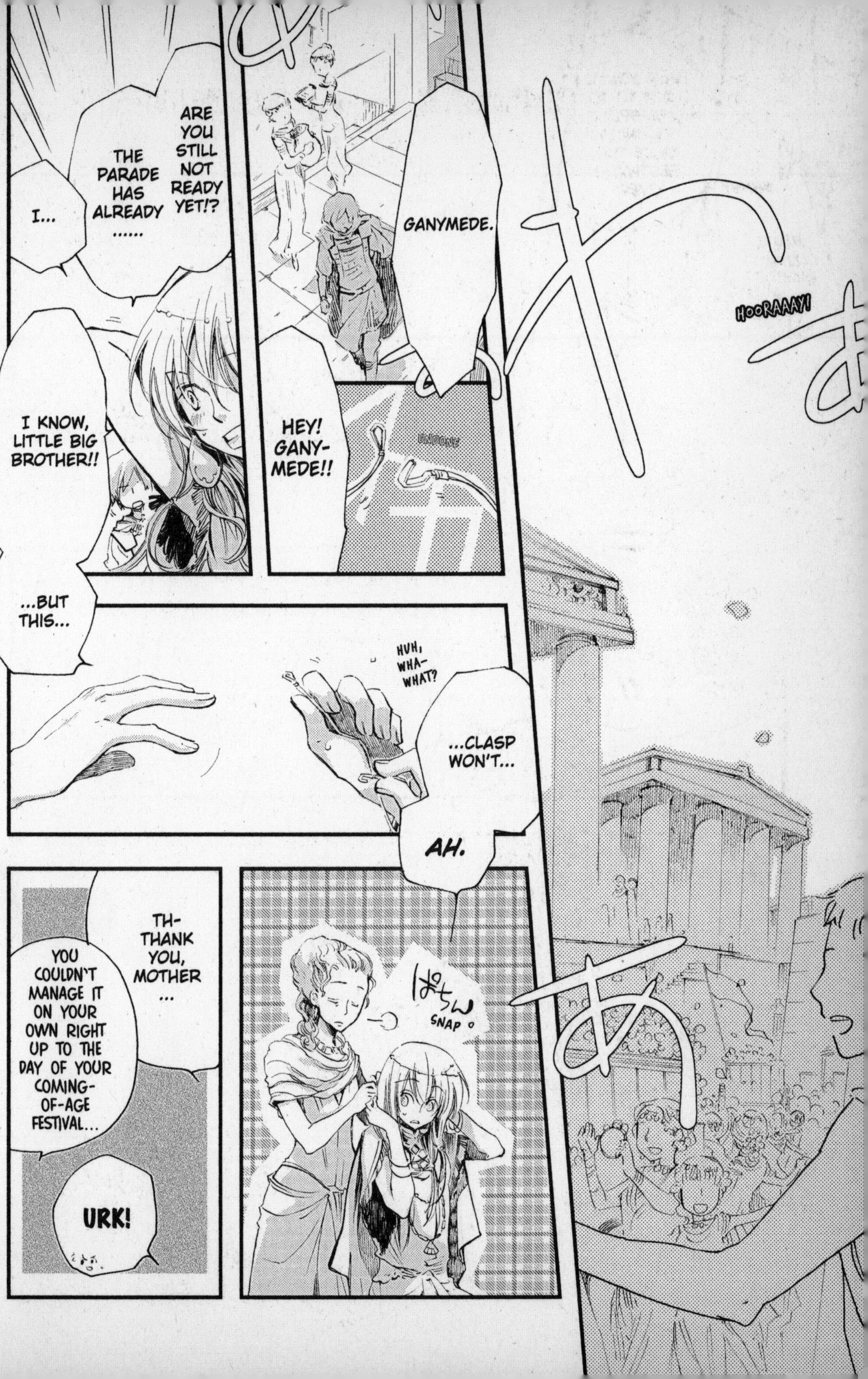
HOORAAAY!
GANYMEDE.
HEY! GANYMEDE!!
UNDONE
ARE YOU STILL NOT READY YET!?
THE PARADE HAS ALREADY ......
I...
I KNOW, LITTLE BIG BROTHER!!
...BUT THIS...
HUH, WHA-WHAT?
...CLASP WON'T...
AH.
ぱちん
SNAP
TH-THANK YOU, MOTHER ...
YOU COULDN'T MANAGE IT ON YOUR OWN RIGHT UP TO THE DAY OF YOUR COMING-OF-AGE FESTIVAL...
URK!

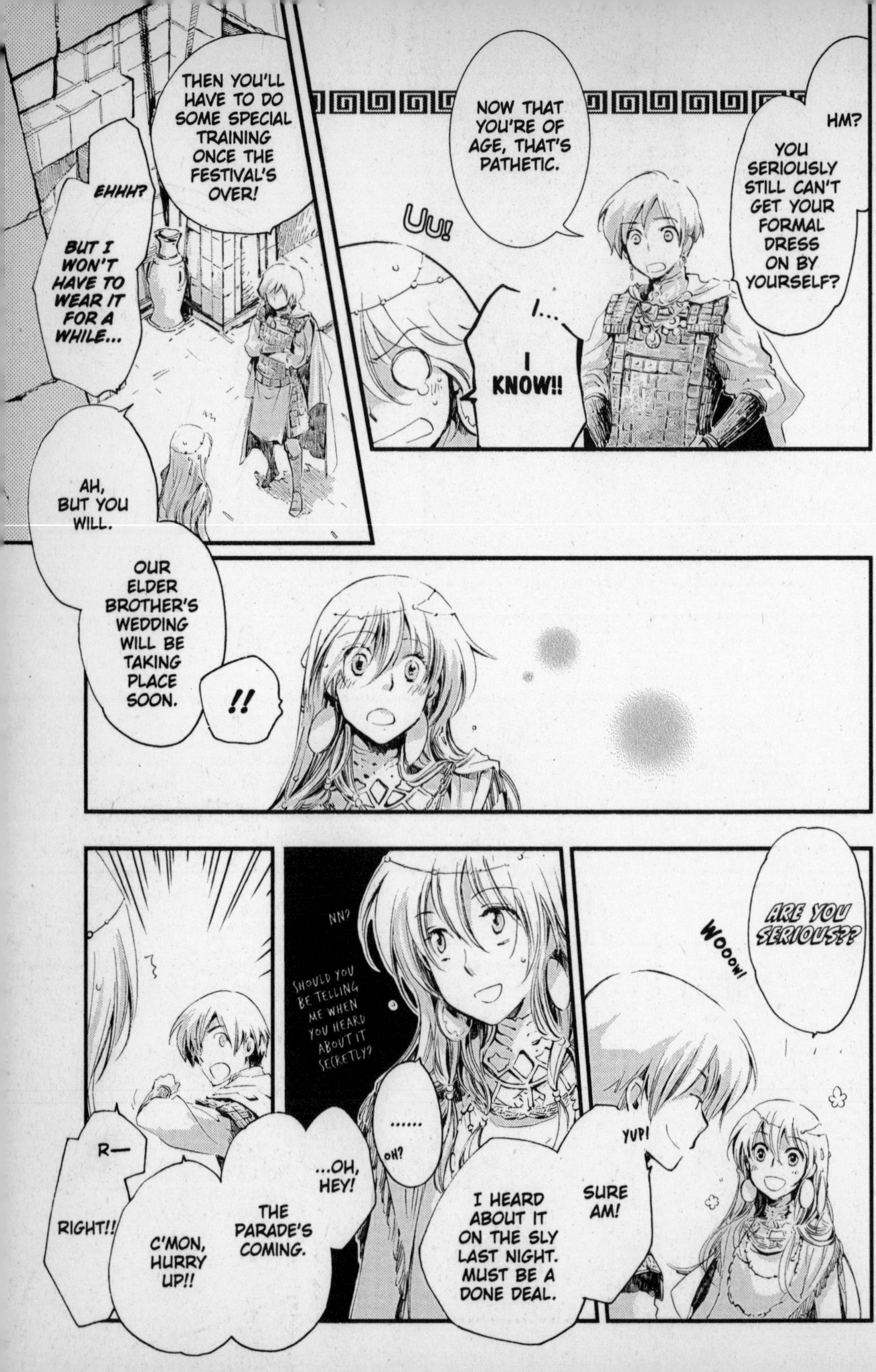
HM?
YOU SERIOUSLY STILL CAN'T GET YOUR FORMAL DRESS ON BY YOURSELF?
NOW THAT YOU'RE OF AGE, THAT'S PATHETIC.
UU!
I... I KNOW!!
THEN YOU'LL HAVE TO DO SOME SPECIAL TRAINING ONCE THE FESTIVAL'S OVER!
EHHH?
BUT I WON'T HAVE TO WEAR IT FOR A WHILE...
AH, BUT YOU WILL.
OUR ELDER BROTHER'S WEDDING WILL BE TAKING PLACE SOON.
!!
ARE YOU SERIOUS??
WOOOW!
YUP!
SURE AM!
I HEARD ABOUT IT ON THE SLY LAST NIGHT. MUST BE A DONE DEAL.
NN?
SHOULD YOU BE TELLING ME WHEN YOU HEARD ABOUT IT SECRETLY?
......
OH?
...OH, HEY!
THE PARADE'S COMING.
R— RIGHT!!
C'MON, HURRY UP!!

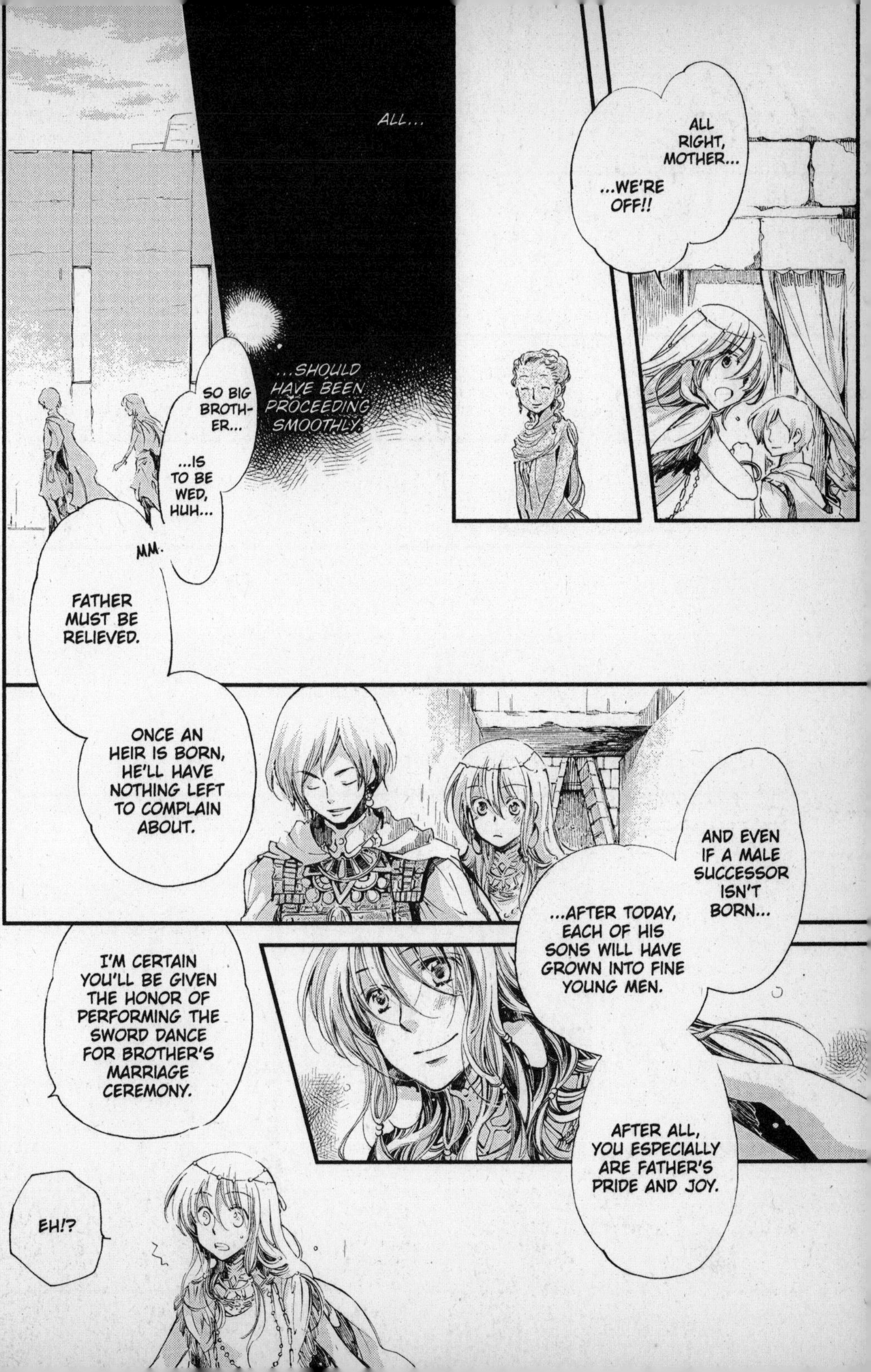
ALL RIGHT, MOTHER...
...WE'RE OFF!!
ALL...
...SHOULD HAVE BEEN PROCEEDING SMOOTHLY.
SO BIG BROTHER...
...IS TO BE WED, HUH...
MM.
FATHER MUST BE RELIEVED.
ONCE AN HEIR IS BORN, HE'LL HAVE NOTHING LEFT TO COMPLAIN ABOUT.
AND EVEN IF A MALE SUCCESSOR ISN'T BORN...
...AFTER TODAY, EACH OF HIS SONS WILL HAVE GROWN INTO FINE YOUNG MEN.
I'M CERTAIN YOU'LL BE GIVEN THE HONOR OF PERFORMING THE SWORD DANCE FOR BROTHER'S MARRIAGE CEREMONY.
AFTER ALL, YOU ESPECIALLY ARE FATHER'S PRIDE AND JOY.
EH!?

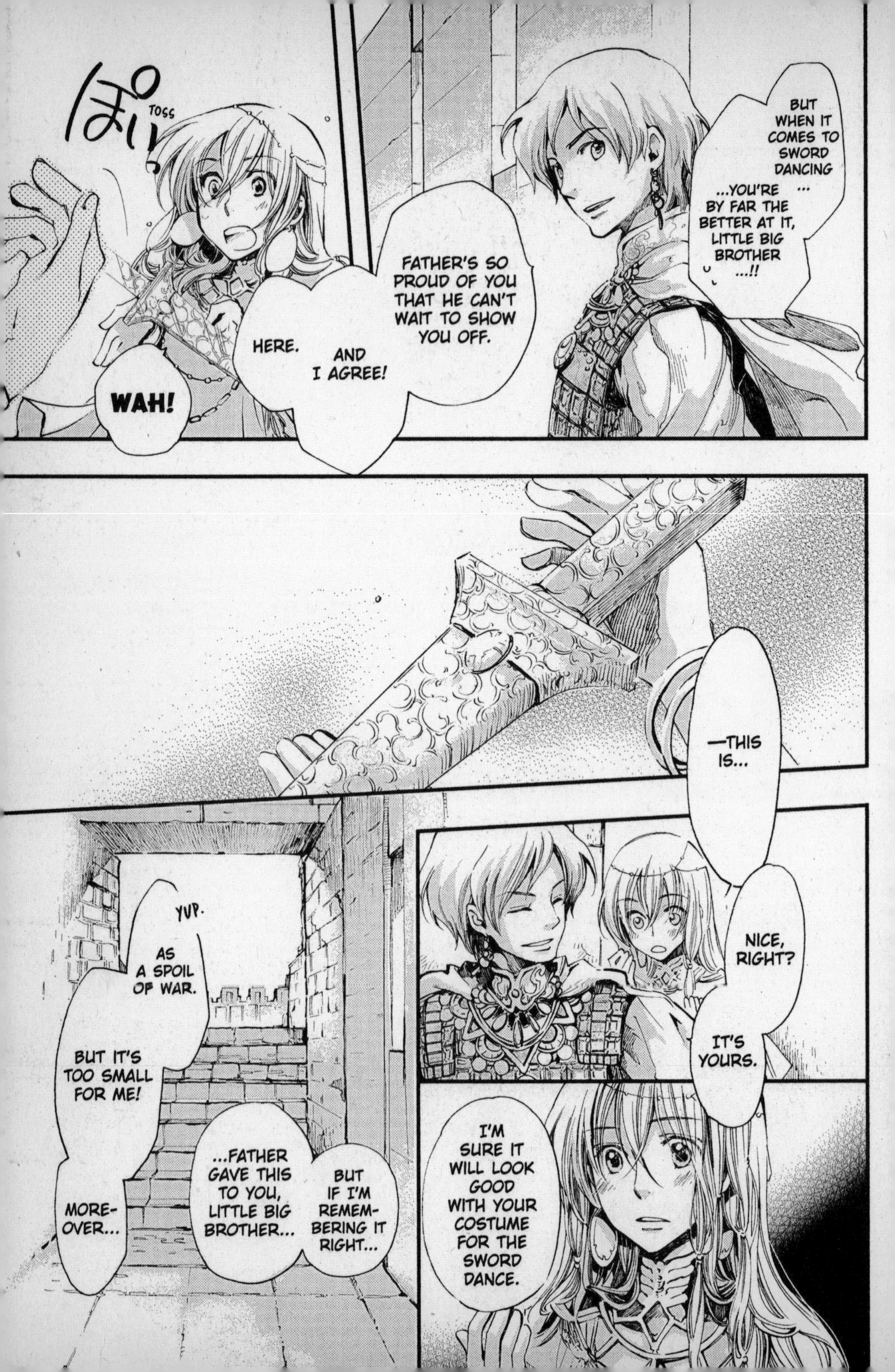
BUT WHEN IT COMES TO SWORD DANCING ...
...YOU'RE BY FAR THE BETTER AT IT, LITTLE BIG BROTHER ...!!
FATHER'S SO PROUD OF YOU THAT HE CAN'T WAIT TO SHOW YOU OFF.
AND I AGREE!
HERE.
ぽい
TOSS
WAH!
—THIS IS...
NICE, RIGHT?
IT'S YOURS.
I'M SURE IT WILL LOOK GOOD WITH YOUR COSTUME FOR THE SWORD DANCE.
BUT IF I'M REMEMBERING IT RIGHT...
...FATHER GAVE THIS TO YOU, LITTLE BIG BROTHER...
YUP.
AS A SPOIL OF WAR.
BUT IT'S TOO SMALL FOR ME!
MORE-OVER...

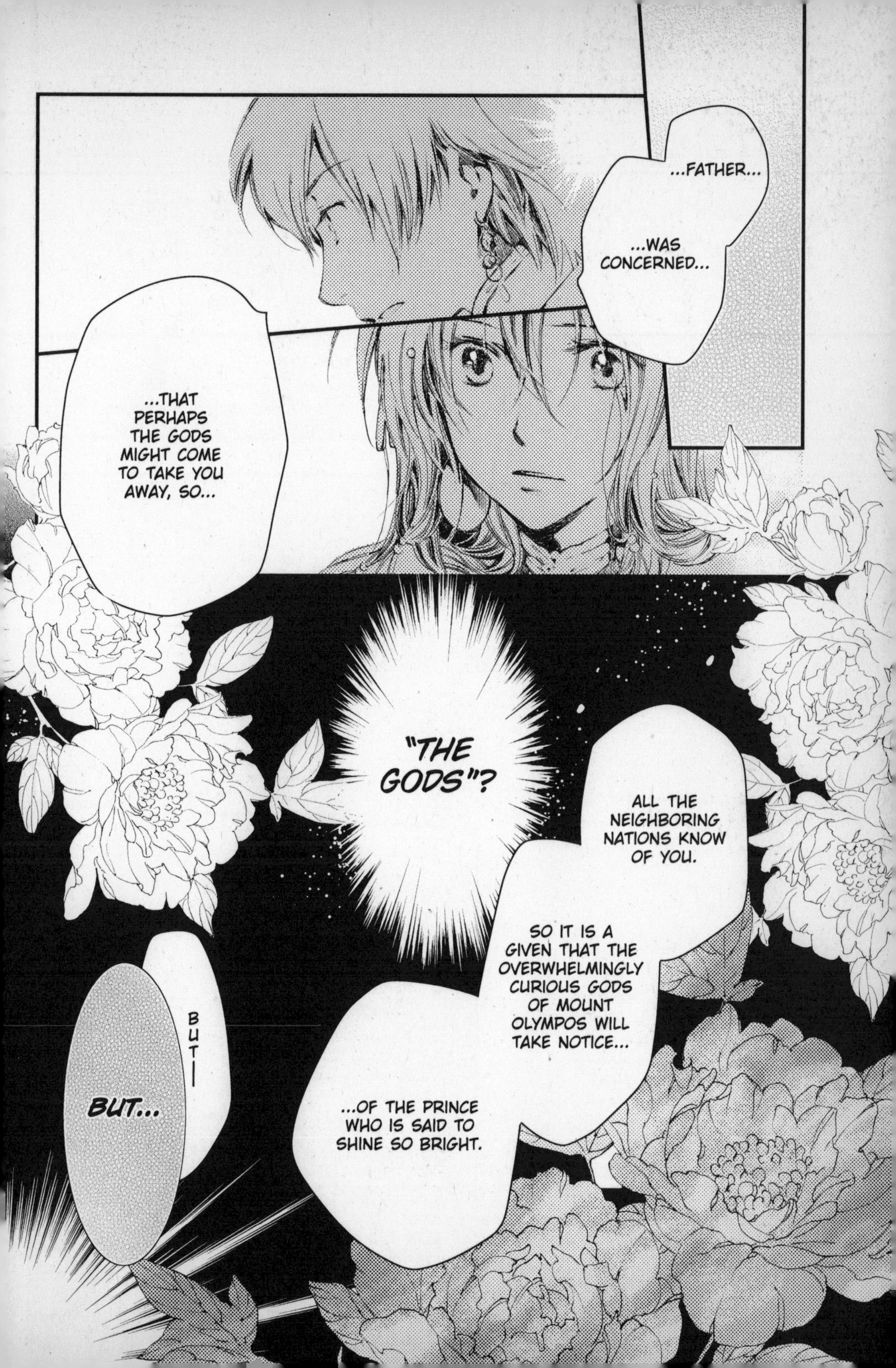
...FATHER...
...WAS CONCERNED...
...THAT PERHAPS THE GODS MIGHT COME TO TAKE YOU AWAY, SO...
"THE GODS"?
ALL THE NEIGHBORING NATIONS KNOW OF YOU.
SO IT IS A GIVEN THAT THE OVERWHELMINGLY CURIOUS GODS OF MOUNT OLYMPOS WILL TAKE NOTICE...
...OF THE PRINCE WHO IS SAID TO SHINE SO BRIGHT.
BUT—
BUT...

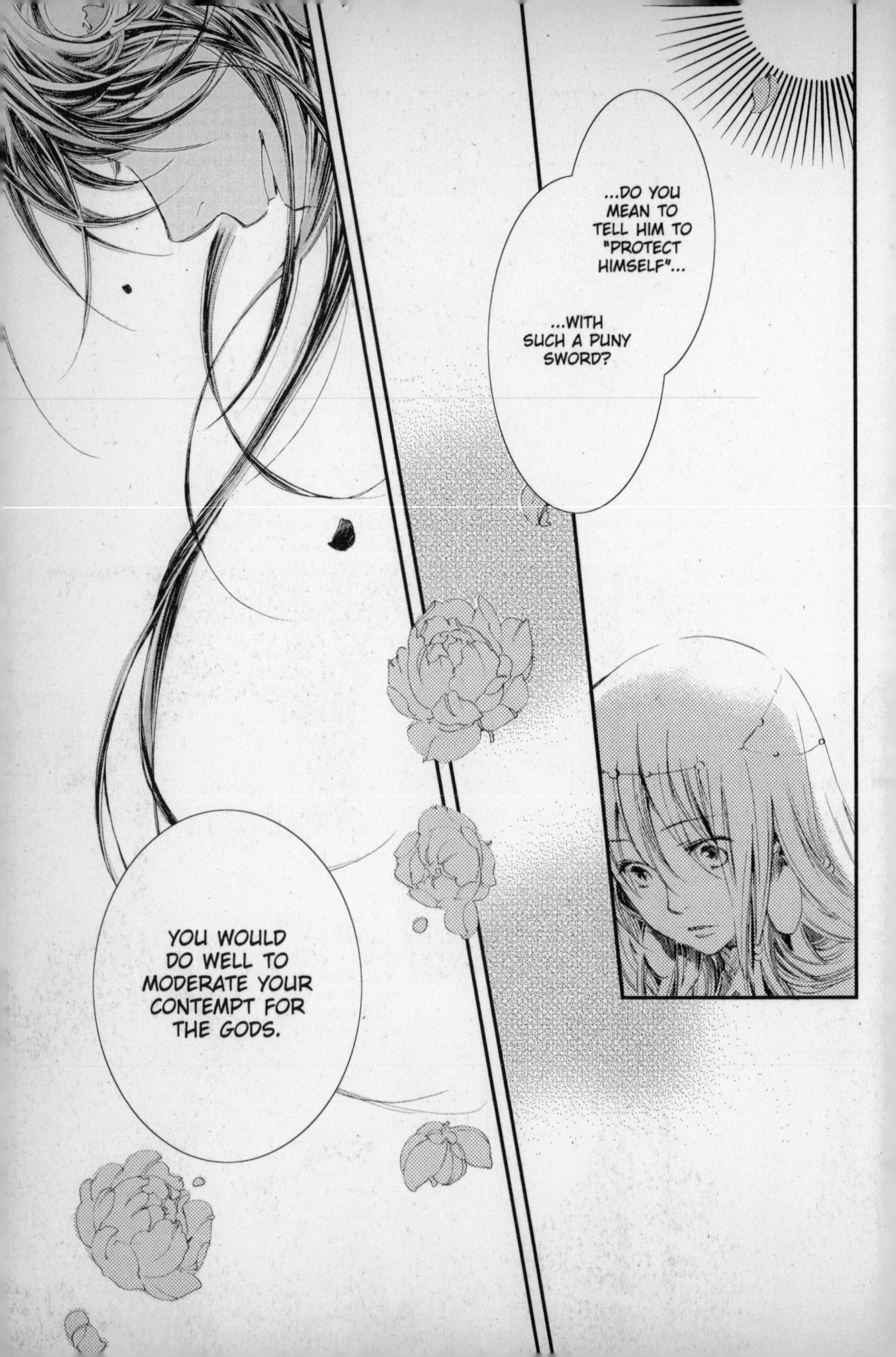
...DO YOU MEAN TO TELL HIM TO "PROTECT HIMSELF"...
...WITH SUCH A PUNY SWORD?
YOU WOULD DO WELL TO MODERATE YOUR CONTEMPT FOR THE GODS.

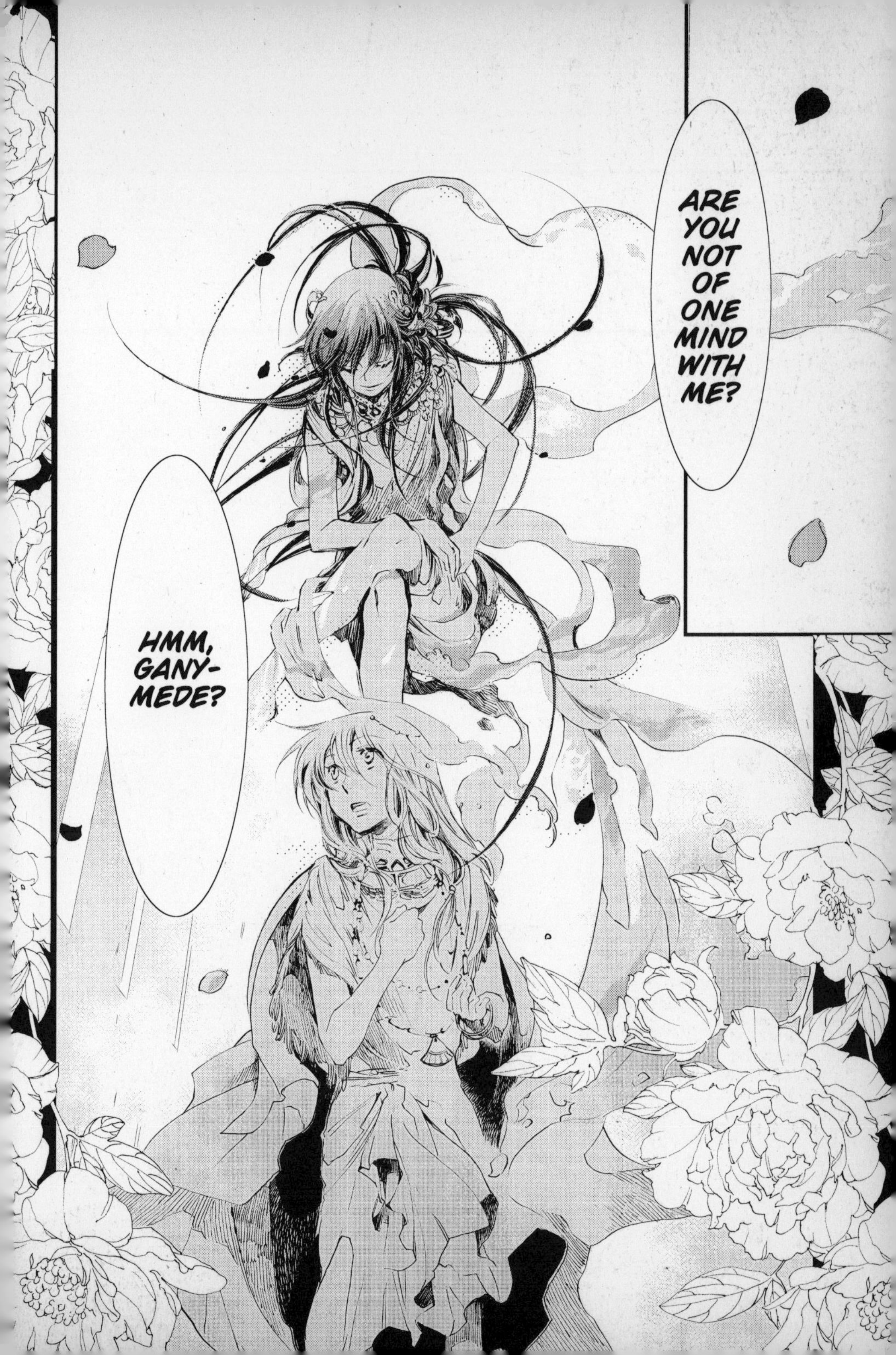
ARE YOU NOT OF ONE MIND WITH ME?
HMM, GANY-MEDE?

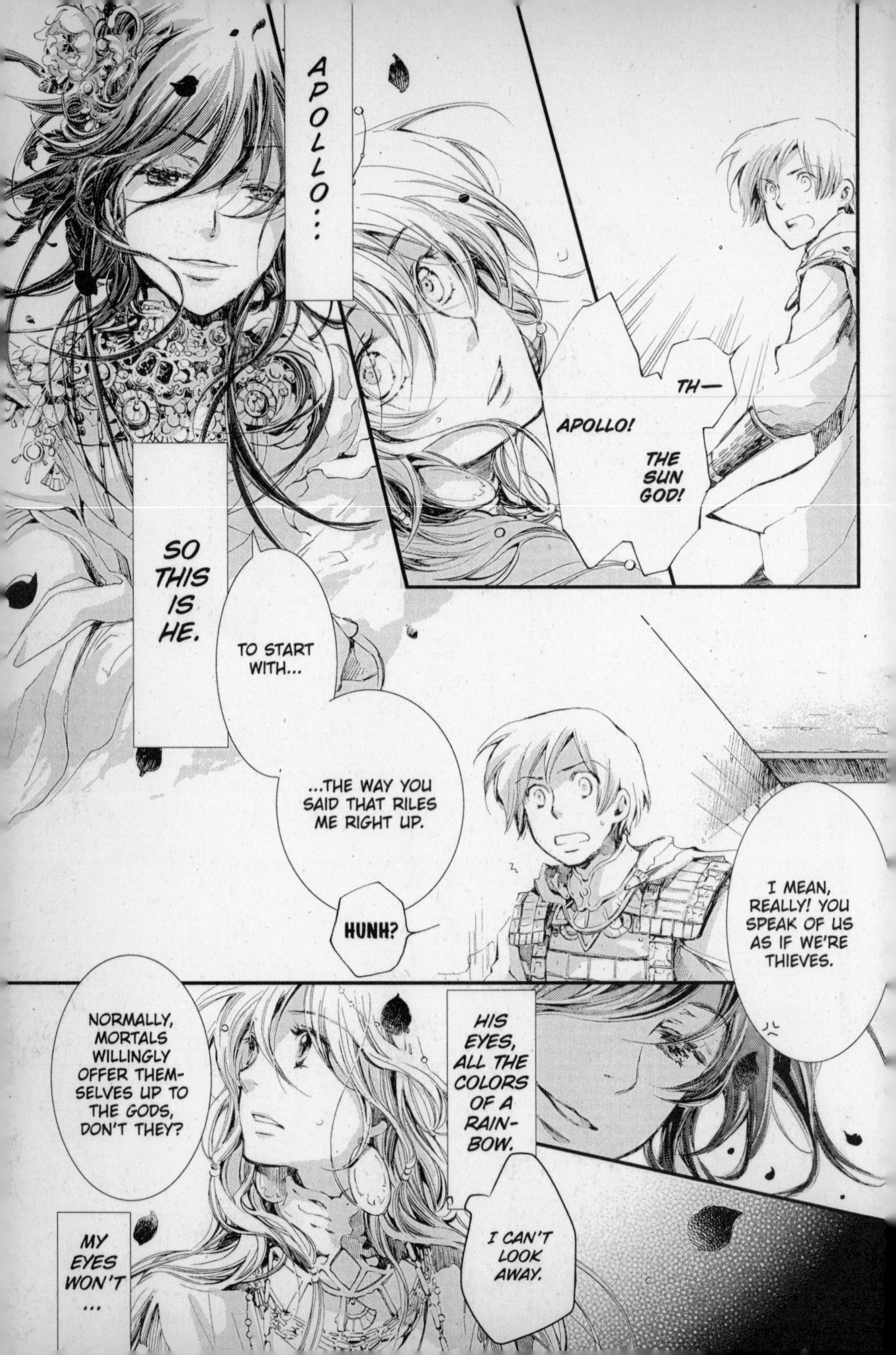
TH—
APOLLO!
THE SUN GOD!
APOLLO...
SO THIS IS HE.
TO START WITH...
...THE WAY YOU SAID THAT RILES ME RIGHT UP.
HUNH?
I MEAN, REALLY! YOU SPEAK OF US AS IF WE'RE THIEVES.
HIS EYES, ALL THE COLORS OF A RAIN-BOW.
NORMALLY, MORTALS WILLINGLY OFFER THEM-SELVES UP TO THE GODS, DON'T THEY?
I CAN'T LOOK AWAY.
MY EYES WON'T ...

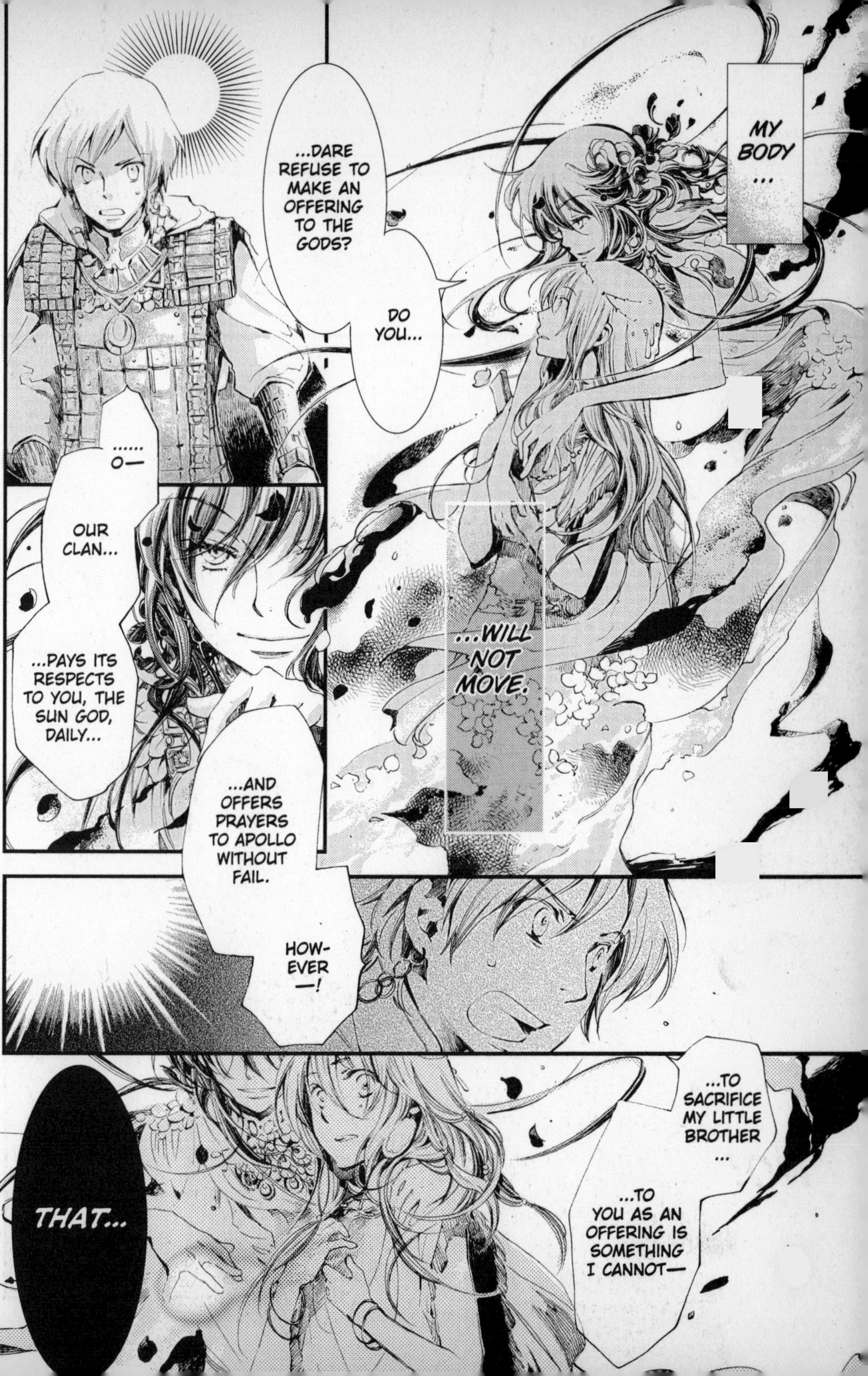

MY BODY ...
...WILL NOT MOVE.
DO YOU...
...DARE REFUSE TO MAKE AN OFFERING TO THE GODS?
...... O—
OUR CLAN...
...PAYS ITS RESPECTS TO YOU, THE SUN GOD, DAILY...
...AND OFFERS PRAYERS TO APOLLO WITHOUT FAIL.
HOW-EVER—!
...TO SACRIFICE MY LITTLE BROTHER ...
...TO YOU AS AN OFFERING IS SOMETHING I CANNOT—
THAT...

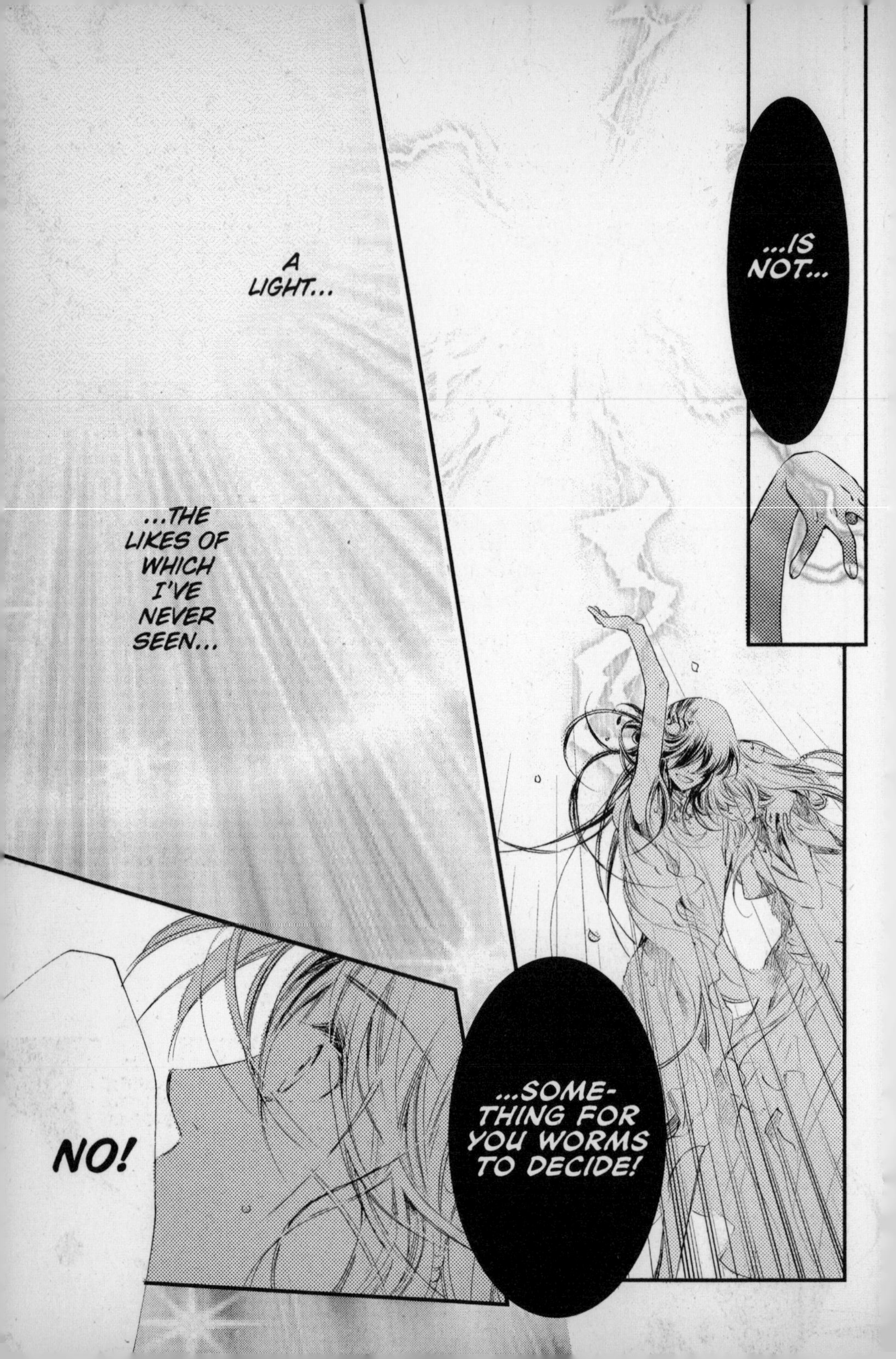
...IS NOT...
...SOME-THING FOR YOU WORMS TO DECIDE!
A LIGHT...
...THE LIKES OF WHICH I'VE NEVER SEEN...
NO!

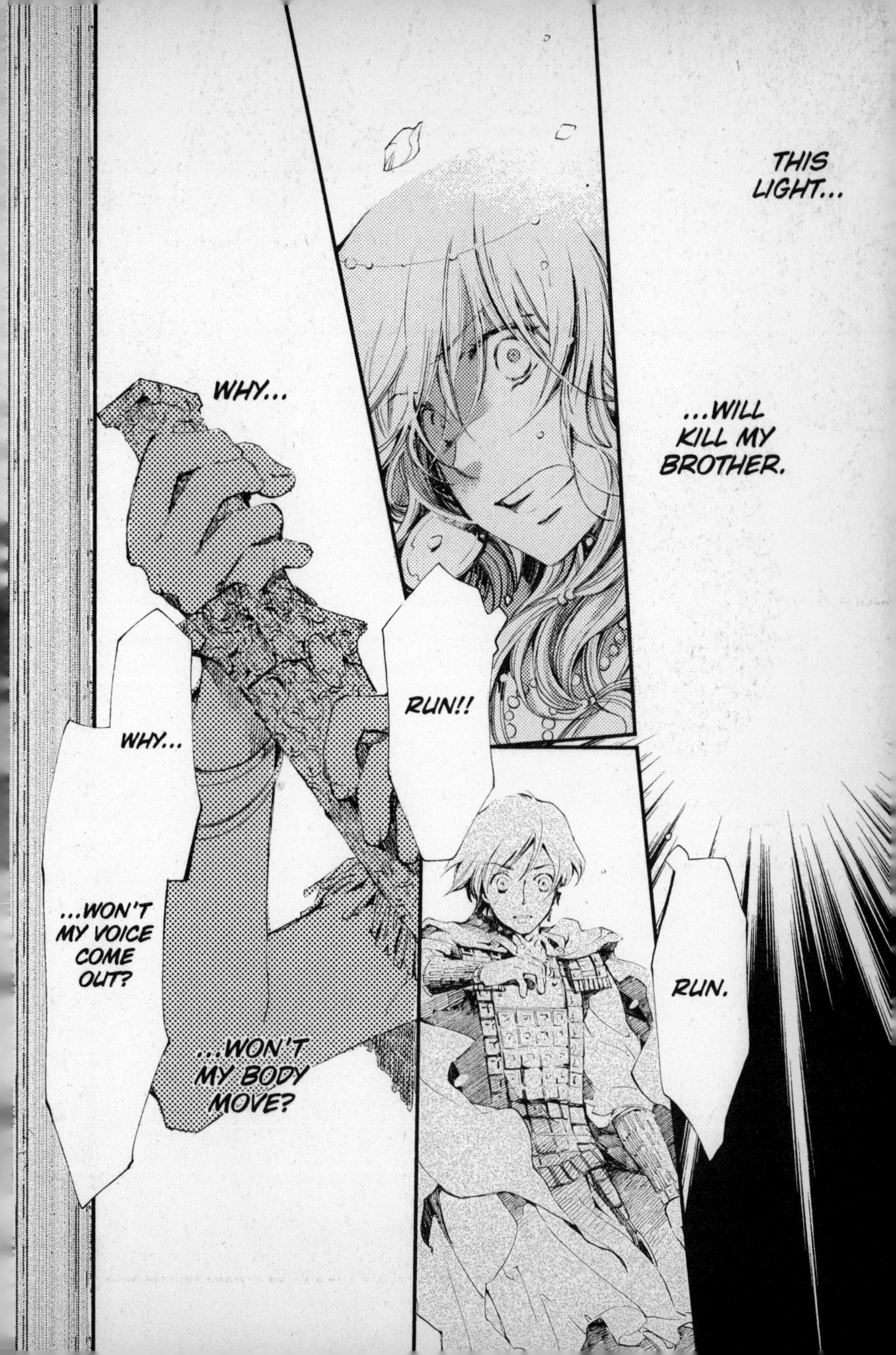
THIS LIGHT...
...WILL KILL MY BROTHER.
RUN.
RUN!!
WHY...
WHY...
...WON'T MY VOICE COME OUT?
...WON'T MY BODY MOVE?

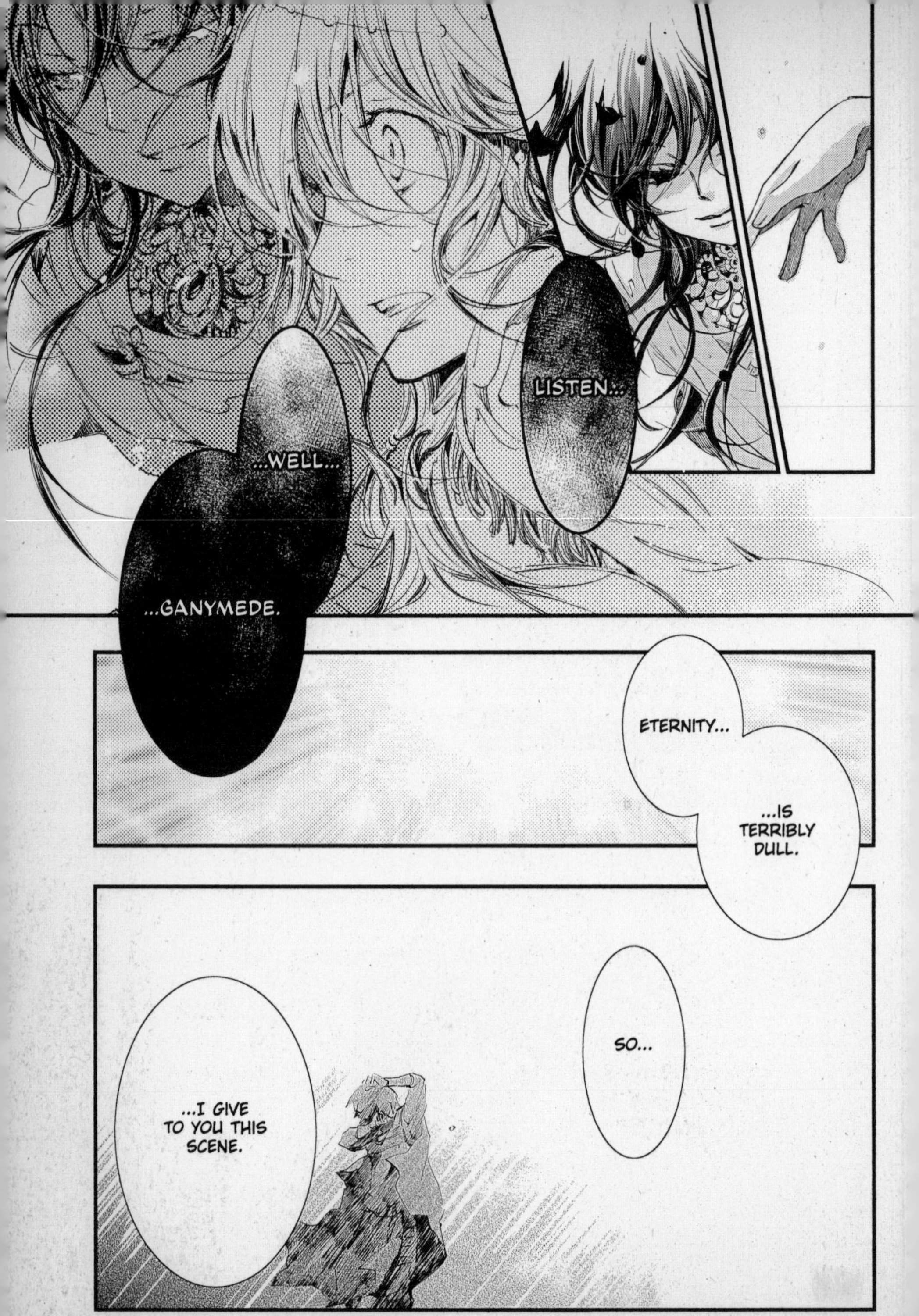
LISTEN...
...WELL...
...GANYMEDE.
ETERNITY...
...IS TERRIBLY DULL.
SO...
...I GIVE TO YOU THIS SCENE.

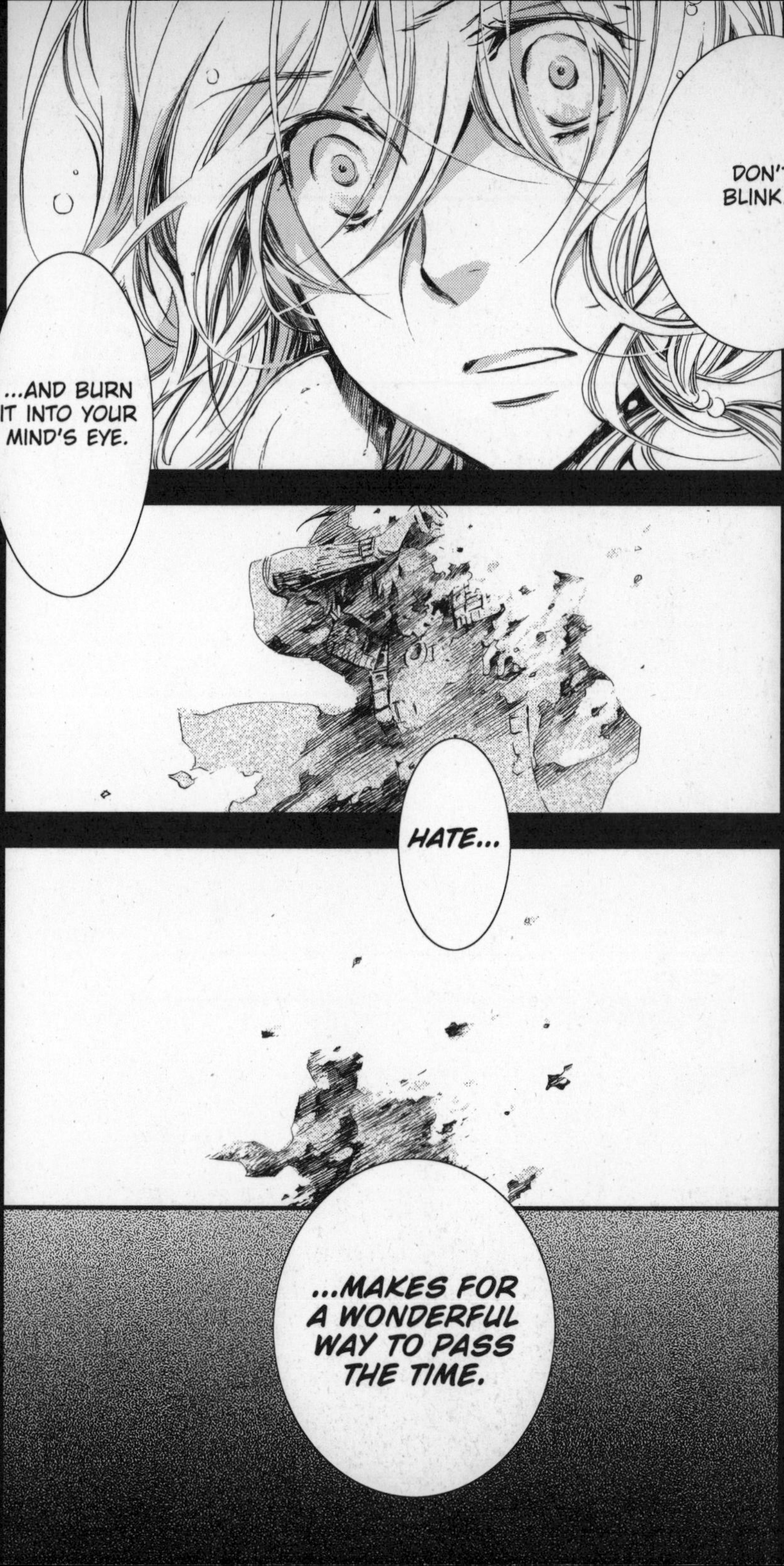
DON'T BLINK...
...AND BURN IT INTO YOUR MIND'S EYE.
HATE...
...MAKES FOR A WONDERFUL WAY TO PASS THE TIME.

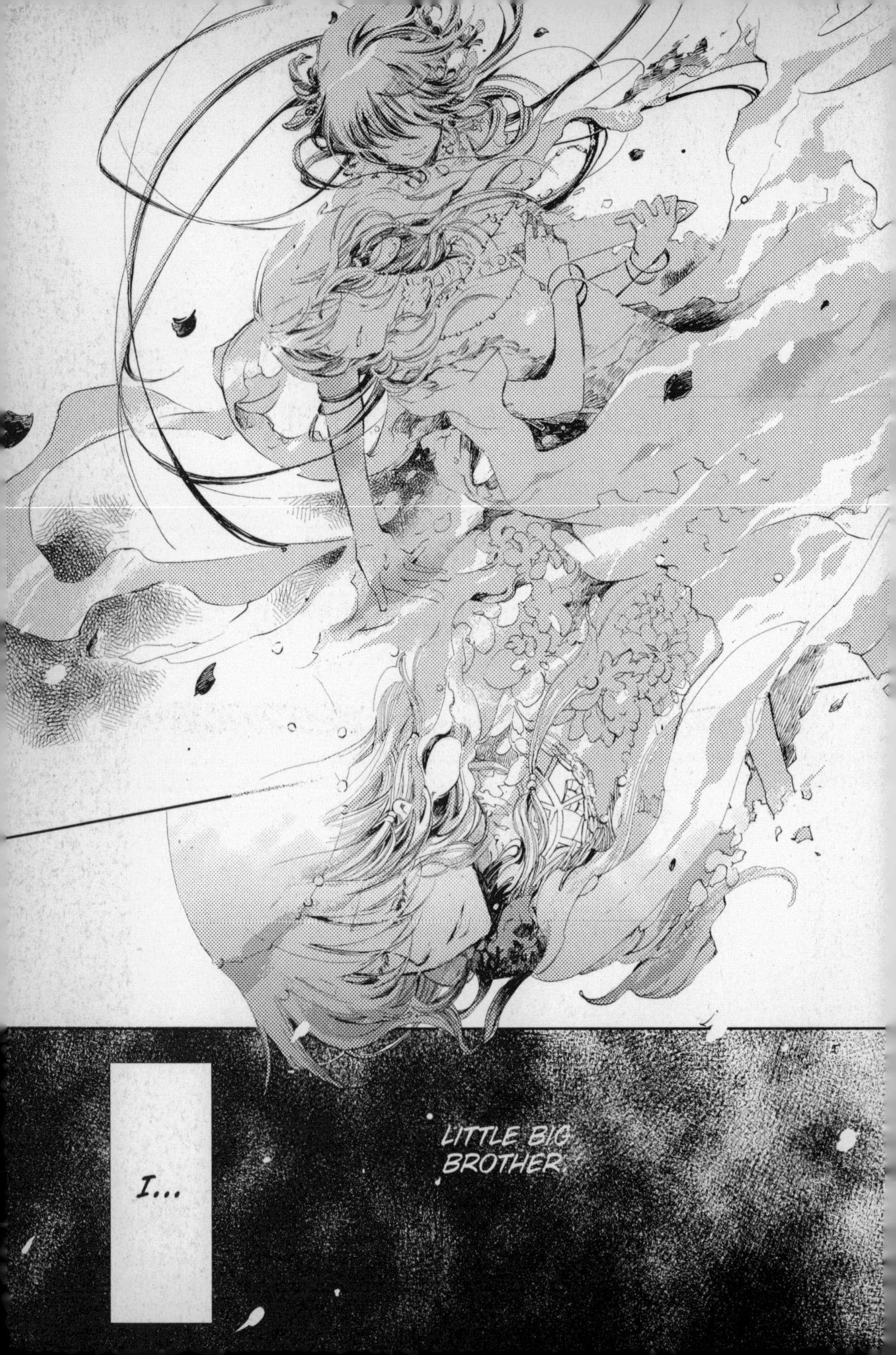
LITTLE BIG BROTHER.
I...

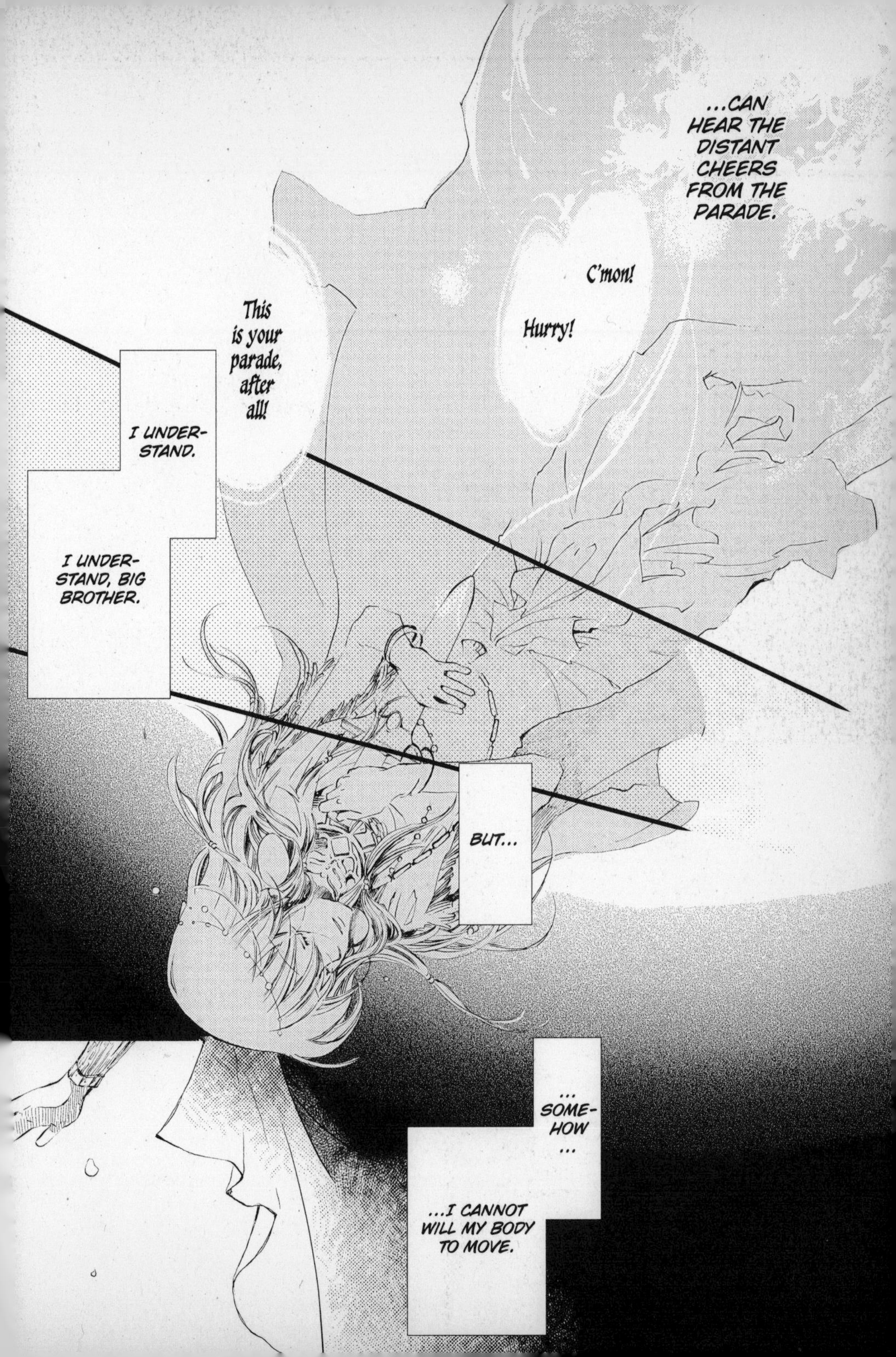
...CAN HEAR THE DISTANT CHEERS FROM THE PARADE.
C'mon!
Hurry!
This is your parade, after all!
I UNDER-STAND.
I UNDER-STAND, BIG BROTHER.
BUT...
...SOME-HOW...
...I CANNOT WILL MY BODY TO MOVE.

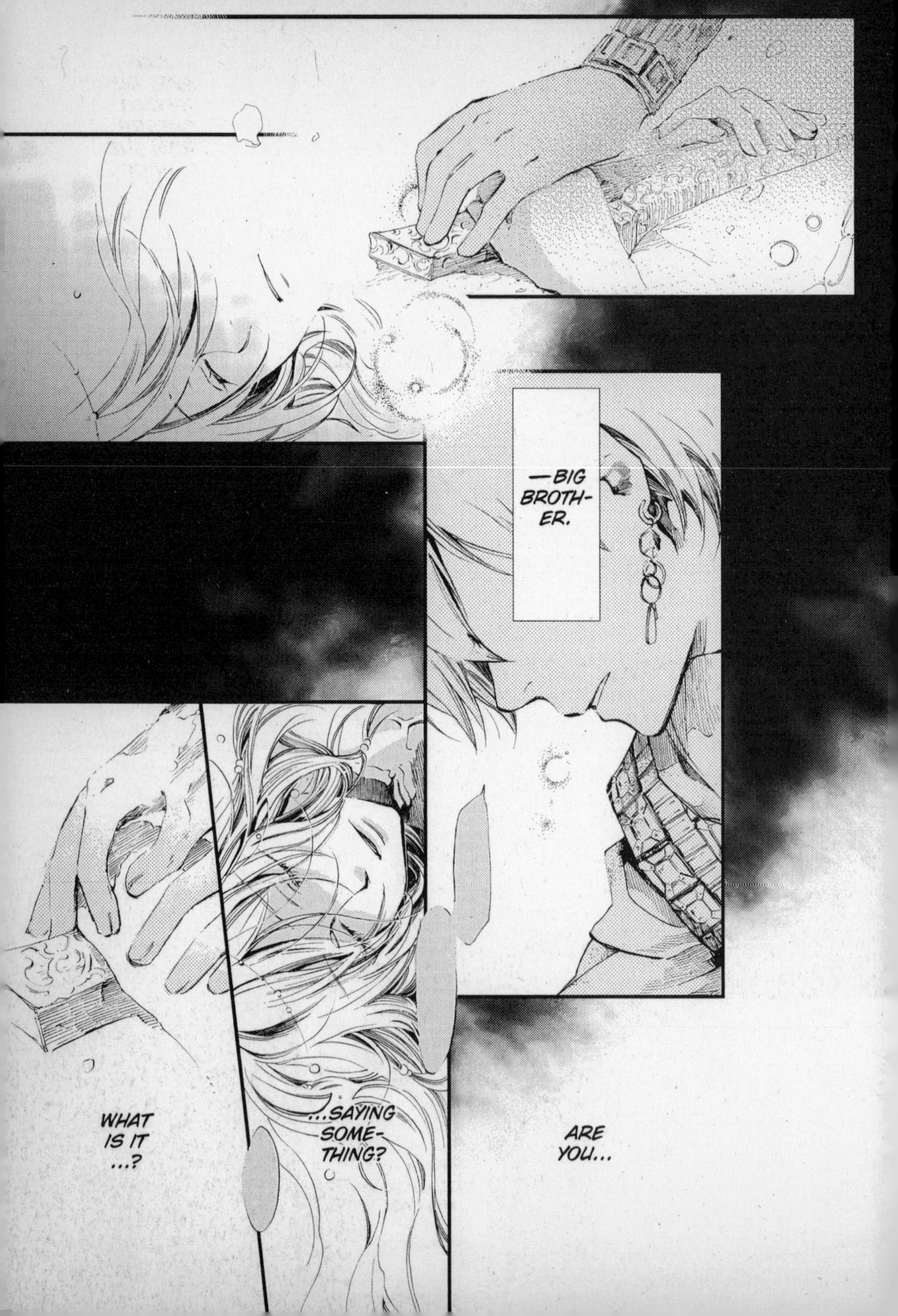
—BIG BROTH-ER.
ARE YOU...
...SAYING SOME-THING?
WHAT IS IT ...?

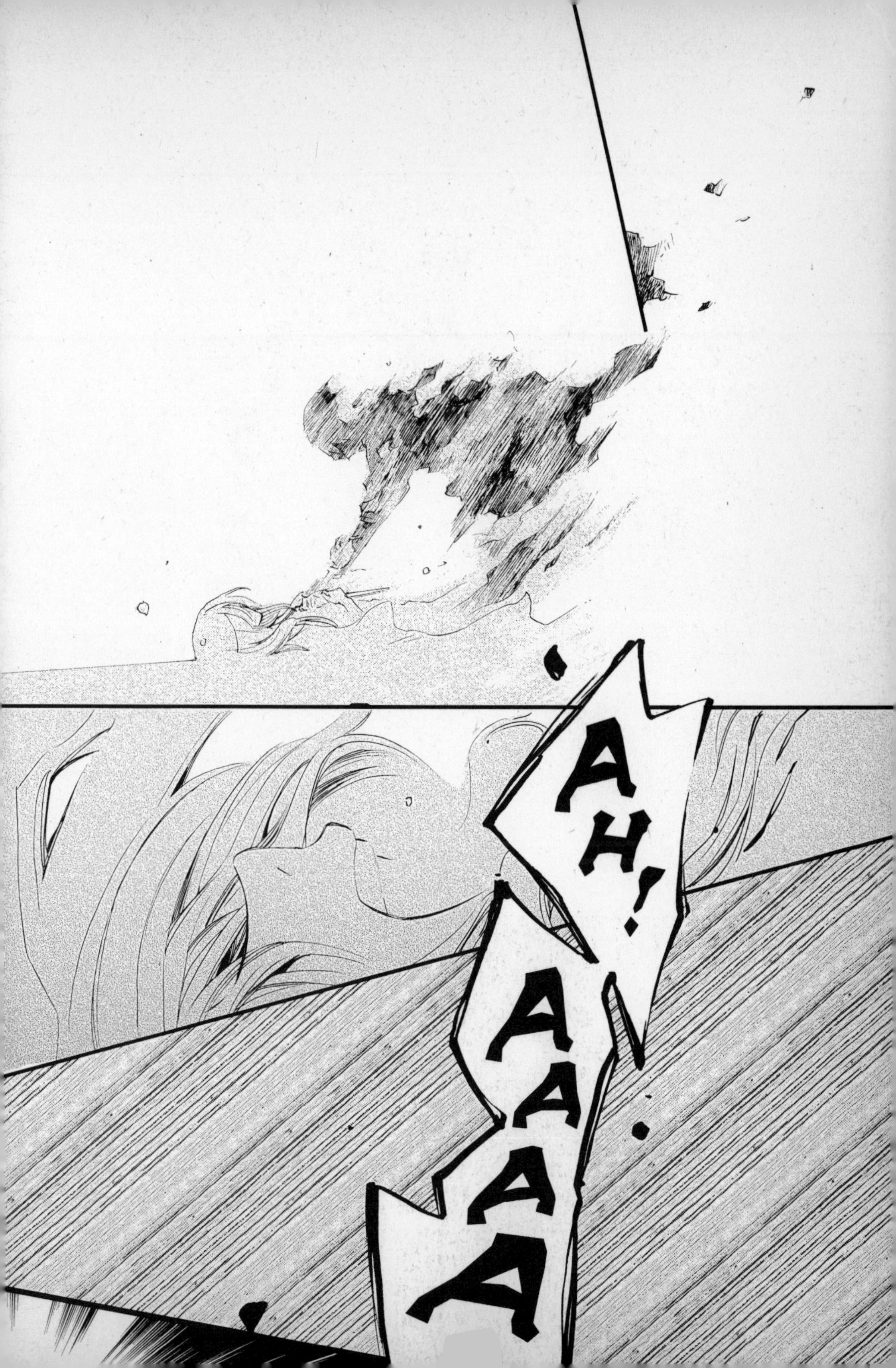
AH! AAAAA

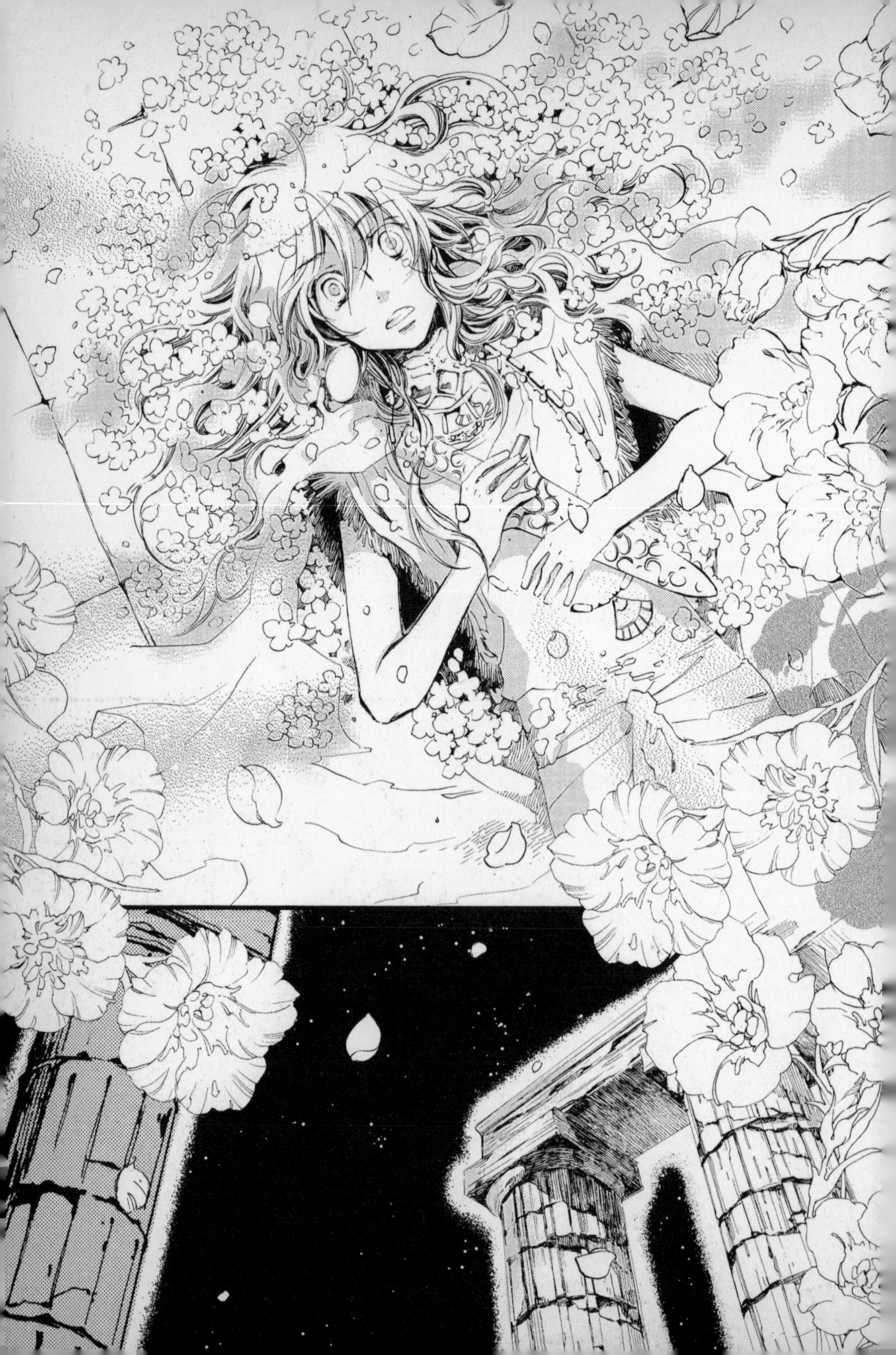

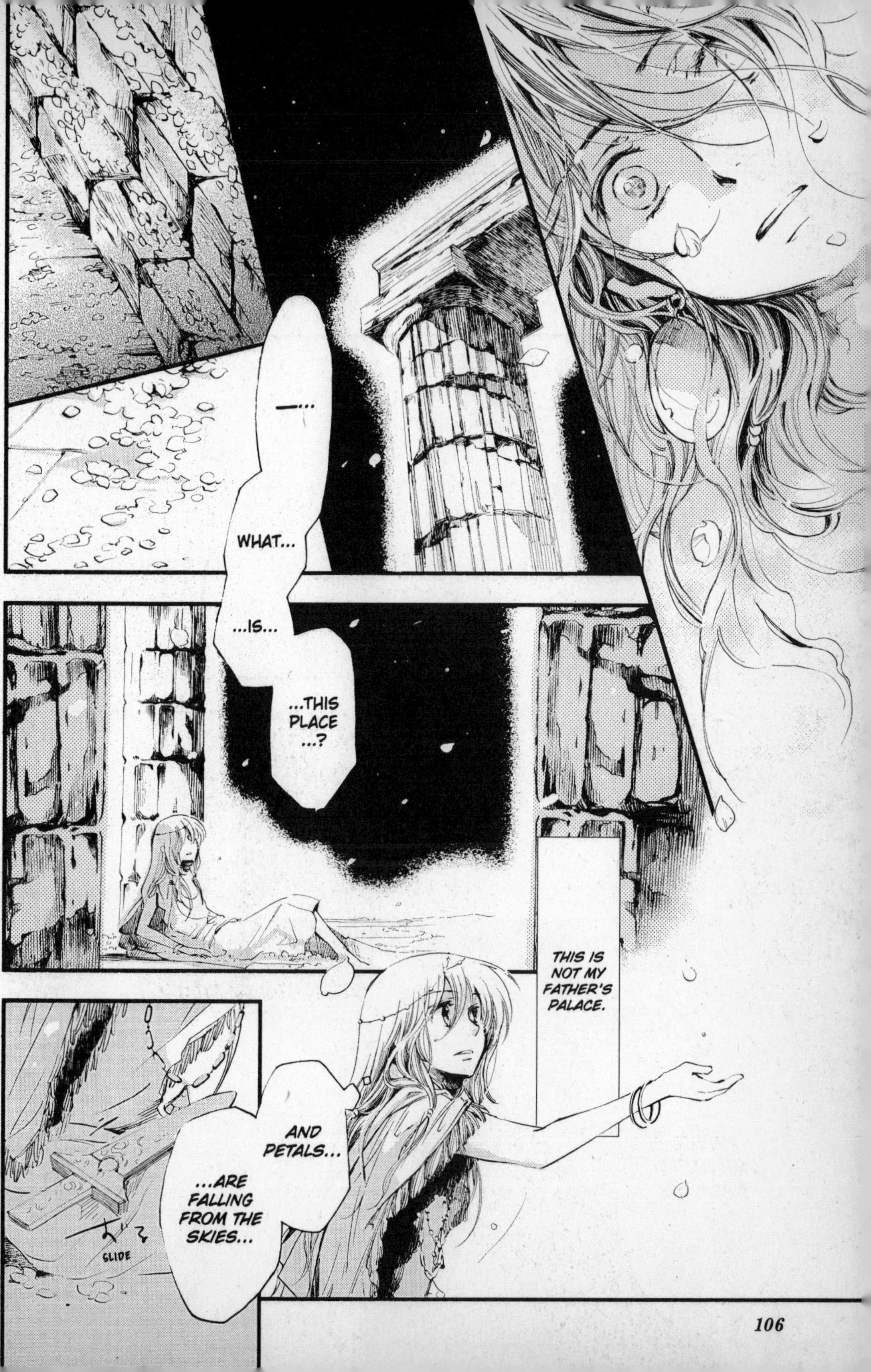
—...
WHAT...
...IS...
...THIS PLACE ...?
THIS IS NOT MY FATHER'S PALACE.
AND PETALS...
...ARE FALLING FROM THE SKIES...
SLIDE

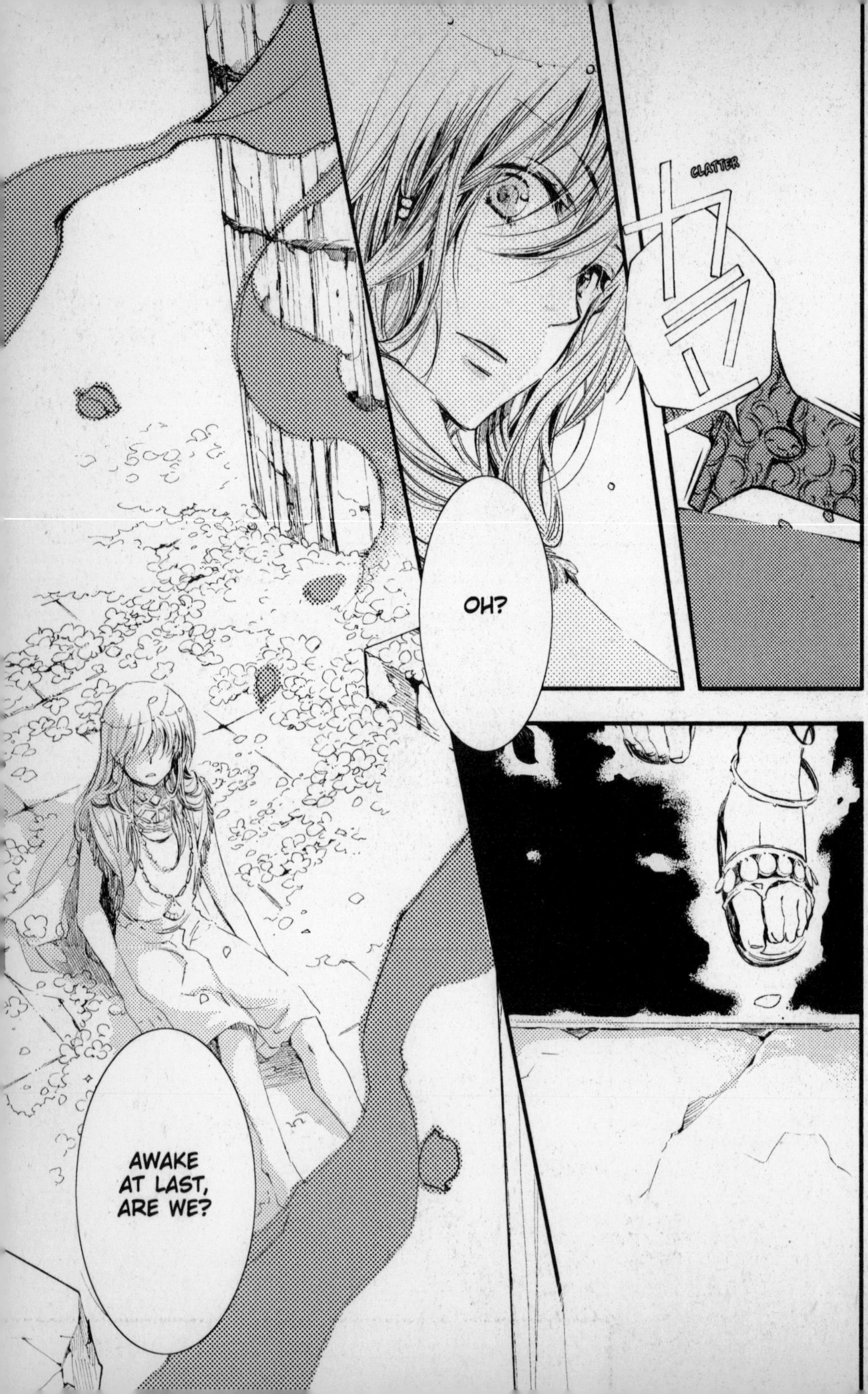
CLATTER
OH?
AWAKE AT LAST, ARE WE?

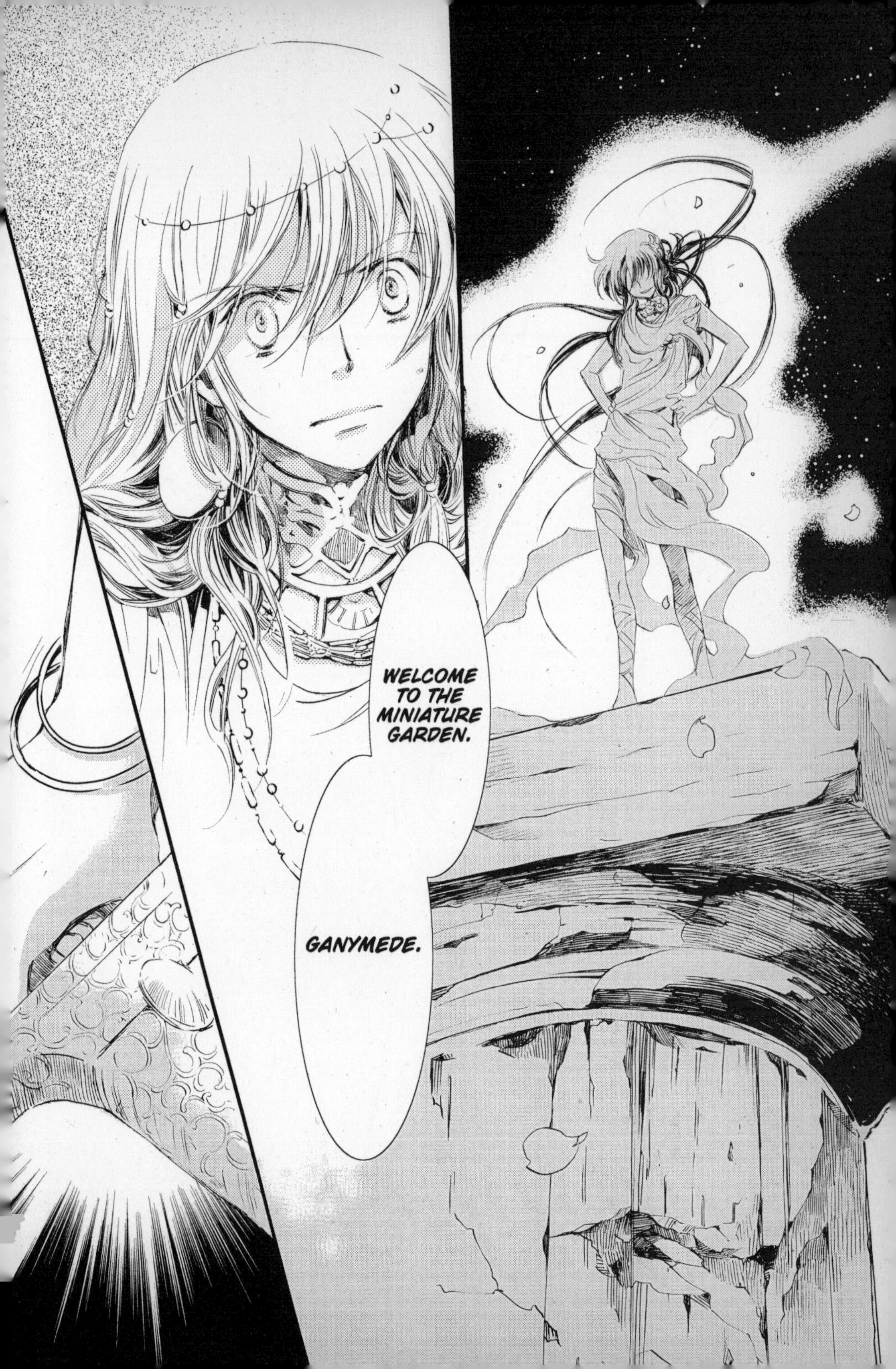
WELCOME TO THE MINIATURE GARDEN.
GANYMEDE.

Olympos

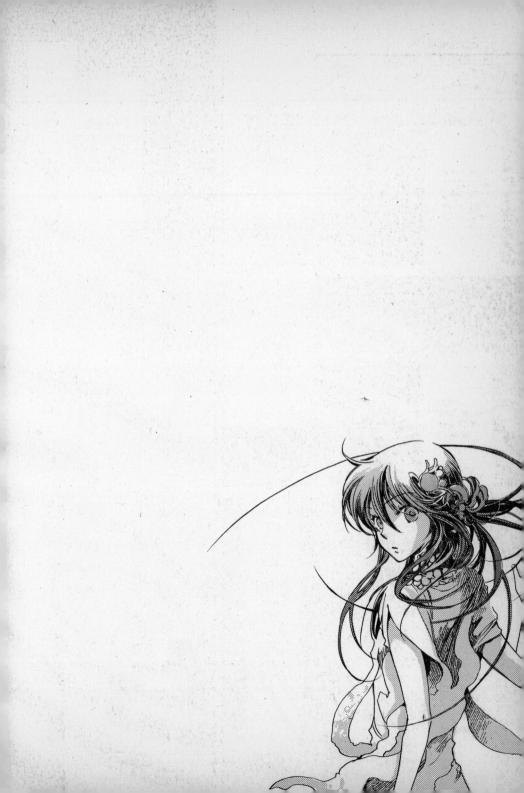

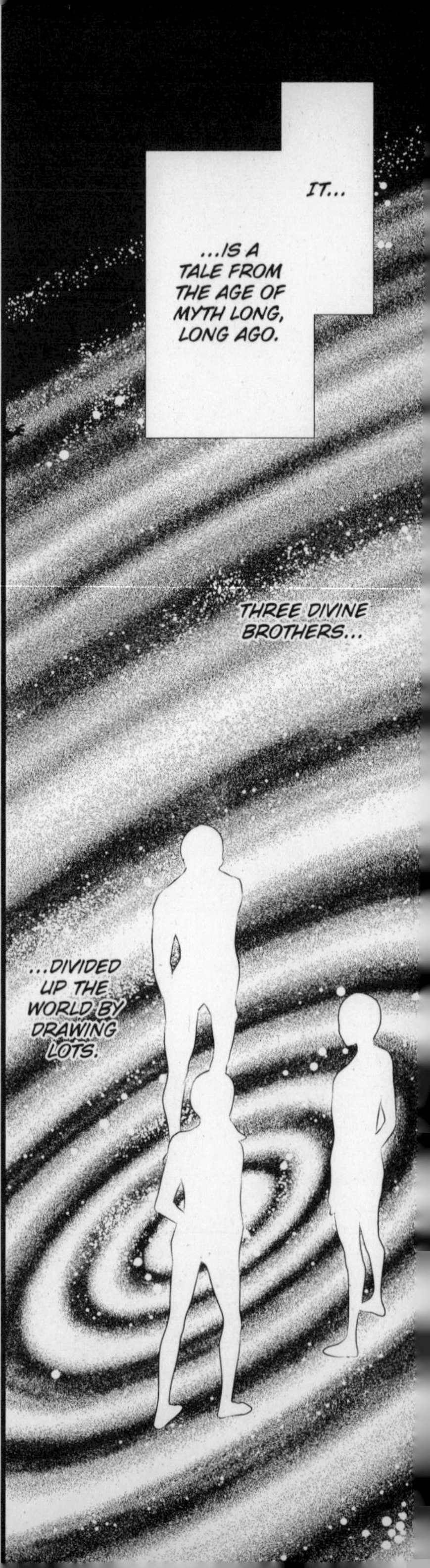
IT...
...IS A TALE FROM THE AGE OF MYTH LONG, LONG AGO.
THREE DIVINE BROTHERS...
...DIVIDED UP THE WORLD BY DRAWING LOTS.

Episode.04

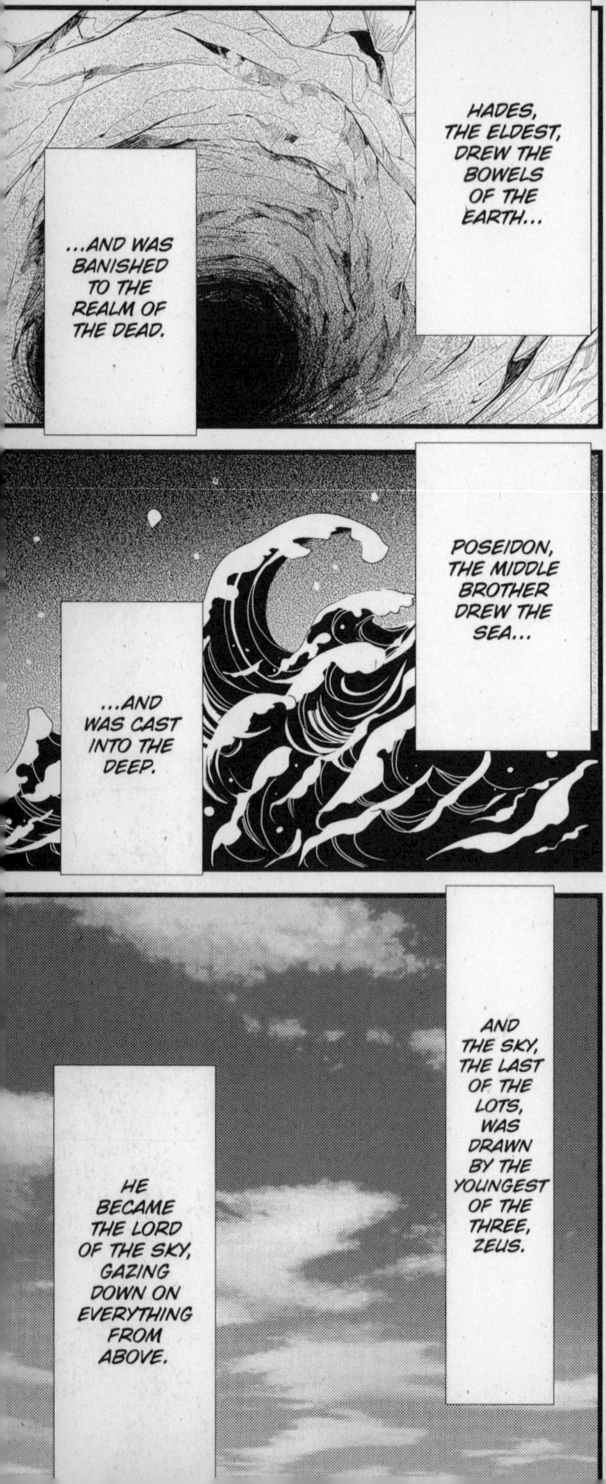
HADES, THE ELDEST, DREW THE BOWELS OF THE EARTH...
...AND WAS BANISHED TO THE REALM OF THE DEAD.
POSEIDON, THE MIDDLE BROTHER DREW THE SEA...
...AND WAS CAST INTO THE DEEP.
AND THE SKY, THE LAST OF THE LOTS, WAS DRAWN BY THE YOUNGEST OF THE THREE, ZEUS.
HE BECAME THE LORD OF THE SKY, GAZING DOWN ON EVERYTHING FROM ABOVE.

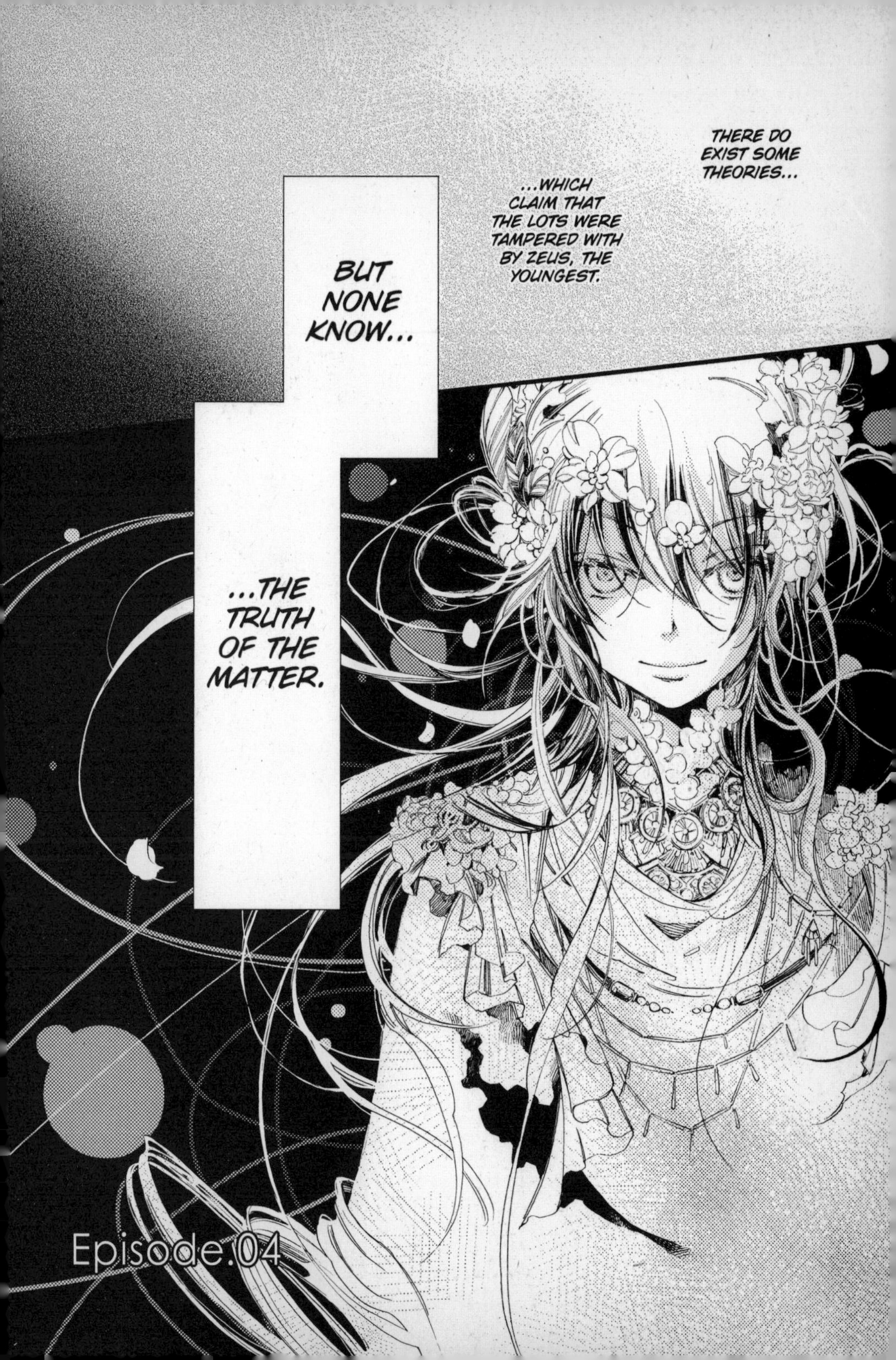
THERE DO EXIST SOME THEORIES...
...WHICH CLAIM THAT THE LOTS WERE TAMPERED WITH BY ZEUS, THE YOUNGEST.
BUT NONE KNOW...
...THE TRUTH OF THE MATTER.
Episode.04

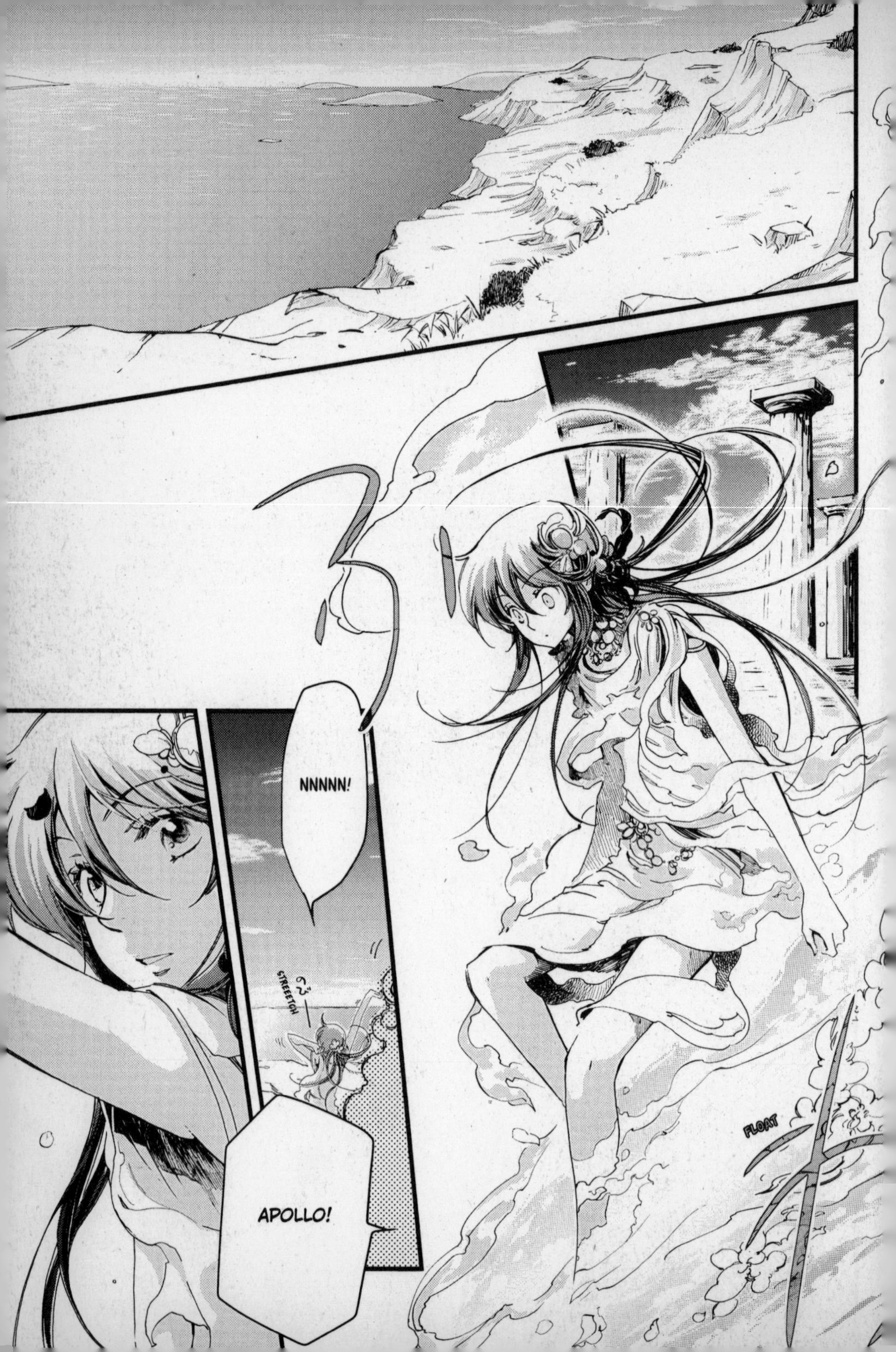
NNNNN!
FLOAT
のび—
STREEETCH
APOLLO!

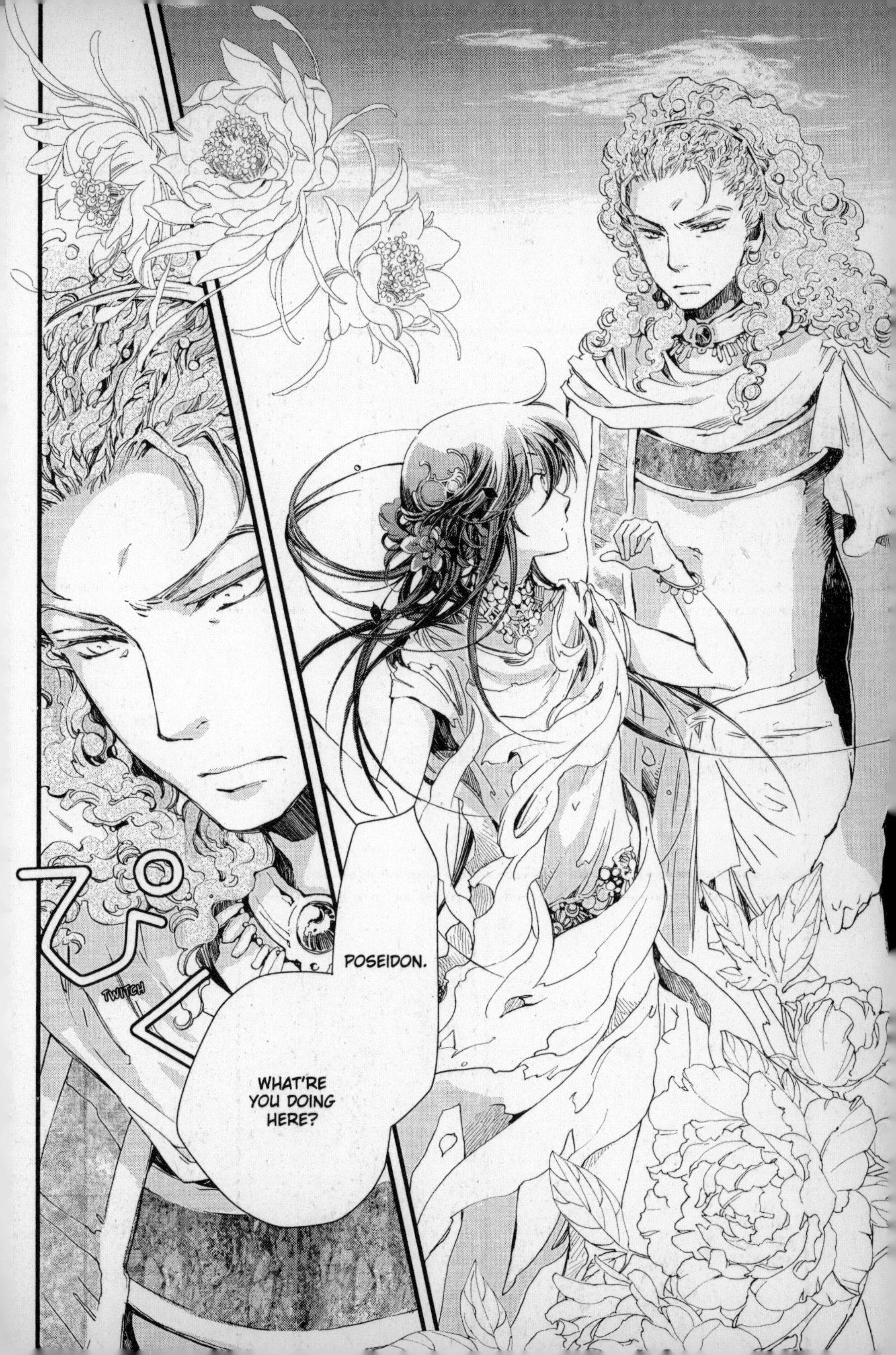
POSEIDON.
WHAT'RE YOU DOING HERE?
TWITCH

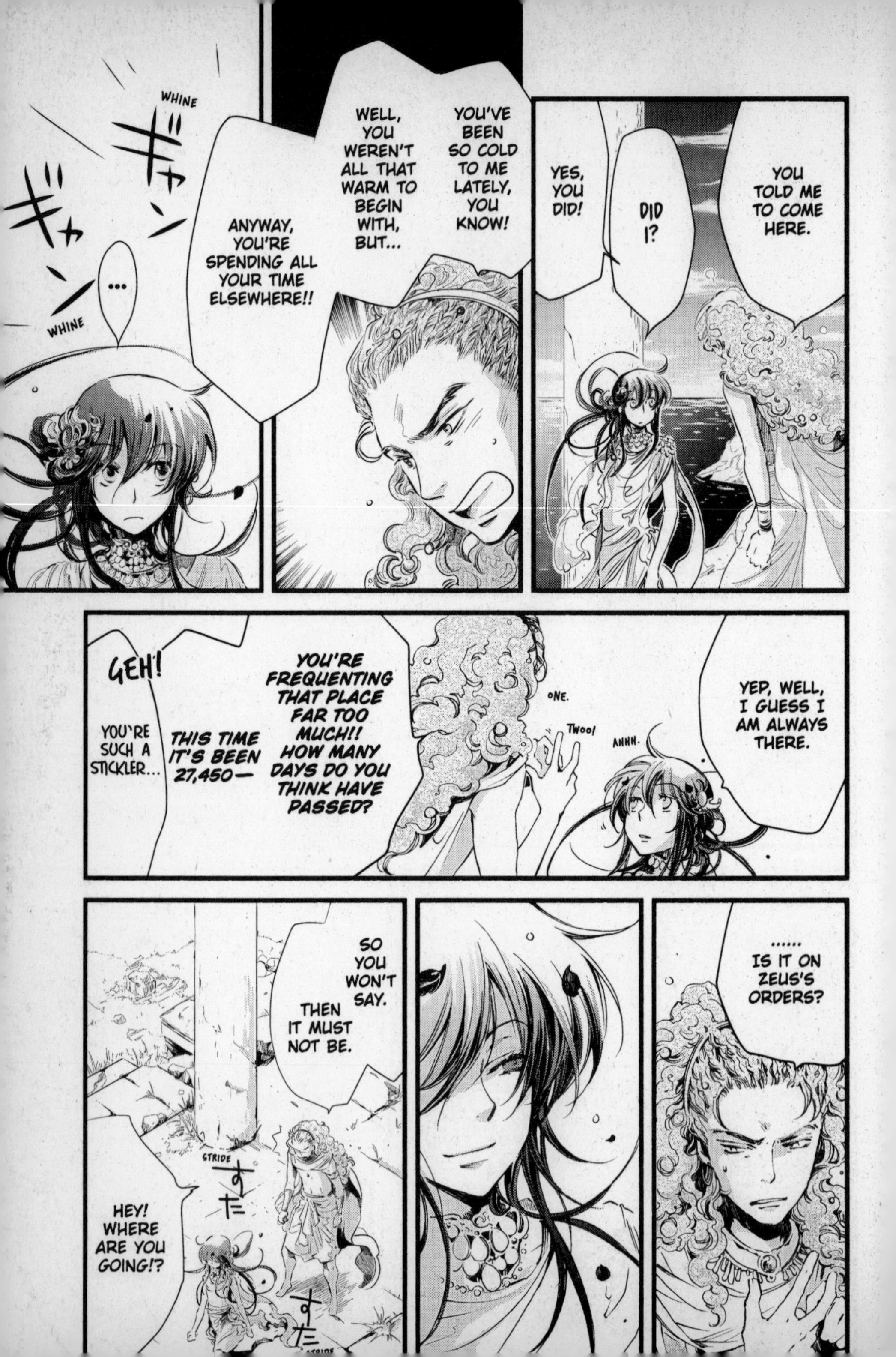
YOU TOLD ME TO COME HERE.
DID I?
YES, YOU DID!
YOU'VE BEEN SO COLD TO ME LATELY, YOU KNOW!
WELL, YOU WEREN'T ALL THAT WARM TO BEGIN WITH, BUT...
ANYWAY, YOU'RE SPENDING ALL YOUR TIME ELSEWHERE!!
WHINE
ギャン
ギャン
WHINE
...
YEP, WELL, I GUESS I AM ALWAYS THERE.
ONE.
TWO!
AHHH.
YOU'RE FREQUENTING THAT PLACE FAR TOO MUCH!! HOW MANY DAYS DO YOU THINK HAVE PASSED?
THIS TIME IT'S BEEN 27,450—
GEH!
YOU'RE SUCH A STICKLER...
......
IS IT ON ZEUS'S ORDERS?
SO YOU WON'T SAY.
THEN IT MUST NOT BE.
STRIDE
すた
すた
HEY! WHERE ARE YOU GOING!?

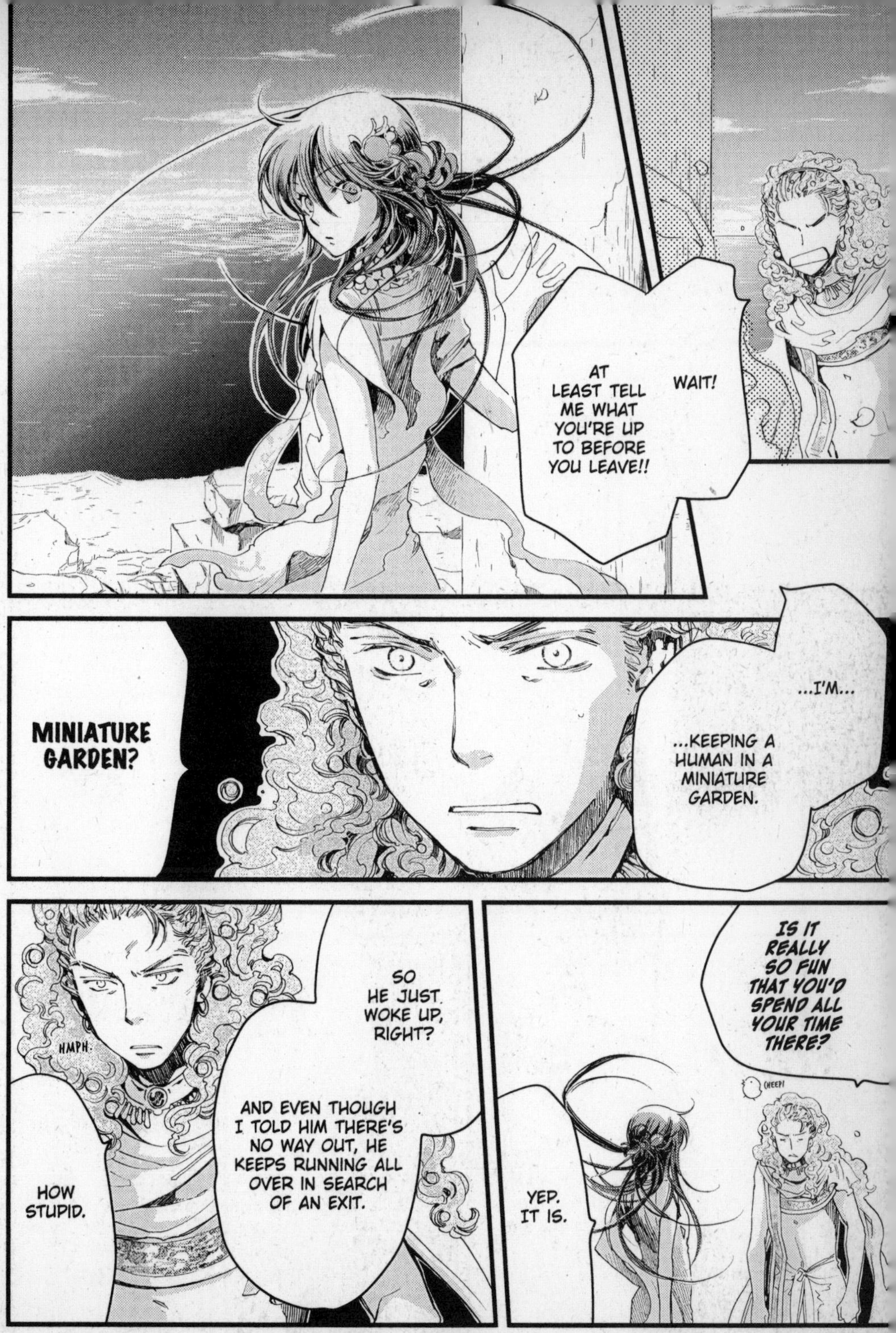
WAIT!
AT LEAST TELL ME WHAT YOU'RE UP TO BEFORE YOU LEAVE!!
...I'M...
...KEEPING A HUMAN IN A MINIATURE GARDEN.
MINIATURE GARDEN?
IS IT REALLY SO FUN THAT YOU'D SPEND ALL YOUR TIME THERE?
CHEEP
YEP. IT IS.
SO HE JUST WOKE UP, RIGHT?
AND EVEN THOUGH I TOLD HIM THERE'S NO WAY OUT, HE KEEPS RUNNING ALL OVER IN SEARCH OF AN EXIT.
HMPH.
HOW STUPID.

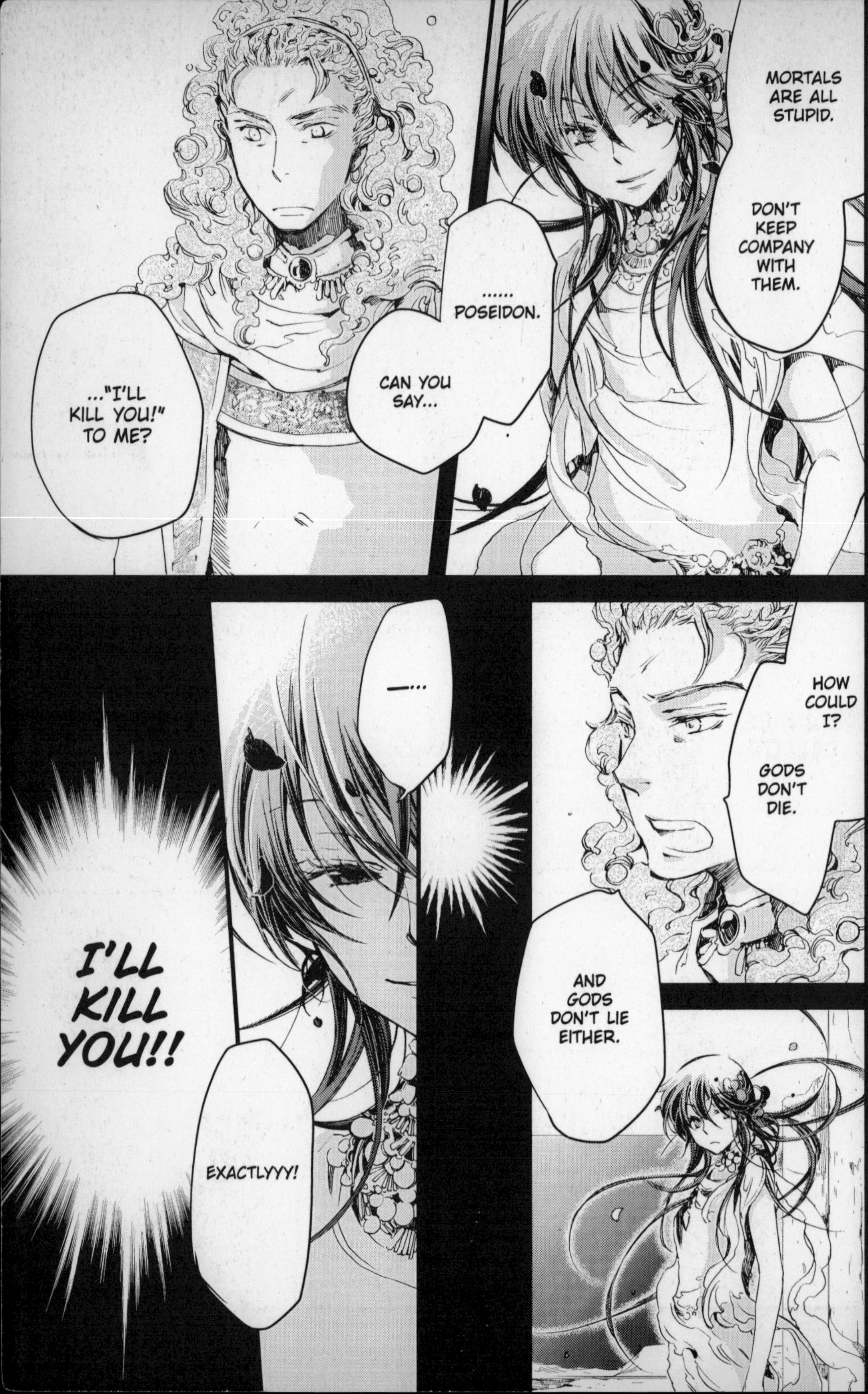
MORTALS ARE ALL STUPID.
DON'T KEEP COMPANY WITH THEM.
......POSEIDON.
CAN YOU SAY...
..."I'LL KILL YOU!" TO ME?
HOW COULD I?
GODS DON'T DIE.
AND GODS DON'T LIE EITHER.
—...
EXACTLYYY!
I'LL KILL YOU!!

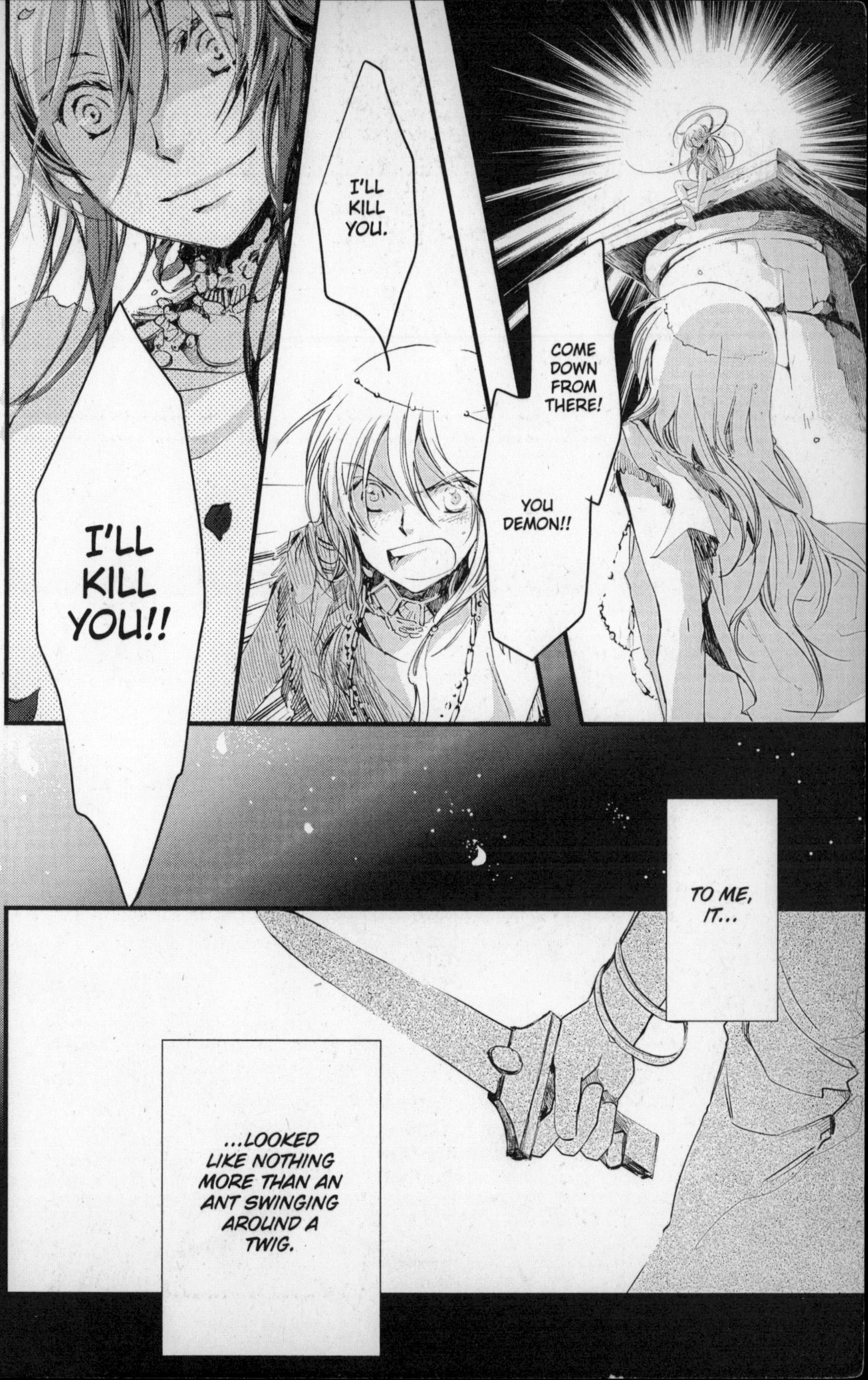
COME DOWN FROM THERE!
YOU DEMON!!
I'LL KILL YOU.
I'LL KILL YOU!!
TO ME, IT...
...LOOKED LIKE NOTHING MORE THAN AN ANT SWINGING AROUND A TWIG.

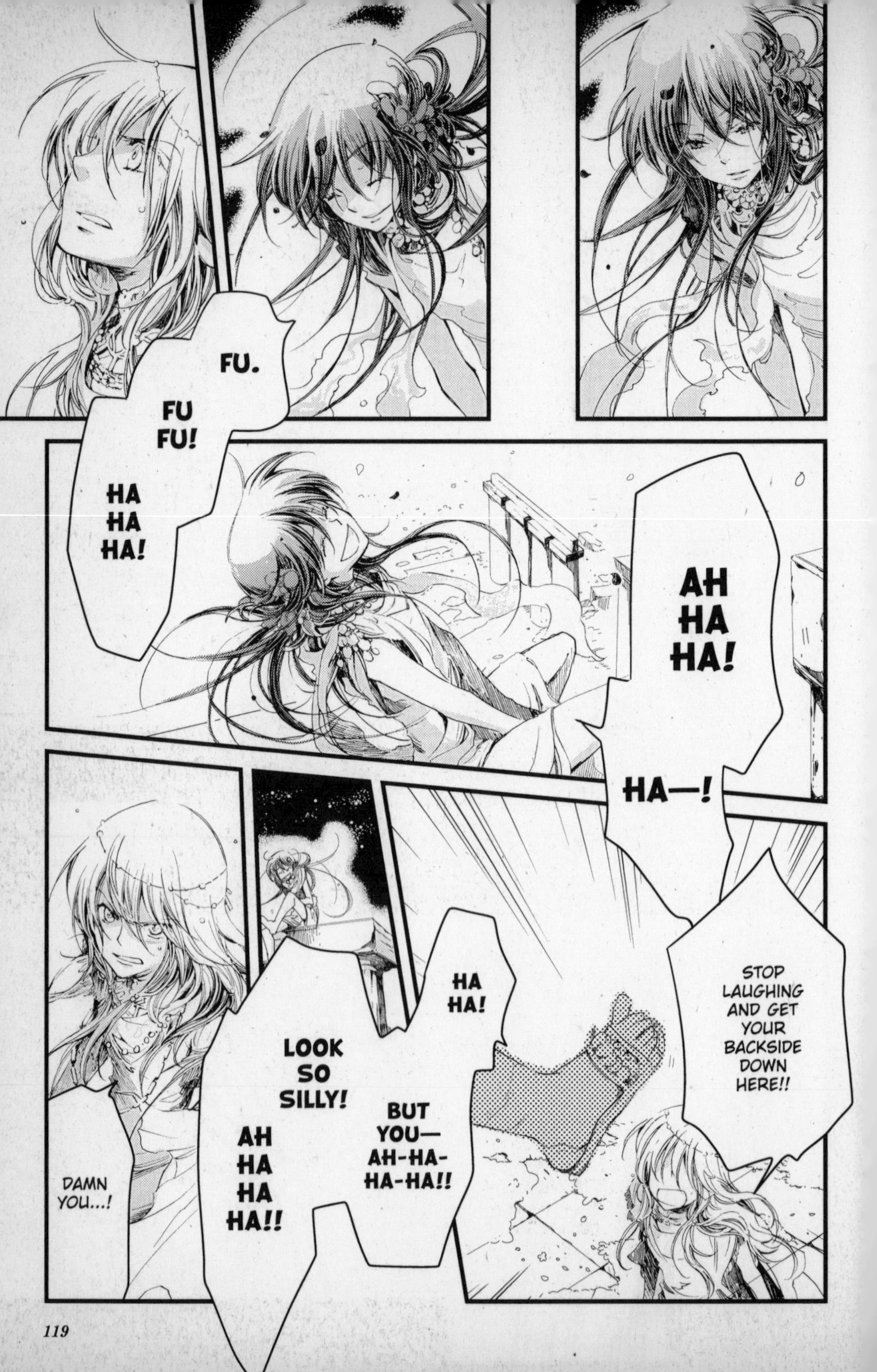
FU.
FU FU!
HA HA HA!
AH HA HA!
HA—!
STOP LAUGHING AND GET YOUR BACKSIDE DOWN HERE!!
HA HA!
BUT YOU— AH-HA-HA-HA!!
LOOK SO SILLY!
AH HA HA HA!!
DAMN YOU...!

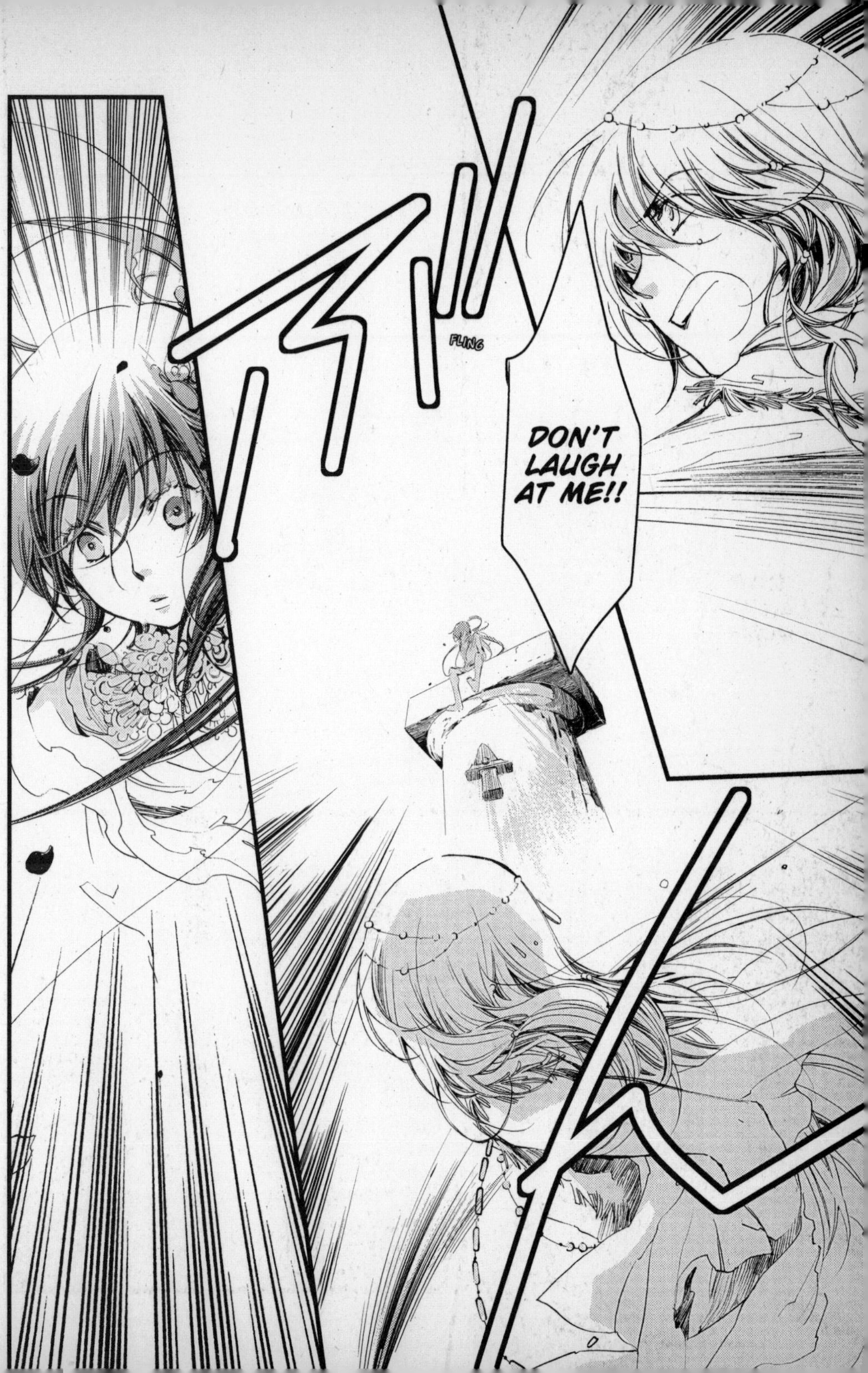
FLING
DON'T LAUGH AT ME!!

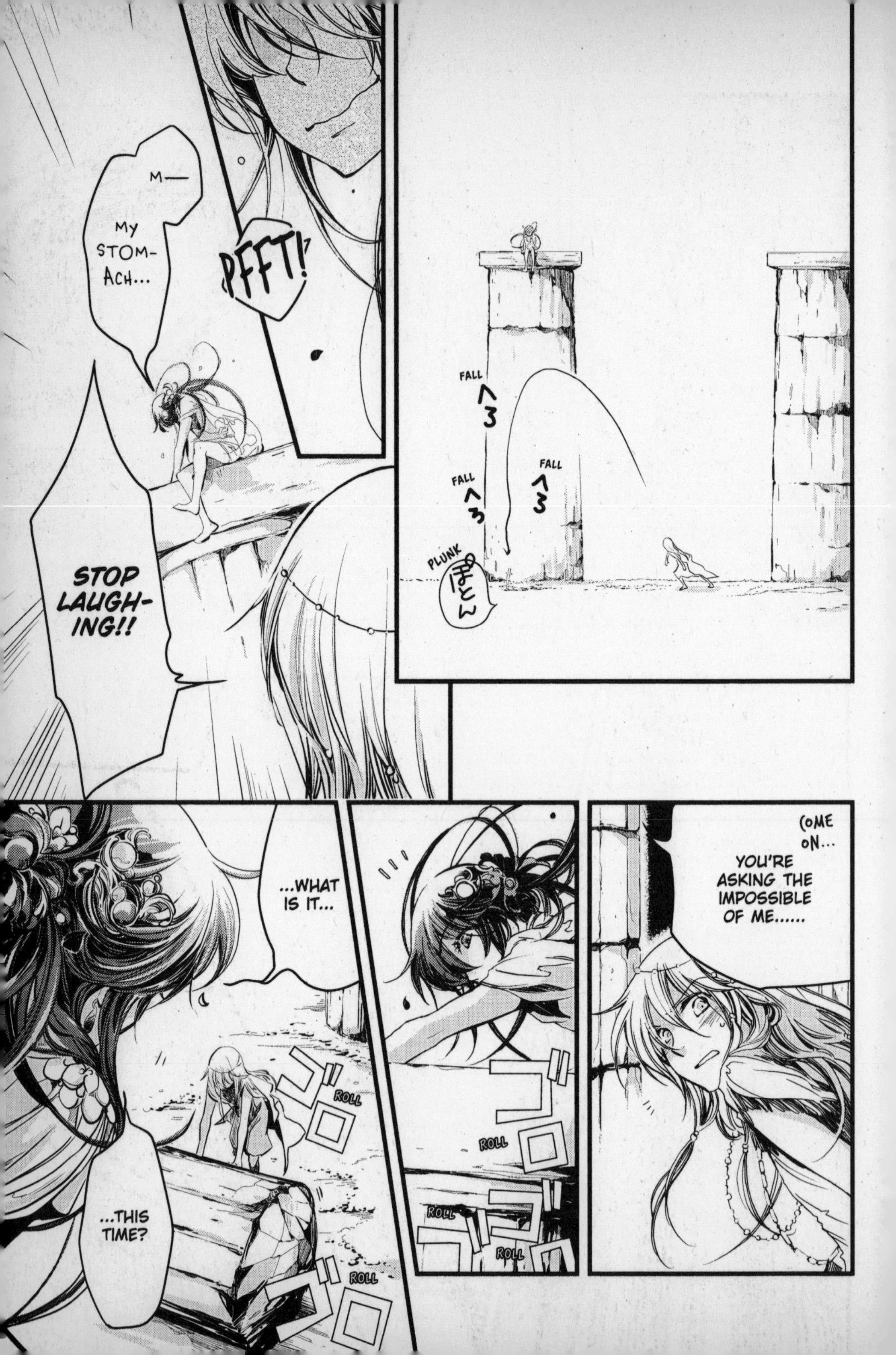
FALL
FALL
FALL
PLUNK
ぽとん
M—
MY STOM-ACH...
PFFT!
STOP LAUGH-ING!!
COME ON...
YOU'RE ASKING THE IMPOSSIBLE OF ME......
ゴロ
ROLL
ゴロ
ROLL
ゴロ
ROLL
ROLL
...WHAT IS IT...
ゴロ
ROLL
...THIS TIME?

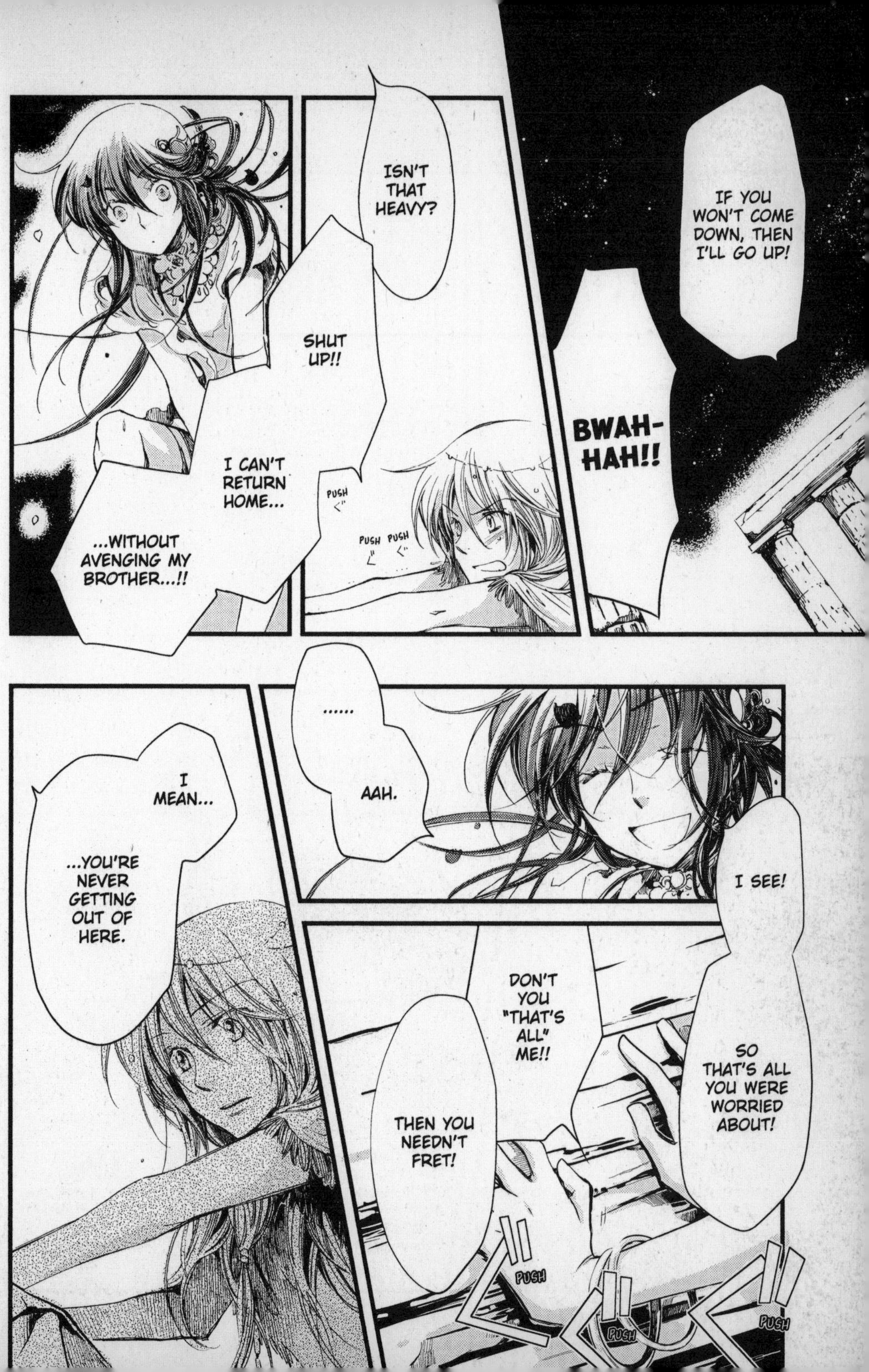
IF YOU WON'T COME DOWN, THEN I'LL GO UP!
BWAH-HAH!!
ISN'T THAT HEAVY?
PUSH
PUSH PUSH
SHUT UP!!
I CAN'T RETURN HOME...
...WITHOUT AVENGING MY BROTHER...!!
......
AAH.
I SEE!
SO THAT'S ALL YOU WERE WORRIED ABOUT!
DON'T YOU "THAT'S ALL" ME!!
THEN YOU NEEDN'T FRET!
PUSH
PUSH
PUSH
I MEAN...
...YOU'RE NEVER GETTING OUT OF HERE.

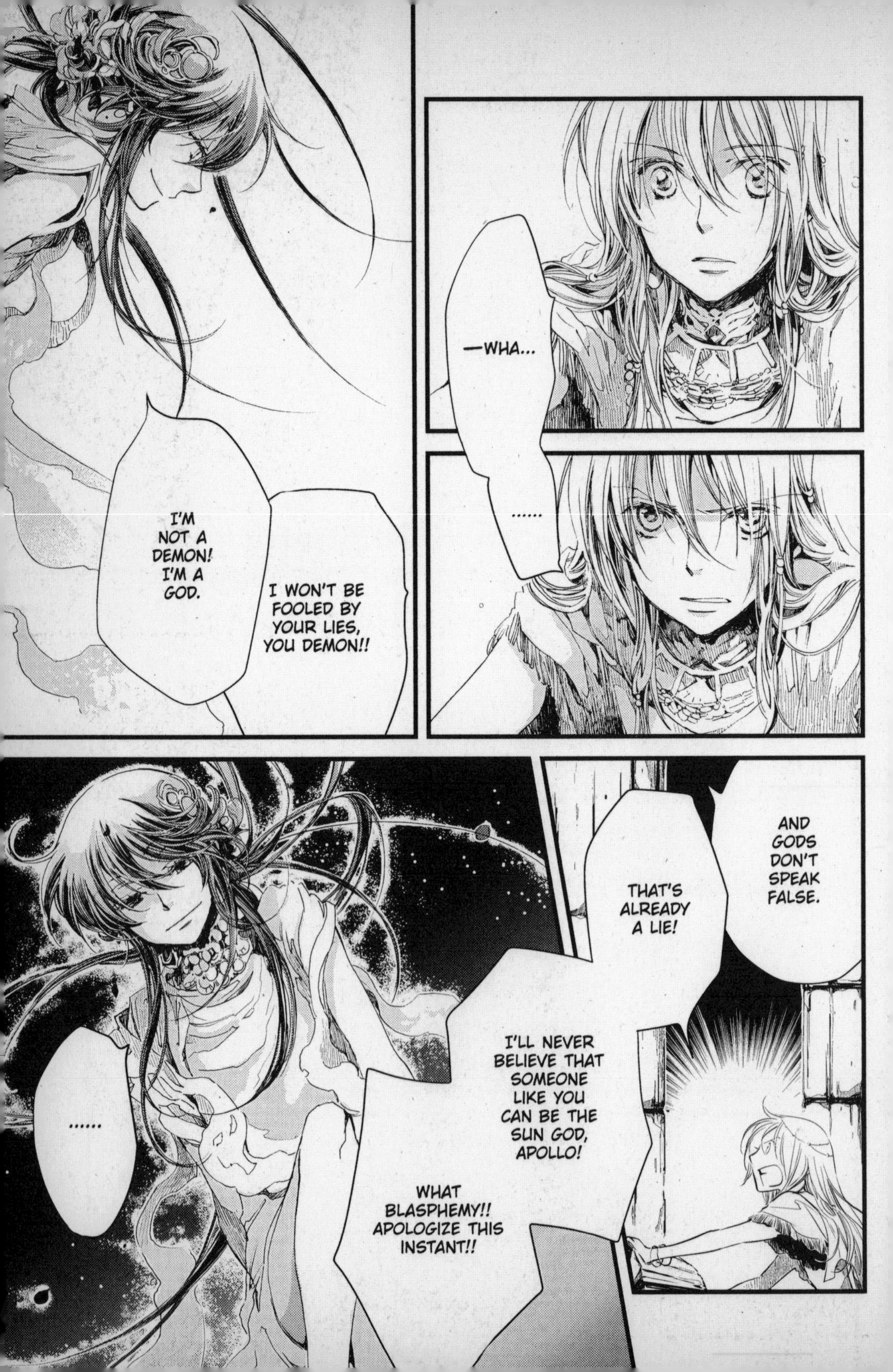
—WHA...
......
I WON'T BE FOOLED BY YOUR LIES, YOU DEMON!!
I'M NOT A DEMON! I'M A GOD.
AND GODS DON'T SPEAK FALSE.
THAT'S ALREADY A LIE!
I'LL NEVER BELIEVE THAT SOMEONE LIKE YOU CAN BE THE SUN GOD, APOLLO!
WHAT BLASPHEMY!! APOLOGIZE THIS INSTANT!!
......

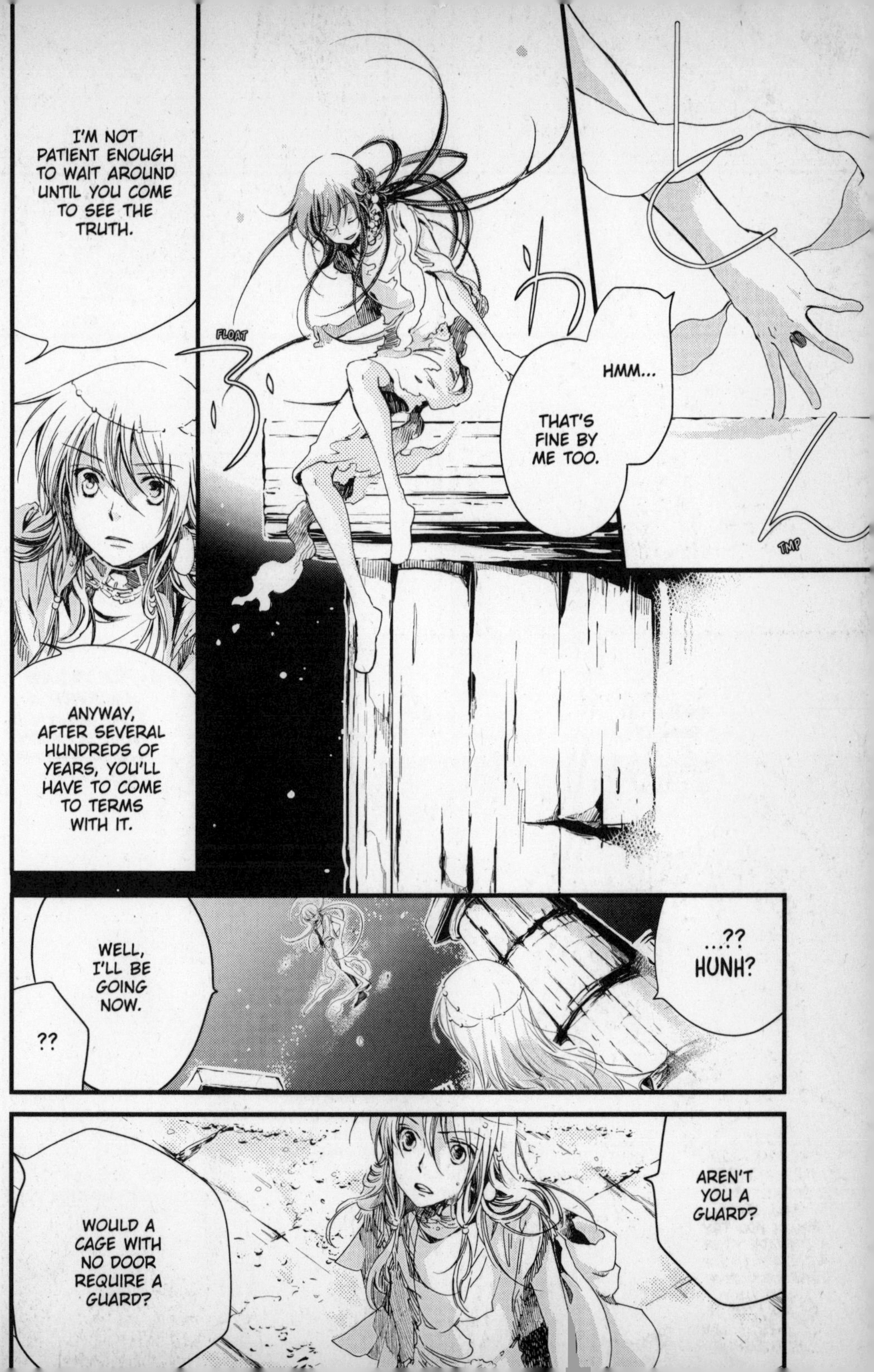
TMP
HMM...
THAT'S FINE BY ME TOO.
FLOAT
I'M NOT PATIENT ENOUGH TO WAIT AROUND UNTIL YOU COME TO SEE THE TRUTH.
ANYWAY, AFTER SEVERAL HUNDREDS OF YEARS, YOU'LL HAVE TO COME TO TERMS WITH IT.
...??
HUNH?
WELL, I'LL BE GOING NOW.
??
AREN'T YOU A GUARD?
WOULD A CAGE WITH NO DOOR REQUIRE A GUARD?

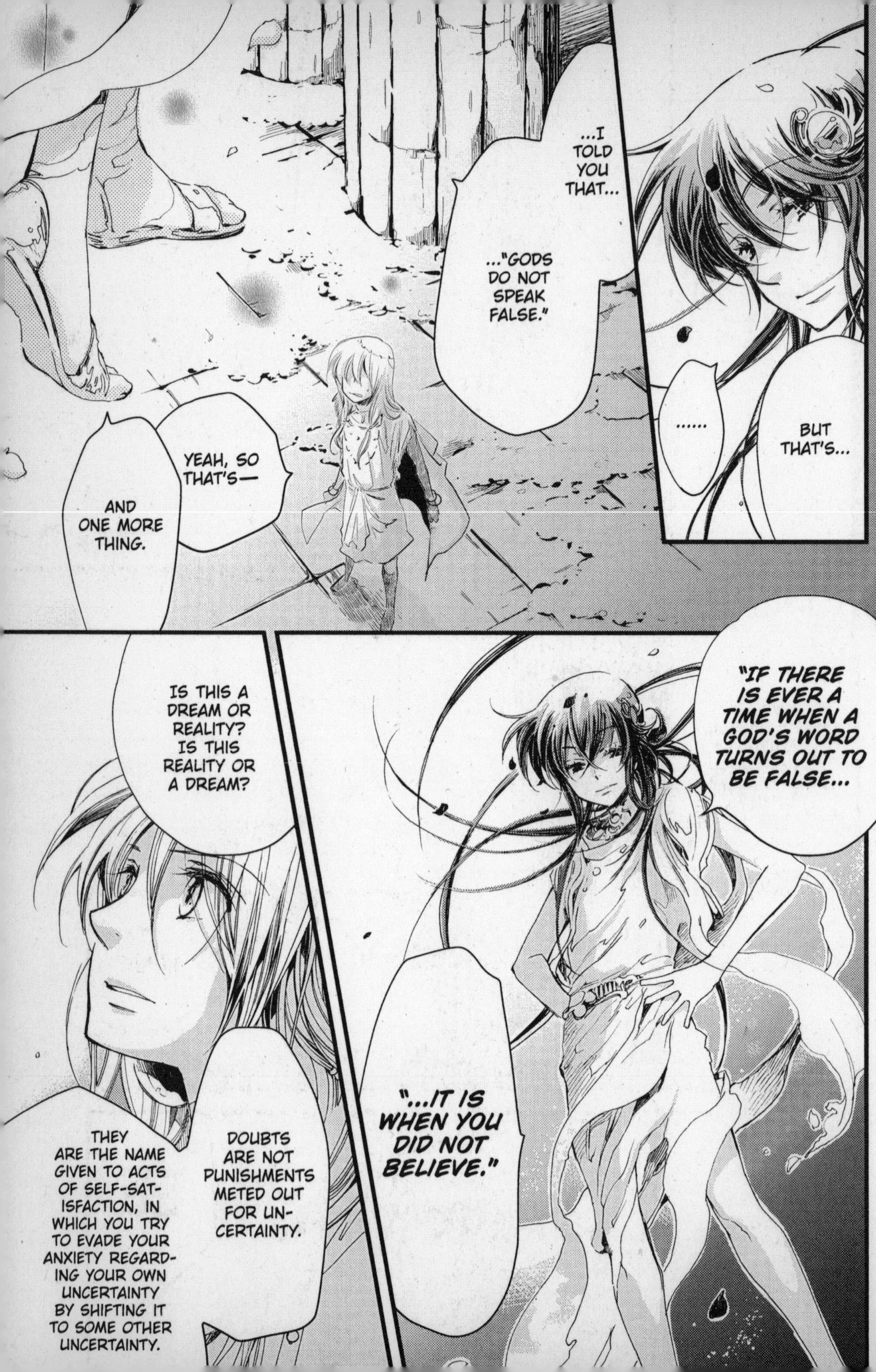
BUT THAT'S...
......
...I TOLD YOU THAT...
..."GODS DO NOT SPEAK FALSE."
YEAH, SO THAT'S—
AND ONE MORE THING.
"IF THERE IS EVER A TIME WHEN A GOD'S WORD TURNS OUT TO BE FALSE...
"...IT IS WHEN YOU DID NOT BELIEVE."
IS THIS A DREAM OR REALITY? IS THIS REALITY OR A DREAM?
DOUBTS ARE NOT PUNISHMENTS METED OUT FOR UN-CERTAINTY.
THEY ARE THE NAME GIVEN TO ACTS OF SELF-SAT-ISFACTION, IN WHICH YOU TRY TO EVADE YOUR ANXIETY REGARD-ING YOUR OWN UNCERTAINTY BY SHIFTING IT TO SOME OTHER UNCERTAINTY.

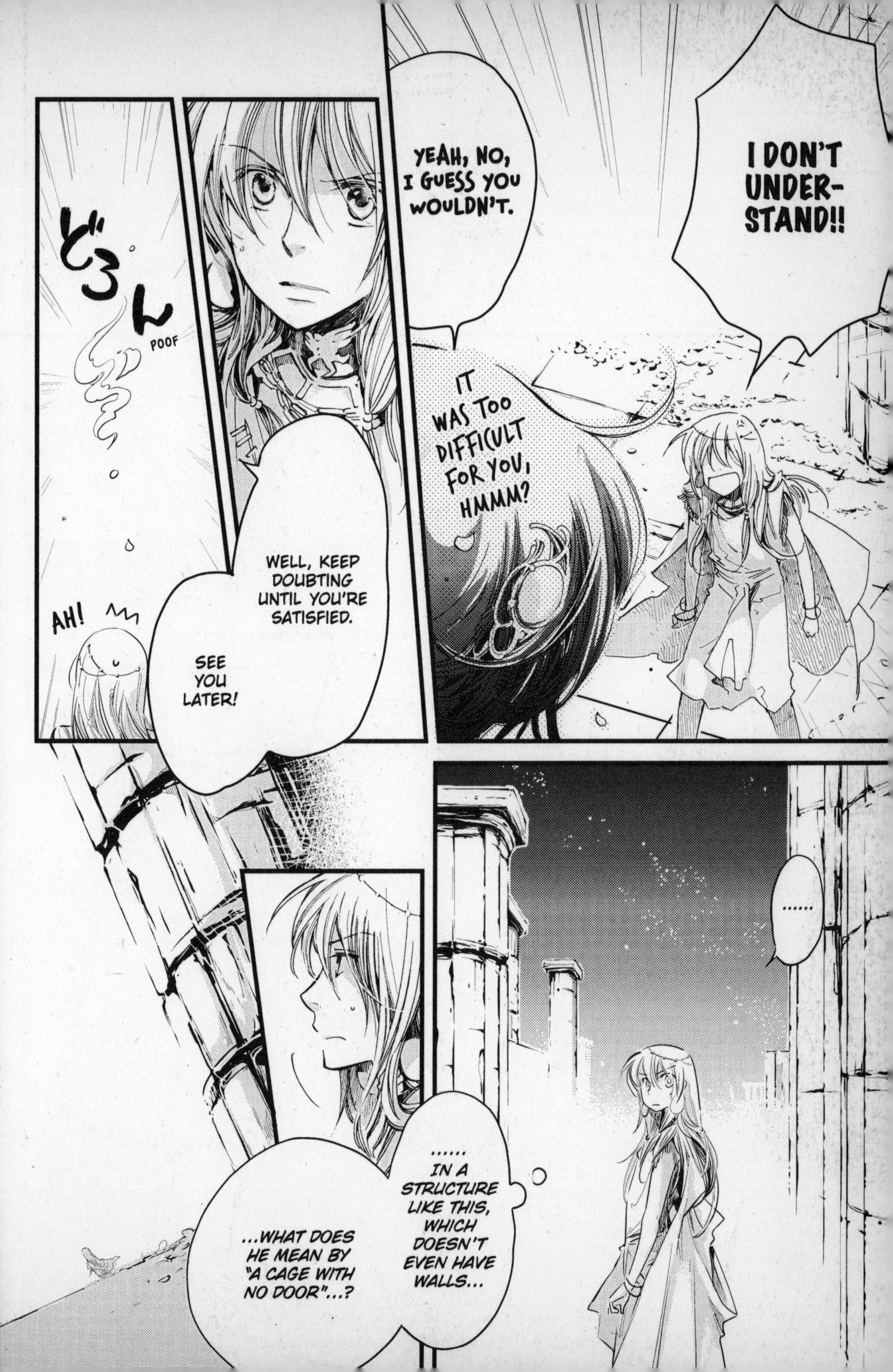
I DON'T UNDER-STAND!!
YEAH, NO, I GUESS YOU WOULDN'T.
IT WAS TOO DIFFICULT FOR YOU, HMMM?
WELL, KEEP DOUBTING UNTIL YOU'RE SATISFIED.
SEE YOU LATER!
どろん
POOF
AH!
......
......
IN A STRUCTURE LIKE THIS, WHICH DOESN'T EVEN HAVE WALLS...
...WHAT DOES HE MEAN BY "A CAGE WITH NO DOOR"...?

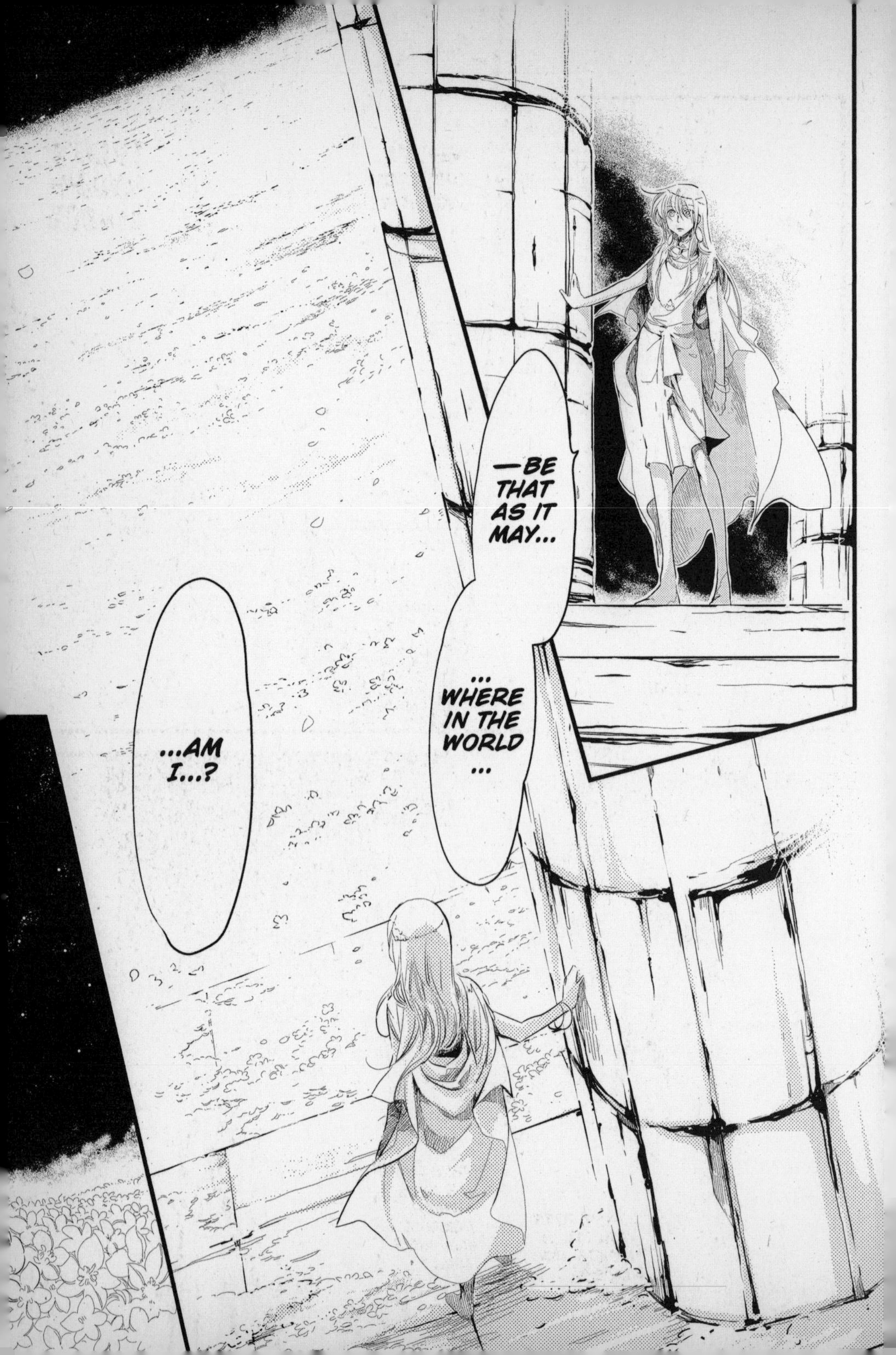
—BE THAT AS IT MAY...
...WHERE IN THE WORLD...
...AM I...?

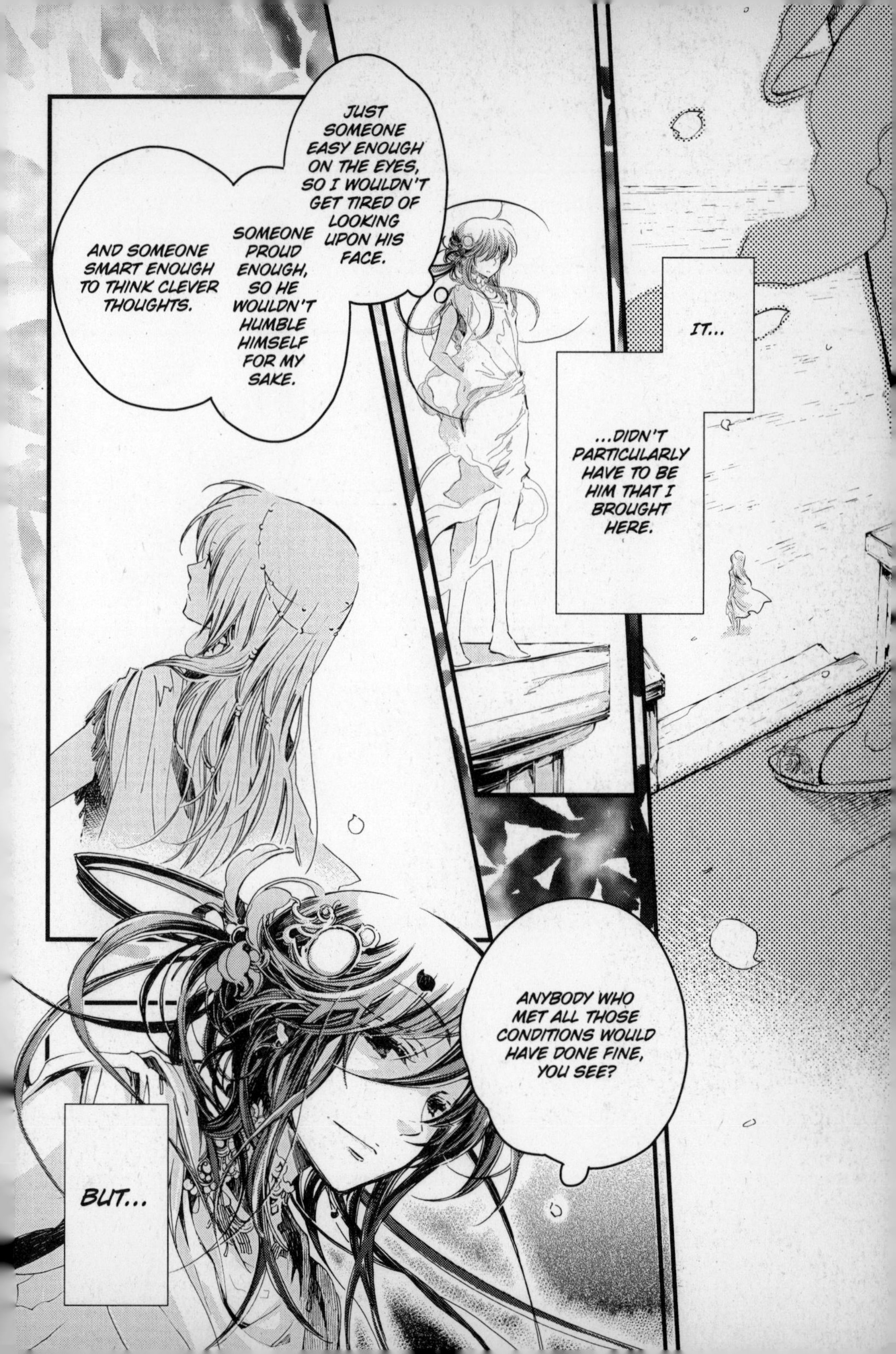
IT...
...DIDN'T PARTICULARLY HAVE TO BE HIM THAT I BROUGHT HERE.
JUST SOMEONE EASY ENOUGH ON THE EYES, SO I WOULDN'T GET TIRED OF LOOKING UPON HIS FACE.
SOMEONE PROUD ENOUGH, SO HE WOULDN'T HUMBLE HIMSELF FOR MY SAKE.
AND SOMEONE SMART ENOUGH TO THINK CLEVER THOUGHTS.
ANYBODY WHO MET ALL THOSE CONDITIONS WOULD HAVE DONE FINE, YOU SEE?
BUT...

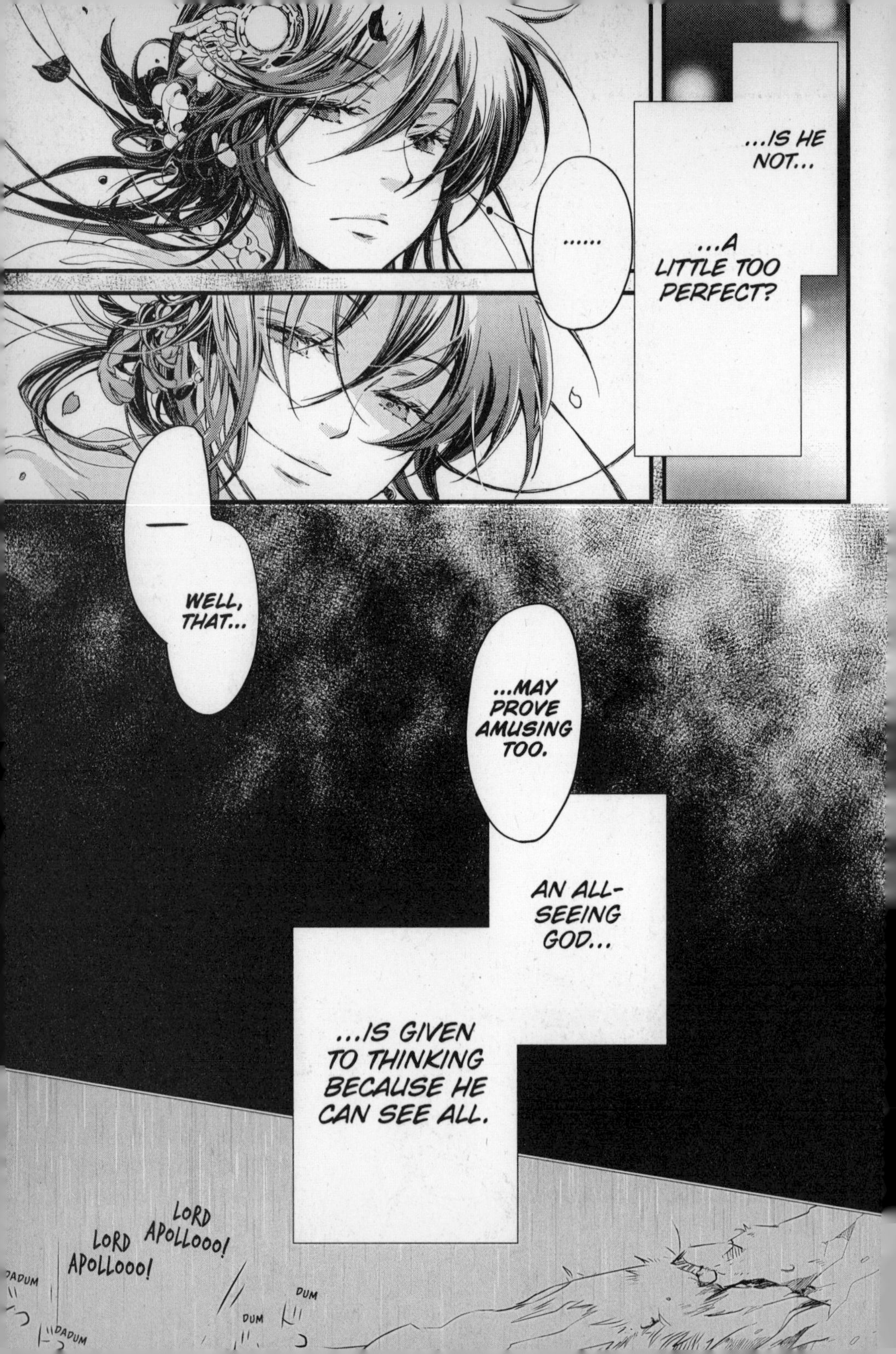
...IS HE NOT...
...A LITTLE TOO PERFECT?
......
— WELL, THAT...
...MAY PROVE AMUSING TOO.
AN ALL-SEEING GOD...
...IS GIVEN TO THINKING BECAUSE HE CAN SEE ALL.
LORD APOLLOOO!
LORD APOLLOOO!
DUM
DUM
DADUM
DADUM

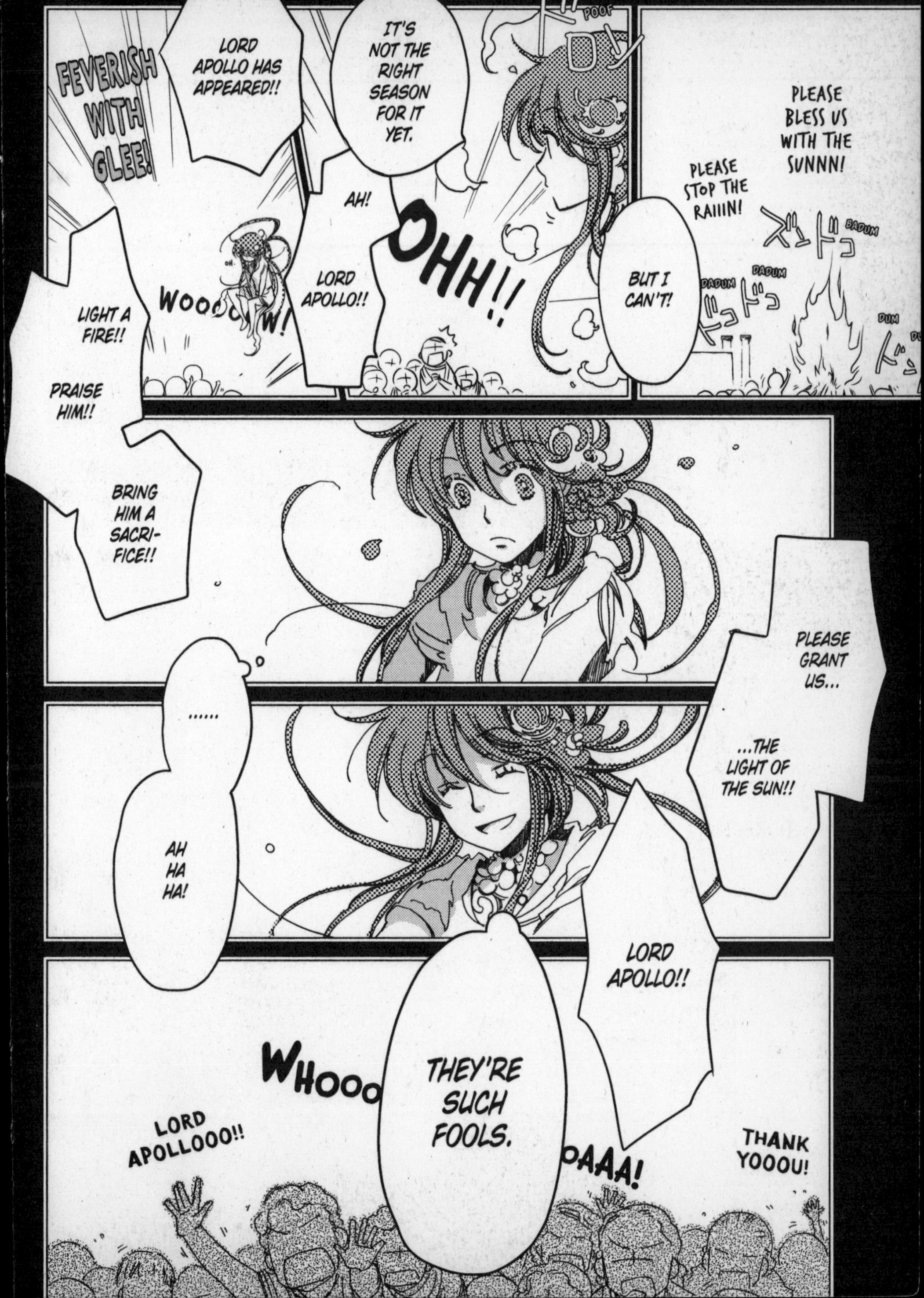
PLEASE BLESS US WITH THE SUNNN!
PLEASE STOP THE RAIIIN!
BADUM
DADUM
DADUM
DUM
POOF
IT'S NOT THE RIGHT SEASON FOR IT YET.
OHH!!
BUT I CAN'T!
AH!
LORD APOLLO!!
LORD APOLLO HAS APPEARED!!
FEVERISH WITH GLEE!
OH.
WOOO
W!
LIGHT A FIRE!!
PRAISE HIM!!
BRING HIM A SACRIFICE!!
PLEASE GRANT US...
......
...THE LIGHT OF THE SUN!!
AH HA HA!
THANK YOOOU!
LORD APOLLO!!
THEY'RE SUCH FOOLS.
WHOOO
OAAA!
LORD APOLLOOO!!

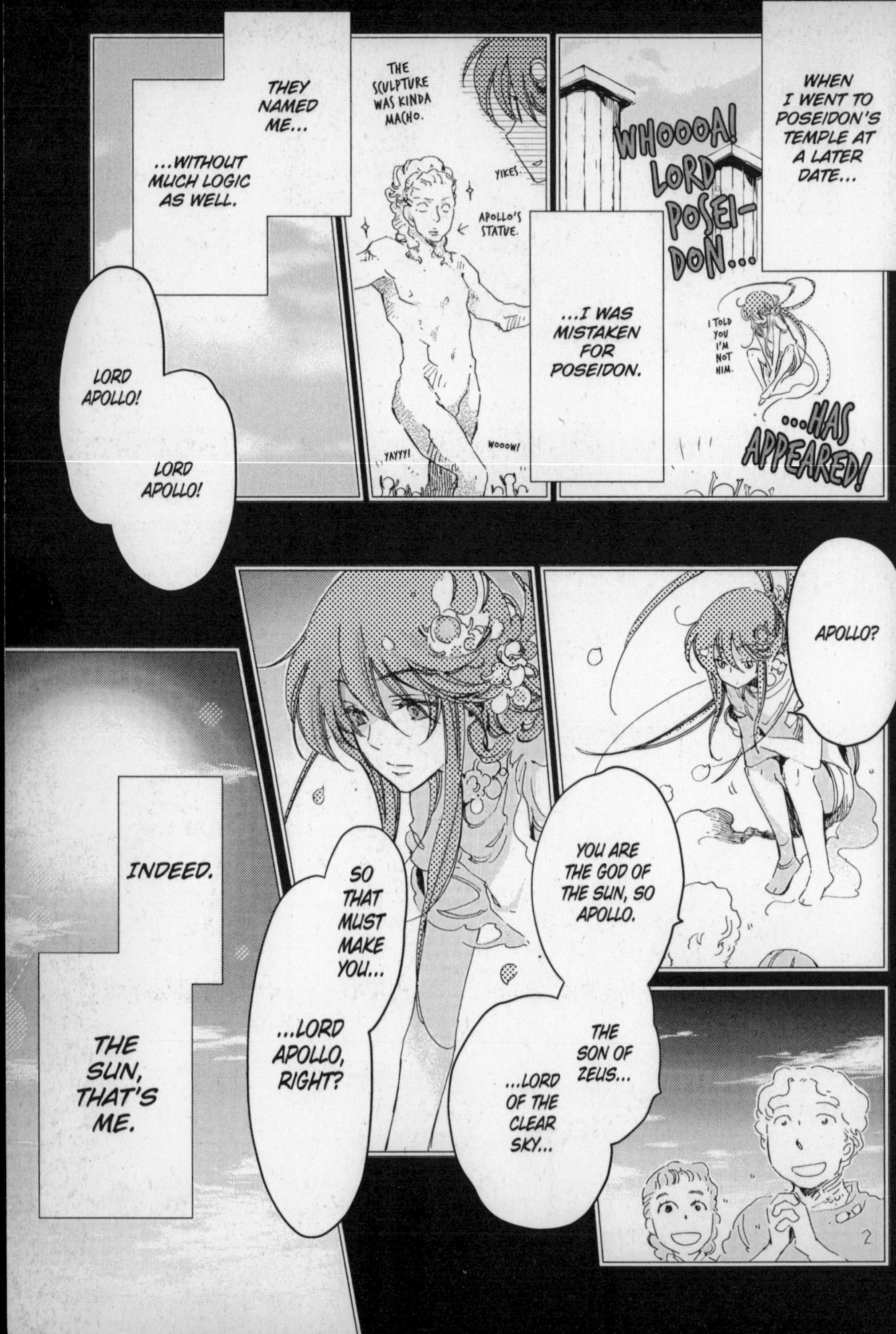
WHEN I WENT TO POSEIDON'S TEMPLE AT A LATER DATE...
WHOOOA! LORD POSEI-DON...
I TOLD YOU I'M NOT HIM.
...HAS APPEARED!
...I WAS MISTAKEN FOR POSEIDON.
THE SCULPTURE WAS KINDA MACHO.
YIKES.
APOLLO'S STATUE.
WOOOW!
YAYYY!
THEY NAMED ME...
...WITHOUT MUCH LOGIC AS WELL.
LORD APOLLO!
LORD APOLLO!
APOLLO?
YOU ARE THE GOD OF THE SUN, SO APOLLO.
THE SON OF ZEUS...
...LORD OF THE CLEAR SKY...
SO THAT MUST MAKE YOU...
...LORD APOLLO, RIGHT?
INDEED.
THE SUN, THAT'S ME.

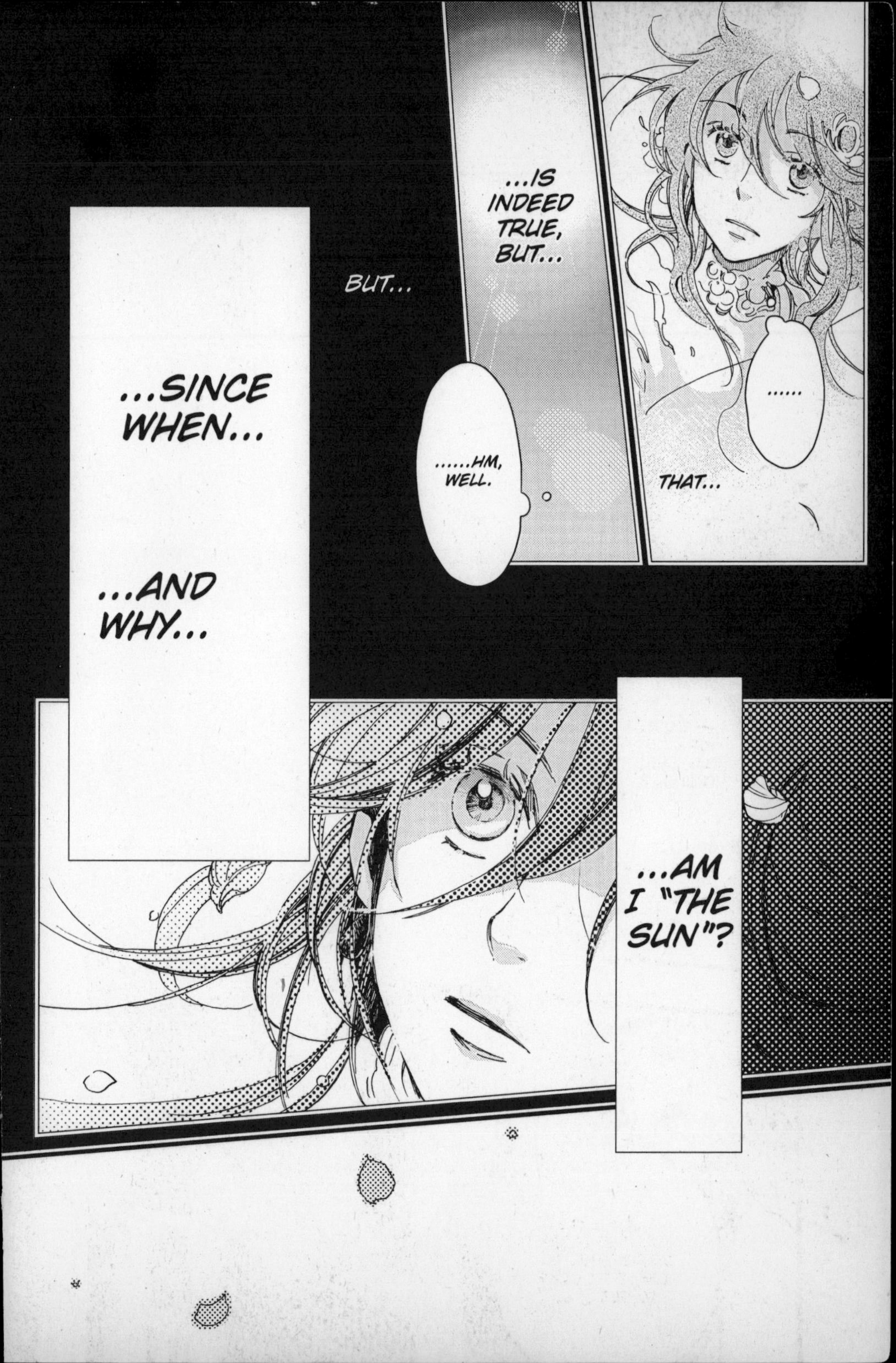
......
THAT...
...IS INDEED TRUE, BUT...
......HM, WELL.
BUT...
...SINCE WHEN...
...AND WHY...
...AM I "THE SUN"?

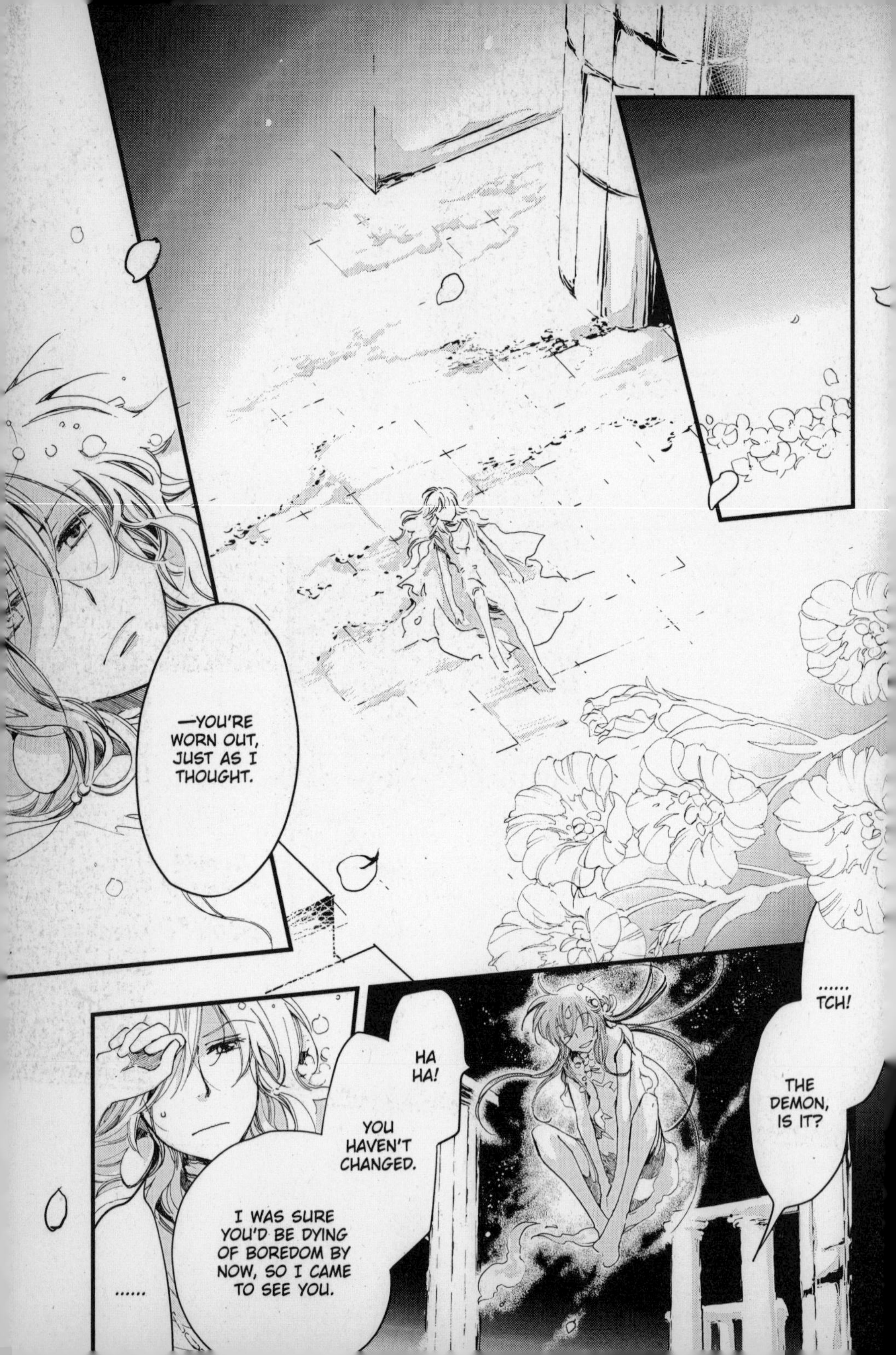
—YOU'RE WORN OUT, JUST AS I THOUGHT.
......TCH!
THE DEMON, IS IT?
HA HA!
YOU HAVEN'T CHANGED.
I WAS SURE YOU'D BE DYING OF BOREDOM BY NOW, SO I CAME TO SEE YOU.
......

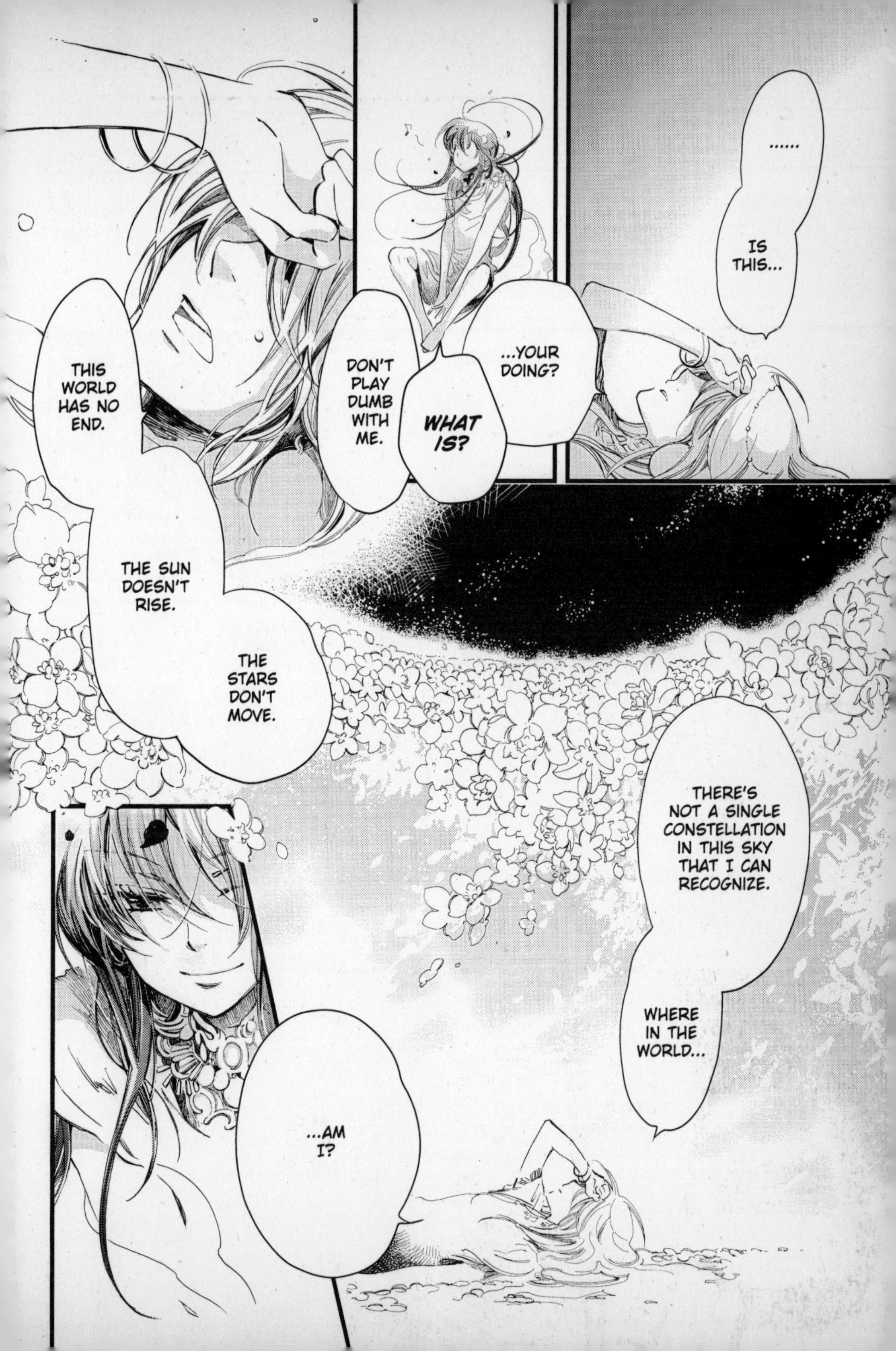
......
IS THIS...
...YOUR DOING?
WHAT IS?
DON'T PLAY DUMB WITH ME.
THIS WORLD HAS NO END.
THE SUN DOESN'T RISE.
THE STARS DON'T MOVE.
THERE'S NOT A SINGLE CONSTELLATION IN THIS SKY THAT I CAN RECOGNIZE.
WHERE IN THE WORLD...
...AM I?

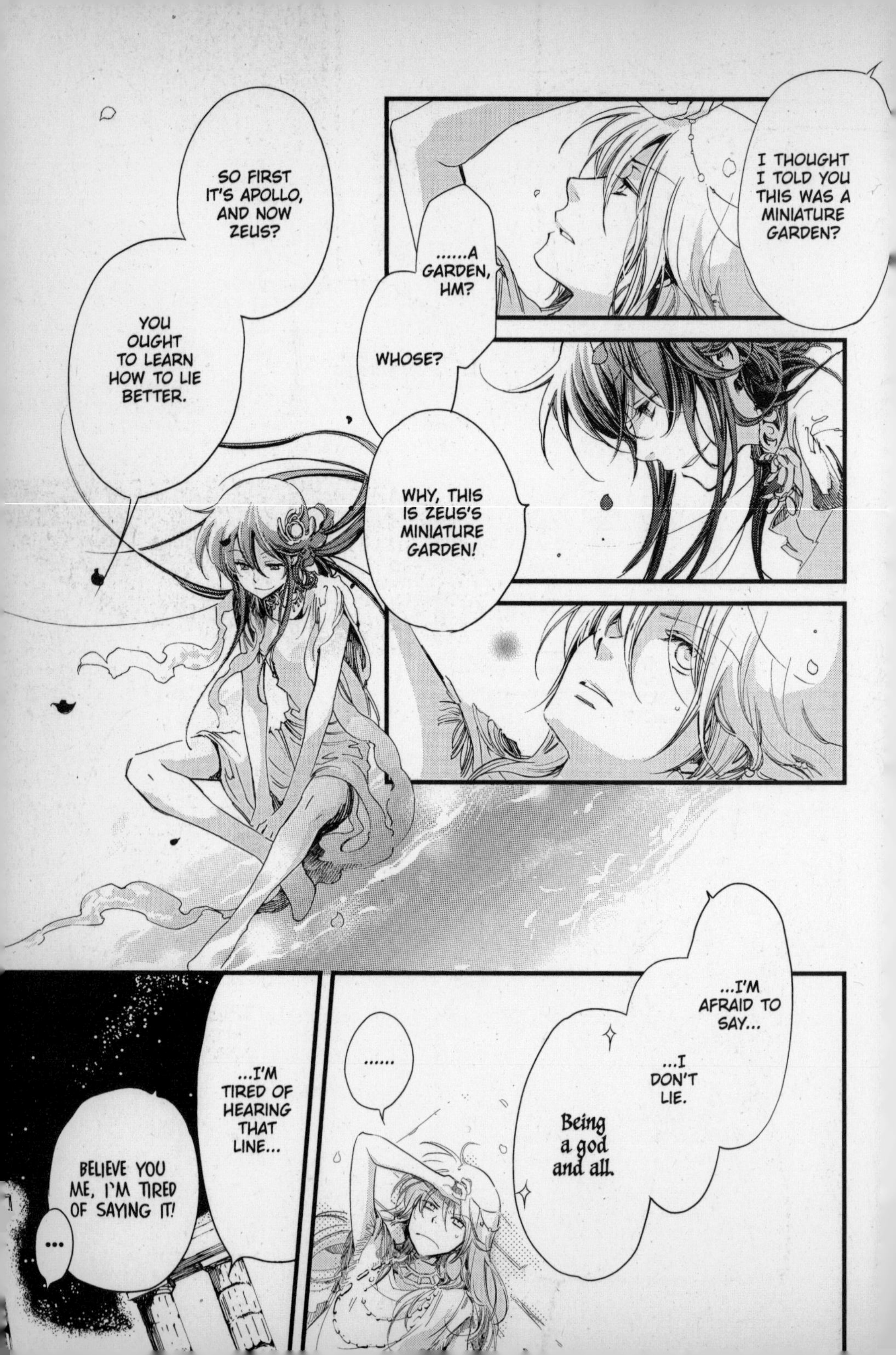
I THOUGHT I TOLD YOU THIS WAS A MINIATURE GARDEN?
......A GARDEN, HM?
WHOSE?
WHY, THIS IS ZEUS'S MINIATURE GARDEN!
SO FIRST IT'S APOLLO, AND NOW ZEUS?
YOU OUGHT TO LEARN HOW TO LIE BETTER.
...I'M AFRAID TO SAY...
...I DON'T LIE.
Being a god and all.
......
...I'M TIRED OF HEARING THAT LINE...
BELIEVE YOU ME, I'M TIRED OF SAYING IT!
...

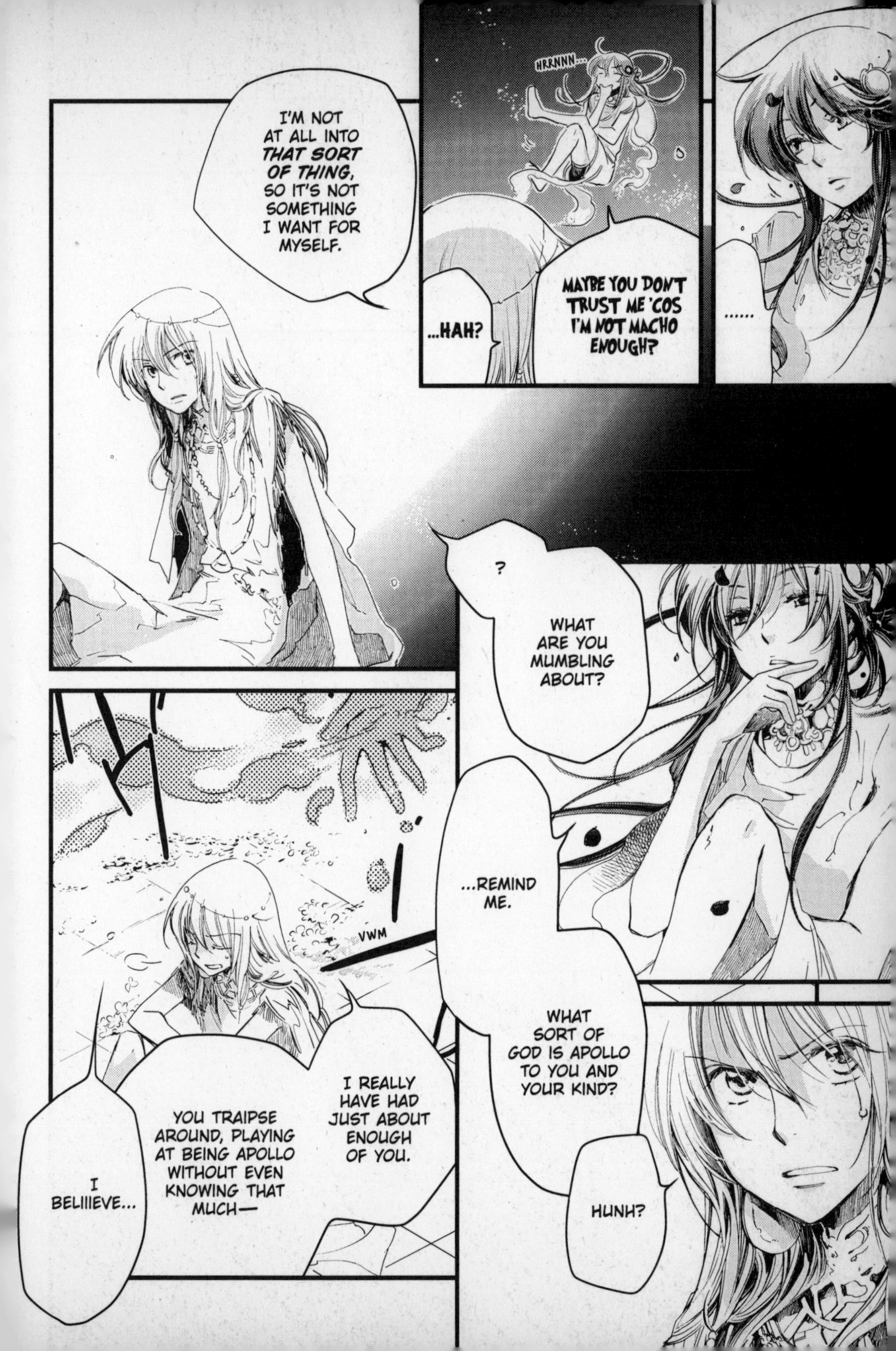
......
HRRNNN...
MAYBE YOU DON'T TRUST ME 'COS I'M NOT MACHO ENOUGH?
...HAH?
I'M NOT AT ALL INTO *THAT SORT OF THING*, SO IT'S NOT SOMETHING I WANT FOR MYSELF.
?
WHAT ARE YOU MUMBLING ABOUT?
...REMIND ME.
WHAT SORT OF GOD IS APOLLO TO YOU AND YOUR KIND?
HUNH?
VWM
I REALLY HAVE HAD JUST ABOUT ENOUGH OF YOU.
YOU TRAIPSE AROUND, PLAYING AT BEING APOLLO WITHOUT EVEN KNOWING THAT MUCH—
I BELIIIEVE...

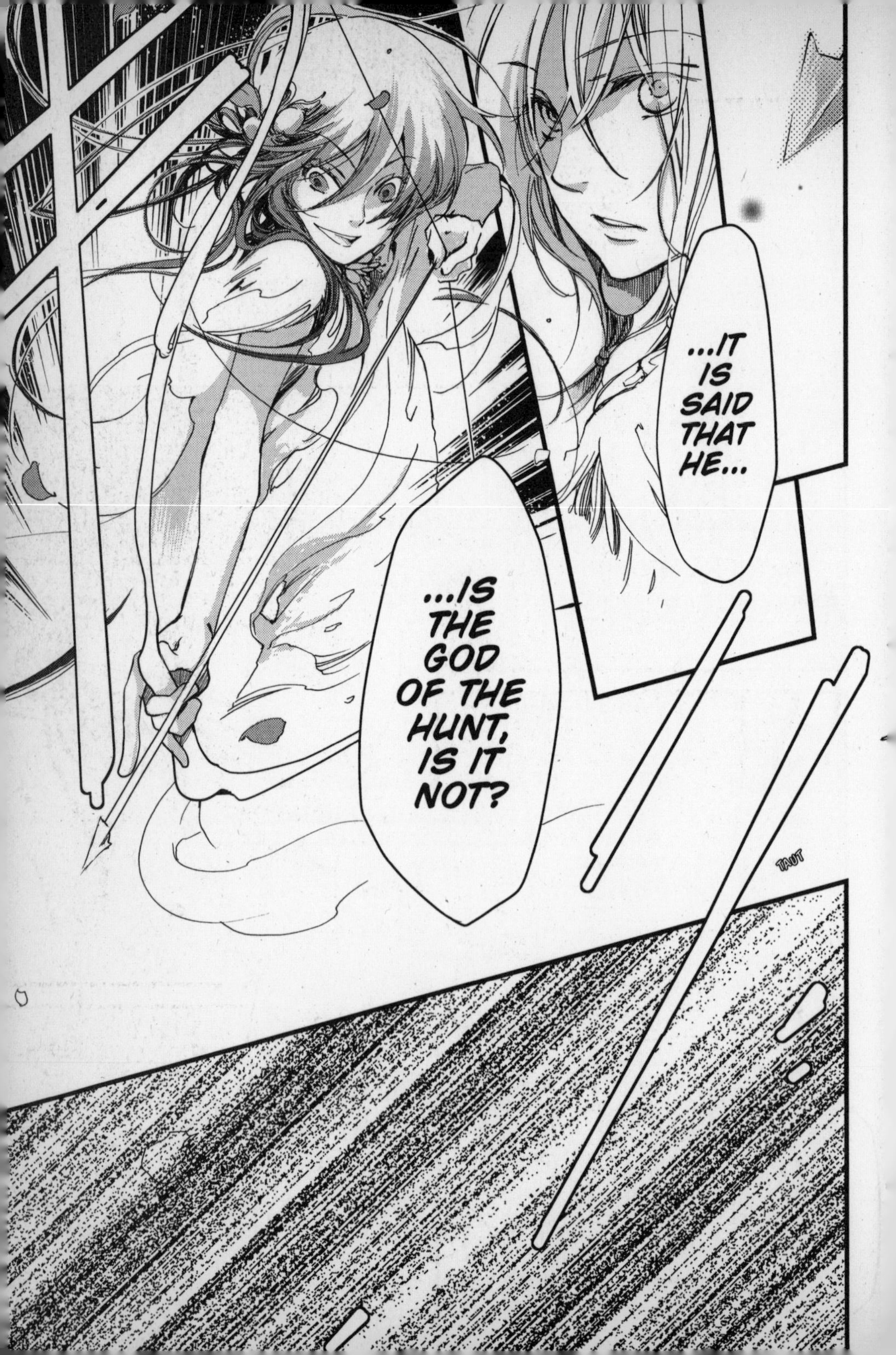
...IT IS SAID THAT HE...
...IS THE GOD OF THE HUNT, IS IT NOT?
TAUT

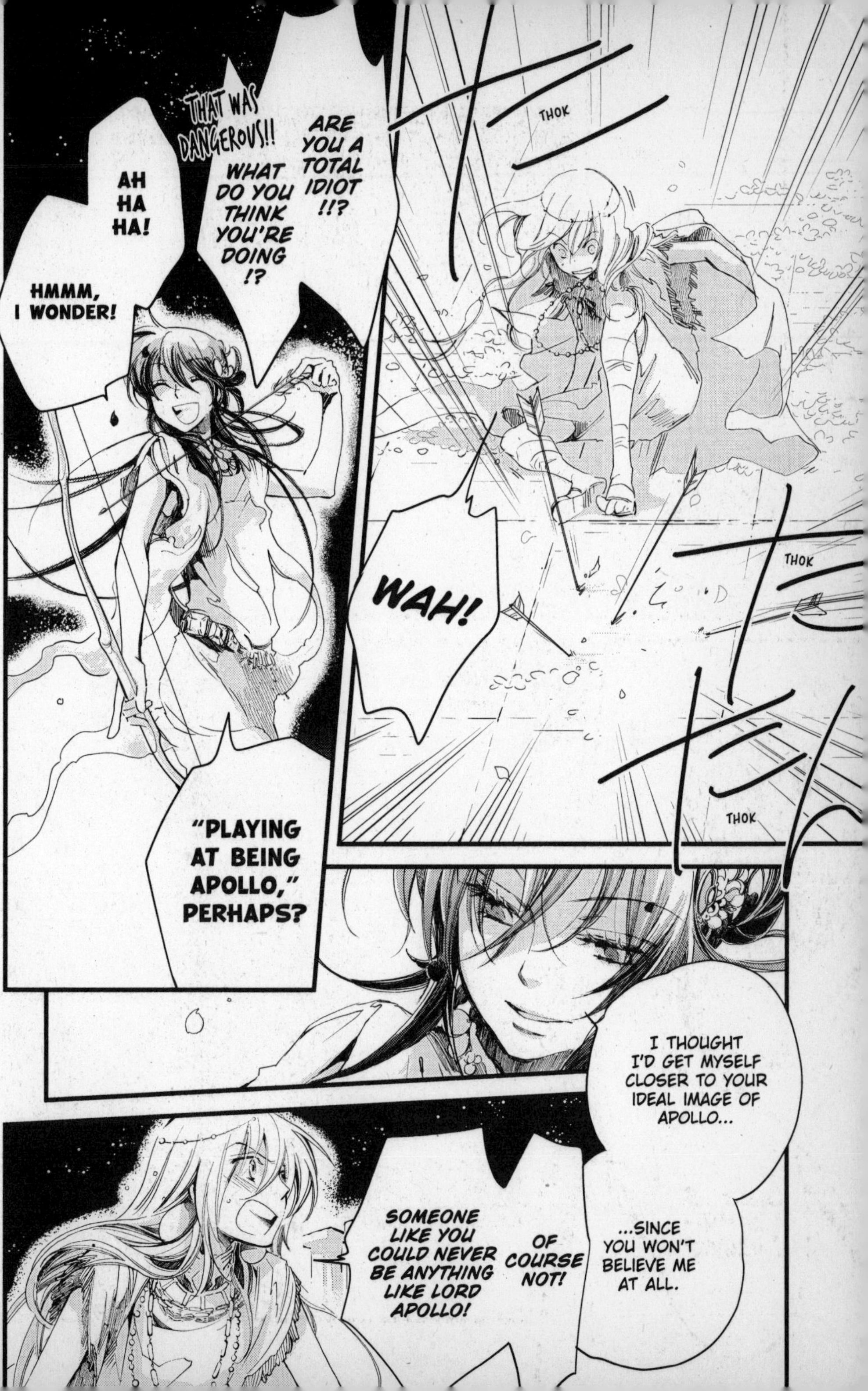
THOK
THOK
THOK
WAH!
THAT WAS DANGEROUS!!
ARE YOU A TOTAL IDIOT !!?
WHAT DO YOU THINK YOU'RE DOING !?
AH HA HA!
HMMM, I WONDER!
"PLAYING AT BEING APOLLO," PERHAPS?
I THOUGHT I'D GET MYSELF CLOSER TO YOUR IDEAL IMAGE OF APOLLO...
...SINCE YOU WON'T BELIEVE ME AT ALL.
OF COURSE NOT!
SOMEONE LIKE YOU COULD NEVER BE ANYTHING LIKE LORD APOLLO!

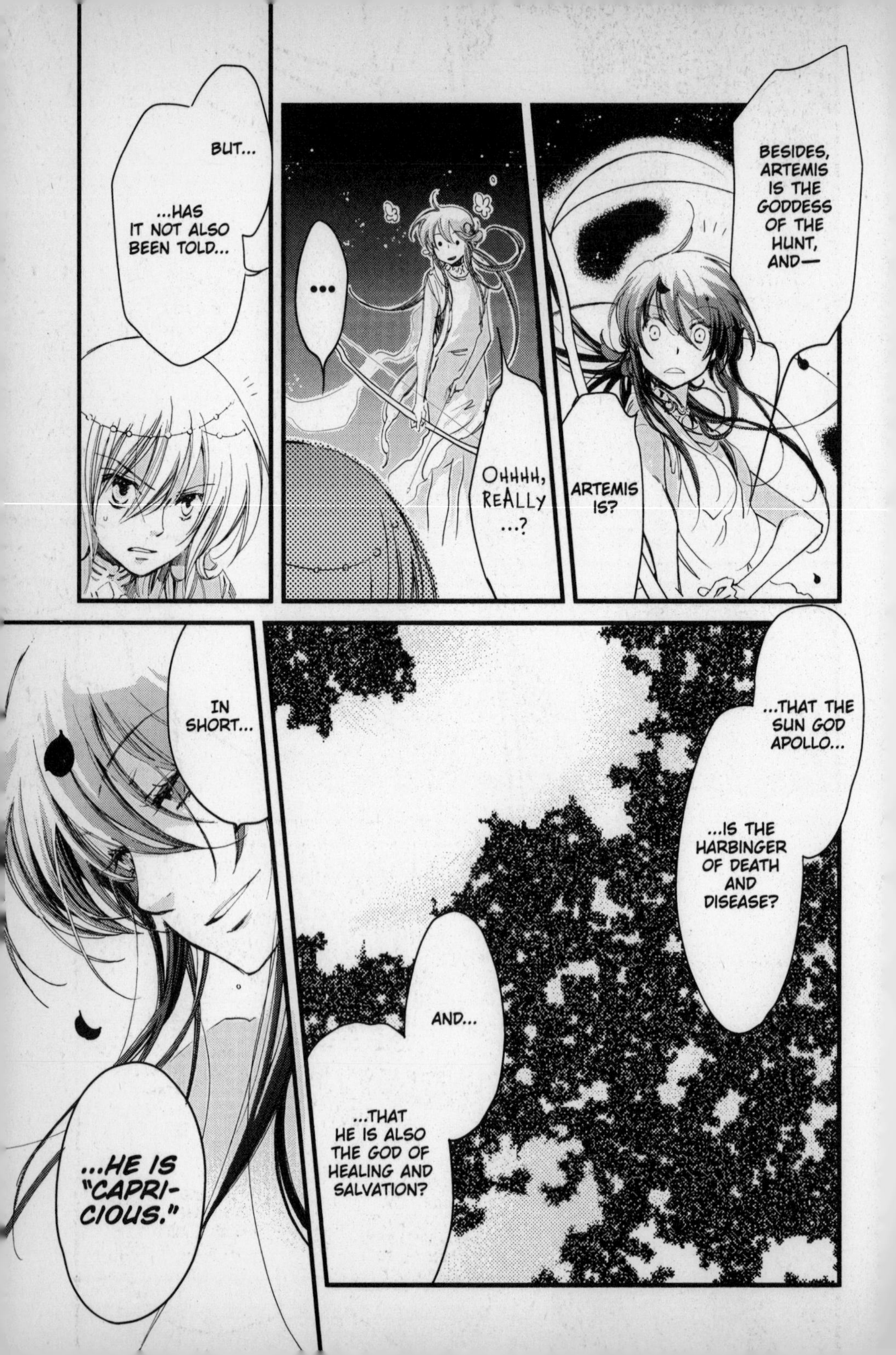
BESIDES, ARTEMIS IS THE GODDESS OF THE HUNT, AND—
ARTEMIS IS?
...
OHHHH, REALLY ...?
BUT...
...HAS IT NOT ALSO BEEN TOLD...
...THAT THE SUN GOD APOLLO...
...IS THE HARBINGER OF DEATH AND DISEASE?
AND...
...THAT HE IS ALSO THE GOD OF HEALING AND SALVATION?
IN SHORT...
...HE IS "CAPRICIOUS."

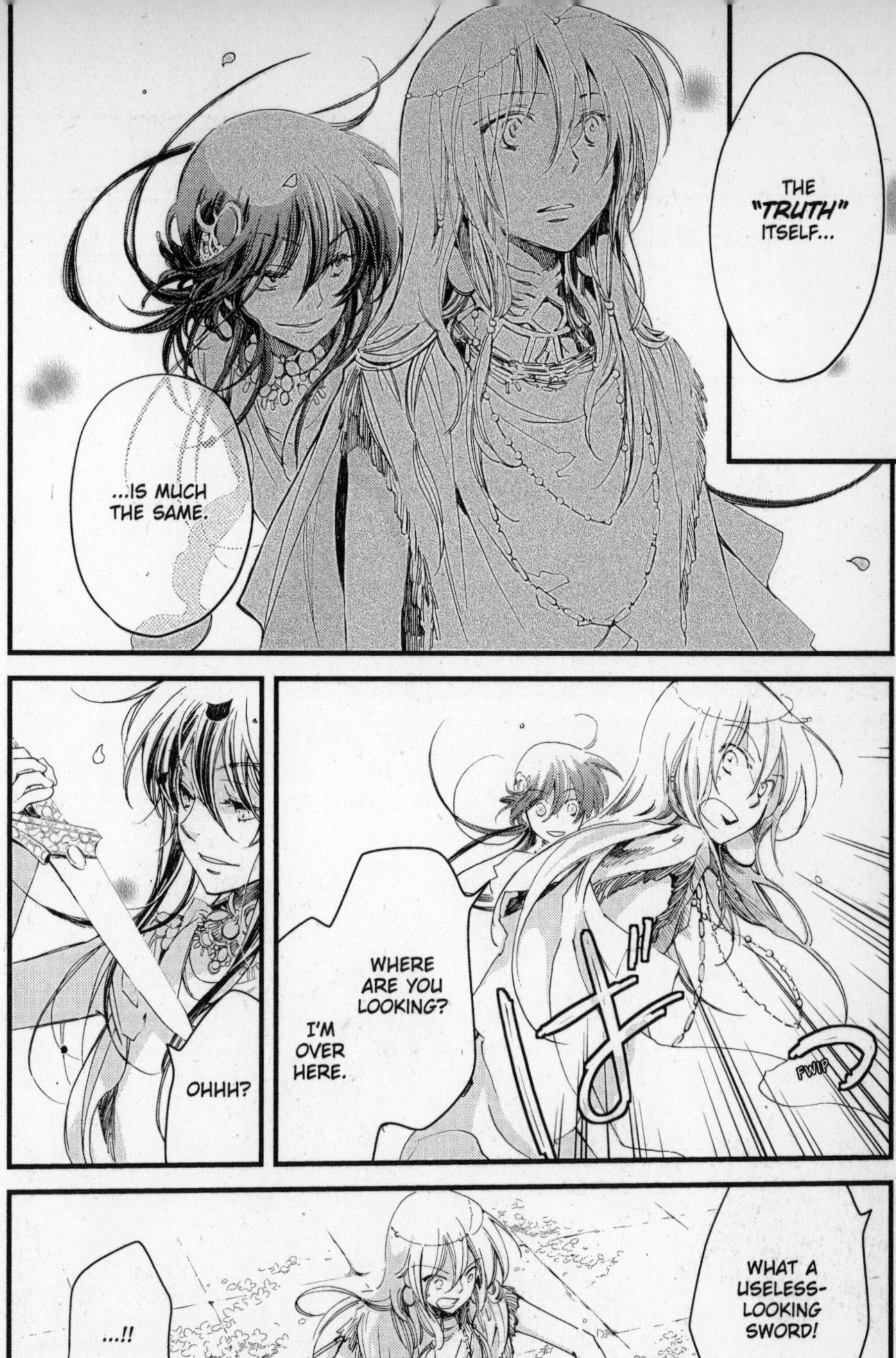
THE "TRUTH" ITSELF...
...IS MUCH THE SAME.
WHERE ARE YOU LOOKING?
I'M OVER HERE.
FWIP
OHHH?
WHAT A USELESS-LOOKING SWORD!
...!!
WHA—

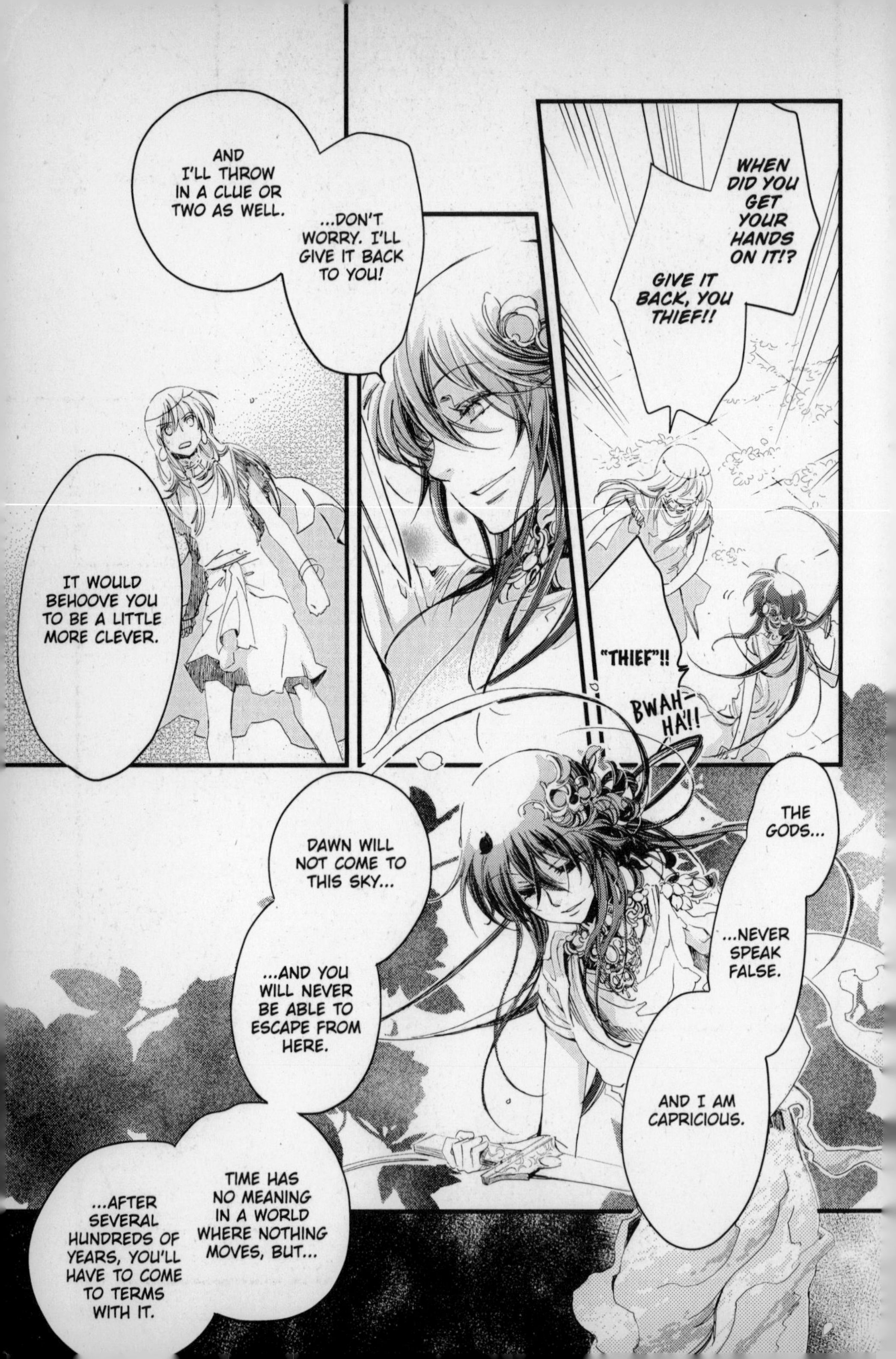
WHEN DID YOU GET YOUR HANDS ON IT!?
GIVE IT BACK, YOU THIEF!!
"THIEF"!!
BWAH-HA!!
...DON'T WORRY. I'LL GIVE IT BACK TO YOU!
AND I'LL THROW IN A CLUE OR TWO AS WELL.
IT WOULD BEHOOVE YOU TO BE A LITTLE MORE CLEVER.
THE GODS...
...NEVER SPEAK FALSE.
AND I AM CAPRICIOUS.
DAWN WILL NOT COME TO THIS SKY...
...AND YOU WILL NEVER BE ABLE TO ESCAPE FROM HERE.
TIME HAS NO MEANING IN A WORLD WHERE NOTHING MOVES, BUT...
...AFTER SEVERAL HUNDREDS OF YEARS, YOU'LL HAVE TO COME TO TERMS WITH IT.

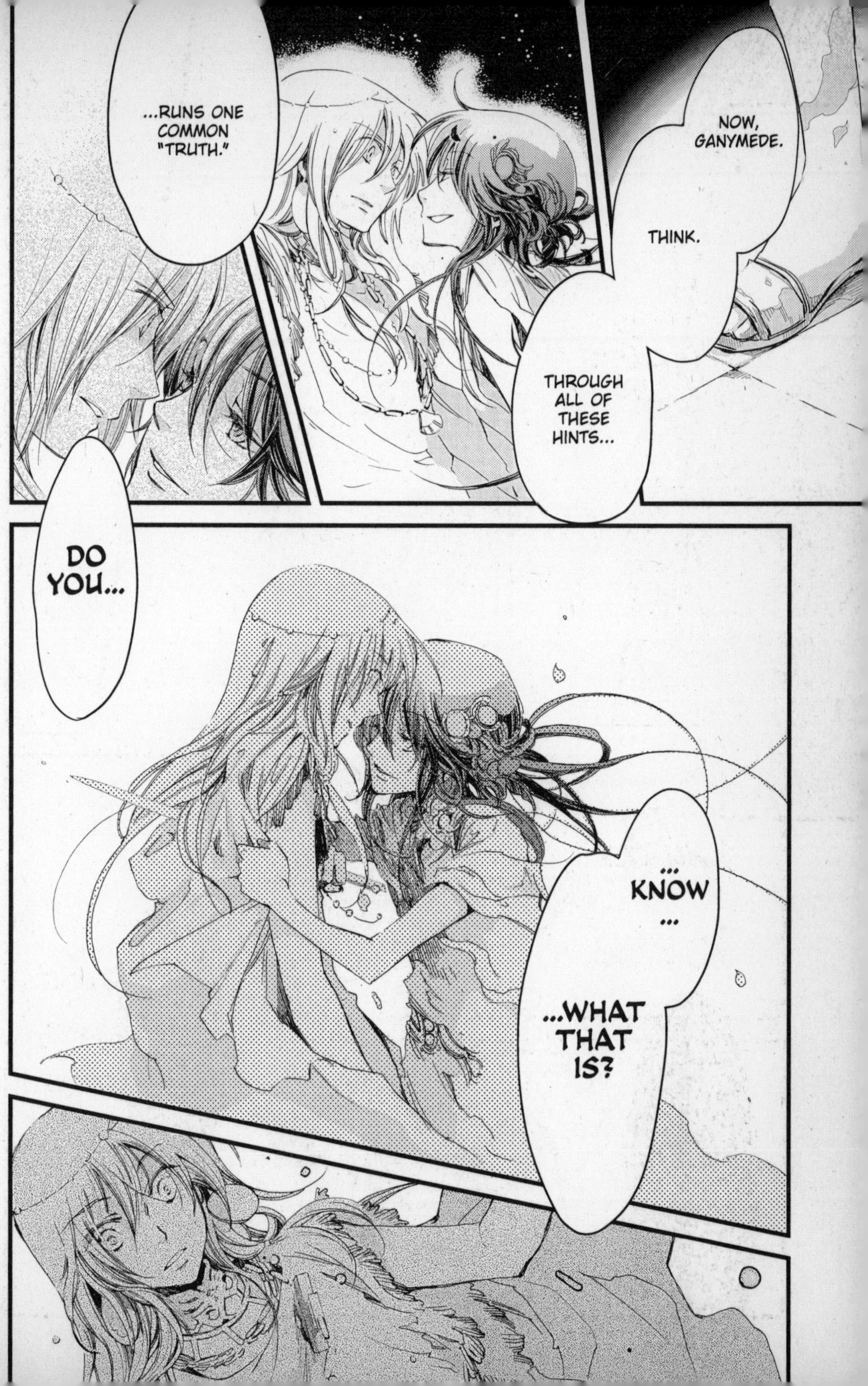
NOW, GANYMEDE.
THINK.
THROUGH ALL OF THESE HINTS...
...RUNS ONE COMMON "TRUTH."
DO YOU...
...KNOW...
...WHAT THAT IS?

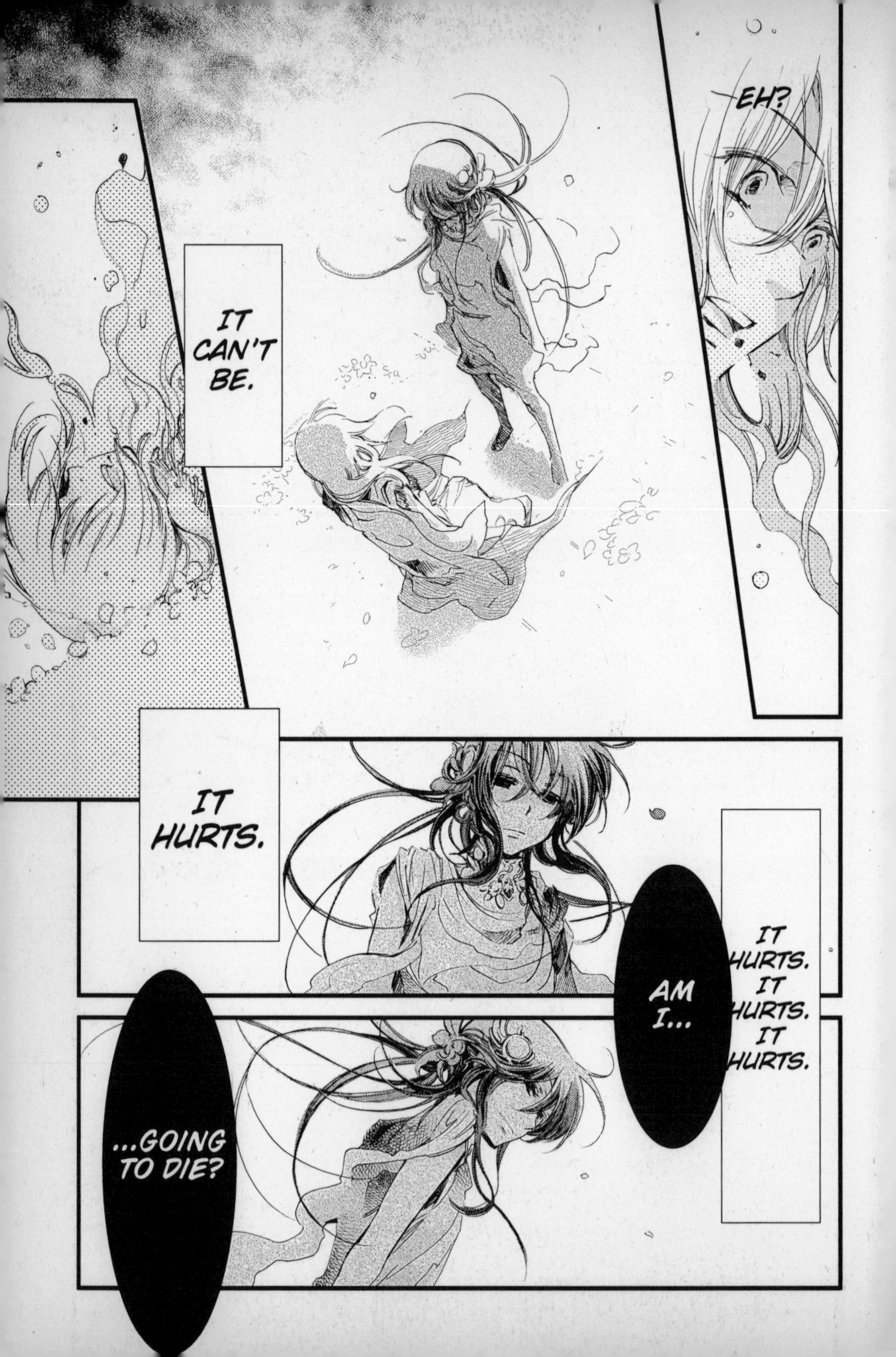
EH?
IT CAN'T BE.
IT HURTS.
IT HURTS. IT HURTS. IT HURTS.
AM I...
...GOING TO DIE?

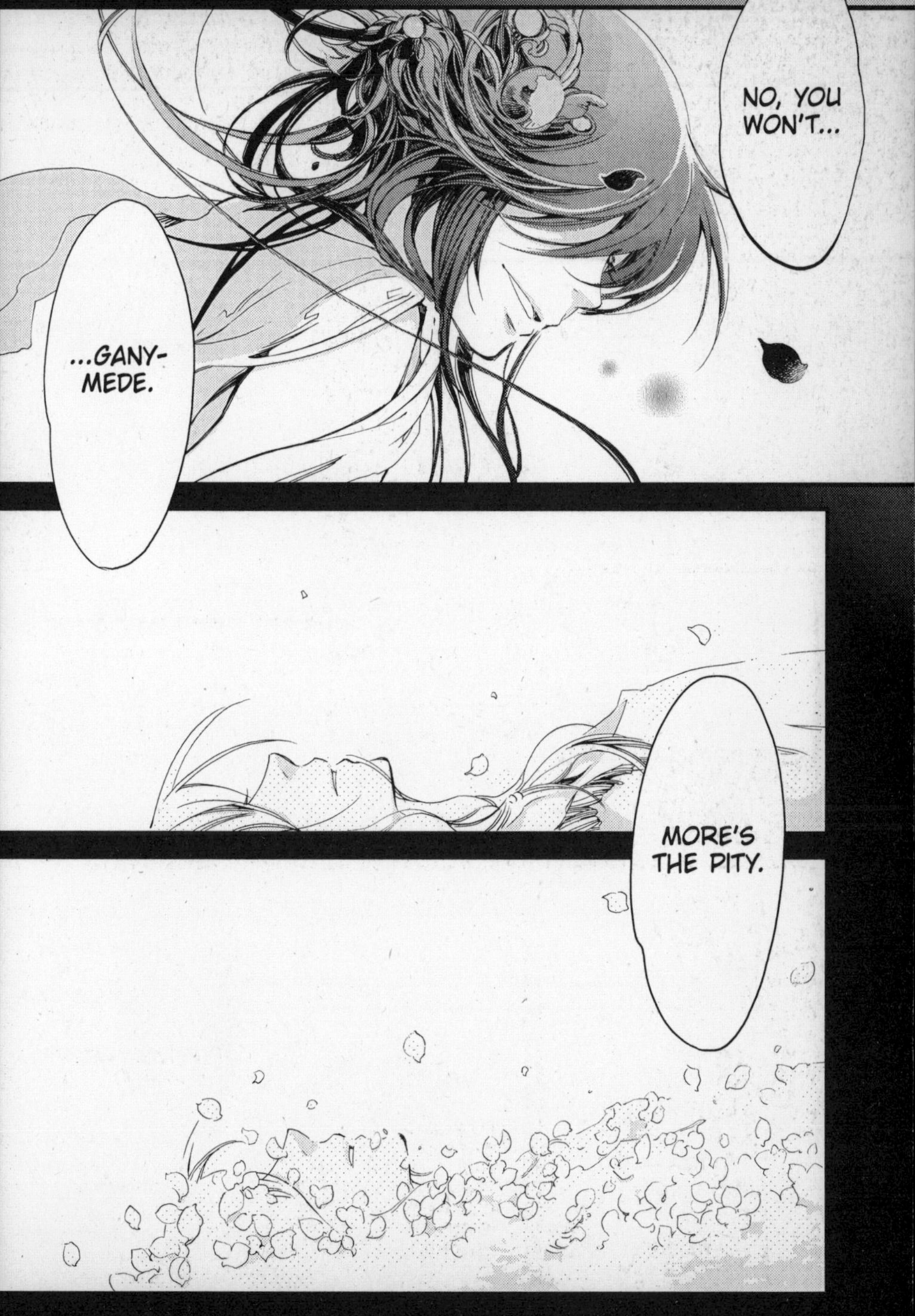
NO, YOU WON'T...
...GANY-MEDE.
MORE'S THE PITY.

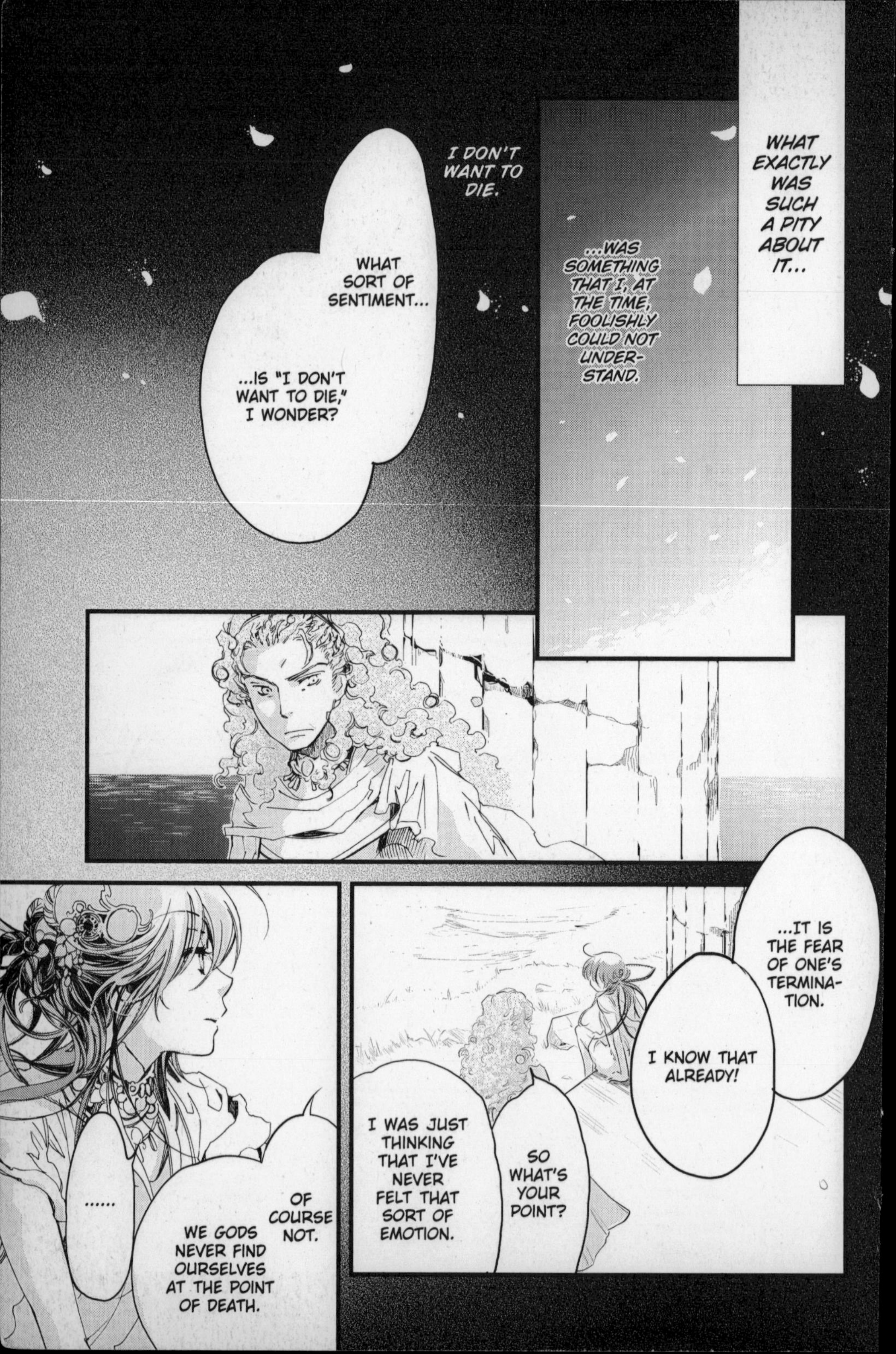
WHAT EXACTLY WAS SUCH A PITY ABOUT IT...
...WAS SOMETHING THAT I, AT THE TIME, FOOLISHLY COULD NOT UNDERSTAND.
I DON'T WANT TO DIE.
WHAT SORT OF SENTIMENT...
...IS "I DON'T WANT TO DIE," I WONDER?
...IT IS THE FEAR OF ONE'S TERMINATION.
I KNOW THAT ALREADY!
SO WHAT'S YOUR POINT?
I WAS JUST THINKING THAT I'VE NEVER FELT THAT SORT OF EMOTION.
OF COURSE NOT.
WE GODS NEVER FIND OURSELVES AT THE POINT OF DEATH.
......

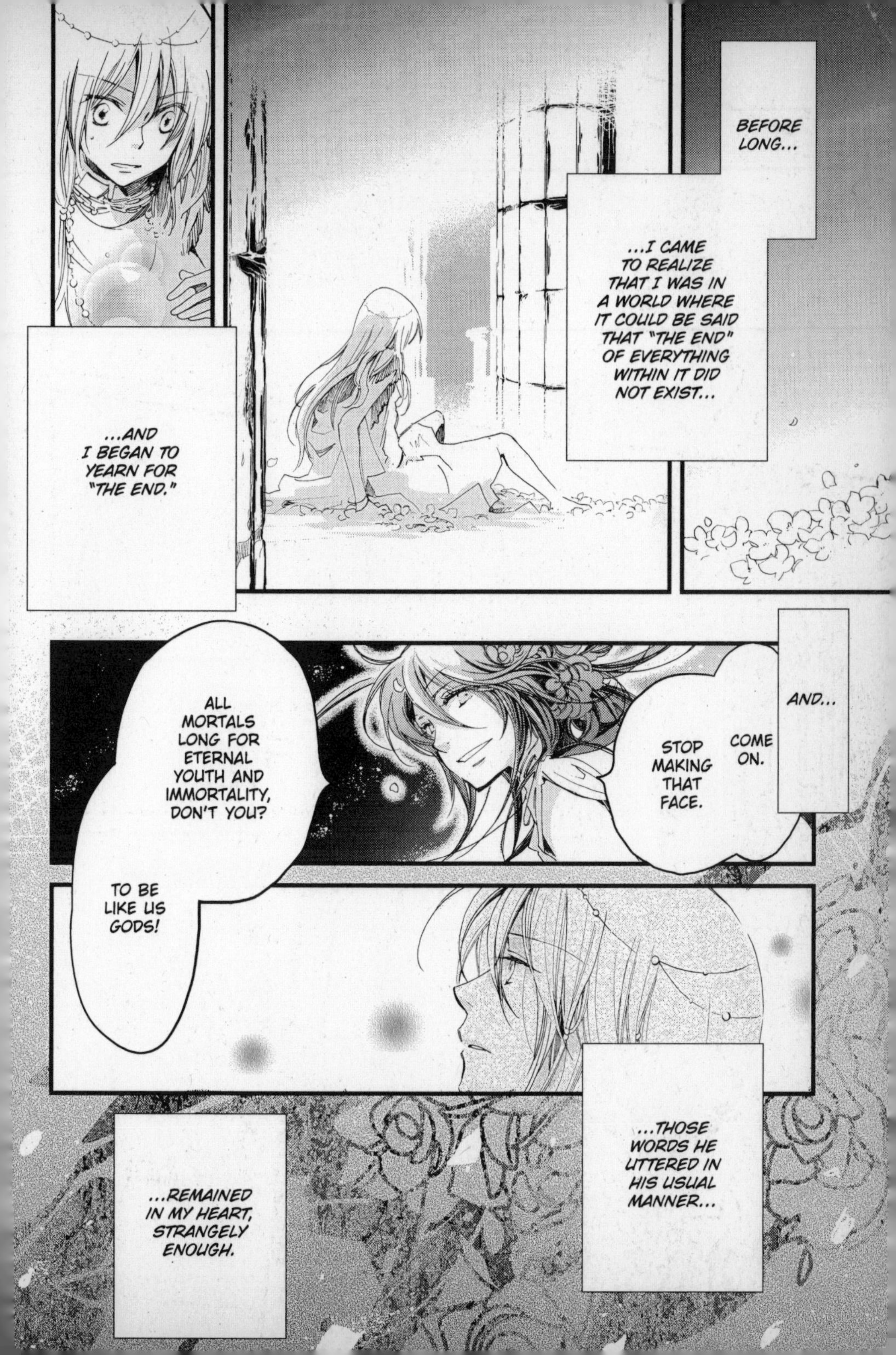
BEFORE LONG...
...I CAME TO REALIZE THAT I WAS IN A WORLD WHERE IT COULD BE SAID THAT "THE END" OF EVERYTHING WITHIN IT DID NOT EXIST...
...AND I BEGAN TO YEARN FOR "THE END."
AND...
COME ON.
STOP MAKING THAT FACE.
ALL MORTALS LONG FOR ETERNAL YOUTH AND IMMORTALITY, DON'T YOU?
TO BE LIKE US GODS!
...THOSE WORDS HE UTTERED IN HIS USUAL MANNER...
...REMAINED IN MY HEART, STRANGELY ENOUGH.

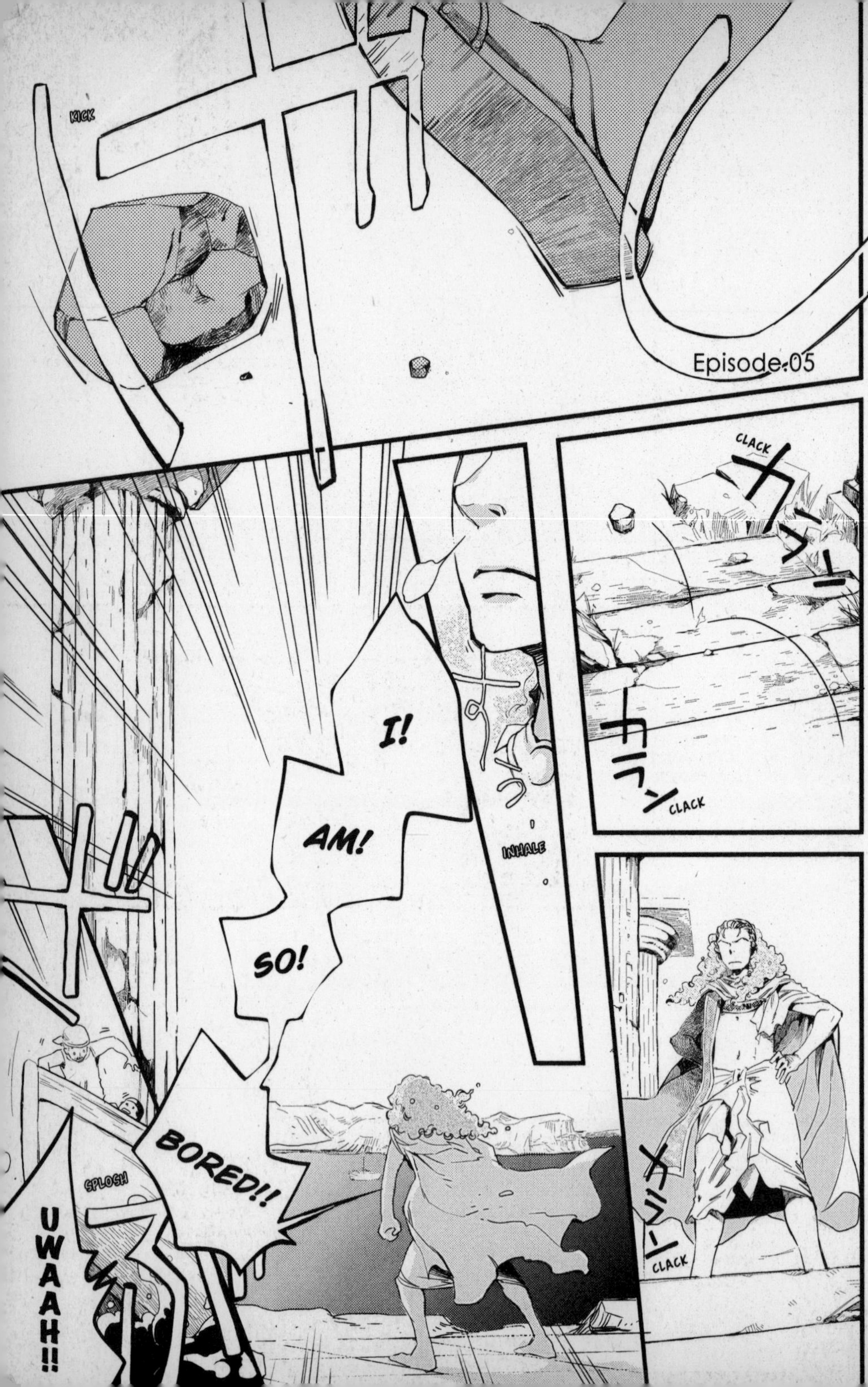

Episode 05
KICK
CLACK
CLACK
INHALE
CLACK
I!
AM!
SO!
BORED!!
SPLOSH
UWAAH!!

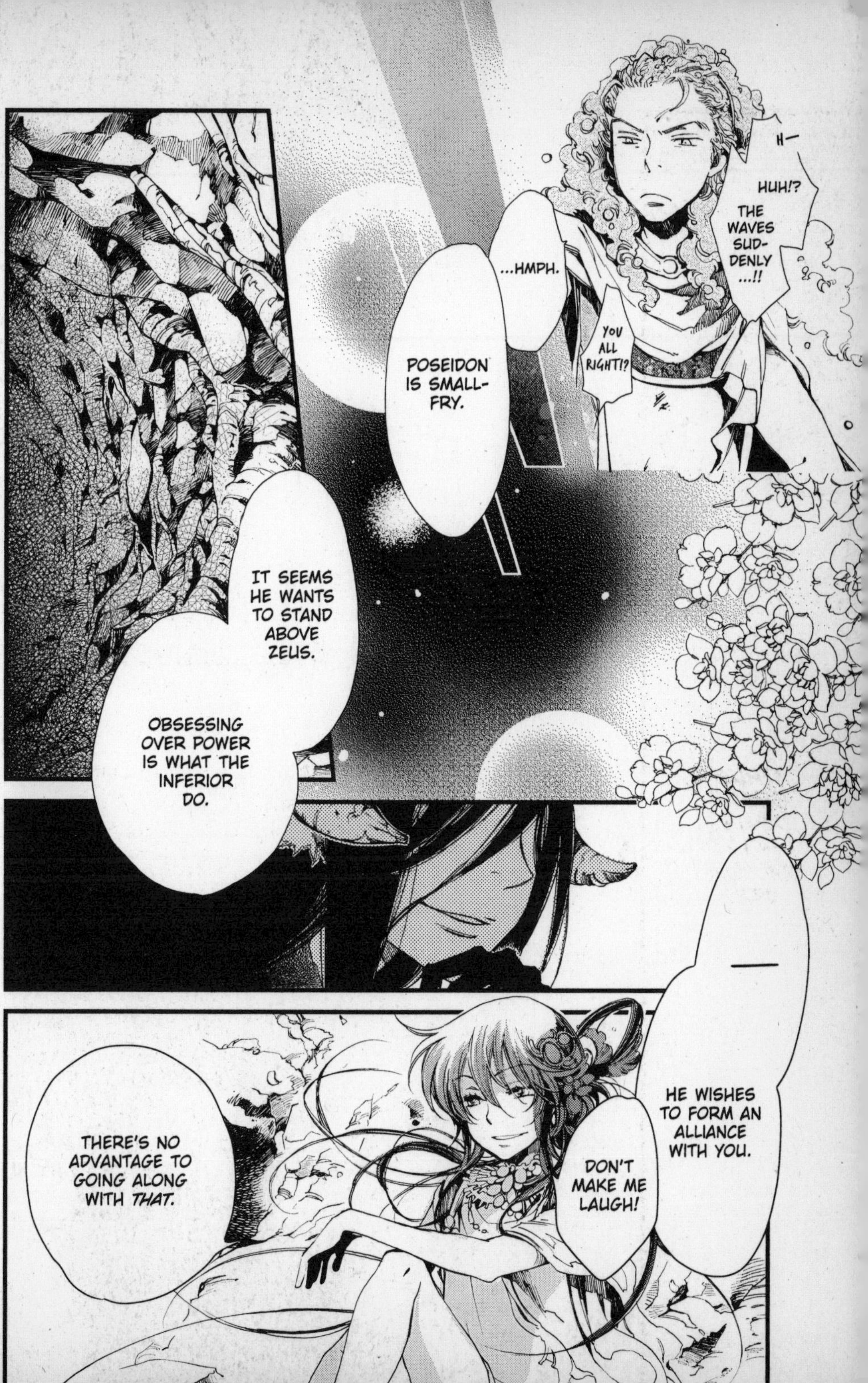
H—
HUH!?
THE WAVES SUDDENLY ...!!
YOU ALL RIGHT!?
...HMPH.
POSEIDON IS SMALL-FRY.
IT SEEMS HE WANTS TO STAND ABOVE ZEUS.
OBSESSING OVER POWER IS WHAT THE INFERIOR DO.
—
HE WISHES TO FORM AN ALLIANCE WITH YOU.
DON'T MAKE ME LAUGH!
THERE'S NO ADVANTAGE TO GOING ALONG WITH *THAT*.

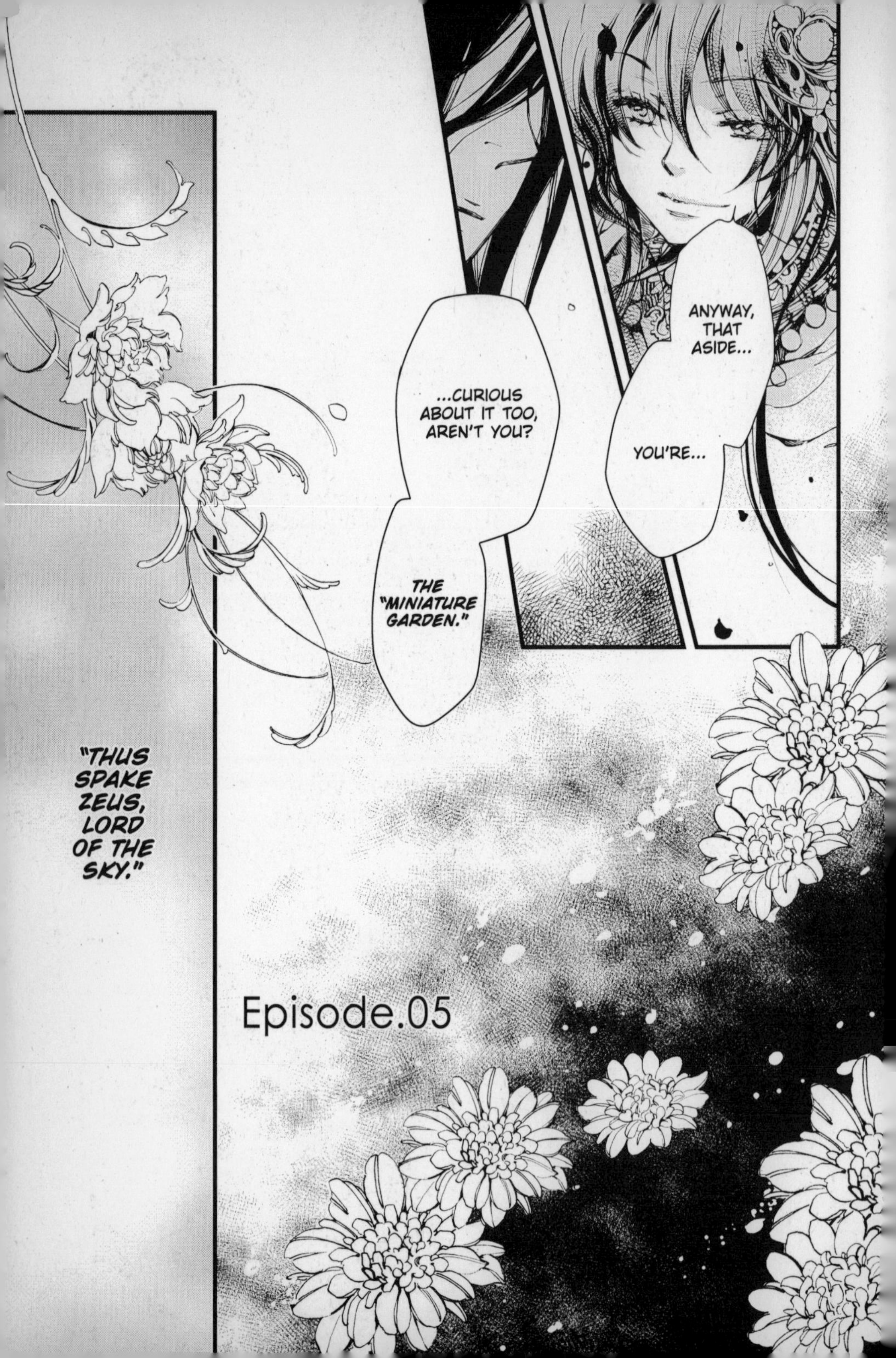
ANYWAY, THAT ASIDE...
YOU'RE...
...CURIOUS ABOUT IT TOO, AREN'T YOU?
THE "MINIATURE GARDEN."
Episode.05
"THUS SPAKE ZEUS, LORD OF THE SKY."

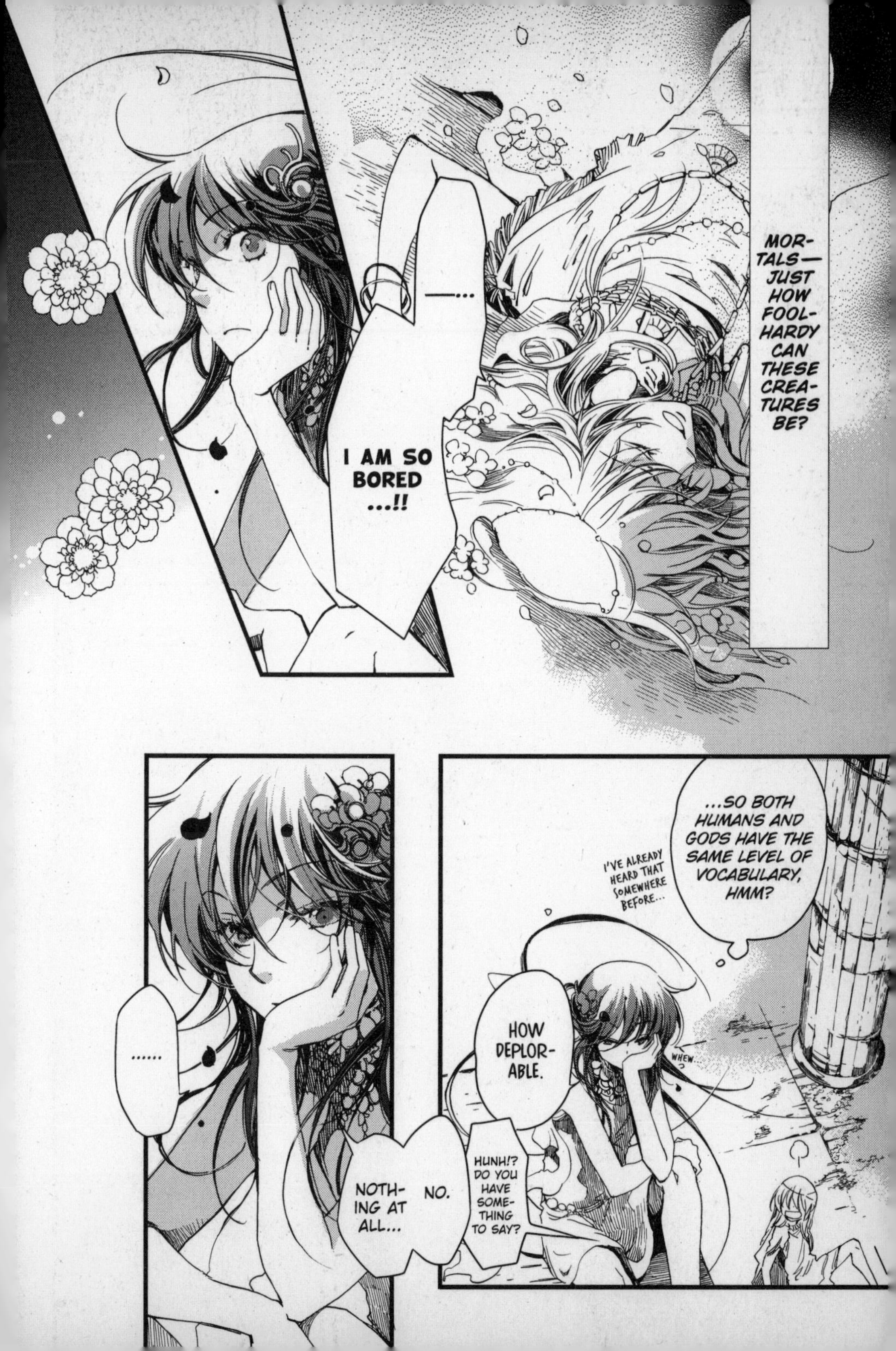

MORTALS—JUST HOW FOOLHARDY CAN THESE CREATURES BE?
——...
I AM SO BORED ...!!
...SO BOTH HUMANS AND GODS HAVE THE SAME LEVEL OF VOCABULARY, HMM?
I'VE ALREADY HEARD THAT SOMEWHERE BEFORE...
HOW DEPLORABLE.
WHEW...
HUNH!? DO YOU HAVE SOMETHING TO SAY?
NO.
NOTHING AT ALL...
......

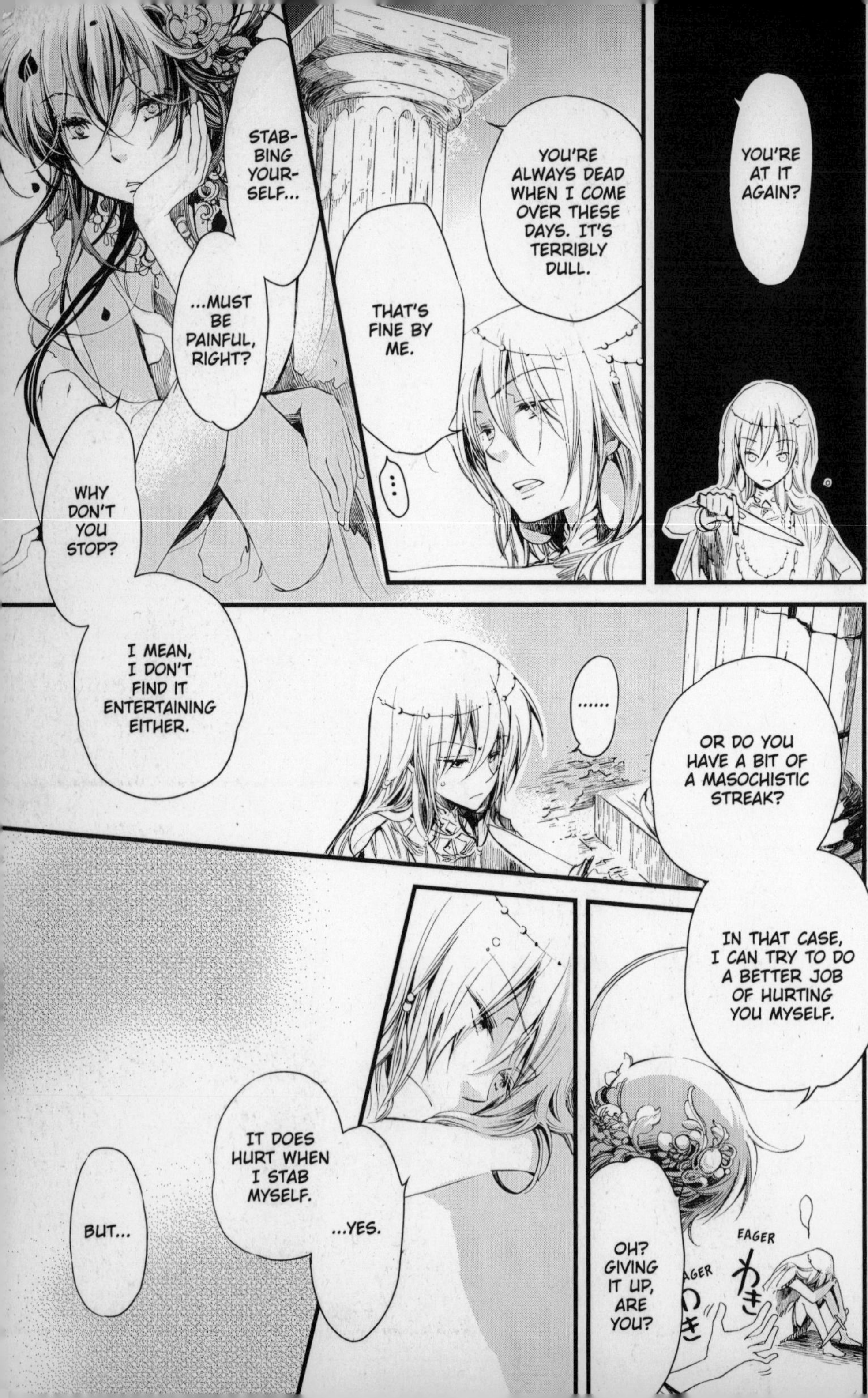
YOU'RE AT IT AGAIN?
YOU'RE ALWAYS DEAD WHEN I COME OVER THESE DAYS. IT'S TERRIBLY DULL.
THAT'S FINE BY ME.
...
STAB-BING YOUR-SELF...
...MUST BE PAINFUL, RIGHT?
WHY DON'T YOU STOP?
I MEAN, I DON'T FIND IT ENTERTAINING EITHER.
OR DO YOU HAVE A BIT OF A MASOCHISTIC STREAK?
......
IN THAT CASE, I CAN TRY TO DO A BETTER JOB OF HURTING YOU MYSELF.
EAGER
わき
OH? GIVING IT UP, ARE YOU?
...YES.
IT DOES HURT WHEN I STAB MYSELF.
BUT...

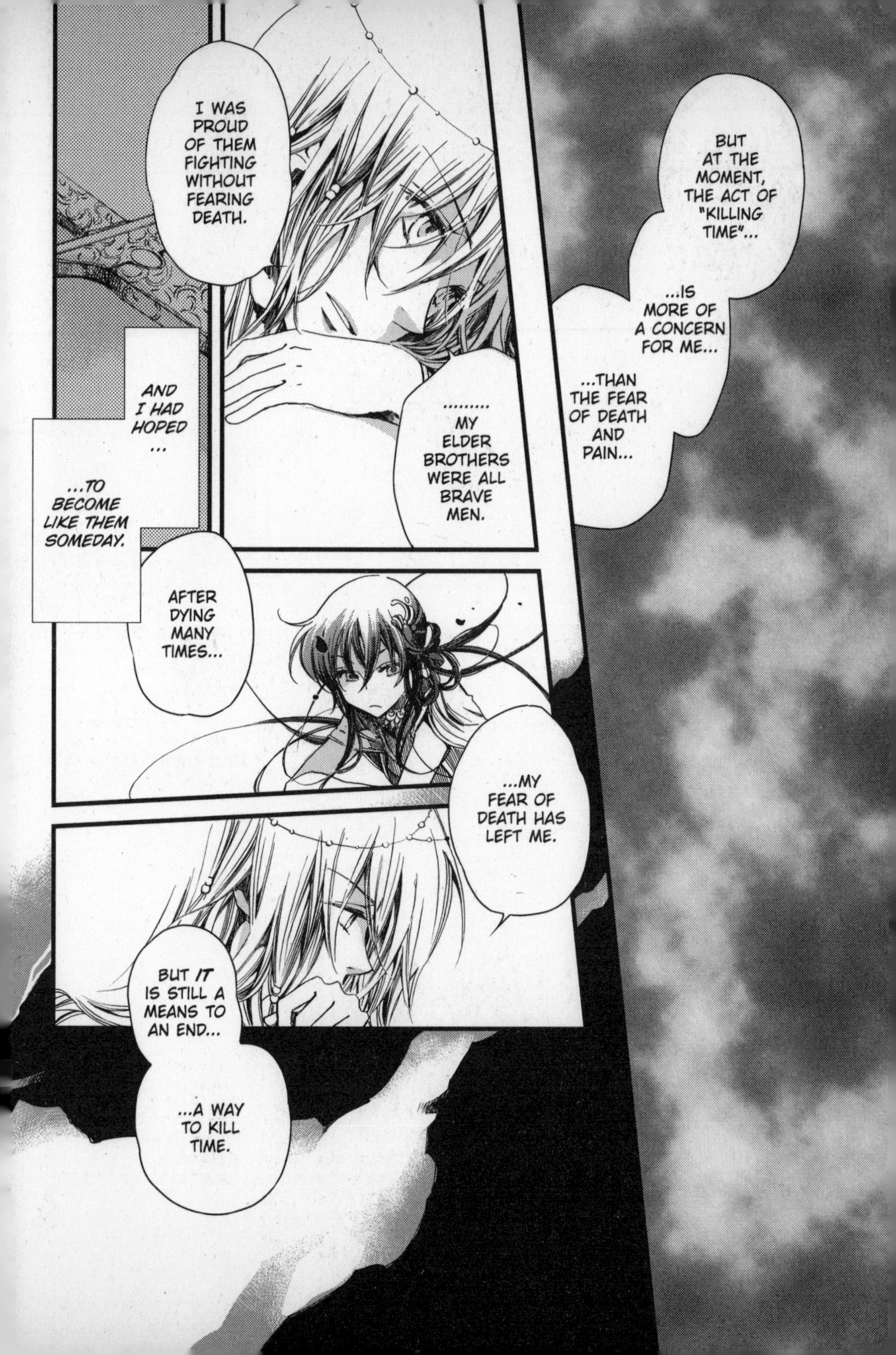
....
MY ELDER BROTHERS WERE ALL BRAVE MEN.
I WAS PROUD OF THEM FIGHTING WITHOUT FEARING DEATH.
AND I HAD HOPED ...
...TO BECOME LIKE THEM SOMEDAY.
AFTER DYING MANY TIMES...
...MY FEAR OF DEATH HAS LEFT ME.
BUT *IT* IS STILL A MEANS TO AN END...
...A WAY TO KILL TIME.
BUT AT THE MOMENT, THE ACT OF "KILLING TIME"...
...IS MORE OF A CONCERN FOR ME...
...THAN THE FEAR OF DEATH AND PAIN...

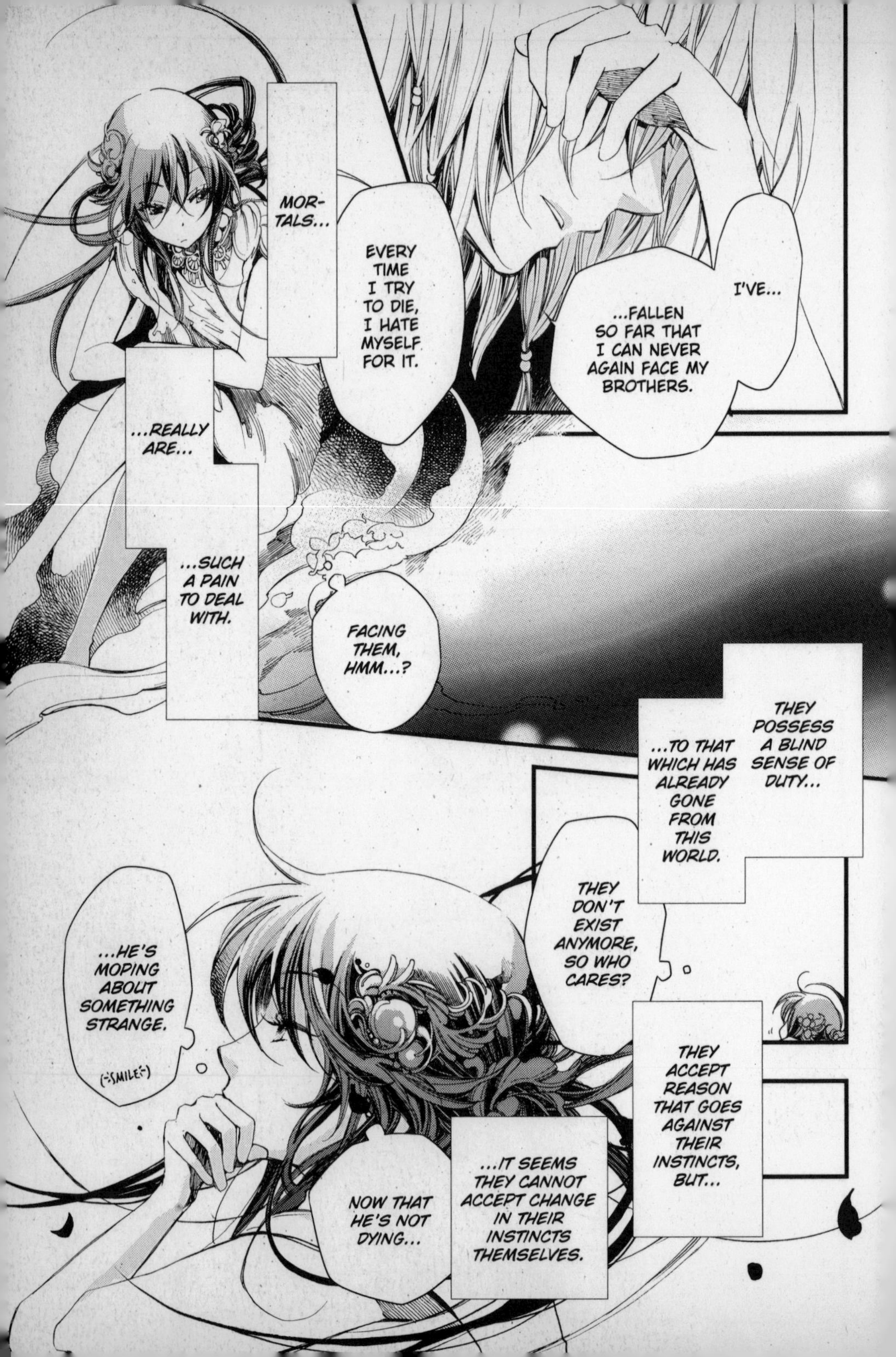
I'VE...
...FALLEN SO FAR THAT I CAN NEVER AGAIN FACE MY BROTHERS.
EVERY TIME I TRY TO DIE, I HATE MYSELF FOR IT.
MOR-TALS...
...REALLY ARE...
...SUCH A PAIN TO DEAL WITH.
FACING THEM, HMM...?
THEY POSSESS A BLIND SENSE OF DUTY...
...TO THAT WHICH HAS ALREADY GONE FROM THIS WORLD.
THEY DON'T EXIST ANYMORE, SO WHO CARES?
THEY ACCEPT REASON THAT GOES AGAINST THEIR INSTINCTS, BUT...
...IT SEEMS THEY CANNOT ACCEPT CHANGE IN THEIR INSTINCTS THEMSELVES.
NOW THAT HE'S NOT DYING...
...HE'S MOPING ABOUT SOMETHING STRANGE.
(SMILE)

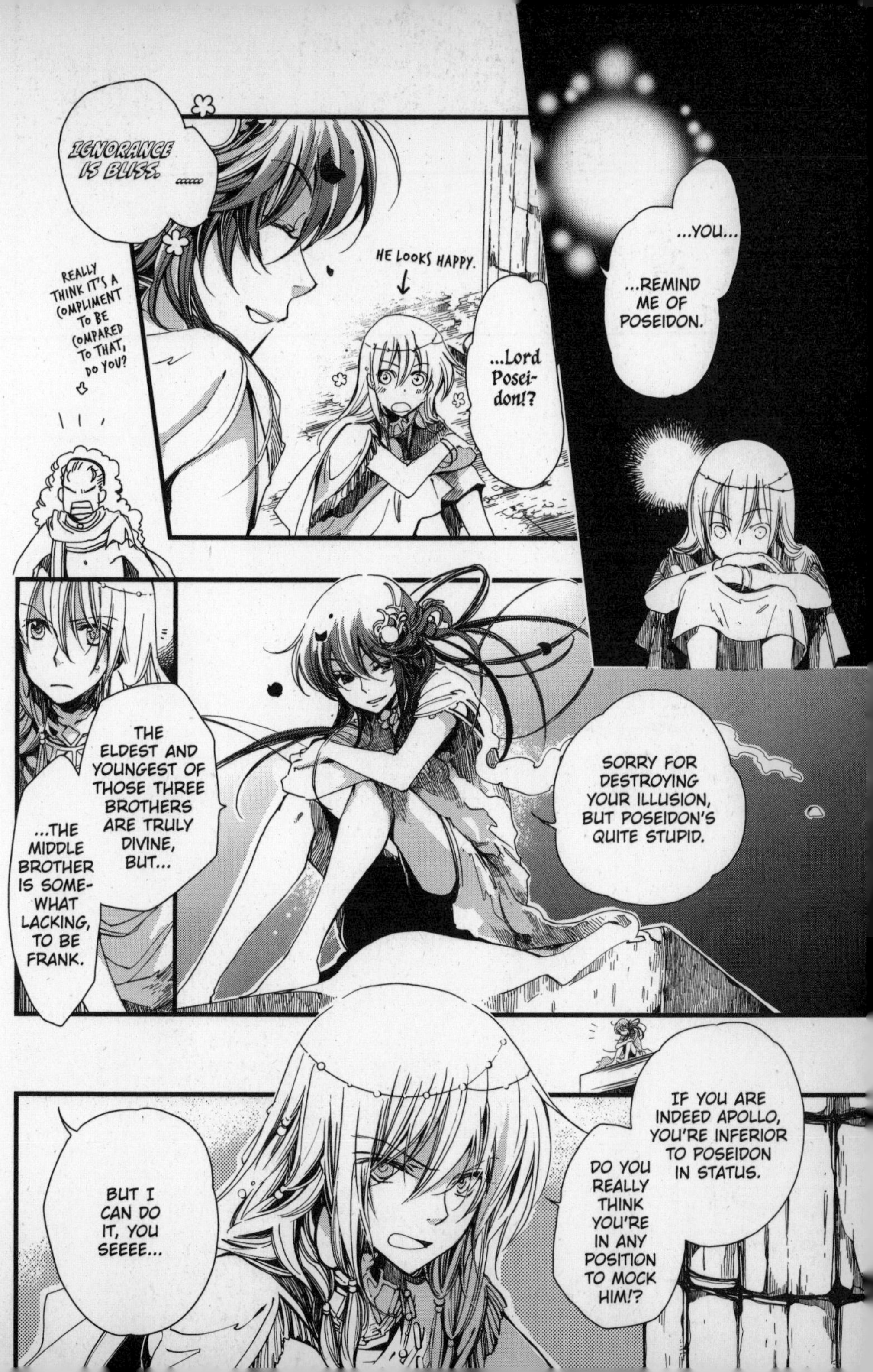
...YOU...
...REMIND ME OF POSEIDON.
...Lord Posei-don!?
HE LOOKS HAPPY.
IGNORANCE IS BLISS. ......
REALLY THINK IT'S A COMPLIMENT TO BE COMPARED TO THAT, DO YOU?
SORRY FOR DESTROYING YOUR ILLUSION, BUT POSEIDON'S QUITE STUPID.
THE ELDEST AND YOUNGEST OF THOSE THREE BROTHERS ARE TRULY DIVINE, BUT...
...THE MIDDLE BROTHER IS SOME-WHAT LACKING, TO BE FRANK.
IF YOU ARE INDEED APOLLO, YOU'RE INFERIOR TO POSEIDON IN STATUS.
DO YOU REALLY THINK YOU'RE IN ANY POSITION TO MOCK HIM!?
BUT I CAN DO IT, YOU SEEEE...

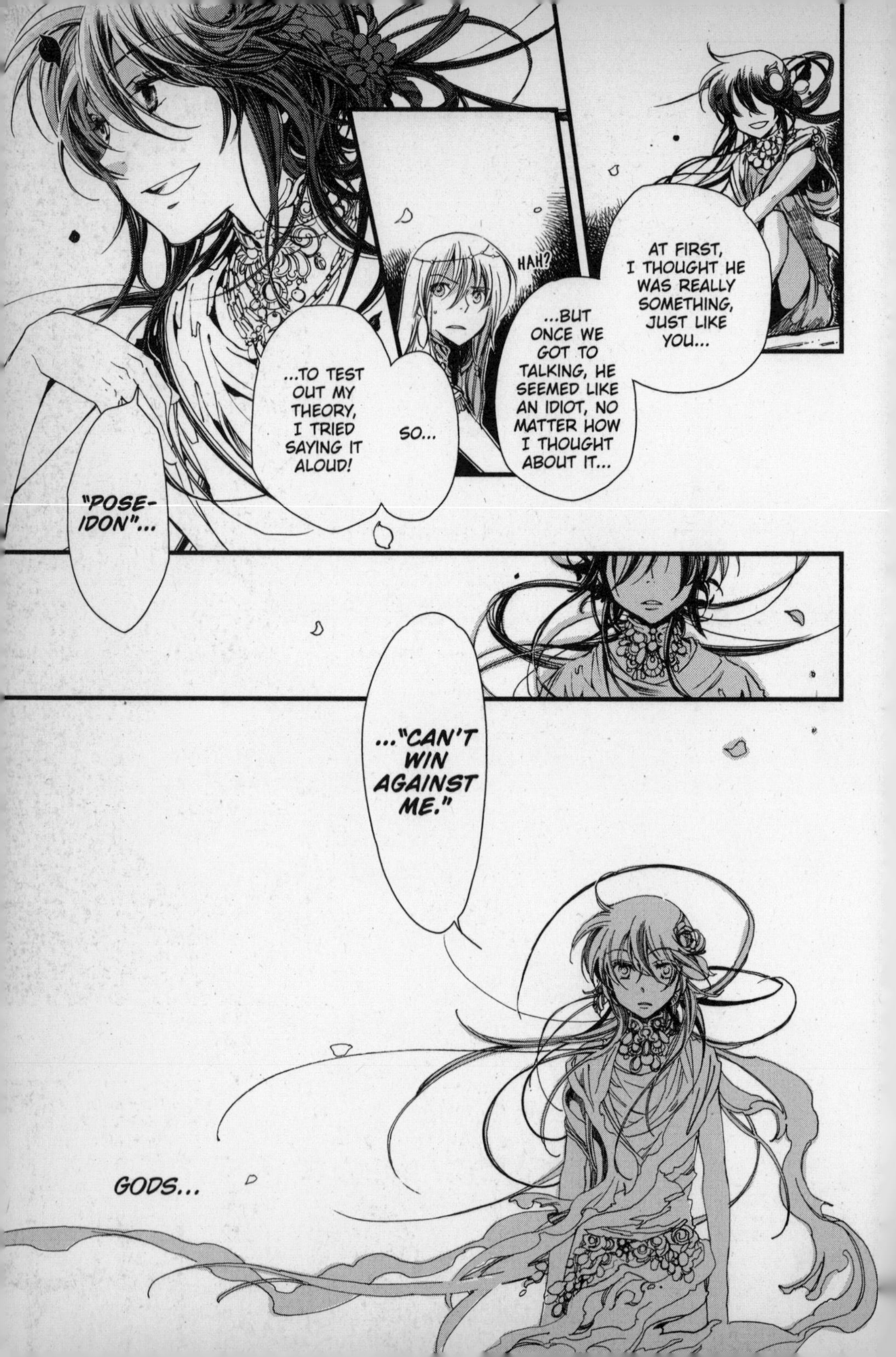
AT FIRST, I THOUGHT HE WAS REALLY SOMETHING, JUST LIKE YOU...
...BUT ONCE WE GOT TO TALKING, HE SEEMED LIKE AN IDIOT, NO MATTER HOW I THOUGHT ABOUT IT...
HAH?
SO...
...TO TEST OUT MY THEORY, I TRIED SAYING IT ALOUD!
"POSE-IDON"...
..."CAN'T WIN AGAINST ME."
GODS...

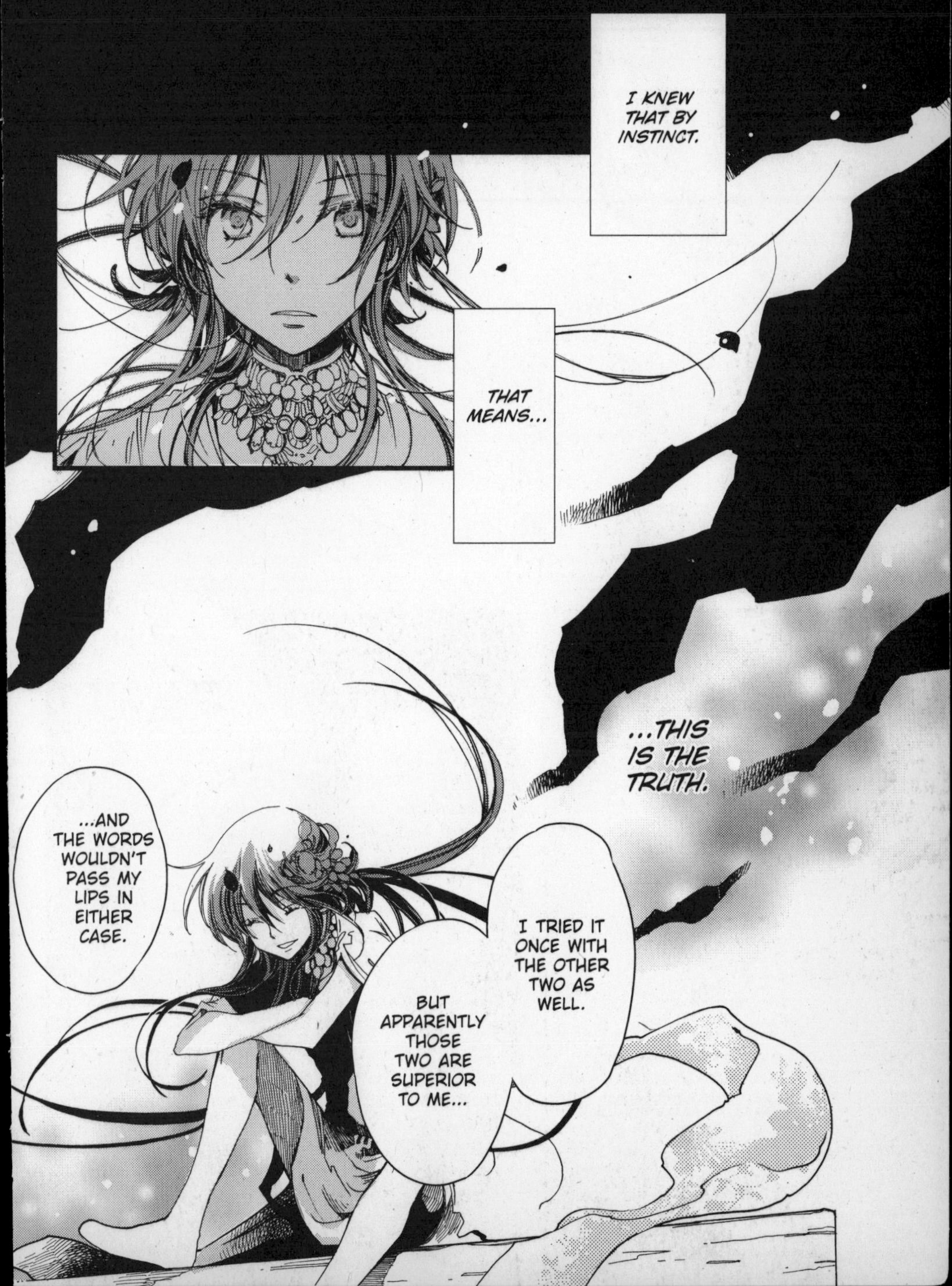
I KNEW THAT BY INSTINCT.
THAT MEANS...
...THIS IS THE TRUTH.
I TRIED IT ONCE WITH THE OTHER TWO AS WELL.
BUT APPARENTLY THOSE TWO ARE SUPERIOR TO ME...
...AND THE WORDS WOULDN'T PASS MY LIPS IN EITHER CASE.

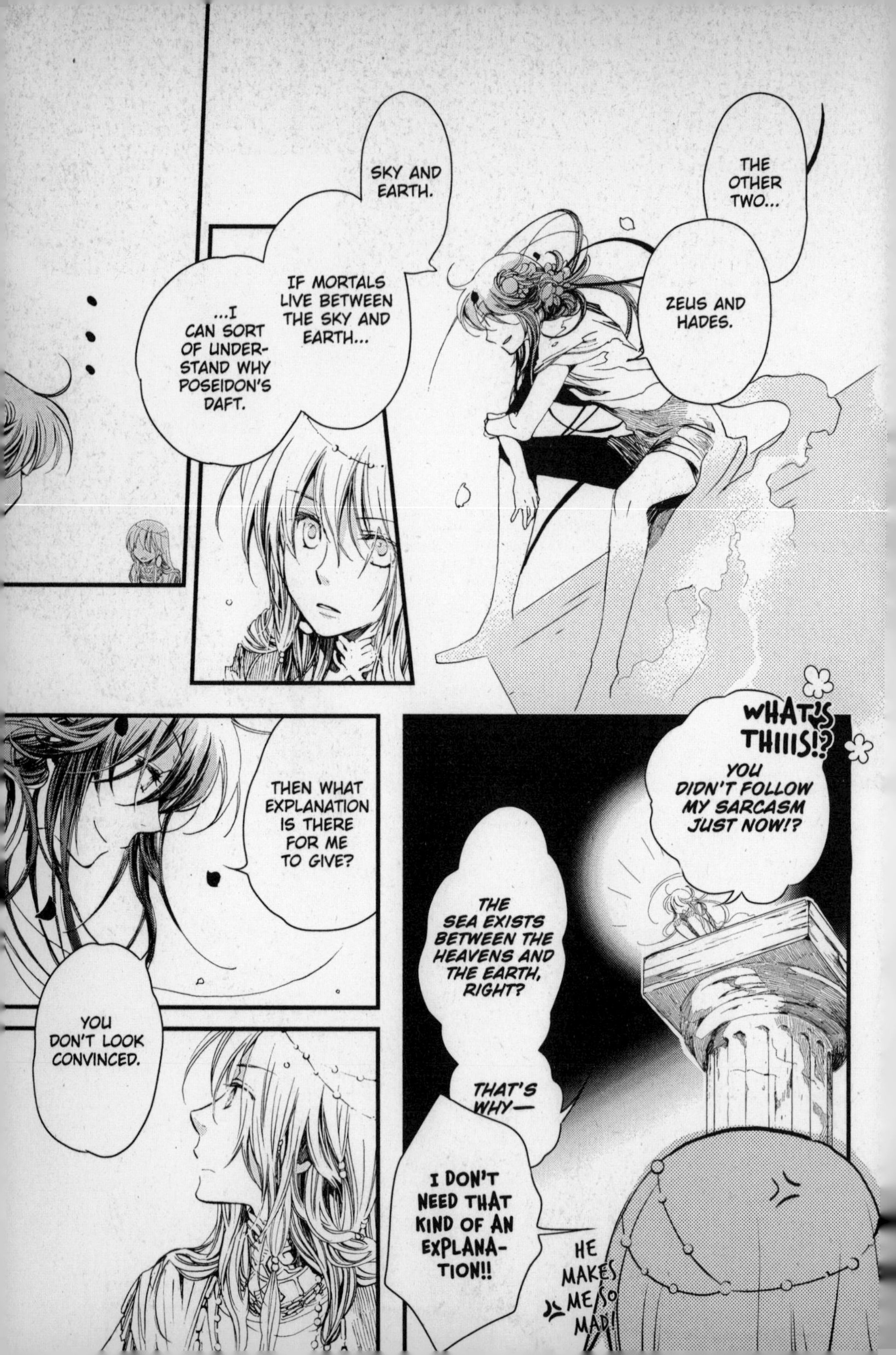
THE OTHER TWO...
ZEUS AND HADES.
SKY AND EARTH.
IF MORTALS LIVE BETWEEN THE SKY AND EARTH...
...I CAN SORT OF UNDER-STAND WHY POSEIDON'S DAFT.
• • •
WHAT'S THIIIS!?
YOU DIDN'T FOLLOW MY SARCASM JUST NOW!?
THE SEA EXISTS BETWEEN THE HEAVENS AND THE EARTH, RIGHT?
THAT'S WHY—
I DON'T NEED THAT KIND OF AN EXPLANA-TION!!
HE MAKES ME SO MAD!
THEN WHAT EXPLANATION IS THERE FOR ME TO GIVE?
YOU DON'T LOOK CONVINCED.

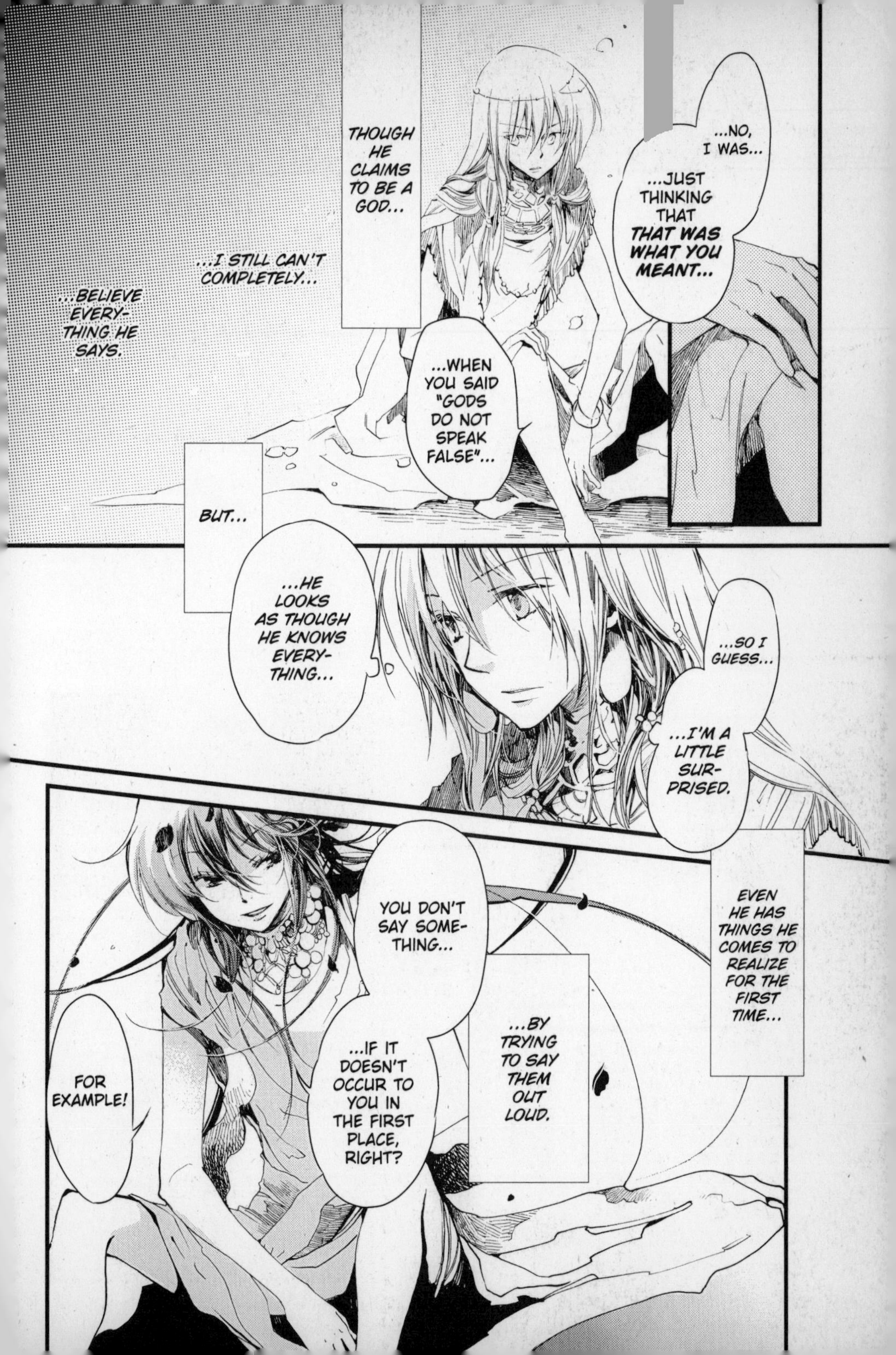

...NO, I WAS...
...JUST THINKING THAT THAT WAS WHAT YOU MEANT...
...WHEN YOU SAID "GODS DO NOT SPEAK FALSE"...
THOUGH HE CLAIMS TO BE A GOD...
...I STILL CAN'T COMPLETELY...
...BELIEVE EVERYTHING HE SAYS.
...SO I GUESS...
...I'M A LITTLE SURPRISED.
BUT...
...HE LOOKS AS THOUGH HE KNOWS EVERYTHING...
EVEN HE HAS THINGS HE COMES TO REALIZE FOR THE FIRST TIME...
...BY TRYING TO SAY THEM OUT LOUD.
YOU DON'T SAY SOMETHING...
...IF IT DOESN'T OCCUR TO YOU IN THE FIRST PLACE, RIGHT?
FOR EXAMPLE!

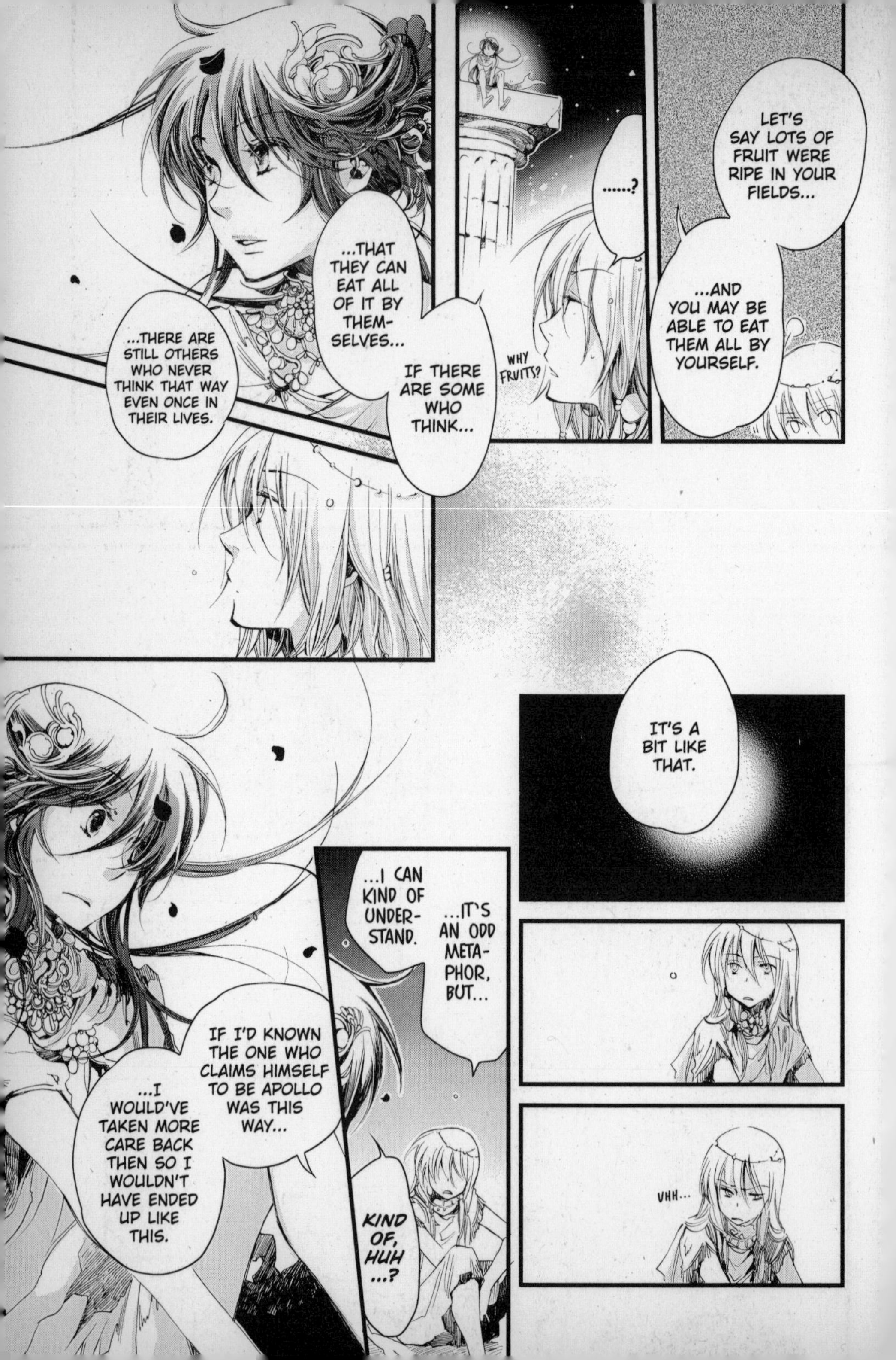
LET'S SAY LOTS OF FRUIT WERE RIPE IN YOUR FIELDS...
...AND YOU MAY BE ABLE TO EAT THEM ALL BY YOURSELF.
......?
WHY FRUITS?
IF THERE ARE SOME WHO THINK...
...THAT THEY CAN EAT ALL OF IT BY THEM-SELVES...
...THERE ARE STILL OTHERS WHO NEVER THINK THAT WAY EVEN ONCE IN THEIR LIVES.
IT'S A BIT LIKE THAT.
UHH...
...IT'S AN ODD META-PHOR, BUT...
...I CAN KIND OF UNDER-STAND.
KIND OF, HUH ...?
IF I'D KNOWN THE ONE WHO CLAIMS HIMSELF TO BE APOLLO WAS THIS WAY...
...I WOULD'VE TAKEN MORE CARE BACK THEN SO I WOULDN'T HAVE ENDED UP LIKE THIS.

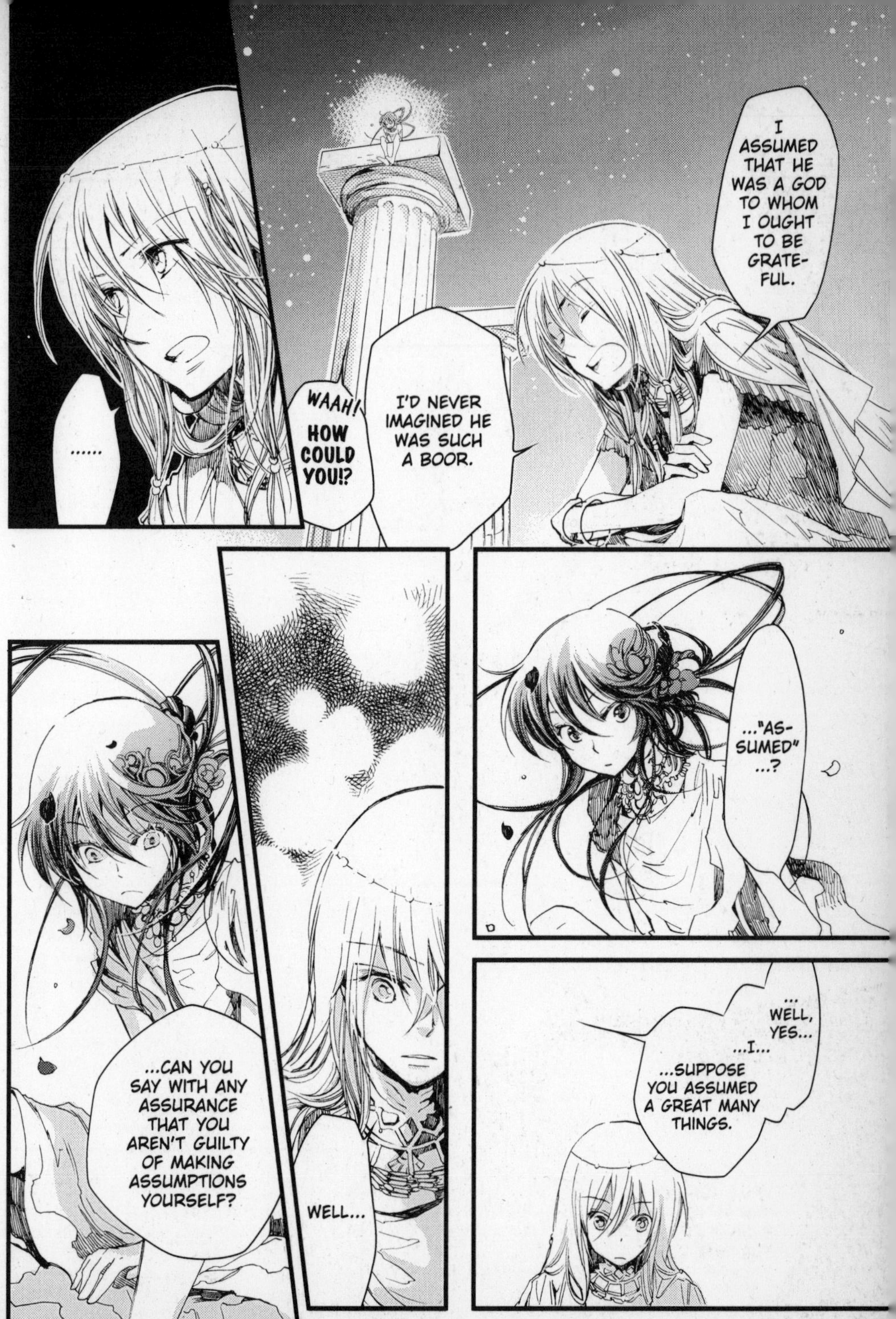
I ASSUMED THAT HE WAS A GOD TO WHOM I OUGHT TO BE GRATEFUL.
I'D NEVER IMAGINED HE WAS SUCH A BOOR.
WAAH! HOW COULD YOU!?
......
..."AS-SUMED" ...?
... WELL, YES...
...I...
...SUPPOSE YOU ASSUMED A GREAT MANY THINGS.
...CAN YOU SAY WITH ANY ASSURANCE THAT YOU AREN'T GUILTY OF MAKING ASSUMPTIONS YOURSELF?
WELL...

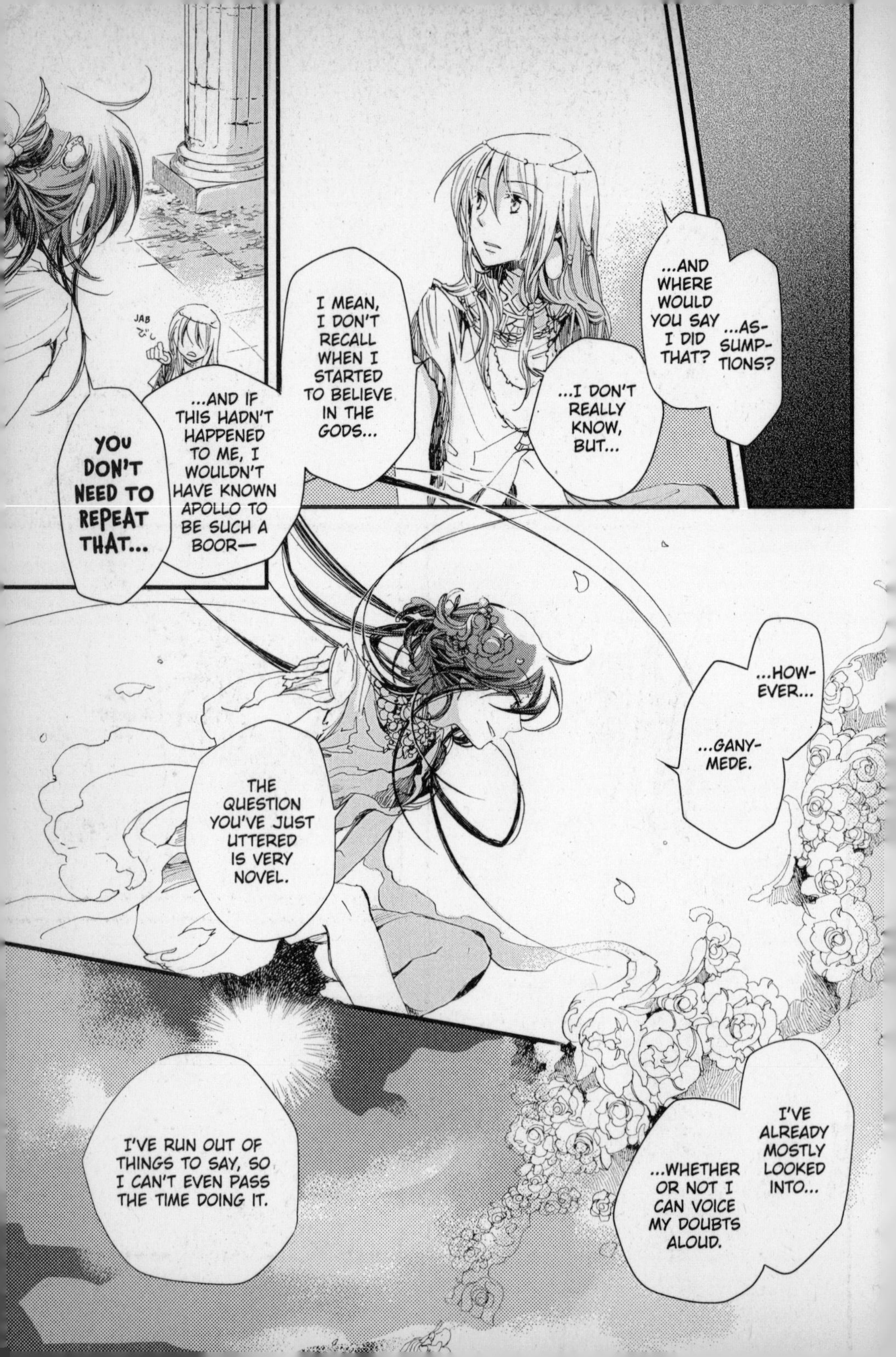
...AND WHERE WOULD YOU SAY I DID THAT?
...AS-SUMP-TIONS?
...I DON'T REALLY KNOW, BUT...
I MEAN, I DON'T RECALL WHEN I STARTED TO BELIEVE IN THE GODS...
...AND IF THIS HADN'T HAPPENED TO ME, I WOULDN'T HAVE KNOWN APOLLO TO BE SUCH A BOOR—
JAB
YOU DON'T NEED TO REPEAT THAT...
...HOW-EVER...
...GANY-MEDE.
THE QUESTION YOU'VE JUST UTTERED IS VERY NOVEL.
I'VE ALREADY MOSTLY LOOKED INTO...
...WHETHER OR NOT I CAN VOICE MY DOUBTS ALOUD.
I'VE RUN OUT OF THINGS TO SAY, SO I CAN'T EVEN PASS THE TIME DOING IT.

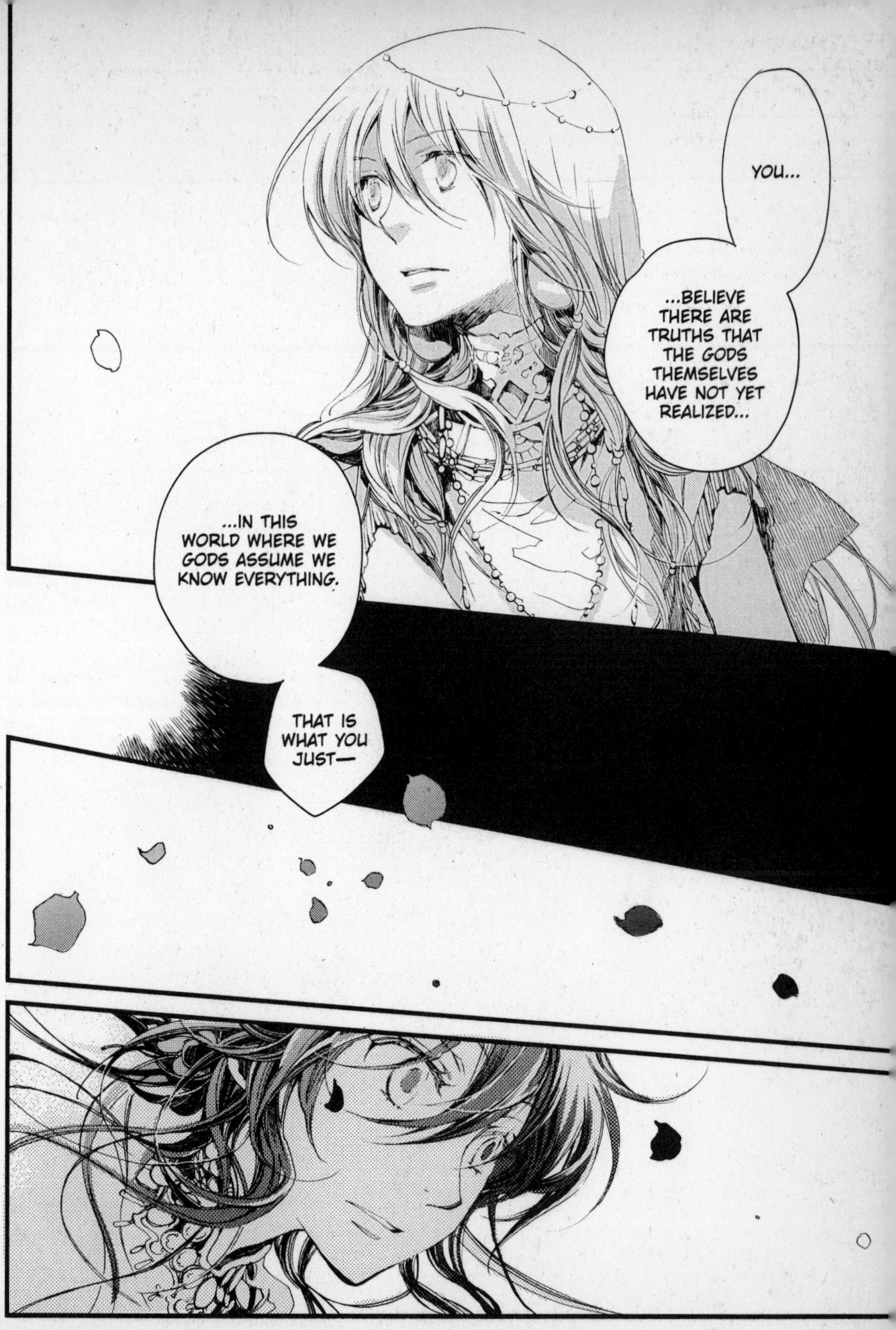
YOU...
...BELIEVE THERE ARE TRUTHS THAT THE GODS THEMSELVES HAVE NOT YET REALIZED...
...IN THIS WORLD WHERE WE GODS ASSUME WE KNOW EVERYTHING.
THAT IS WHAT YOU JUST—

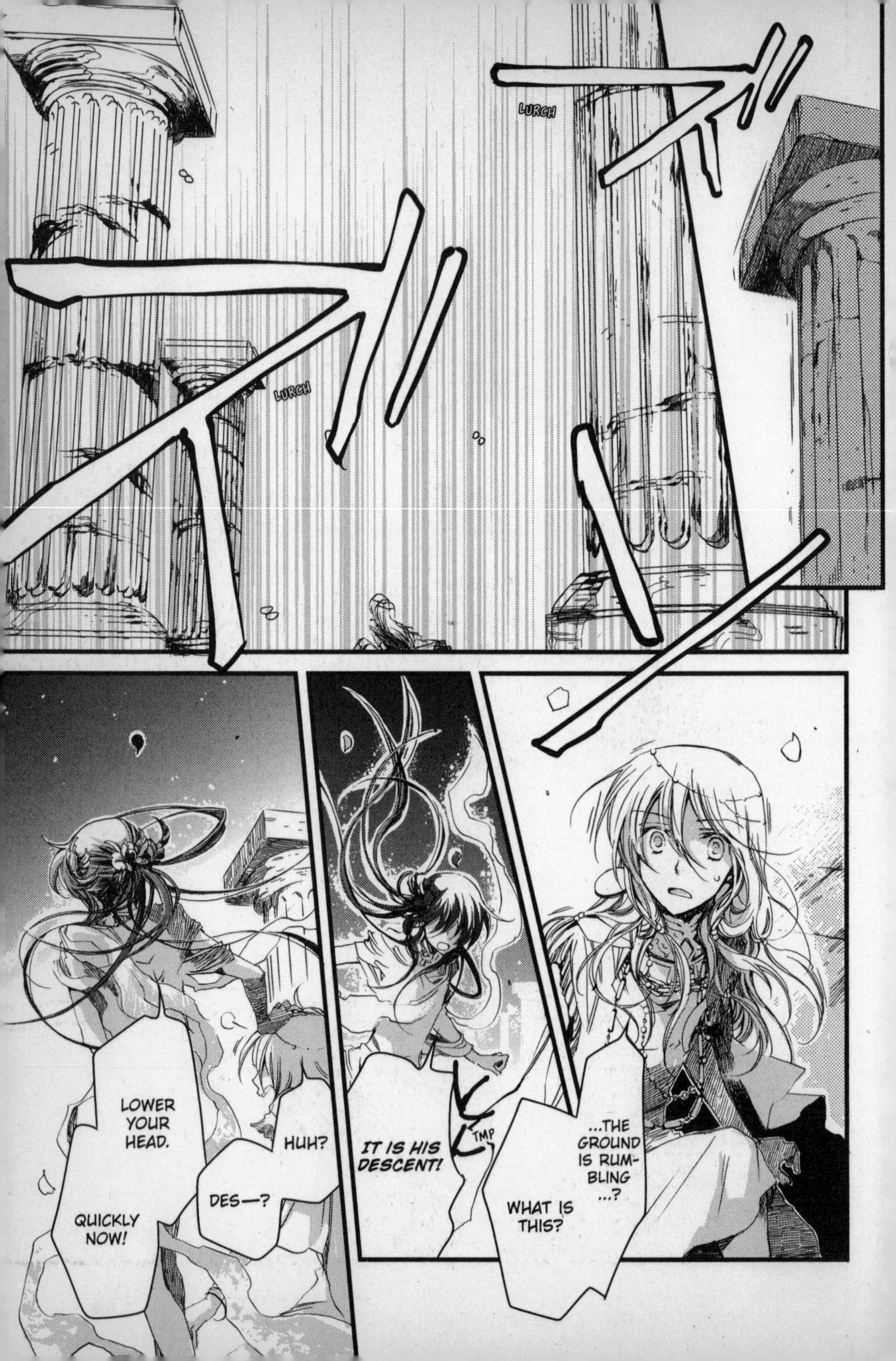
LURCH
LURCH
...THE GROUND IS RUMBLING...?
WHAT IS THIS?
IT IS HIS DESCENT!
TMP
HUH?
DES—?
LOWER YOUR HEAD.
QUICKLY NOW!

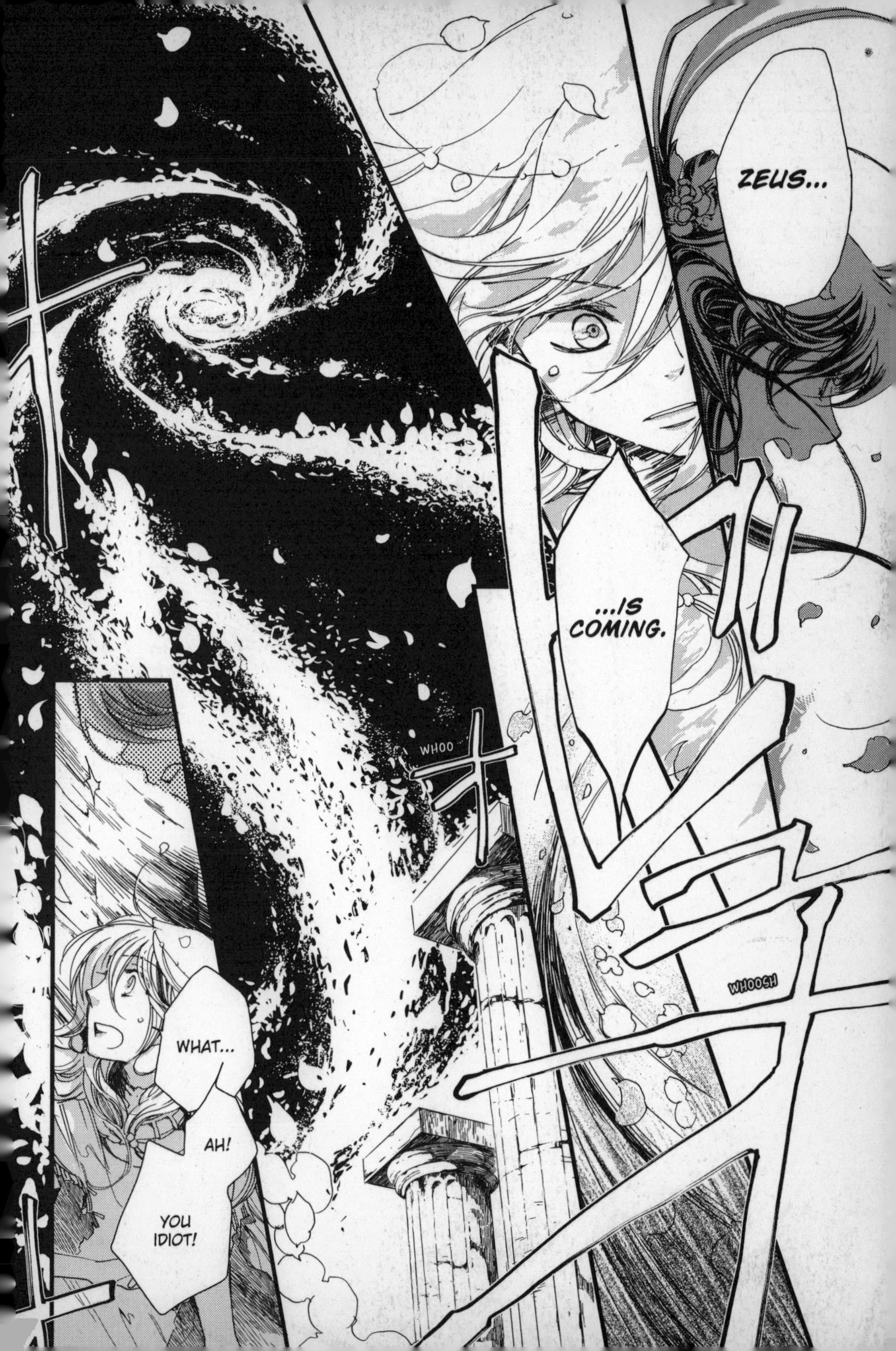
ZEUS...
...IS COMING.
WHOOSH
WHOO
WHAT...
AH!
YOU IDIOT!

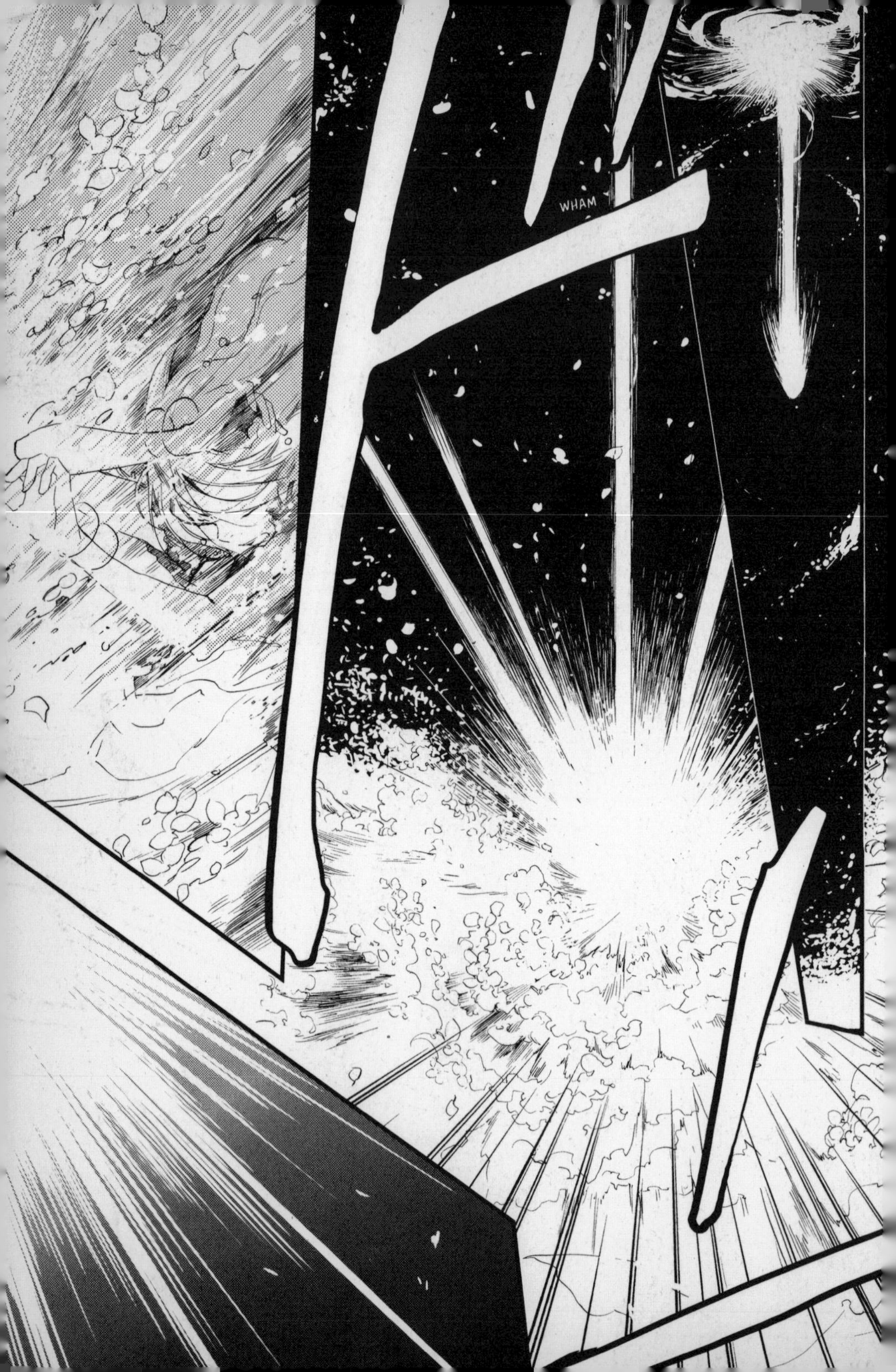
WHAM

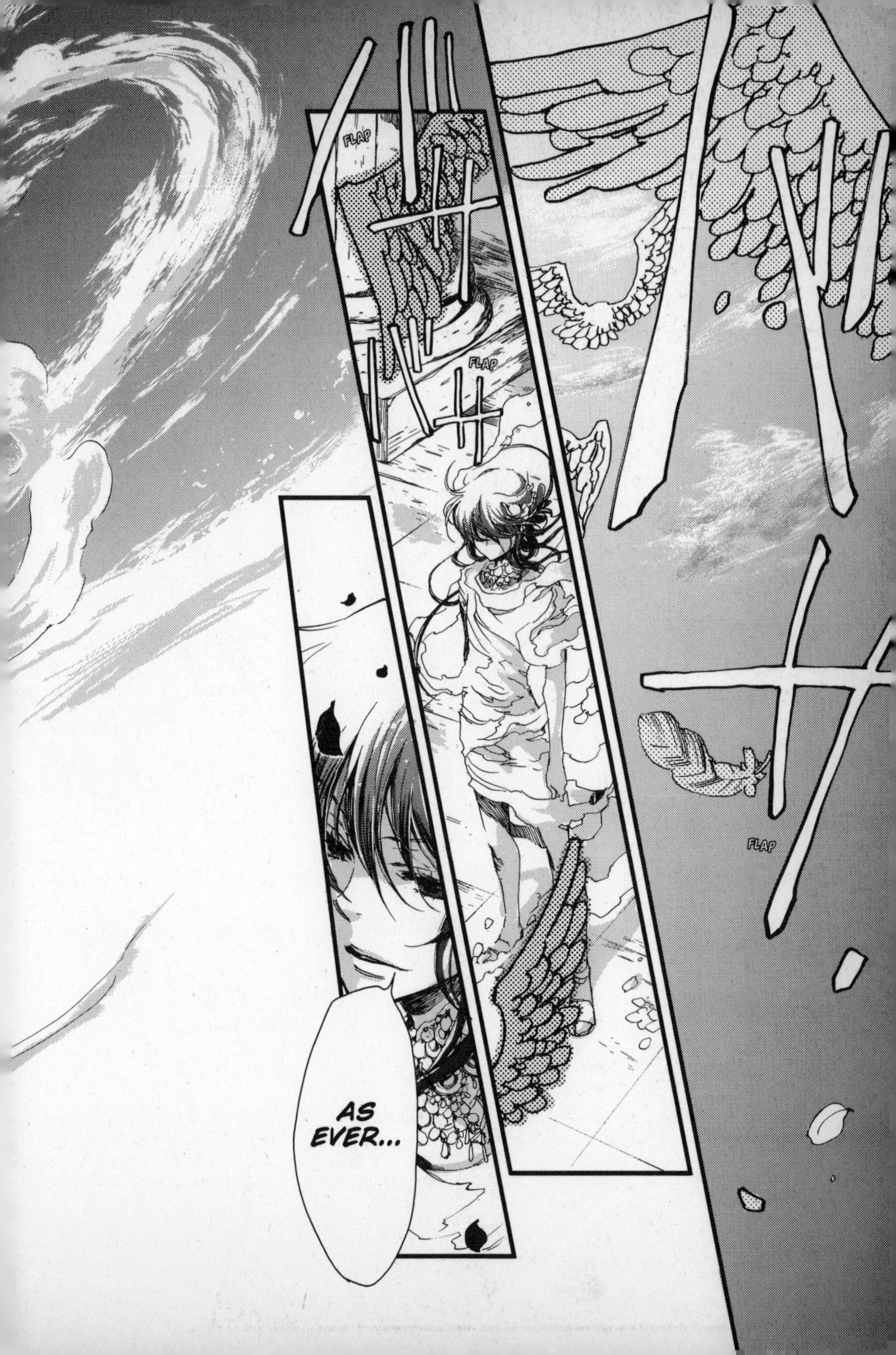
FLAP
FLAP
FLAP
AS EVER...

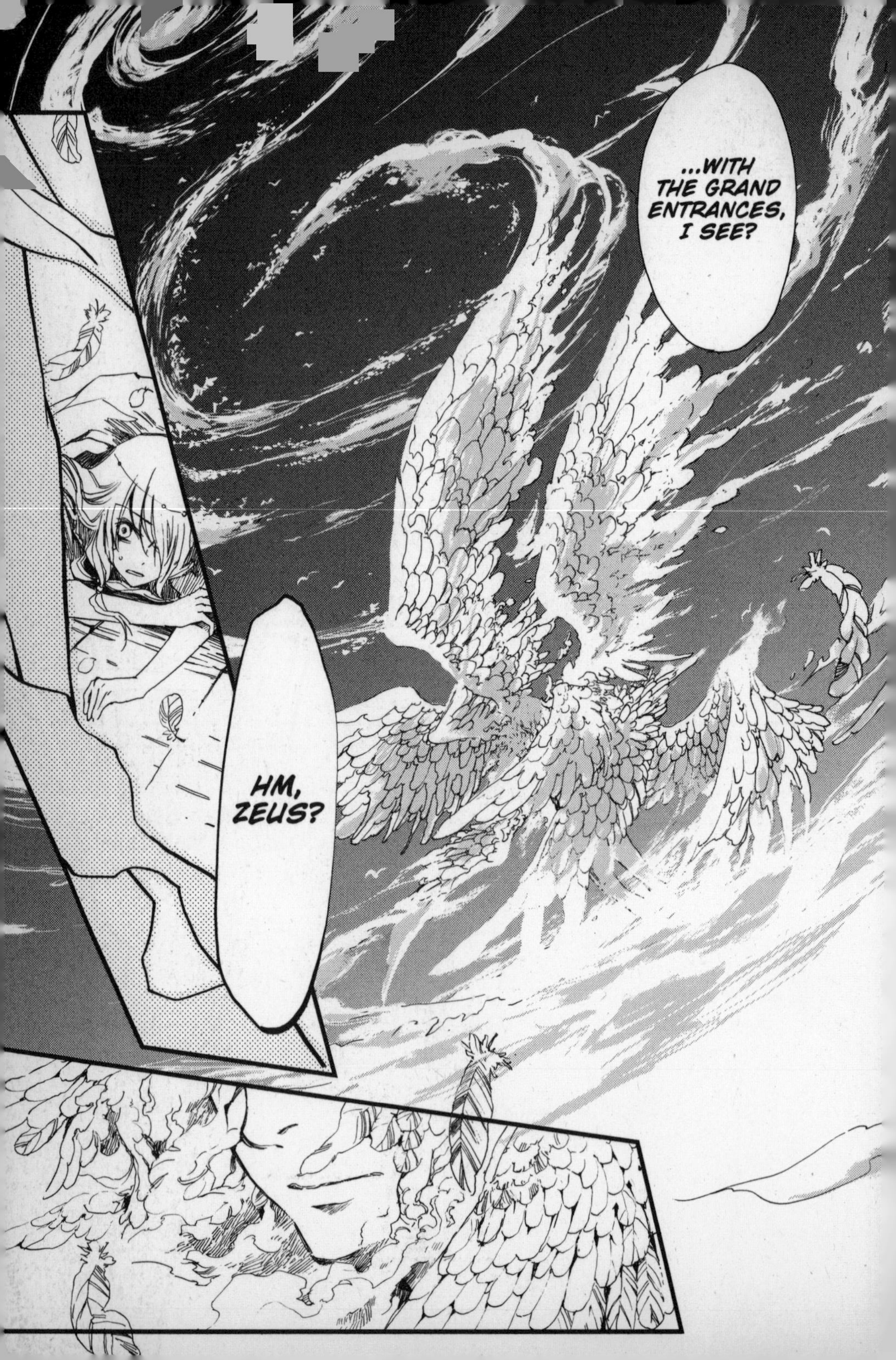
...WITH THE GRAND ENTRANCES, I SEE?
HM, ZEUS?

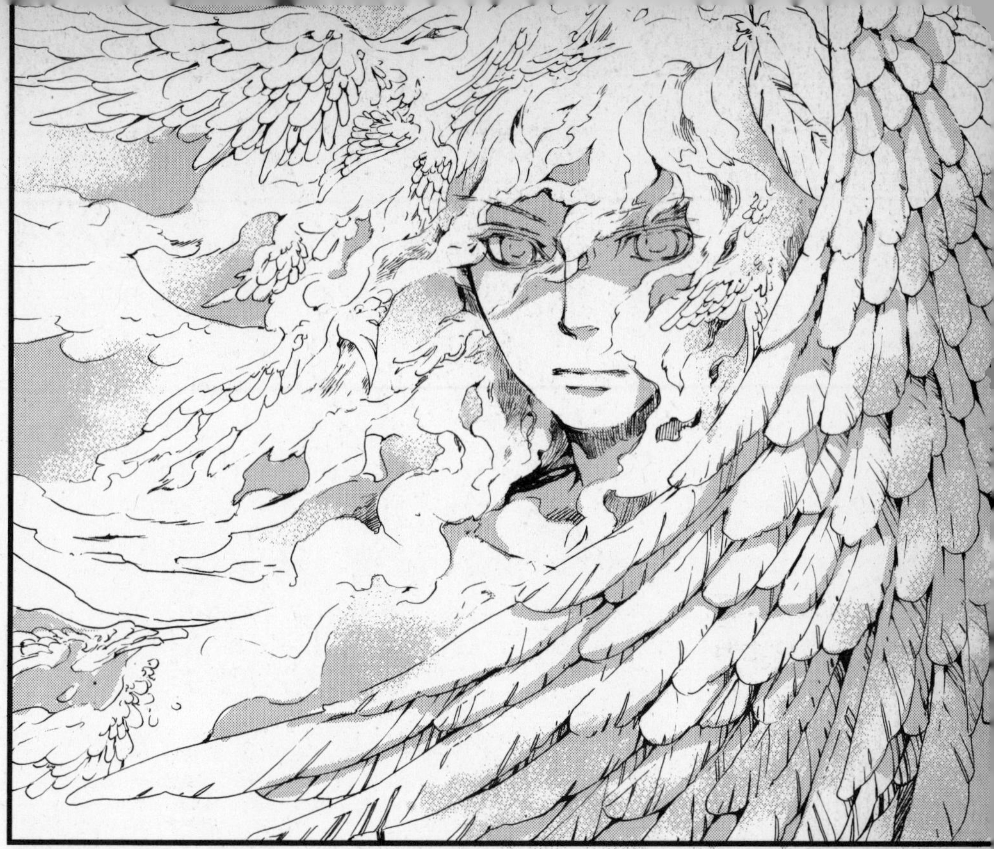
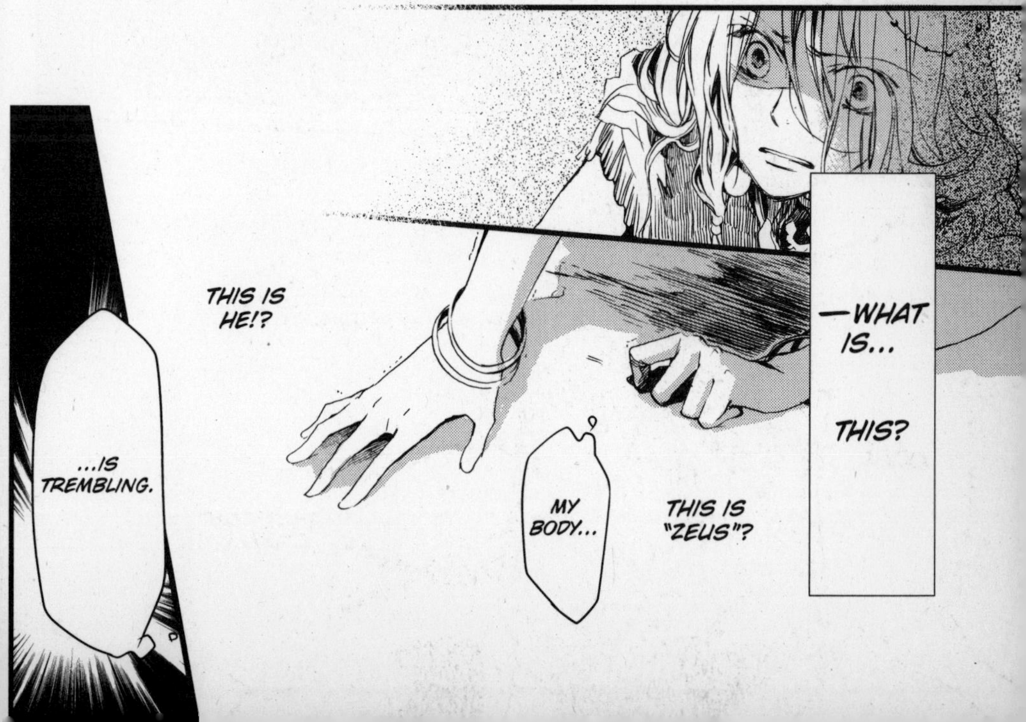
—WHAT IS...
THIS?
THIS IS "ZEUS"?
MY BODY...
THIS IS HE!?
...IS TREMBLING.

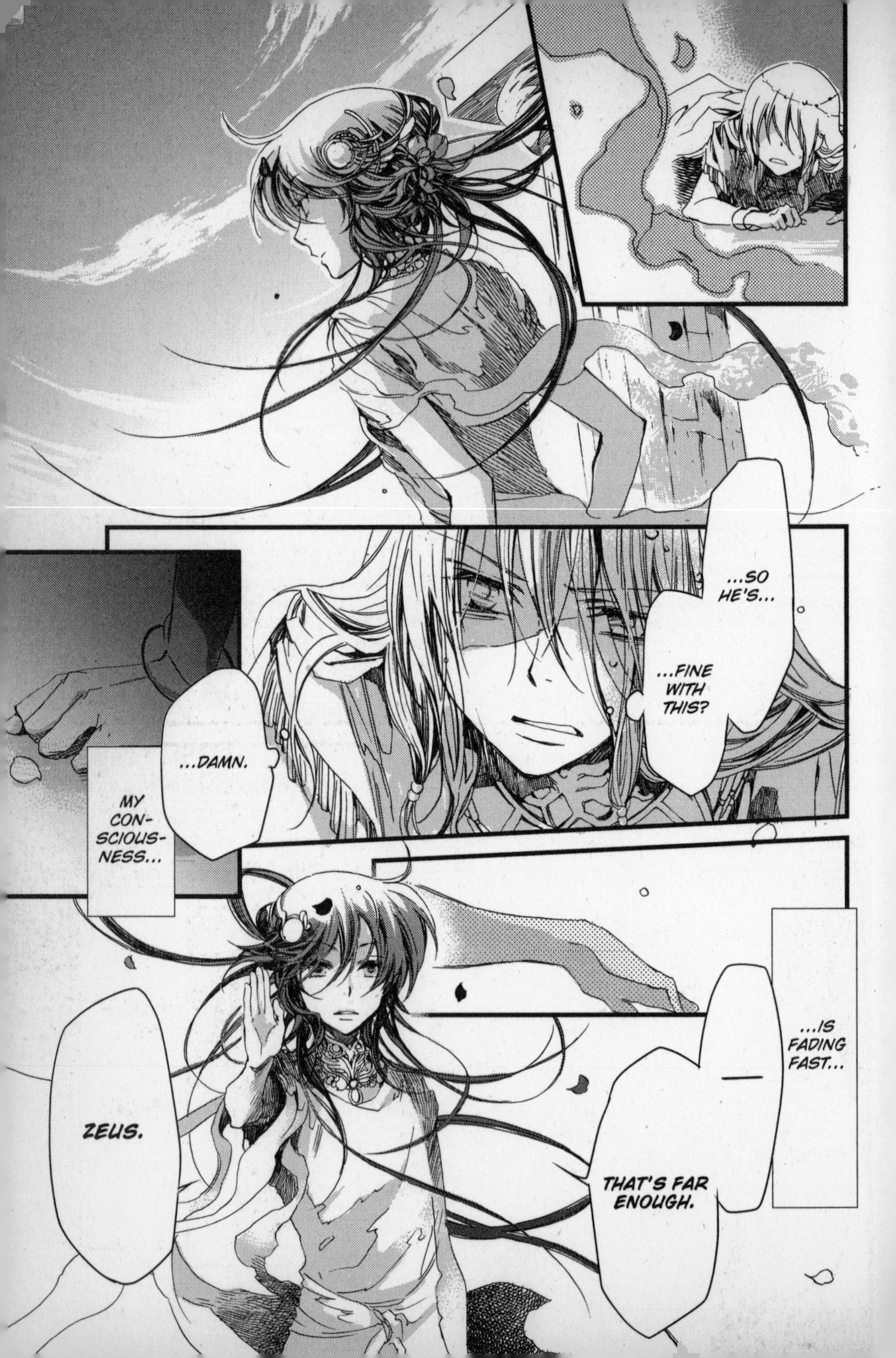
...SO HE'S...
...FINE WITH THIS?
...DAMN.
MY CON-SCIOUS-NESS...
...IS FADING FAST...
— THAT'S FAR ENOUGH.
ZEUS.

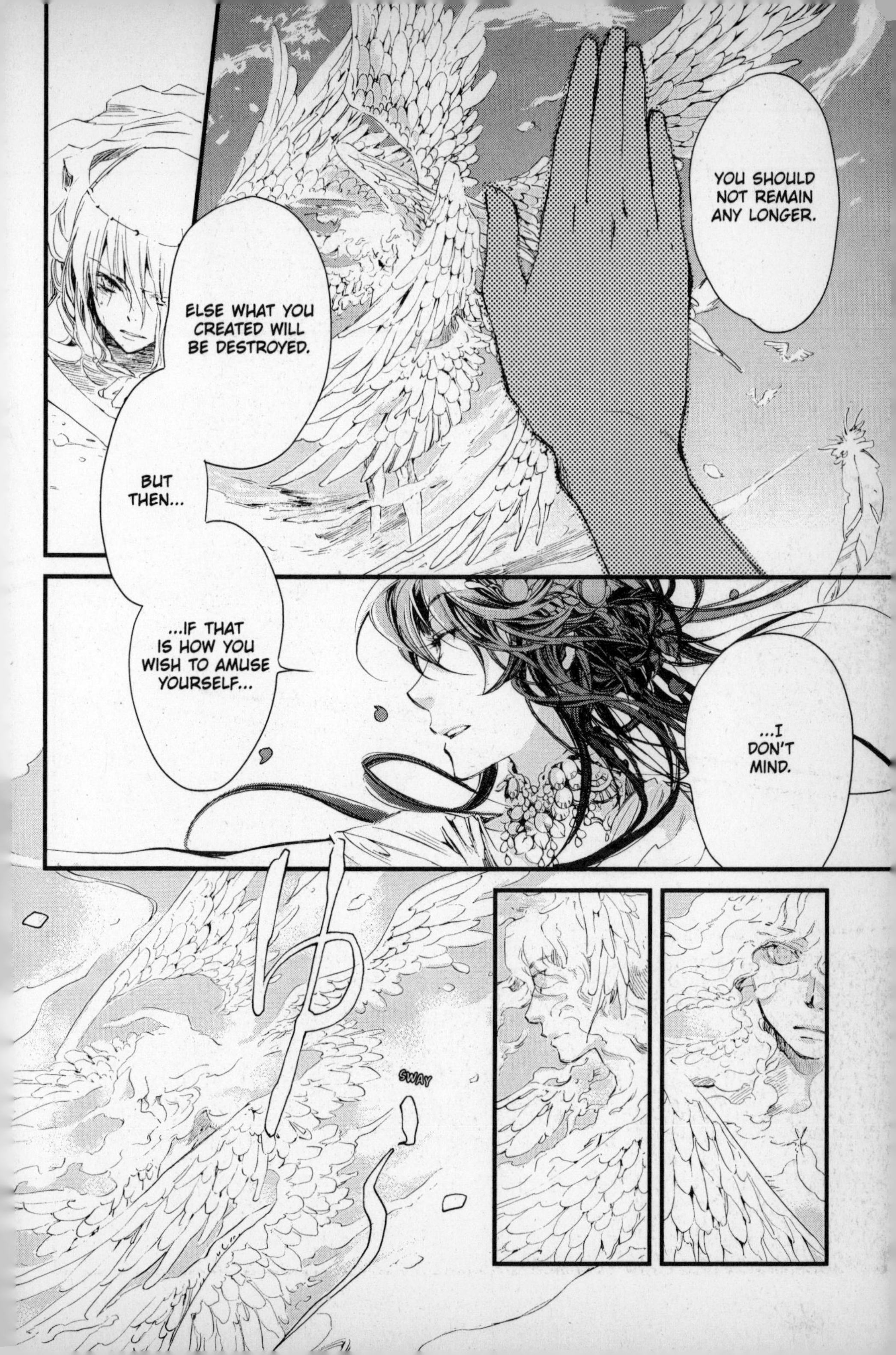
YOU SHOULD NOT REMAIN ANY LONGER.
ELSE WHAT YOU CREATED WILL BE DESTROYED.
BUT THEN...
...IF THAT IS HOW YOU WISH TO AMUSE YOURSELF...
...I DON'T MIND.
SWAY

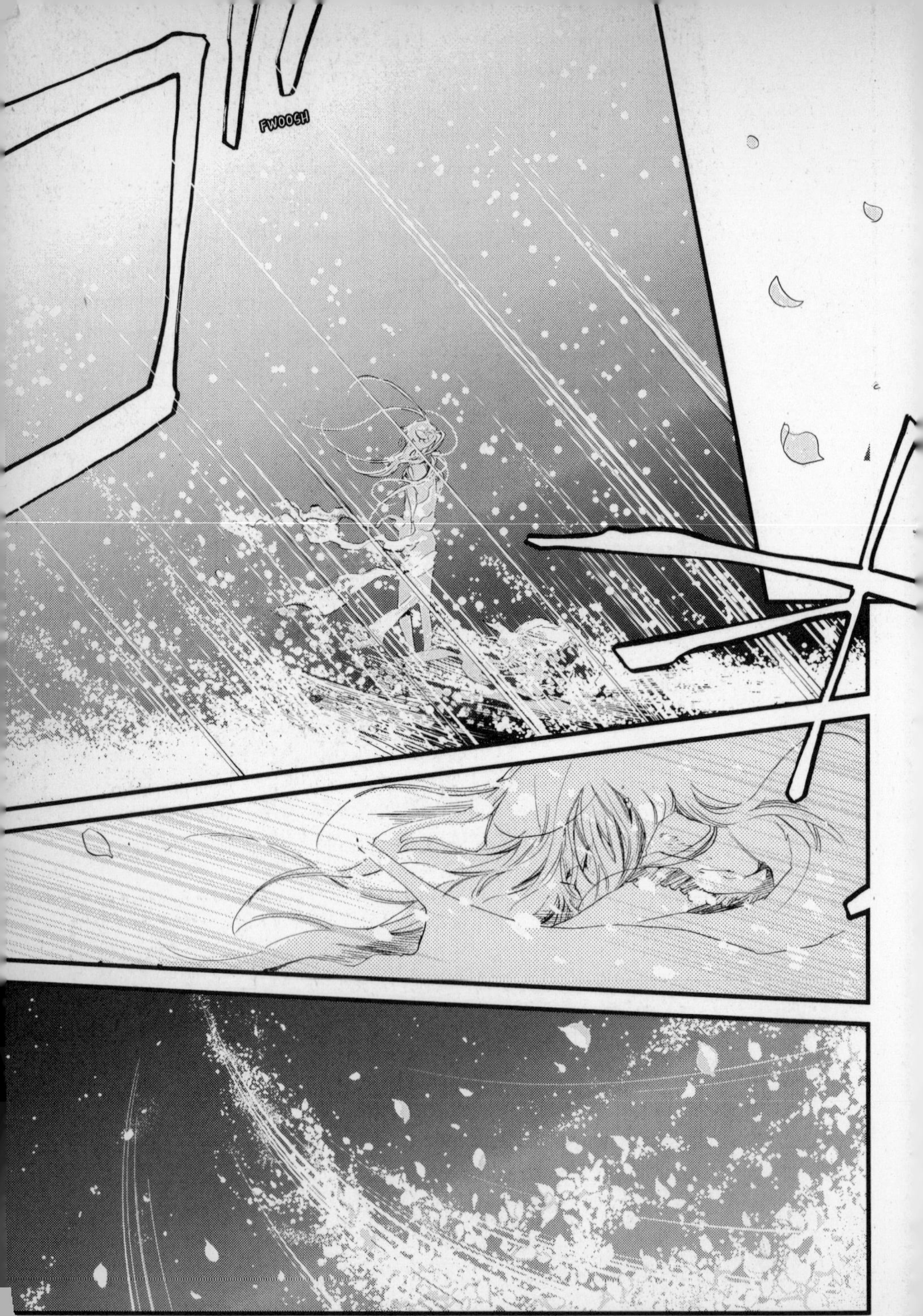
FWOOSH

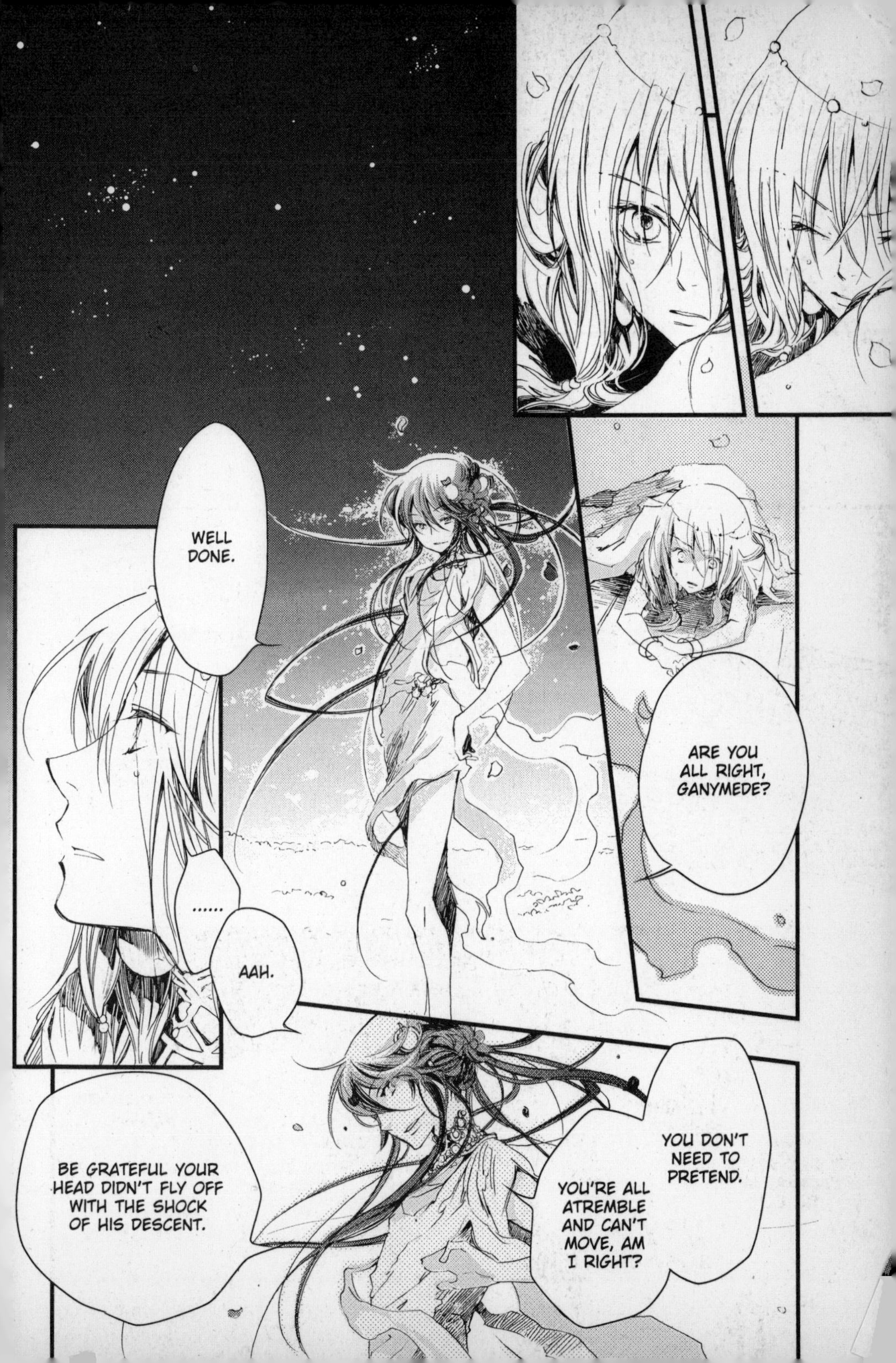
ARE YOU ALL RIGHT, GANYMEDE?
WELL DONE.
......
AAH.
YOU DON'T NEED TO PRETEND.
YOU'RE ALL ATREMBLE AND CAN'T MOVE, AM I RIGHT?
BE GRATEFUL YOUR HEAD DIDN'T FLY OFF WITH THE SHOCK OF HIS DESCENT.

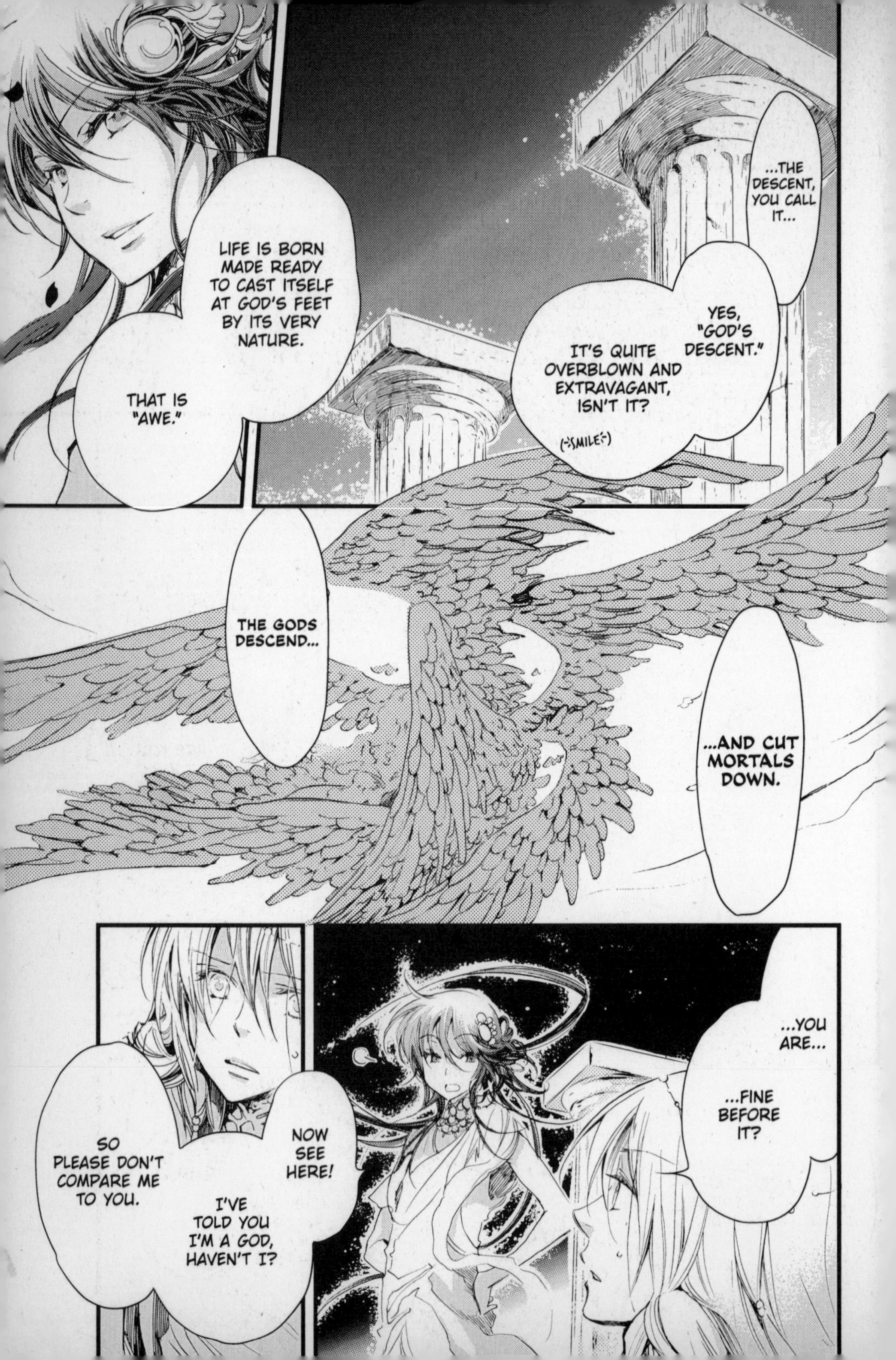
...THE DESCENT, YOU CALL IT...
YES, "GOD'S DESCENT."
IT'S QUITE OVERBLOWN AND EXTRAVAGANT, ISN'T IT?
(-SMILE-)
LIFE IS BORN MADE READY TO CAST ITSELF AT GOD'S FEET BY ITS VERY NATURE.
THAT IS "AWE."
THE GODS DESCEND...
...AND CUT MORTALS DOWN.
...YOU ARE...
...FINE BEFORE IT?
NOW SEE HERE!
I'VE TOLD YOU I'M A GOD, HAVEN'T I?
SO PLEASE DON'T COMPARE ME TO YOU.

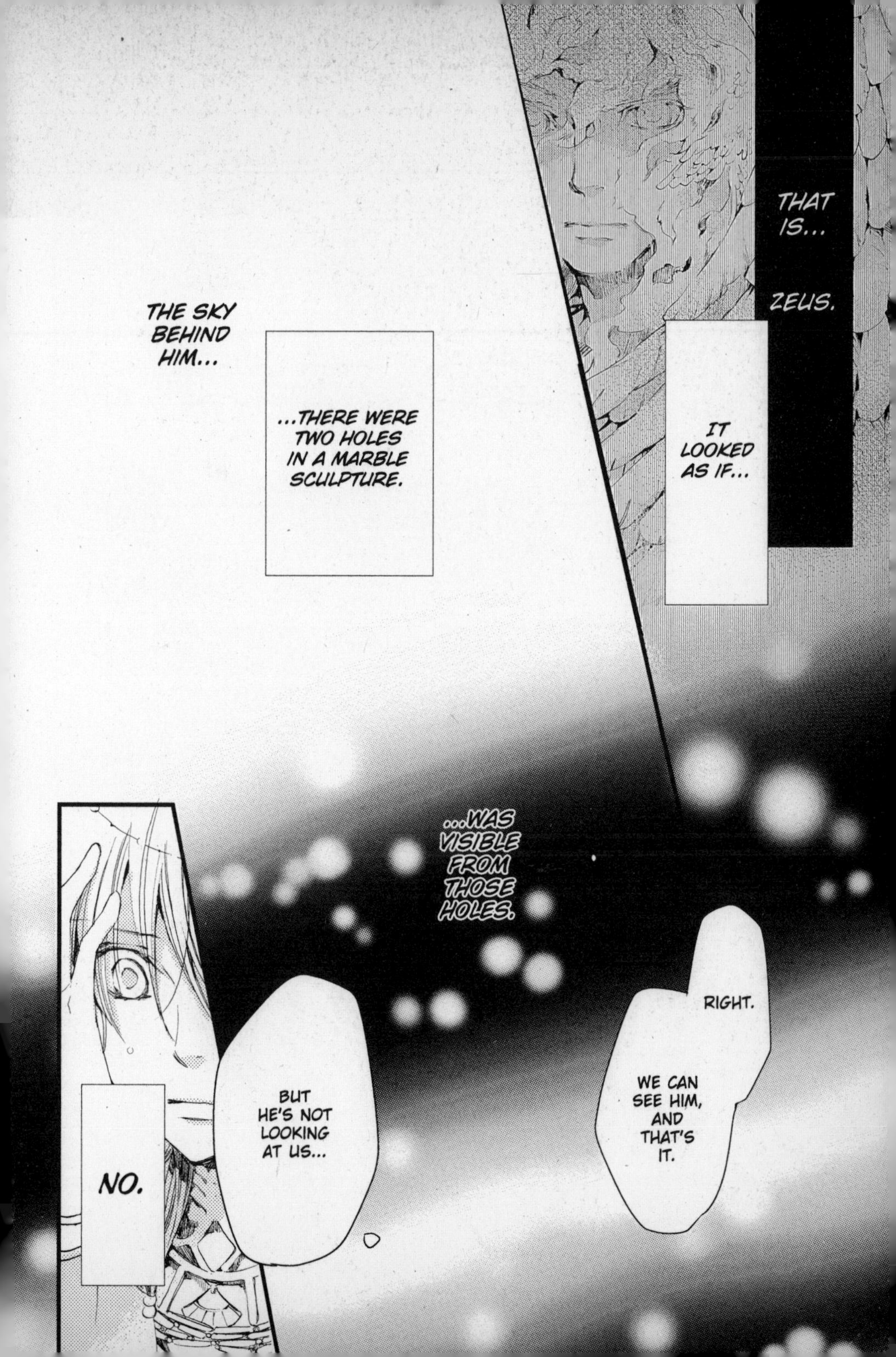
THAT IS...
ZEUS.
IT LOOKED AS IF...
...THERE WERE TWO HOLES IN A MARBLE SCULPTURE.
THE SKY BEHIND HIM...
...WAS VISIBLE FROM THOSE HOLES.
RIGHT.
WE CAN SEE HIM, AND THAT'S IT.
BUT HE'S NOT LOOKING AT US...
NO.

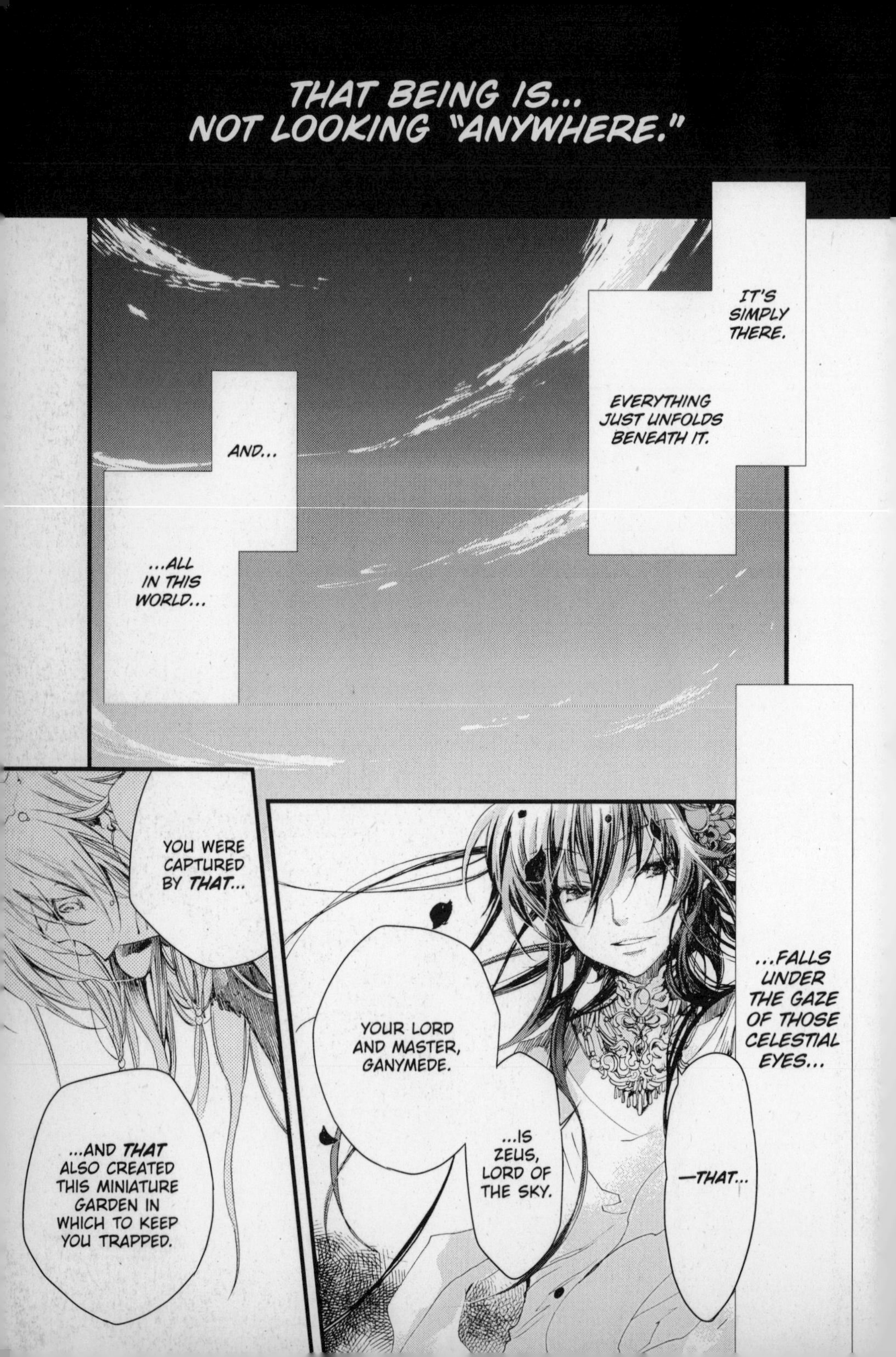
THAT BEING IS... NOT LOOKING "ANYWHERE."
IT'S SIMPLY THERE.
EVERYTHING JUST UNFOLDS BENEATH IT.
AND...
...ALL IN THIS WORLD...
...FALLS UNDER THE GAZE OF THOSE CELESTIAL EYES...
—THAT...
...IS ZEUS, LORD OF THE SKY.
YOUR LORD AND MASTER, GANYMEDE.
YOU WERE CAPTURED BY *THAT*...
...AND *THAT* ALSO CREATED THIS MINIATURE GARDEN IN WHICH TO KEEP YOU TRAPPED.

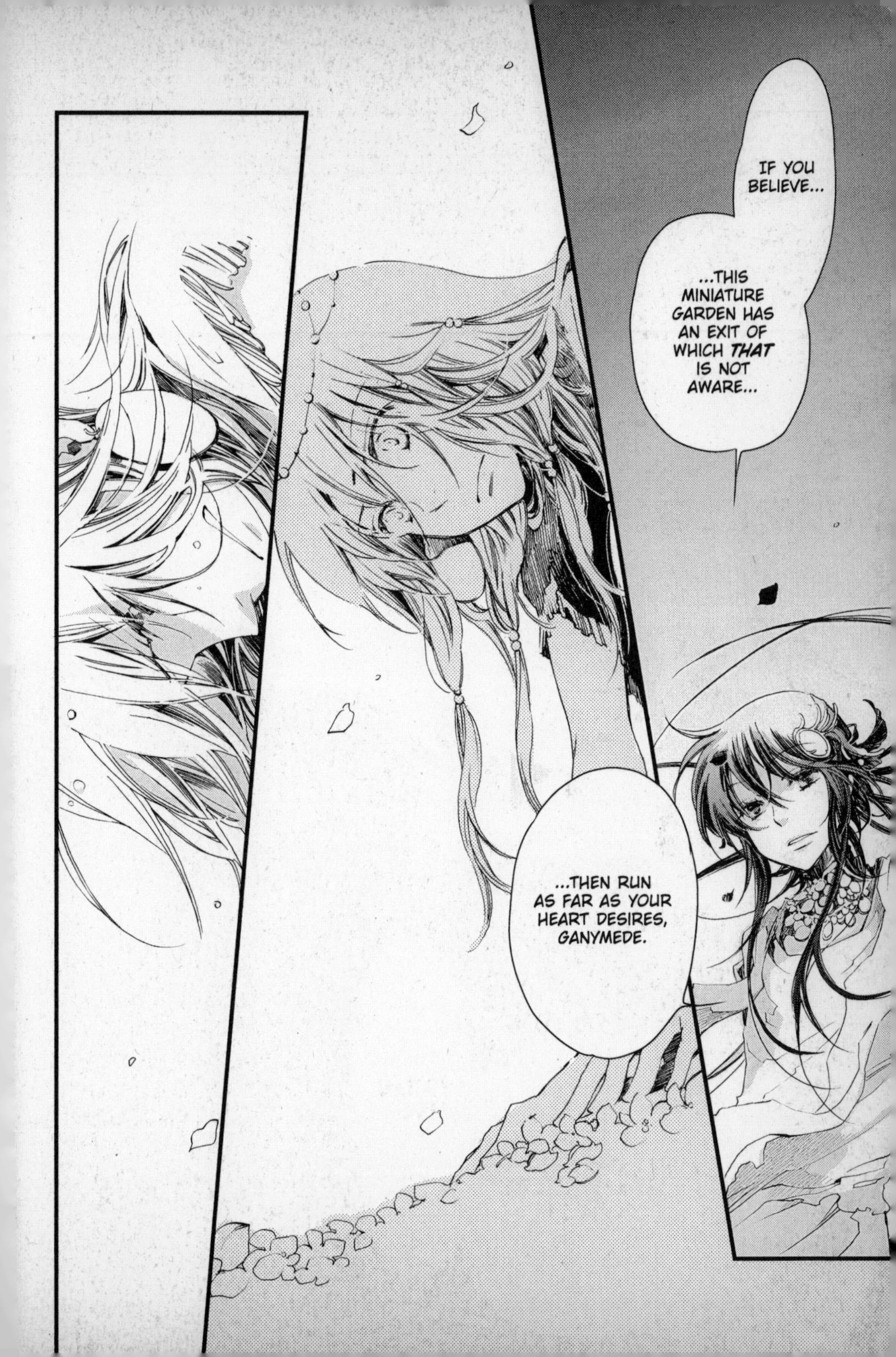
IF YOU BELIEVE...
...THIS MINIATURE GARDEN HAS AN EXIT OF WHICH *THAT* IS NOT AWARE...
...THEN RUN AS FAR AS YOUR HEART DESIRES, GANYMEDE.

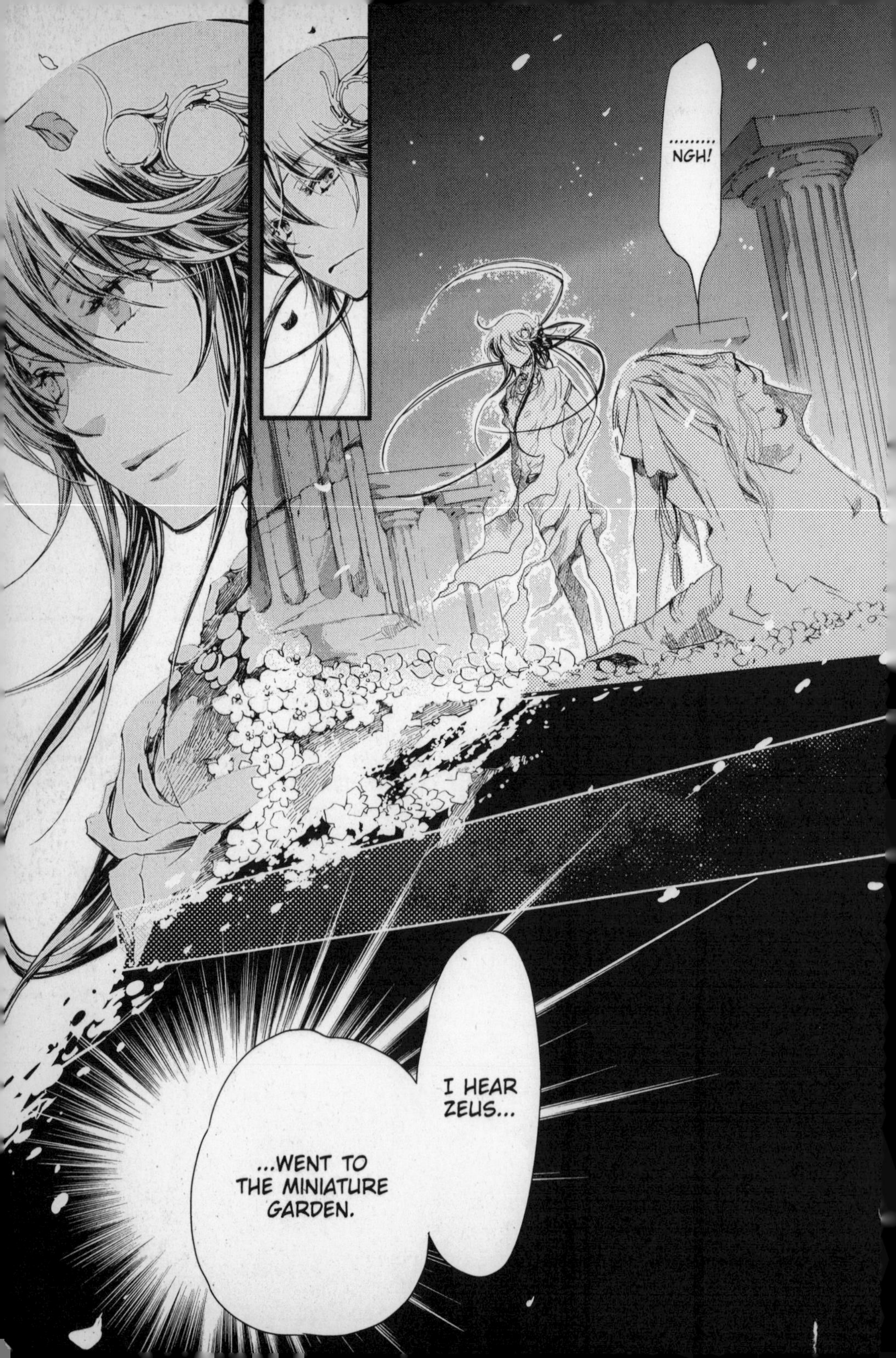

....
NGH!
I HEAR ZEUS...
...WENT TO THE MINIATURE GARDEN.

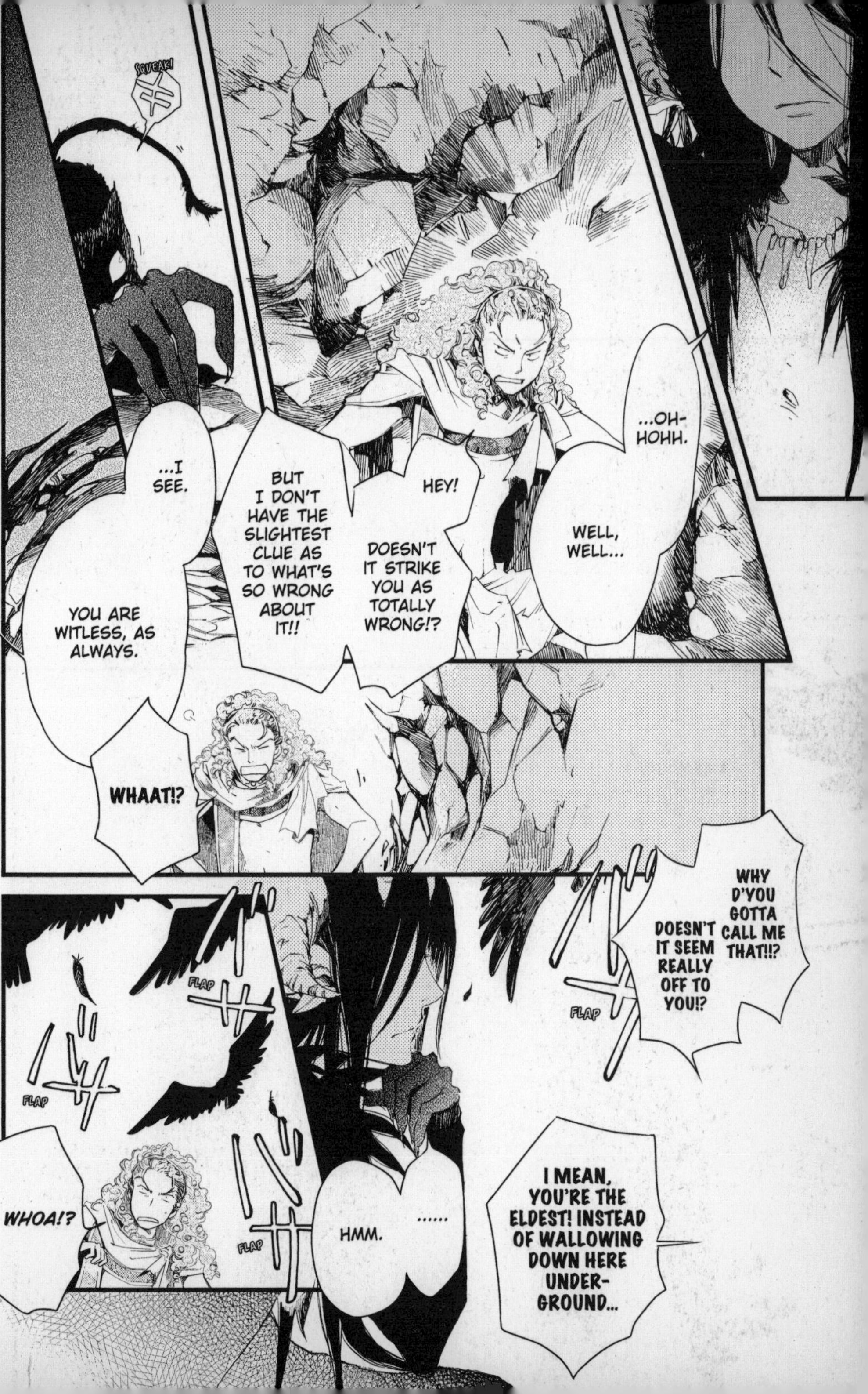
...OH-HOHH.
WELL, WELL...
HEY!
DOESN'T IT STRIKE YOU AS TOTALLY WRONG!?
BUT I DON'T HAVE THE SLIGHTEST CLUE AS TO WHAT'S SO WRONG ABOUT IT!!
SQUEAK!
...I SEE.
YOU ARE WITLESS, AS ALWAYS.
WHAAT!?
WHY D'YOU GOTTA CALL ME THAT!!?
DOESN'T IT SEEM REALLY OFF TO YOU!?
FLAP
I MEAN, YOU'RE THE ELDEST! INSTEAD OF WALLOWING DOWN HERE UNDER-GROUND...
......
HMM.
FLAP
FLAP
FLAP
WHOA!?

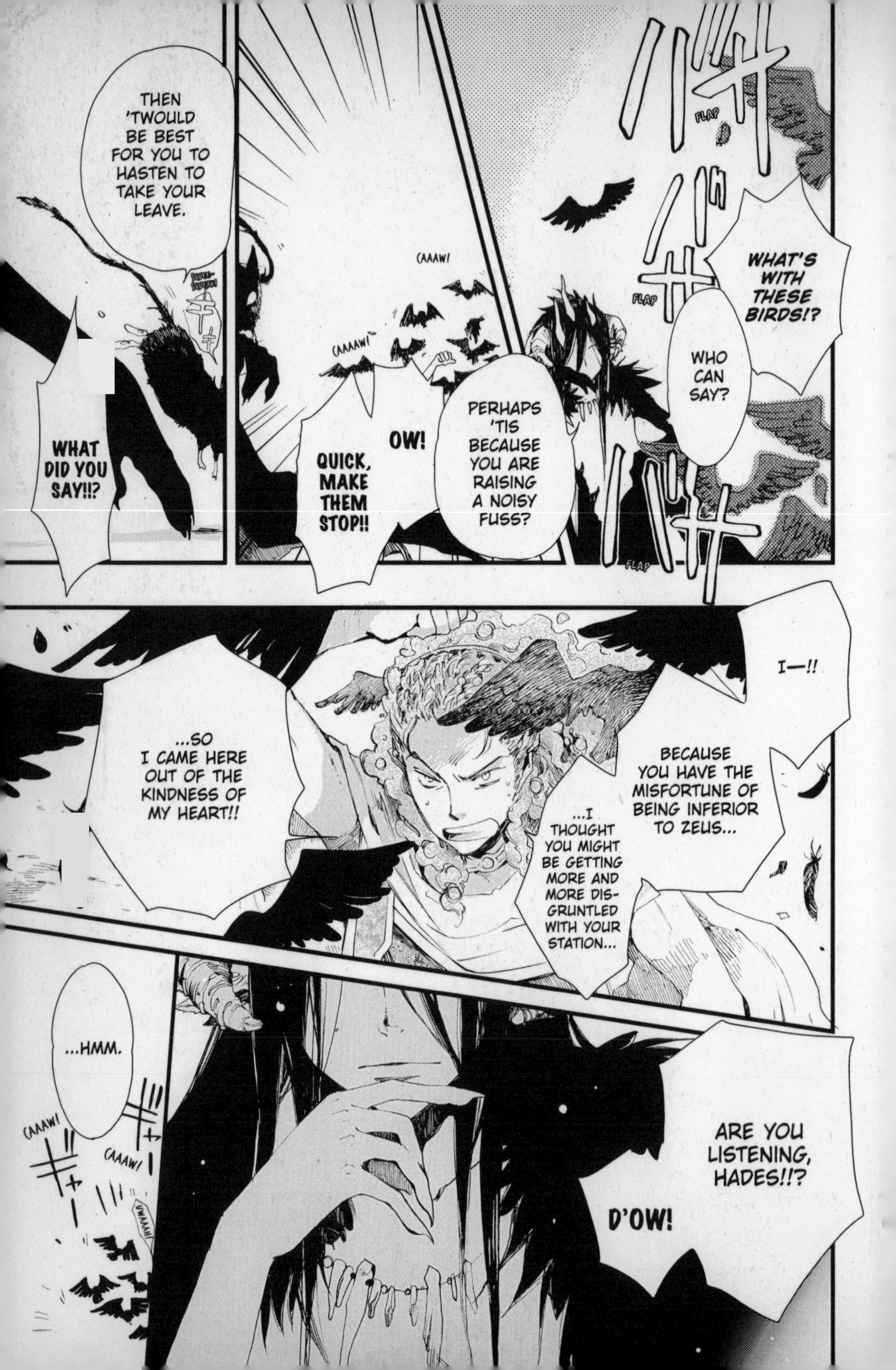
FLAP
WHAT'S WITH THESE BIRDS!?
FLAP
WHO CAN SAY?
FLAP
PERHAPS 'TIS BECAUSE YOU ARE RAISING A NOISY FUSS?
CAAAW!
CAAAAW!
OW!
QUICK, MAKE THEM STOP!!
THEN 'TWOULD BE BEST FOR YOU TO HASTEN TO TAKE YOUR LEAVE.
WHAT DID YOU SAY!!?
I—!!
BECAUSE YOU HAVE THE MISFORTUNE OF BEING INFERIOR TO ZEUS...
...I THOUGHT YOU MIGHT BE GETTING MORE AND MORE DIS-GRUNTLED WITH YOUR STATION...
...SO I CAME HERE OUT OF THE KINDNESS OF MY HEART!!
ARE YOU LISTENING, HADES!!?
D'OW!
...HMM.
CAAAW!
CAAAW!

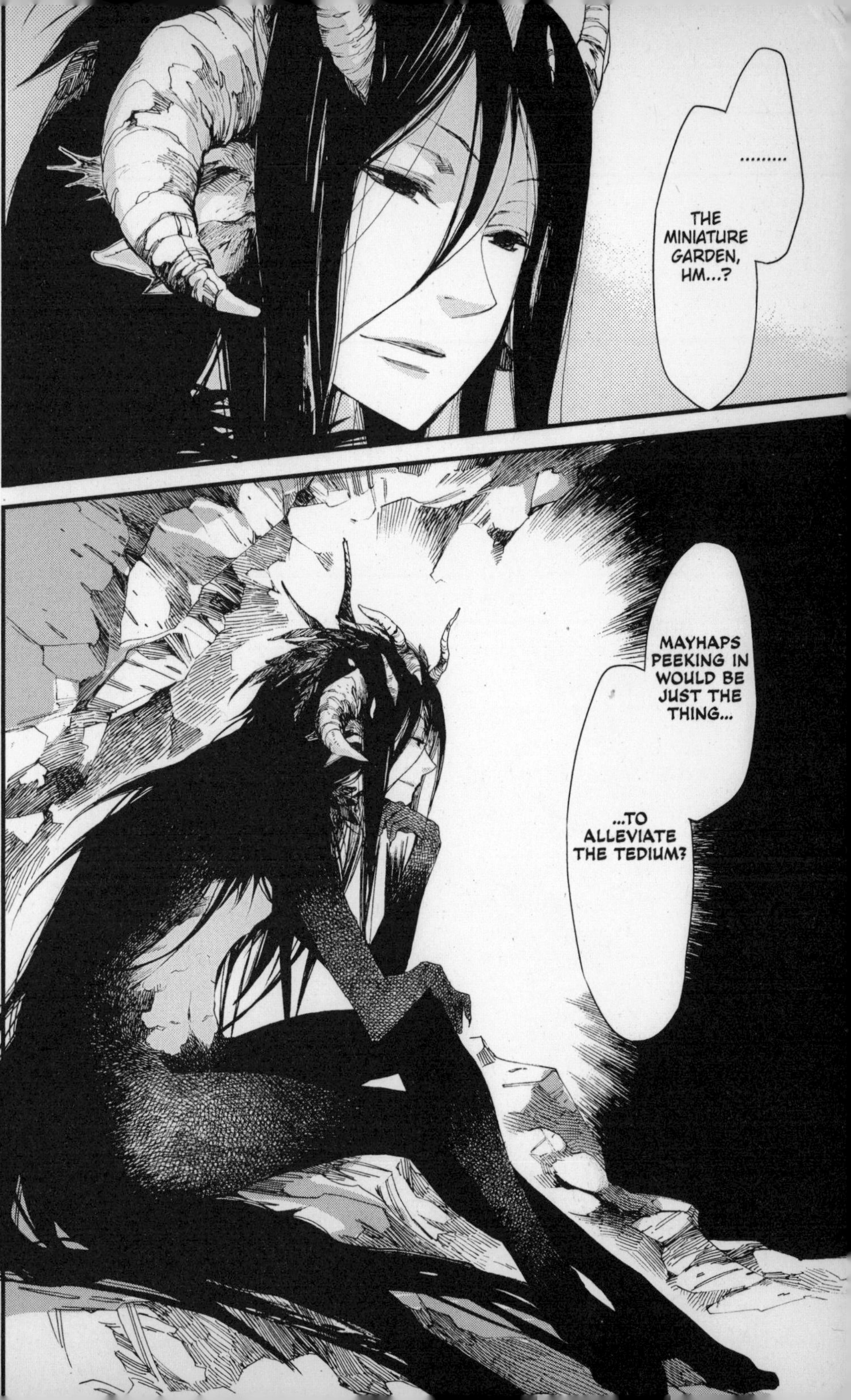
....
THE MINIATURE GARDEN, HM...?
MAYHAPS PEEKING IN WOULD BE JUST THE THING...
...TO ALLEVIATE THE TEDIUM?

Olympos

APOLLO LOOKED LIKE THIS IN THE VEEEERY BEGINNING. (-`SMILE´-)

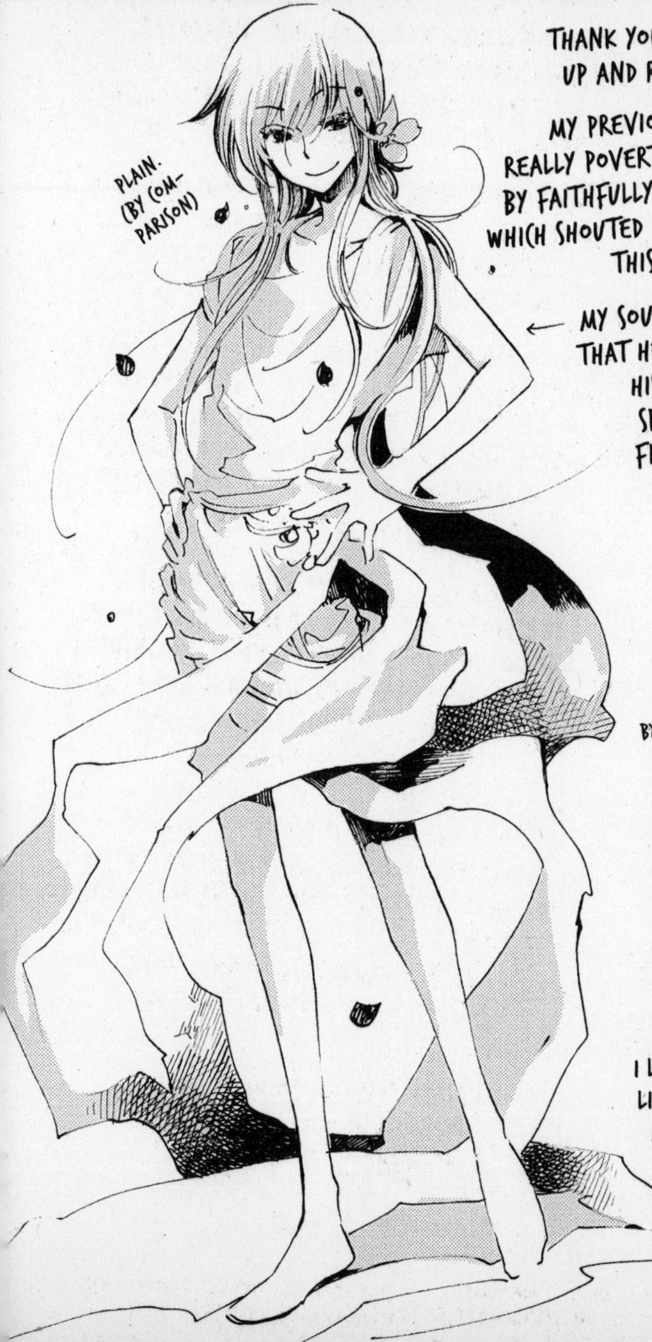
PLAIN. (BY COMPARISON)

WELL, HELLO THERE. I'M AKI.

THANK YOU SO MUCH FOR PICKING UP AND READING THIS MANGA!

MY PREVIOUS MANGA WAS FULL OF REALLY POVERTY-STRICKEN CHARACTERS, SO BY FAITHFULLY FOLLOWING MY INSTINCTS—WHICH SHOUTED "I WANNA DRAW SPARKLES!!"—THIS MANGA WAS BORN.

← MY SOUL SHOUTED SO LOUDLY THAT HE WENT FROM THIS TO HIS PRESENT FORM. SPARKLE-SPARKLE! FLITTER-FLUTTER!

BY THE WAY...

AS I'M DRAWING THIS, A CERTAIN POP IDOL IS TOURING ALL OVER JAPAN. BUT I'M NOT A GROUPIE, OKAAAY!? IDOLS ARE JUST GREAT, THEY REALLY ARE!! THE WAY THEY CAN WEAR SHINY COSTUMES LIKE NORMAL CLOTHES IS THE PART ABOUT THEM I LIKE BEST!!! (SERIOUSLY?)

I LOVE BEAUTIFUL PEOPLE WHO LOOK LIKE THEY HAVE MYSTERY TO THEM, AND WHO SPARKLE AND FLUTTER.

TOTALLY!! (-`SMILE´-)

I EDITED THE PAGES HERE AND THERE FOR THE COLLECTED GRAPHIC NOVEL... BUT THE PLACES I COULDN'T DO MUCH ABOUT BEFORE ARE STILL THAT WAY EVEN AFTER THE CORRECTIONS... IT'S TOUGH TO DRAW WHAT'S IN MY HEAD! GAAAH!

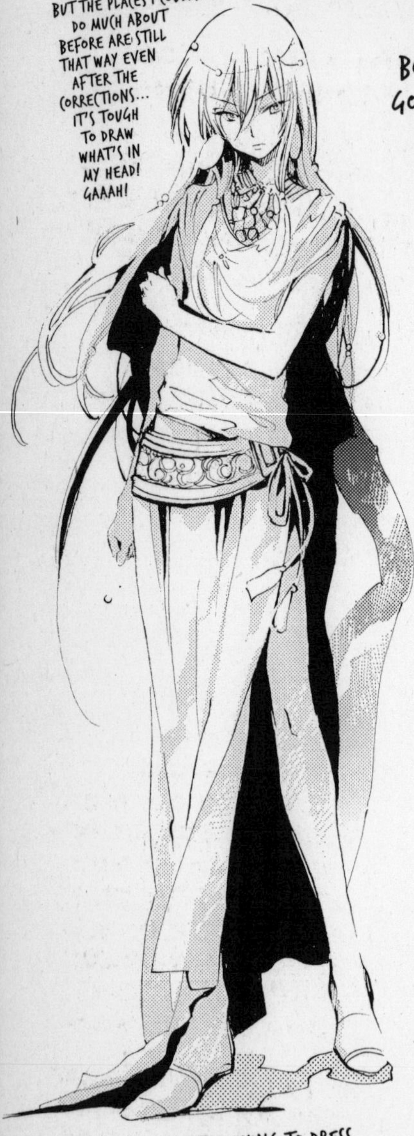

I'M STILL DYING TO DRESS HIM UP IN DIFFERENT CLOTHES! (-SMILE-)

WELL, "DIFFERENT" SIMPLY MEANS THAT THE DETAILS KINDA DIFFER.

TO DRAW THIS STORY, I DID READ ALL KINDS OF BOOKS ON GREEK MYTHOLOGY, BUT THEY WERE ALL SO GOSSIPY! (-SMILE-) THEY WERE FULL OF GODS I WANTED TO PAT ON THE BACK WHILE SMILING AND SAYING, "YEAH, YOU GUYS ARE PRETTY INTERESTING!! ☆"

SO I USED THE "APPARENTLY ALL GODS HAVE TOO MUCH TIME ON THEIR HANDS" BIT AS MY JUMPING-OFF POINT, GALLANTLY IGNORING THE REST. GOOD-BYE TO HISTORICAL SETTINGS. (-SMILE-)

FOR PEOPLE WHO ARE FOND OF PURE GREEK MYTH, THIS MANGA HAS TURNED OUT TO BE A "WHAT THE HECK!?" KIND OF WORK. SO I THINK IT WOULD BE BEST IF YOU CONSIDER THIS MANGA AN ALTERNATE VERSION, IN WHICH ONLY THE NAMES AND SETTINGS HAVE BEEN BORROWED.

I PERSONALLY CAME UP WITH THE LOGIC IN THE STORY, SO I GUESS THE READERS WILL HAVE VARIOUS OPINIONS ABOUT IT. I'D BE GRATEFUL IF SOMEONE WHO READS THIS MANGA IS MOVED BY IT IN ANY WAY, TAKING BOTH THE GOOD AND THE BAD TOGETHER.

HOW PEOPLE FEEL ABOUT THIS MANGA IS UP TO EACH PERSON, AND I HAVE NO CONTROL OVER THAT. IDEALLY, I'D LIKE FOR US BOTH REACH A PLACE WE LIKE, BUT I SHOULDN'T HOPE FOR TOO MUCH, HUH? (-SMILE-) I SHOULD PROBABLY AIM FOR AN "IT'S NOT ALL THAT BAD."

WELL, THEN! I HOPE WE CAN MEET AGAIN IN A PLACE WE BOTH LIKE (OR AS CLOSE AS WE CAN GET TO ONE).

-AKI

NOTE: MY HANDWRITING IS SLIIIIIGHTLY TILTED—NOT 'COS I GOOFED DURING MY SCANNING, BUT 'COS THIS IS HOW I WRITE. I CAN'T SEEM TO FIX IT...

Of Gods & Mortals

A brief mythological and historical background

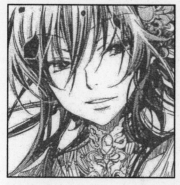

Apollo

Son of Zeus and twin brother of Artemis, Apollo was heralded and worshipped as the god of many things. Music, prophecy, archery, healing, poetry, shepherding, the warding off of evil, and the protection of youth, among others, were all part of his domain. He was also known for being the god of plague and disease, and the god of the truth and the light, and often conflated with Helios, the sun god. Depicted as a handsome young man with long tresses, Apollo can be found in many works of the arts with a bow and arrows, laurel, a swan, and/or a lyre, all of which which are among his symbols. Truly his father's son, Apollo, like Zeus, was fond of amorous encounters with males and females alike, and he too fathered many a child. Beautiful and sometimes cruel, Apollo could be capricious and possessed a violent temper, despite his overall beneficent presence. It is said that Apollo, along with Poseidon, built the walls of the ancient city of Troy. But due to a conflict that arose on the matter of payment for this service, the two gods grew to hate the Trojans, fighting against them in the Trojan War that laid the city to waste.

Ganymede

A young Trojan prince whose beauty was said to surpass all others, Ganymede, son of the king of Troy, caught the eye of Zeus while tending his flock on Mount Ida. He was then spirited away to Mount Olympos to serve as an immortal cupbearer in the heavens—though whether he was taken by Zeus himself, Zeus in the form of an eagle, or Zeus's eagle messenger is unclear. He was said to be a favorite of Zeus's and Zeus's lover. Ganymede's father, distraught by the loss of his son, was bribed by Zeus with the assurance that his son was granted immortality and a gift of divine horses. Ganymede, who was taken to fill the cups of the immortals in the sky, is sometimes said to be the constellation Aquarius, the water-bearer.

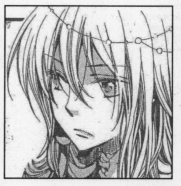

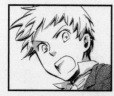

Heinz

The person on whom Heinz is based is Heinrich Schliemann (full name: Johann Ludwig Heinrich Julius Schliemann), a German amateur archaeologist who began excavating the ruins of the ancient city of Troy in 1871.

Hades

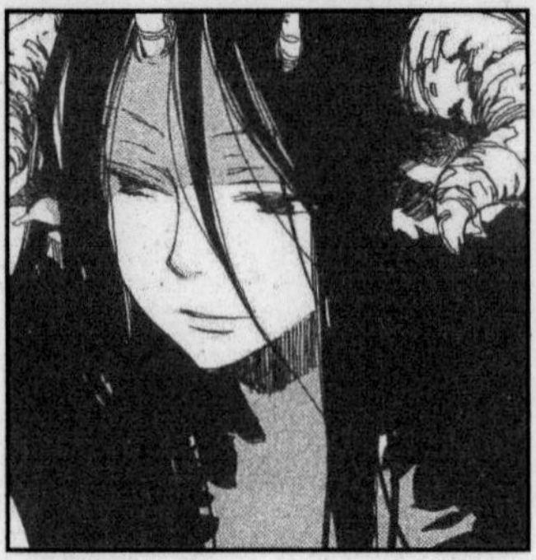

The ancient Greek god of the underworld and the eldest of the three divine brothers who came to rule the world after overthrowing the Titans of Greek myth. Hades arguably drew the worst lot in the lottery with his brothers to divide up all of the cosmos. As a result, he became the king of the shades, ruling over the realm of the dead, which was said to exist somewhere unseen within the Earth itself. No stranger to greed, Hades was said to always be seeking ways to increase the number of his subjects. Strict, aloof, and wrathful, he was not fond of allowing anyone to leave his realm. He was also the god of the riches of the Earth, for example good soil, and precious stones and metals. Though feared by mortals, Hades was not aggressively evil and maintained a kind of balance in the world.

Poseidon

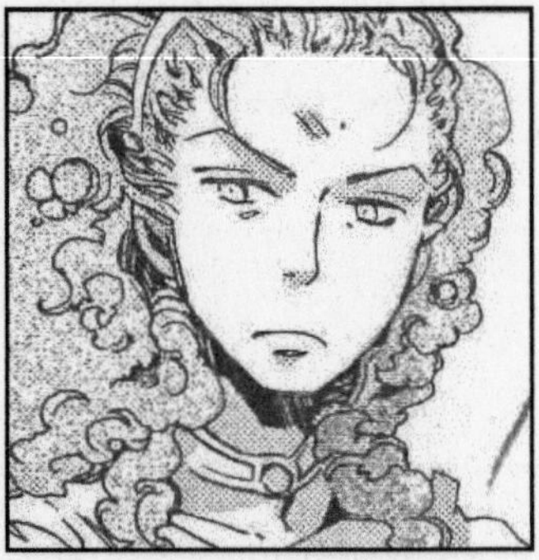

The middle brother and the god of the seas and rivers, a title he gained from the lottery with his brothers. A god of an argumentative stripe, he was said to have had a difficult personality and would attempt to overthrow other gods and take the countries over which they ruled. He was also the god of floods, droughts, and earthquakes—which he could initiate with his legendary trident—and horses, which he created in order to impress the goddess Demeter. He was equal to Zeus in terms of rank and took offense at being ordered around by his younger brother, but he was also known to give in to Zeus's demands. One of these demands sent Poseidon and Apollo to build the walls of the ancient city of Troy, but a conflict between the gods and the Trojan leader they had assisted led Poseidon to despise the Trojans and fight against them in the Trojan War.

Zeus

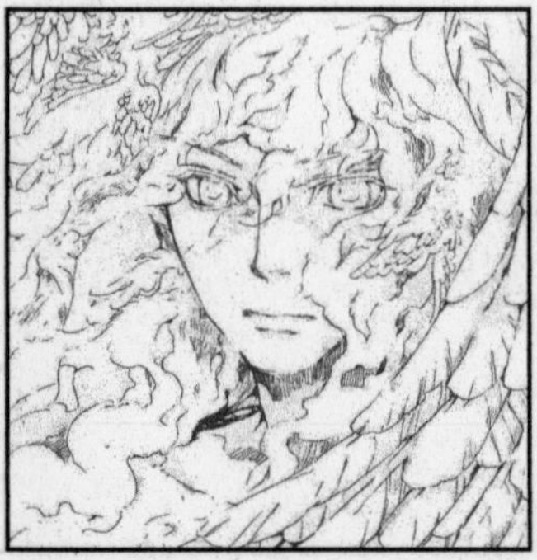

The youngest of the three divine brother-gods, who through the drawing of lots became the lord of the heavens and upper realms, and supreme ruler of Mount Olympos and the gods who resided there. Seen as the omnipotent king and father of both gods and mortals, the regal Zeus was also considered the god of the weather, of law and order, and of fate. One of his most noted characteristics was his roving eye; there was no shortage of romantic escapades in which Zeus took part. He had numerous offspring, both mortal and immortal (and legitimate and illegitimate), including Apollo and Artemis. The thunderbolt and the eagle are among the most recognizable symbols of Zeus, the latter being Zeus's messenger and, as in the case of Ganymede, his agent of abduction. It is said that Zeus, who had fallen in love with the young prince, sent his eagle or became one himself to pluck Ganymede from the mortal plane and take the boyto the heavens to serve him in immortality as a cupbearer and lover. The Trojan War is said to be entirely of Zeus's manufacture.

Olympos

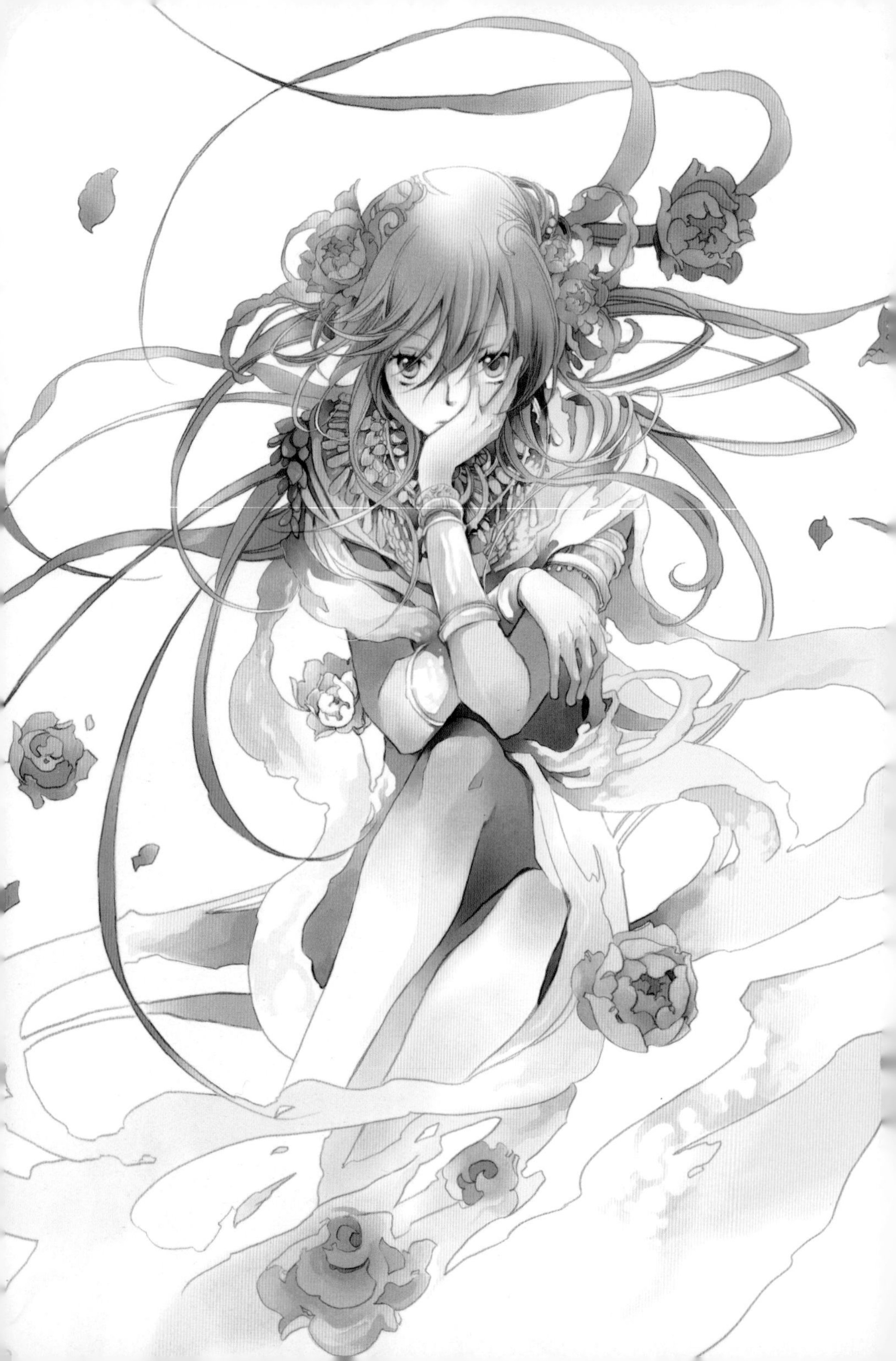

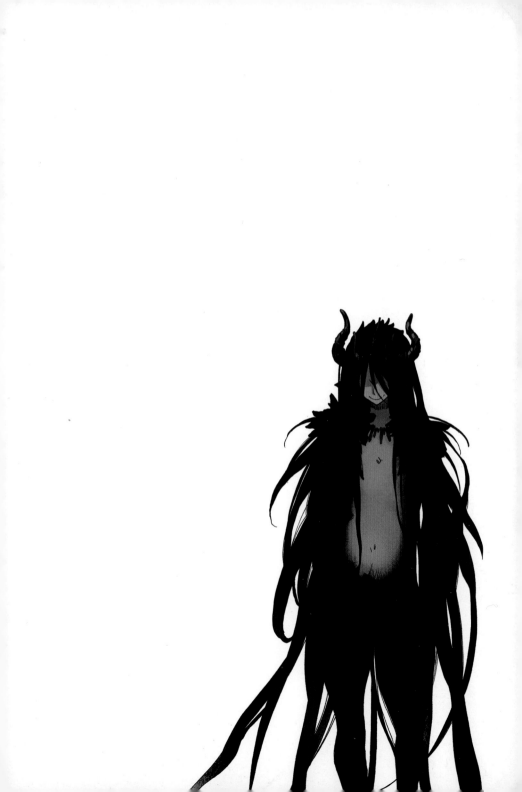

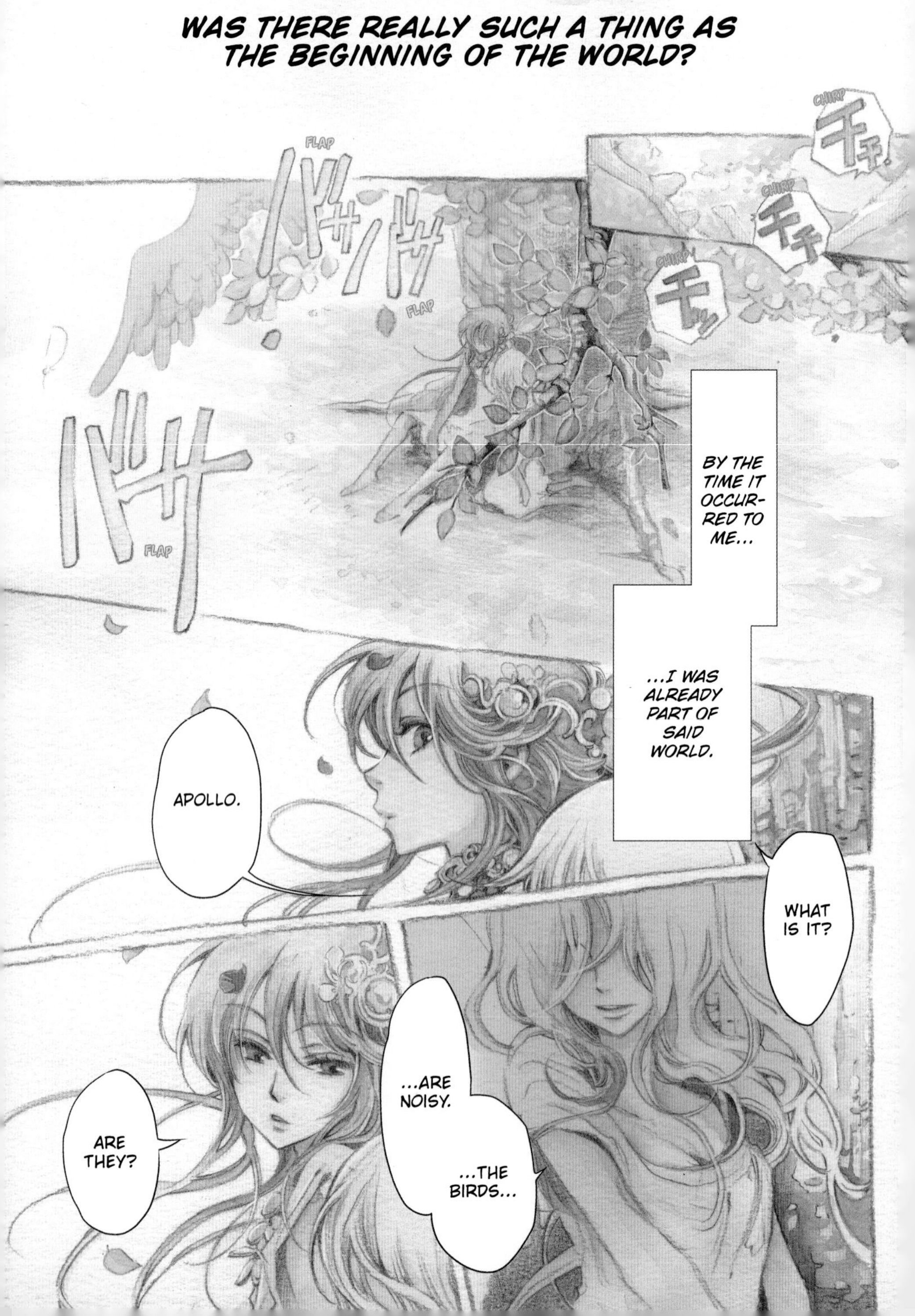
WAS THERE REALLY SUCH A THING AS THE BEGINNING OF THE WORLD?
CHIRP
CHIRP
CHIRP
FLAP
FLAP
FLAP
BY THE TIME IT OCCURRED TO ME...
...I WAS ALREADY PART OF SAID WORLD.
APOLLO.
WHAT IS IT?
...ARE NOISY.
...THE BIRDS...
ARE THEY?

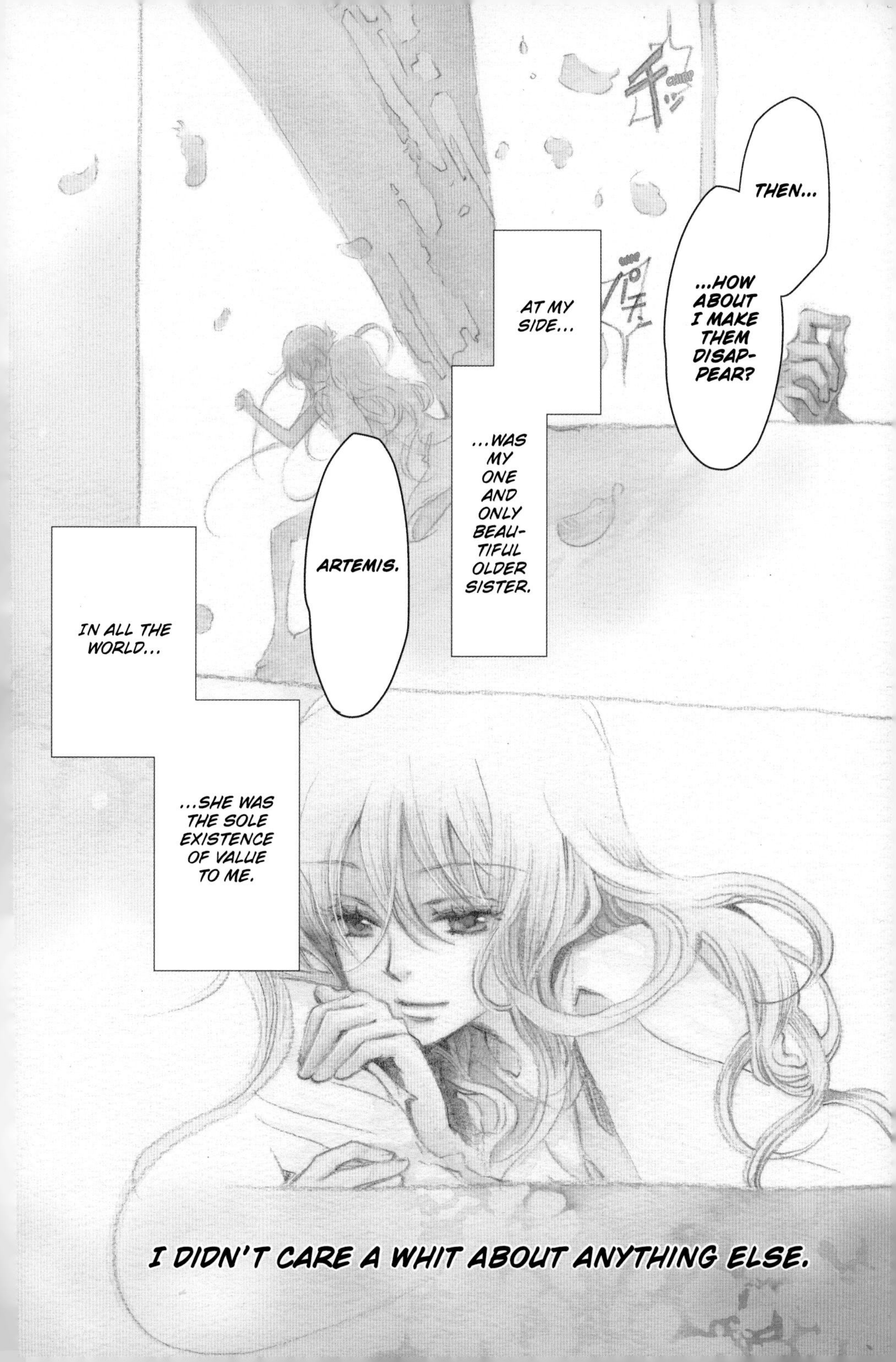
THEN...
...HOW ABOUT I MAKE THEM DISAP-PEAR?
AT MY SIDE...
...WAS MY ONE AND ONLY BEAU-TIFUL OLDER SISTER.
ARTEMIS.
IN ALL THE WORLD...
...SHE WAS THE SOLE EXISTENCE OF VALUE TO ME.
I DIDN'T CARE A WHIT ABOUT ANYTHING ELSE.

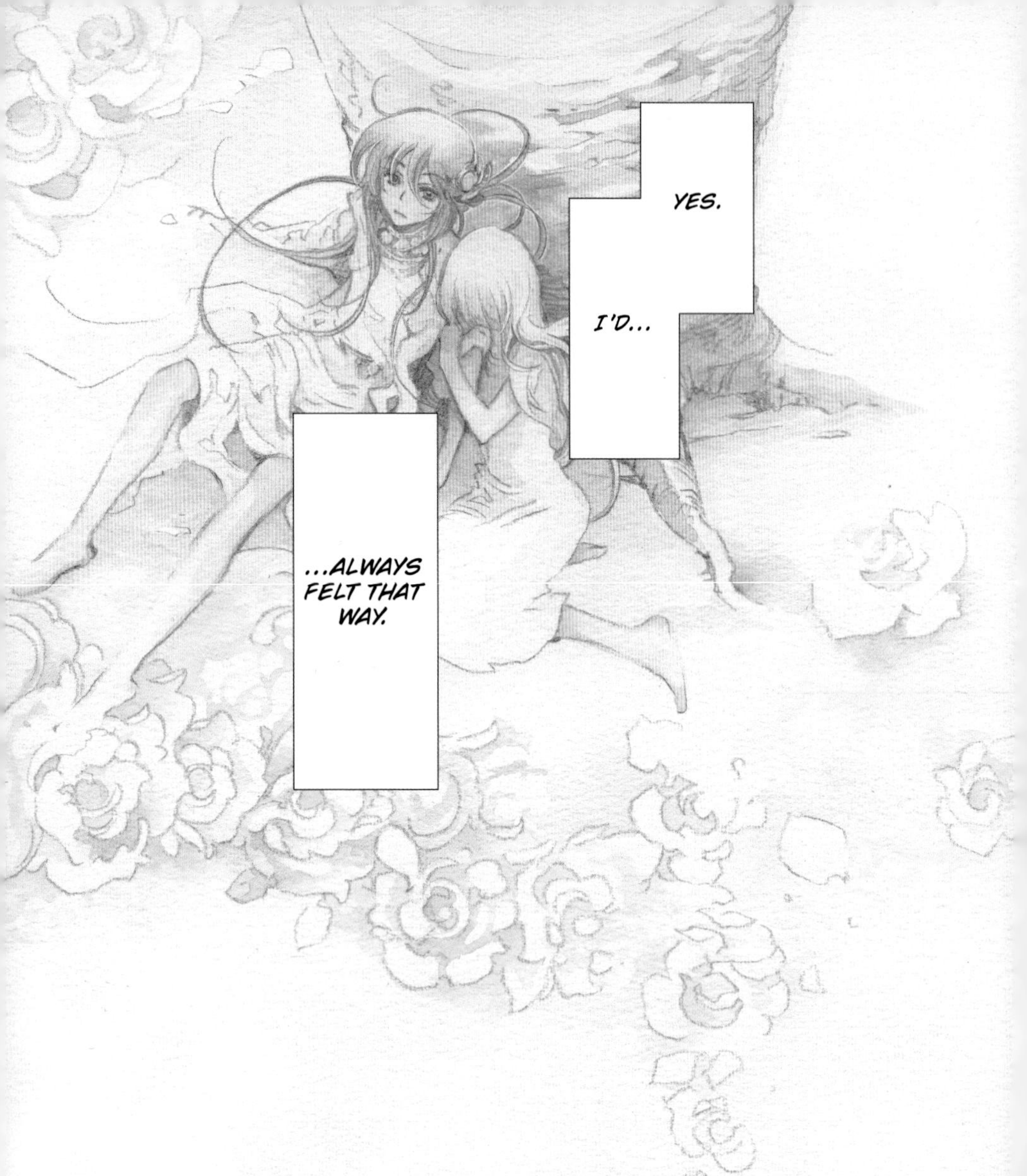
YES.
I'D...
...ALWAYS FELT THAT WAY.

Episode.06

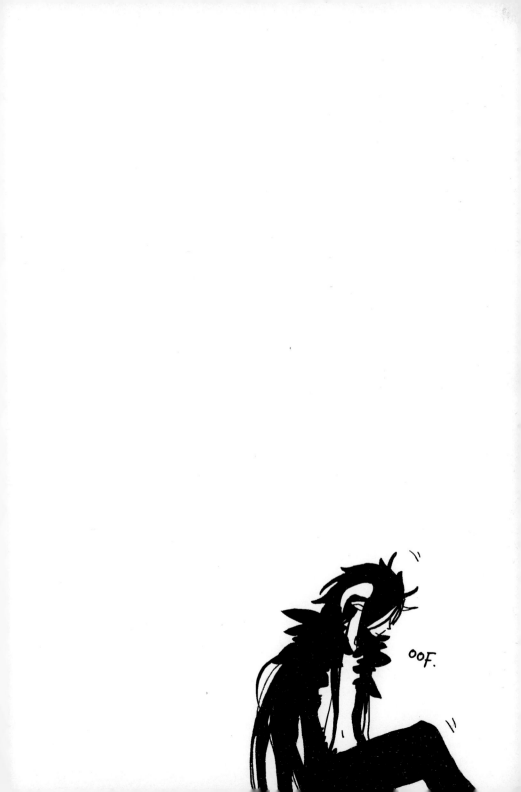

OOF.

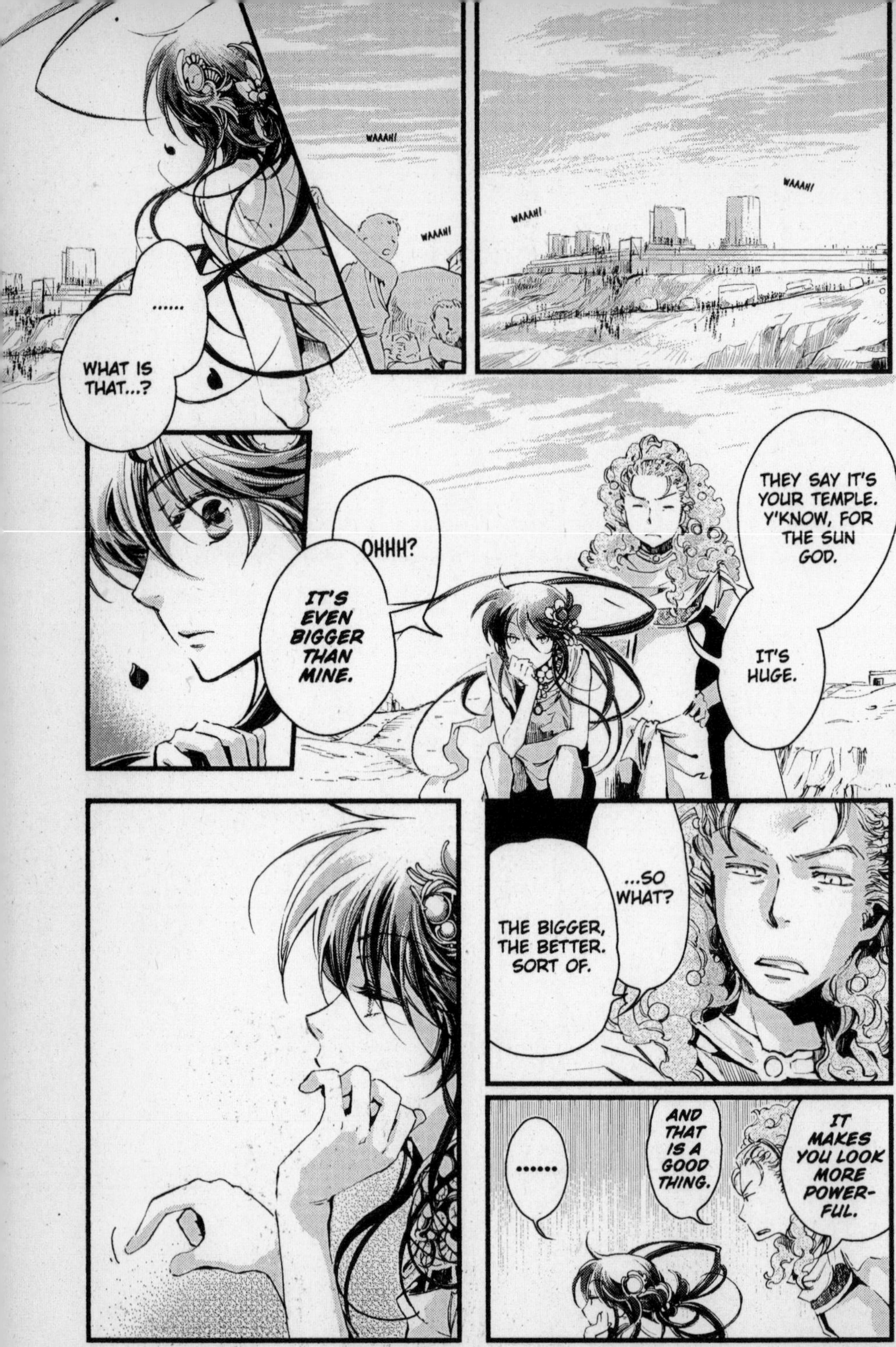
WAAAH!
WAAAH!
WAAAH!
WAAAH!
......
WHAT IS THAT...?
THEY SAY IT'S YOUR TEMPLE. Y'KNOW, FOR THE SUN GOD.
IT'S HUGE.
OHHH?
IT'S EVEN BIGGER THAN MINE.
...SO WHAT?
THE BIGGER, THE BETTER. SORT OF.
IT MAKES YOU LOOK MORE POWER-FUL.
AND THAT IS A GOOD THING.
......

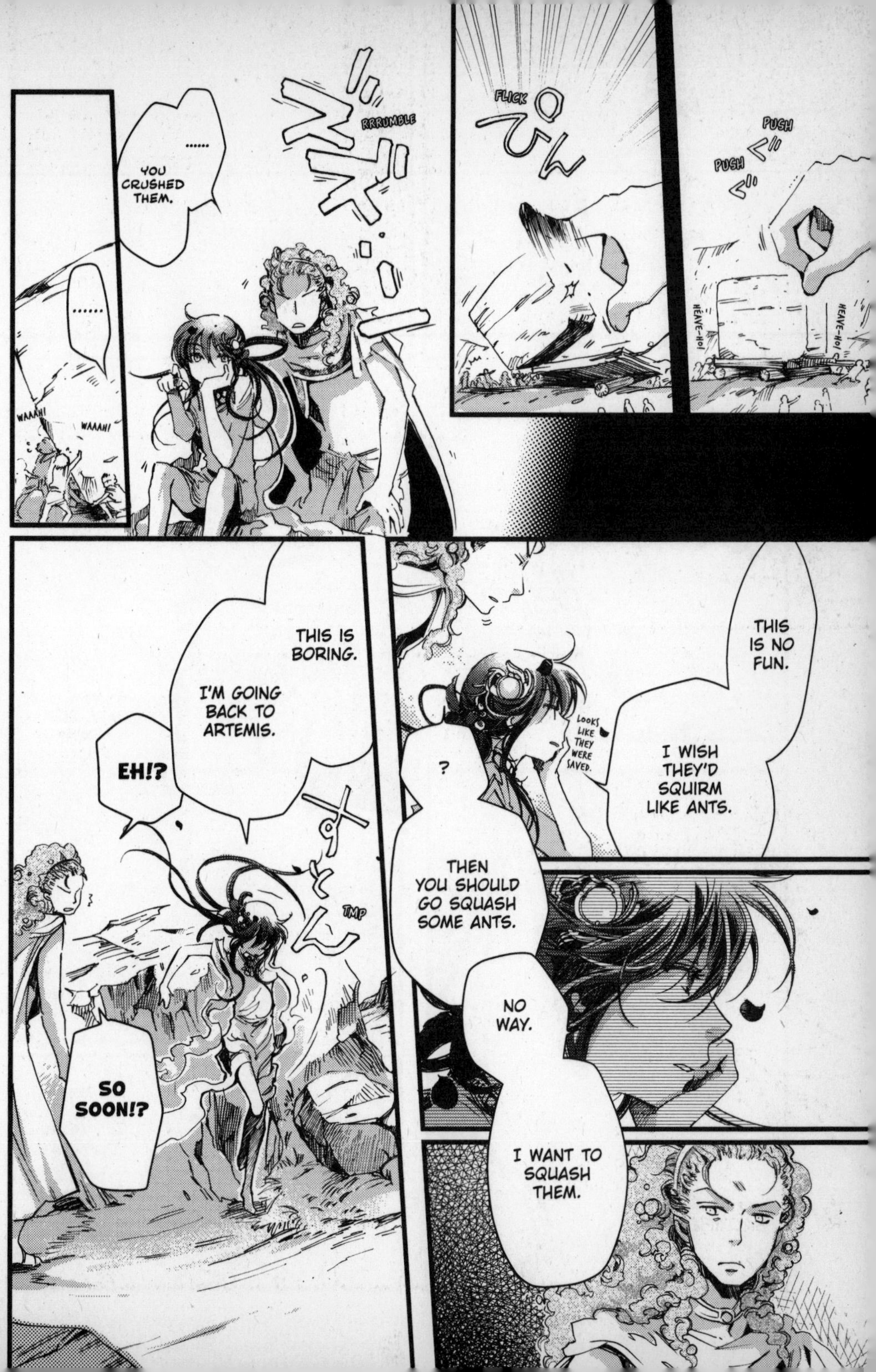

PUSH
PUSH
HEAVE-HO!
HEAVE-HO!
FLICK
RRRUMBLE
......
YOU CRUSHED THEM.
......
WAAAH!
WAAAH!
THIS IS NO FUN.
I WISH THEY'D SQUIRM LIKE ANTS.
LOOKS LIKE THEY WERE SAVED.
?
THEN YOU SHOULD GO SQUASH SOME ANTS.
NO WAY.
I WANT TO SQUASH THEM.
THIS IS BORING.
I'M GOING BACK TO ARTEMIS.
EH!?
TMP
SO SOON!?

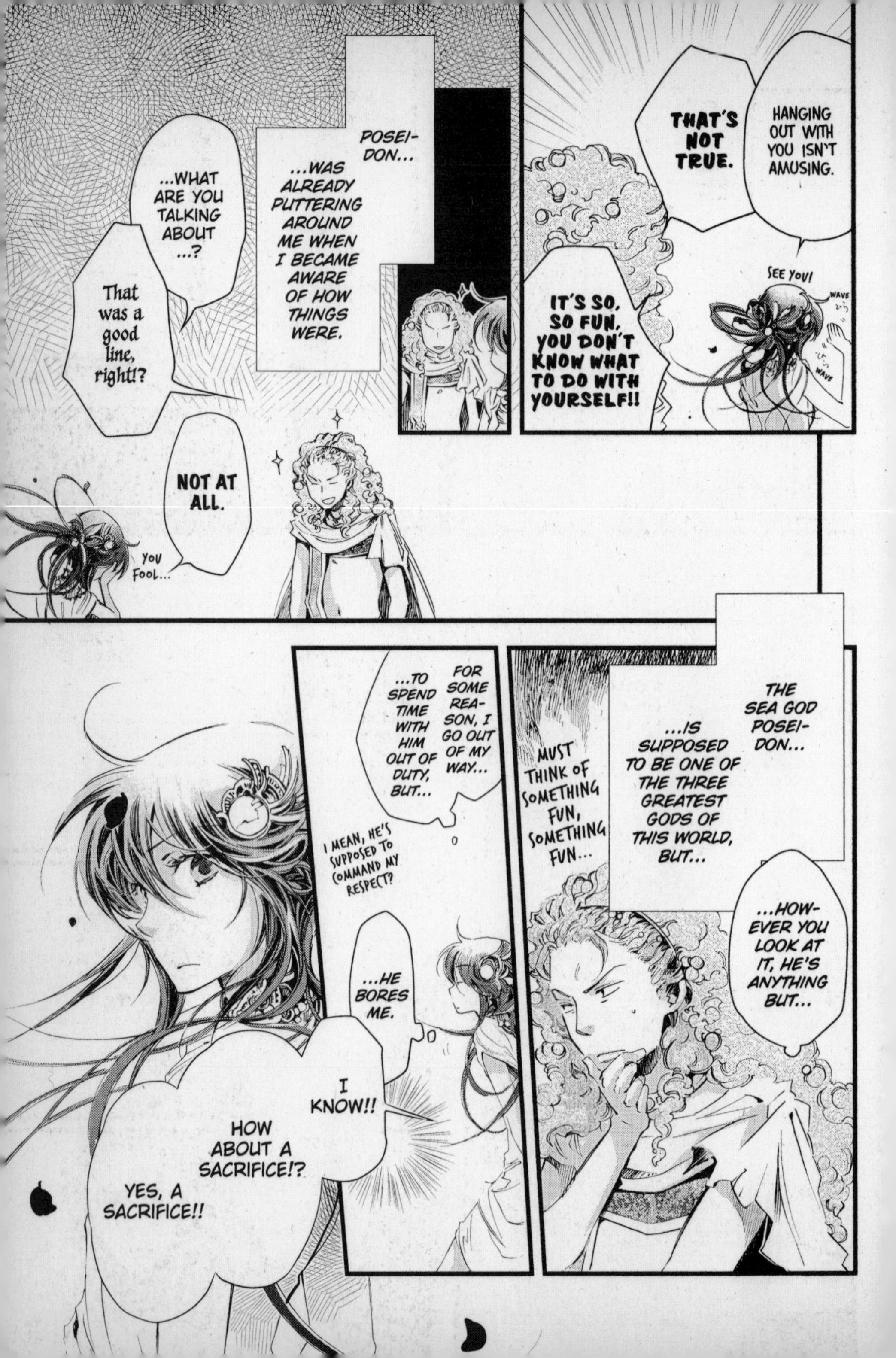
HANGING OUT WITH YOU ISN'T AMUSING.
THAT'S NOT TRUE.
IT'S SO, SO FUN, YOU DON'T KNOW WHAT TO DO WITH YOURSELF!!
SEE YOU!
WAVE
WAVE
POSEI-DON...
...WAS ALREADY PUTTERING AROUND ME WHEN I BECAME AWARE OF HOW THINGS WERE.
...WHAT ARE YOU TALKING ABOUT ...?
That was a good line, right!?
NOT AT ALL.
YOU FOOL...
THE SEA GOD POSEI-DON...
...IS SUPPOSED TO BE ONE OF THE THREE GREATEST GODS OF THIS WORLD, BUT...
...HOW-EVER YOU LOOK AT IT, HE'S ANYTHING BUT...
MUST THINK OF SOMETHING FUN, SOMETHING FUN...
FOR SOME REA-SON, I GO OUT OF MY WAY...
...TO SPEND TIME WITH HIM OUT OF DUTY, BUT...
I MEAN, HE'S SUPPOSED TO COMMAND MY RESPECT?
...HE BORES ME.
I KNOW!!
HOW ABOUT A SACRIFICE!?
YES, A SACRIFICE!!

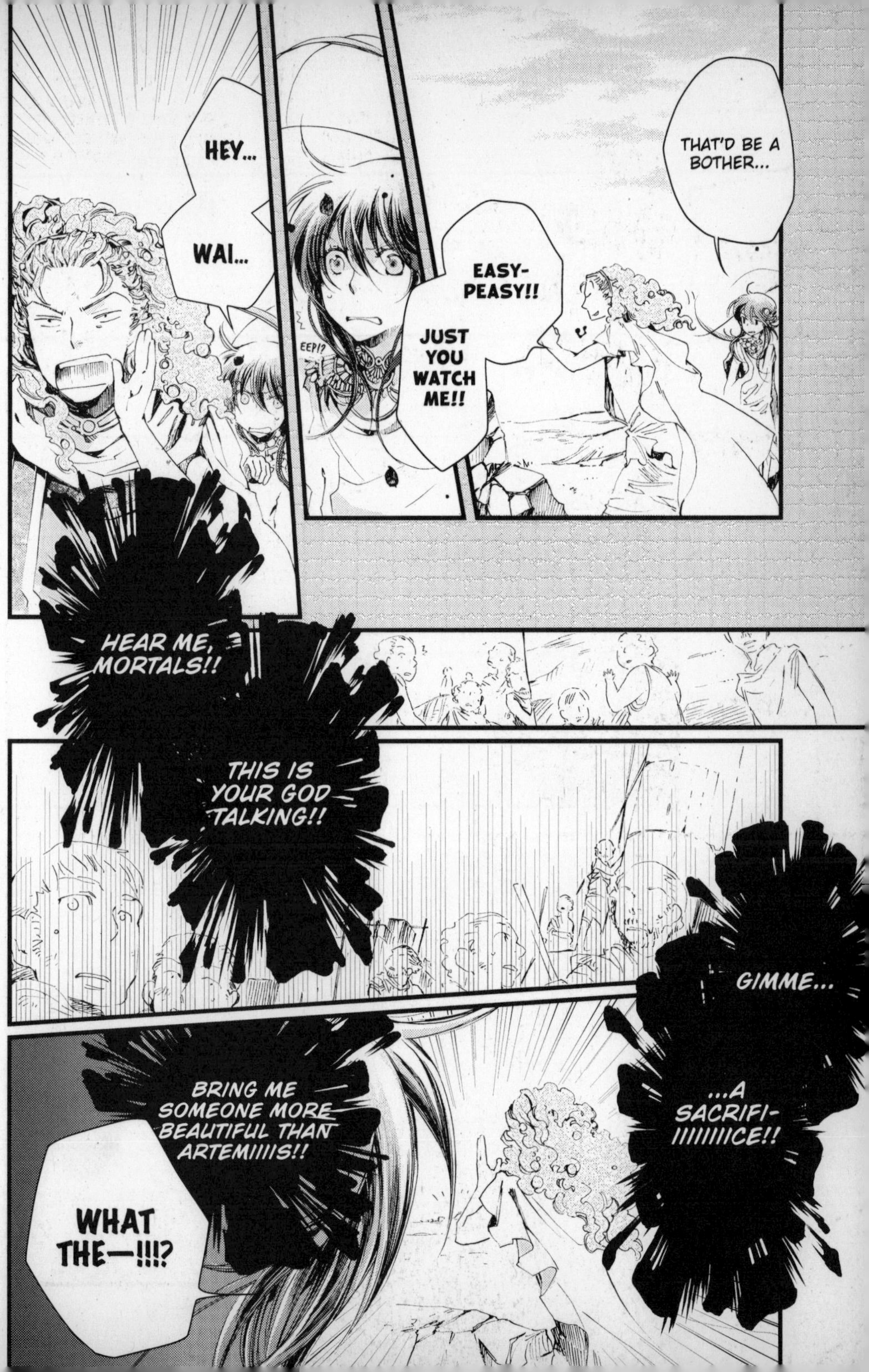
THAT'D BE A BOTHER...
EASY-PEASY!!
JUST YOU WATCH ME!!
EEP!?
HEY...
WAI...
HEAR ME, MORTALS!!
THIS IS YOUR GOD TALKING!!
GIMME...
...A SACRIFI-IIIIIIIICE!!
BRING ME SOMEONE MORE BEAUTIFUL THAN ARTEMIIIIS!!
WHAT THE—!!!?

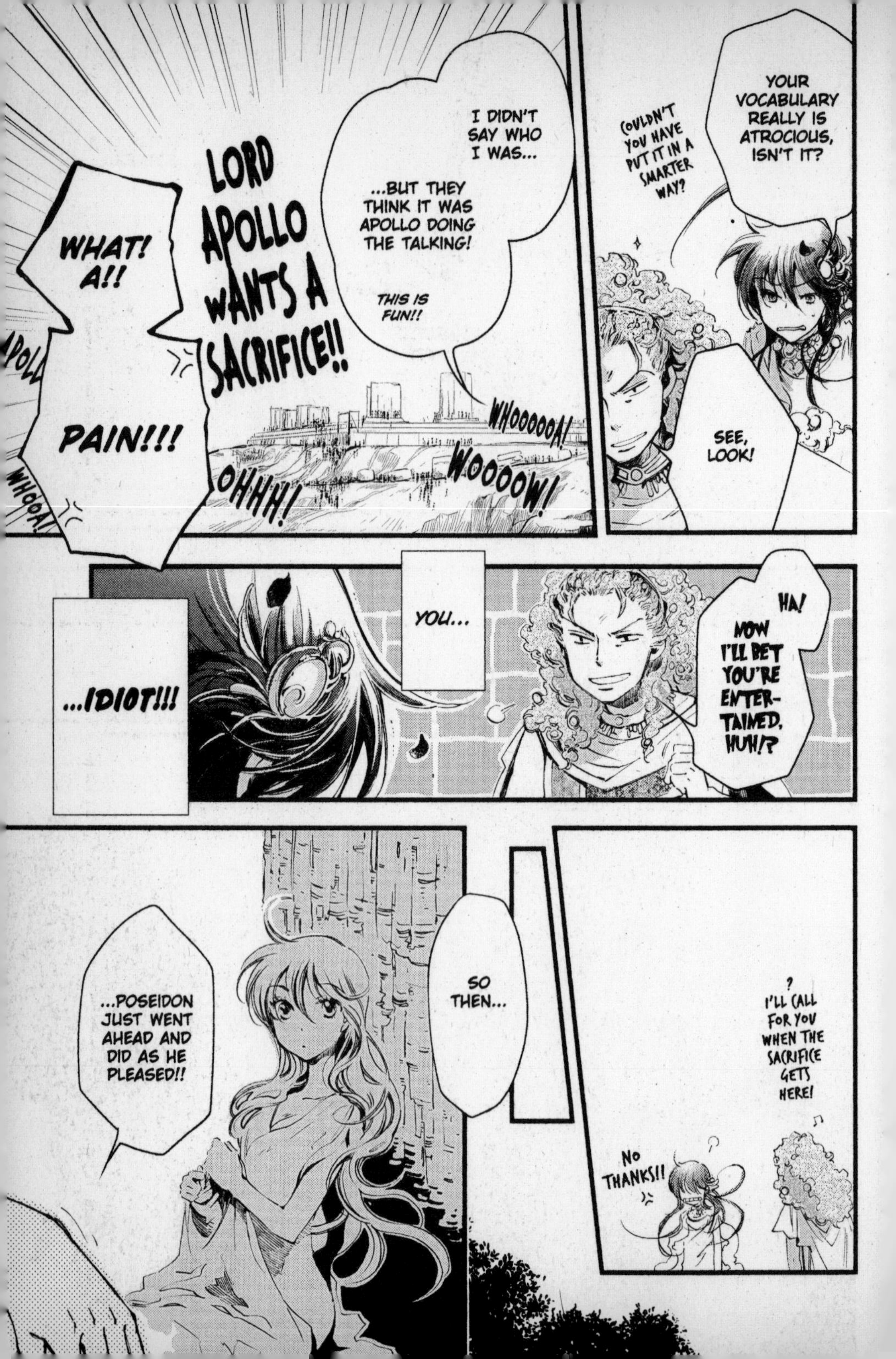
YOUR VOCABULARY REALLY IS ATROCIOUS, ISN'T IT?
COULDN'T YOU HAVE PUT IT IN A SMARTER WAY?
SEE, LOOK!
I DIDN'T SAY WHO I WAS...
...BUT THEY THINK IT WAS APOLLO DOING THE TALKING!
THIS IS FUN!!
WHOOOOOA!
WOOOOW!
LORD APOLLO WANTS A SACRIFICE!!
OHHH!
WHAT! A!! PAIN!!!
HA! NOW I'LL BET YOU'RE ENTER-TAINED, HUH!?
YOU...
...IDIOT!!!
?
I'LL CALL FOR YOU WHEN THE SACRIFICE GETS HERE!
NO THANKS!!
SO THEN...
...POSEIDON JUST WENT AHEAD AND DID AS HE PLEASED!!

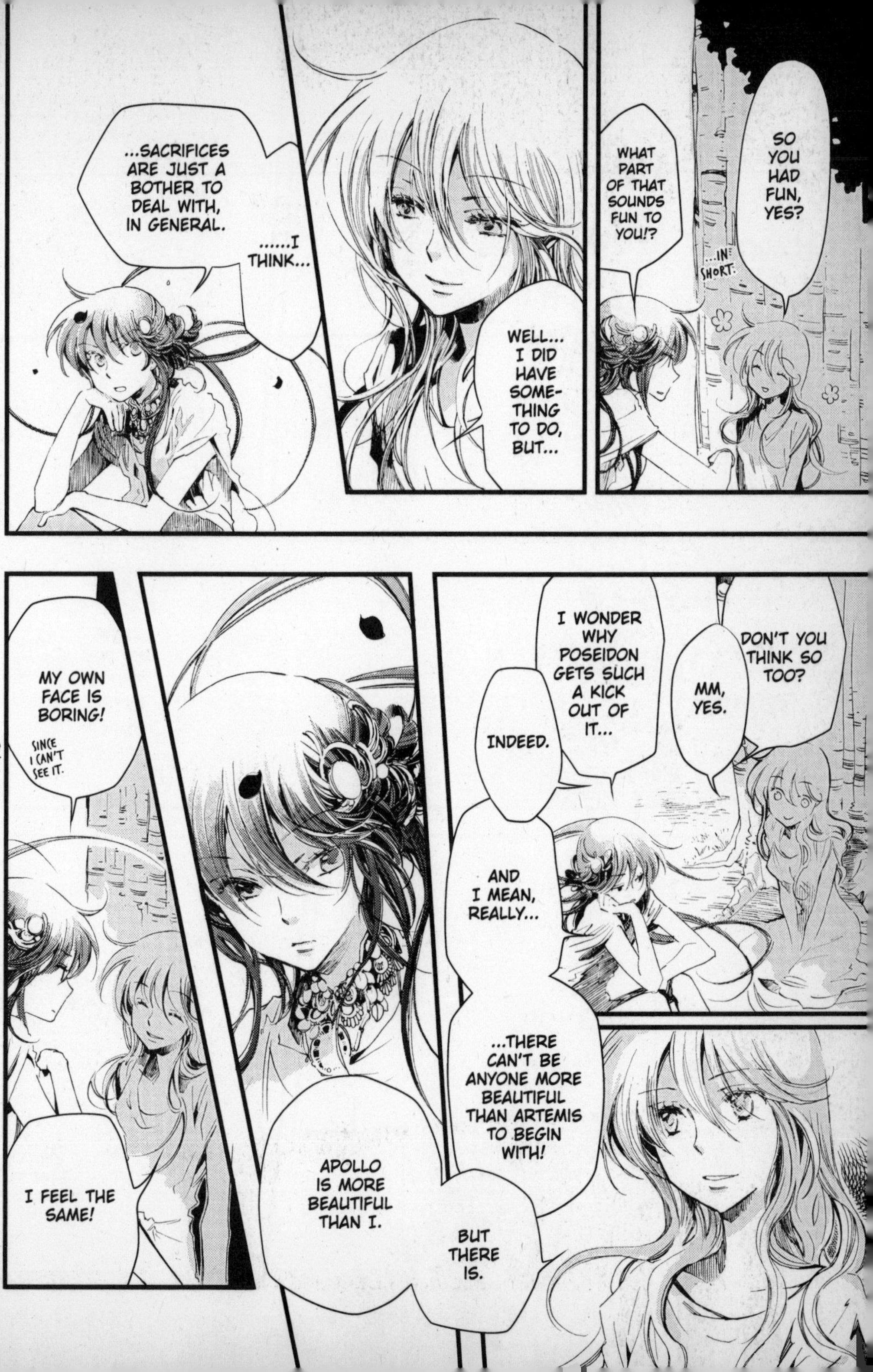
SO YOU HAD FUN, YES?
...IN SHORT.
WHAT PART OF THAT SOUNDS FUN TO YOU!?
WELL... I DID HAVE SOME-THING TO DO, BUT...
......I THINK...
...SACRIFICES ARE JUST A BOTHER TO DEAL WITH, IN GENERAL.
DON'T YOU THINK SO TOO?
MM, YES.
I WONDER WHY POSEIDON GETS SUCH A KICK OUT OF IT...
INDEED.
AND I MEAN, REALLY...
...THERE CAN'T BE ANYONE MORE BEAUTIFUL THAN ARTEMIS TO BEGIN WITH!
BUT THERE IS.
APOLLO IS MORE BEAUTIFUL THAN I.
MY OWN FACE IS BORING!
SINCE I CAN'T SEE IT.
I FEEL THE SAME!

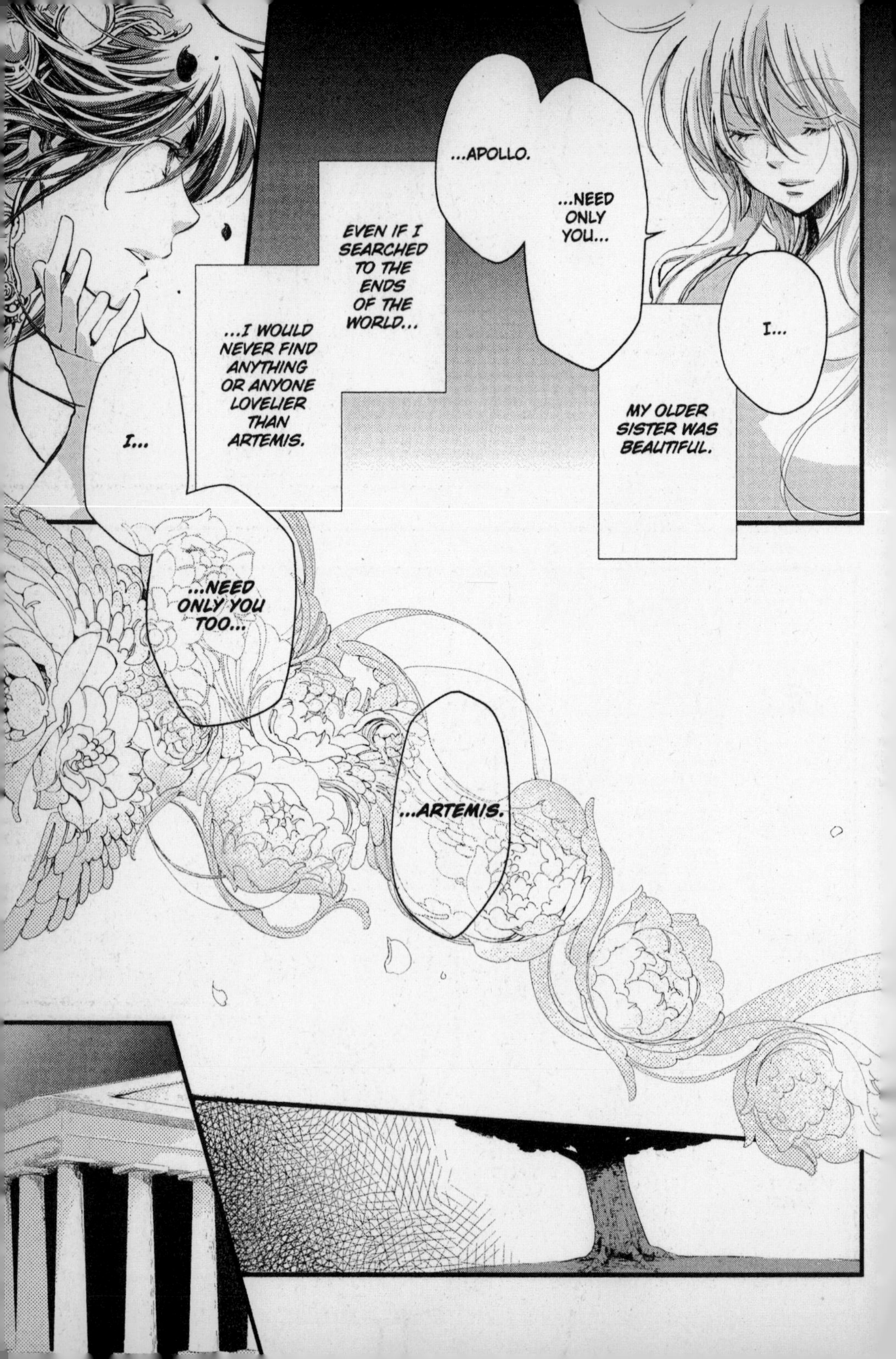
I...
...NEED ONLY YOU...
...APOLLO.
MY OLDER SISTER WAS BEAUTIFUL.
EVEN IF I SEARCHED TO THE ENDS OF THE WORLD...
...I WOULD NEVER FIND ANYTHING OR ANYONE LOVELIER THAN ARTEMIS.
I...
...NEED ONLY YOU TOO...
...ARTEMIS.

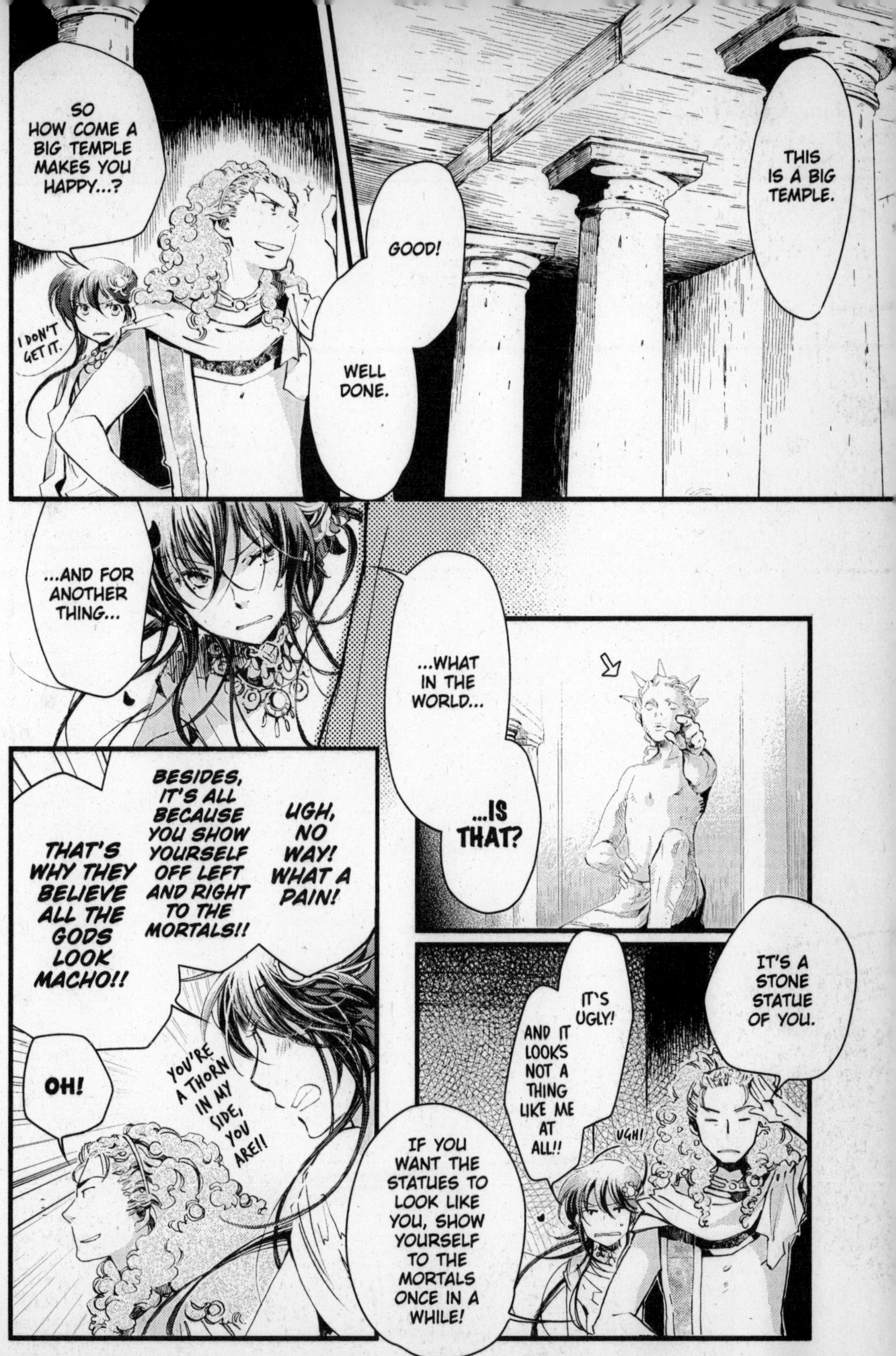
THIS IS A BIG TEMPLE.
GOOD!
WELL DONE.
SO HOW COME A BIG TEMPLE MAKES YOU HAPPY...?
I DON'T GET IT.
...AND FOR ANOTHER THING...
...WHAT IN THE WORLD...
...IS THAT?
IT'S A STONE STATUE OF YOU.
IT'S UGLY!
AND IT LOOKS NOT A THING LIKE ME AT ALL!!
UGH!
IF YOU WANT THE STATUES TO LOOK LIKE YOU, SHOW YOURSELF TO THE MORTALS ONCE IN A WHILE!
UGH, NO WAY! WHAT A PAIN!
BESIDES, IT'S ALL BECAUSE YOU SHOW YOURSELF OFF LEFT AND RIGHT TO THE MORTALS!!
THAT'S WHY THEY BELIEVE ALL THE GODS LOOK MACHO!!
YOU'RE A THORN IN MY SIDE, YOU ARE!!
OH!

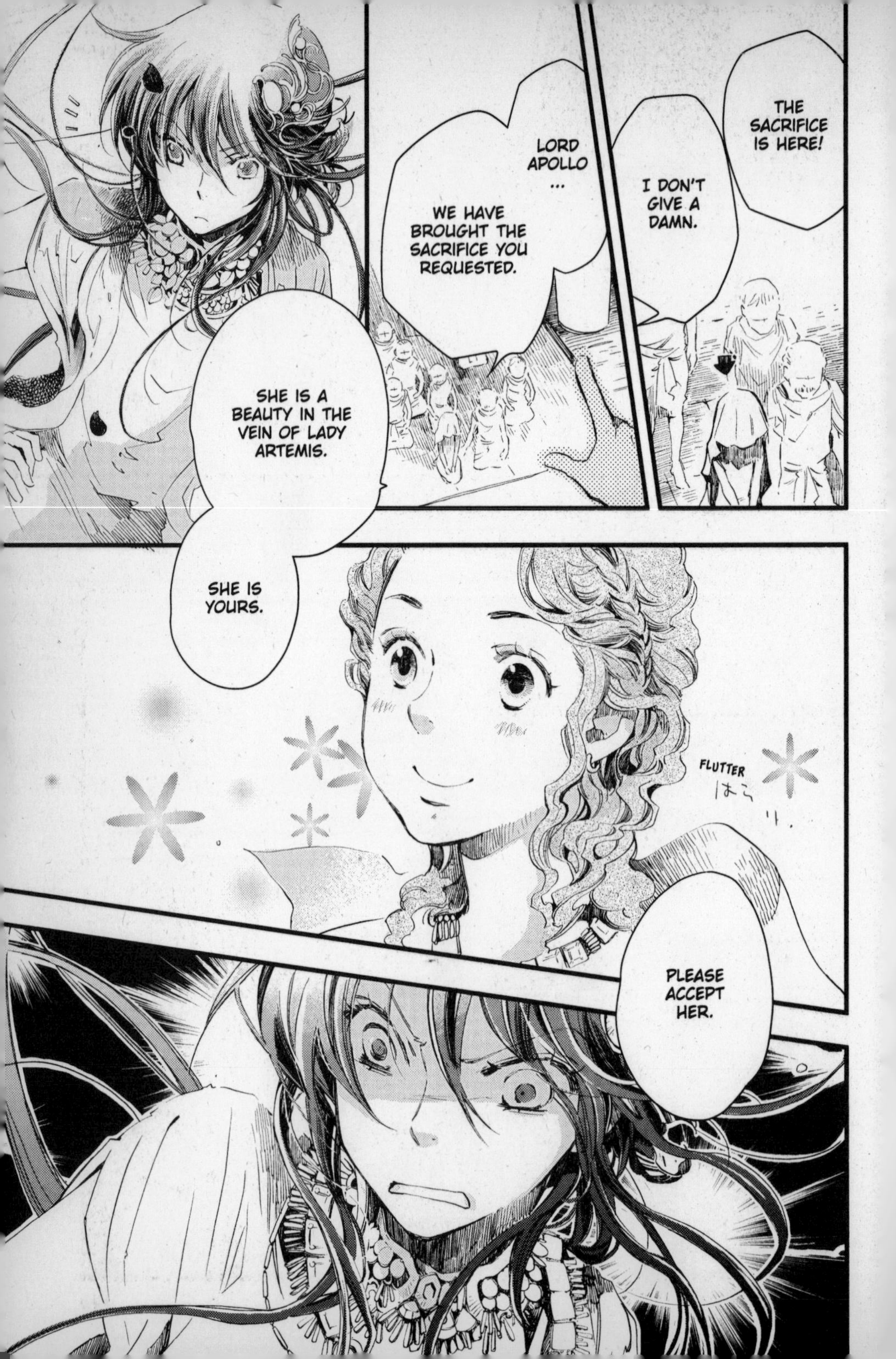
THE SACRIFICE IS HERE!
I DON'T GIVE A DAMN.
LORD APOLLO ...
WE HAVE BROUGHT THE SACRIFICE YOU REQUESTED.
SHE IS A BEAUTY IN THE VEIN OF LADY ARTEMIS.
SHE IS YOURS.
FLUTTER
はらり
PLEASE ACCEPT HER.

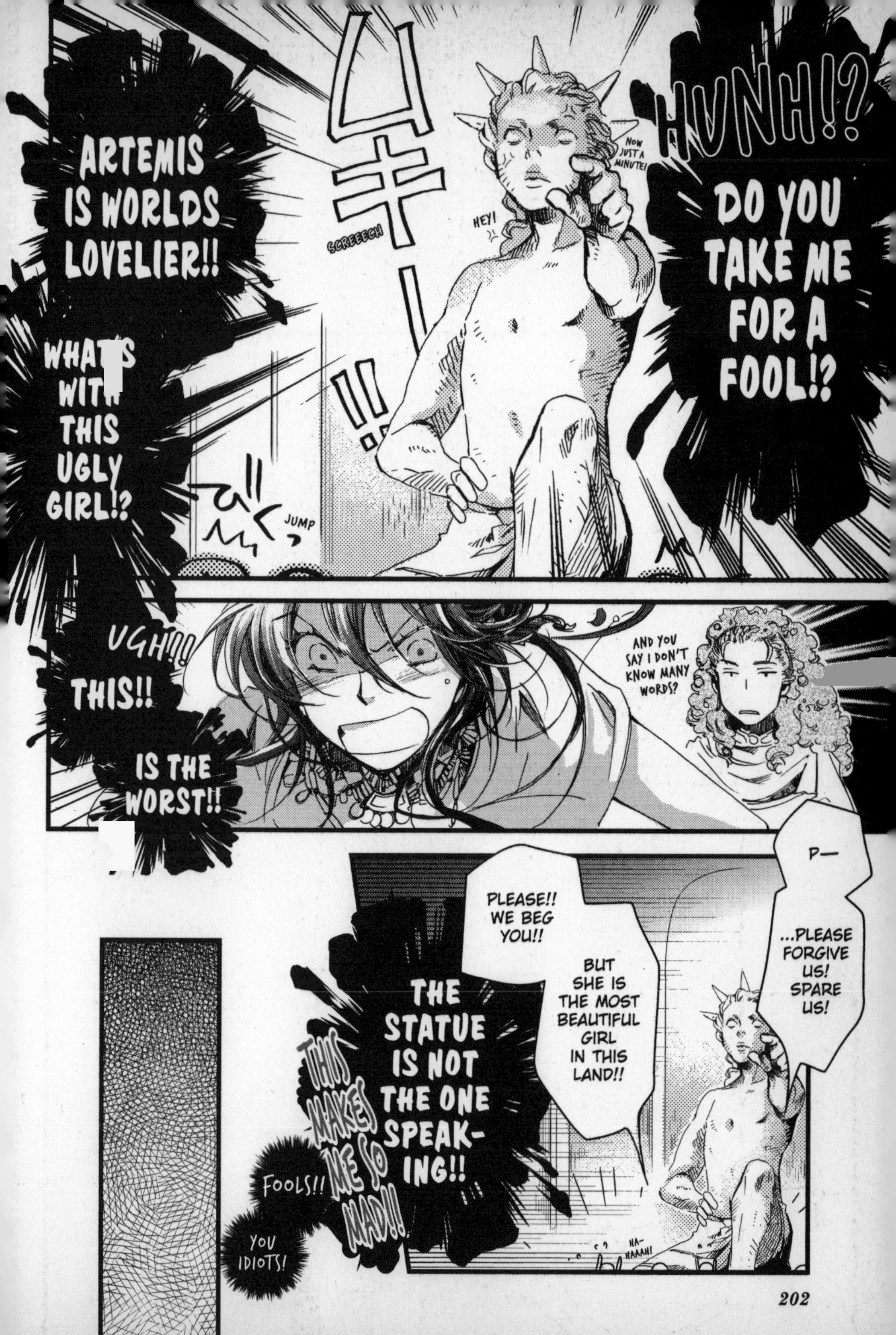
HUNH!?
DO YOU TAKE ME FOR A FOOL!?
NOW JUST A MINUTE!
HEY!
SCREEECH
ARTEMIS IS WORLDS LOVELIER!!
WHATS WITH THIS UGLY GIRL!?
JUMP
AND YOU SAY I DON'T KNOW MANY WORDS?
UGH!!!
THIS!!
IS THE WORST!!
P—
...PLEASE FORGIVE US! SPARE US!
PLEASE!! WE BEG YOU!!
BUT SHE IS THE MOST BEAUTIFUL GIRL IN THIS LAND!!
HA-HAAAH!
THE STATUE IS NOT THE ONE SPEAK-ING!!
THIS MAKES ME SO MAD!!
FOOLS!!
YOU IDIOTS!

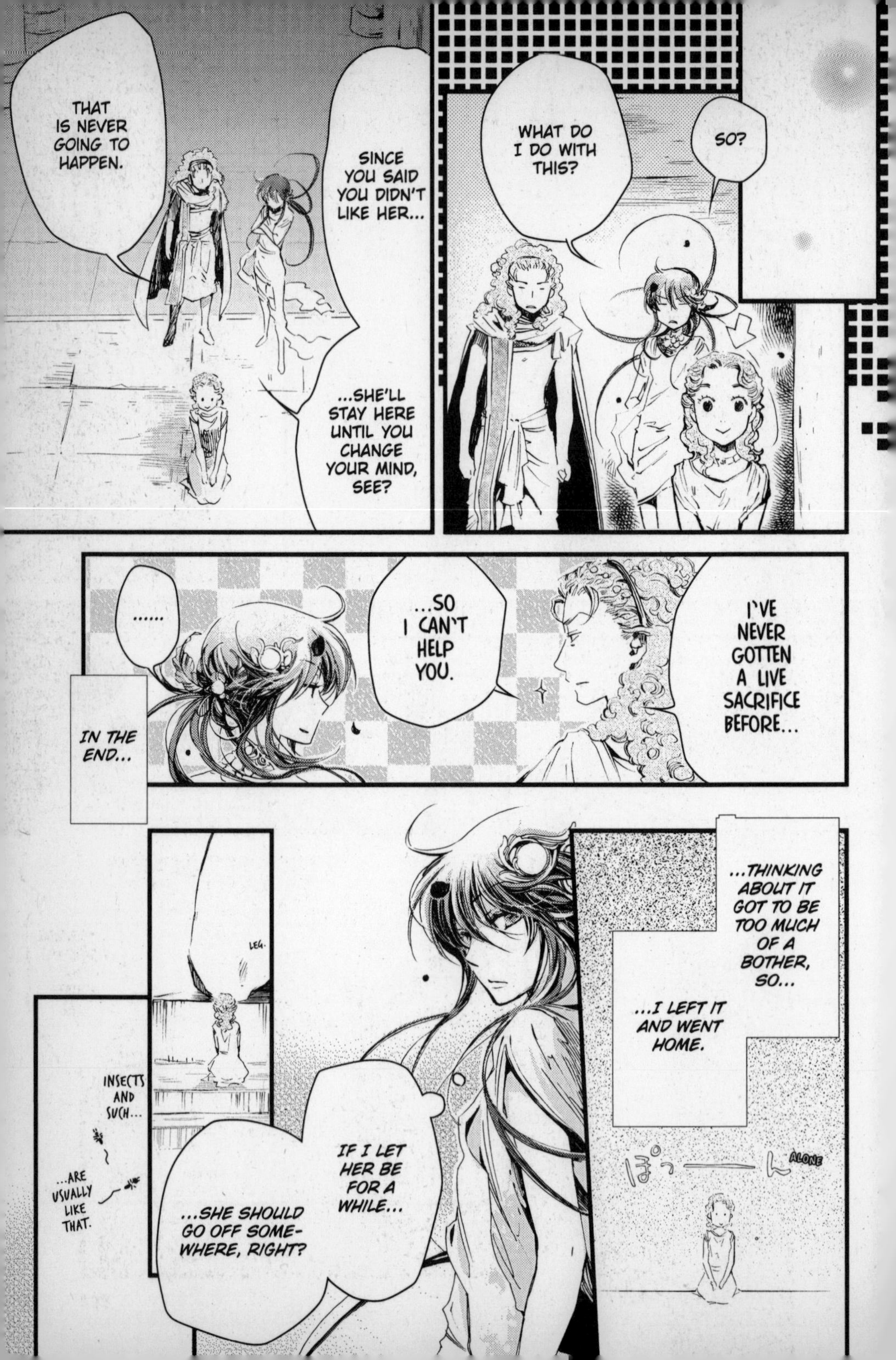
SO?
WHAT DO I DO WITH THIS?
SINCE YOU SAID YOU DIDN'T LIKE HER...
...SHE'LL STAY HERE UNTIL YOU CHANGE YOUR MIND, SEE?
THAT IS NEVER GOING TO HAPPEN.
I'VE NEVER GOTTEN A LIVE SACRIFICE BEFORE...
...SO I CAN'T HELP YOU.
......
IN THE END...
...THINKING ABOUT IT GOT TO BE TOO MUCH OF A BOTHER, SO...
...I LEFT IT AND WENT HOME.
ぽつーーん
ALONE
IF I LET HER BE FOR A WHILE...
...SHE SHOULD GO OFF SOMEWHERE, RIGHT?
LEG.
INSECTS AND SUCH...
...ARE USUALLY LIKE THAT.

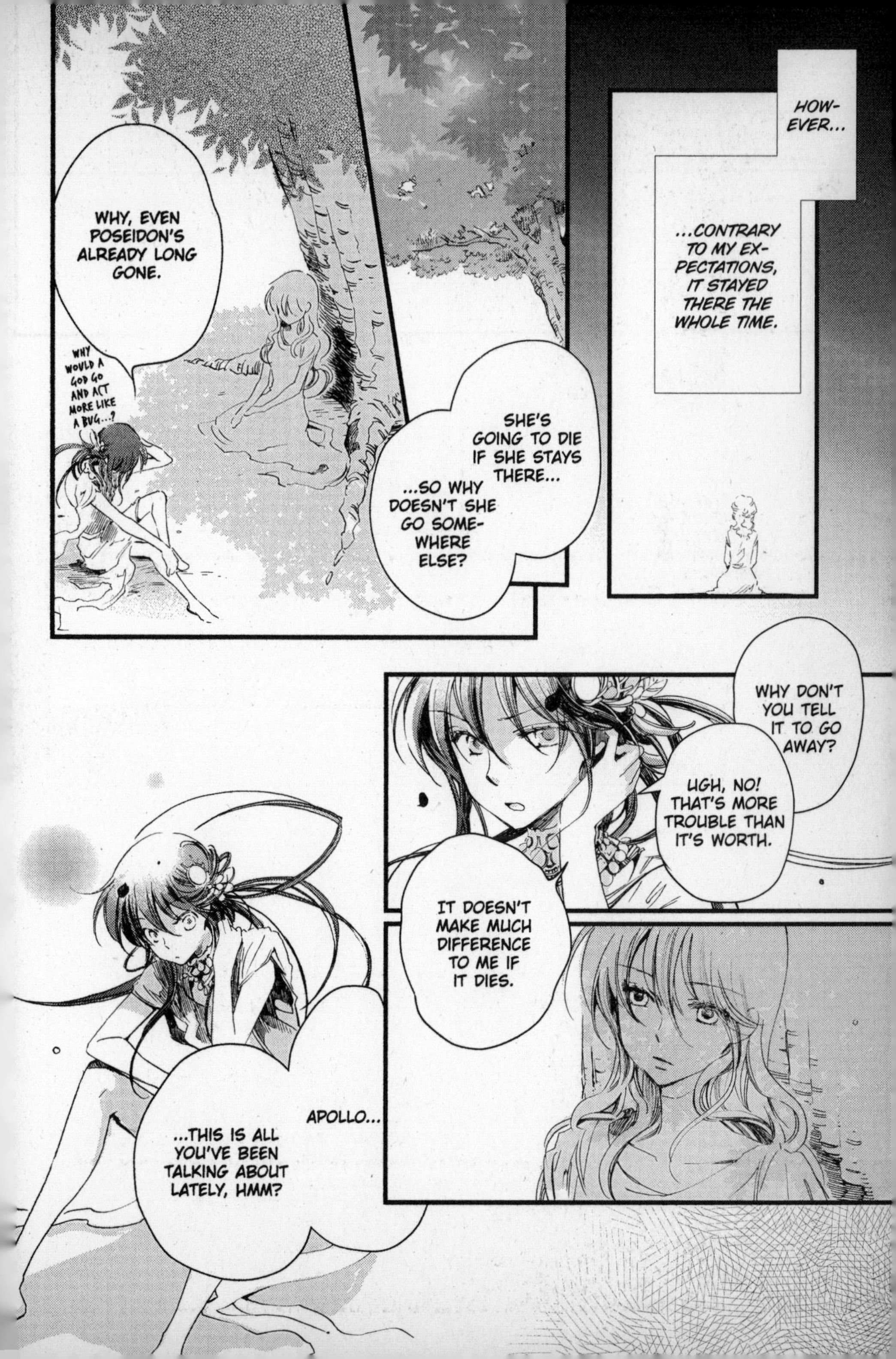
HOW-EVER...
...CONTRARY TO MY EX-PECTATIONS, IT STAYED THERE THE WHOLE TIME.
SHE'S GOING TO DIE IF SHE STAYS THERE...
...SO WHY DOESN'T SHE GO SOME-WHERE ELSE?
WHY, EVEN POSEIDON'S ALREADY LONG GONE.
WHY WOULD A GOD GO AND ACT MORE LIKE A BUG...?
WHY DON'T YOU TELL IT TO GO AWAY?
UGH, NO! THAT'S MORE TROUBLE THAN IT'S WORTH.
IT DOESN'T MAKE MUCH DIFFERENCE TO ME IF IT DIES.
APOLLO...
...THIS IS ALL YOU'VE BEEN TALKING ABOUT LATELY, HMM?

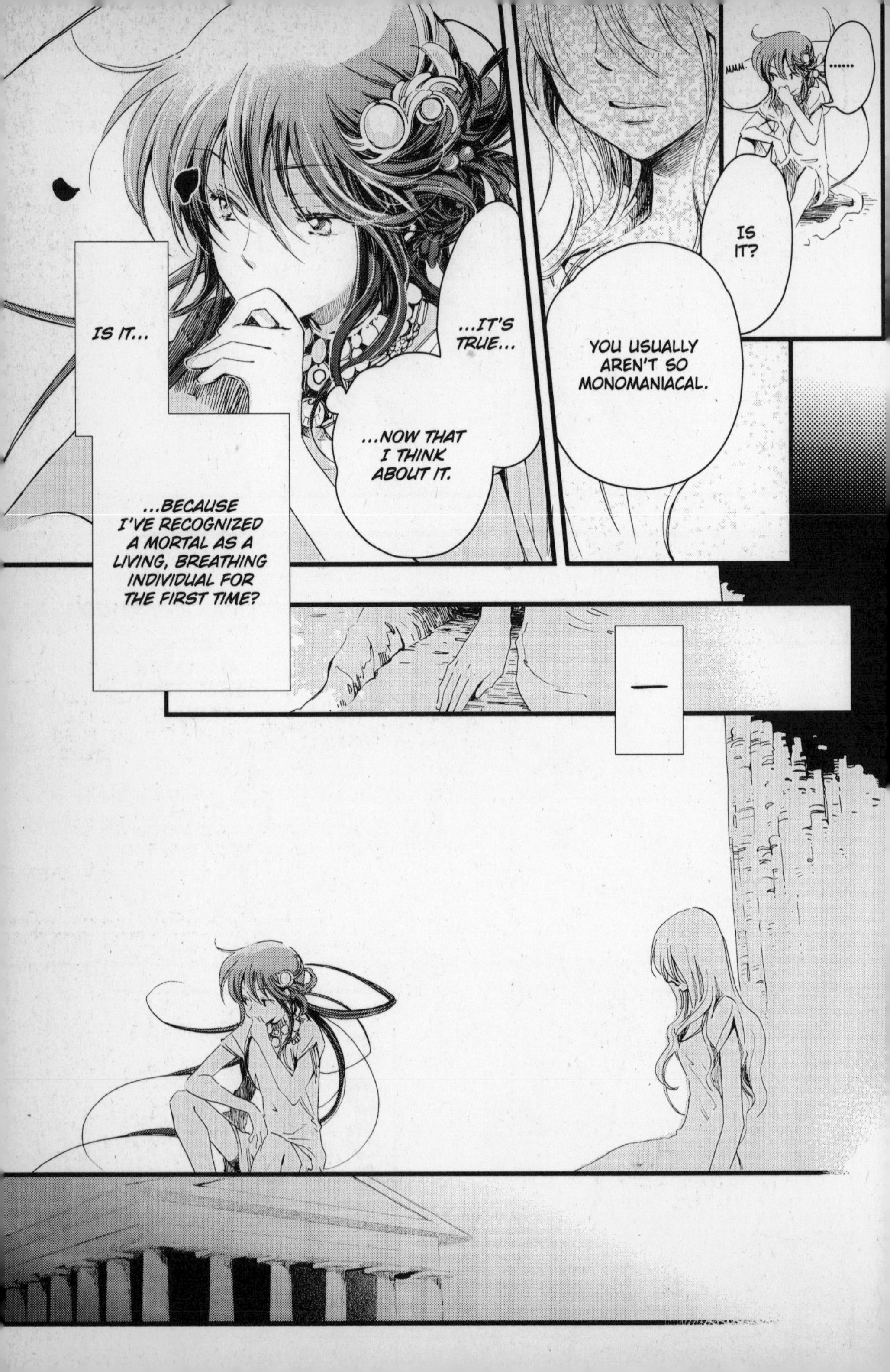
......
MMM.
IS IT?
YOU USUALLY AREN'T SO MONOMANIACAL.
...IT'S TRUE...
...NOW THAT I THINK ABOUT IT.
IS IT...
...BECAUSE I'VE RECOGNIZED A MORTAL AS A LIVING, BREATHING INDIVIDUAL FOR THE FIRST TIME?
—

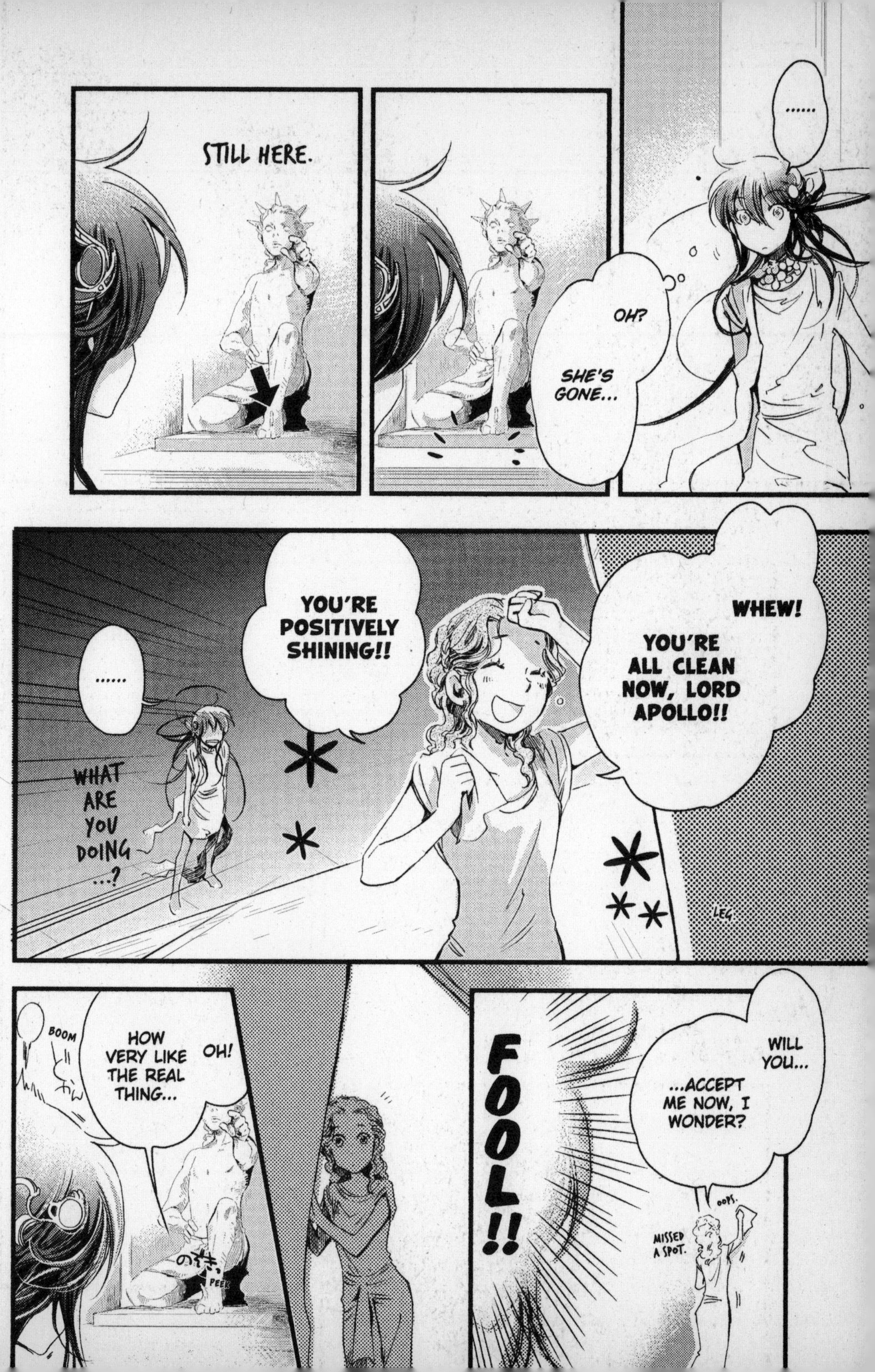
......
OH?
SHE'S GONE...
STILL HERE.
WHEW!
YOU'RE ALL CLEAN NOW, LORD APOLLO!!
YOU'RE POSITIVELY SHINING!!
......
WHAT ARE YOU DOING ...?
WILL YOU...
...ACCEPT ME NOW, I WONDER?
OOPS.
MISSED A SPOT.
FOOL!!
OH!
HOW VERY LIKE THE REAL THING...
BOOM
PEEK

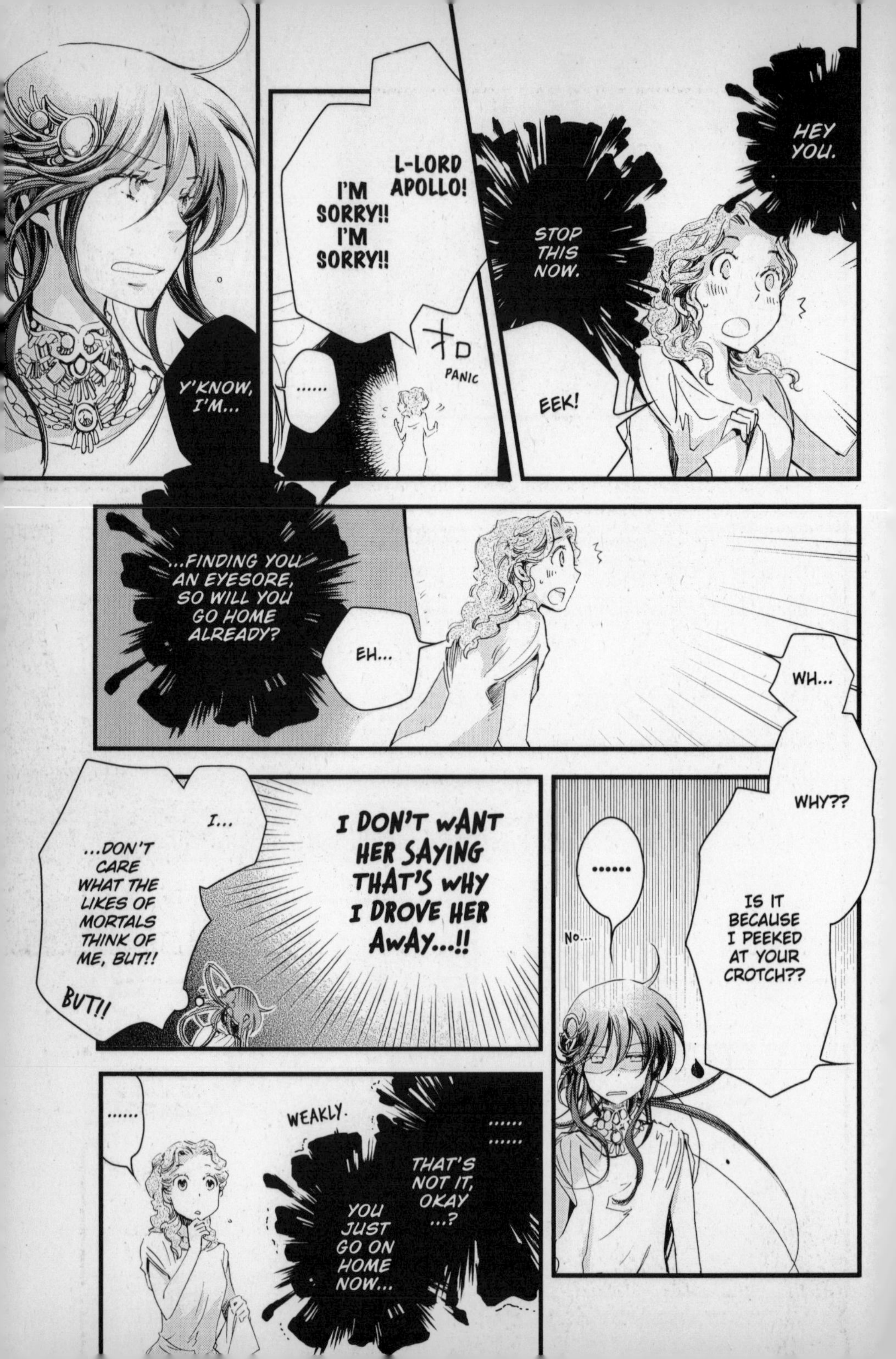
HEY YOU.
STOP THIS NOW.
EEK!
L-LORD APOLLO!
I'M SORRY!! I'M SORRY!!
PANIC
......
Y'KNOW, I'M...
...FINDING YOU AN EYESORE, SO WILL YOU GO HOME ALREADY?
EH...
WH...
WHY??
IS IT BECAUSE I PEEKED AT YOUR CROTCH??
......
No...
I DON'T WANT HER SAYING THAT'S WHY I DROVE HER AWAY...!!
I...
...DON'T CARE WHAT THE LIKES OF MORTALS THINK OF ME, BUT!!
BUT!!
....
THAT'S NOT IT, OKAY ...?
YOU JUST GO ON HOME NOW...
WEAKLY.
......

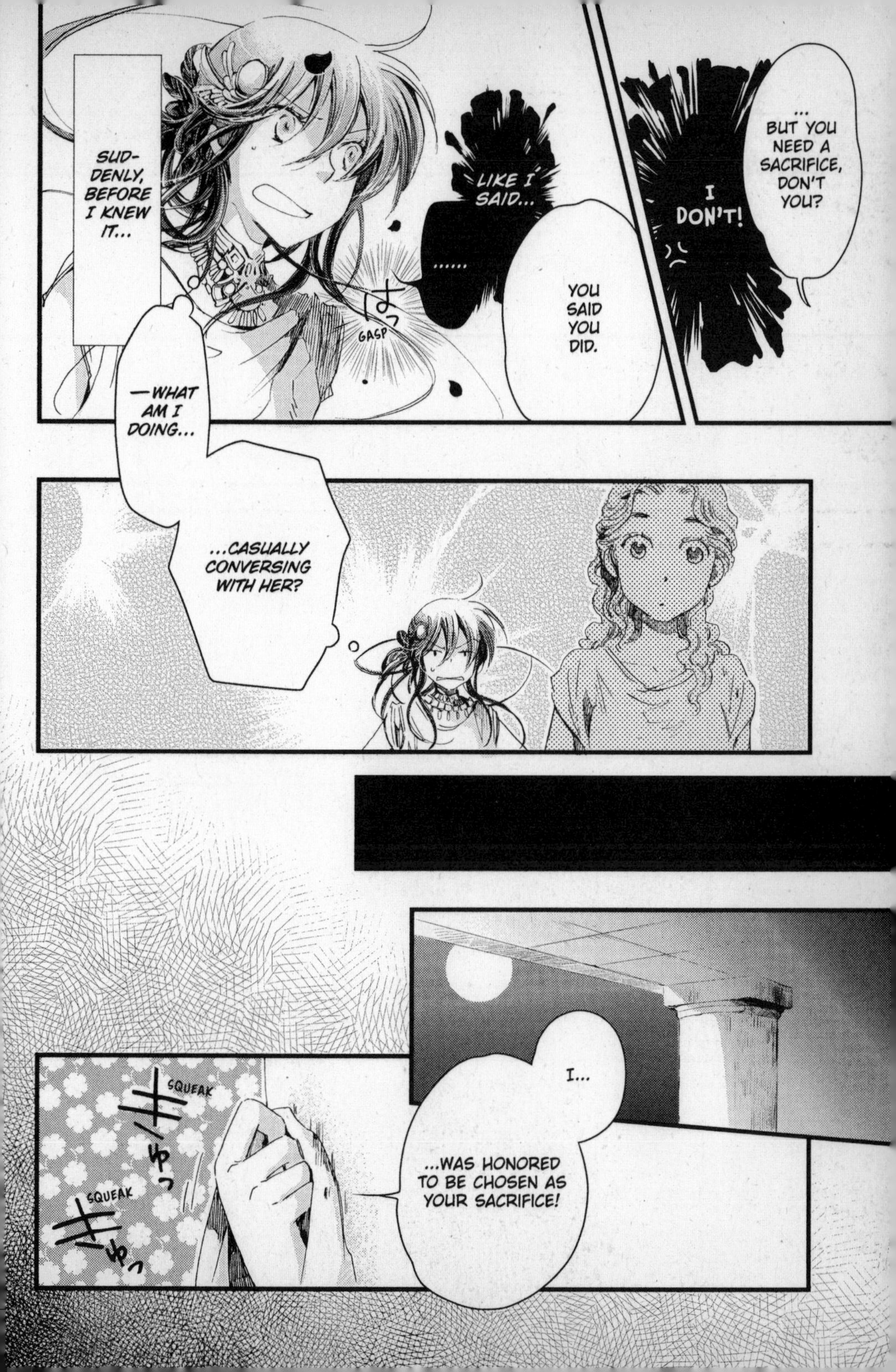

...
BUT YOU NEED A SACRIFICE, DON'T YOU?
I DON'T!
YOU SAID YOU DID.
LIKE I SAID...
......
GASP
SUD-DENLY, BEFORE I KNEW IT...
—WHAT AM I DOING...
...CASUALLY CONVERSING WITH HER?
I...
...WAS HONORED TO BE CHOSEN AS YOUR SACRIFICE!
SQUEAK
SQUEAK

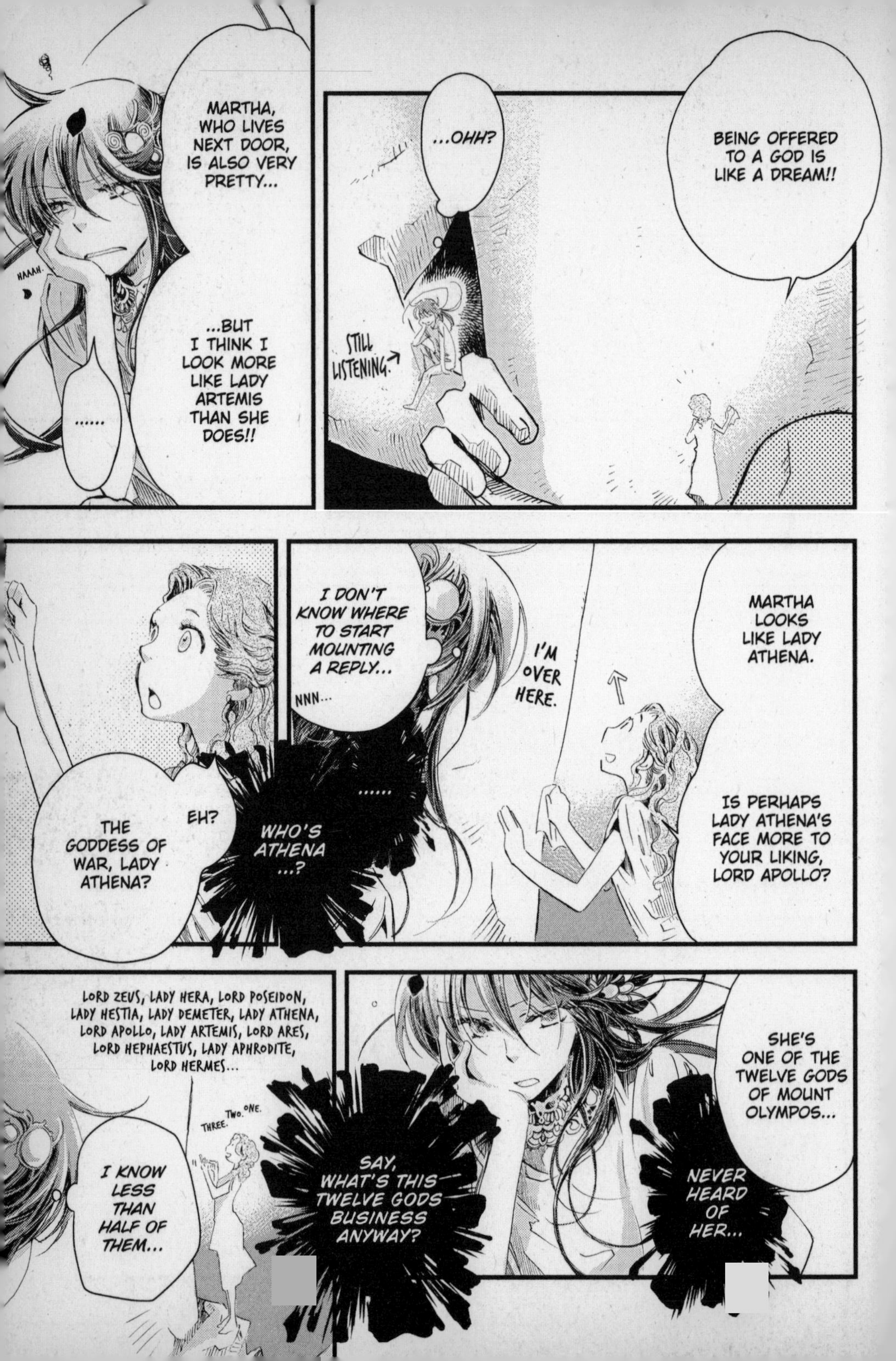
BEING OFFERED TO A GOD IS LIKE A DREAM!!
...OHH?
STILL LISTENING.
MARTHA, WHO LIVES NEXT DOOR, IS ALSO VERY PRETTY...
...BUT I THINK I LOOK MORE LIKE LADY ARTEMIS THAN SHE DOES!!
HAAAH.
......
MARTHA LOOKS LIKE LADY ATHENA.
IS PERHAPS LADY ATHENA'S FACE MORE TO YOUR LIKING, LORD APOLLO?
I'M OVER HERE.
I DON'T KNOW WHERE TO START MOUNTING A REPLY...
NNN...
......
WHO'S ATHENA ...?
EH?
THE GODDESS OF WAR, LADY ATHENA?
SHE'S ONE OF THE TWELVE GODS OF MOUNT OLYMPOS...
NEVER HEARD OF HER...
SAY, WHAT'S THIS TWELVE GODS BUSINESS ANYWAY?
LORD ZEUS, LADY HERA, LORD POSEIDON, LADY HESTIA, LADY DEMETER, LADY ATHENA, LORD APOLLO, LADY ARTEMIS, LORD ARES, LORD HEPHAESTUS, LADY APHRODITE, LORD HERMES...
THREE. TWO. ONE.
I KNOW LESS THAN HALF OF THEM...

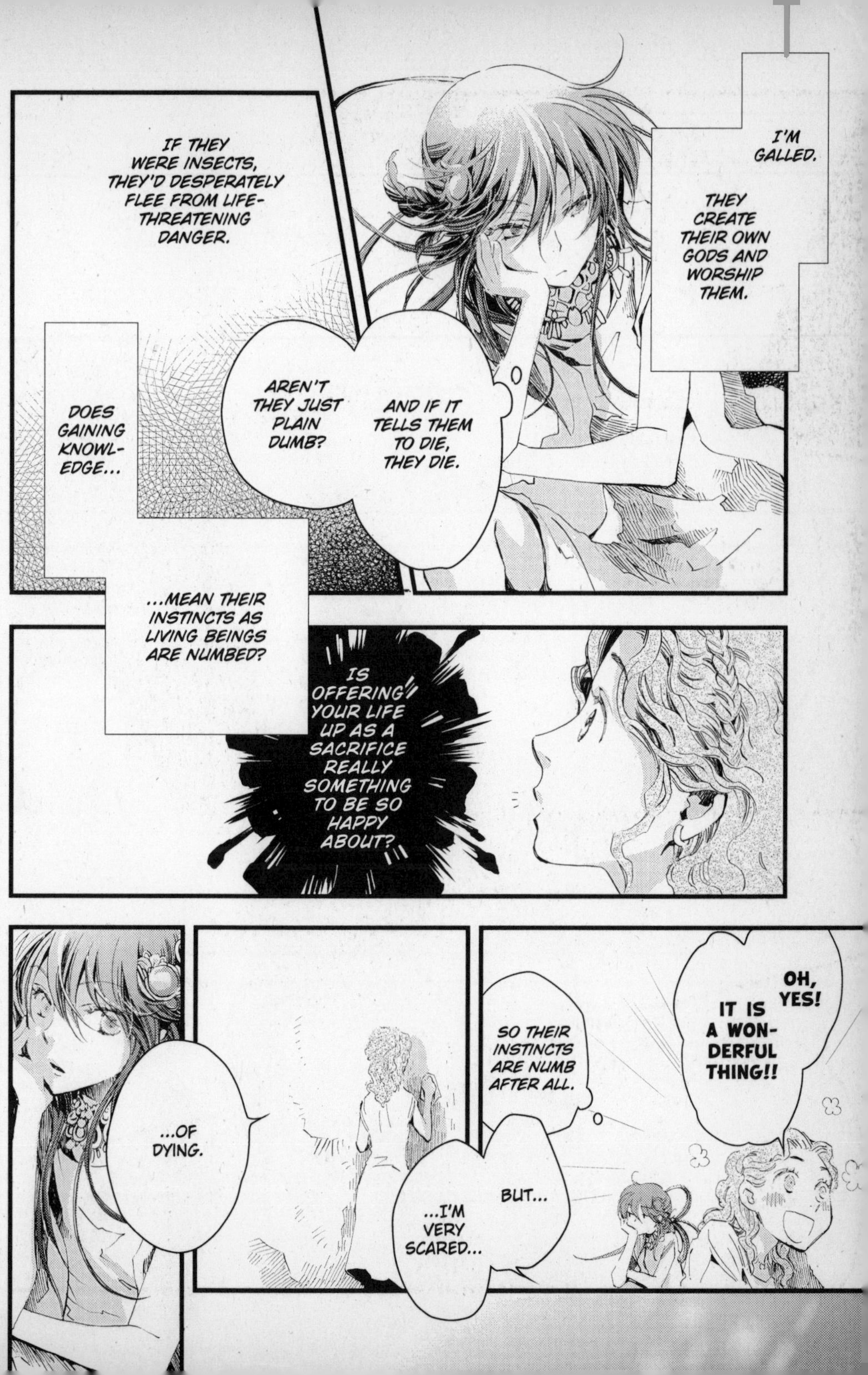
I'M GALLED.
THEY CREATE THEIR OWN GODS AND WORSHIP THEM.
AND IF IT TELLS THEM TO DIE, THEY DIE.
AREN'T THEY JUST PLAIN DUMB?
IF THEY WERE INSECTS, THEY'D DESPERATELY FLEE FROM LIFE-THREATENING DANGER.
DOES GAINING KNOWL-EDGE...
...MEAN THEIR INSTINCTS AS LIVING BEINGS ARE NUMBED?
IS OFFERING YOUR LIFE UP AS A SACRIFICE REALLY SOMETHING TO BE SO HAPPY ABOUT?
OH, YES!
IT IS A WON-DERFUL THING!!
SO THEIR INSTINCTS ARE NUMB AFTER ALL.
BUT...
...I'M VERY SCARED...
...OF DYING.

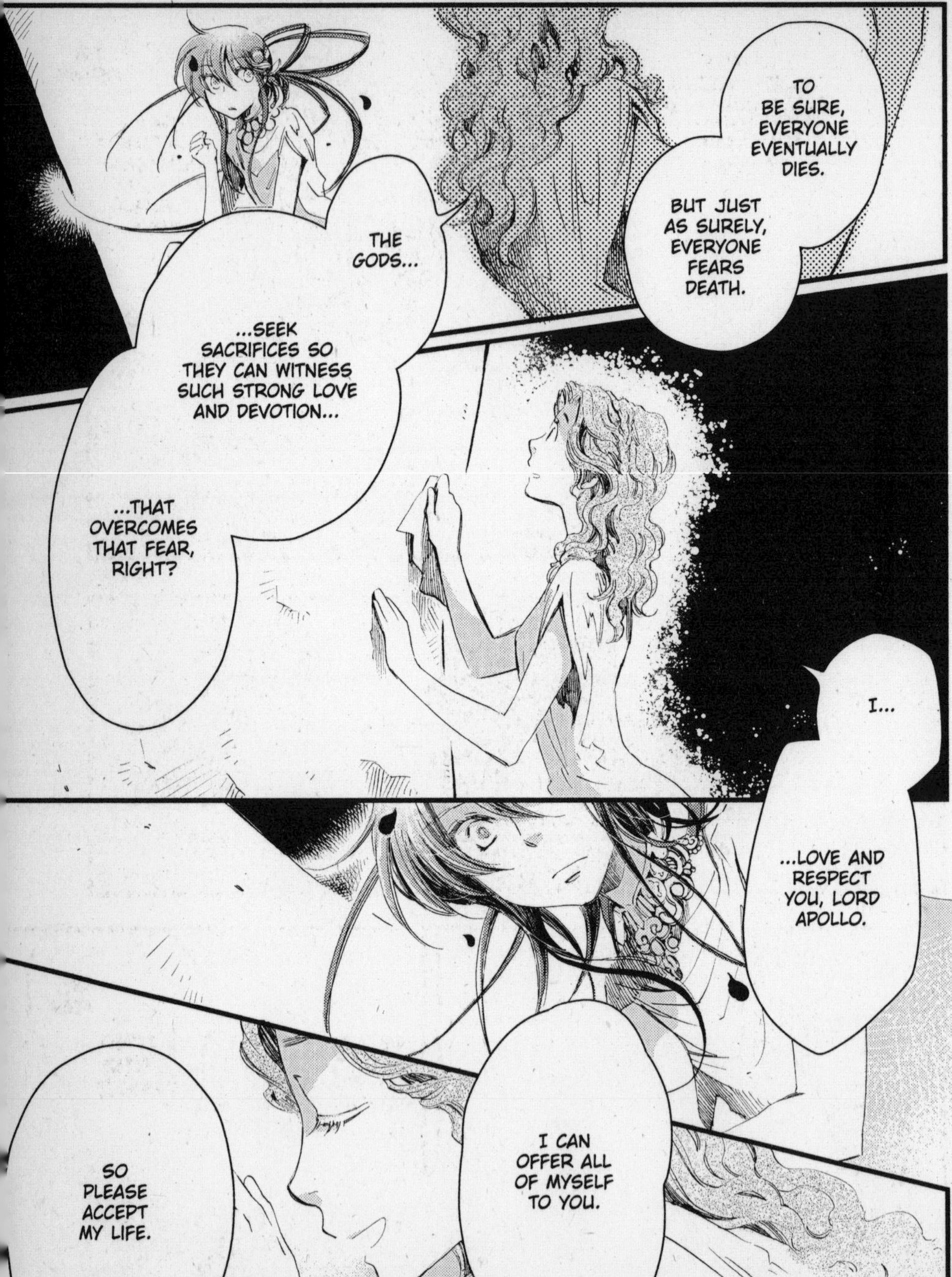
TO BE SURE, EVERYONE EVENTUALLY DIES.
BUT JUST AS SURELY, EVERYONE FEARS DEATH.
THE GODS...
...SEEK SACRIFICES SO THEY CAN WITNESS SUCH STRONG LOVE AND DEVOTION...
...THAT OVERCOMES THAT FEAR, RIGHT?
I...
...LOVE AND RESPECT YOU, LORD APOLLO.
I CAN OFFER ALL OF MYSELF TO YOU.
SO PLEASE ACCEPT MY LIFE.

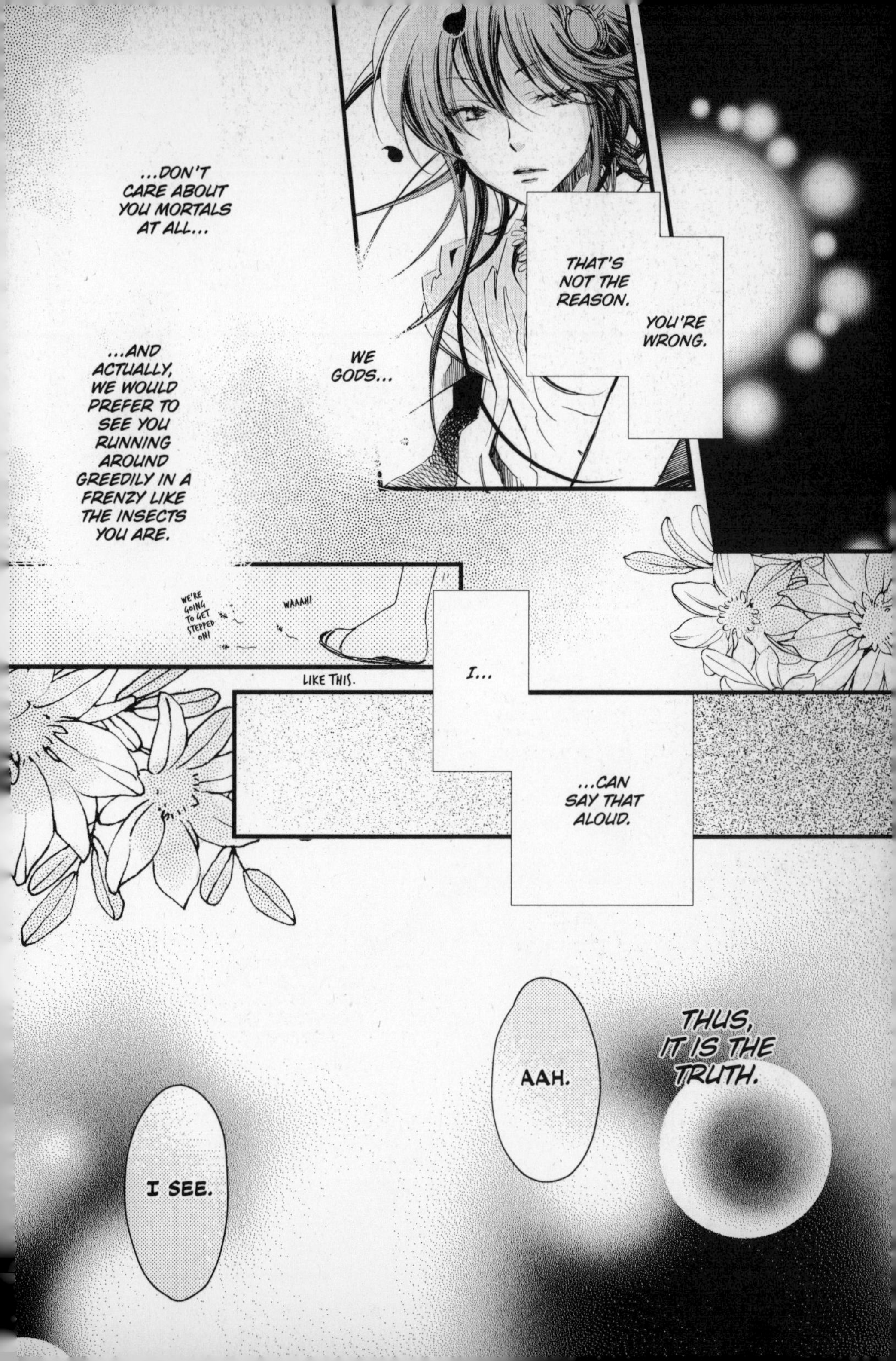
THAT'S NOT THE REASON.
YOU'RE WRONG.
WE GODS...
...DON'T CARE ABOUT YOU MORTALS AT ALL...
...AND ACTUALLY, WE WOULD PREFER TO SEE YOU RUNNING AROUND GREEDILY IN A FRENZY LIKE THE INSECTS YOU ARE.
I...
WAAAH!
WE'RE GOING TO GET STEPPED ON!
LIKE THIS.
...CAN SAY THAT ALOUD.
THUS, IT IS THE TRUTH.
AAH.
I SEE.

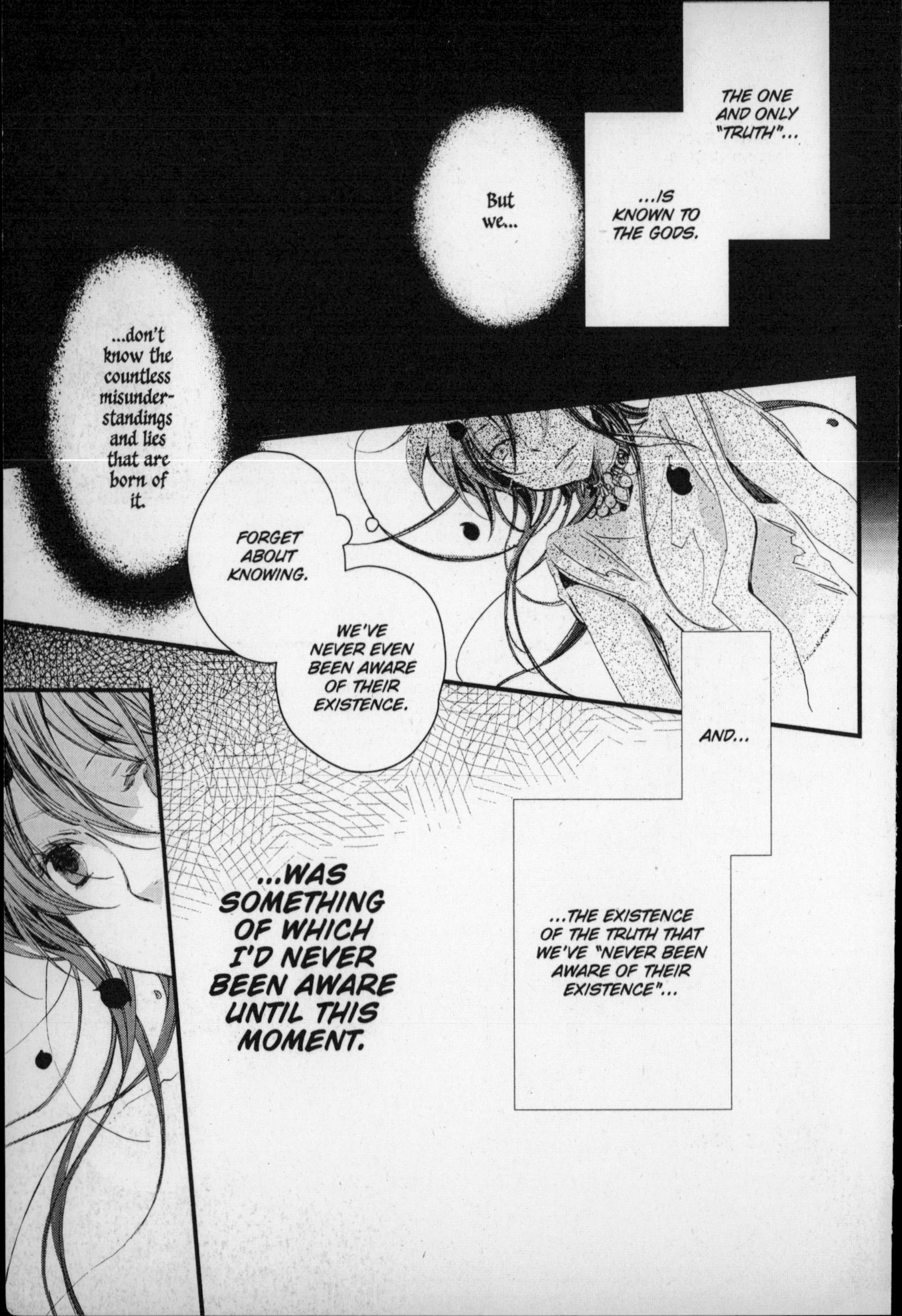
THE ONE AND ONLY "TRUTH"...
...IS KNOWN TO THE GODS.
But we...
...don't know the countless misunder-standings and lies that are born of it.
FORGET ABOUT KNOWING.
WE'VE NEVER EVEN BEEN AWARE OF THEIR EXISTENCE.
AND...
...THE EXISTENCE OF THE TRUTH THAT WE'VE "NEVER BEEN AWARE OF THEIR EXISTENCE"...
...WAS SOMETHING OF WHICH I'D NEVER BEEN AWARE UNTIL THIS MOMENT.

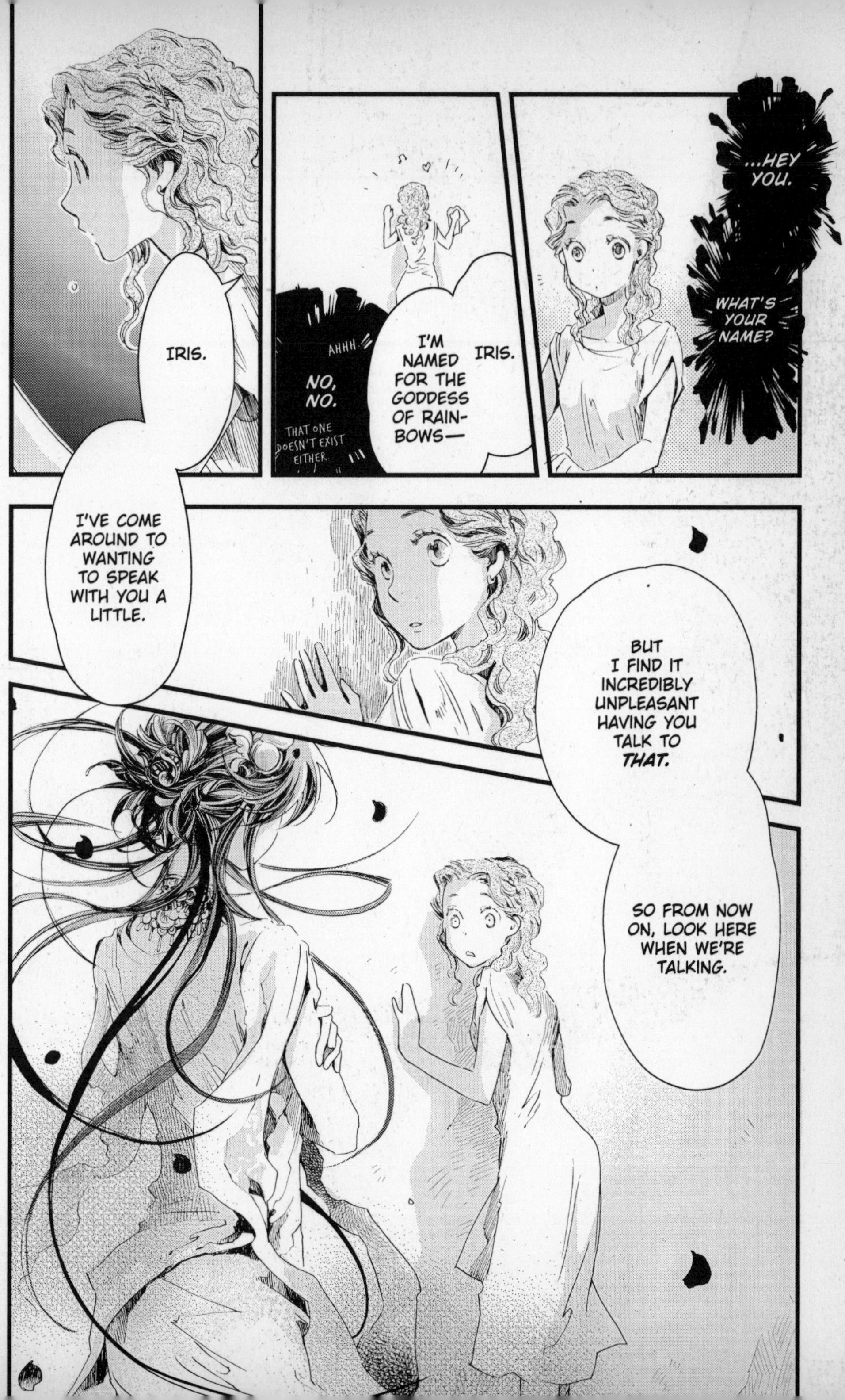
...HEY YOU.
WHAT'S YOUR NAME?
IRIS.
I'M NAMED FOR THE GODDESS OF RAIN-BOWS—
AHHH
NO, NO.
THAT ONE DOESN'T EXIST EITHER.
IRIS.
I'VE COME AROUND TO WANTING TO SPEAK WITH YOU A LITTLE.
BUT I FIND IT INCREDIBLY UNPLEASANT HAVING YOU TALK TO *THAT.*
SO FROM NOW ON, LOOK HERE WHEN WE'RE TALKING.

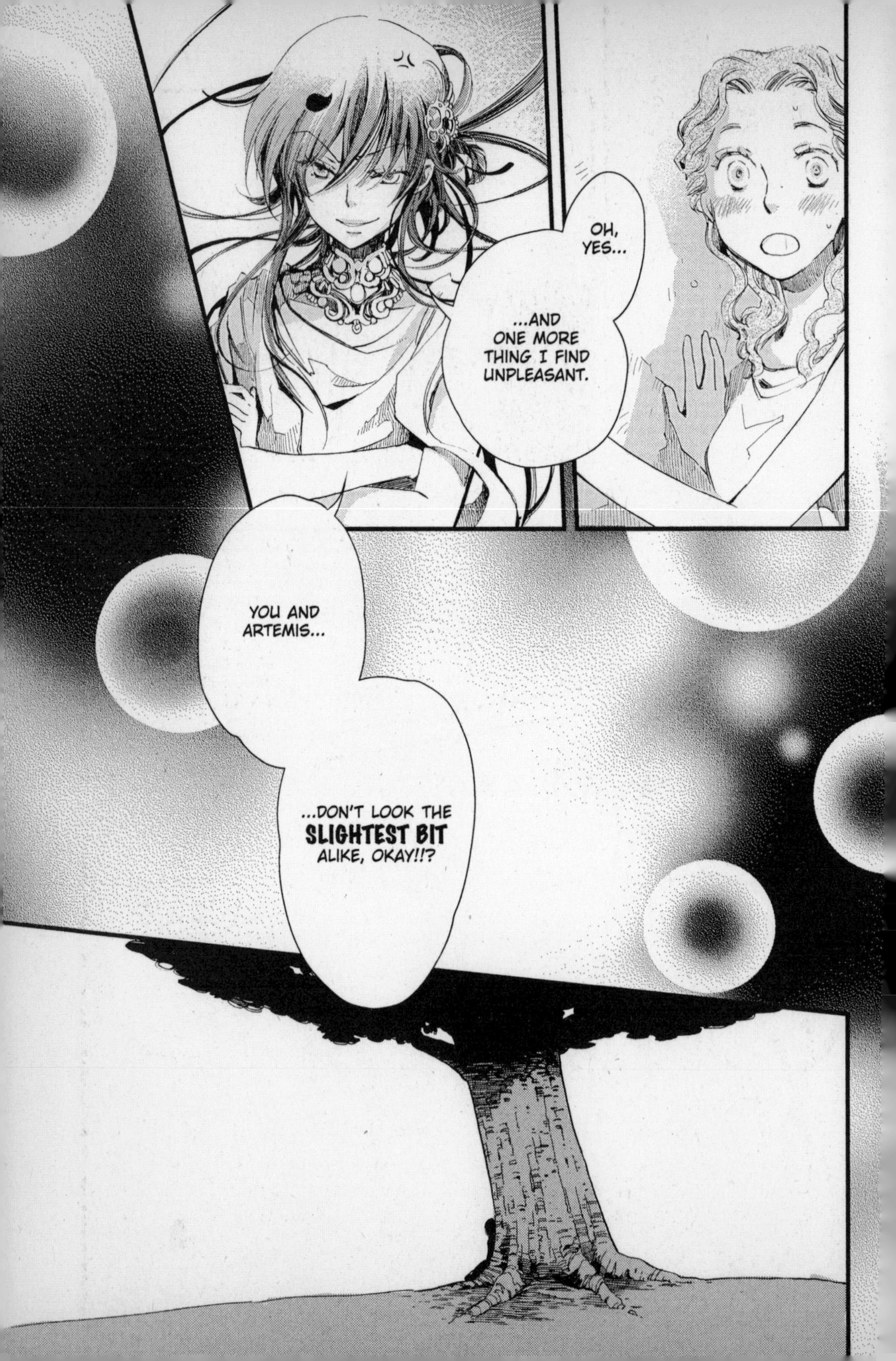
OH, YES...
...AND ONE MORE THING I FIND UNPLEASANT.
YOU AND ARTEMIS...
...DON'T LOOK THE SLIGHTEST BIT ALIKE, OKAY!!?

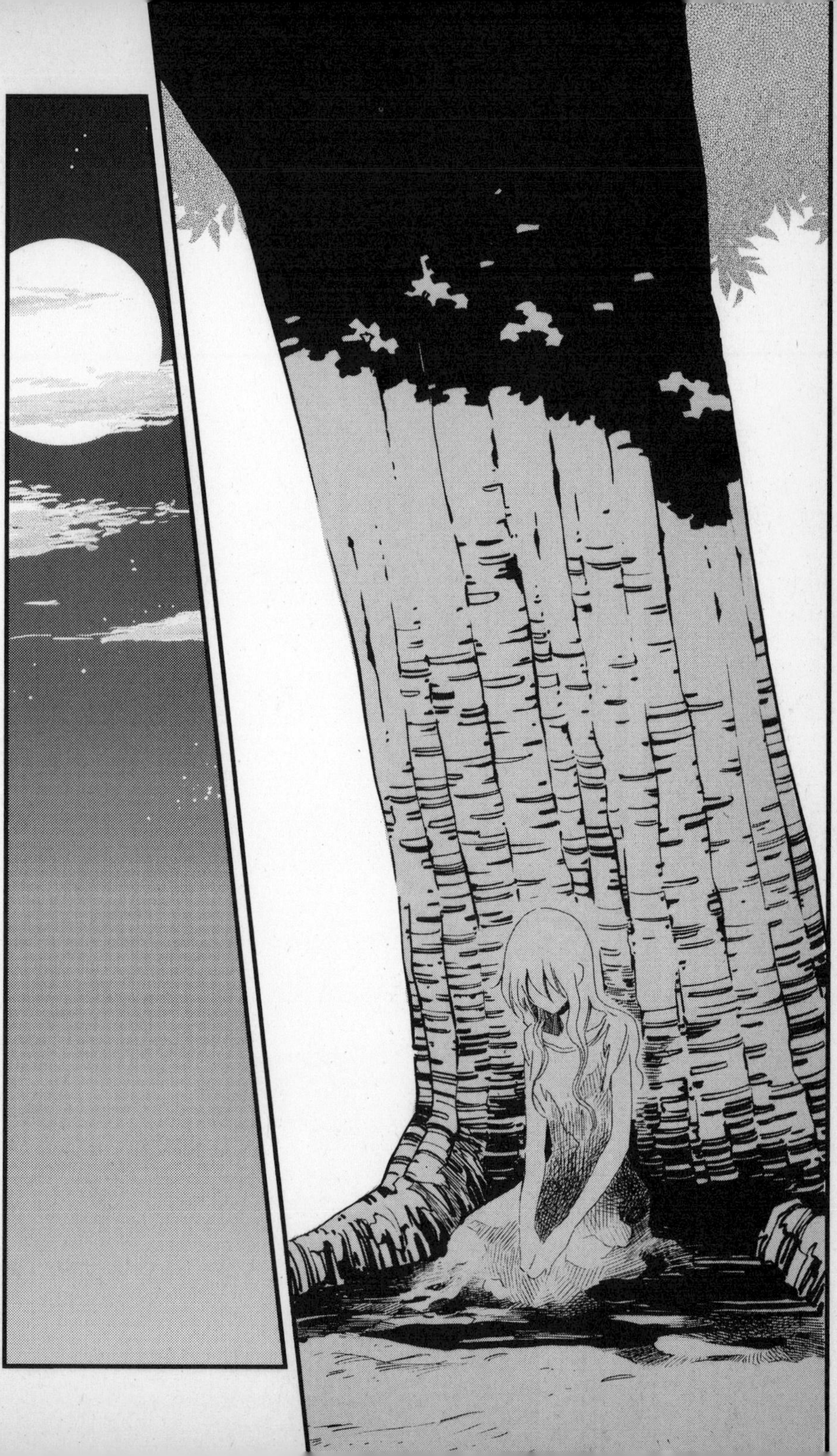

FLUTTER
ひら
FLUTTER
ひら
FLUTTER
ひら

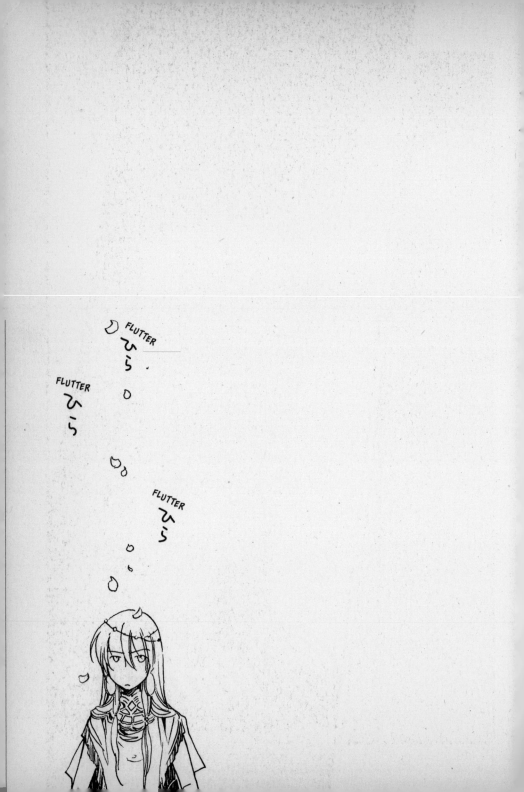

Olympos

Episode.07

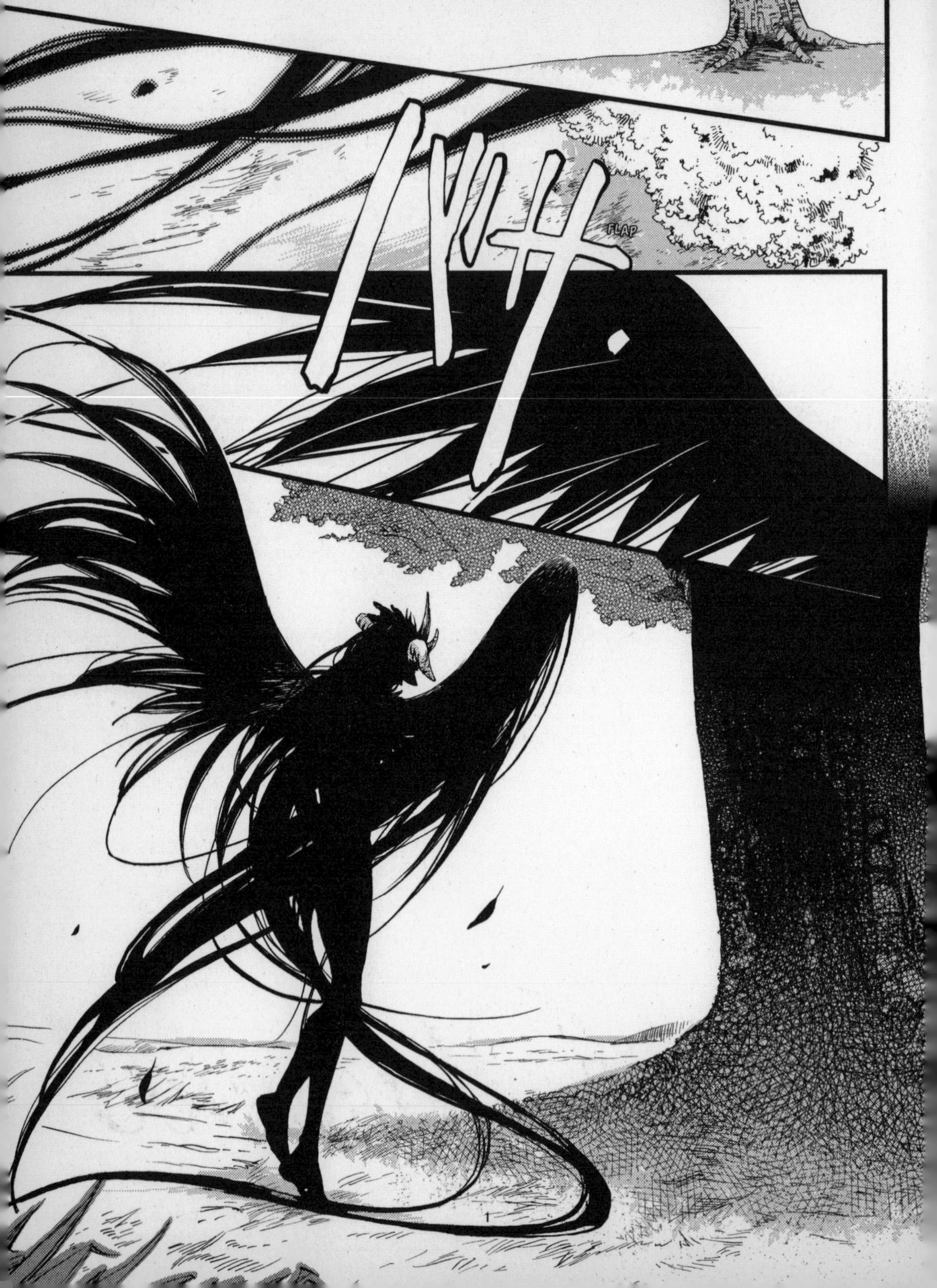
FLAP

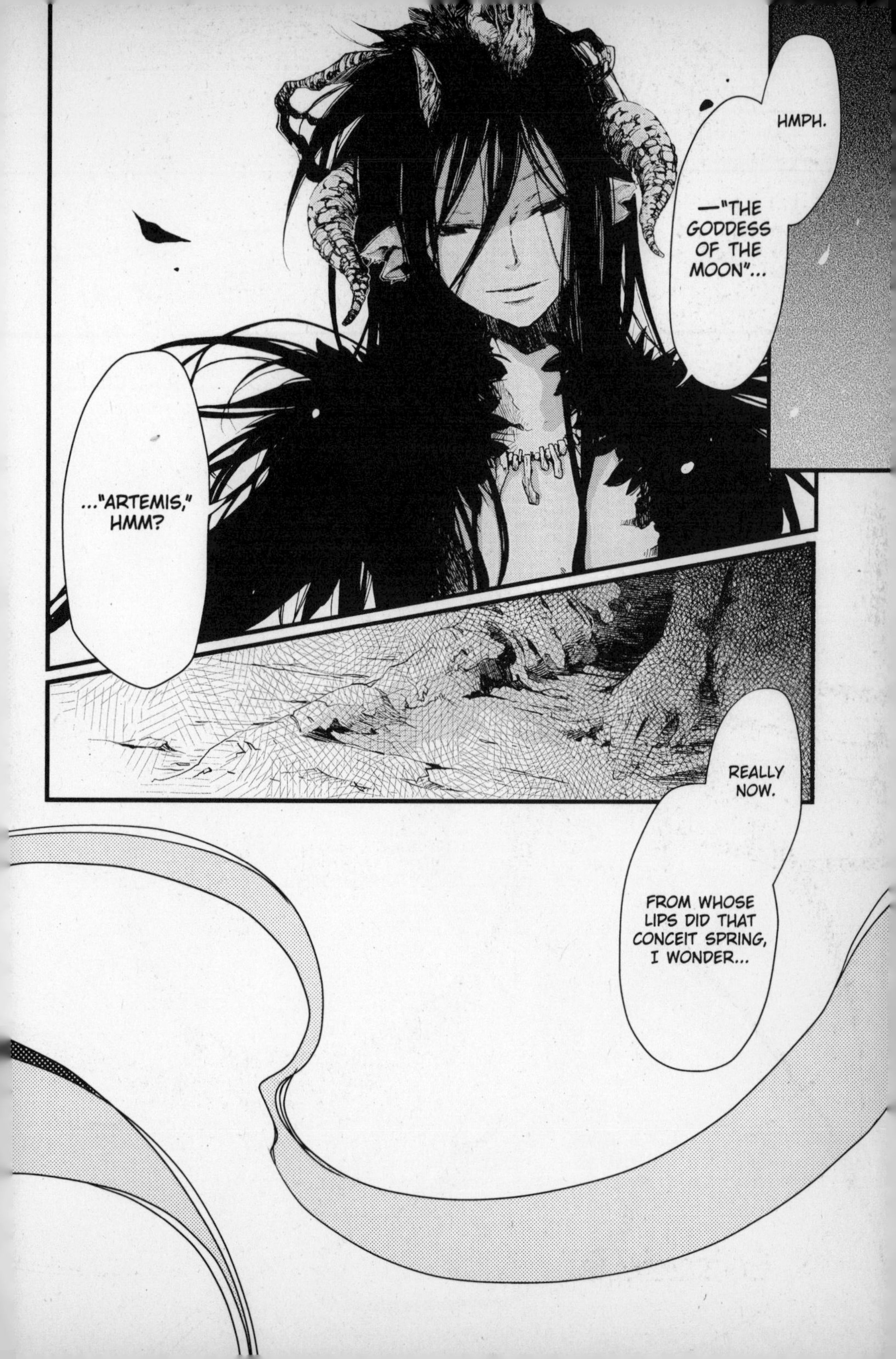
HMPH.
—"THE GODDESS OF THE MOON"...
..."ARTEMIS," HMM?
REALLY NOW.
FROM WHOSE LIPS DID THAT CONCEIT SPRING, I WONDER...

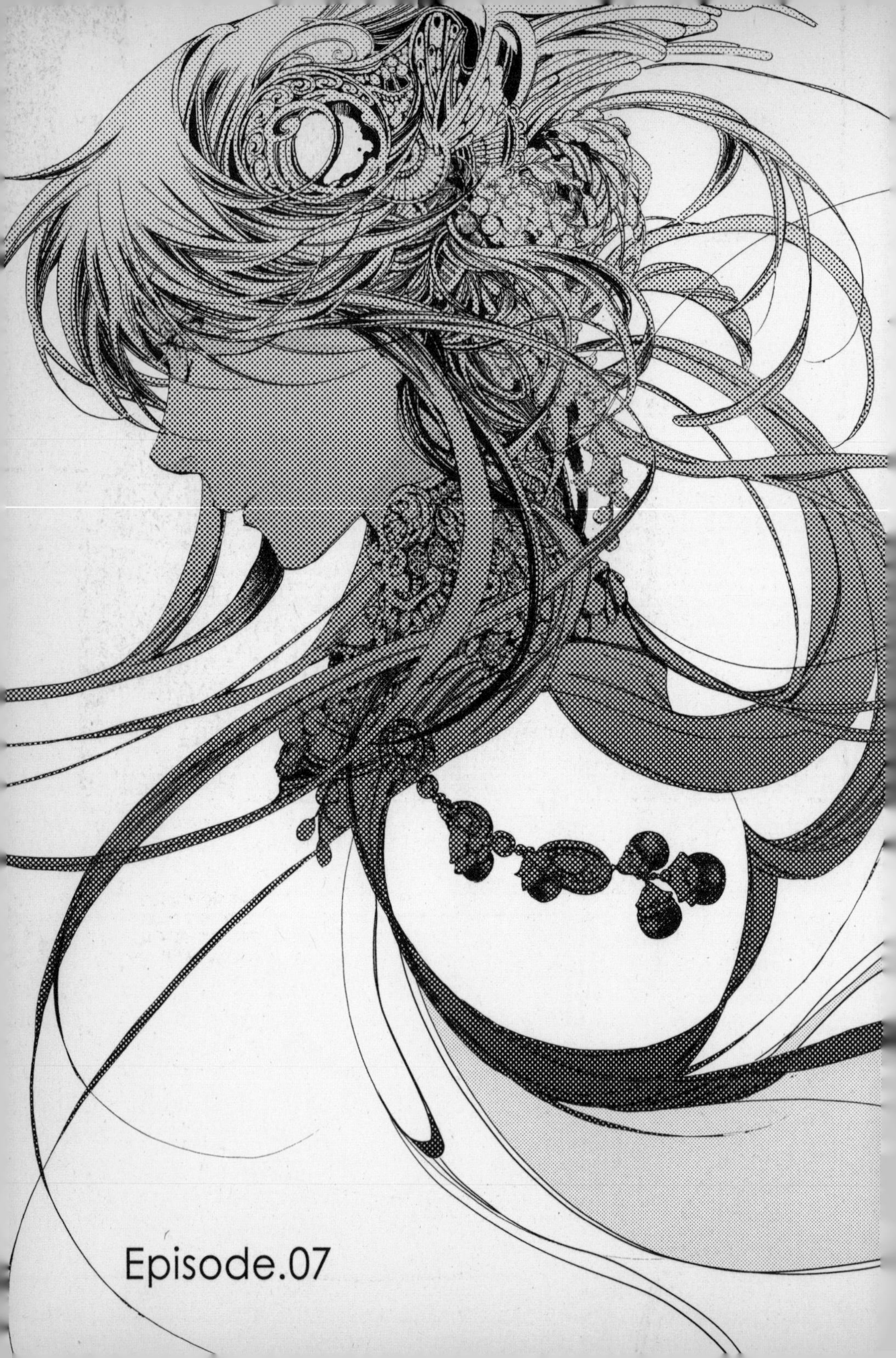
Episode.07

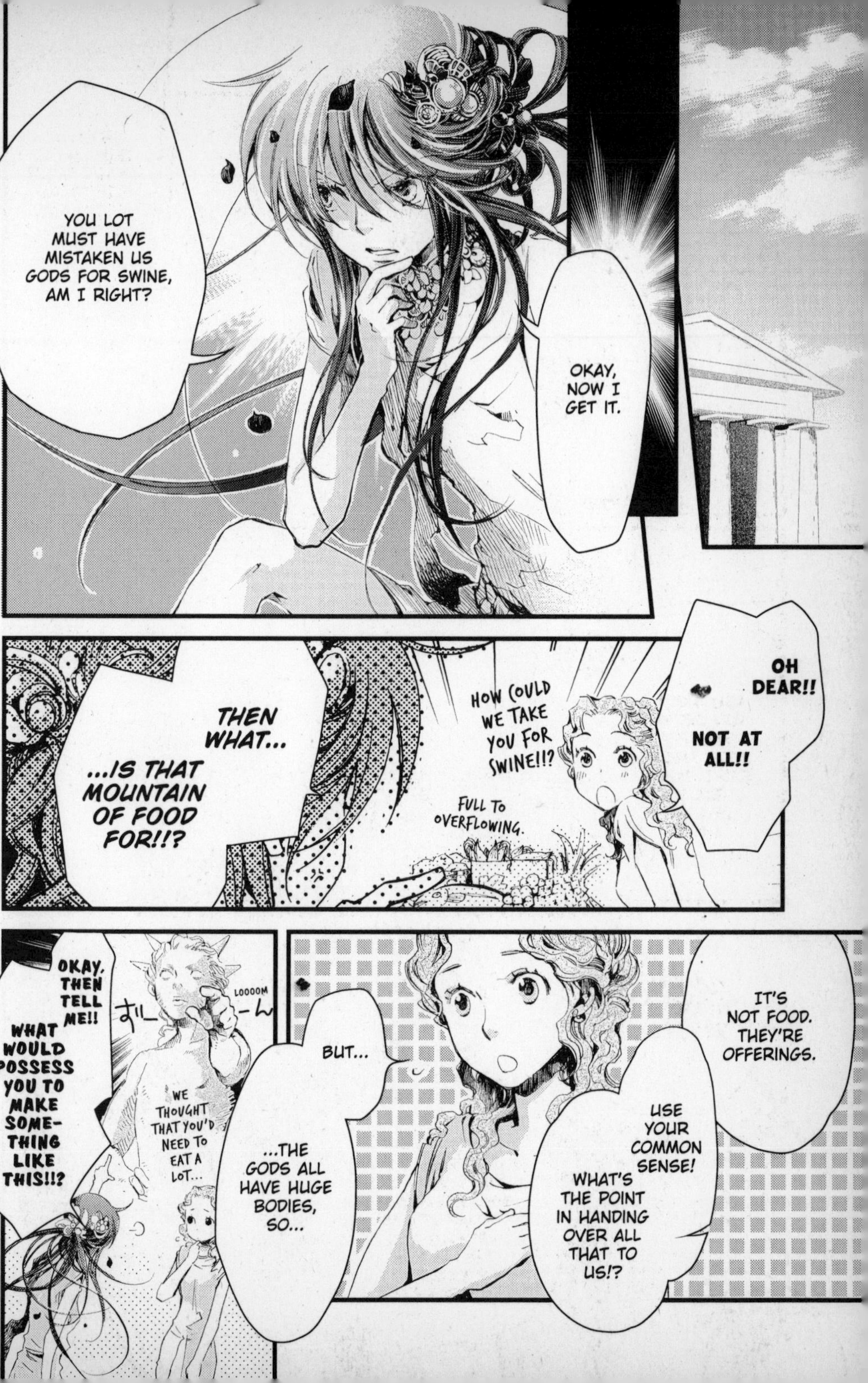
OKAY, NOW I GET IT.
YOU LOT MUST HAVE MISTAKEN US GODS FOR SWINE, AM I RIGHT?
OH DEAR!! NOT AT ALL!!
HOW COULD WE TAKE YOU FOR SWINE!!?
FULL TO OVERFLOWING.
THEN WHAT...
...IS THAT MOUNTAIN OF FOOD FOR!!?
IT'S NOT FOOD. THEY'RE OFFERINGS.
USE YOUR COMMON SENSE!
WHAT'S THE POINT IN HANDING OVER ALL THAT TO US!?
BUT...
...THE GODS ALL HAVE HUGE BODIES, SO...
LOOOOM
OKAY, THEN TELL ME!!
WHAT WOULD POSSESS YOU TO MAKE SOME-THING LIKE THIS!!?
WE THOUGHT THAT YOU'D NEED TO EAT A LOT...

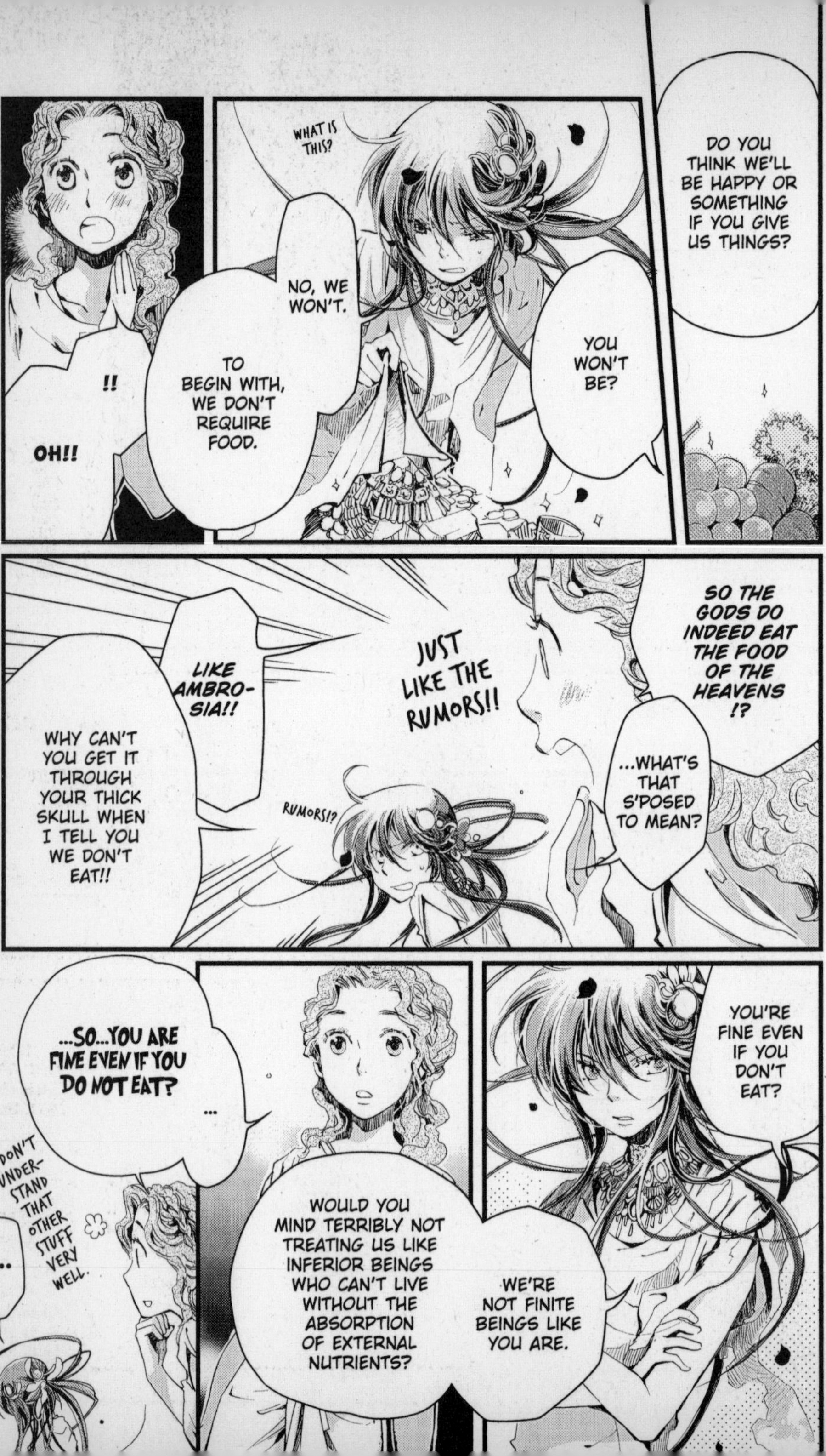
DO YOU THINK WE'LL BE HAPPY OR SOMETHING IF YOU GIVE US THINGS?
YOU WON'T BE?
WHAT IS THIS?
NO, WE WON'T.
TO BEGIN WITH, WE DON'T REQUIRE FOOD.
!!
OH!!
SO THE GODS DO INDEED EAT THE FOOD OF THE HEAVENS !?
JUST LIKE THE RUMORS!!
...WHAT'S THAT S'POSED TO MEAN?
RUMORS!?
LIKE AMBROSIA!!
WHY CAN'T YOU GET IT THROUGH YOUR THICK SKULL WHEN I TELL YOU WE DON'T EAT!!
YOU'RE FINE EVEN IF YOU DON'T EAT?
WE'RE NOT FINITE BEINGS LIKE YOU ARE.
WOULD YOU MIND TERRIBLY NOT TREATING US LIKE INFERIOR BEINGS WHO CAN'T LIVE WITHOUT THE ABSORPTION OF EXTERNAL NUTRIENTS?
...SO...YOU ARE FINE EVEN IF YOU DO NOT EAT?
...
I DON'T UNDER-STAND THAT OTHER STUFF VERY WELL.
...

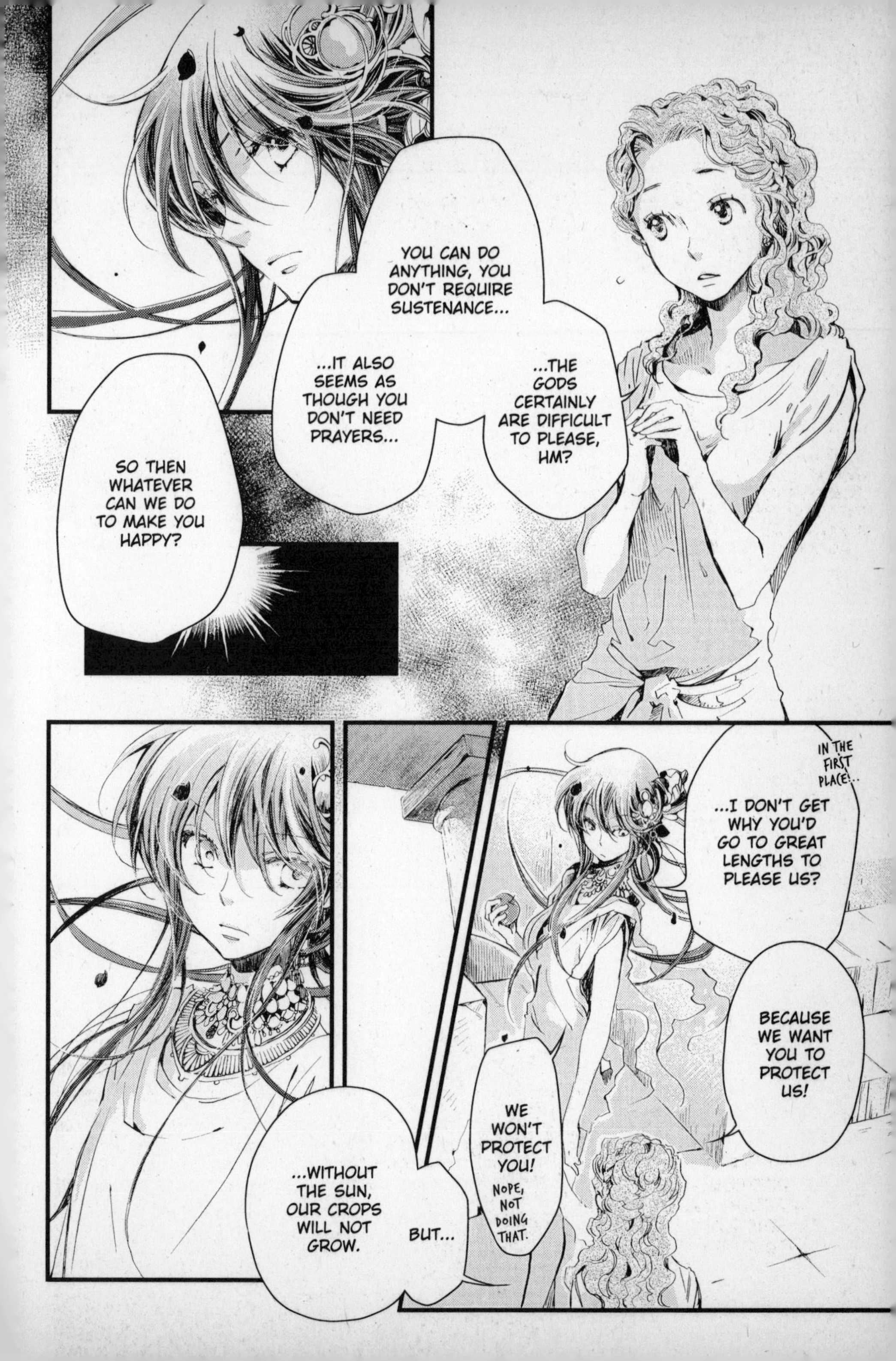
YOU CAN DO ANYTHING, YOU DON'T REQUIRE SUSTENANCE...
...THE GODS CERTAINLY ARE DIFFICULT TO PLEASE, HM?
...IT ALSO SEEMS AS THOUGH YOU DON'T NEED PRAYERS...
SO THEN WHATEVER CAN WE DO TO MAKE YOU HAPPY?
IN THE FIRST PLACE...
...I DON'T GET WHY YOU'D GO TO GREAT LENGTHS TO PLEASE US?
BECAUSE WE WANT YOU TO PROTECT US!
WE WON'T PROTECT YOU!
NOPE, NOT DOING THAT.
BUT...
...WITHOUT THE SUN, OUR CROPS WILL NOT GROW.

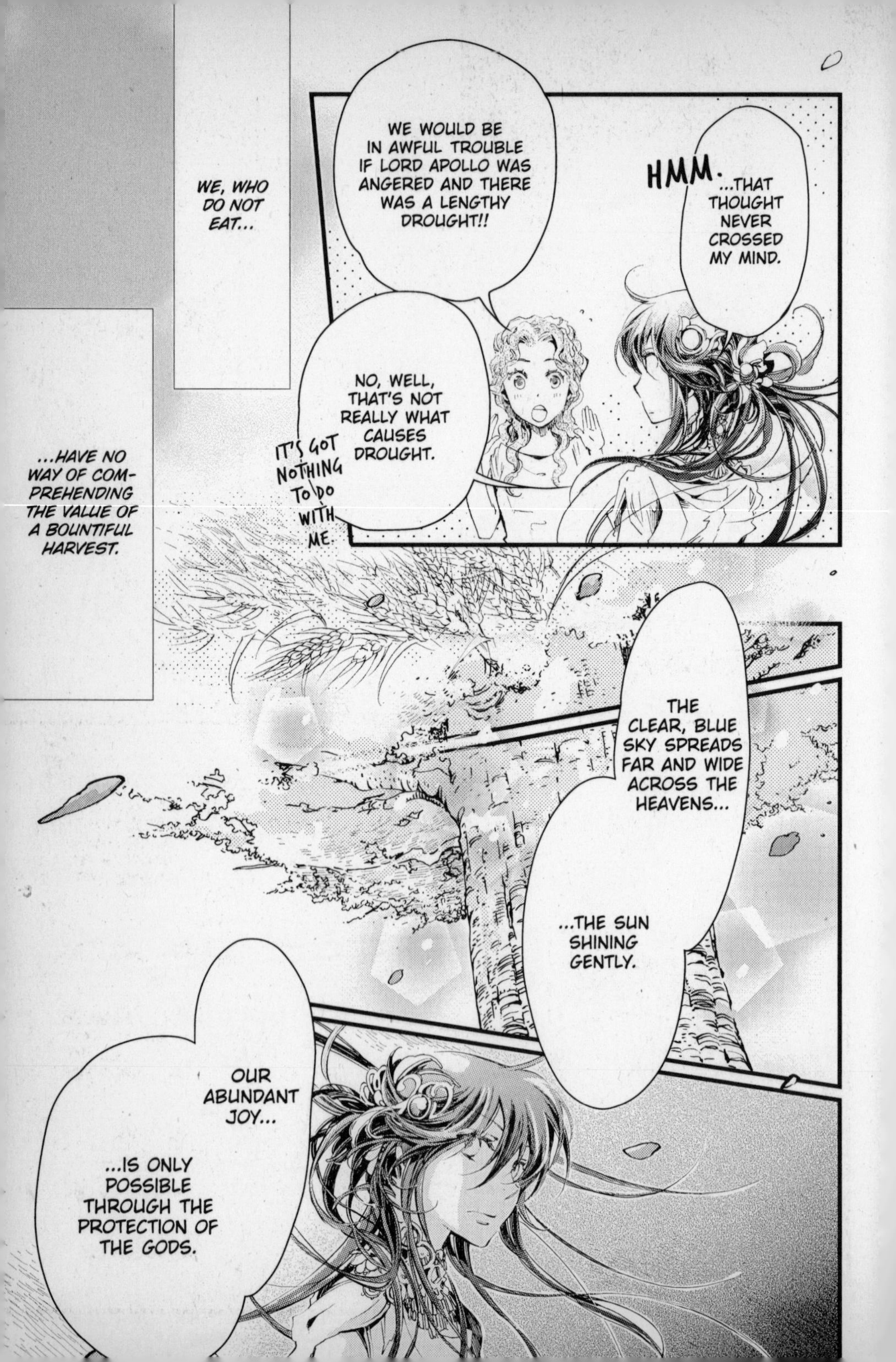
WE WOULD BE IN AWFUL TROUBLE IF LORD APOLLO WAS ANGERED AND THERE WAS A LENGTHY DROUGHT!!
HMM.
...THAT THOUGHT NEVER CROSSED MY MIND.
NO, WELL, THAT'S NOT REALLY WHAT CAUSES DROUGHT.
IT'S GOT NOTHING TO DO WITH ME.
WE, WHO DO NOT EAT...
...HAVE NO WAY OF COM-PREHENDING THE VALUE OF A BOUNTIFUL HARVEST.
THE CLEAR, BLUE SKY SPREADS FAR AND WIDE ACROSS THE HEAVENS...
...THE SUN SHINING GENTLY.
OUR ABUNDANT JOY...
...IS ONLY POSSIBLE THROUGH THE PROTECTION OF THE GODS.

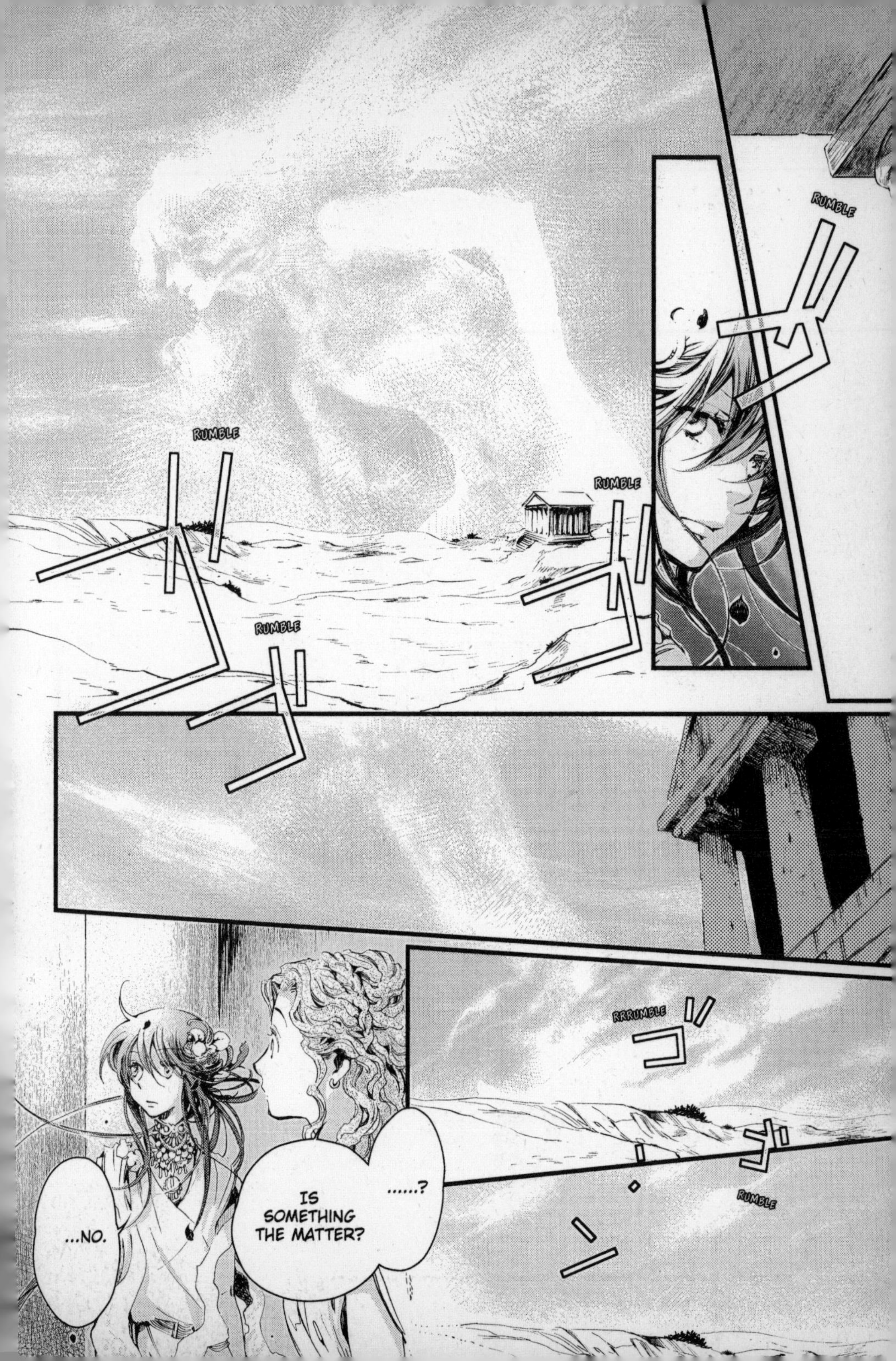
RUMBLE
RUMBLE
RUMBLE
RUMBLE
RRRUMBLE
RUMBLE
......?
IS SOMETHING THE MATTER?
...NO.

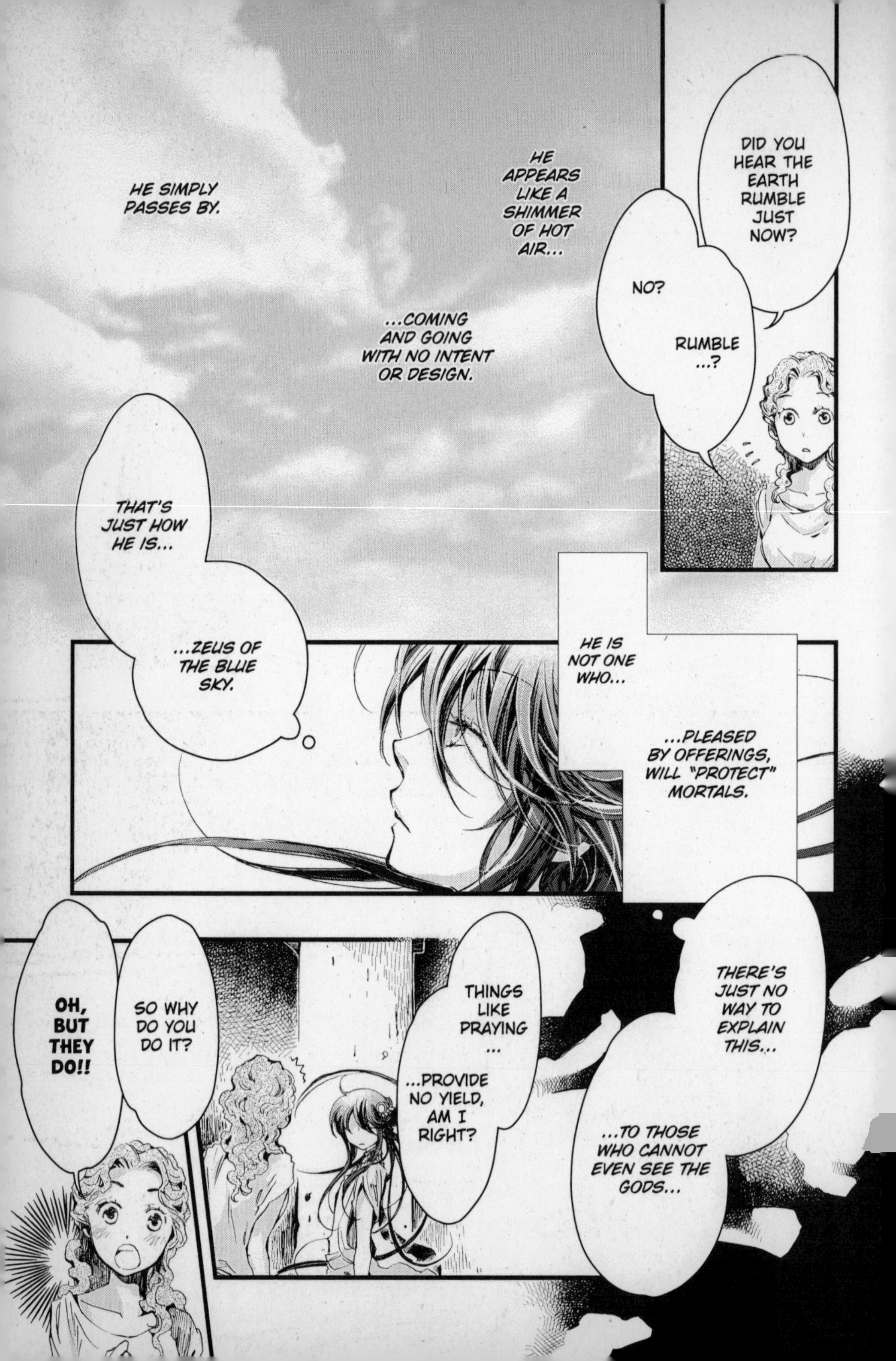
DID YOU HEAR THE EARTH RUMBLE JUST NOW?
NO?
RUMBLE ...?
HE APPEARS LIKE A SHIMMER OF HOT AIR...
HE SIMPLY PASSES BY.
...COMING AND GOING WITH NO INTENT OR DESIGN.
THAT'S JUST HOW HE IS...
...ZEUS OF THE BLUE SKY.
HE IS NOT ONE WHO...
...PLEASED BY OFFERINGS, WILL "PROTECT" MORTALS.
THERE'S JUST NO WAY TO EXPLAIN THIS...
...TO THOSE WHO CANNOT EVEN SEE THE GODS...
THINGS LIKE PRAYING ...
...PROVIDE NO YIELD, AM I RIGHT?
SO WHY DO YOU DO IT?
OH, BUT THEY DO!!

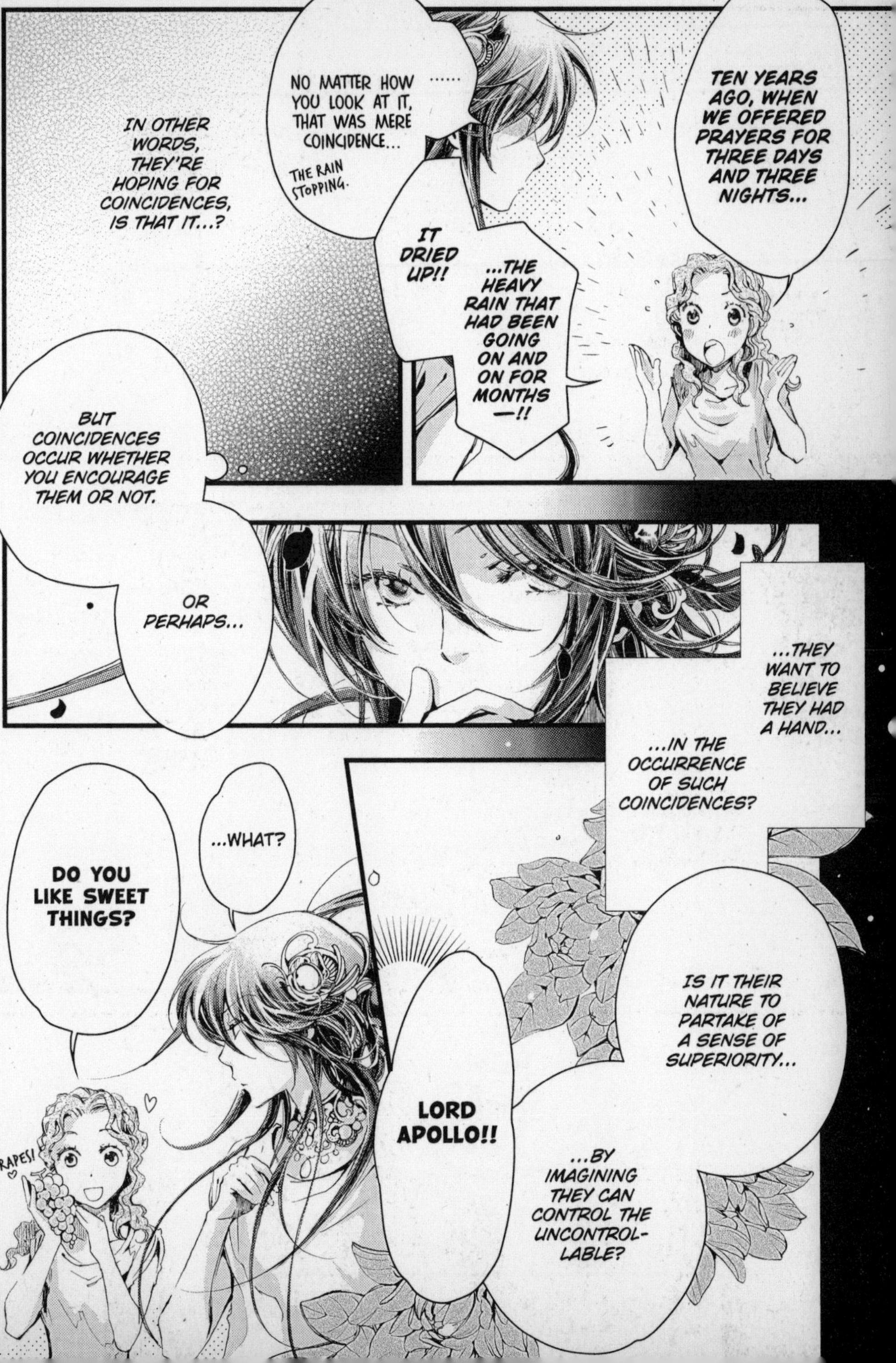

TEN YEARS AGO, WHEN WE OFFERED PRAYERS FOR THREE DAYS AND THREE NIGHTS...
...THE HEAVY RAIN THAT HAD BEEN GOING ON AND ON FOR MONTHS—!!
IT DRIED UP!!
NO MATTER HOW YOU LOOK AT IT, THAT WAS MERE COINCIDENCE...
THE RAIN STOPPING.
......
IN OTHER WORDS, THEY'RE HOPING FOR COINCIDENCES, IS THAT IT...?
BUT COINCIDENCES OCCUR WHETHER YOU ENCOURAGE THEM OR NOT.
OR PERHAPS...
...THEY WANT TO BELIEVE THEY HAD A HAND...
...IN THE OCCURRENCE OF SUCH COINCIDENCES?
IS IT THEIR NATURE TO PARTAKE OF A SENSE OF SUPERIORITY...
...BY IMAGINING THEY CAN CONTROL THE UNCONTROL-LABLE?
LORD APOLLO!!
...WHAT?
DO YOU LIKE SWEET THINGS?
GRAPES!

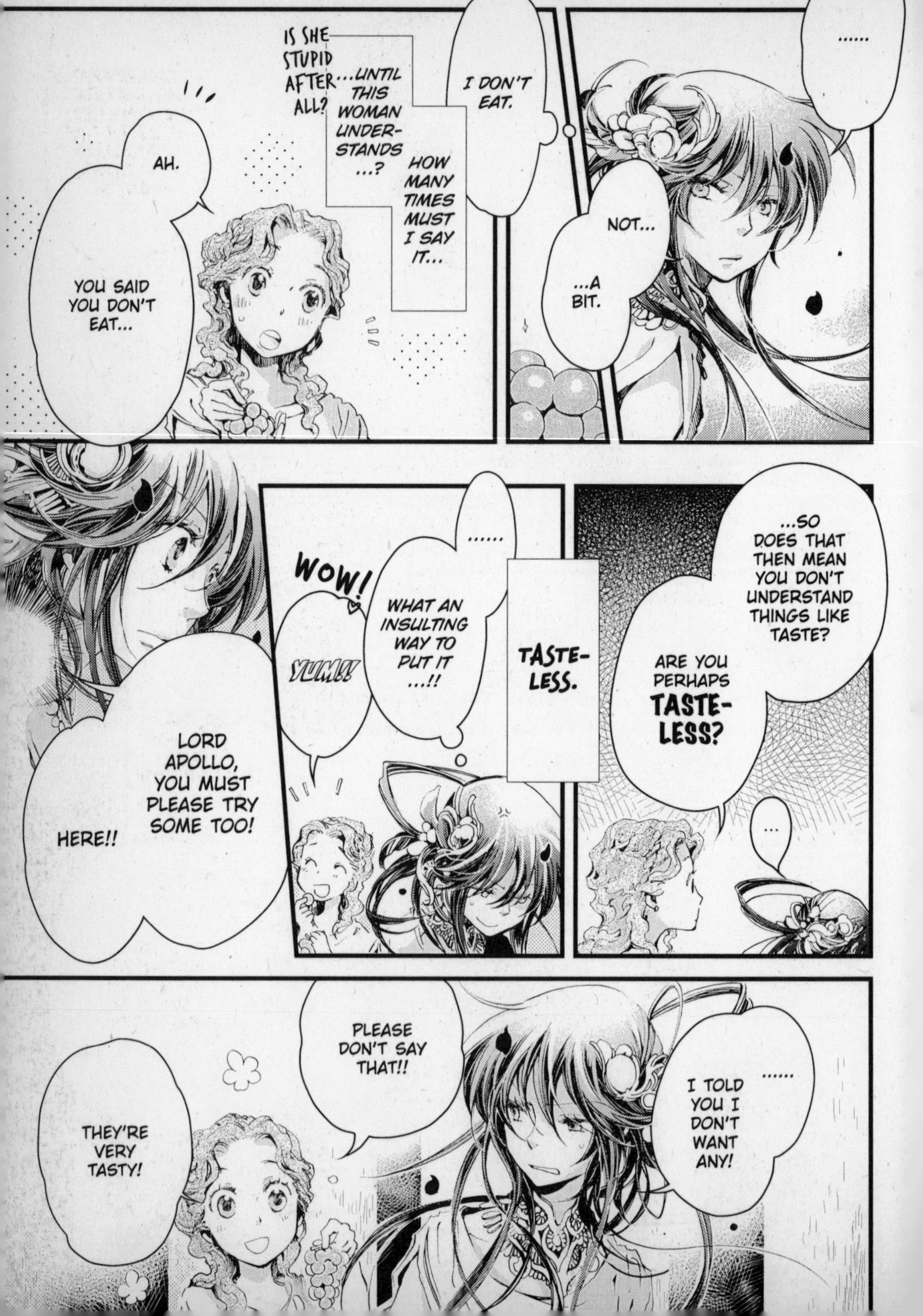
......
NOT...
...A BIT.
I DON'T EAT.
HOW MANY TIMES MUST I SAY IT...
...UNTIL THIS WOMAN UNDERSTANDS ...?
IS SHE STUPID AFTER ALL?
AH.
YOU SAID YOU DON'T EAT...
...SO DOES THAT THEN MEAN YOU DON'T UNDERSTAND THINGS LIKE TASTE?
ARE YOU PERHAPS **TASTE-LESS?**
...
TASTE-LESS.
......
WHAT AN INSULTING WAY TO PUT IT ...!!
WOW!
YUM!!
LORD APOLLO, YOU MUST PLEASE TRY SOME TOO!
HERE!!
......
I TOLD YOU I DON'T WANT ANY!
PLEASE DON'T SAY THAT!!
THEY'RE VERY TASTY!

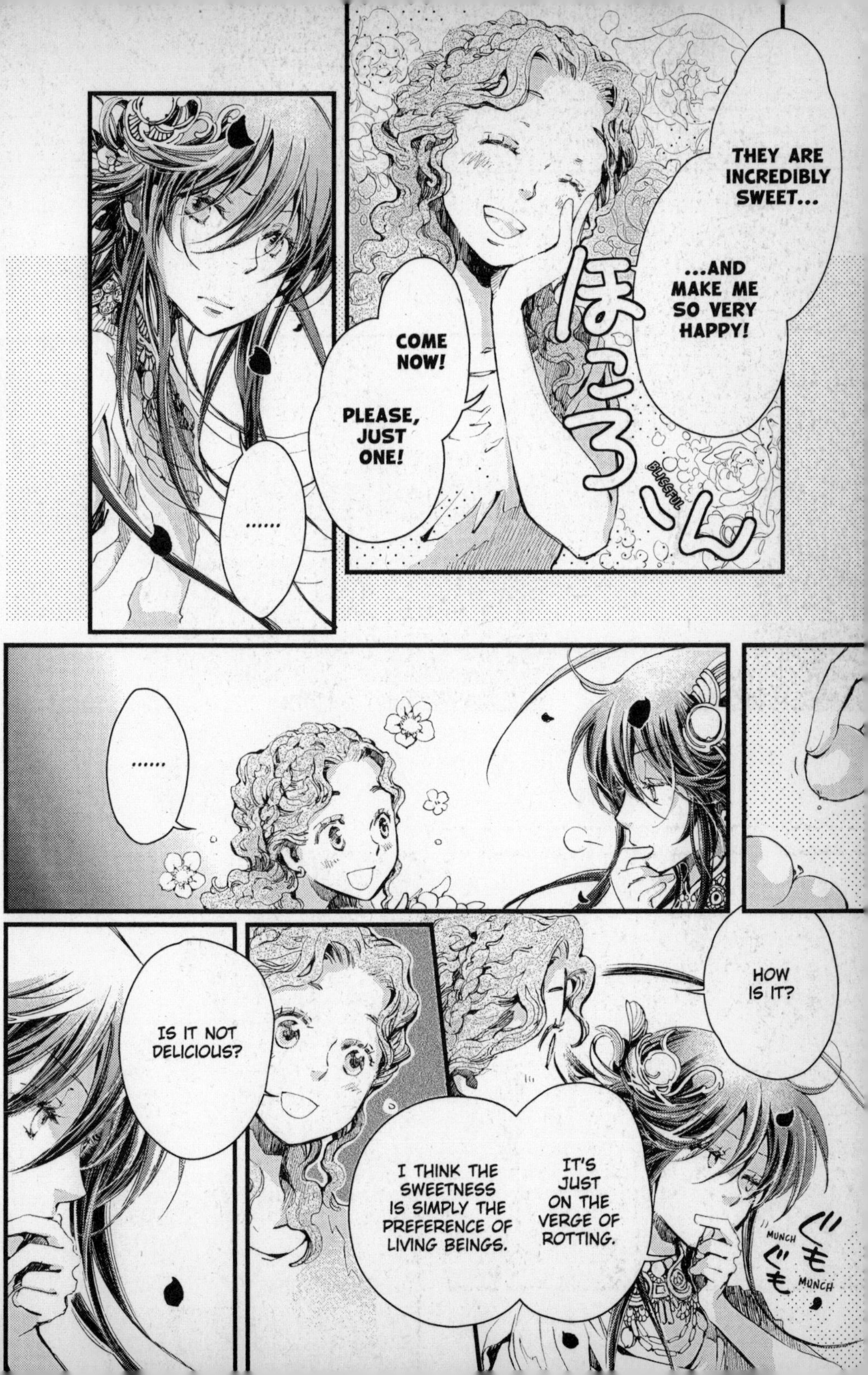
THEY ARE INCREDIBLY SWEET...
...AND MAKE ME SO VERY HAPPY!
ほっこりん
BLISSFUL
COME NOW!
PLEASE, JUST ONE!
......
......
HOW IS IT?
もぐもぐ
MUNCH MUNCH
IT'S JUST ON THE VERGE OF ROTTING.
I THINK THE SWEETNESS IS SIMPLY THE PREFERENCE OF LIVING BEINGS.
IS IT NOT DELICIOUS?

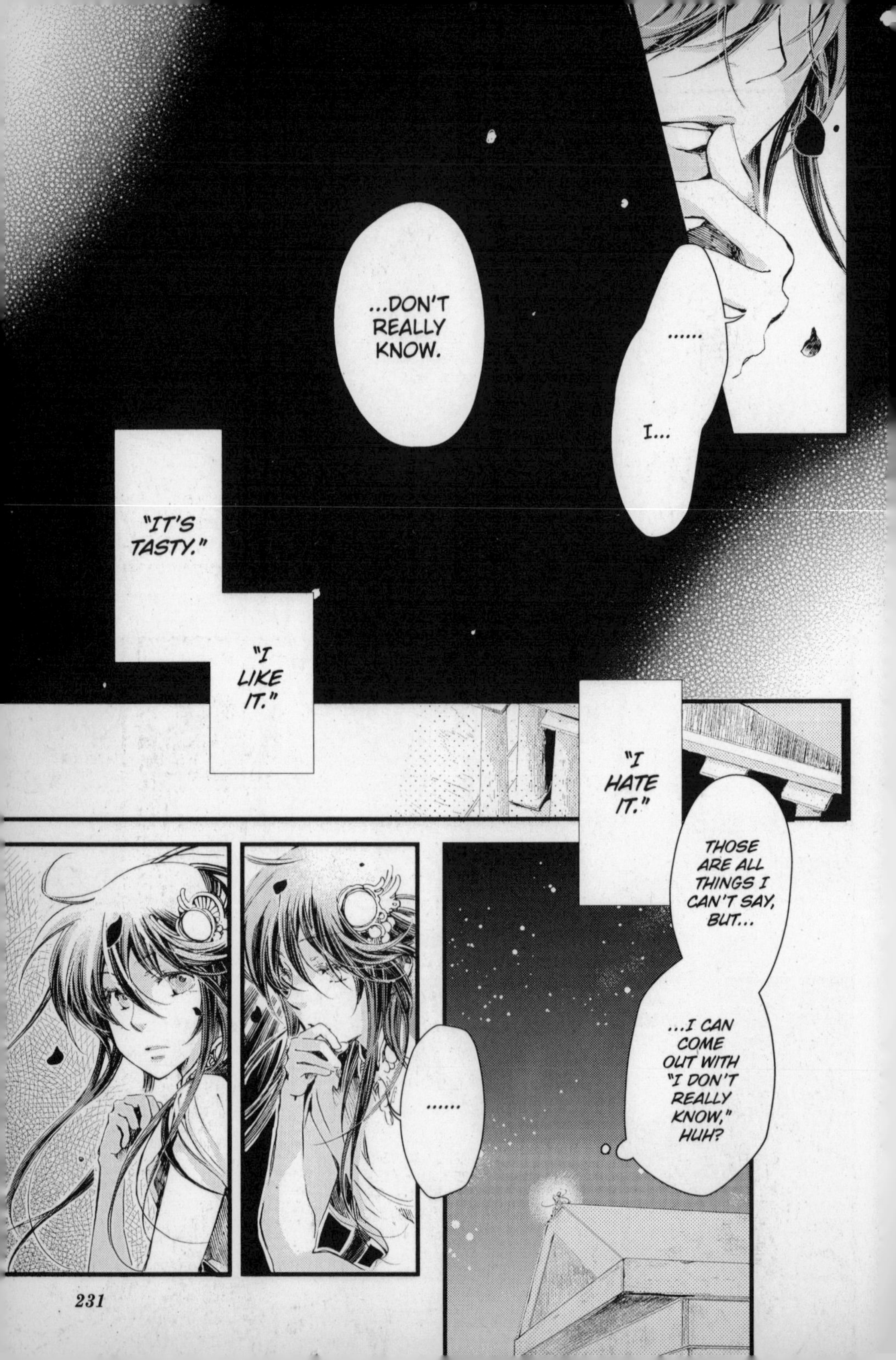
......
I...
...DON'T REALLY KNOW.
"IT'S TASTY."
"I LIKE IT."
"I HATE IT."
THOSE ARE ALL THINGS I CAN'T SAY, BUT...
...I CAN COME OUT WITH "I DON'T REALLY KNOW," HUH?
......

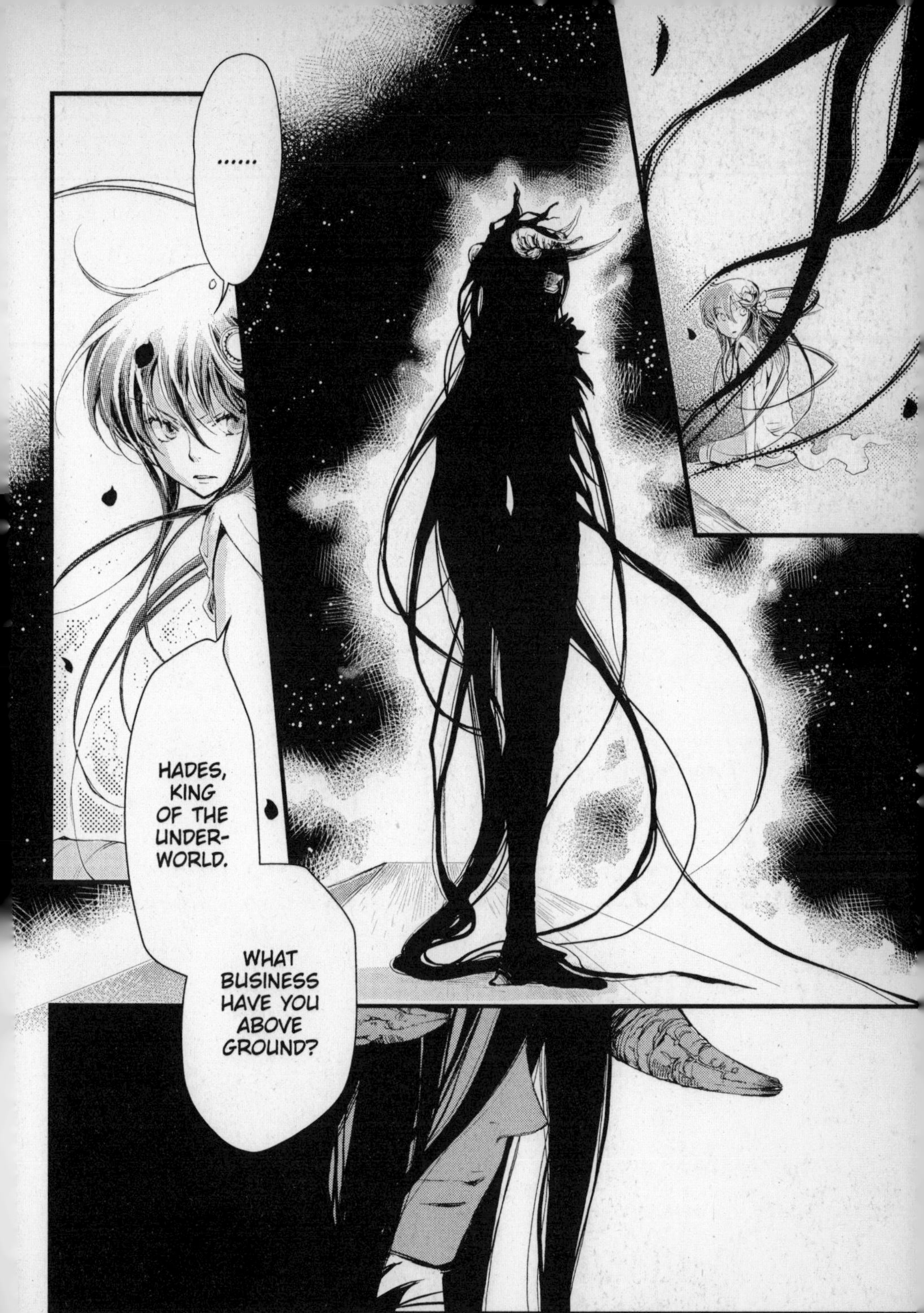
......
HADES, KING OF THE UNDER-WORLD.
WHAT BUSINESS HAVE YOU ABOVE GROUND?

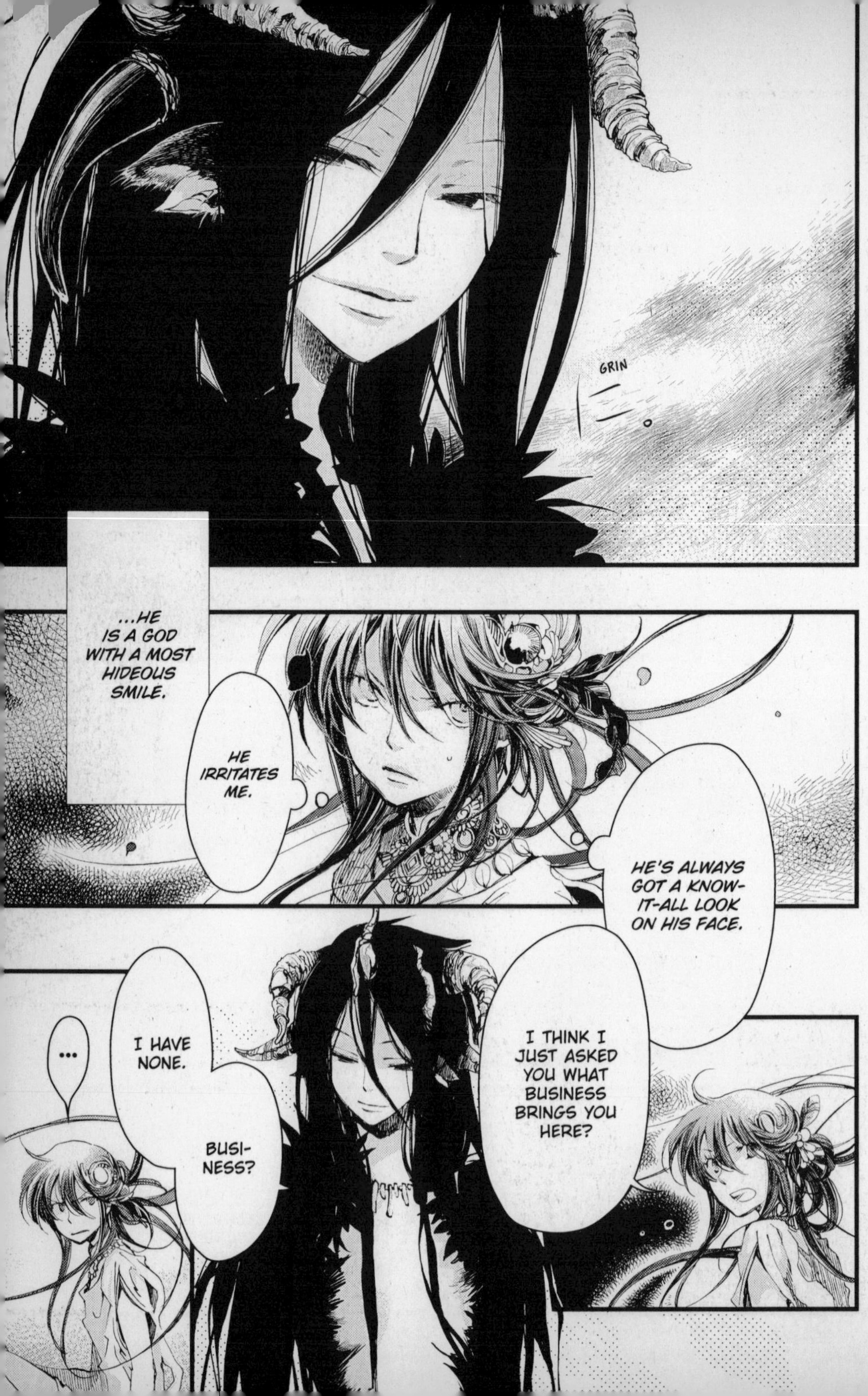
GRIN
...HE IS A GOD WITH A MOST HIDEOUS SMILE.
HE'S ALWAYS GOT A KNOW-IT-ALL LOOK ON HIS FACE.
HE IRRITATES ME.
I THINK I JUST ASKED YOU WHAT BUSINESS BRINGS YOU HERE?
BUSI-NESS?
I HAVE NONE.
...

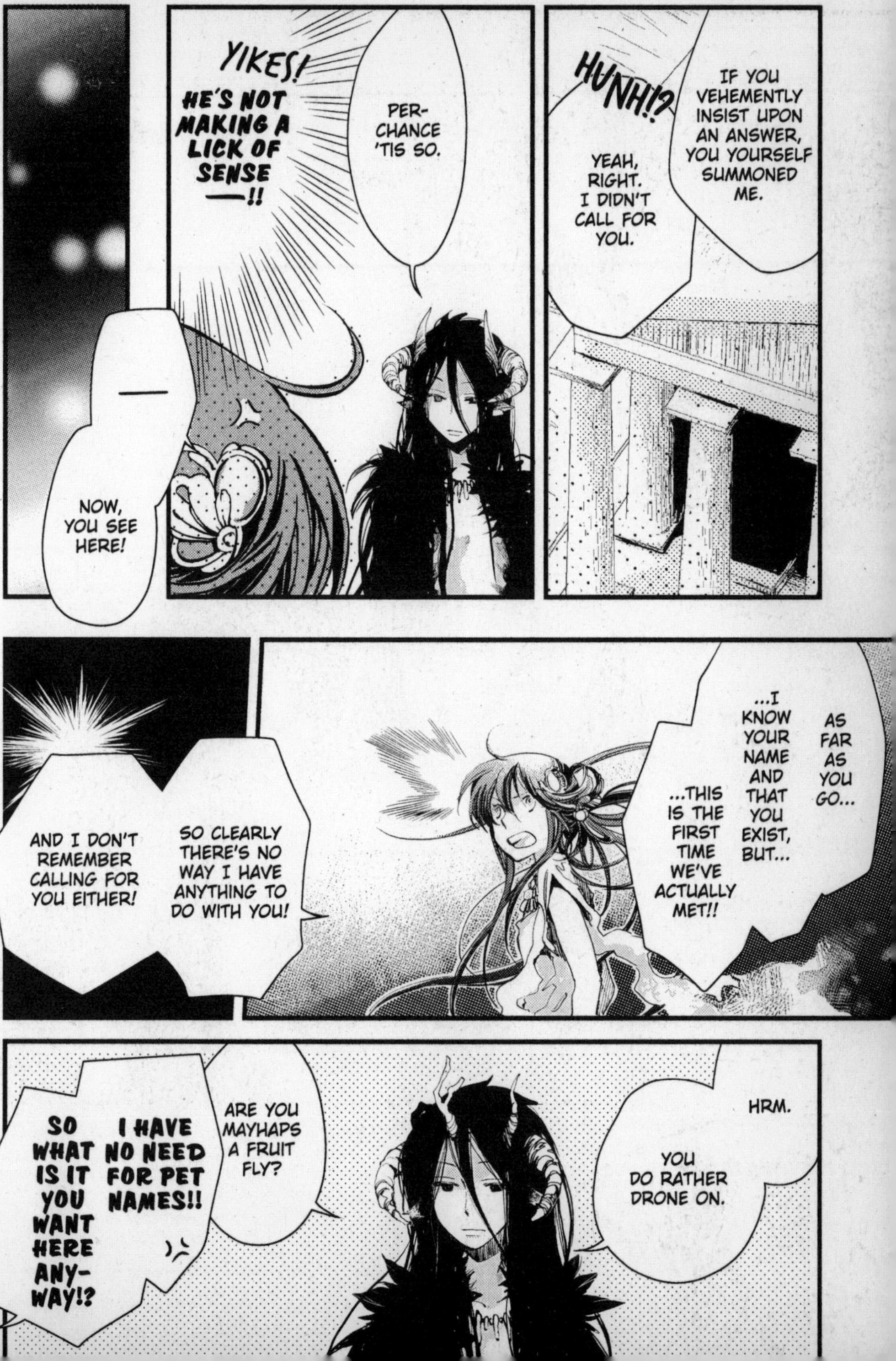
IF YOU VEHEMENTLY INSIST UPON AN ANSWER, YOU YOURSELF SUMMONED ME.
HUNH!?
YEAH, RIGHT. I DIDN'T CALL FOR YOU.
PER-CHANCE 'TIS SO.
YIKES!
HE'S NOT MAKING A LICK OF SENSE —!!
—
NOW, YOU SEE HERE!
AS FAR AS YOU GO...
...I KNOW YOUR NAME AND THAT YOU EXIST, BUT...
...THIS IS THE FIRST TIME WE'VE ACTUALLY MET!!
SO CLEARLY THERE'S NO WAY I HAVE ANYTHING TO DO WITH YOU!
AND I DON'T REMEMBER CALLING FOR YOU EITHER!
HRM.
YOU DO RATHER DRONE ON.
ARE YOU MAYHAPS A FRUIT FLY?
I HAVE NO NEED FOR PET NAMES!!
SO WHAT IS IT YOU WANT HERE ANY-WAY!?

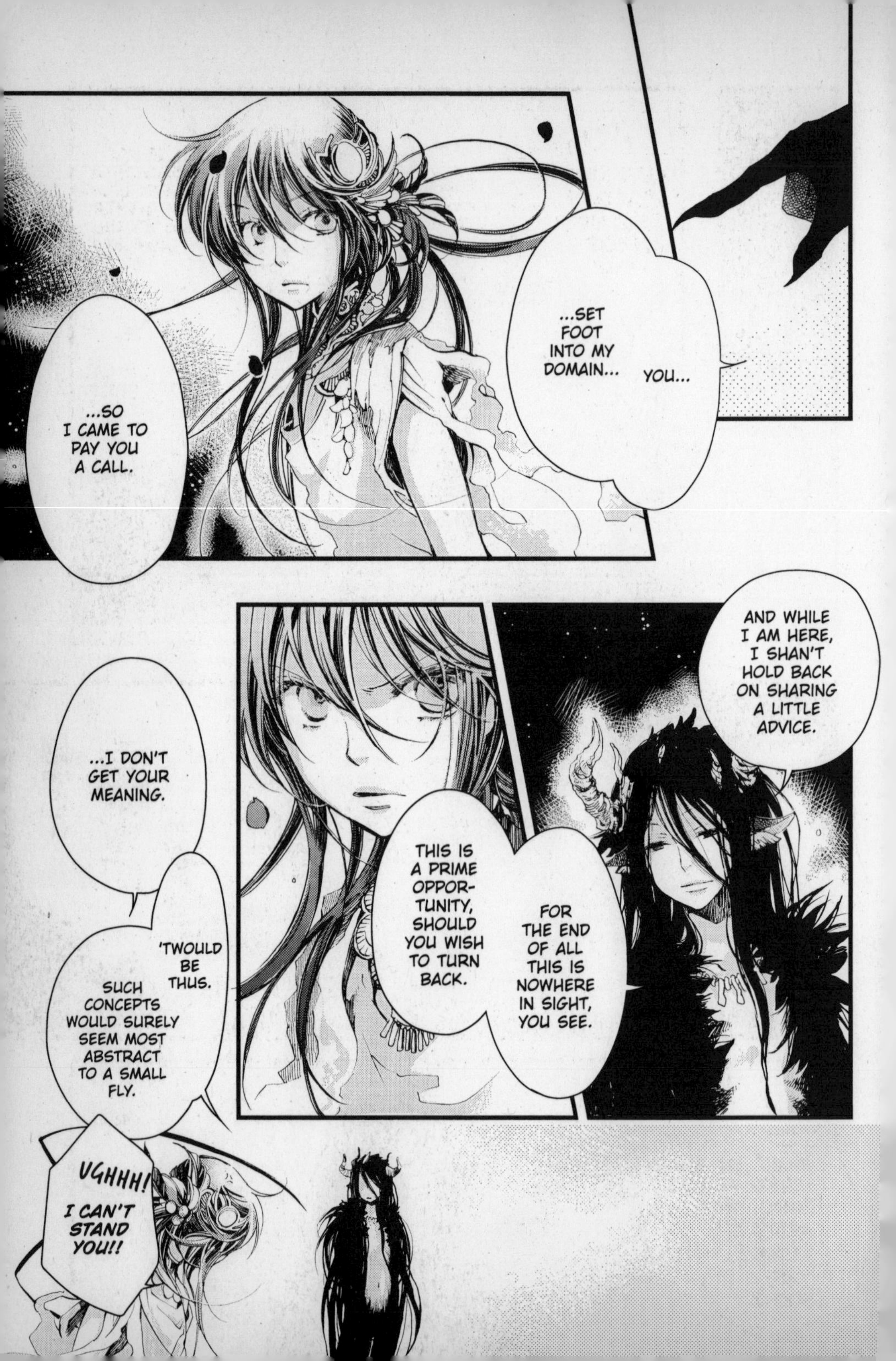

YOU...
...SET FOOT INTO MY DOMAIN...
...SO I CAME TO PAY YOU A CALL.
AND WHILE I AM HERE, I SHAN'T HOLD BACK ON SHARING A LITTLE ADVICE.
FOR THE END OF ALL THIS IS NOWHERE IN SIGHT, YOU SEE.
THIS IS A PRIME OPPOR-TUNITY, SHOULD YOU WISH TO TURN BACK.
...I DON'T GET YOUR MEANING.
'TWOULD BE THUS.
SUCH CONCEPTS WOULD SURELY SEEM MOST ABSTRACT TO A SMALL FLY.
UGHHH! I CAN'T STAND YOU!!

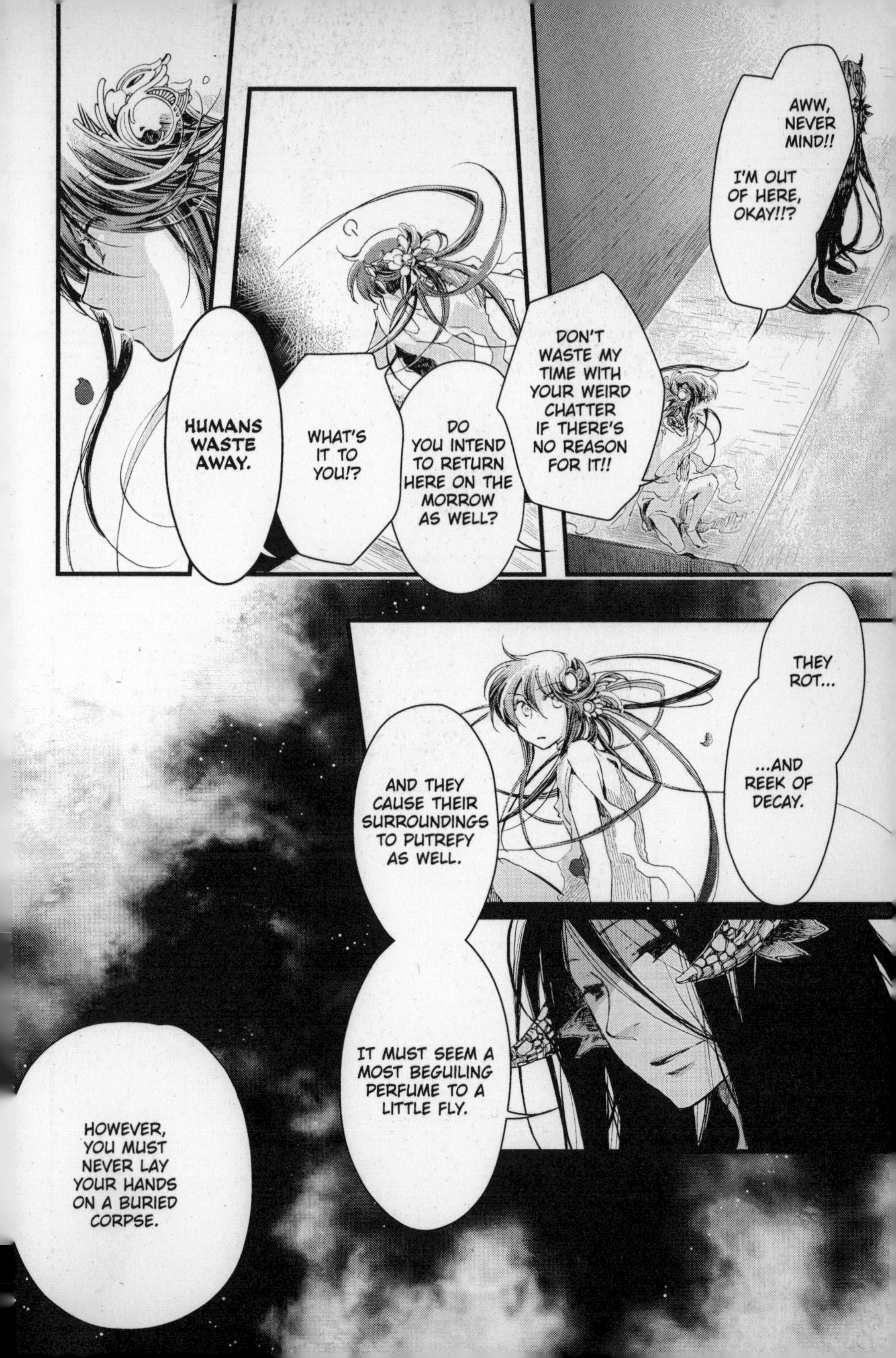
AWW, NEVER MIND!!
I'M OUT OF HERE, OKAY!!?
DON'T WASTE MY TIME WITH YOUR WEIRD CHATTER IF THERE'S NO REASON FOR IT!!
DO YOU INTEND TO RETURN HERE ON THE MORROW AS WELL?
WHAT'S IT TO YOU!?
HUMANS WASTE AWAY.
THEY ROT...
...AND REEK OF DECAY.
AND THEY CAUSE THEIR SURROUNDINGS TO PUTREFY AS WELL.
IT MUST SEEM A MOST BEGUILING PERFUME TO A LITTLE FLY.
HOWEVER, YOU MUST NEVER LAY YOUR HANDS ON A BURIED CORPSE.

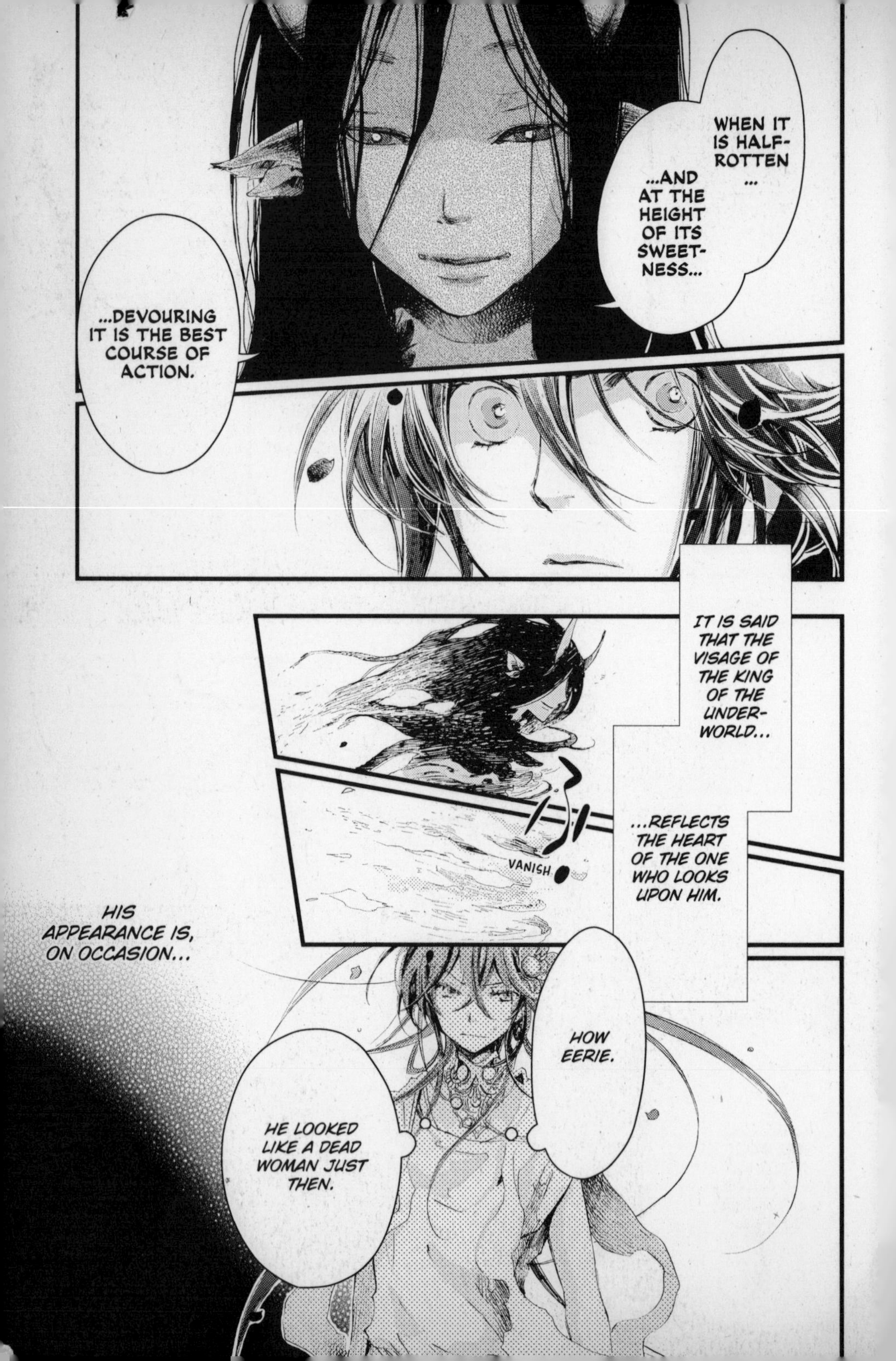
WHEN IT IS HALF-ROTTEN...
...AND AT THE HEIGHT OF ITS SWEETNESS...
...DEVOURING IT IS THE BEST COURSE OF ACTION.
IT IS SAID THAT THE VISAGE OF THE KING OF THE UNDERWORLD...
VANISH
...REFLECTS THE HEART OF THE ONE WHO LOOKS UPON HIM.
HIS APPEARANCE IS, ON OCCASION...
HOW EERIE.
HE LOOKED LIKE A DEAD WOMAN JUST THEN.

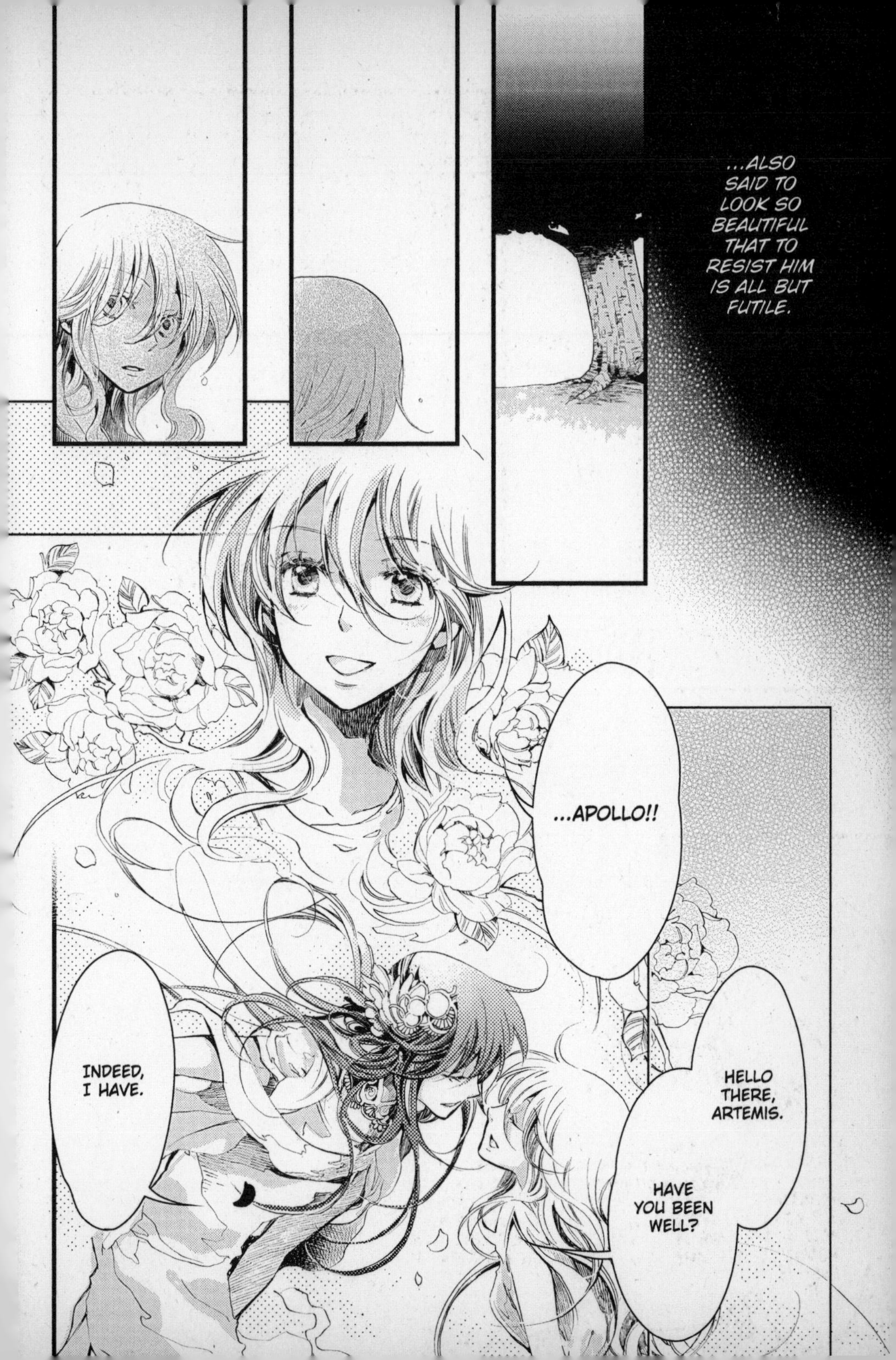

...ALSO SAID TO LOOK SO BEAUTIFUL THAT TO RESIST HIM IS ALL BUT FUTILE.
...APOLLO!!
HELLO THERE, ARTEMIS.
HAVE YOU BEEN WELL?
INDEED, I HAVE.

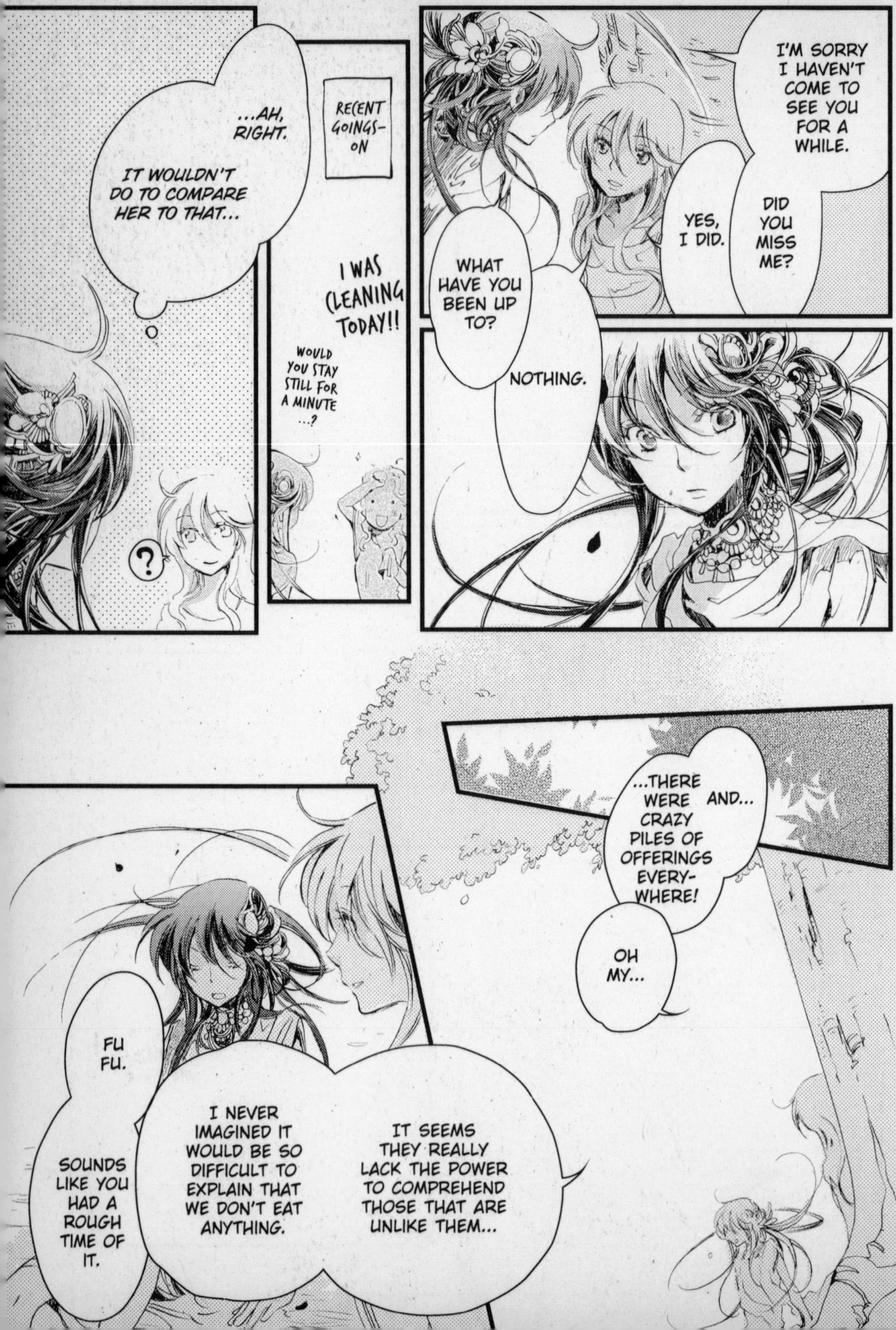

I'M SORRY I HAVEN'T COME TO SEE YOU FOR A WHILE.
DID YOU MISS ME?
YES, I DID.
WHAT HAVE YOU BEEN UP TO?
NOTHING.
RECENT GOINGS-ON
I WAS CLEANING TODAY!!
WOULD YOU STAY STILL FOR A MINUTE ...?
...AH, RIGHT.
IT WOULDN'T DO TO COMPARE HER TO THAT...
AND...
...THERE WERE CRAZY PILES OF OFFERINGS EVERY-WHERE!
OH MY...
IT SEEMS THEY REALLY LACK THE POWER TO COMPREHEND THOSE THAT ARE UNLIKE THEM...
I NEVER IMAGINED IT WOULD BE SO DIFFICULT TO EXPLAIN THAT WE DON'T EAT ANYTHING.
FU FU.
SOUNDS LIKE YOU HAD A ROUGH TIME OF IT.

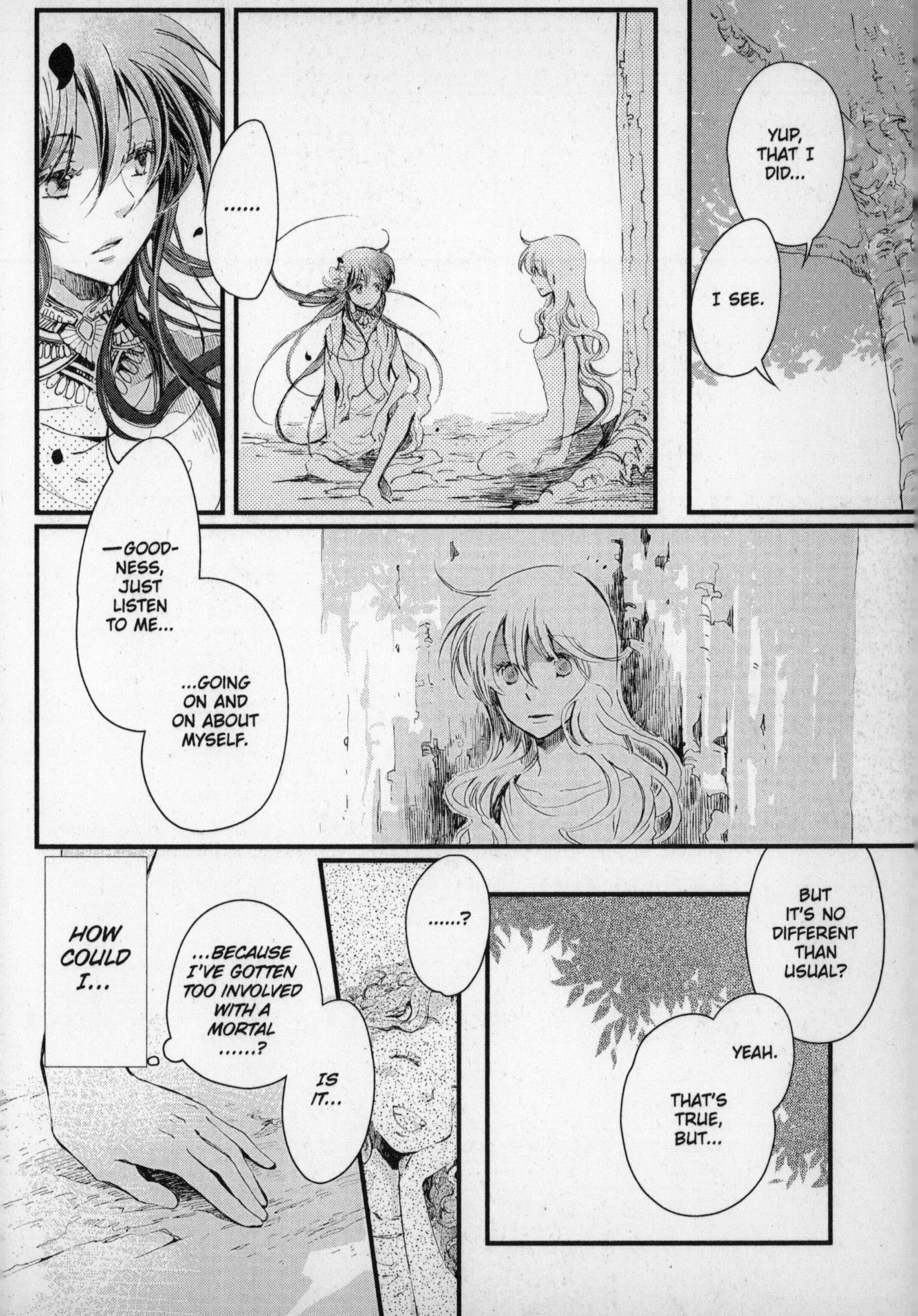
YUP, THAT I DID...
I SEE.
......
—GOOD-NESS, JUST LISTEN TO ME...
...GOING ON AND ON ABOUT MYSELF.
BUT IT'S NO DIFFERENT THAN USUAL?
YEAH.
THAT'S TRUE, BUT...
......?
IS IT...
...BECAUSE I'VE GOTTEN TOO INVOLVED WITH A MORTAL ......?
HOW COULD I...

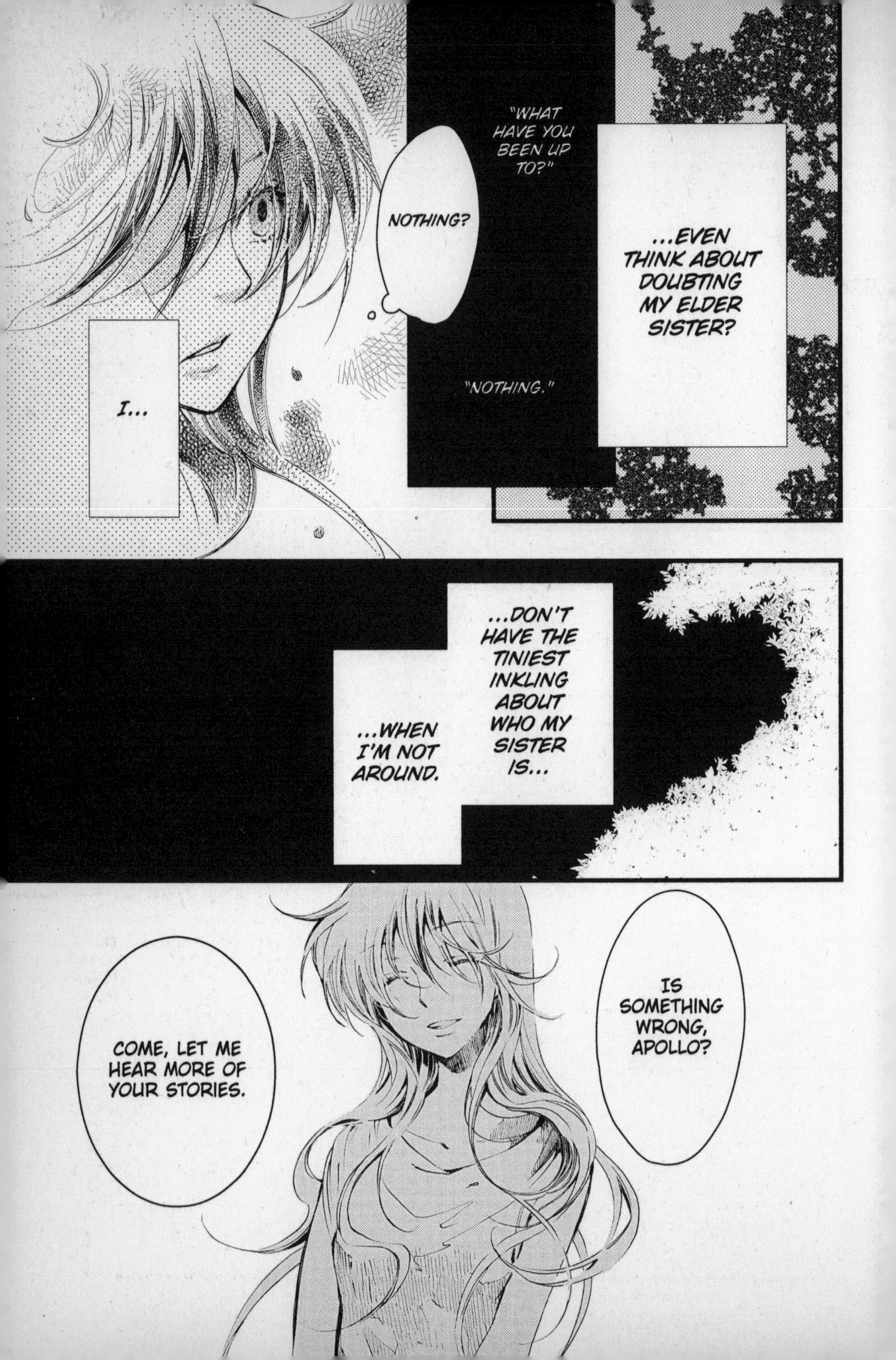
...EVEN THINK ABOUT DOUBTING MY ELDER SISTER?
"WHAT HAVE YOU BEEN UP TO?"
"NOTHING."
NOTHING?
I...
...DON'T HAVE THE TINIEST INKLING ABOUT WHO MY SISTER IS...
...WHEN I'M NOT AROUND.
IS SOMETHING WRONG, APOLLO?
COME, LET ME HEAR MORE OF YOUR STORIES.

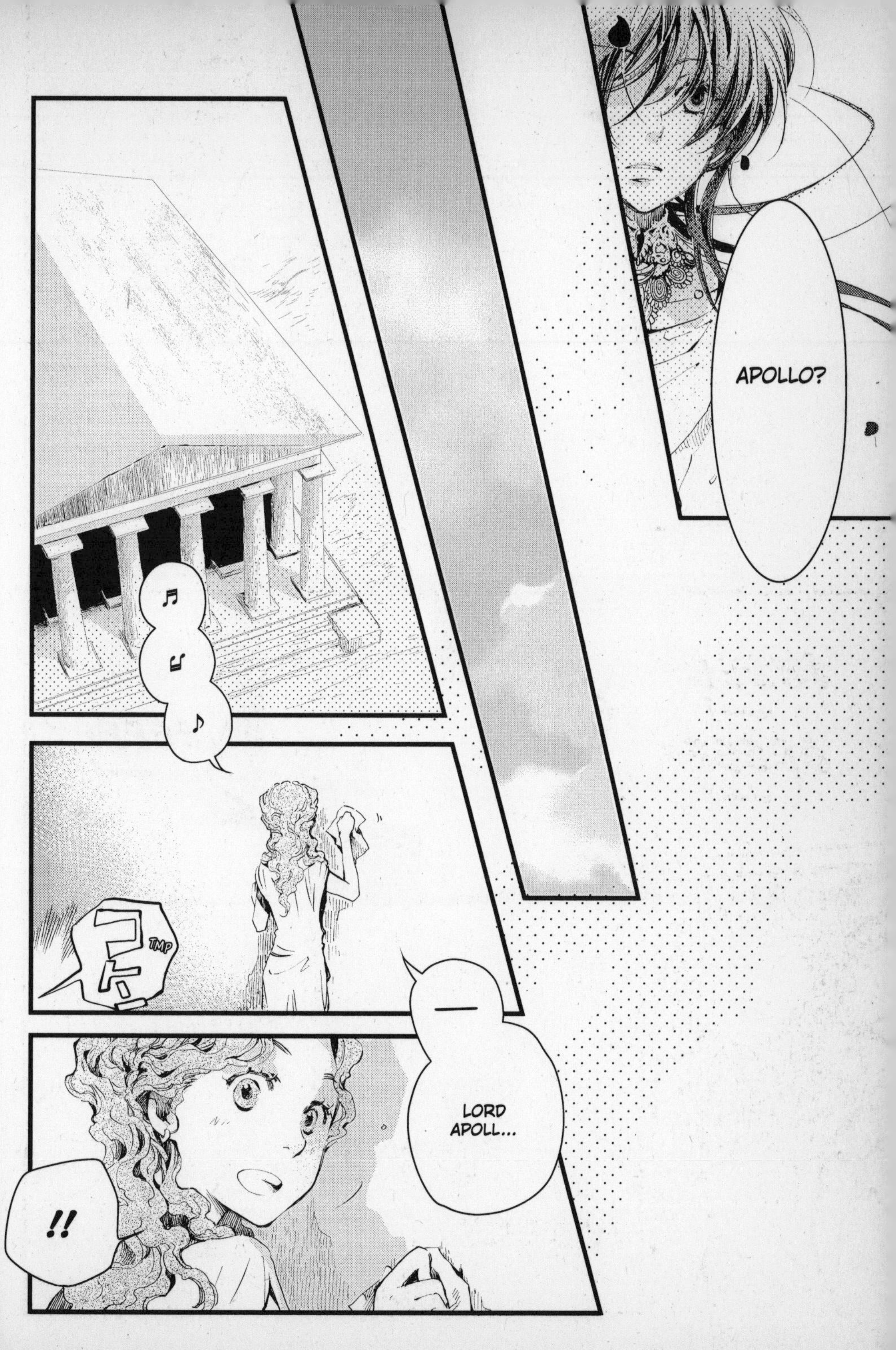
APOLLO?
♬ ♫ ♪
TMP
—
LORD APOLL...
!!

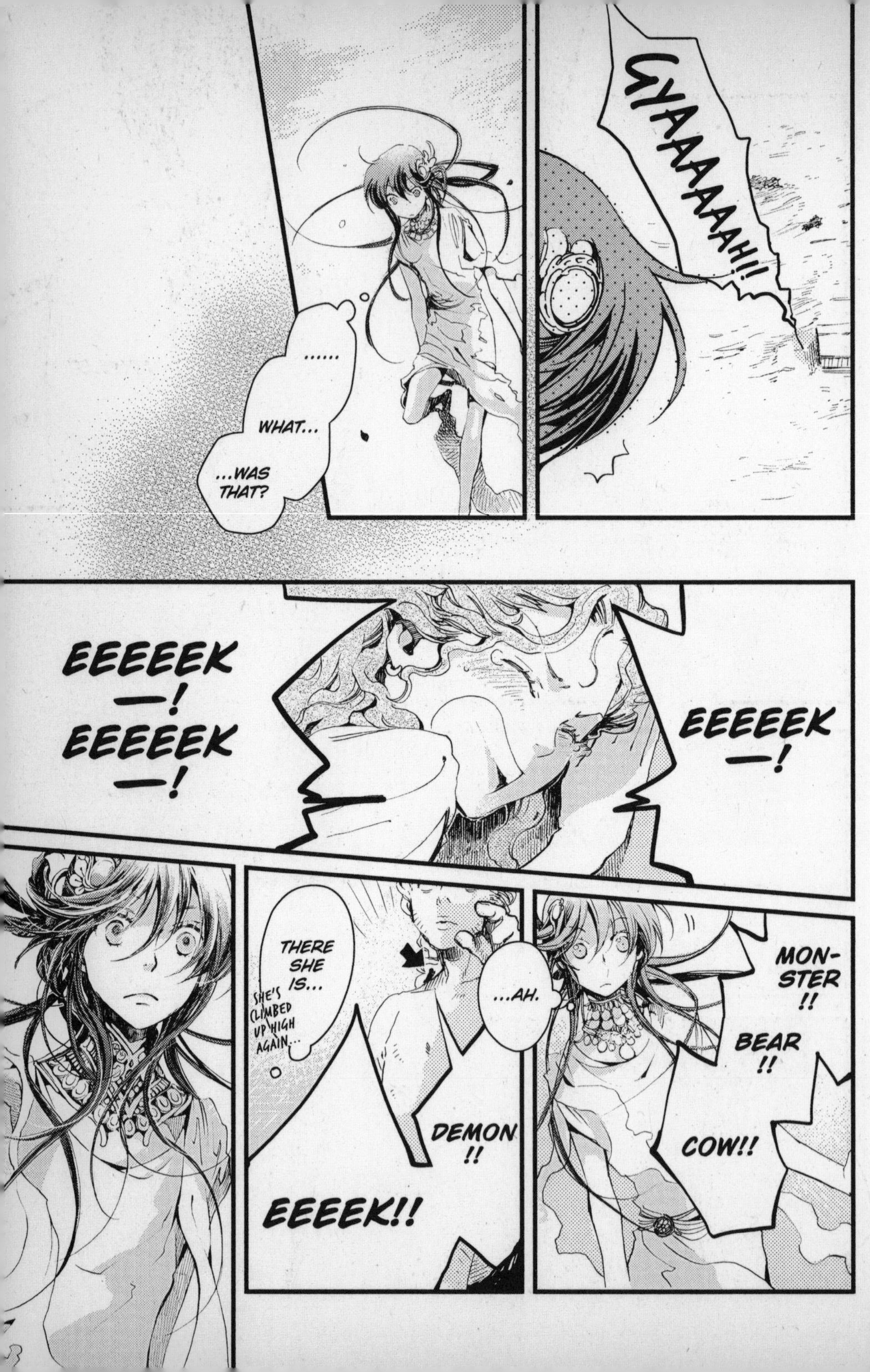
GYAAAAAAH!!
......
WHAT...
...WAS THAT?
EEEEEK—!
EEEEEK—! EEEEEK—!
MON-STER!!
BEAR!!
COW!!
...AH.
THERE SHE IS...
SHE'S CLIMBED UP HIGH AGAIN...
DEMON!!
EEEEK!!

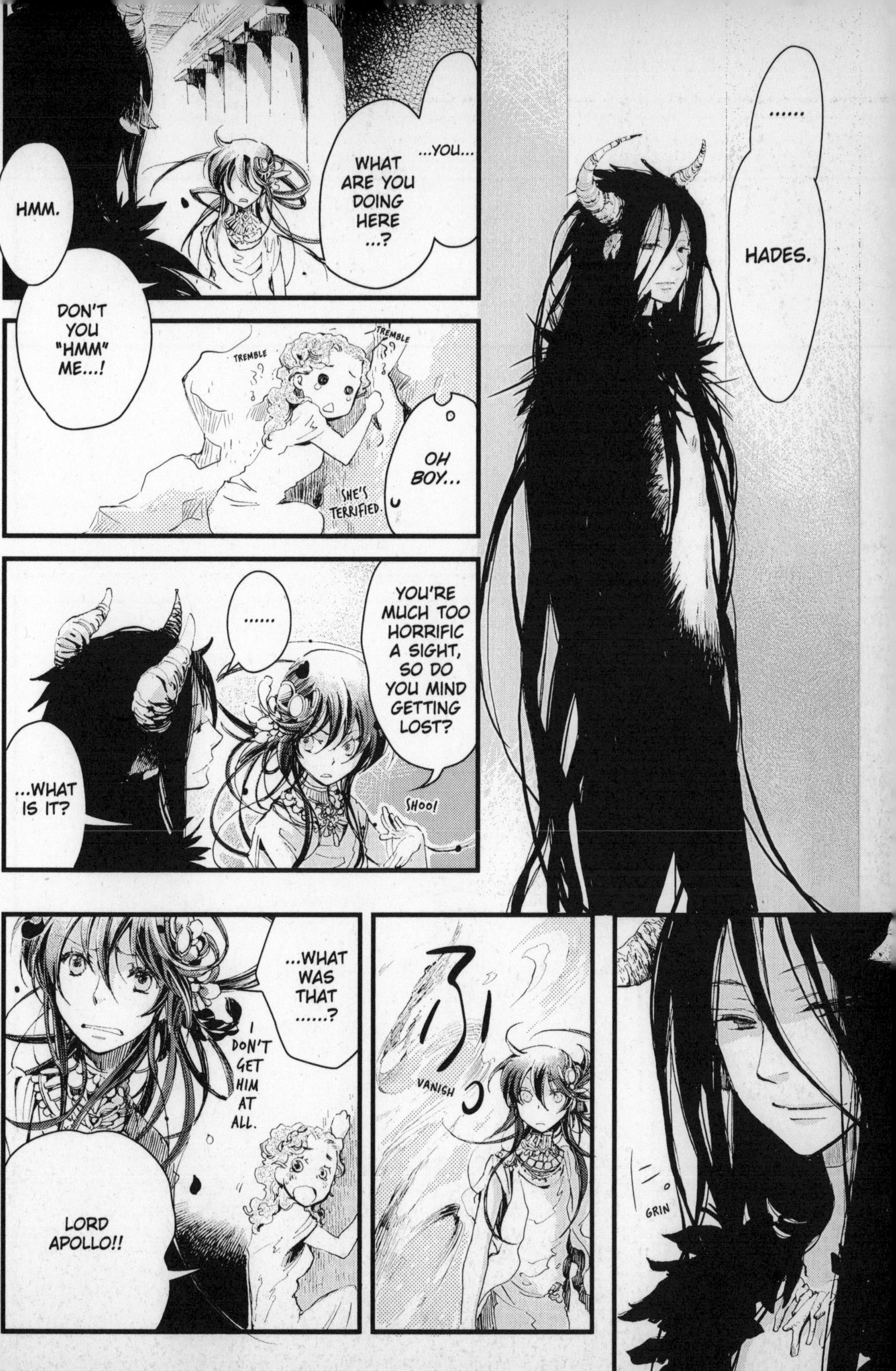

......
HADES.
...YOU...
WHAT ARE YOU DOING HERE ...?
HMM.
DON'T YOU "HMM" ME...!
TREMBLE
TREMBLE
OH BOY...
SHE'S TERRIFIED.
YOU'RE MUCH TOO HORRIFIC A SIGHT, SO DO YOU MIND GETTING LOST?
......
...WHAT IS IT?
SHOO!
GRIN
ふ
VANISH
...WHAT WAS THAT ......?
I DON'T GET HIM AT ALL.
LORD APOLLO!!

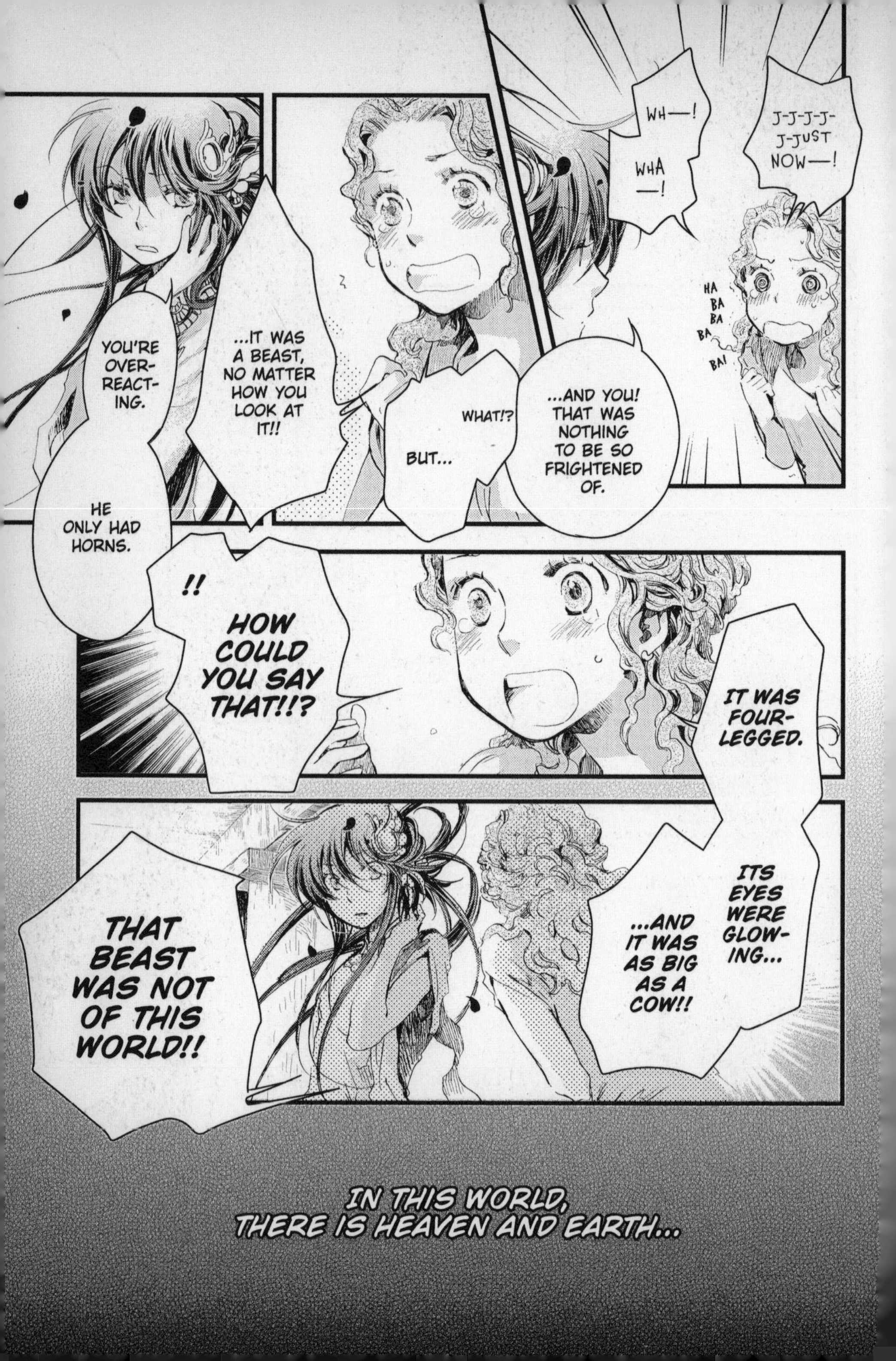
J-J-J-J-J-JUST NOW—!
HA BA BA BA BA!
WH—! WHA—!
...AND YOU! THAT WAS NOTHING TO BE SO FRIGHTENED OF.
WHAT!?
BUT...
...IT WAS A BEAST, NO MATTER HOW YOU LOOK AT IT!!
YOU'RE OVER-REACTING.
HE ONLY HAD HORNS.
!! HOW COULD YOU SAY THAT!!?
IT WAS FOUR-LEGGED.
ITS EYES WERE GLOWING...
...AND IT WAS AS BIG AS A COW!!
THAT BEAST WAS NOT OF THIS WORLD!!
IN THIS WORLD, THERE IS HEAVEN AND EARTH...

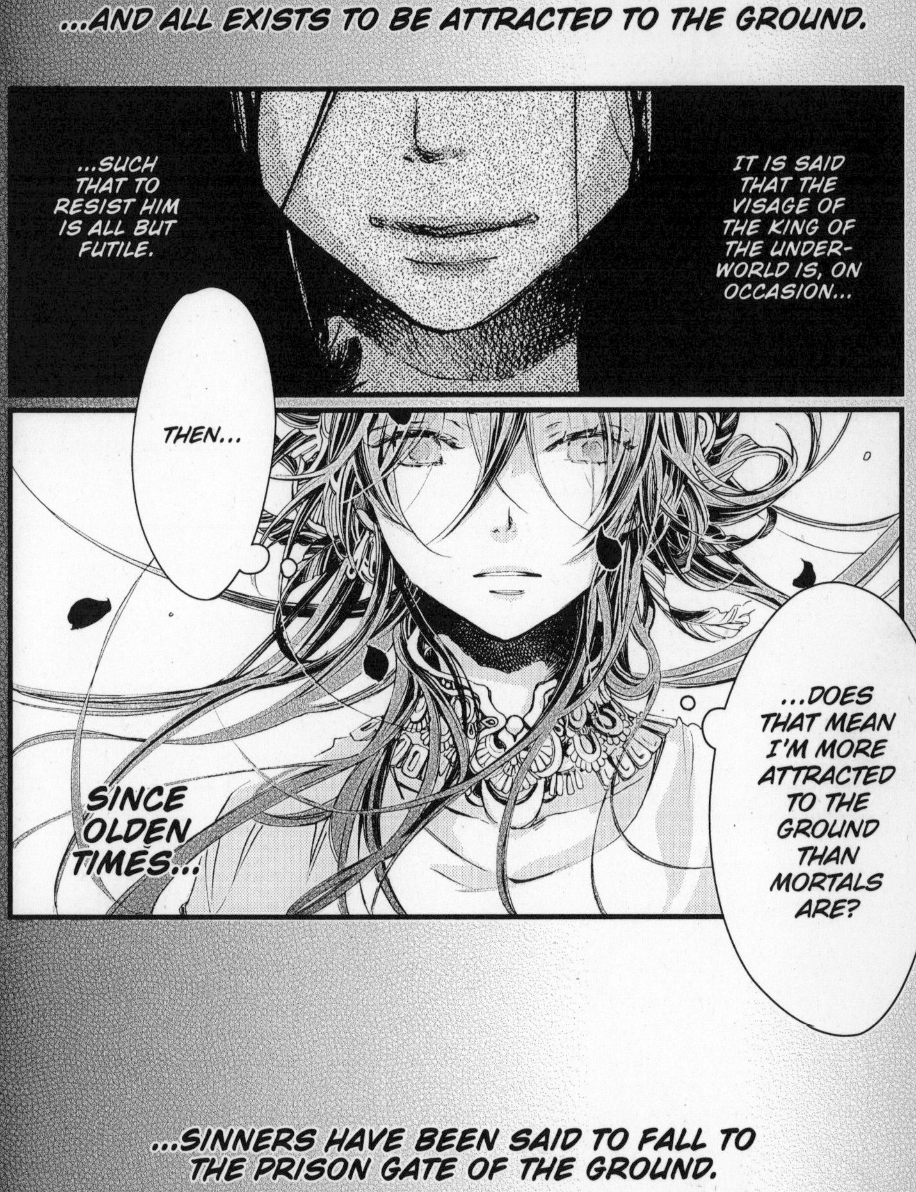
...AND ALL EXISTS TO BE ATTRACTED TO THE GROUND.
IT IS SAID THAT THE VISAGE OF THE KING OF THE UNDER-WORLD IS, ON OCCASION...
...SUCH THAT TO RESIST HIM IS ALL BUT FUTILE.
THEN...
...DOES THAT MEAN I'M MORE ATTRACTED TO THE GROUND THAN MORTALS ARE?
SINCE OLDEN TIMES...
...SINNERS HAVE BEEN SAID TO FALL TO THE PRISON GATE OF THE GROUND.

Olympos

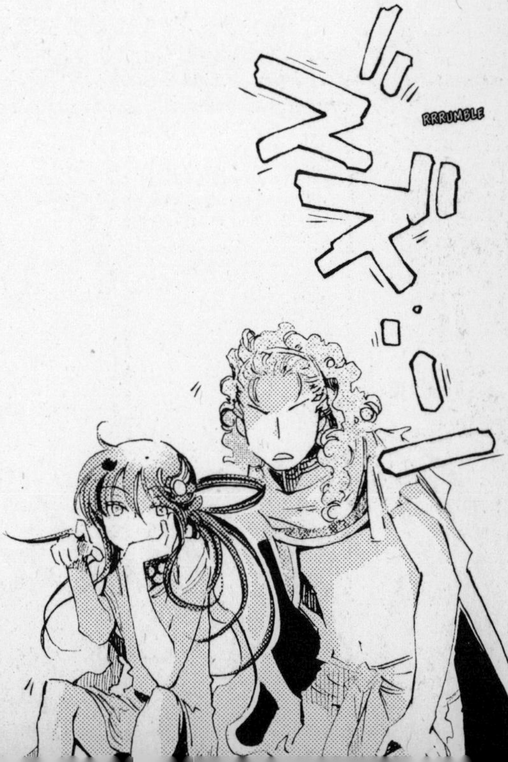

ズズ…ン
RRRUMBLE

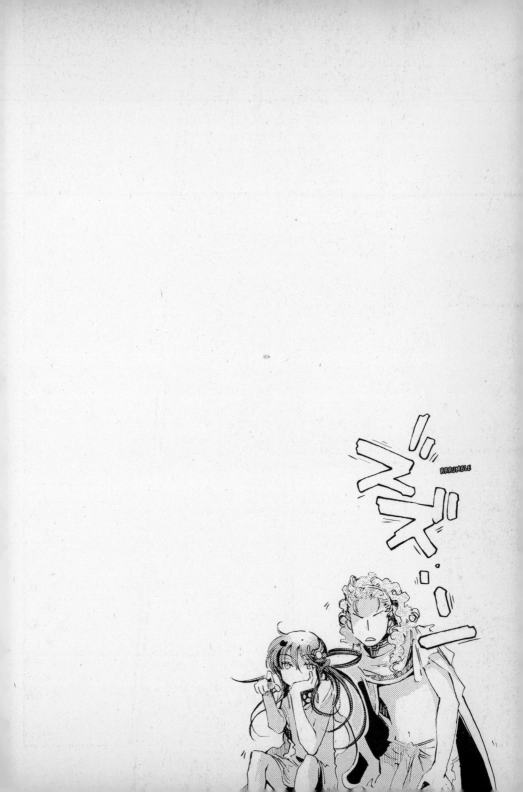

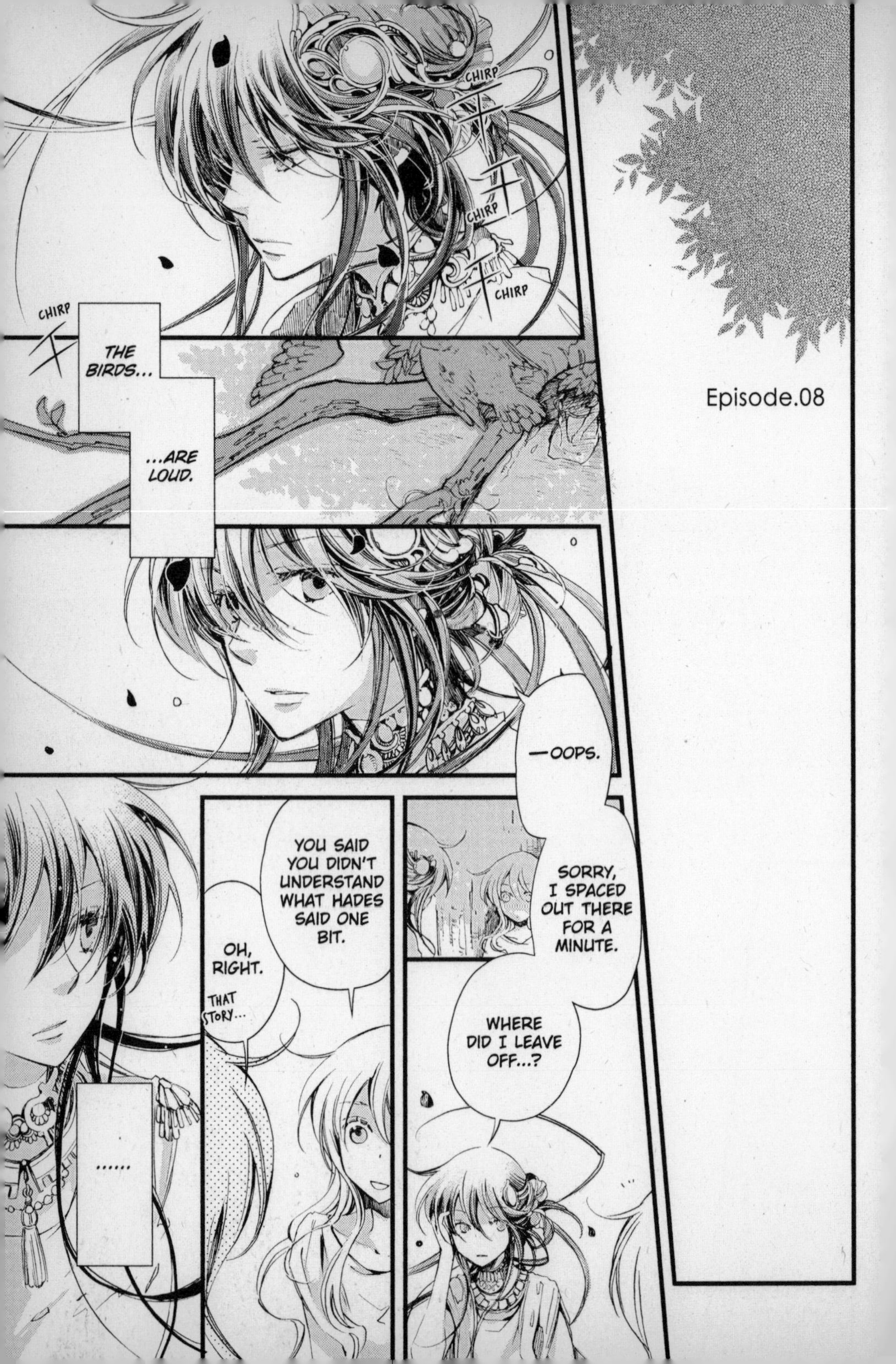
Episode.08
CHIRP
CHIRP
CHIRP
CHIRP
THE BIRDS...
...ARE LOUD.
—OOPS.
SORRY, I SPACED OUT THERE FOR A MINUTE.
WHERE DID I LEAVE OFF...?
YOU SAID YOU DIDN'T UNDERSTAND WHAT HADES SAID ONE BIT.
OH, RIGHT.
THAT STORY...
......

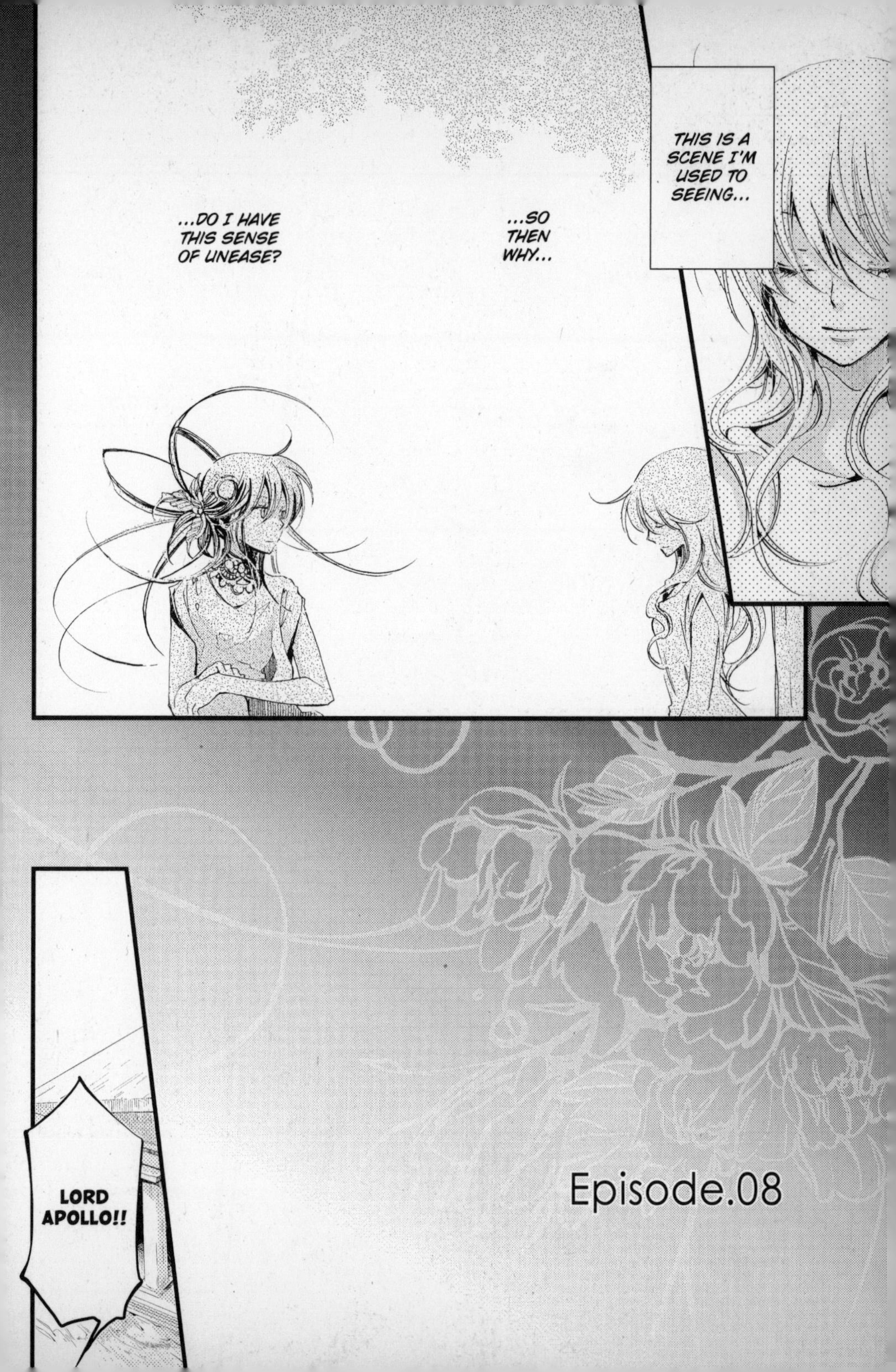
THIS IS A SCENE I'M USED TO SEEING...
...SO THEN WHY...
...DO I HAVE THIS SENSE OF UNEASE?
Episode.08
LORD APOLLO!!

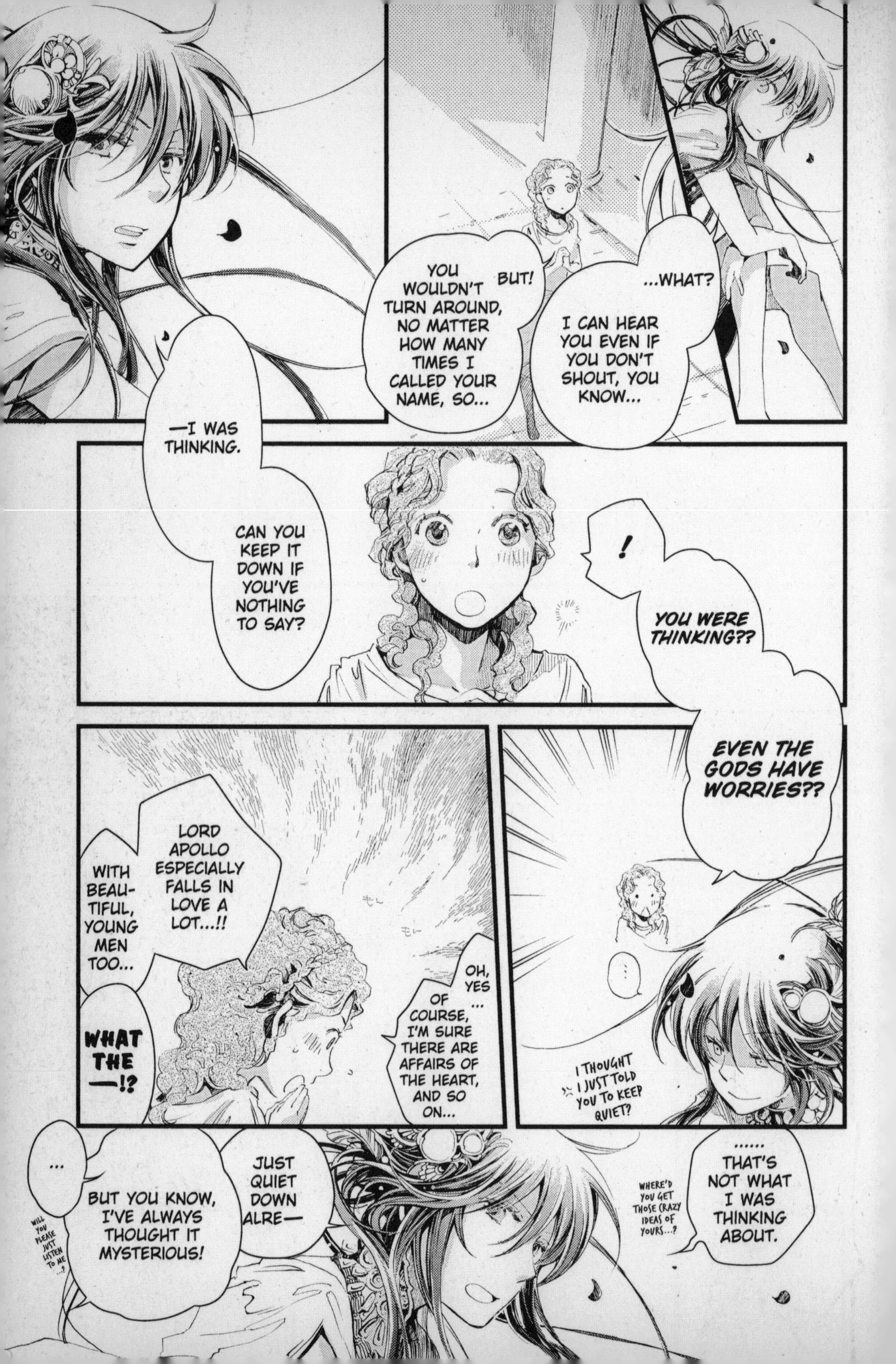
...WHAT?
I CAN HEAR YOU EVEN IF YOU DON'T SHOUT, YOU KNOW...
BUT!
YOU WOULDN'T TURN AROUND, NO MATTER HOW MANY TIMES I CALLED YOUR NAME, SO...
—I WAS THINKING.
CAN YOU KEEP IT DOWN IF YOU'VE NOTHING TO SAY?
!
YOU WERE THINKING??
EVEN THE GODS HAVE WORRIES??
...
I THOUGHT I JUST TOLD YOU TO KEEP QUIET?
OH, YES... OF COURSE, I'M SURE THERE ARE AFFAIRS OF THE HEART, AND SO ON...
LORD APOLLO ESPECIALLY FALLS IN LOVE A LOT...!!
WITH BEAU-TIFUL, YOUNG MEN TOO...
WHAT THE—!?
...... THAT'S NOT WHAT I WAS THINKING ABOUT.
WHERE'D YOU GET THOSE CRAZY IDEAS OF YOURS...?
JUST QUIET DOWN ALRE—
...
BUT YOU KNOW, I'VE ALWAYS THOUGHT IT MYSTERIOUS!
WILL YOU PLEASE JUST LISTEN TO ME...?

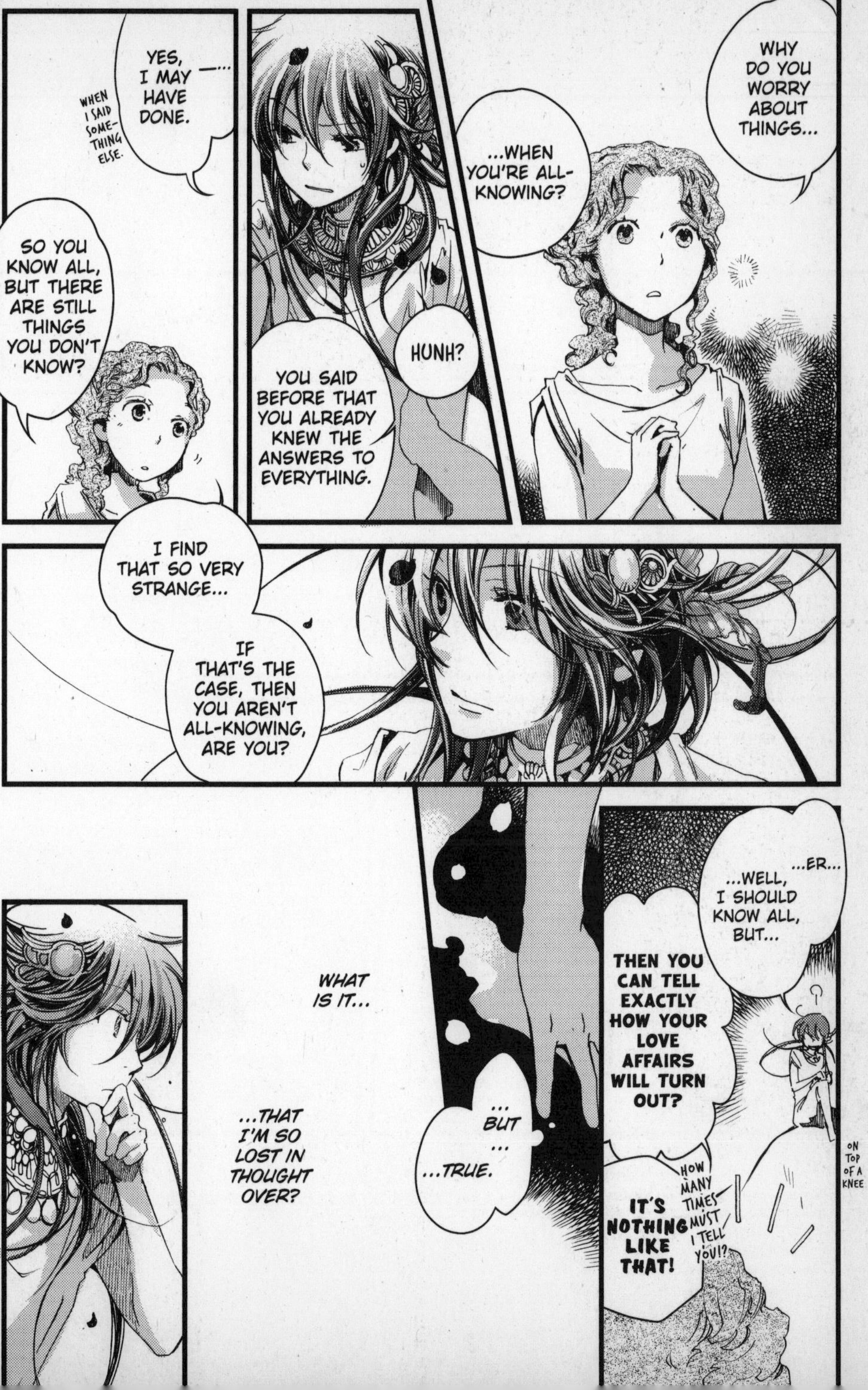
WHY DO YOU WORRY ABOUT THINGS...
...WHEN YOU'RE ALL-KNOWING?
HUNH?
YOU SAID BEFORE THAT YOU ALREADY KNEW THE ANSWERS TO EVERYTHING.
YES, I MAY HAVE DONE. —...
WHEN I SAID SOMETHING ELSE.
SO YOU KNOW ALL, BUT THERE ARE STILL THINGS YOU DON'T KNOW?
I FIND THAT SO VERY STRANGE...
IF THAT'S THE CASE, THEN YOU AREN'T ALL-KNOWING, ARE YOU?
...ER...
...WELL, I SHOULD KNOW ALL, BUT...
THEN YOU CAN TELL EXACTLY HOW YOUR LOVE AFFAIRS WILL TURN OUT?
IT'S NOTHING LIKE THAT!
HOW MANY TIMES MUST I TELL YOU!?
ON TOP OF A KNEE
... BUT ...
...TRUE.
WHAT IS IT...
...THAT I'M SO LOST IN THOUGHT OVER?

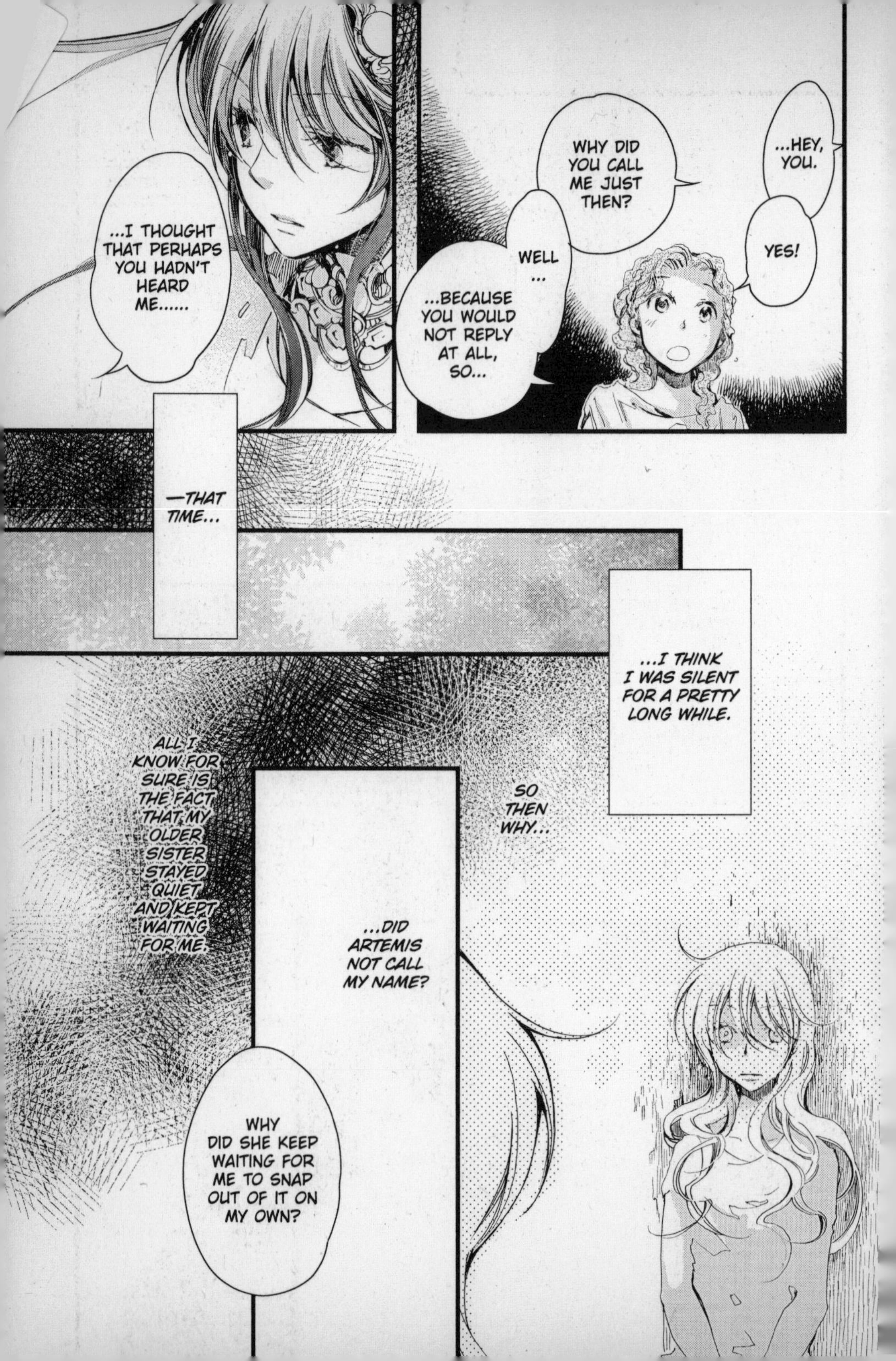
...HEY, YOU.
YES!
WHY DID YOU CALL ME JUST THEN?
WELL...
...BECAUSE YOU WOULD NOT REPLY AT ALL, SO...
...I THOUGHT THAT PERHAPS YOU HADN'T HEARD ME......
—THAT TIME...
...I THINK I WAS SILENT FOR A PRETTY LONG WHILE.
SO THEN WHY...
...DID ARTEMIS NOT CALL MY NAME?
ALL I KNOW FOR SURE IS THE FACT THAT MY OLDER SISTER STAYED QUIET AND KEPT WAITING FOR ME.
WHY DID SHE KEEP WAITING FOR ME TO SNAP OUT OF IT ON MY OWN?

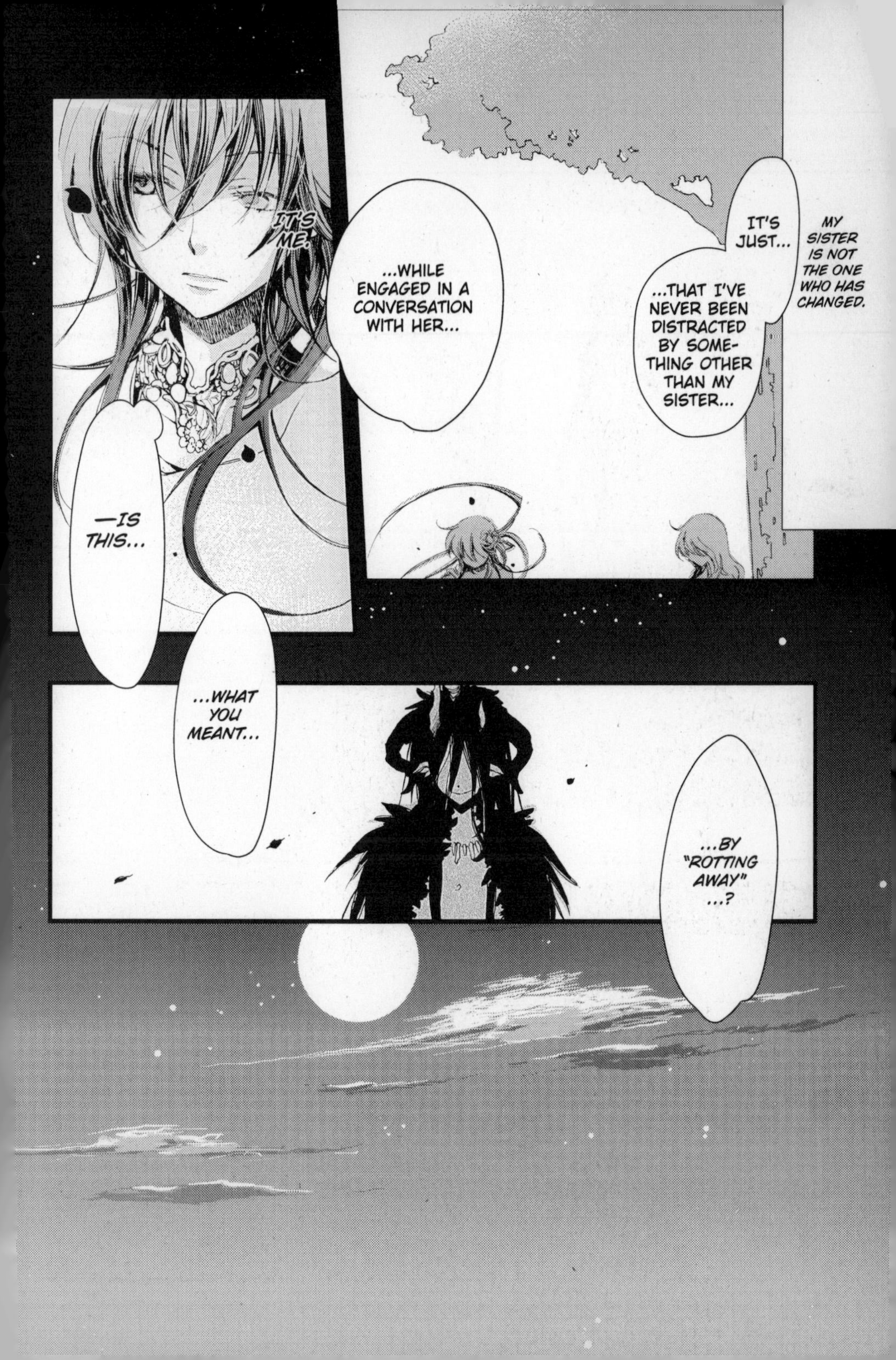
MY SISTER IS NOT THE ONE WHO HAS CHANGED.
IT'S JUST...
...THAT I'VE NEVER BEEN DISTRACTED BY SOME-THING OTHER THAN MY SISTER...
...WHILE ENGAGED IN A CONVERSATION WITH HER...
IT'S ME.
—IS THIS...
...WHAT YOU MEANT...
...BY "ROTTING AWAY" ...?

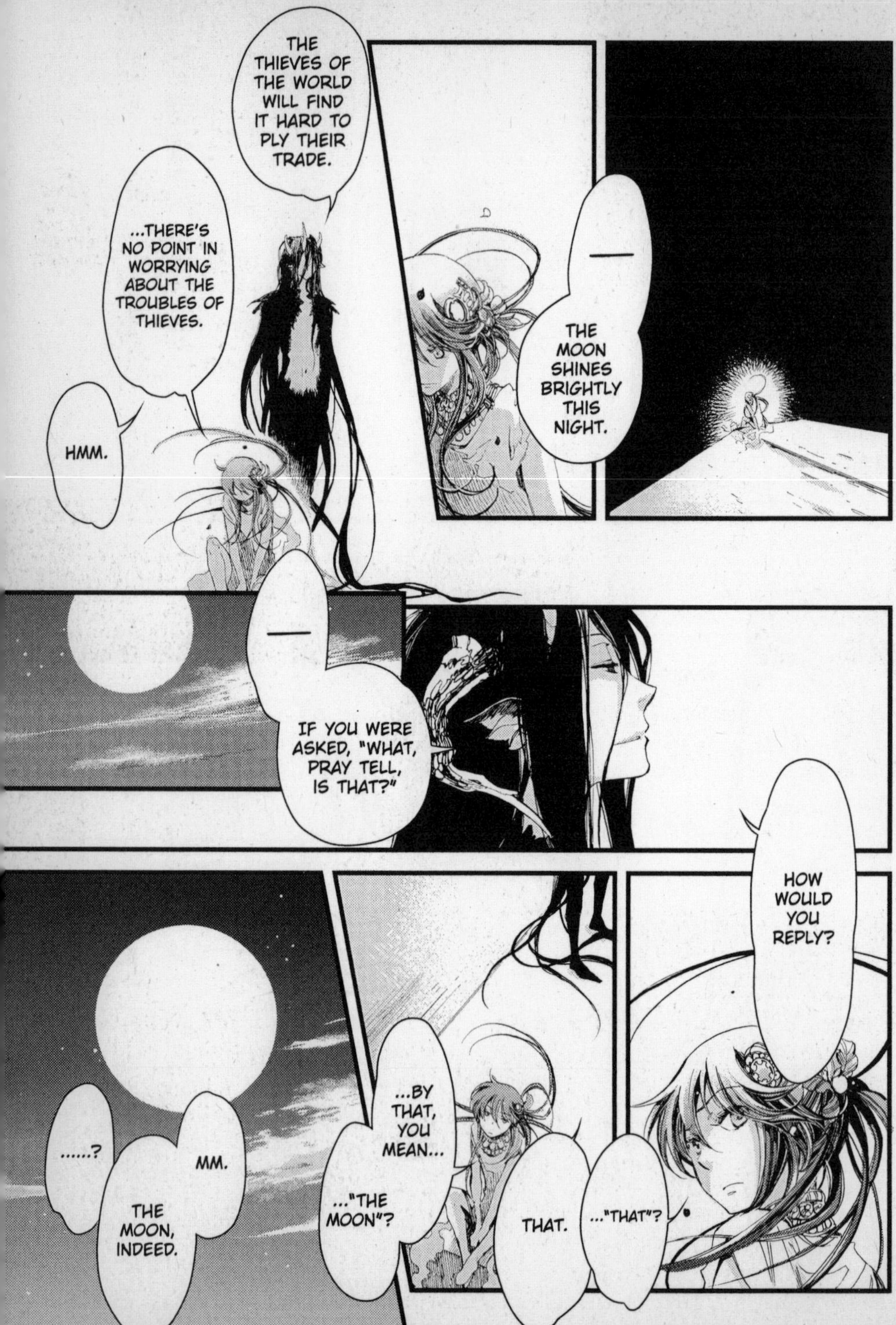
—
THE MOON SHINES BRIGHTLY THIS NIGHT.
THE THIEVES OF THE WORLD WILL FIND IT HARD TO PLY THEIR TRADE.
...THERE'S NO POINT IN WORRYING ABOUT THE TROUBLES OF THIEVES.
HMM.
—
IF YOU WERE ASKED, "WHAT, PRAY TELL, IS THAT?"
HOW WOULD YOU REPLY?
..."THAT"?
THAT.
...BY THAT, YOU MEAN...
..."THE MOON"?
MM.
THE MOON, INDEED.
......?

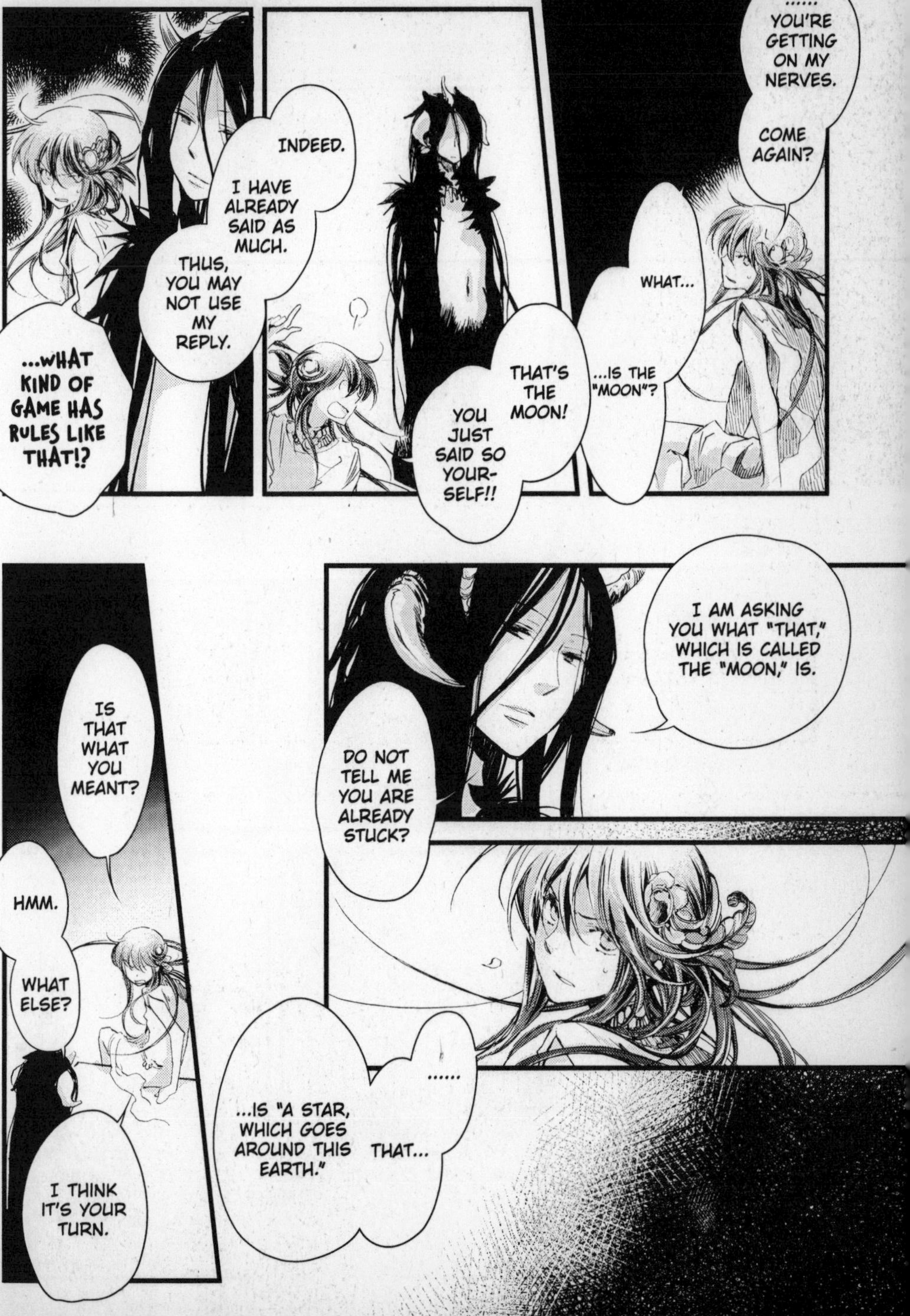

...... YOU'RE GETTING ON MY NERVES.
COME AGAIN?
WHAT...
...IS THE "MOON"?
THAT'S THE MOON!
YOU JUST SAID SO YOURSELF!!
INDEED.
I HAVE ALREADY SAID AS MUCH.
THUS, YOU MAY NOT USE MY REPLY.
...WHAT KIND OF GAME HAS RULES LIKE THAT!?
I AM ASKING YOU WHAT "THAT," WHICH IS CALLED THE "MOON," IS.
DO NOT TELL ME YOU ARE ALREADY STUCK?
......
THAT...
...IS "A STAR, WHICH GOES AROUND THIS EARTH."
IS THAT WHAT YOU MEANT?
HMM.
WHAT ELSE?
I THINK IT'S YOUR TURN.

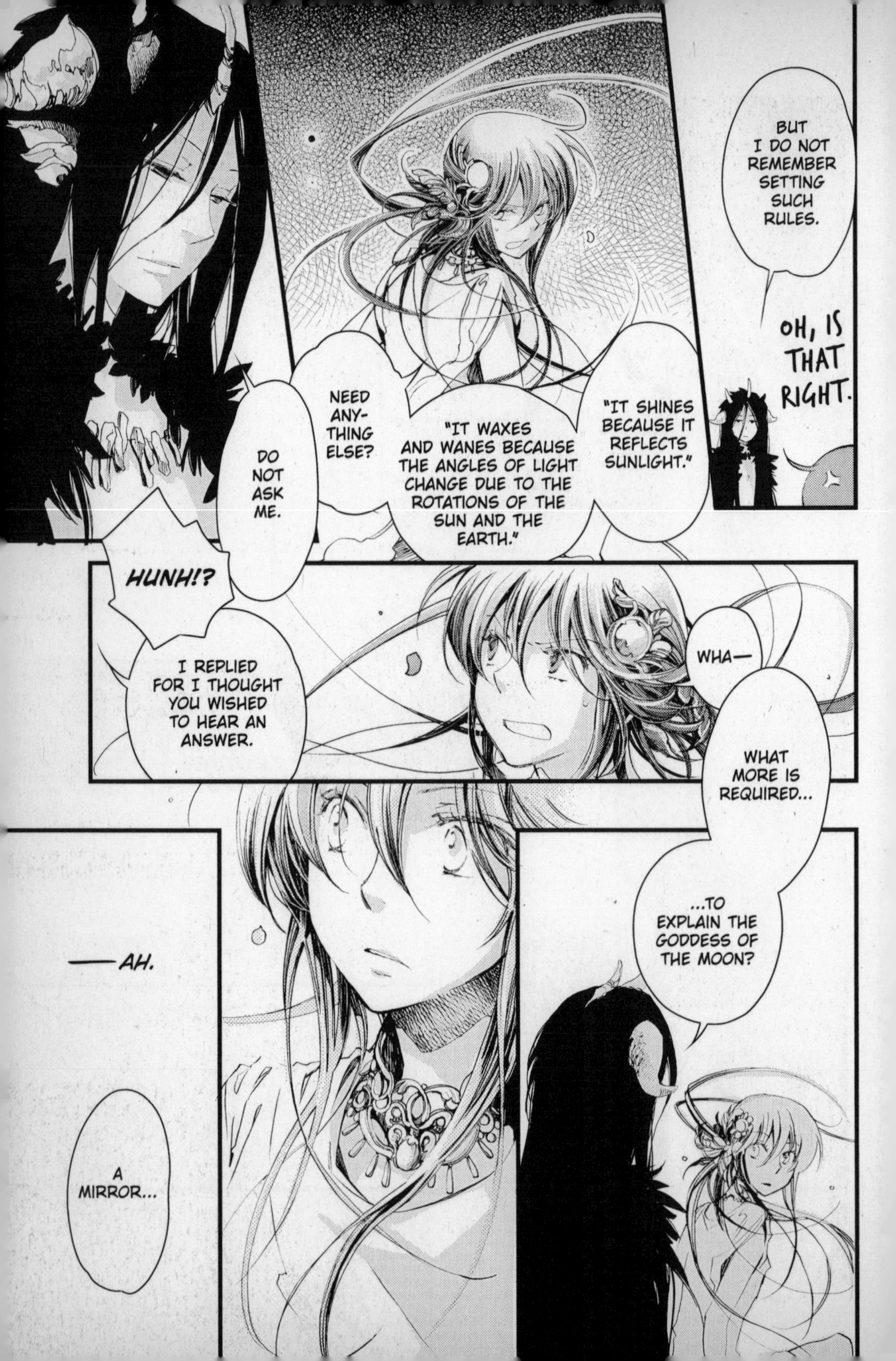
BUT I DO NOT REMEMBER SETTING SUCH RULES.
OH, IS THAT RIGHT.
"IT SHINES BECAUSE IT REFLECTS SUNLIGHT."
"IT WAXES AND WANES BECAUSE THE ANGLES OF LIGHT CHANGE DUE TO THE ROTATIONS OF THE SUN AND THE EARTH."
NEED ANYTHING ELSE?
DO NOT ASK ME.
HUNH!?
I REPLIED FOR I THOUGHT YOU WISHED TO HEAR AN ANSWER.
WHA—
WHAT MORE IS REQUIRED...
...TO EXPLAIN THE GODDESS OF THE MOON?
—AH.
A MIRROR...

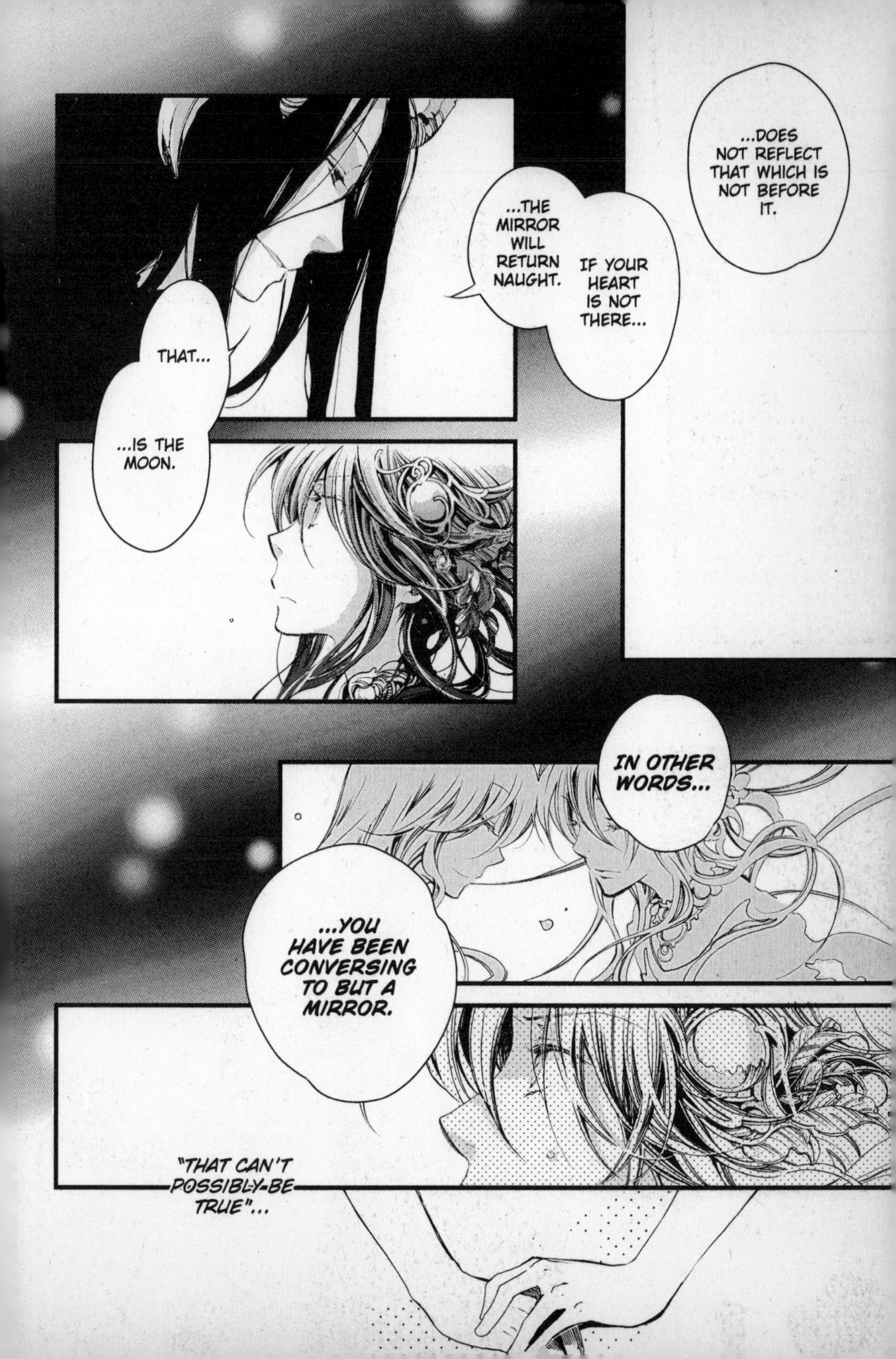
...DOES NOT REFLECT THAT WHICH IS NOT BEFORE IT.
IF YOUR HEART IS NOT THERE...
...THE MIRROR WILL RETURN NAUGHT.
THAT...
...IS THE MOON.
IN OTHER WORDS...
...YOU HAVE BEEN CONVERSING TO BUT A MIRROR.
"THAT CAN'T POSSIBLY BE TRUE"...

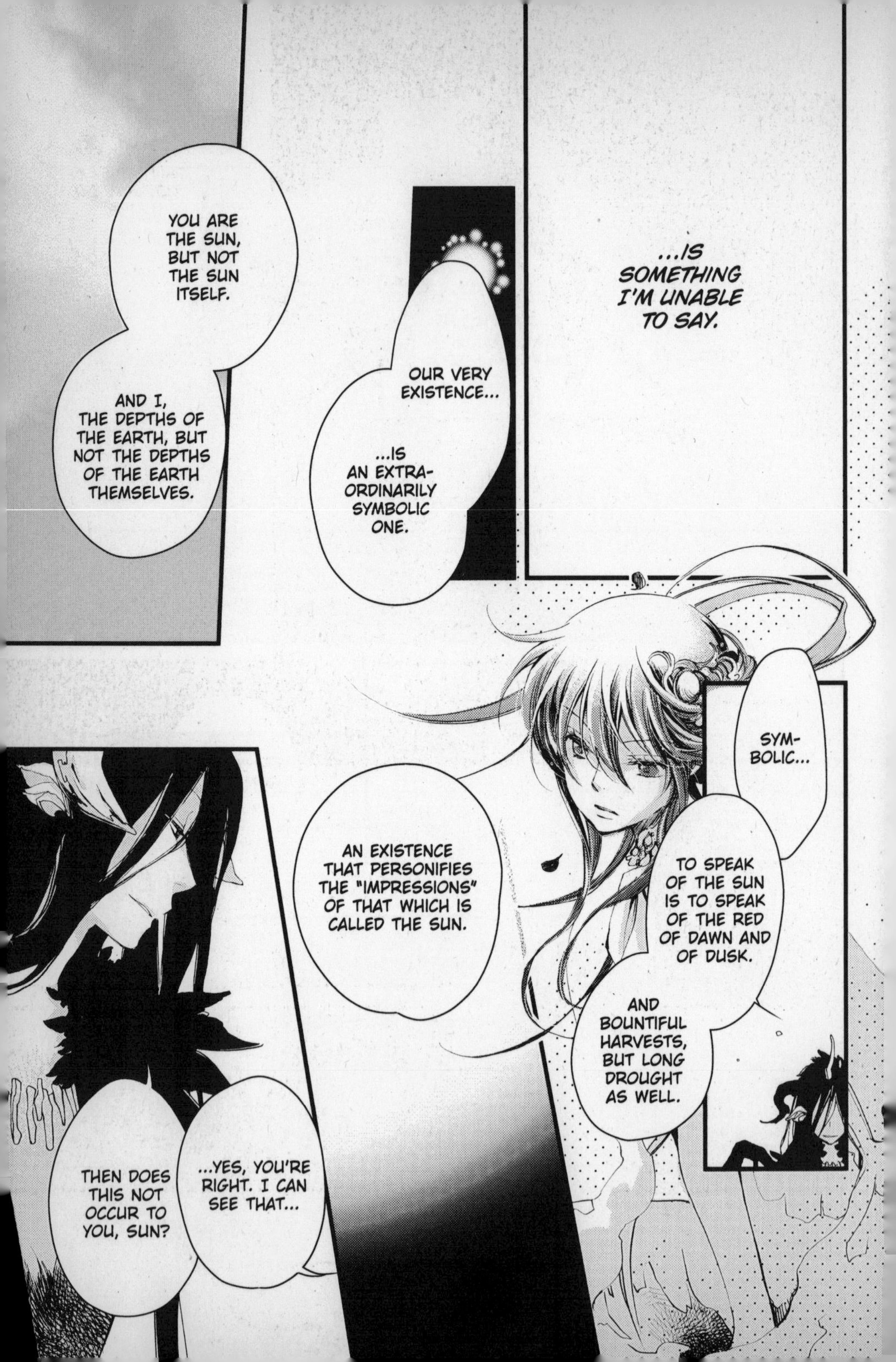
...IS SOMETHING I'M UNABLE TO SAY.
OUR VERY EXISTENCE...
...IS AN EXTRA-ORDINARILY SYMBOLIC ONE.
YOU ARE THE SUN, BUT NOT THE SUN ITSELF.
AND I, THE DEPTHS OF THE EARTH, BUT NOT THE DEPTHS OF THE EARTH THEMSELVES.
SYM-BOLIC...
TO SPEAK OF THE SUN IS TO SPEAK OF THE RED OF DAWN AND OF DUSK.
AND BOUNTIFUL HARVESTS, BUT LONG DROUGHT AS WELL.
AN EXISTENCE THAT PERSONIFIES THE "IMPRESSIONS" OF THAT WHICH IS CALLED THE SUN.
...YES, YOU'RE RIGHT. I CAN SEE THAT...
THEN DOES THIS NOT OCCUR TO YOU, SUN?

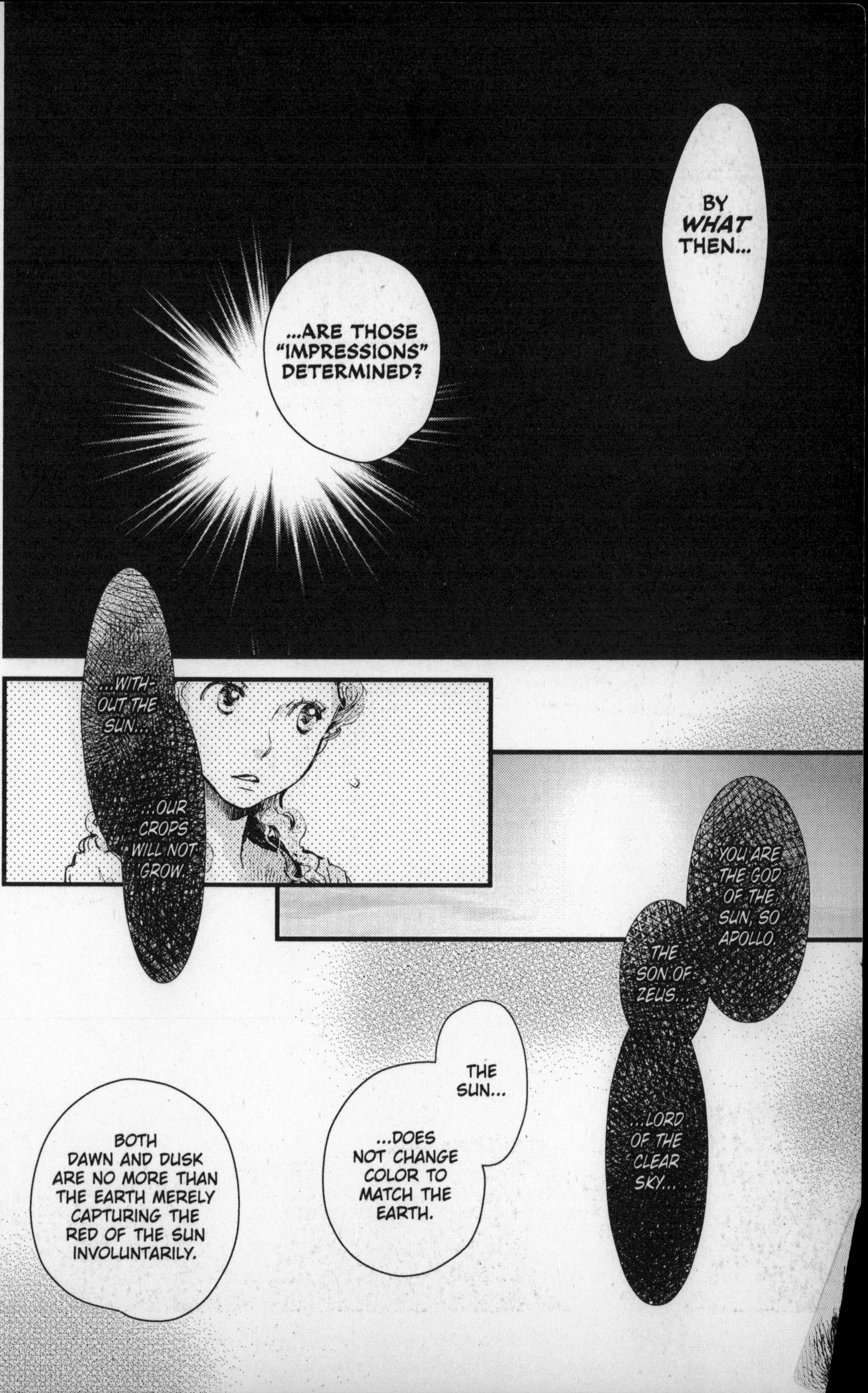
BY WHAT THEN...
...ARE THOSE "IMPRESSIONS" DETERMINED?
YOU ARE THE GOD OF THE SUN, SO APOLLO.
THE SON OF ZEUS...
...LORD OF THE CLEAR SKY...
...WITH-OUT THE SUN...
...OUR CROPS WILL NOT GROW.
THE SUN...
...DOES NOT CHANGE COLOR TO MATCH THE EARTH.
BOTH DAWN AND DUSK ARE NO MORE THAN THE EARTH MERELY CAPTURING THE RED OF THE SUN INVOLUNTARILY.

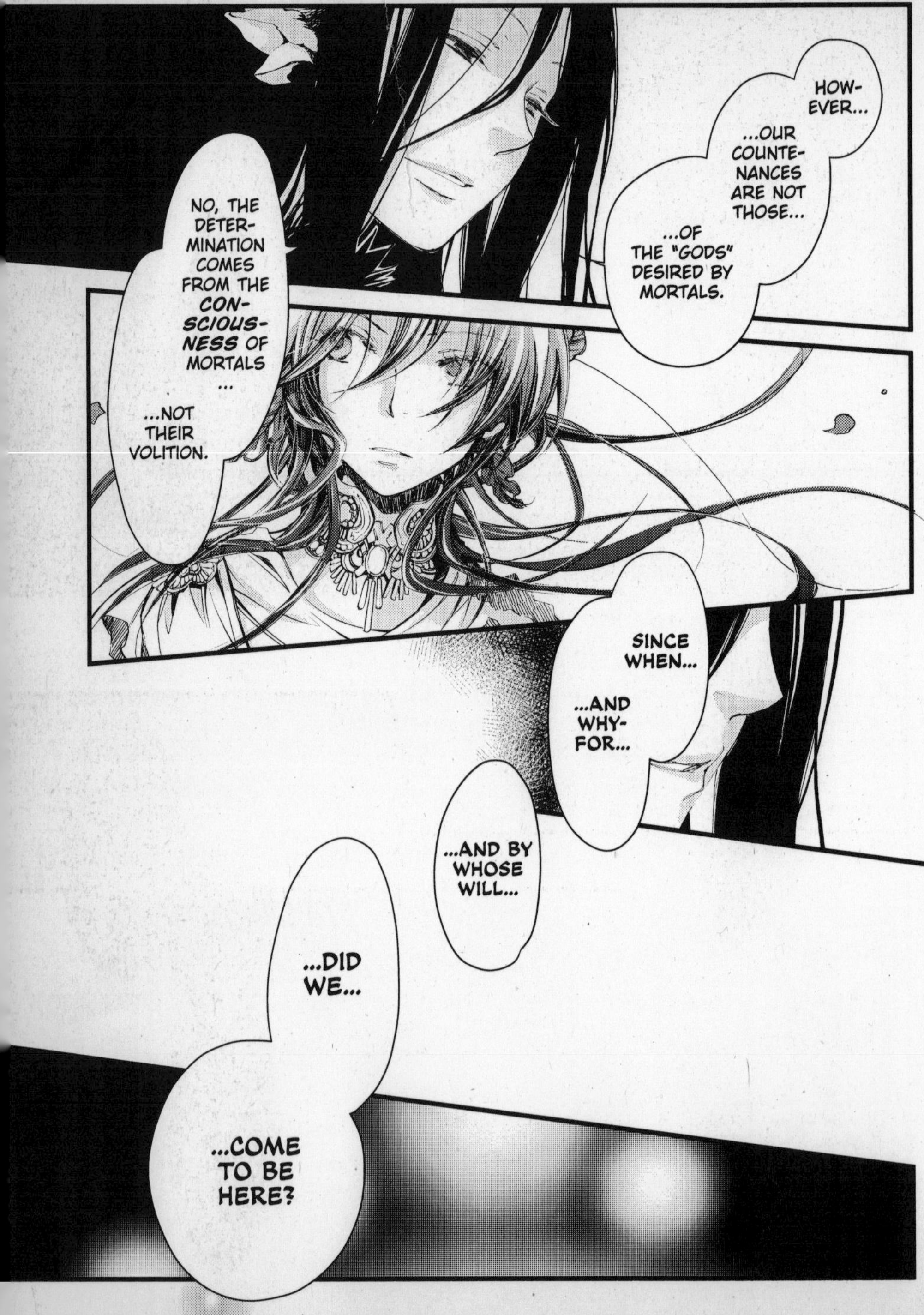
HOW-EVER...
...OUR COUNTE-NANCES ARE NOT THOSE...
...OF THE "GODS" DESIRED BY MORTALS.
NO, THE DETER-MINATION COMES FROM THE ***CON-SCIOUS-NESS*** OF MORTALS...
...NOT THEIR VOLITION.
SINCE WHEN...
...AND WHY-FOR...
...AND BY WHOSE WILL...
...DID WE...
...COME TO BE HERE?

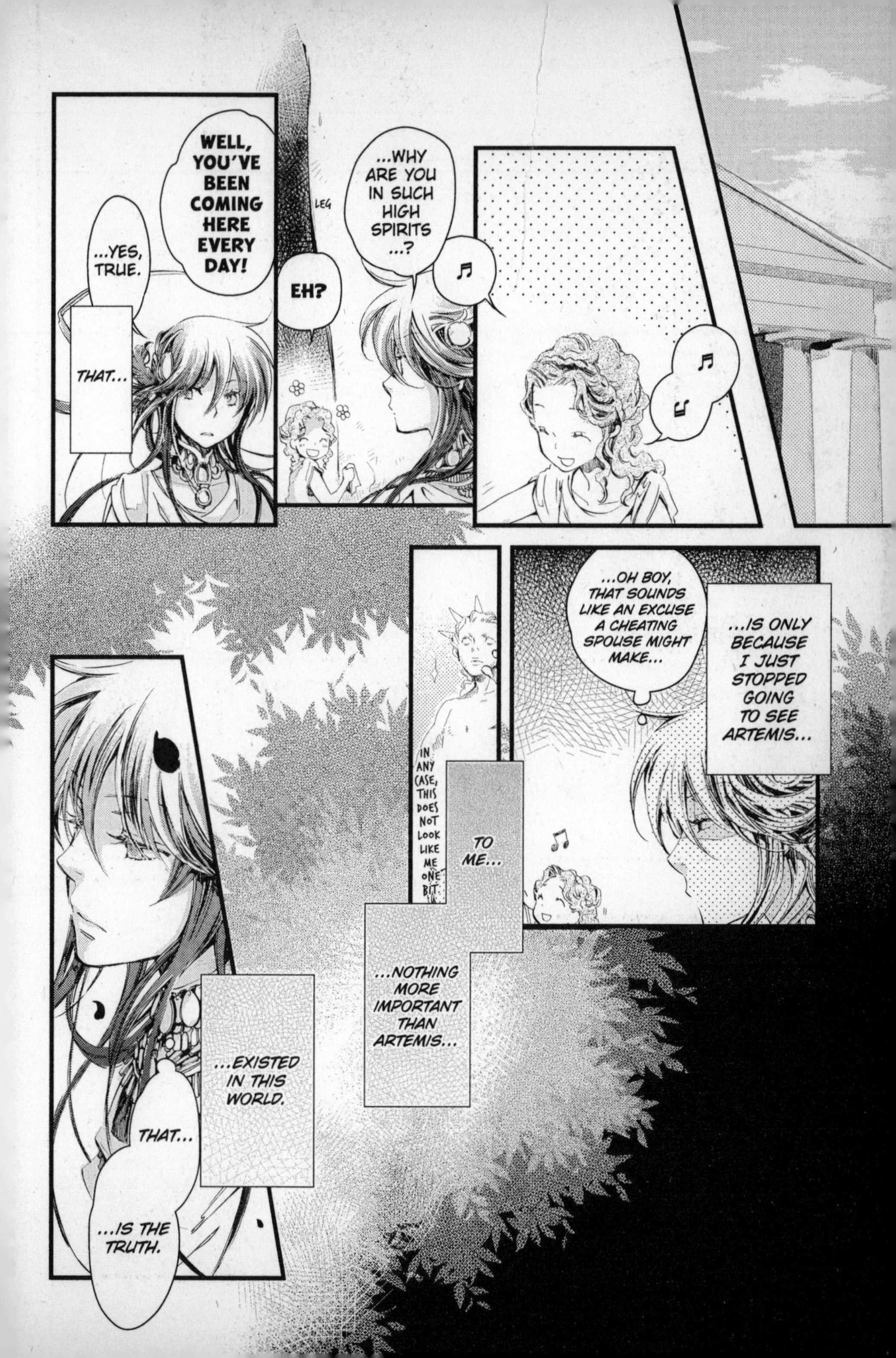
♪
♪
♪
♪
...WHY ARE YOU IN SUCH HIGH SPIRITS ...?
LEG
EH?
WELL, YOU'VE BEEN COMING HERE EVERY DAY!
...YES, TRUE.
THAT...
...IS ONLY BECAUSE I JUST STOPPED GOING TO SEE ARTEMIS...
...OH BOY, THAT SOUNDS LIKE AN EXCUSE A CHEATING SPOUSE MIGHT MAKE...
♪
IN ANY CASE, THIS DOES NOT LOOK LIKE ME ONE BIT.
TO ME...
...NOTHING MORE IMPORTANT THAN ARTEMIS...
...EXISTED IN THIS WORLD.
THAT...
...IS THE TRUTH.

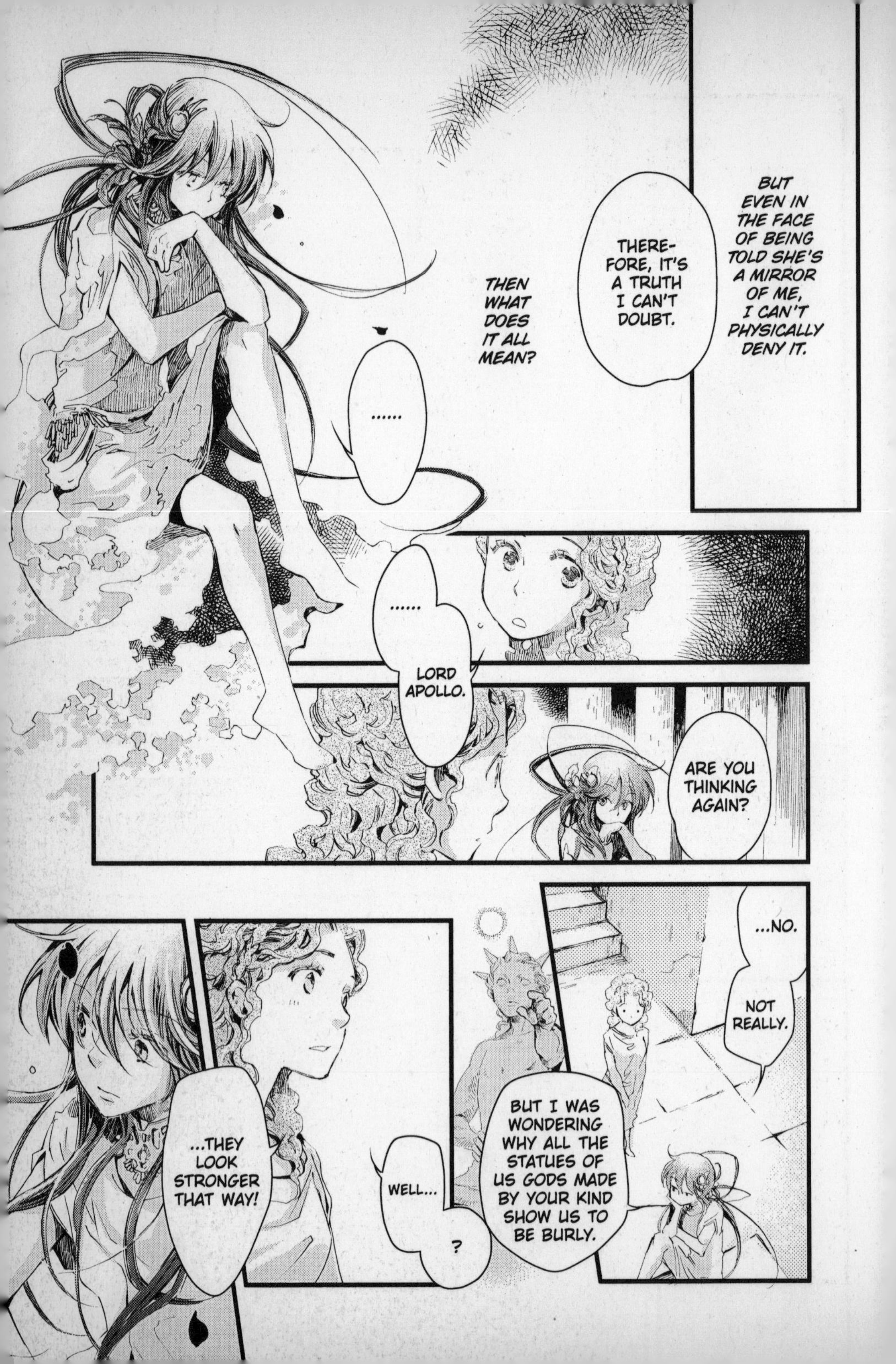
BUT EVEN IN THE FACE OF BEING TOLD SHE'S A MIRROR OF ME, I CAN'T PHYSICALLY DENY IT.
THERE-FORE, IT'S A TRUTH I CAN'T DOUBT.
THEN WHAT DOES IT ALL MEAN?
......
......
LORD APOLLO.
ARE YOU THINKING AGAIN?
...NO.
NOT REALLY.
BUT I WAS WONDERING WHY ALL THE STATUES OF US GODS MADE BY YOUR KIND SHOW US TO BE BURLY.
?
WELL...
...THEY LOOK STRONGER THAT WAY!

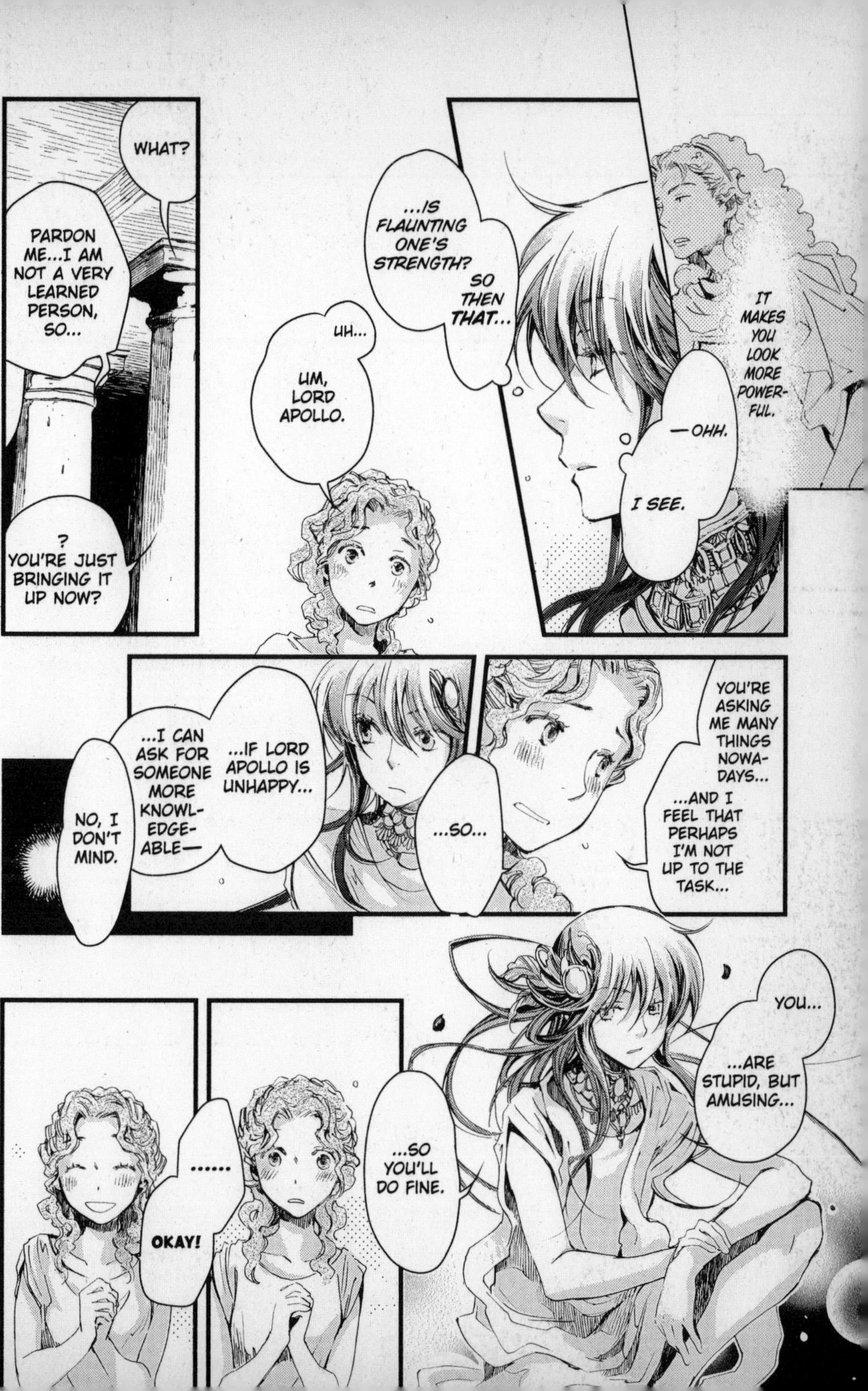
IT MAKES YOU LOOK MORE POWER-FUL.
—OHH.
I SEE.
...IS FLAUNTING ONE'S STRENGTH? SO THEN THAT...
UH...
UM, LORD APOLLO.
WHAT?
PARDON ME...I AM NOT A VERY LEARNED PERSON, SO...
? YOU'RE JUST BRINGING IT UP NOW?
YOU'RE ASKING ME MANY THINGS NOWA-DAYS...
...AND I FEEL THAT PERHAPS I'M NOT UP TO THE TASK...
...SO...
...IF LORD APOLLO IS UNHAPPY...
...I CAN ASK FOR SOMEONE MORE KNOWL-EDGE-ABLE—
NO, I DON'T MIND.
YOU...
...ARE STUPID, BUT AMUSING...
...SO YOU'LL DO FINE.
......
OKAY!

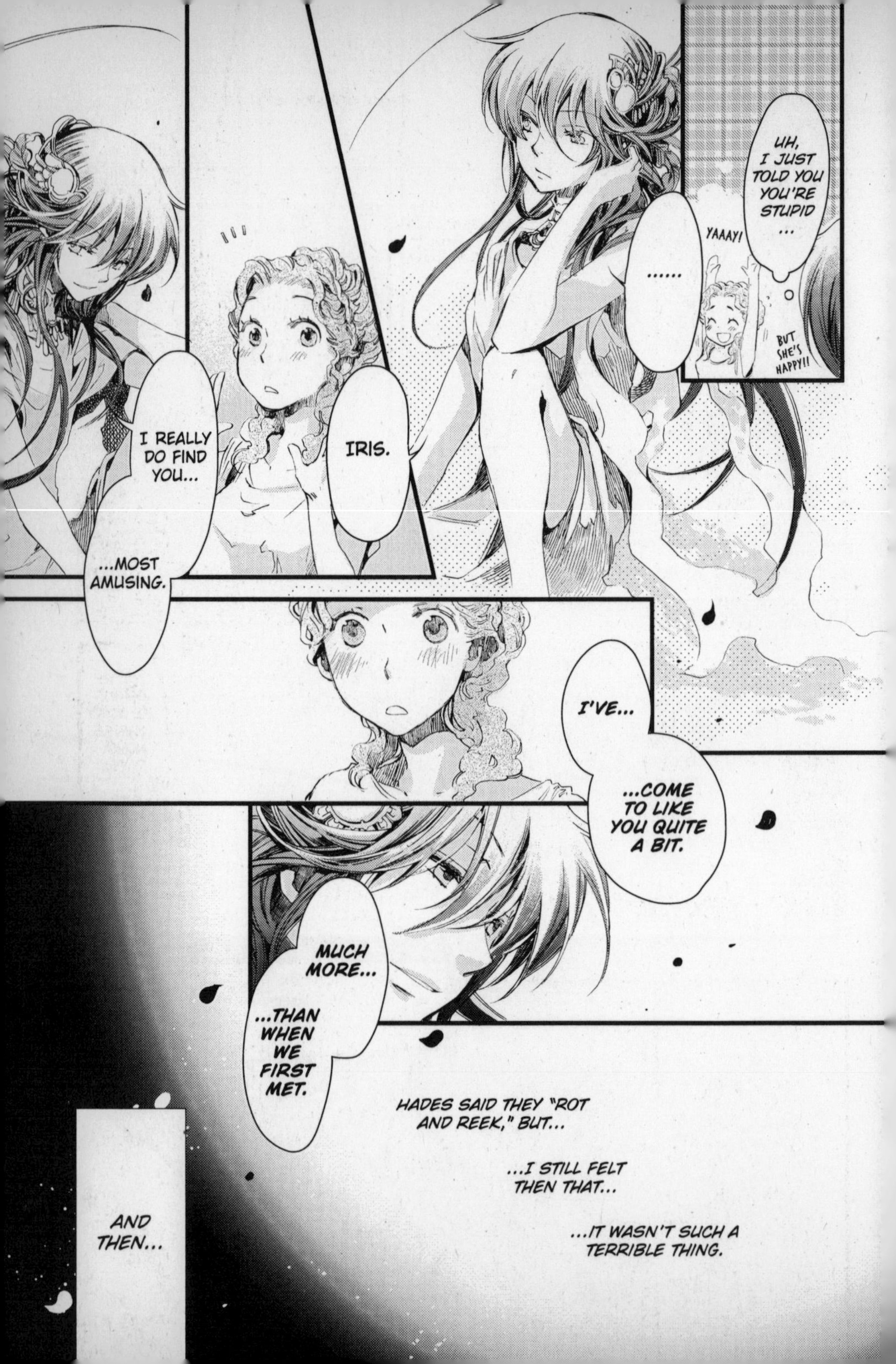
......
UH, I JUST TOLD YOU YOU'RE STUPID...
YAAAY!
BUT SHE'S HAPPY!!
IRIS.
I REALLY DO FIND YOU...
...MOST AMUSING.
I'VE...
...COME TO LIKE YOU QUITE A BIT.
MUCH MORE...
...THAN WHEN WE FIRST MET.
HADES SAID THEY "ROT AND REEK," BUT...
...I STILL FELT THEN THAT...
...IT WASN'T SUCH A TERRIBLE THING.
AND THEN...

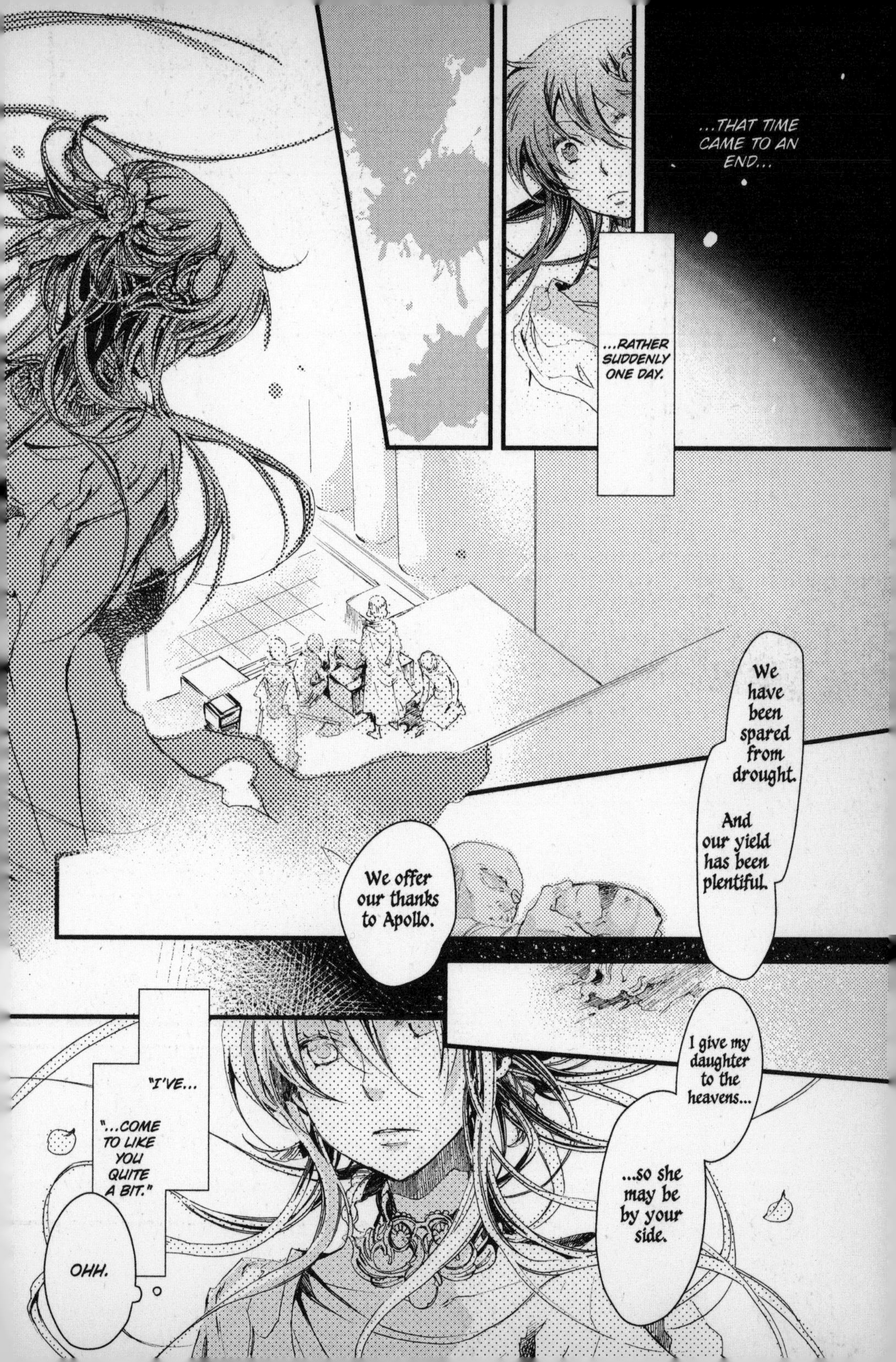
...THAT TIME CAME TO AN END...
...RATHER SUDDENLY ONE DAY.
We have been spared from drought.
And our yield has been plentiful.
We offer our thanks to Apollo.
I give my daughter to the heavens...
...so she may be by your side.
"I'VE...
"...COME TO LIKE YOU QUITE A BIT."
OHH.

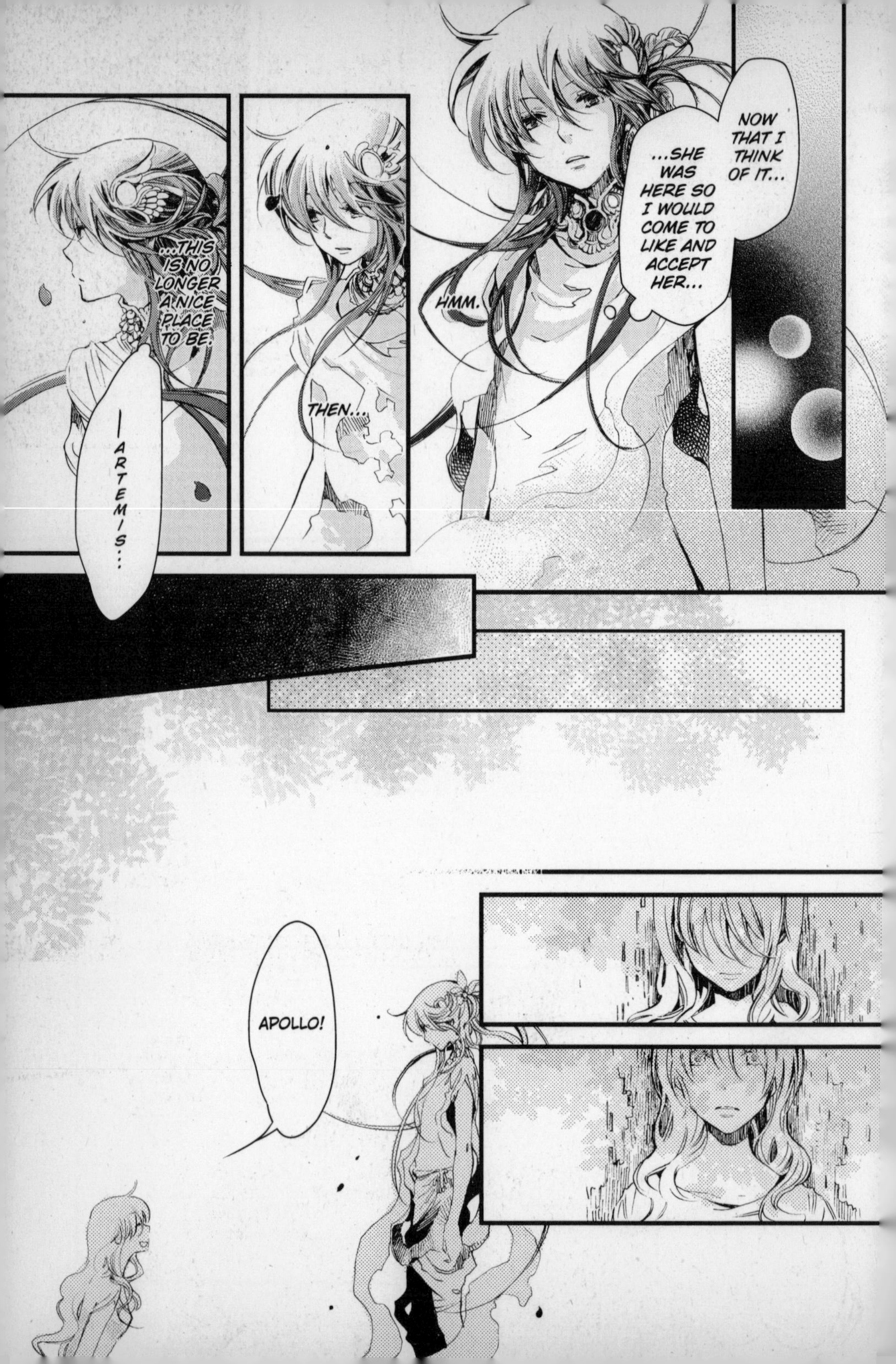
NOW THAT I THINK OF IT...
...SHE WAS HERE SO I WOULD COME TO LIKE AND ACCEPT HER...
HMM.
THEN...
...THIS IS NO LONGER A NICE PLACE TO BE.
—ARTEMIS...
APOLLO!

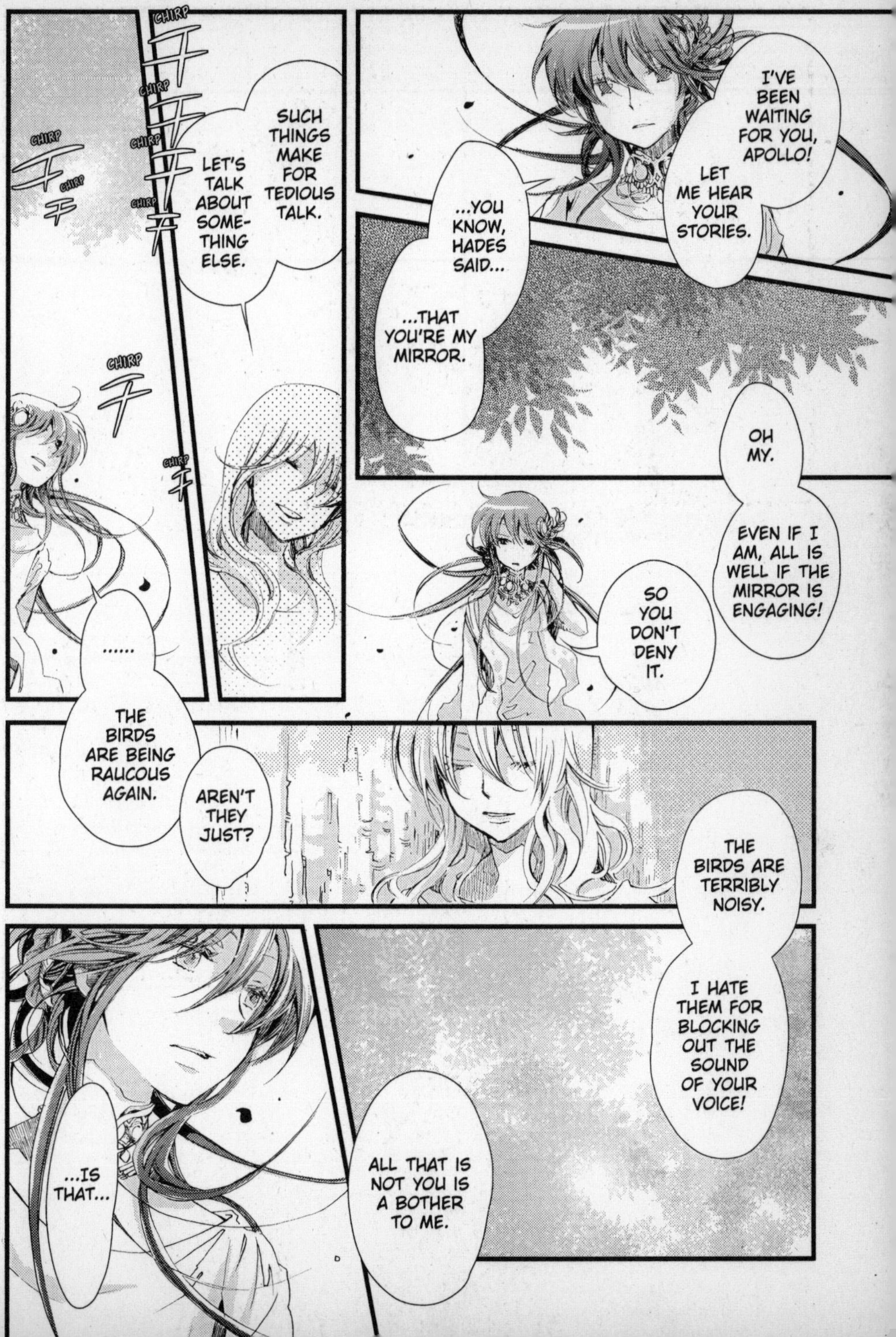
I'VE BEEN WAITING FOR YOU, APOLLO!
LET ME HEAR YOUR STORIES.
...YOU KNOW, HADES SAID...
...THAT YOU'RE MY MIRROR.
OH MY.
EVEN IF I AM, ALL IS WELL IF THE MIRROR IS ENGAGING!
SO YOU DON'T DENY IT.
CHIRP
CHIRP
CHIRP
CHIRP
SUCH THINGS MAKE FOR TEDIOUS TALK.
LET'S TALK ABOUT SOME-THING ELSE.
CHIRP
CHIRP
CHIRP
CHIRP
......
THE BIRDS ARE BEING RAUCOUS AGAIN.
AREN'T THEY JUST?
THE BIRDS ARE TERRIBLY NOISY.
I HATE THEM FOR BLOCKING OUT THE SOUND OF YOUR VOICE!
ALL THAT IS NOT YOU IS A BOTHER TO ME.
...IS THAT...

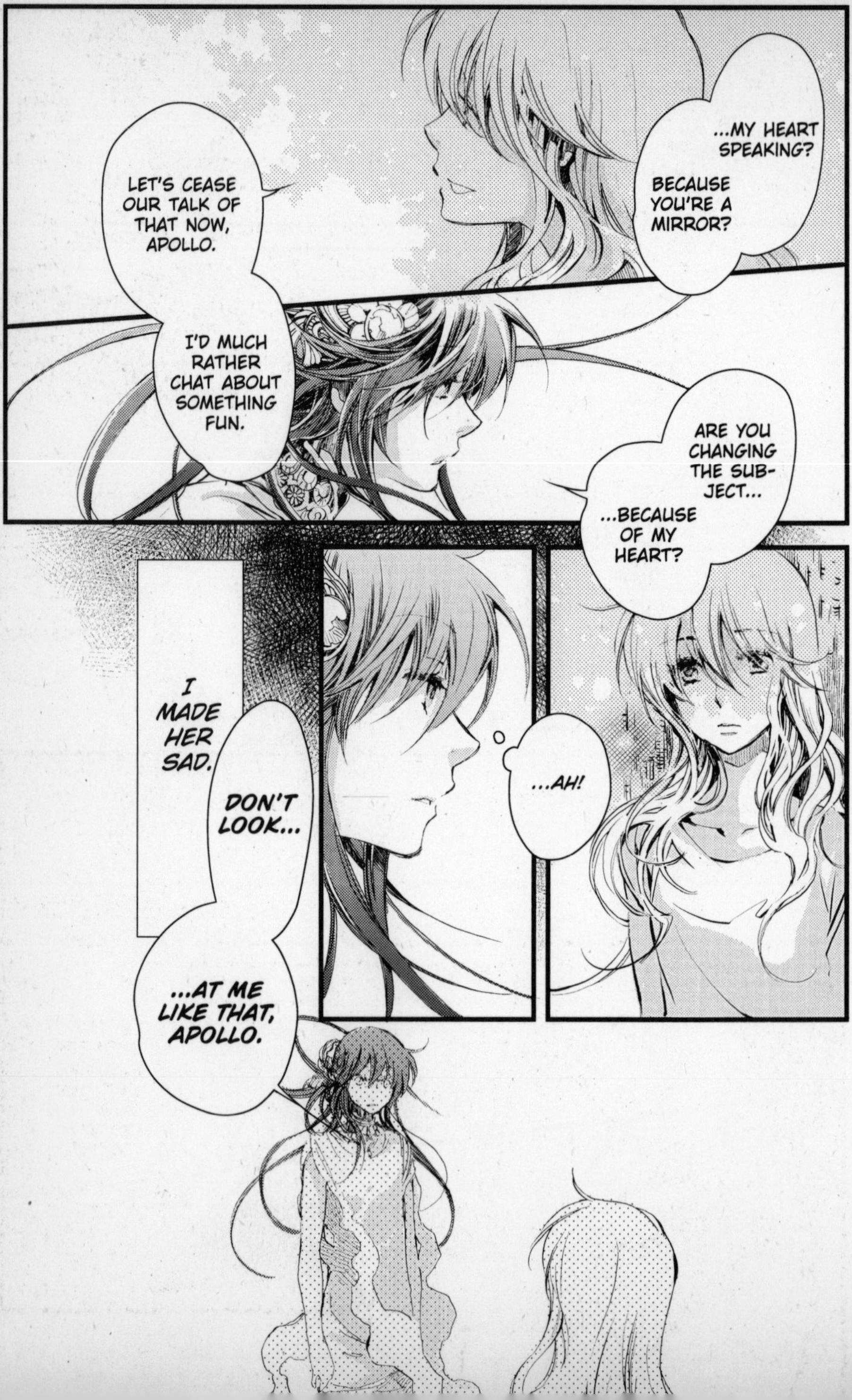
...MY HEART SPEAKING?
BECAUSE YOU'RE A MIRROR?
LET'S CEASE OUR TALK OF THAT NOW, APOLLO.
I'D MUCH RATHER CHAT ABOUT SOMETHING FUN.
ARE YOU CHANGING THE SUB-JECT...
...BECAUSE OF MY HEART?
...AH!
I MADE HER SAD.
DON'T LOOK...
...AT ME LIKE THAT, APOLLO.

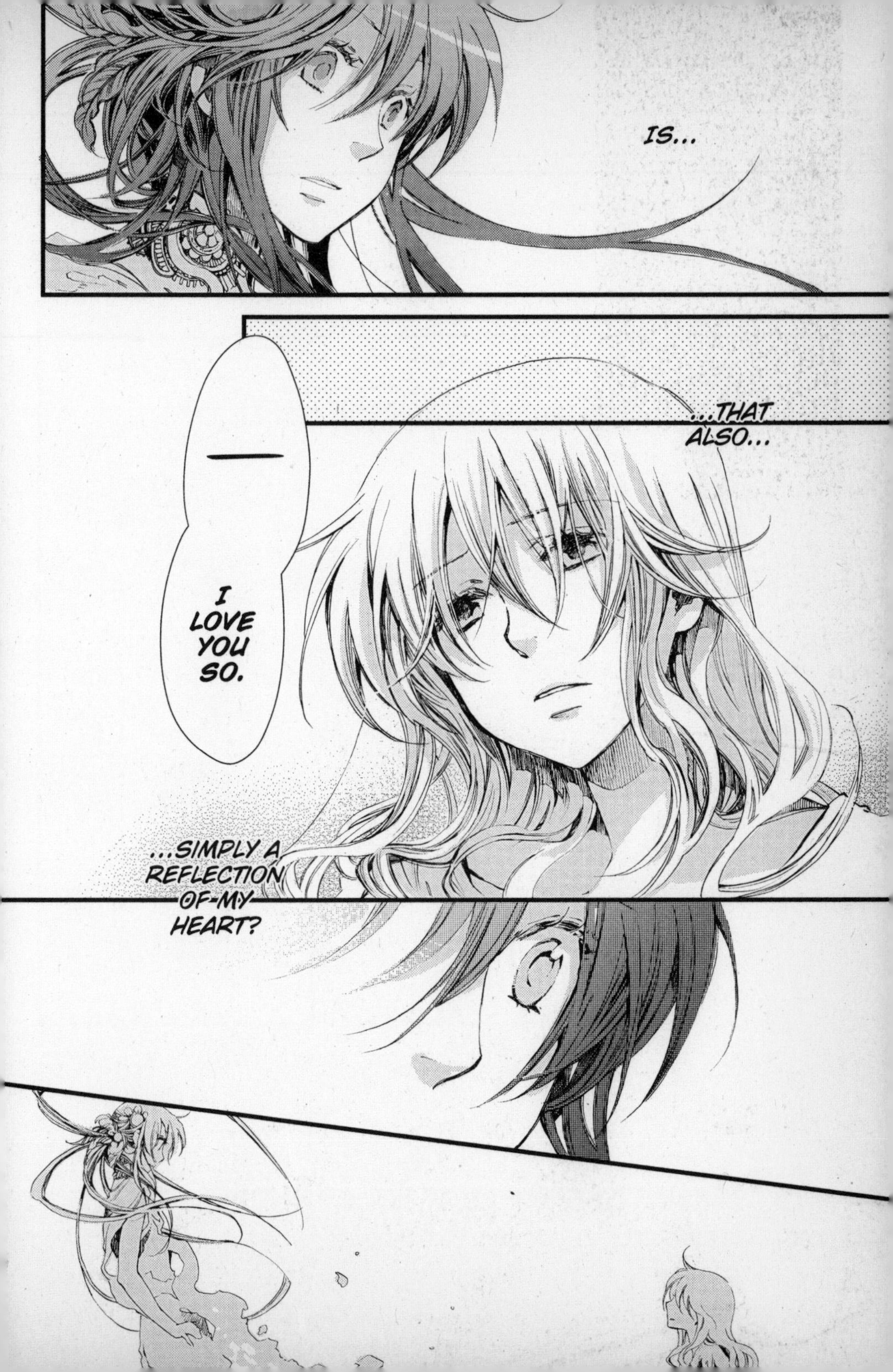
IS...
...THAT ALSO...
—
I LOVE YOU SO.
...SIMPLY A REFLECTION OF MY HEART?

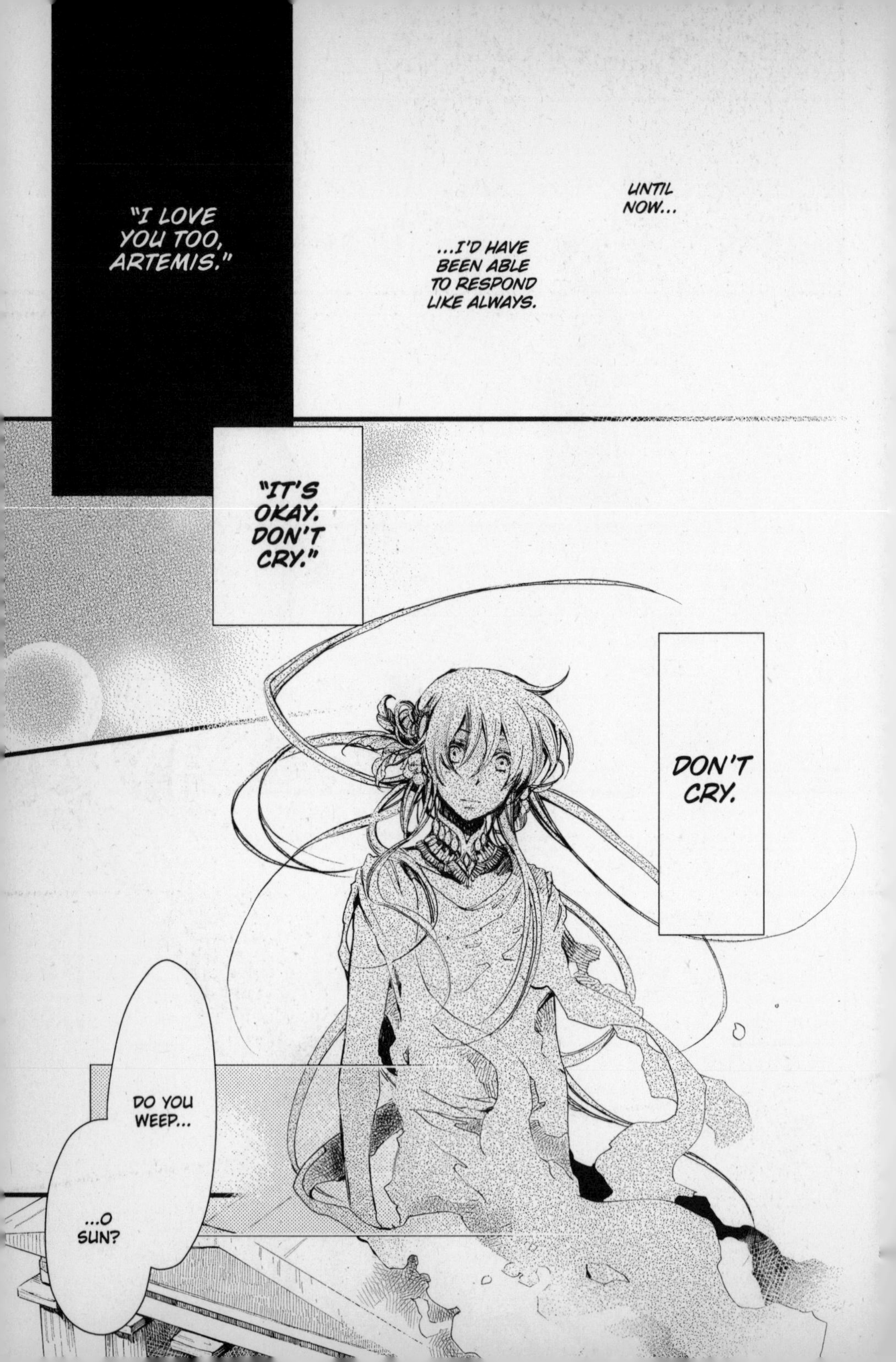
UNTIL NOW...
...I'D HAVE BEEN ABLE TO RESPOND LIKE ALWAYS.
"I LOVE YOU TOO, ARTEMIS."
"IT'S OKAY. DON'T CRY."
DON'T CRY.
DO YOU WEEP...
...O SUN?

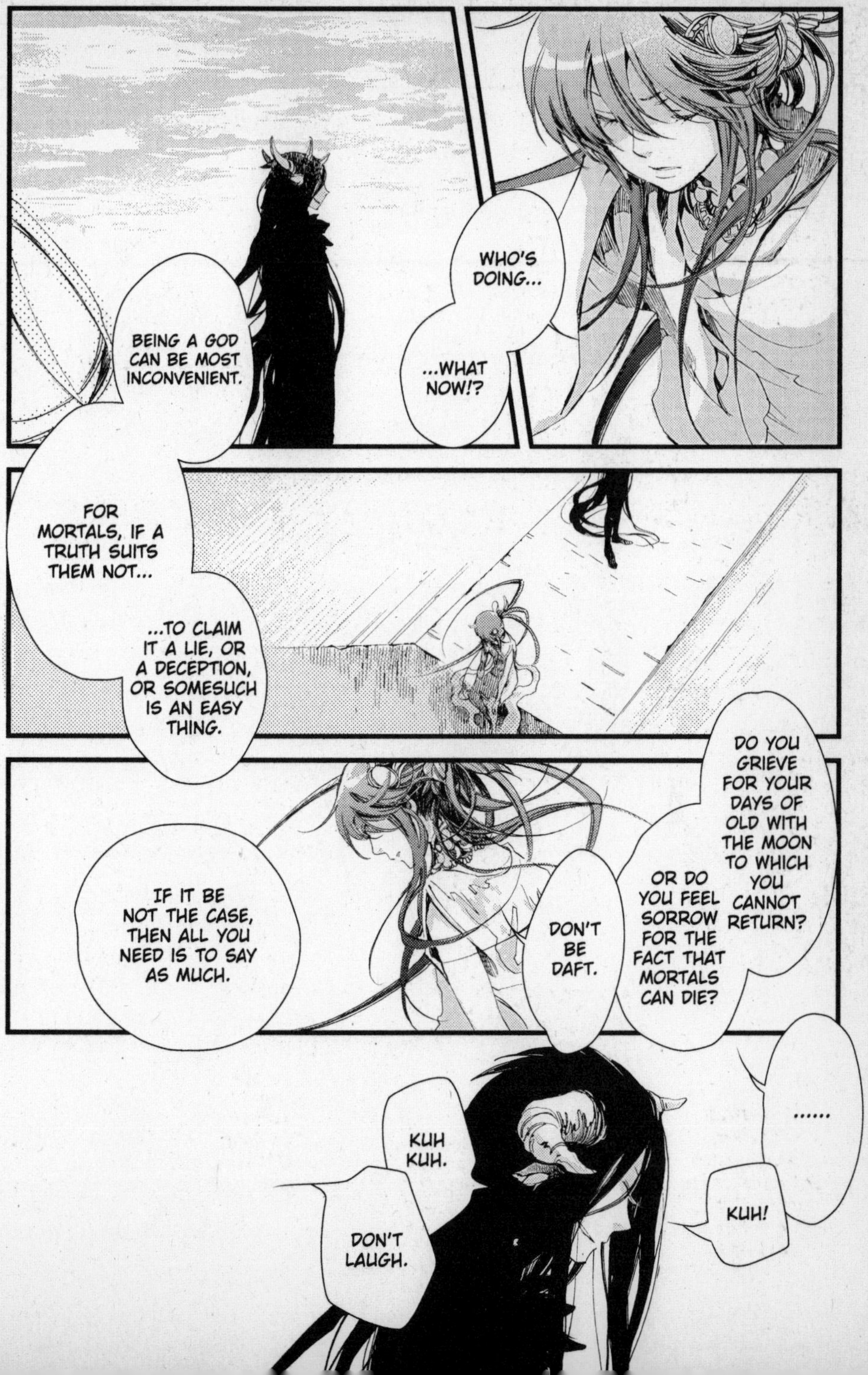
WHO'S DOING...
...WHAT NOW!?
BEING A GOD CAN BE MOST INCONVENIENT.
FOR MORTALS, IF A TRUTH SUITS THEM NOT...
...TO CLAIM IT A LIE, OR A DECEPTION, OR SOMESUCH IS AN EASY THING.
DO YOU GRIEVE FOR YOUR DAYS OF OLD WITH THE MOON TO WHICH YOU CANNOT RETURN?
OR DO YOU FEEL SORROW FOR THE FACT THAT MORTALS CAN DIE?
DON'T BE DAFT.
IF IT BE NOT THE CASE, THEN ALL YOU NEED IS TO SAY AS MUCH.
......
KUH!
KUH KUH.
DON'T LAUGH.

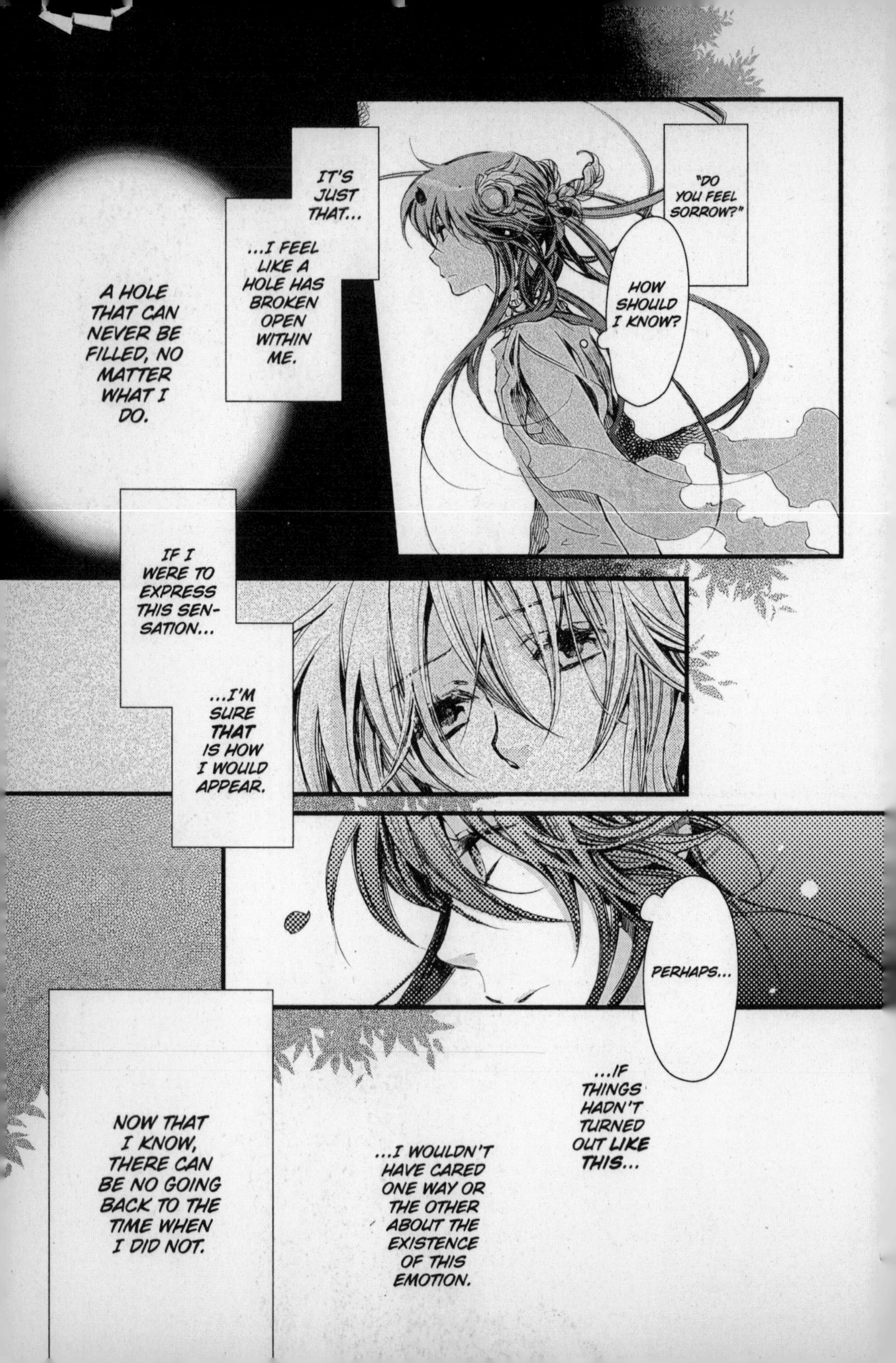
"DO YOU FEEL SORROW?"
HOW SHOULD I KNOW?
IT'S JUST THAT...
...I FEEL LIKE A HOLE HAS BROKEN OPEN WITHIN ME.
A HOLE THAT CAN NEVER BE FILLED, NO MATTER WHAT I DO.
IF I WERE TO EXPRESS THIS SENSATION...
...I'M SURE THAT IS HOW I WOULD APPEAR.
PERHAPS...
...IF THINGS HADN'T TURNED OUT LIKE THIS...
...I WOULDN'T HAVE CARED ONE WAY OR THE OTHER ABOUT THE EXISTENCE OF THIS EMOTION.
NOW THAT I KNOW, THERE CAN BE NO GOING BACK TO THE TIME WHEN I DID NOT.

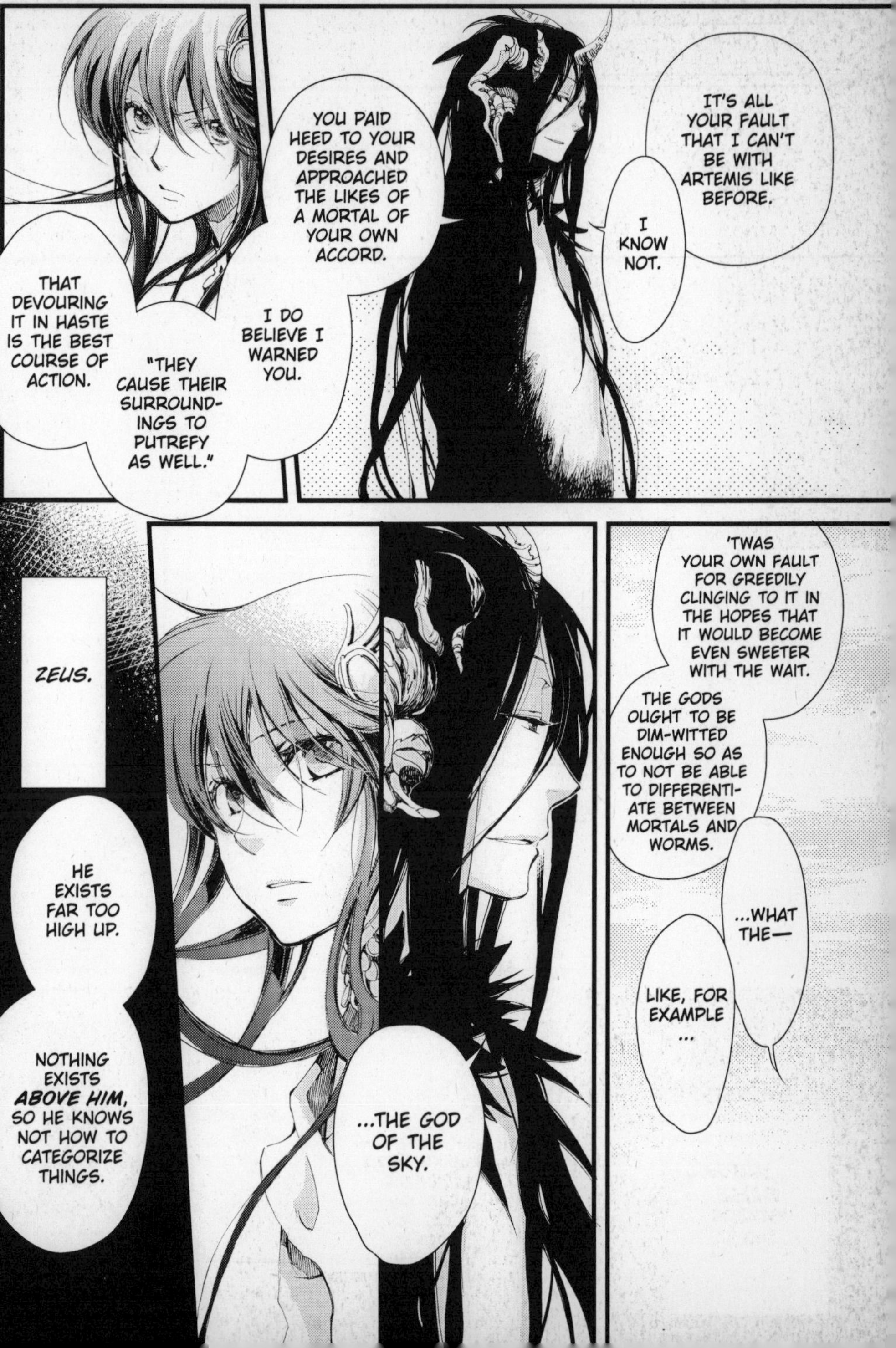
IT'S ALL YOUR FAULT THAT I CAN'T BE WITH ARTEMIS LIKE BEFORE.
I KNOW NOT.
YOU PAID HEED TO YOUR DESIRES AND APPROACHED THE LIKES OF A MORTAL OF YOUR OWN ACCORD.
I DO BELIEVE I WARNED YOU.
"THEY CAUSE THEIR SURROUND-INGS TO PUTREFY AS WELL."
THAT DEVOURING IT IN HASTE IS THE BEST COURSE OF ACTION.
'TWAS YOUR OWN FAULT FOR GREEDILY CLINGING TO IT IN THE HOPES THAT IT WOULD BECOME EVEN SWEETER WITH THE WAIT.
THE GODS OUGHT TO BE DIM-WITTED ENOUGH SO AS TO NOT BE ABLE TO DIFFERENTI-ATE BETWEEN MORTALS AND WORMS.
...WHAT THE—
LIKE, FOR EXAMPLE ...
...THE GOD OF THE SKY.
ZEUS.
HE EXISTS FAR TOO HIGH UP.
NOTHING EXISTS ***ABOVE HIM***, SO HE KNOWS NOT HOW TO CATEGORIZE THINGS.

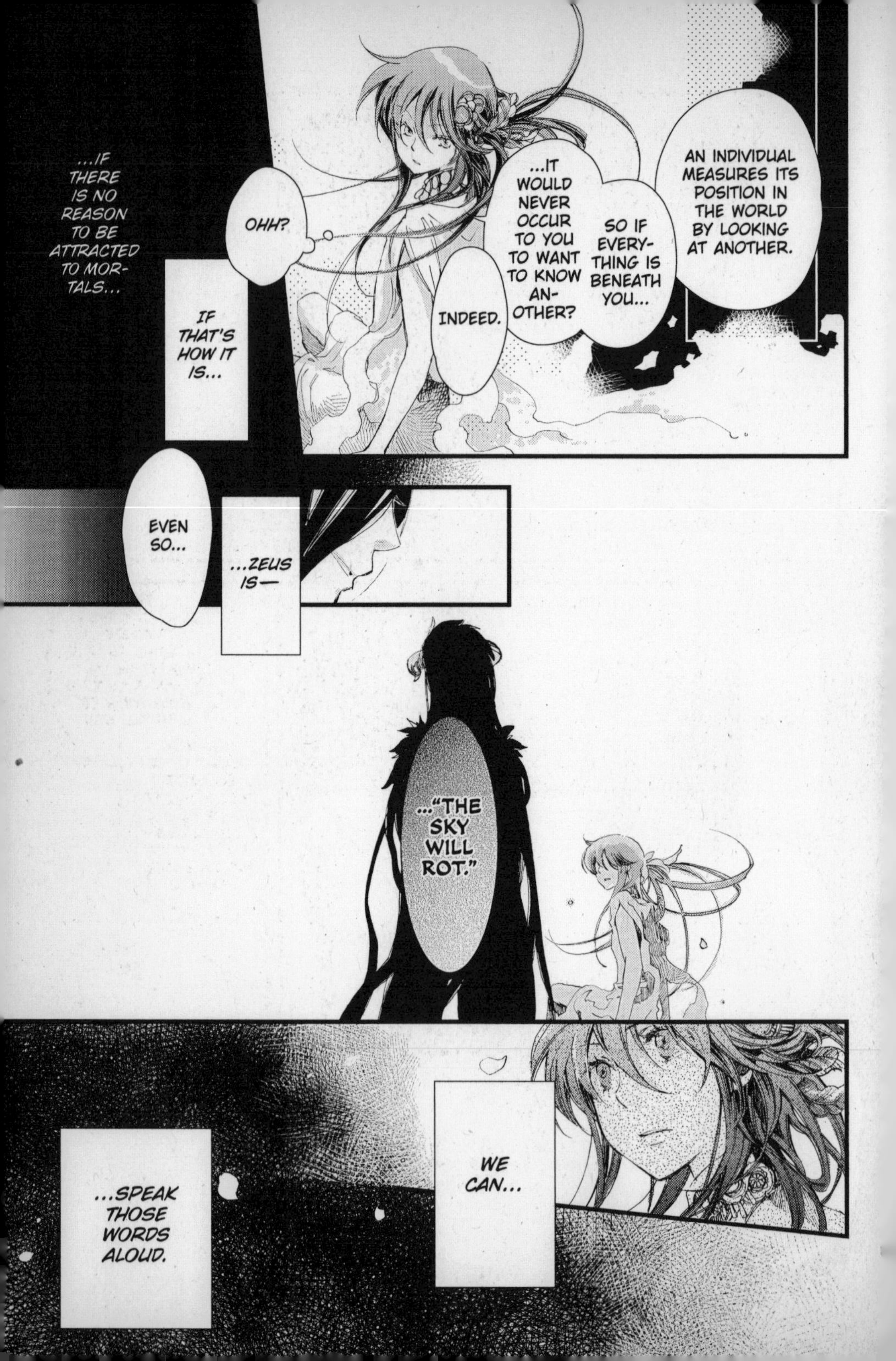
AN INDIVIDUAL MEASURES ITS POSITION IN THE WORLD BY LOOKING AT ANOTHER.
SO IF EVERYTHING IS BENEATH YOU...
...IT WOULD NEVER OCCUR TO YOU TO WANT TO KNOW ANOTHER?
INDEED.
OHH?
...IF THERE IS NO REASON TO BE ATTRACTED TO MORTALS...
IF THAT'S HOW IT IS...
EVEN SO...
...ZEUS IS—
..."THE SKY WILL ROT."
WE CAN...
...SPEAK THOSE WORDS ALOUD.

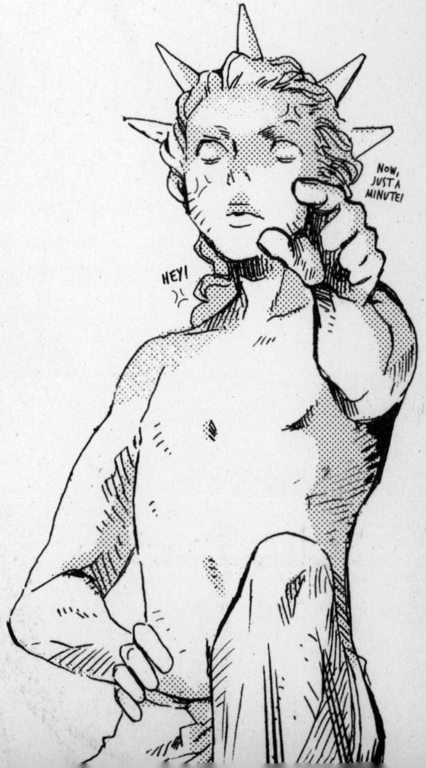
NOW, JUST A MINUTE!
HEY!

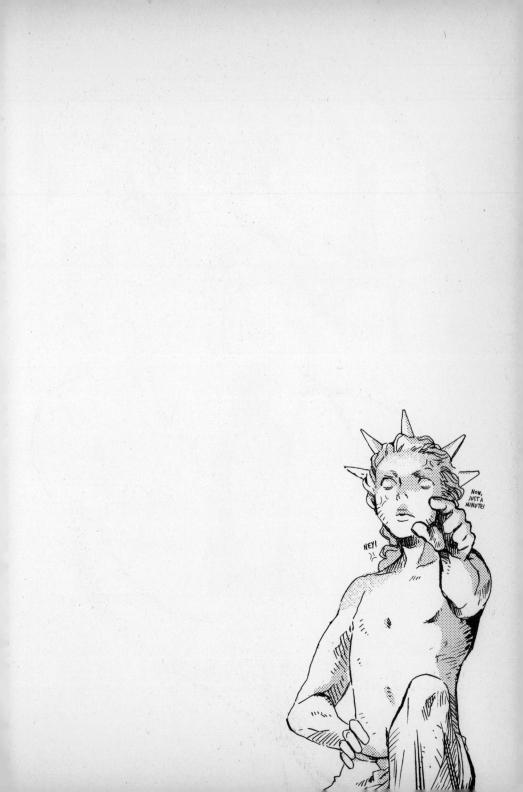

Episode.09

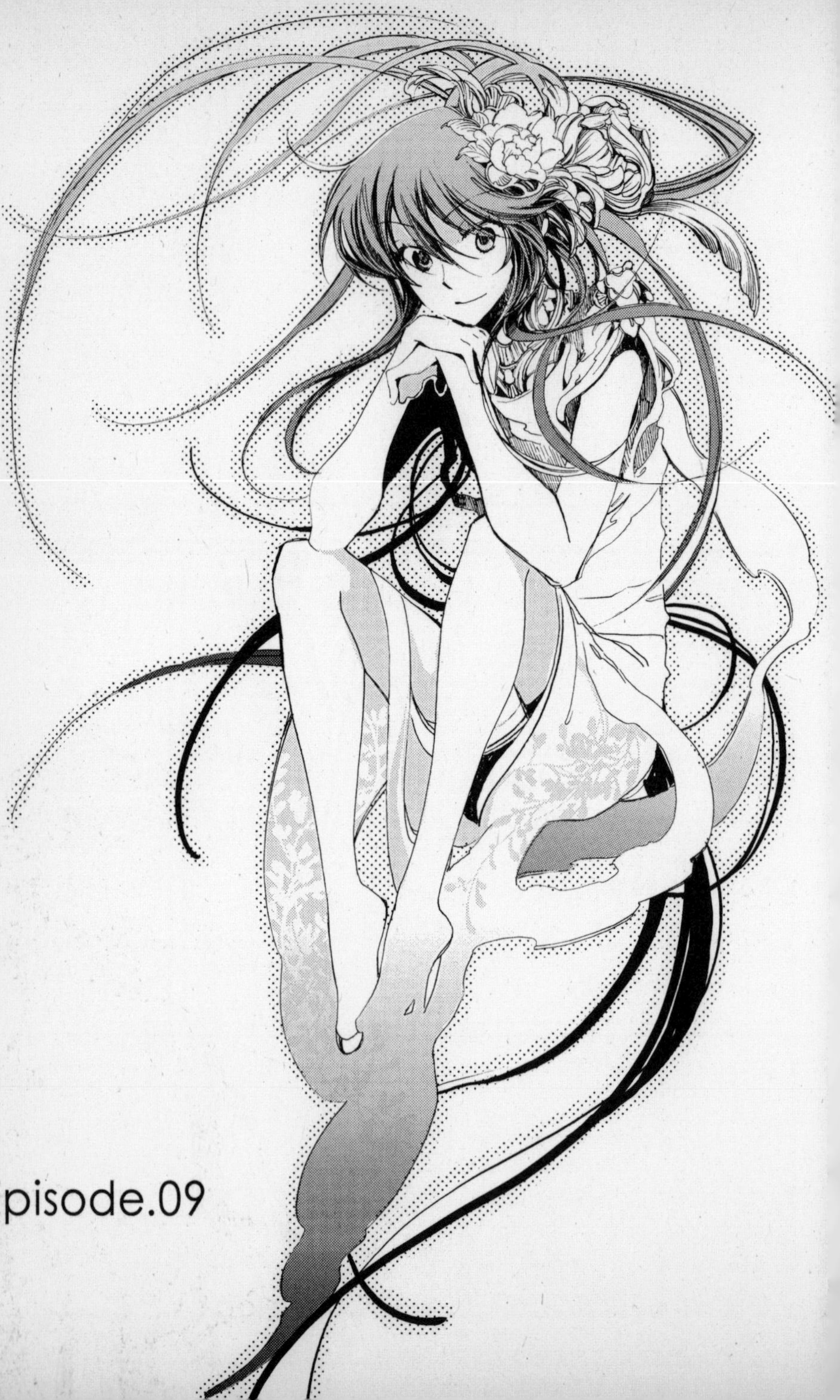

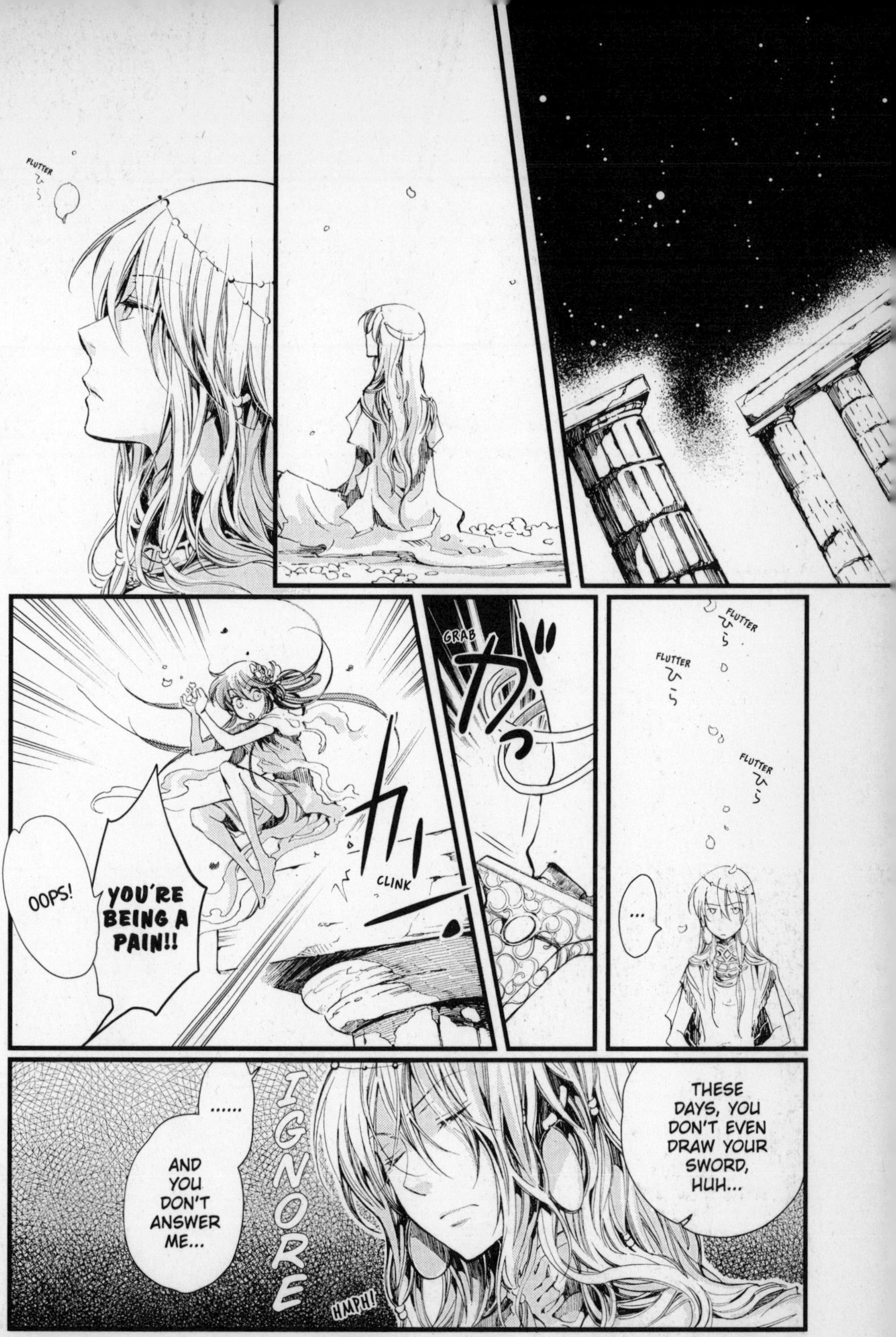
FLUTTER
FLUTTER
FLUTTER
FLUTTER
...
GRAB
CLINK
YOU'RE BEING A PAIN!!
OOPS!
THESE DAYS, YOU DON'T EVEN DRAW YOUR SWORD, HUH...
IGNORE
HMPH!
......
AND YOU DON'T ANSWER ME...

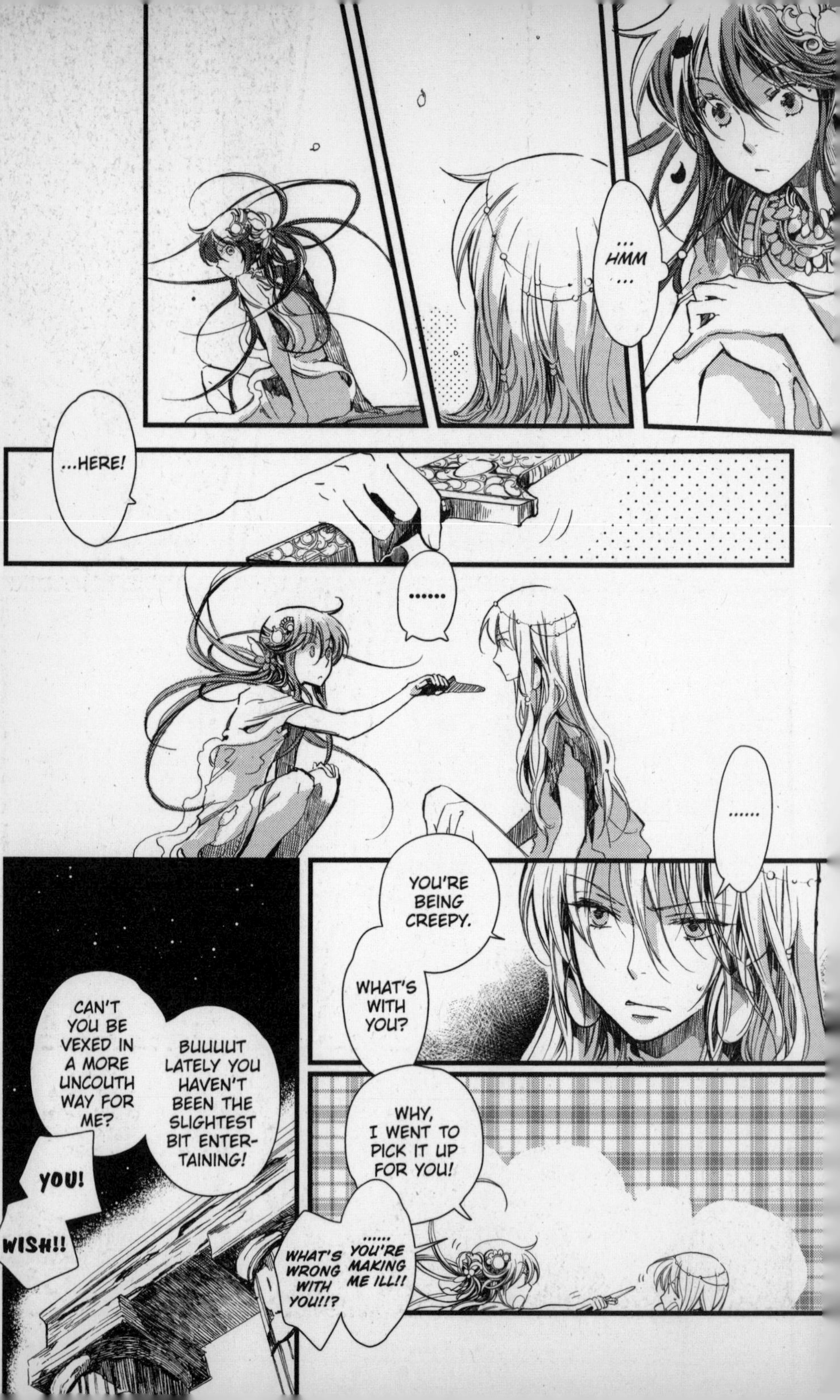

...HMM...
...HERE!
......
......
YOU'RE BEING CREEPY.
WHAT'S WITH YOU?
WHY, I WENT TO PICK IT UP FOR YOU!
......YOU'RE MAKING ME ILL!!
WHAT'S WRONG WITH YOU!!?
BUUUUT LATELY YOU HAVEN'T BEEN THE SLIGHTEST BIT ENTER-TAINING!
CAN'T YOU BE VEXED IN A MORE UNCOUTH WAY FOR ME?
YOU!
WISH!!

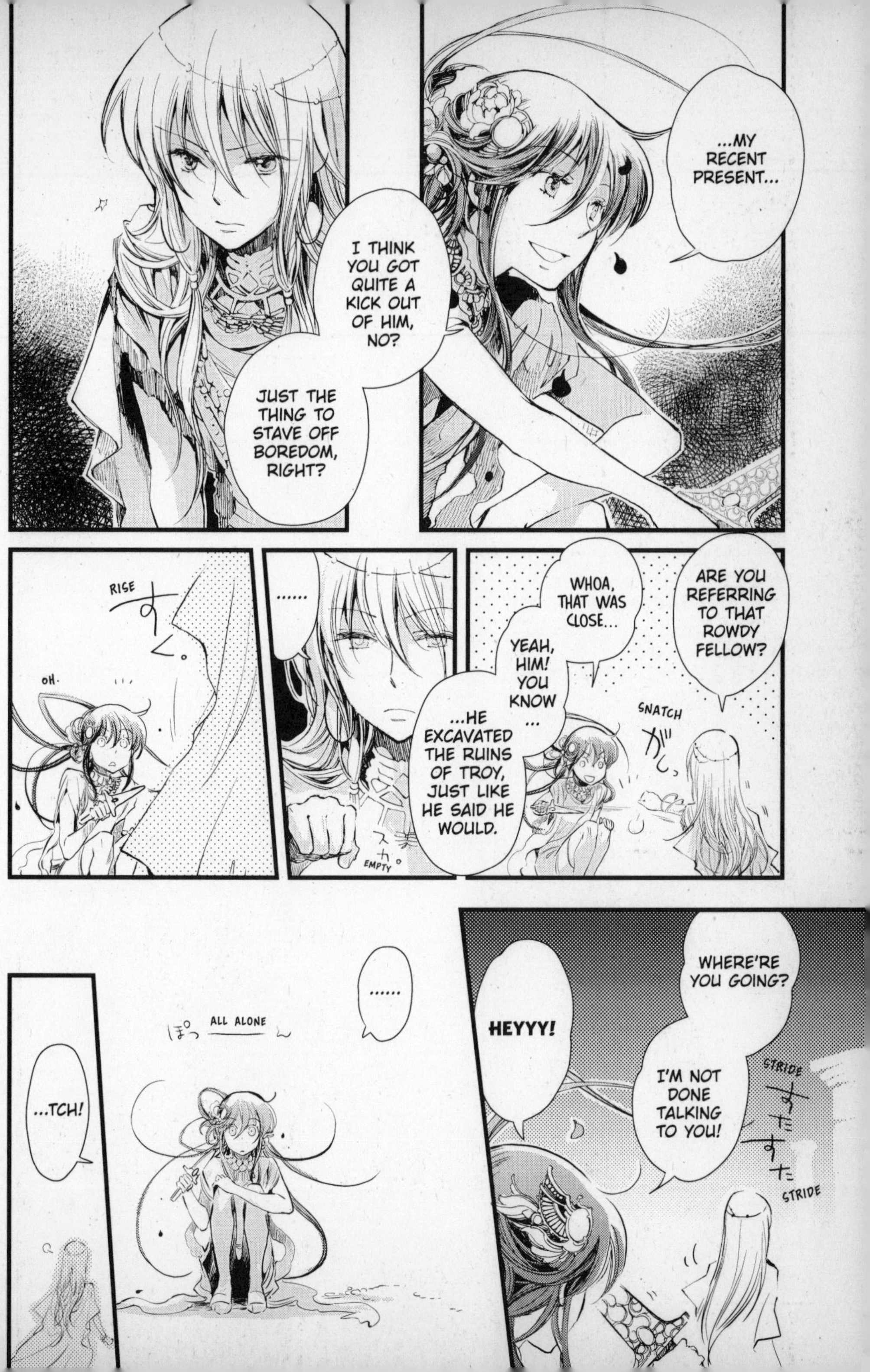
...MY RECENT PRESENT...
I THINK YOU GOT QUITE A KICK OUT OF HIM, NO?
JUST THE THING TO STAVE OFF BOREDOM, RIGHT?
ARE YOU REFERRING TO THAT ROWDY FELLOW?
WHOA, THAT WAS CLOSE...
SNATCH
YEAH, HIM! YOU KNOW...
...HE EXCAVATED THE RUINS OF TROY, JUST LIKE HE SAID HE WOULD.
......
EMPTY
RISE
OH.
WHERE'RE YOU GOING?
HEYYY!
STRIDE
I'M NOT DONE TALKING TO YOU!
STRIDE
......
ALL ALONE
...TCH!

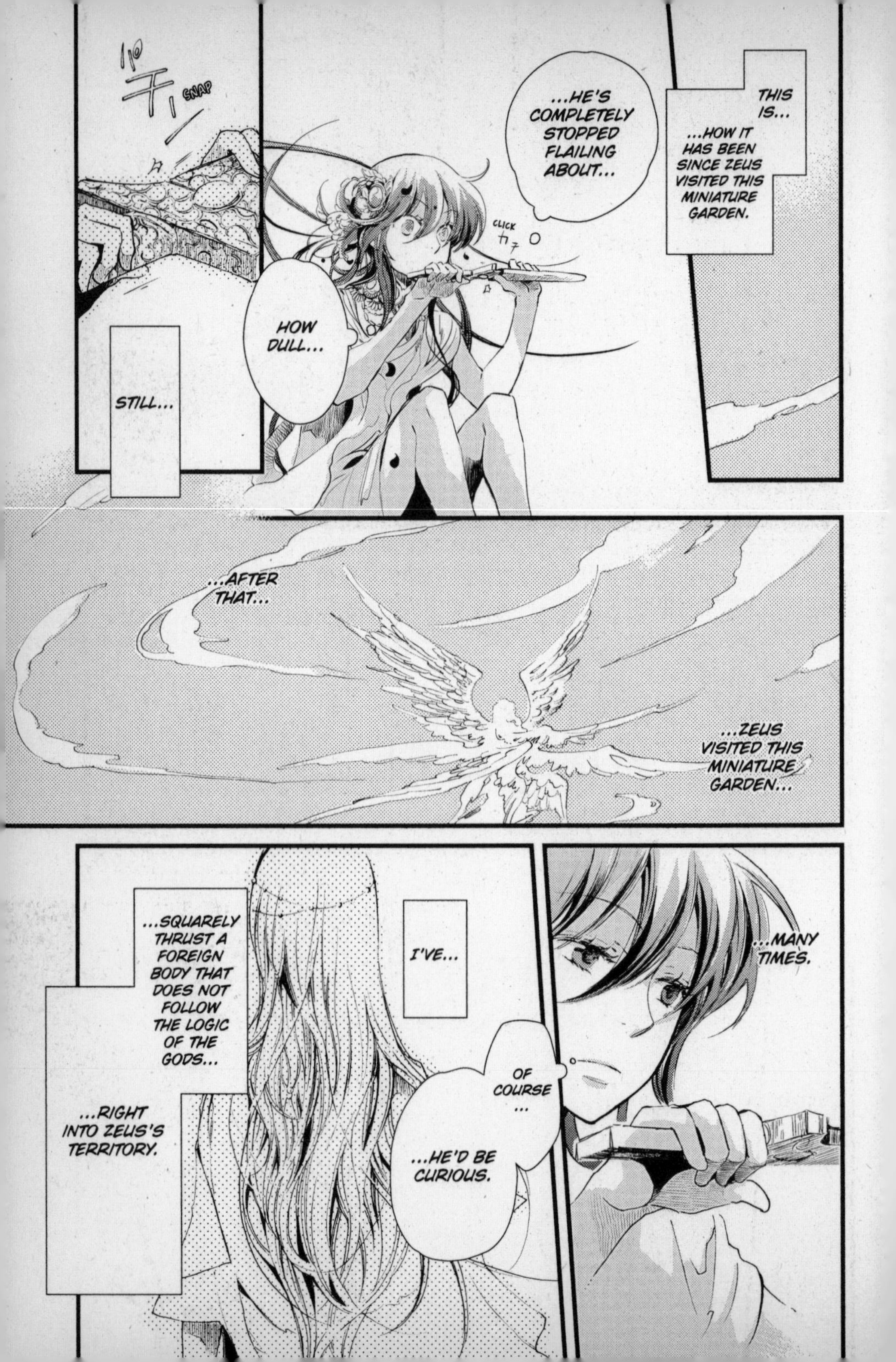
THIS IS...
...HOW IT HAS BEEN SINCE ZEUS VISITED THIS MINIATURE GARDEN.
...HE'S COMPLETELY STOPPED FLAILING ABOUT...
CLICK
HOW DULL...
SNAP
STILL...
...AFTER THAT...
...ZEUS VISITED THIS MINIATURE GARDEN...
...MANY TIMES.
OF COURSE...
...HE'D BE CURIOUS.
I'VE...
...SQUARELY THRUST A FOREIGN BODY THAT DOES NOT FOLLOW THE LOGIC OF THE GODS...
...RIGHT INTO ZEUS'S TERRITORY.

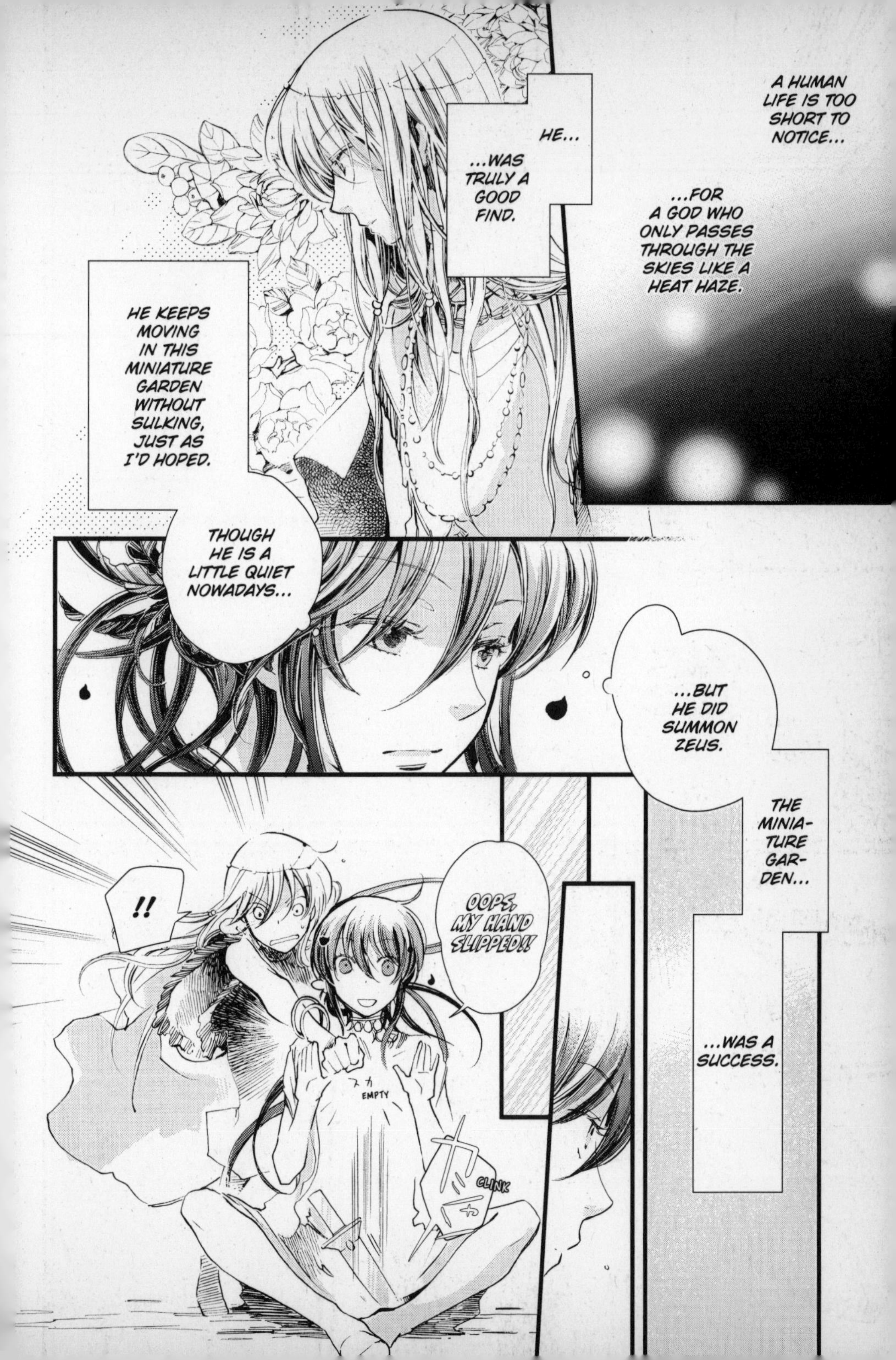
A HUMAN LIFE IS TOO SHORT TO NOTICE...
...FOR A GOD WHO ONLY PASSES THROUGH THE SKIES LIKE A HEAT HAZE.
HE...
...WAS TRULY A GOOD FIND.
HE KEEPS MOVING IN THIS MINIATURE GARDEN WITHOUT SULKING, JUST AS I'D HOPED.
THOUGH HE IS A LITTLE QUIET NOWADAYS...
...BUT HE DID SUMMON ZEUS.
THE MINIA-TURE GAR-DEN...
...WAS A SUCCESS.
OOPS, MY HAND SLIPPED!!
!!
EMPTY
CLINK

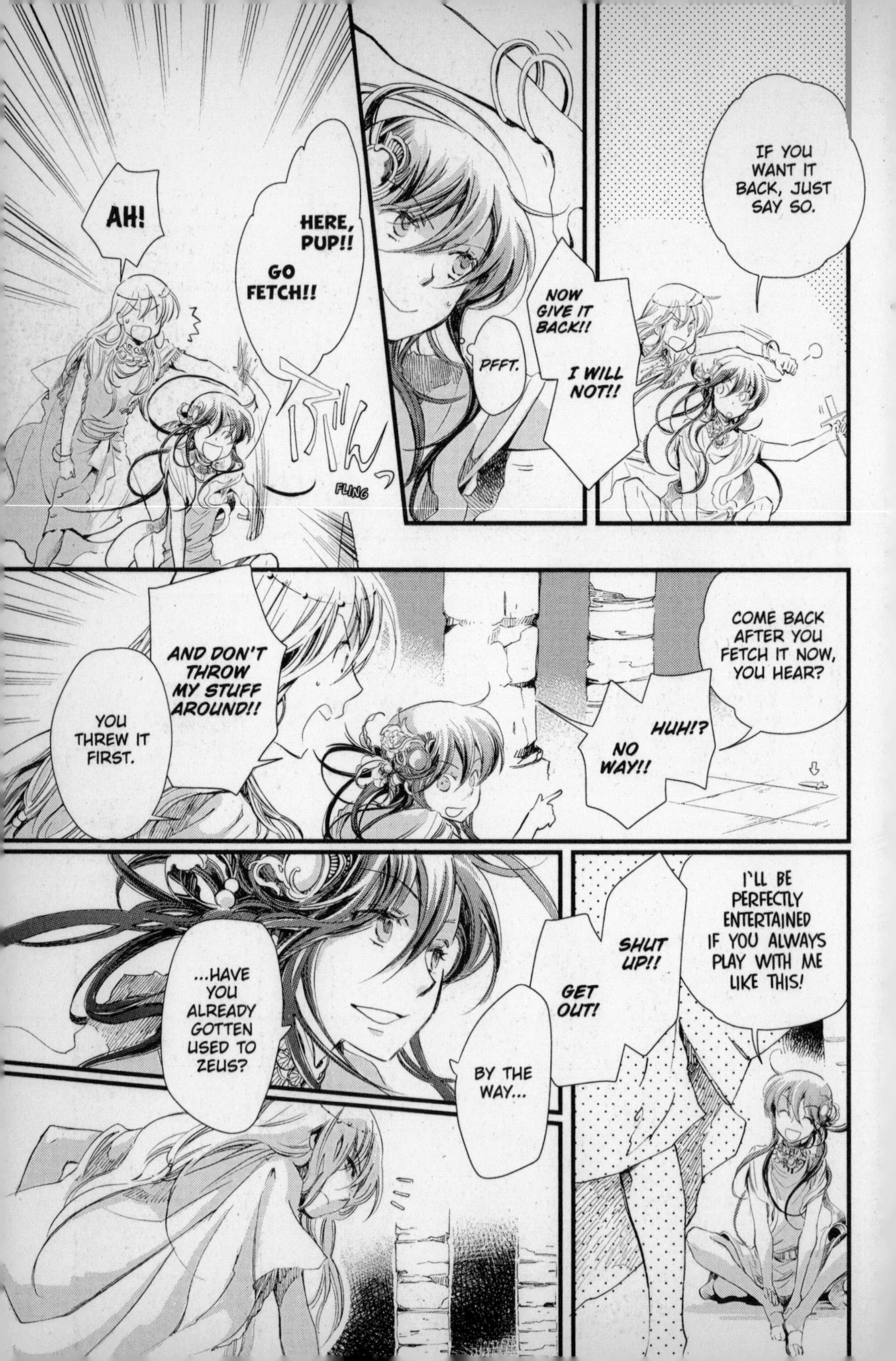

IF YOU WANT IT BACK, JUST SAY SO.
NOW GIVE IT BACK!!
I WILL NOT!!
PFFT.
HERE, PUP!!
GO FETCH!!
FLING
AH!
COME BACK AFTER YOU FETCH IT NOW, YOU HEAR?
HUH!?
NO WAY!!
AND DON'T THROW MY STUFF AROUND!!
YOU THREW IT FIRST.
I'LL BE PERFECTLY ENTERTAINED IF YOU ALWAYS PLAY WITH ME LIKE THIS!
SHUT UP!!
GET OUT!
BY THE WAY...
...HAVE YOU ALREADY GOTTEN USED TO ZEUS?

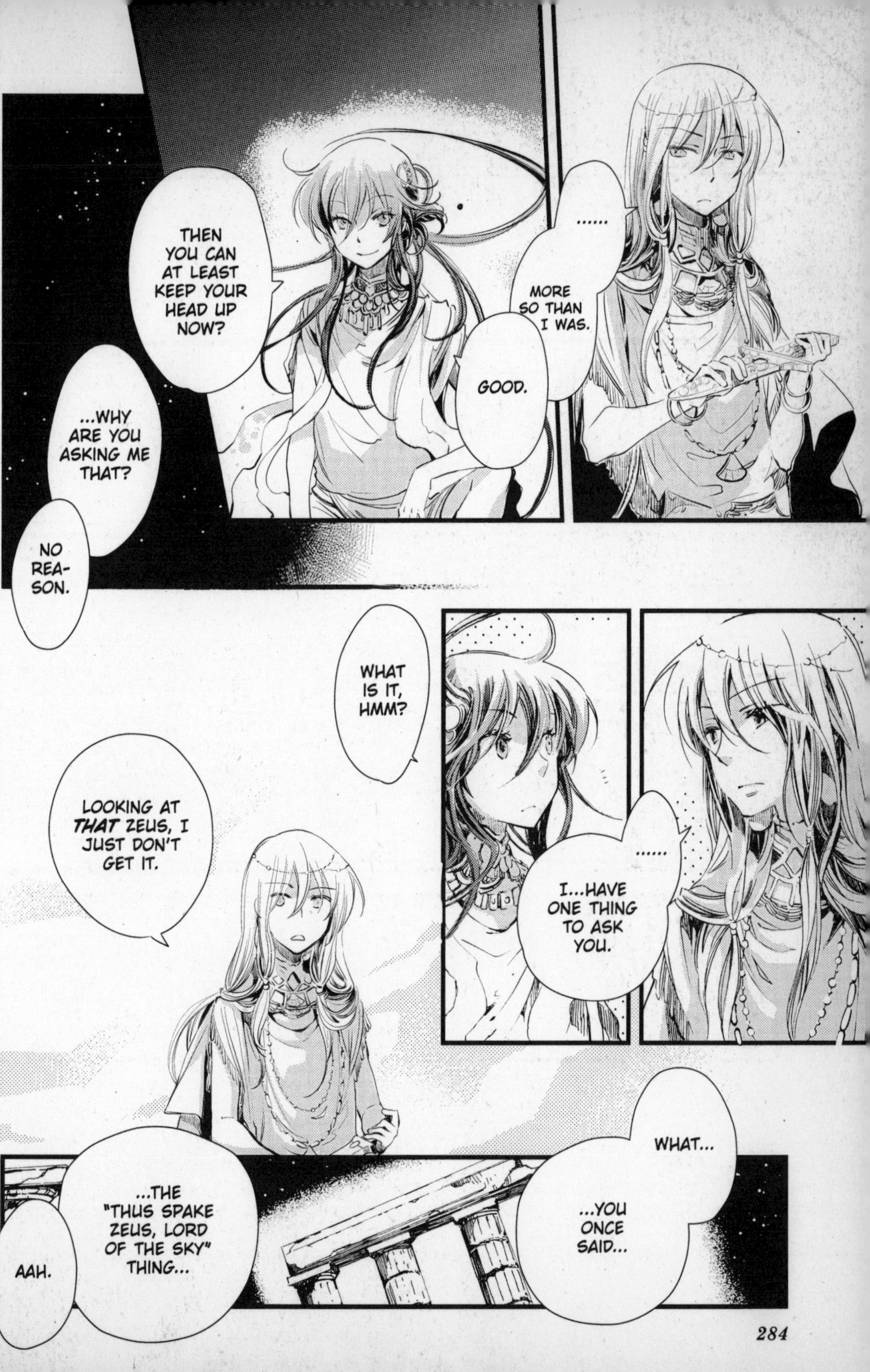

THEN YOU CAN AT LEAST KEEP YOUR HEAD UP NOW?
......
MORE SO THAN I WAS.
GOOD.
...WHY ARE YOU ASKING ME THAT?
NO REA-SON.
......
I...HAVE ONE THING TO ASK YOU.
WHAT IS IT, HMM?
LOOKING AT *THAT* ZEUS, I JUST DON'T GET IT.
WHAT...
...YOU ONCE SAID...
...THE "THUS SPAKE ZEUS, LORD OF THE SKY" THING...
AAH.

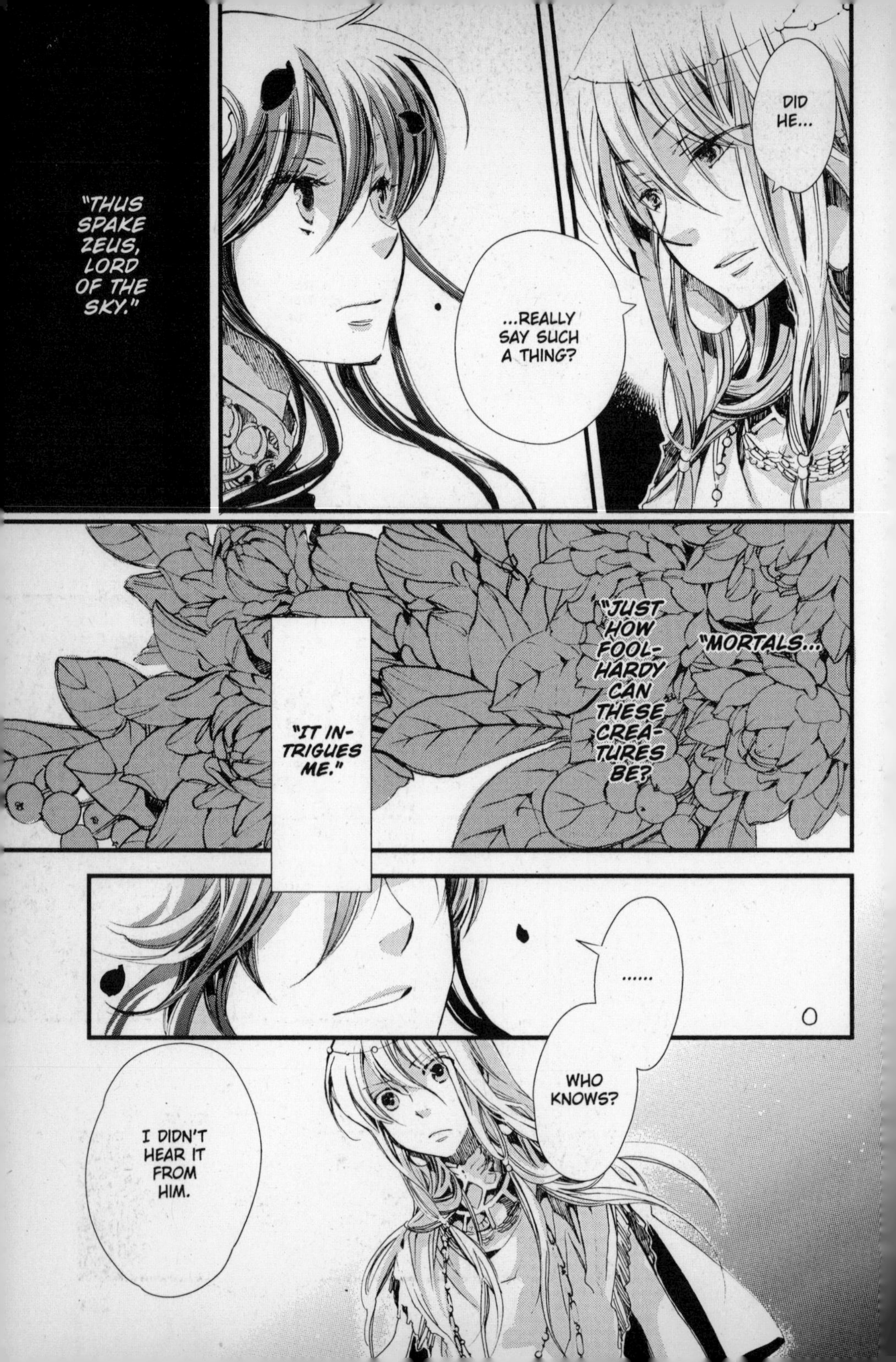
DID HE...
...REALLY SAY SUCH A THING?
"THUS SPAKE ZEUS, LORD OF THE SKY."
"MORTALS...
"JUST HOW FOOL-HARDY CAN THESE CREA-TURES BE?
"IT IN-TRIGUES ME."
......
WHO KNOWS?
I DIDN'T HEAR IT FROM HIM.

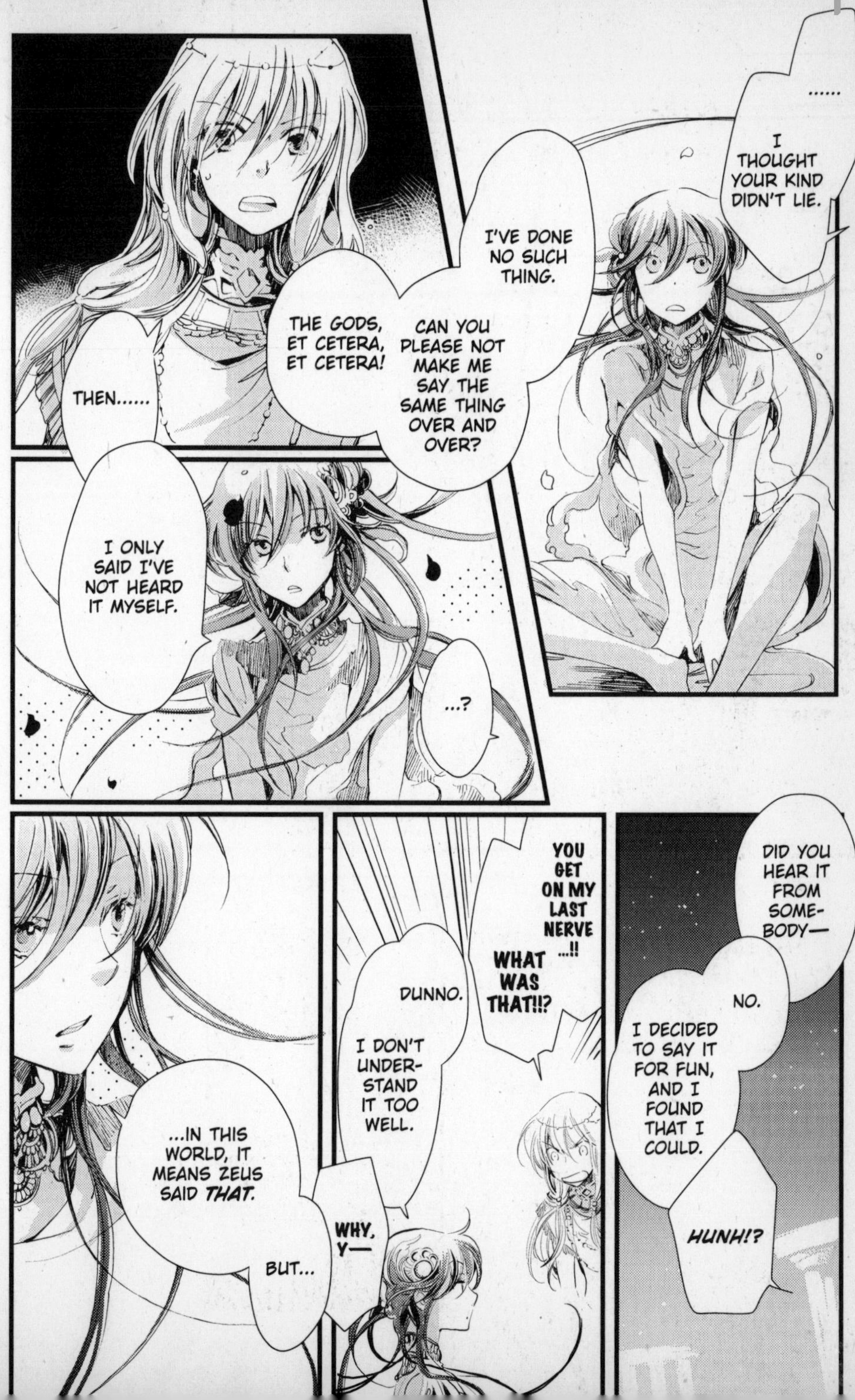
......
I THOUGHT YOUR KIND DIDN'T LIE.
I'VE DONE NO SUCH THING.
CAN YOU PLEASE NOT MAKE ME SAY THE SAME THING OVER AND OVER?
THE GODS, ET CETERA, ET CETERA!
THEN......
I ONLY SAID I'VE NOT HEARD IT MYSELF.
...?
DID YOU HEAR IT FROM SOME-BODY—
NO.
I DECIDED TO SAY IT FOR FUN, AND I FOUND THAT I COULD.
HUNH!?
YOU GET ON MY LAST NERVE...!!
WHAT WAS THAT!!?
DUNNO.
I DON'T UNDER-STAND IT TOO WELL.
WHY, Y—
BUT...
...IN THIS WORLD, IT MEANS ZEUS SAID *THAT*.

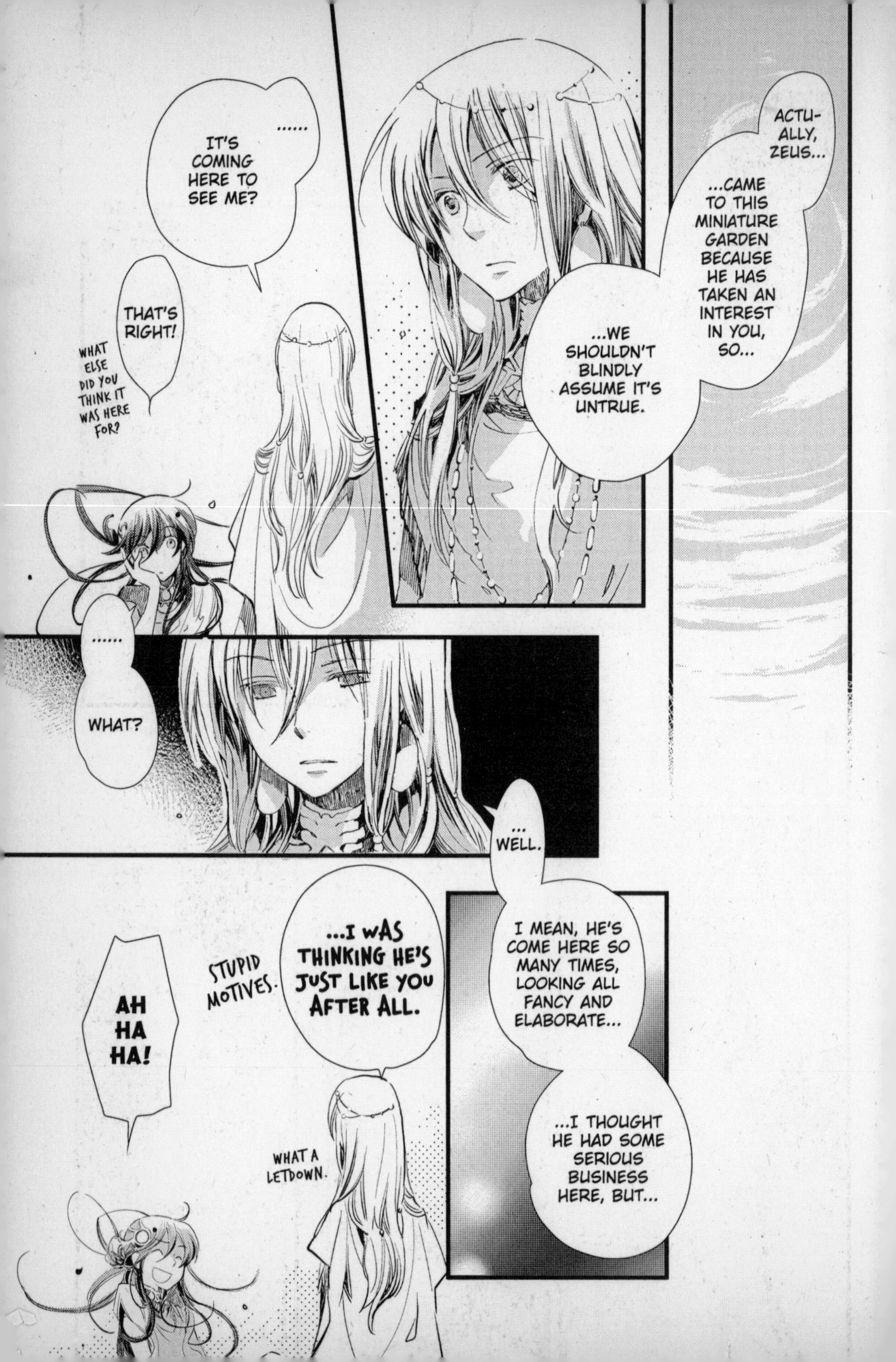
ACTU-ALLY, ZEUS...
...CAME TO THIS MINIATURE GARDEN BECAUSE HE HAS TAKEN AN INTEREST IN YOU, SO...
...WE SHOULDN'T BLINDLY ASSUME IT'S UNTRUE.
......
IT'S COMING HERE TO SEE ME?
THAT'S RIGHT!
WHAT ELSE DID YOU THINK IT WAS HERE FOR?
......
WHAT?
... WELL.
I MEAN, HE'S COME HERE SO MANY TIMES, LOOKING ALL FANCY AND ELABORATE...
...I THOUGHT HE HAD SOME SERIOUS BUSINESS HERE, BUT...
WHAT A LETDOWN.
...I WAS THINKING HE'S JUST LIKE YOU AFTER ALL.
STUPID MOTIVES.
AH HA HA!

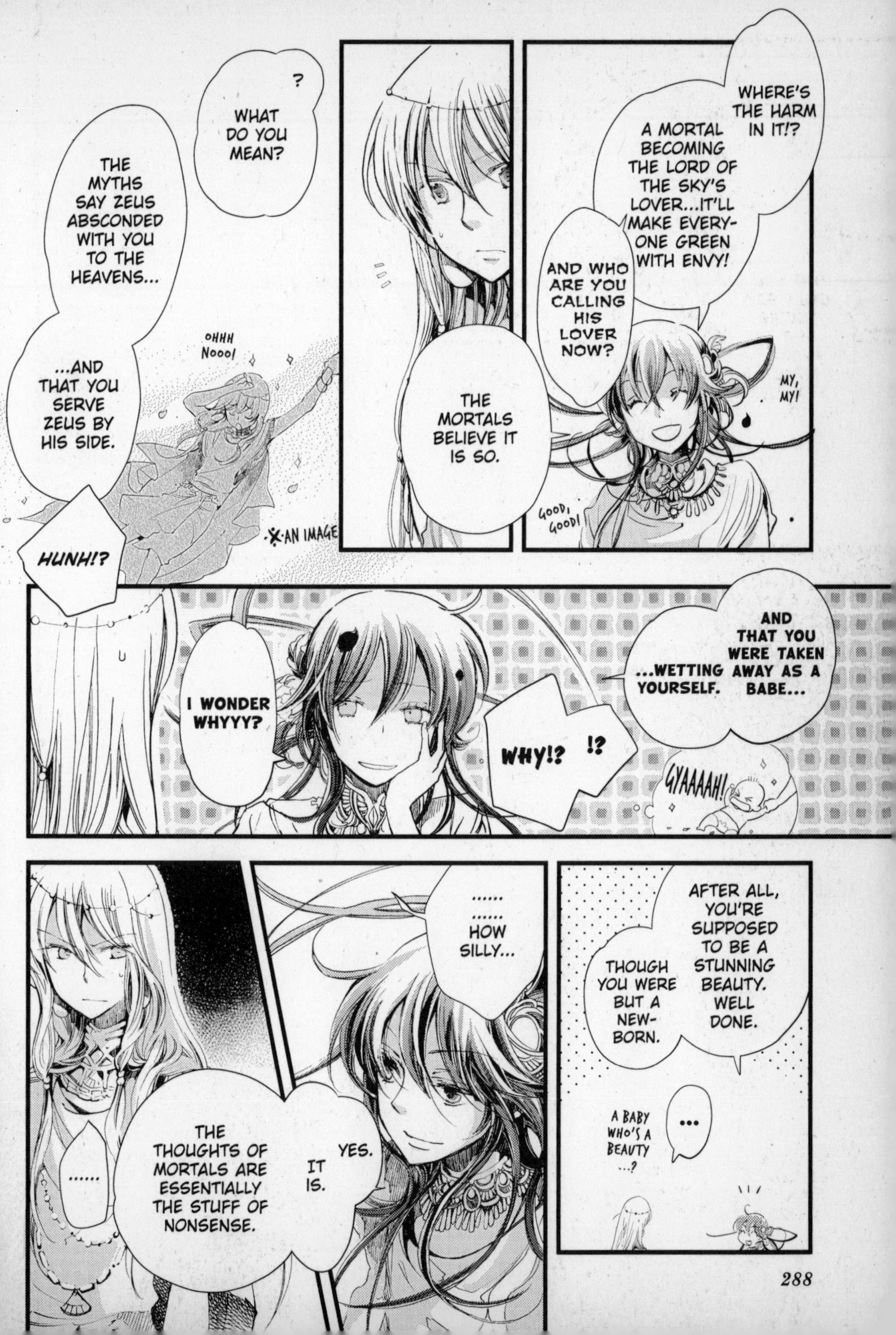
WHERE'S THE HARM IN IT!?
A MORTAL BECOMING THE LORD OF THE SKY'S LOVER...IT'LL MAKE EVERY-ONE GREEN WITH ENVY!
AND WHO ARE YOU CALLING HIS LOVER NOW?
MY, MY!
GOOD, GOOD!
THE MORTALS BELIEVE IT IS SO.
?
WHAT DO YOU MEAN?
THE MYTHS SAY ZEUS ABSCONDED WITH YOU TO THE HEAVENS...
...AND THAT YOU SERVE ZEUS BY HIS SIDE.
OHHH NOOO!
※AN IMAGE
HUNH!?
AND THAT YOU WERE TAKEN AWAY AS A BABE...
...WETTING YOURSELF.
GYAAAAH!
!?
WHY!?
I WONDER WHYYY?
AFTER ALL, YOU'RE SUPPOSED TO BE A STUNNING BEAUTY. WELL DONE.
THOUGH YOU WERE BUT A NEW-BORN.
...
A BABY WHO'S A BEAUTY ...?
.... HOW SILLY...
YES. IT IS.
THE THOUGHTS OF MORTALS ARE ESSENTIALLY THE STUFF OF NONSENSE.
......

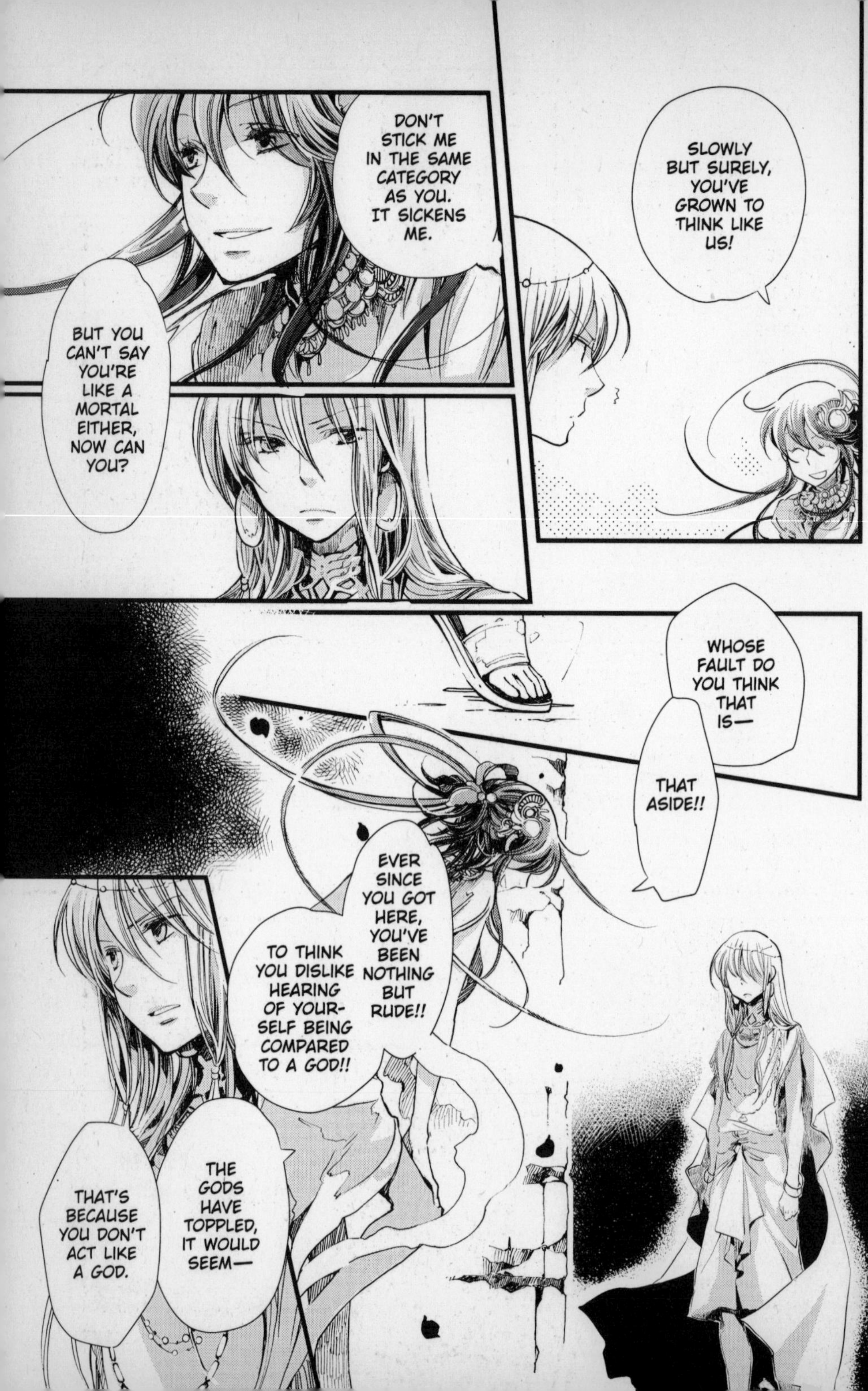
SLOWLY BUT SURELY, YOU'VE GROWN TO THINK LIKE US!
DON'T STICK ME IN THE SAME CATEGORY AS YOU. IT SICKENS ME.
BUT YOU CAN'T SAY YOU'RE LIKE A MORTAL EITHER, NOW CAN YOU?
WHOSE FAULT DO YOU THINK THAT IS—
THAT ASIDE!!
EVER SINCE YOU GOT HERE, YOU'VE BEEN NOTHING BUT RUDE!!
TO THINK YOU DISLIKE HEARING OF YOUR-SELF BEING COMPARED TO A GOD!!
THE GODS HAVE TOPPLED, IT WOULD SEEM—
THAT'S BECAUSE YOU DON'T ACT LIKE A GOD.

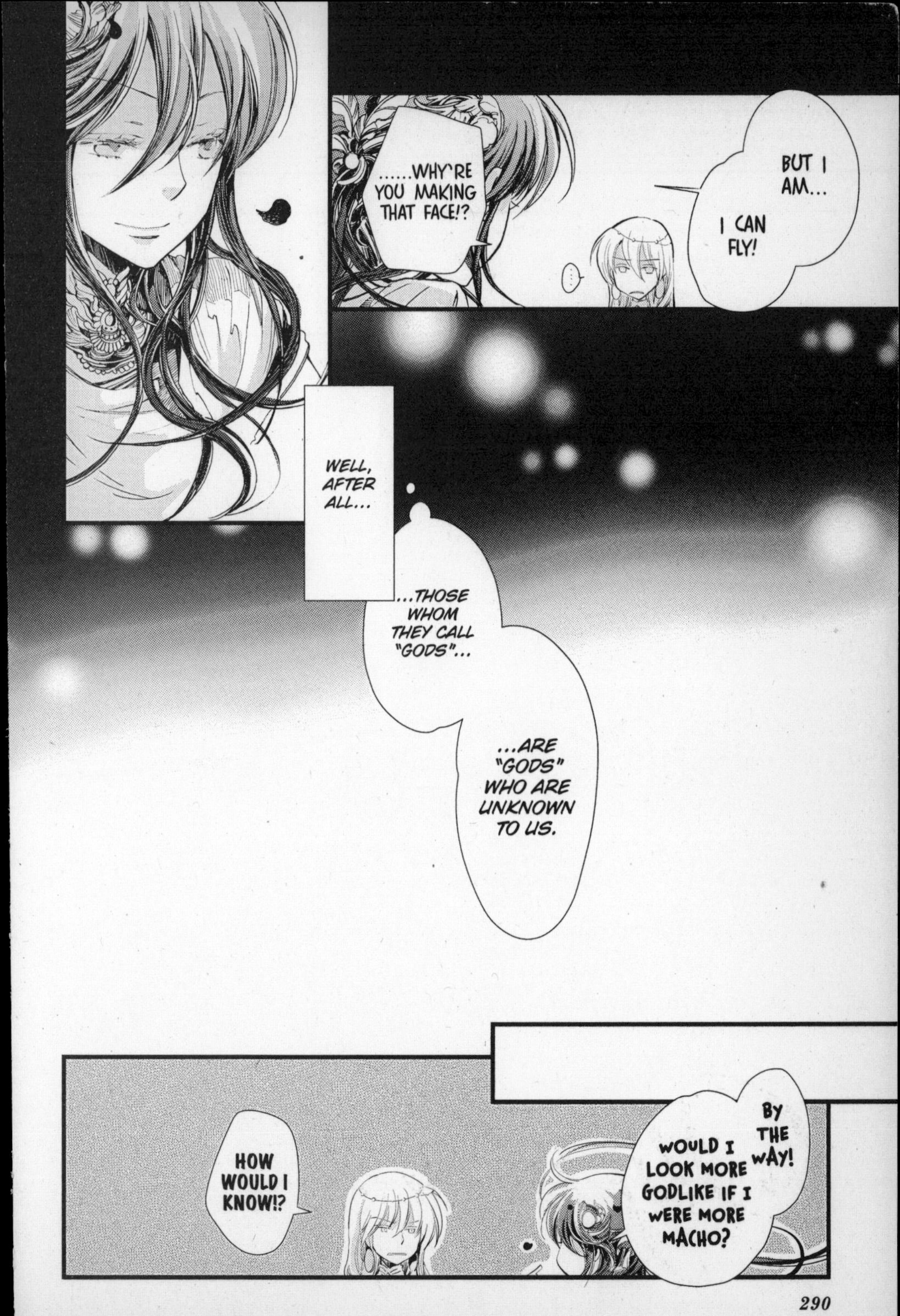
BUT I AM...
I CAN FLY!
......WHY'RE YOU MAKING THAT FACE!?
...
WELL, AFTER ALL...
...THOSE WHOM THEY CALL "GODS"...
...ARE "GODS" WHO ARE UNKNOWN TO US.
BY THE WAY!
WOULD I LOOK MORE GODLIKE IF I WERE MORE MACHO?
HOW WOULD I KNOW!?

Olympos

TREMBLE
TREMBLE
SHE'S TERRIFIED.

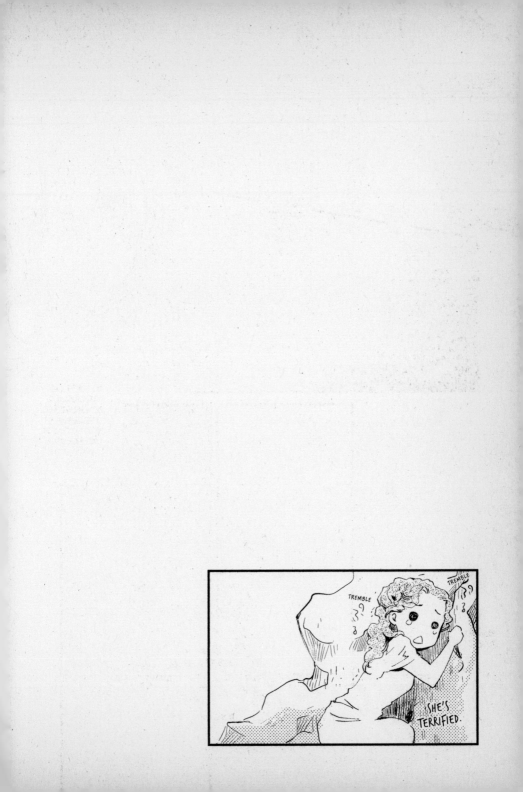

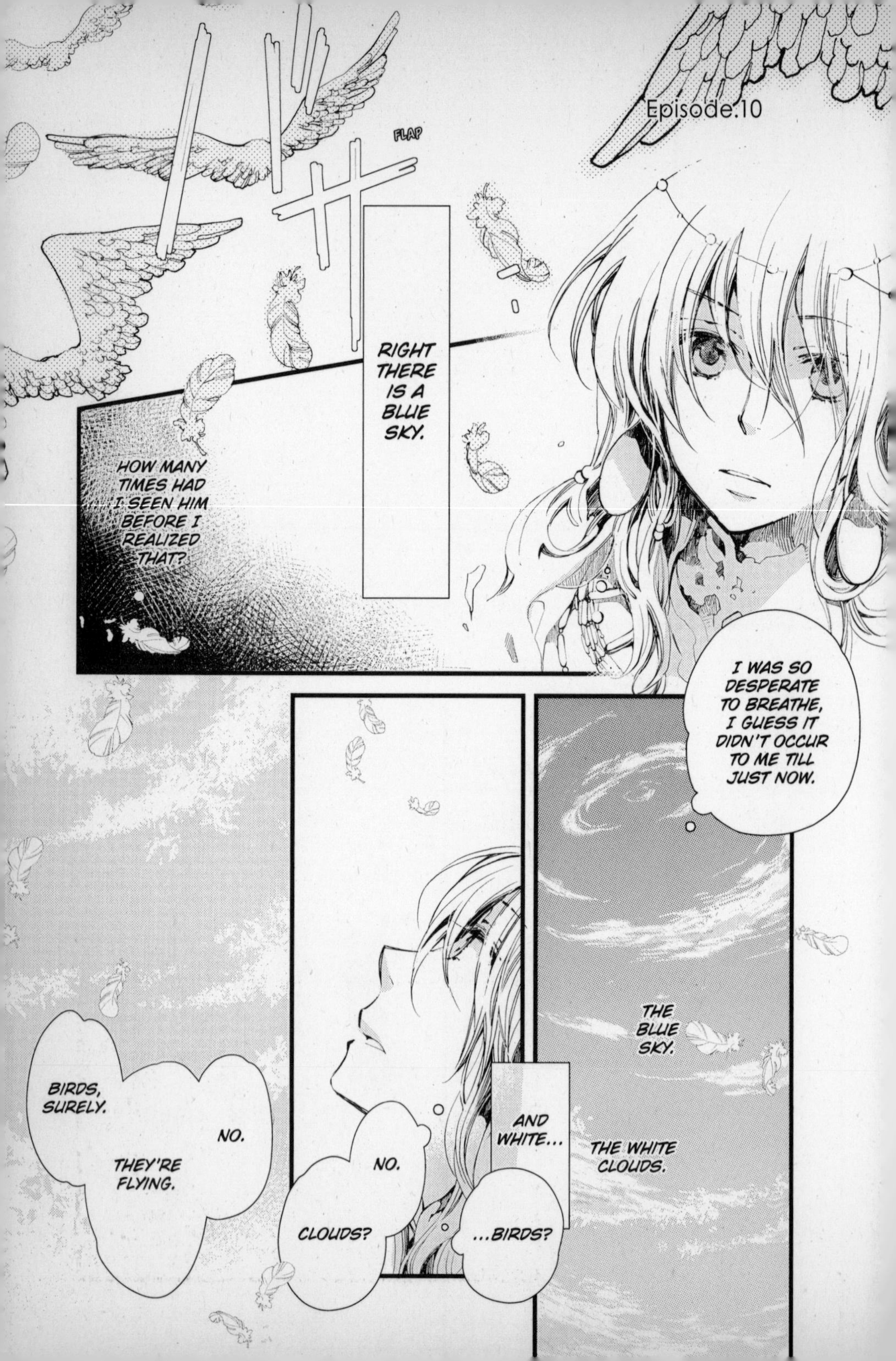
Episode.10
FLAP
RIGHT THERE IS A BLUE SKY.
HOW MANY TIMES HAD I SEEN HIM BEFORE I REALIZED THAT?
I WAS SO DESPERATE TO BREATHE, I GUESS IT DIDN'T OCCUR TO ME TILL JUST NOW.
THE BLUE SKY.
THE WHITE CLOUDS.
AND WHITE...
...BIRDS?
NO.
CLOUDS?
BIRDS, SURELY.
NO.
THEY'RE FLYING.

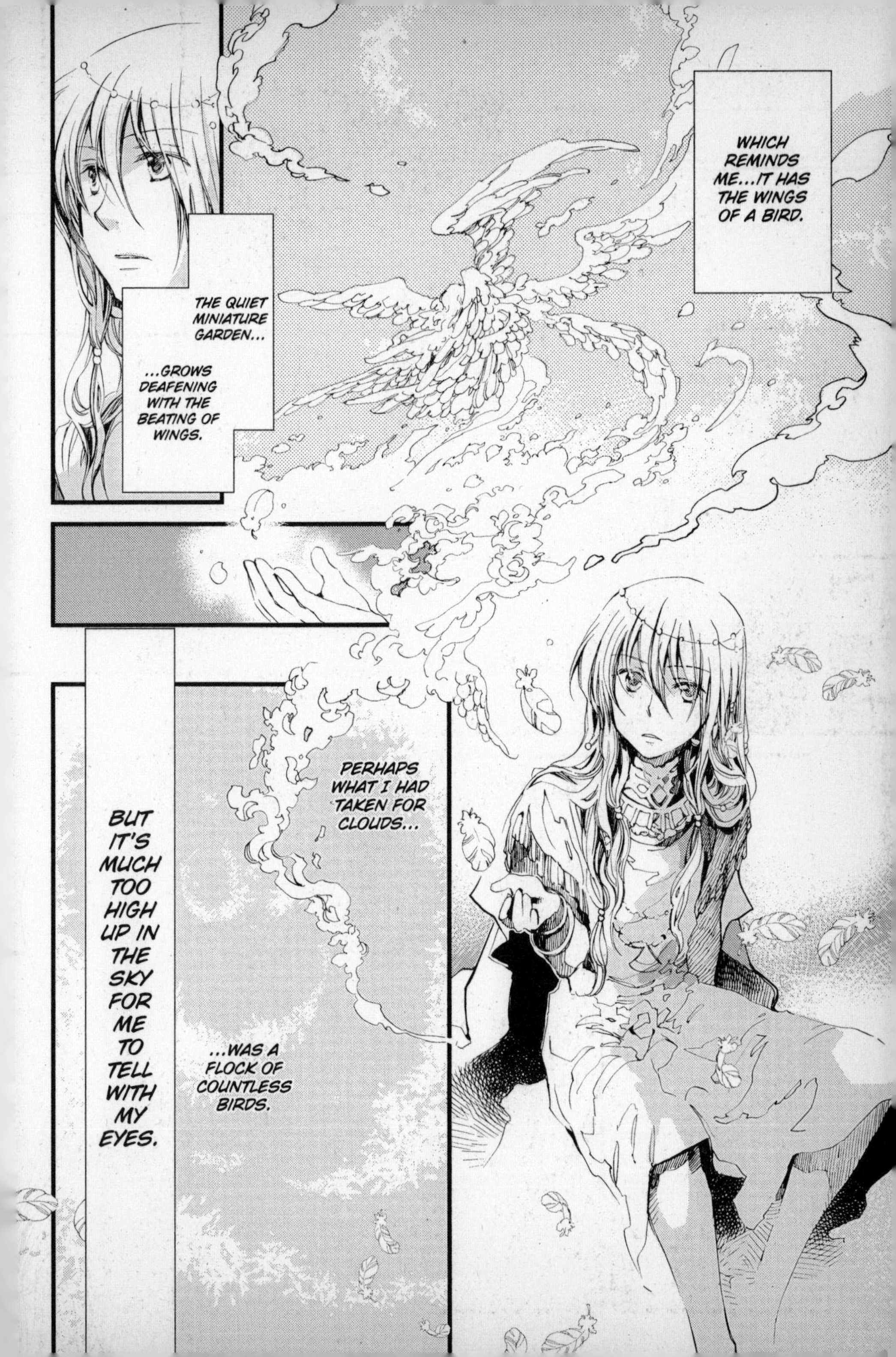
WHICH REMINDS ME...IT HAS THE WINGS OF A BIRD.
THE QUIET MINIATURE GARDEN...
...GROWS DEAFENING WITH THE BEATING OF WINGS.
PERHAPS WHAT I HAD TAKEN FOR CLOUDS...
...WAS A FLOCK OF COUNTLESS BIRDS.
BUT IT'S MUCH TOO HIGH UP IN THE SKY FOR ME TO TELL WITH MY EYES.

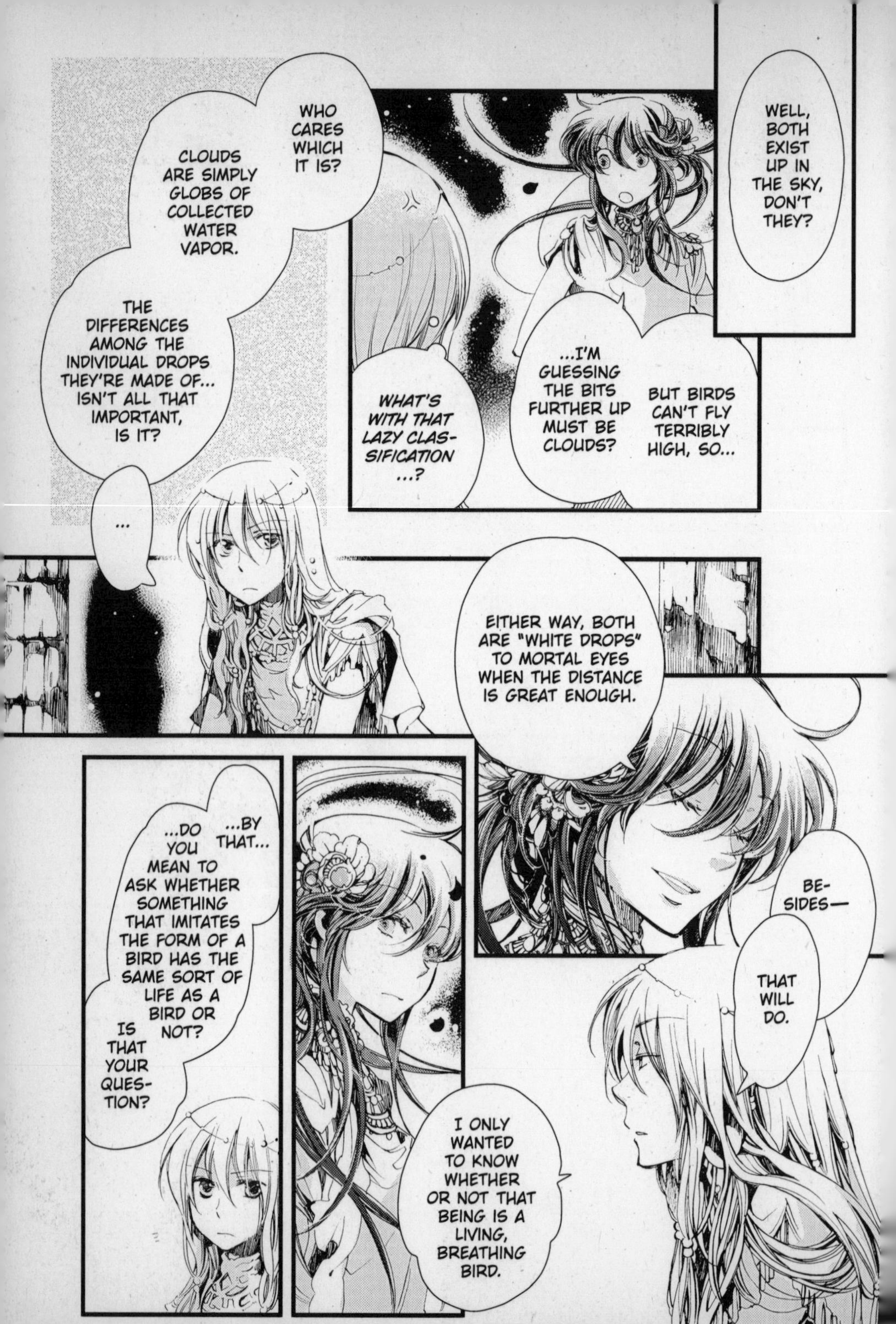
WELL, BOTH EXIST UP IN THE SKY, DON'T THEY?
BUT BIRDS CAN'T FLY TERRIBLY HIGH, SO...
...I'M GUESSING THE BITS FURTHER UP MUST BE CLOUDS?
WHAT'S WITH THAT LAZY CLAS-SIFICATION ...?
WHO CARES WHICH IT IS?
CLOUDS ARE SIMPLY GLOBS OF COLLECTED WATER VAPOR.
THE DIFFERENCES AMONG THE INDIVIDUAL DROPS THEY'RE MADE OF... ISN'T ALL THAT IMPORTANT, IS IT?
...
EITHER WAY, BOTH ARE "WHITE DROPS" TO MORTAL EYES WHEN THE DISTANCE IS GREAT ENOUGH.
BE-SIDES—
THAT WILL DO.
I ONLY WANTED TO KNOW WHETHER OR NOT THAT BEING IS A LIVING, BREATHING BIRD.
...BY THAT...
...DO YOU MEAN TO ASK WHETHER SOMETHING THAT IMITATES THE FORM OF A BIRD HAS THE SAME SORT OF LIFE AS A BIRD OR NOT?
IS THAT YOUR QUES-TION?

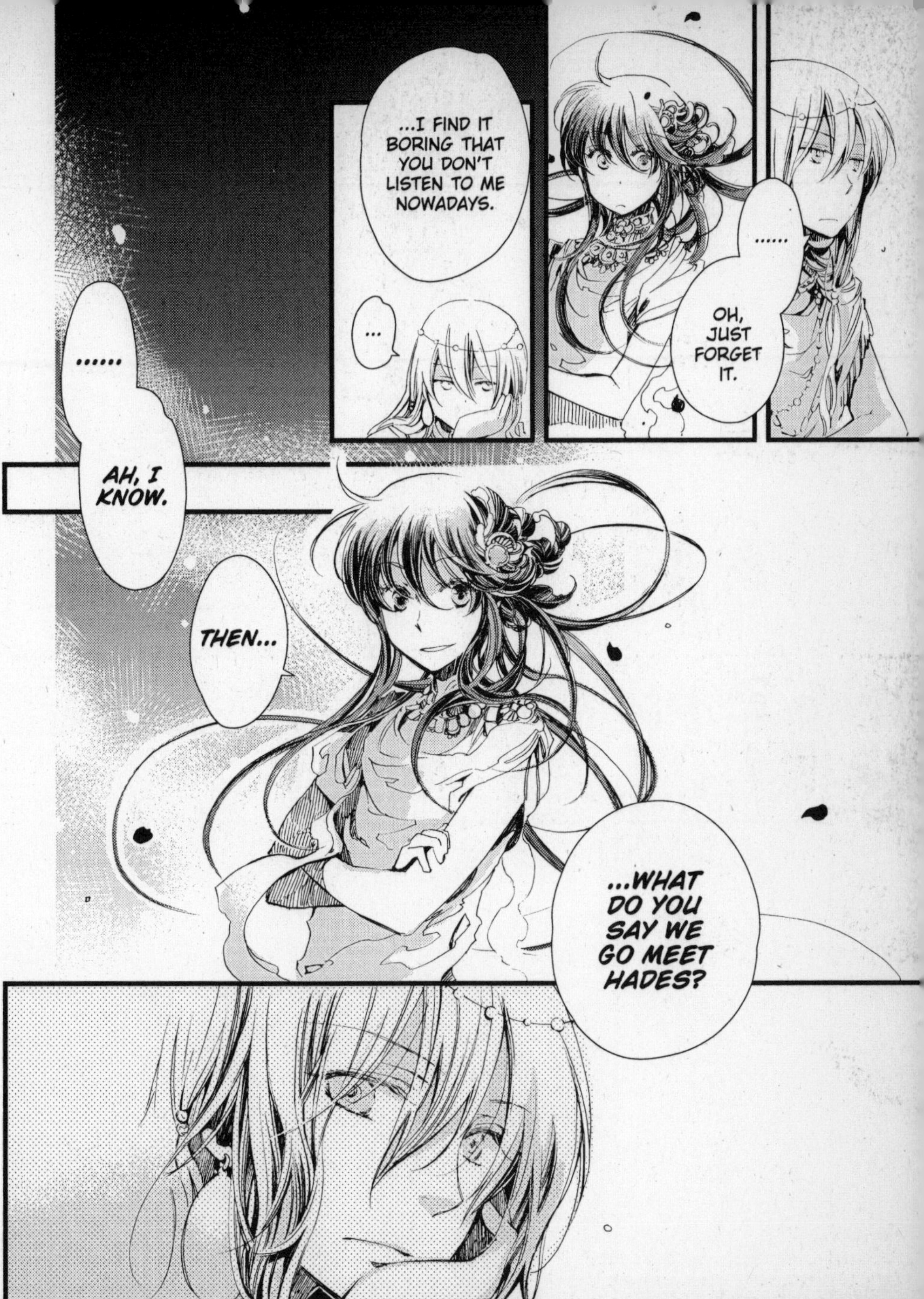
......
OH, JUST FORGET IT.
...I FIND IT BORING THAT YOU DON'T LISTEN TO ME NOWADAYS.
...
......
AH, I KNOW.
THEN...
...WHAT DO YOU SAY WE GO MEET HADES?

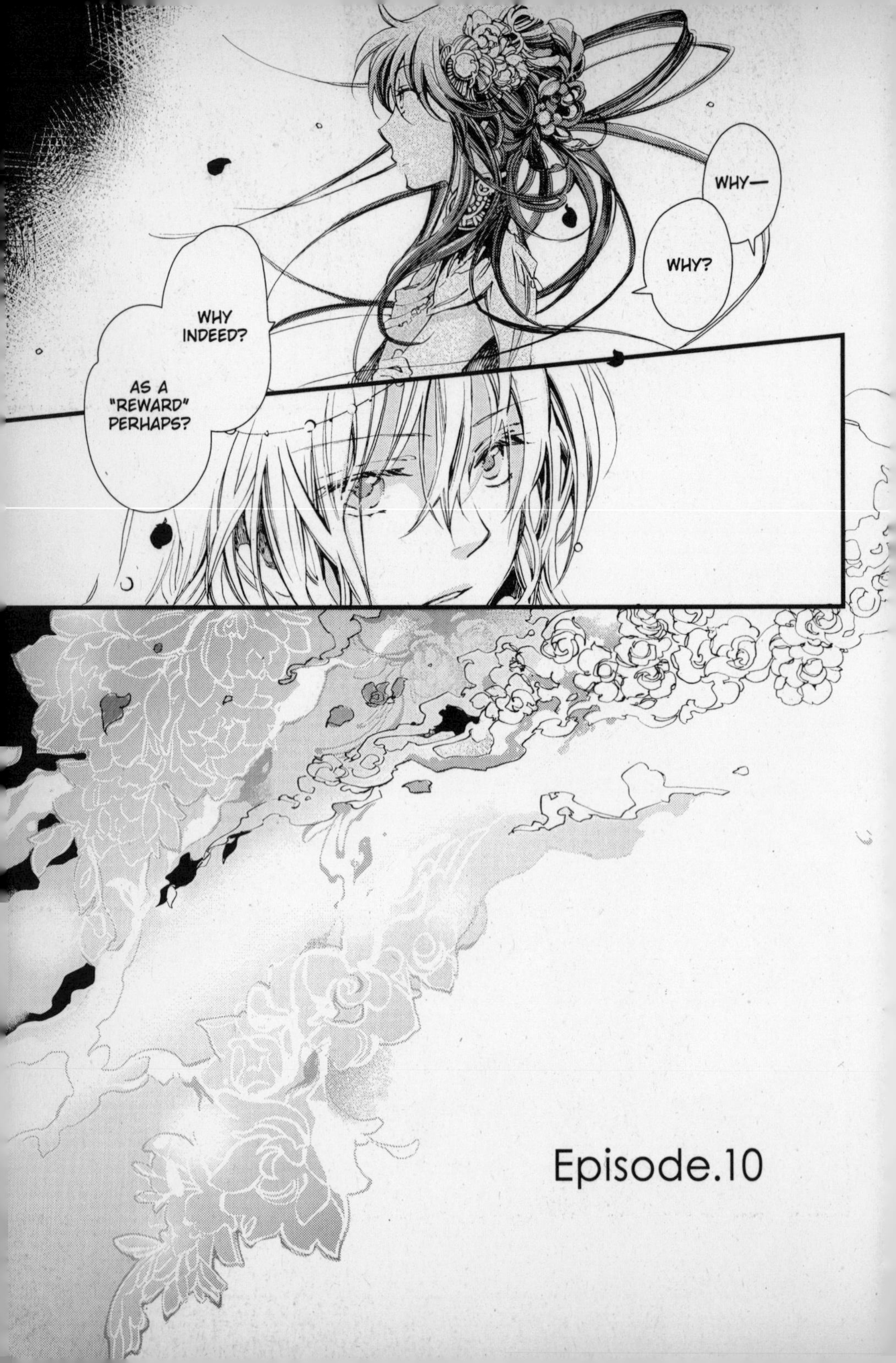
WHY—
WHY?
WHY INDEED?
AS A "REWARD" PERHAPS?
Episode.10

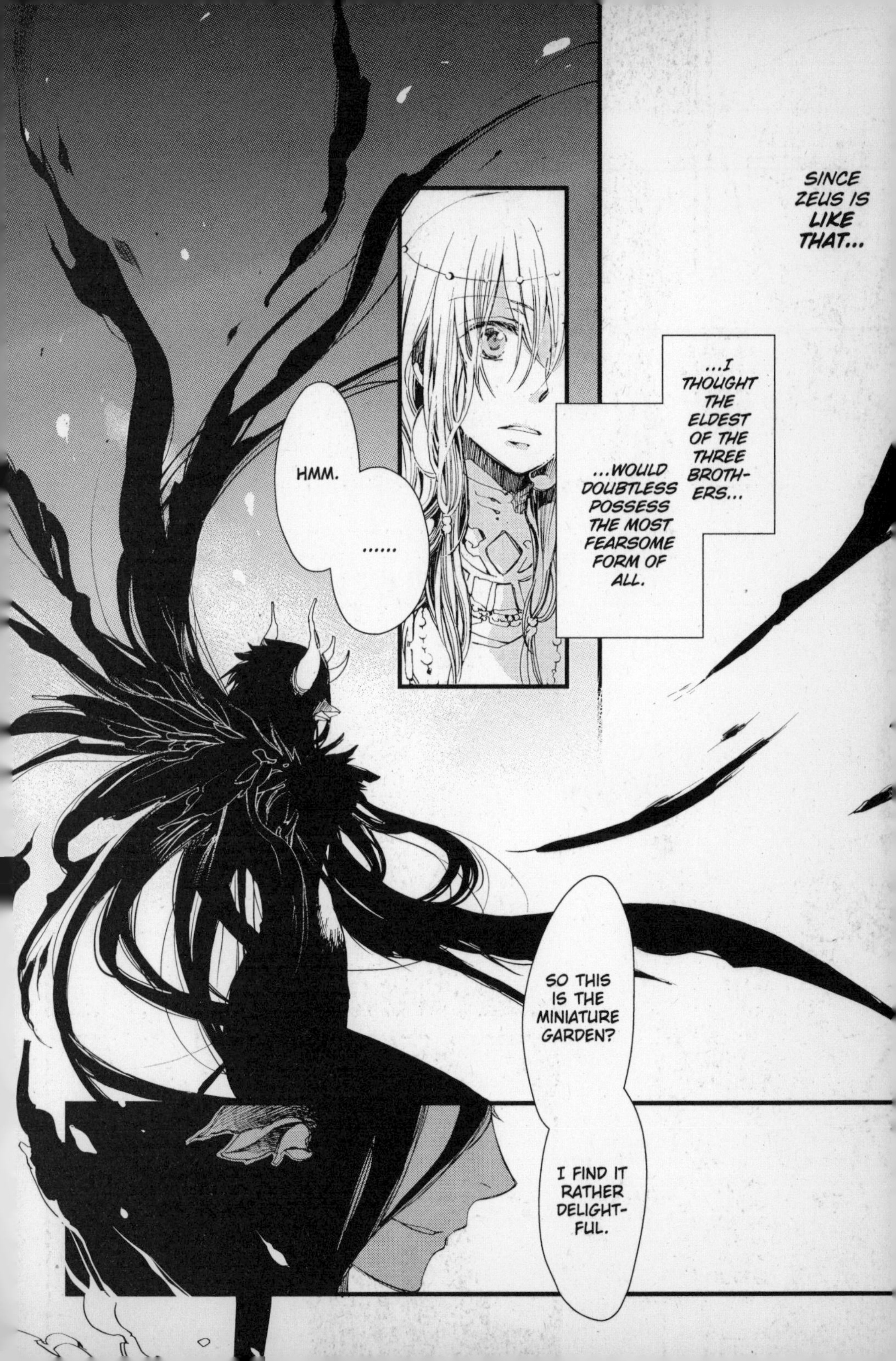
SINCE ZEUS IS LIKE THAT...
...I THOUGHT THE ELDEST OF THE THREE BROTH-ERS...
...WOULD DOUBTLESS POSSESS THE MOST FEARSOME FORM OF ALL.
HMM.
......
SO THIS IS THE MINIATURE GARDEN?
I FIND IT RATHER DELIGHT-FUL.

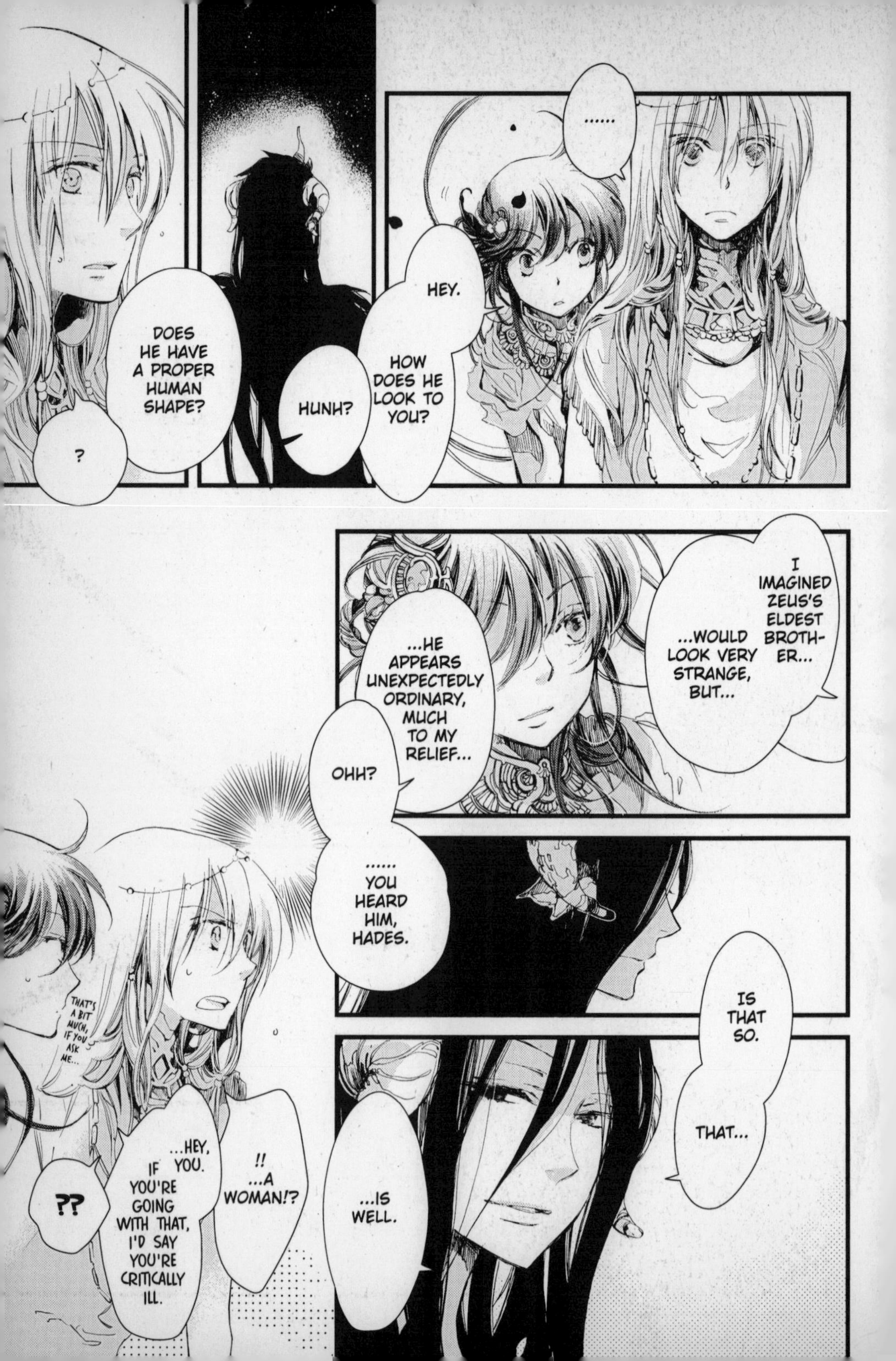
......
HEY.
HOW DOES HE LOOK TO YOU?
HUNH?
DOES HE HAVE A PROPER HUMAN SHAPE?
?
I IMAGINED ZEUS'S ELDEST BROTHER...
...WOULD LOOK VERY STRANGE, BUT...
...HE APPEARS UNEXPECTEDLY ORDINARY, MUCH TO MY RELIEF...
OHH?
...... YOU HEARD HIM, HADES.
IS THAT SO.
THAT...
...IS WELL.
!! ...A WOMAN!?
...HEY, YOU. IF YOU'RE GOING WITH THAT, I'D SAY YOU'RE CRITICALLY ILL.
??
THAT'S A BIT MUCH, IF YOU ASK ME...

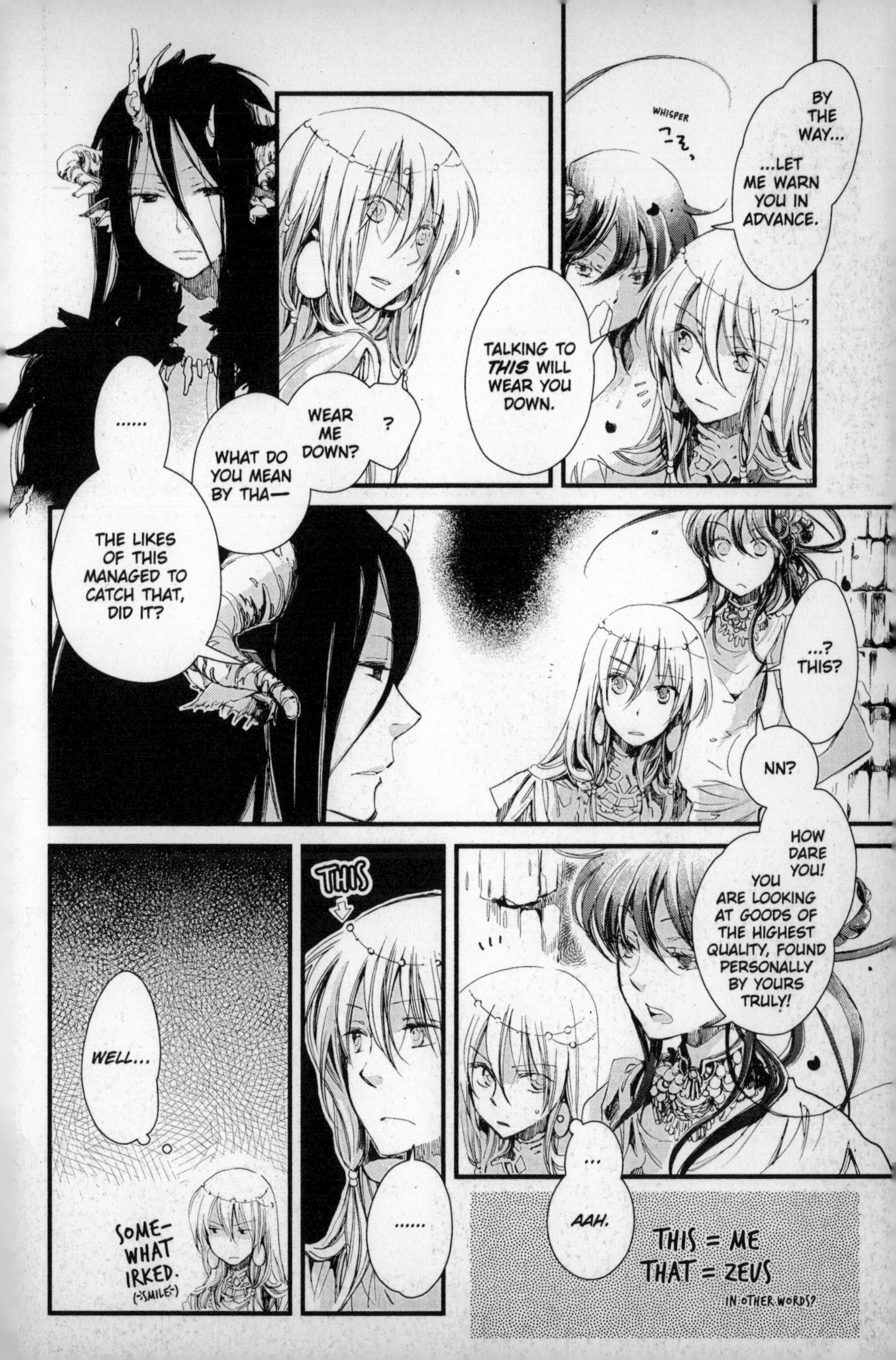
BY THE WAY...
...LET ME WARN YOU IN ADVANCE.
WHISPER
TALKING TO THIS WILL WEAR YOU DOWN.
WEAR ME DOWN?
?
WHAT DO YOU MEAN BY THA—
......
THE LIKES OF THIS MANAGED TO CATCH THAT, DID IT?
...? THIS?
NN?
HOW DARE YOU! YOU ARE LOOKING AT GOODS OF THE HIGHEST QUALITY, FOUND PERSONALLY BY YOURS TRULY!
...
AAH.
THIS = ME
THAT = ZEUS
IN OTHER WORDS?
THIS
......
WELL...
SOME-WHAT IRKED.
(SMILE)

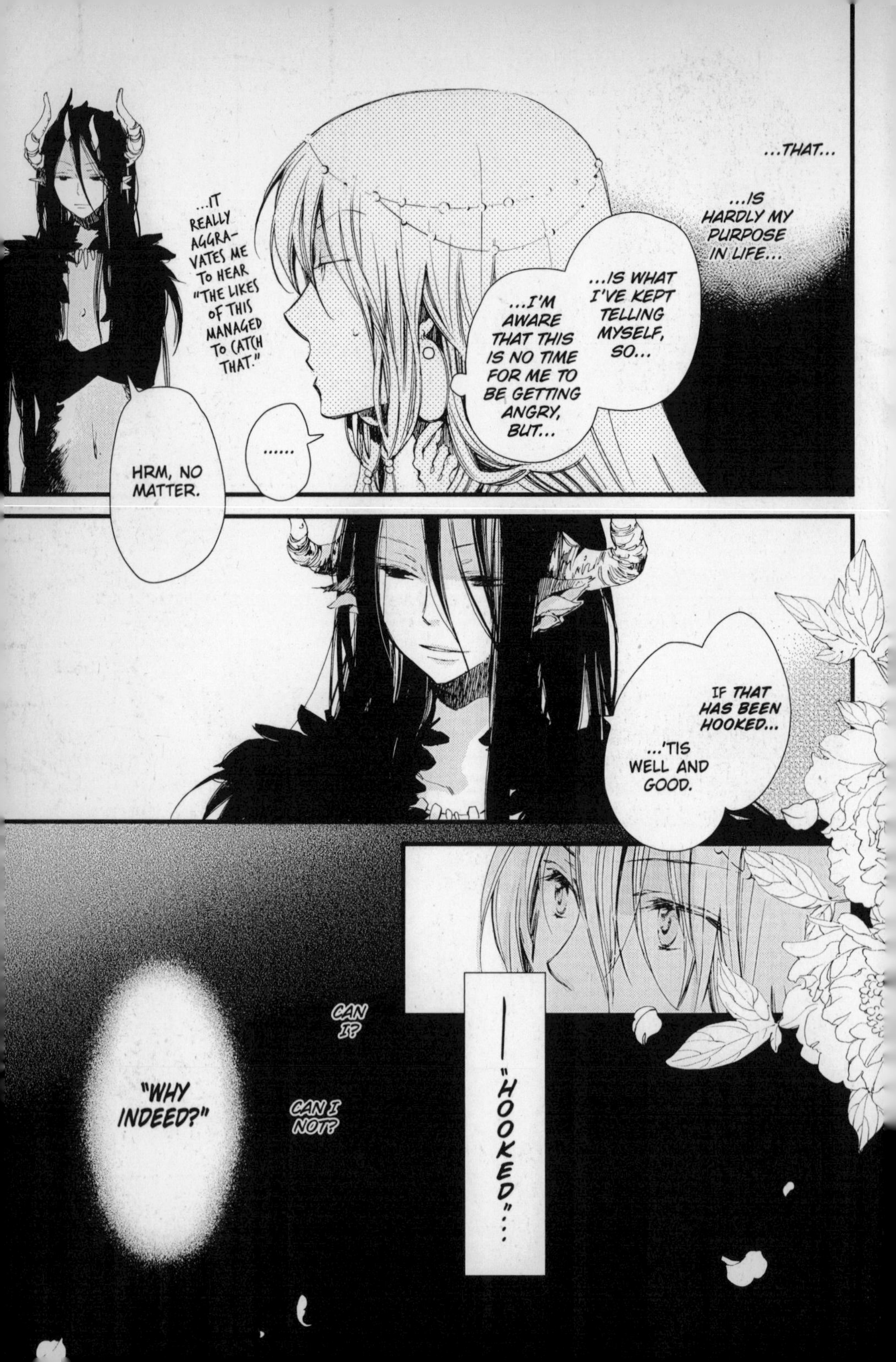
...THAT...
...IS HARDLY MY PURPOSE IN LIFE...
...IS WHAT I'VE KEPT TELLING MYSELF, SO...
...I'M AWARE THAT THIS IS NO TIME FOR ME TO BE GETTING ANGRY, BUT...
......
...IT REALLY AGGRAVATES ME TO HEAR "THE LIKES OF THIS MANAGED TO CATCH THAT."
HRM, NO MATTER.
IF THAT HAS BEEN HOOKED...
...'TIS WELL AND GOOD.
—"HOOKED"...
CAN I?
CAN I NOT?
"WHY INDEED?"

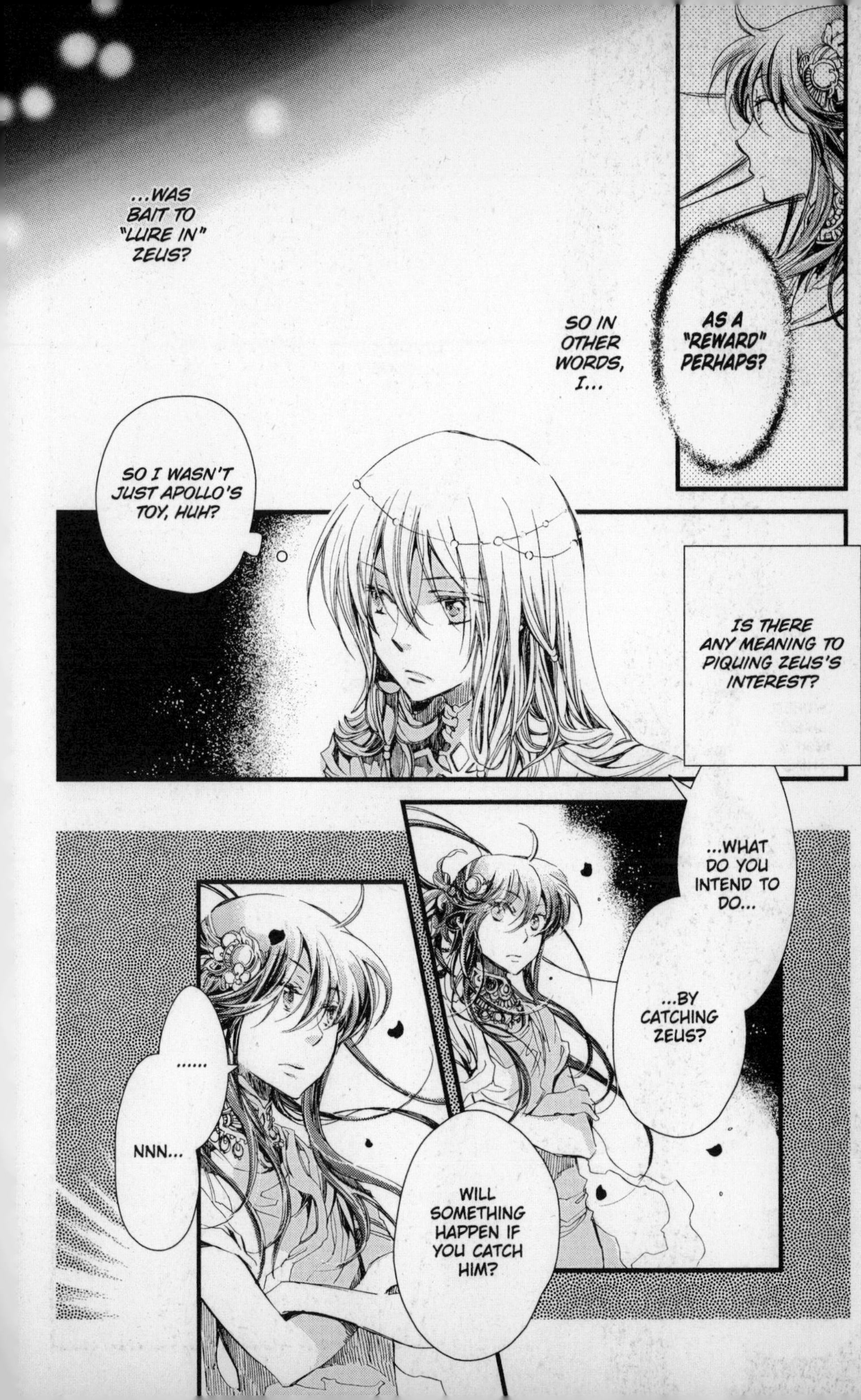
AS A "REWARD" PERHAPS?
SO IN OTHER WORDS, I...
...WAS BAIT TO "LURE IN" ZEUS?
IS THERE ANY MEANING TO PIQUING ZEUS'S INTEREST?
SO I WASN'T JUST APOLLO'S TOY, HUH?
...WHAT DO YOU INTEND TO DO...
...BY CATCHING ZEUS?
WILL SOMETHING HAPPEN IF YOU CATCH HIM?
......
NNN...

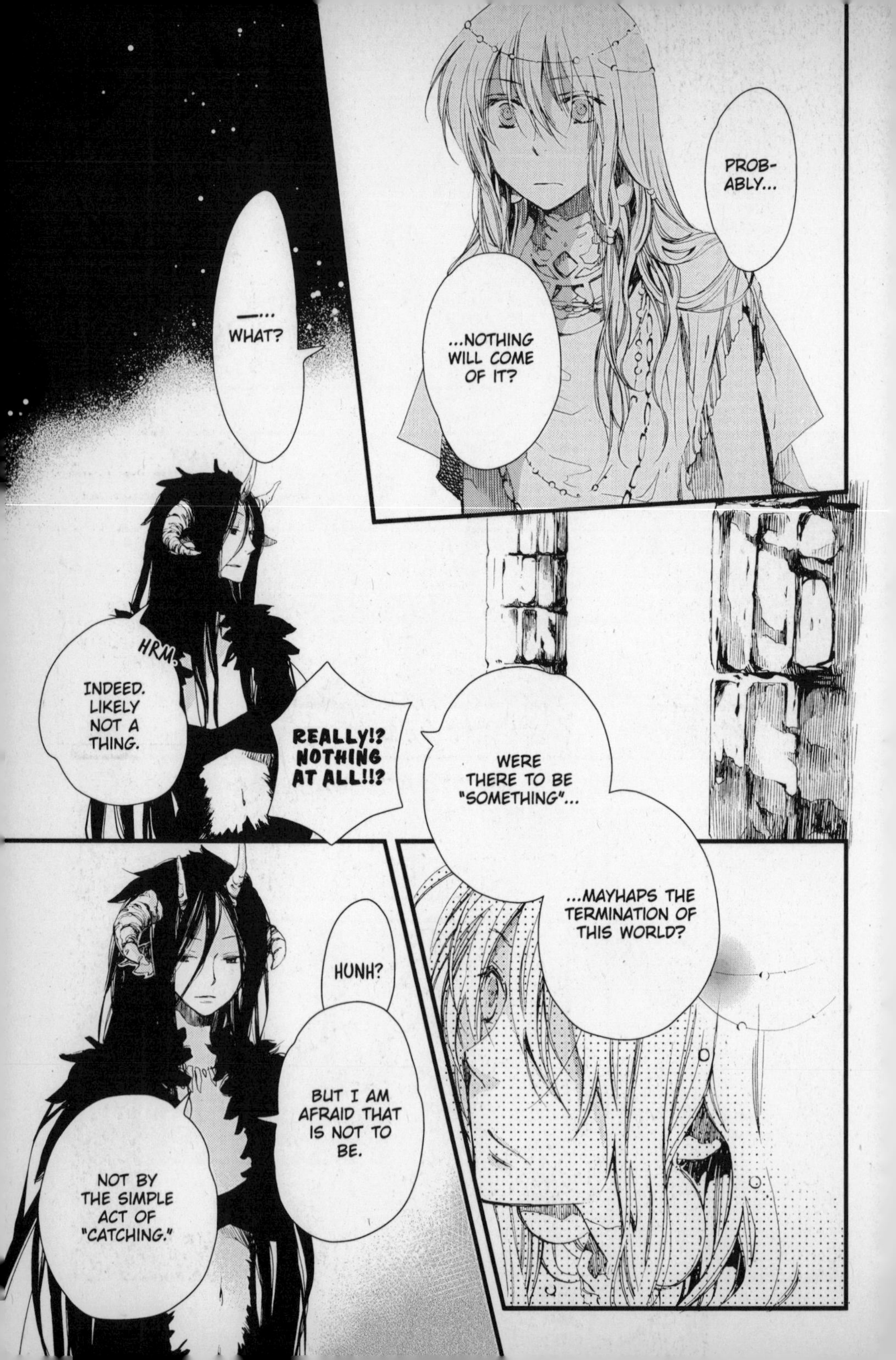
PROB-ABLY...
...NOTHING WILL COME OF IT?
—... WHAT?
REALLY!? NOTHING AT ALL!!?
HRM.
INDEED. LIKELY NOT A THING.
WERE THERE TO BE "SOMETHING"...
...MAYHAPS THE TERMINATION OF THIS WORLD?
HUNH?
BUT I AM AFRAID THAT IS NOT TO BE.
NOT BY THE SIMPLE ACT OF "CATCHING."

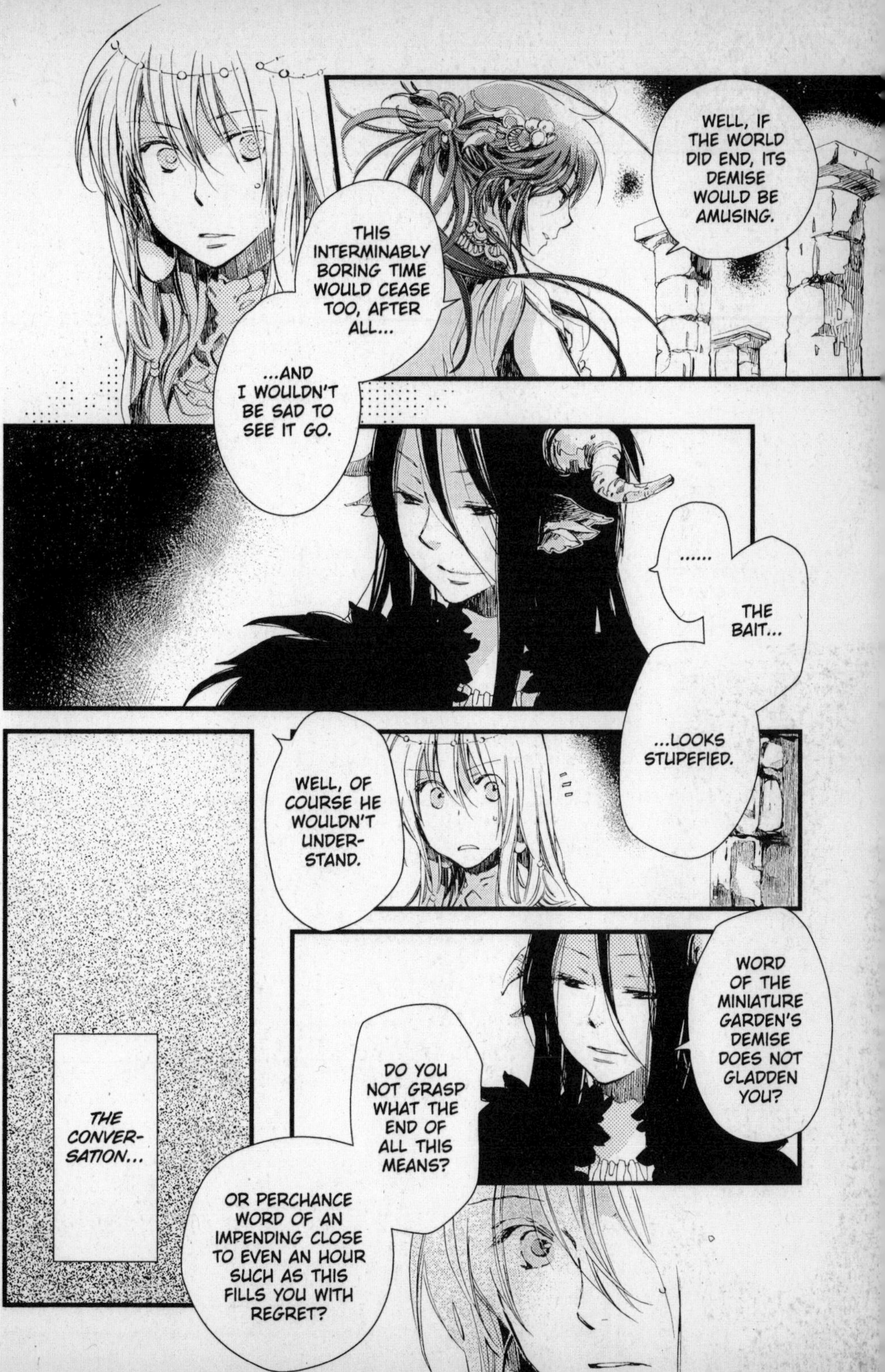
WELL, IF THE WORLD DID END, ITS DEMISE WOULD BE AMUSING.
THIS INTERMINABLY BORING TIME WOULD CEASE TOO, AFTER ALL...
...AND I WOULDN'T BE SAD TO SEE IT GO.
......
THE BAIT...
...LOOKS STUPEFIED.
WELL, OF COURSE HE WOULDN'T UNDER-STAND.
WORD OF THE MINIATURE GARDEN'S DEMISE DOES NOT GLADDEN YOU?
DO YOU NOT GRASP WHAT THE END OF ALL THIS MEANS?
OR PERCHANCE WORD OF AN IMPENDING CLOSE TO EVEN AN HOUR SUCH AS THIS FILLS YOU WITH REGRET?
THE CONVER-SATION...

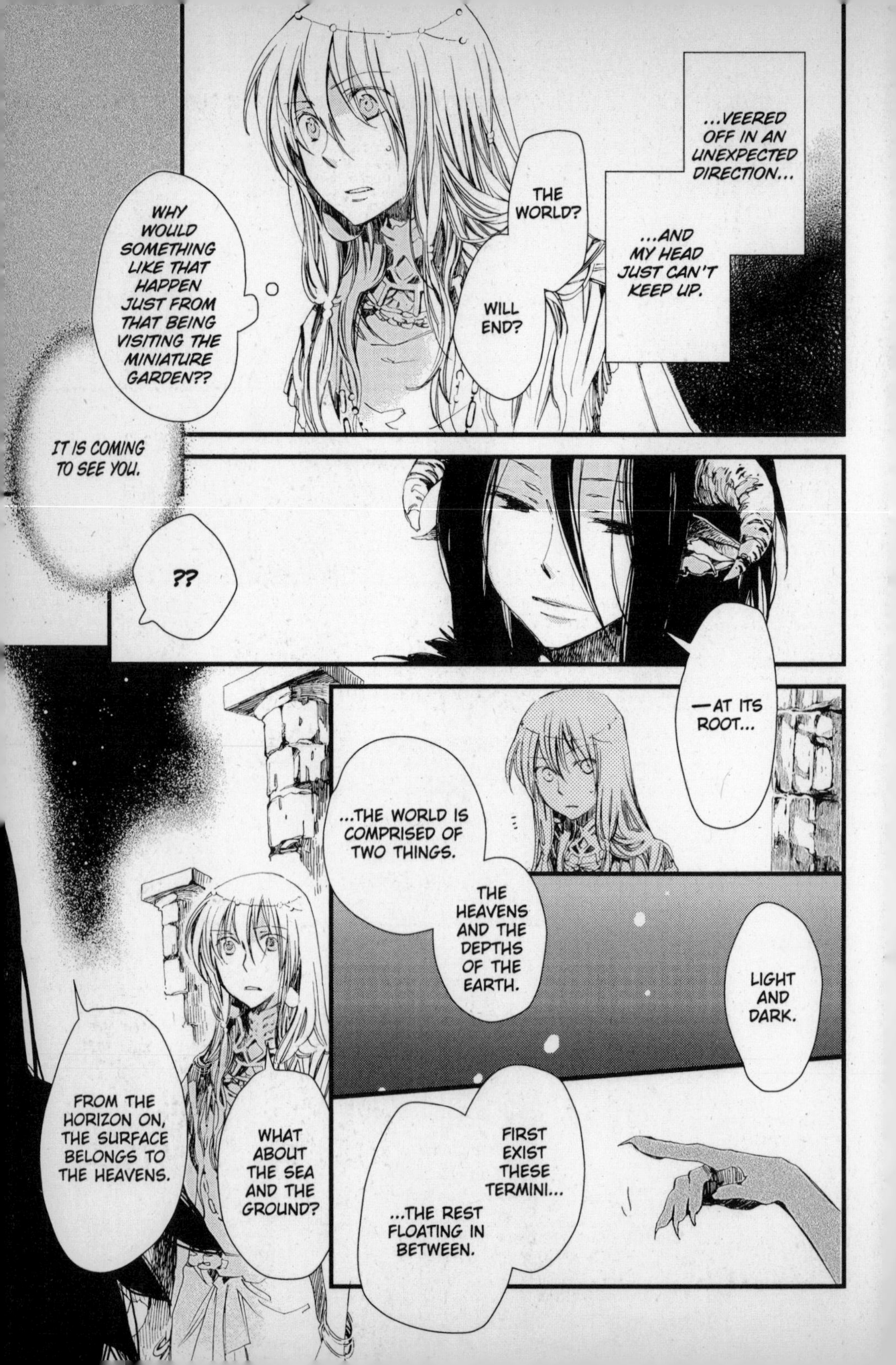
...VEERED OFF IN AN UNEXPECTED DIRECTION...
...AND MY HEAD JUST CAN'T KEEP UP.
THE WORLD?
WILL END?
WHY WOULD SOMETHING LIKE THAT HAPPEN JUST FROM THAT BEING VISITING THE MINIATURE GARDEN??
IT IS COMING TO SEE YOU.
??
—AT ITS ROOT...
...THE WORLD IS COMPRISED OF TWO THINGS.
LIGHT AND DARK.
THE HEAVENS AND THE DEPTHS OF THE EARTH.
FIRST EXIST THESE TERMINI...
...THE REST FLOATING IN BETWEEN.
WHAT ABOUT THE SEA AND THE GROUND?
FROM THE HORIZON ON, THE SURFACE BELONGS TO THE HEAVENS.

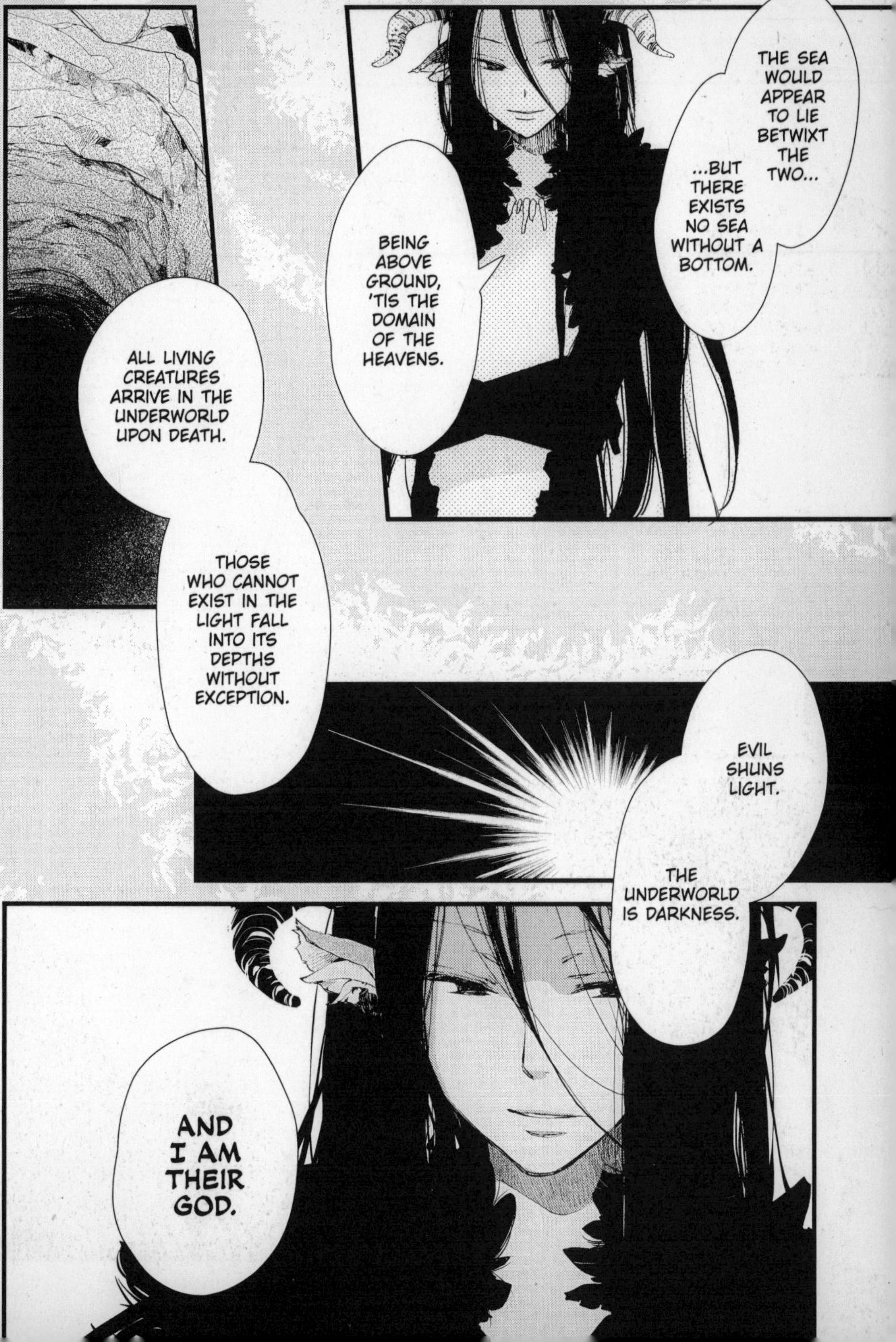
THE SEA WOULD APPEAR TO LIE BETWIXT THE TWO...
...BUT THERE EXISTS NO SEA WITHOUT A BOTTOM.
BEING ABOVE GROUND, 'TIS THE DOMAIN OF THE HEAVENS.
ALL LIVING CREATURES ARRIVE IN THE UNDERWORLD UPON DEATH.
THOSE WHO CANNOT EXIST IN THE LIGHT FALL INTO ITS DEPTHS WITHOUT EXCEPTION.
EVIL SHUNS LIGHT.
THE UNDERWORLD IS DARKNESS.
AND I AM THEIR GOD.

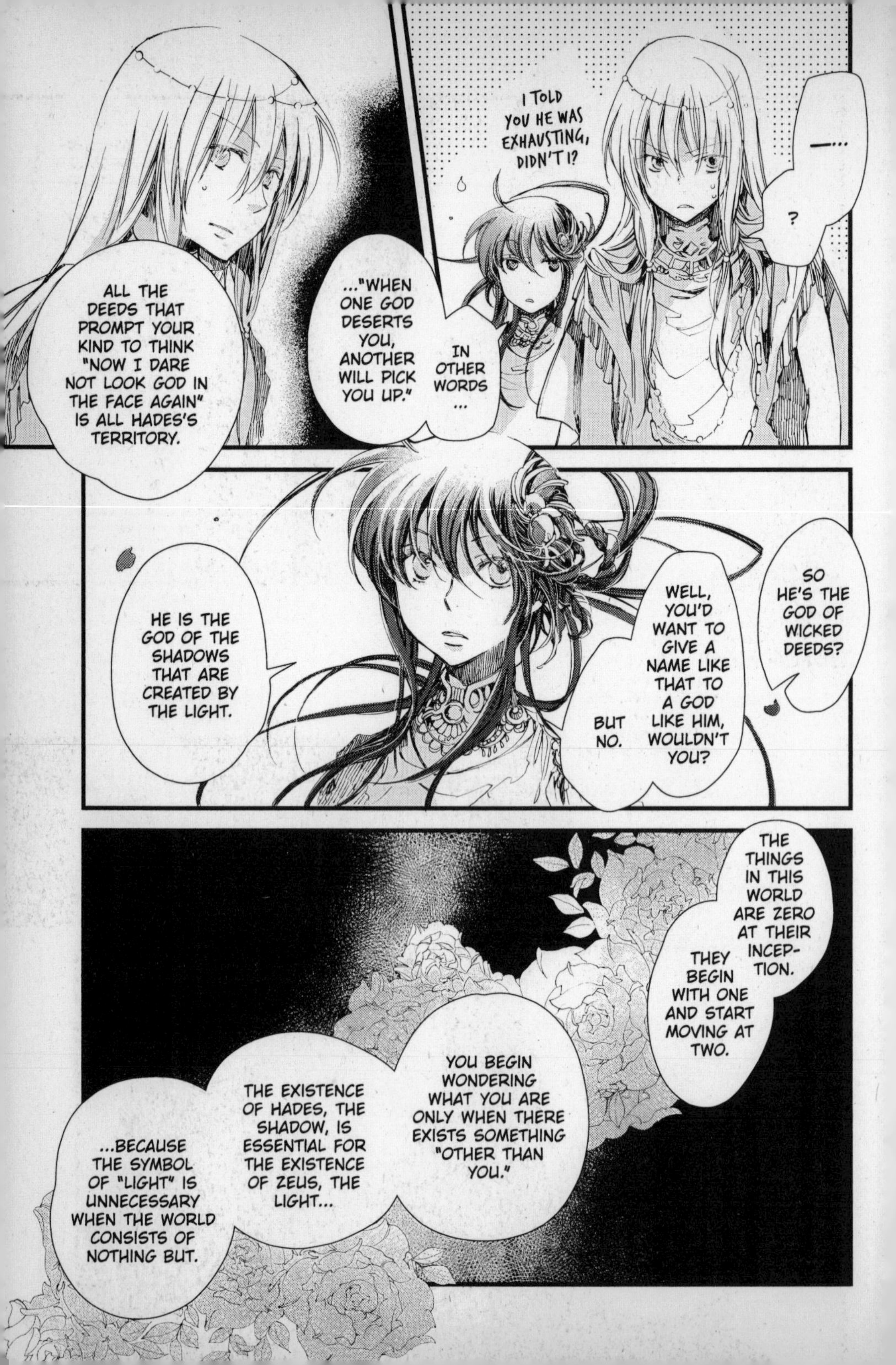
—...
?
I TOLD YOU HE WAS EXHAUSTING, DIDN'T I?
IN OTHER WORDS...
..."WHEN ONE GOD DESERTS YOU, ANOTHER WILL PICK YOU UP."
ALL THE DEEDS THAT PROMPT YOUR KIND TO THINK "NOW I DARE NOT LOOK GOD IN THE FACE AGAIN" IS ALL HADES'S TERRITORY.
SO HE'S THE GOD OF WICKED DEEDS?
WELL, YOU'D WANT TO GIVE A NAME LIKE THAT TO A GOD LIKE HIM, WOULDN'T YOU?
BUT NO.
HE IS THE GOD OF THE SHADOWS THAT ARE CREATED BY THE LIGHT.
THE THINGS IN THIS WORLD ARE ZERO AT THEIR INCEPTION.
THEY BEGIN WITH ONE AND START MOVING AT TWO.
YOU BEGIN WONDERING WHAT YOU ARE ONLY WHEN THERE EXISTS SOMETHING "OTHER THAN YOU."
THE EXISTENCE OF HADES, THE SHADOW, IS ESSENTIAL FOR THE EXISTENCE OF ZEUS, THE LIGHT...
...BECAUSE THE SYMBOL OF "LIGHT" IS UNNECESSARY WHEN THE WORLD CONSISTS OF NOTHING BUT.

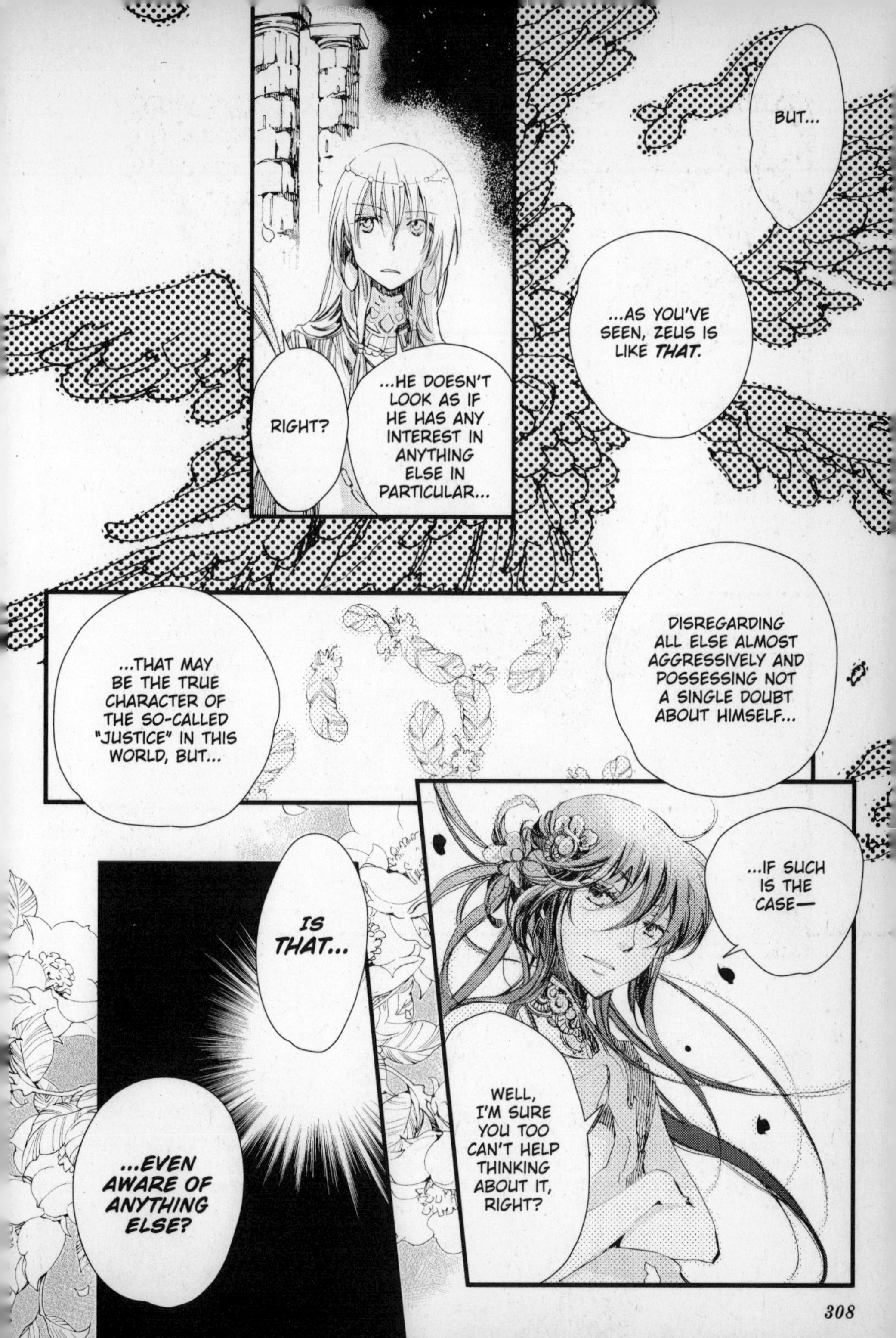
BUT...
...AS YOU'VE SEEN, ZEUS IS LIKE *THAT.*
...HE DOESN'T LOOK AS IF HE HAS ANY INTEREST IN ANYTHING ELSE IN PARTICULAR...
RIGHT?
DISREGARDING ALL ELSE ALMOST AGGRESSIVELY AND POSSESSING NOT A SINGLE DOUBT ABOUT HIMSELF...
...THAT MAY BE THE TRUE CHARACTER OF THE SO-CALLED "JUSTICE" IN THIS WORLD, BUT...
...IF SUCH IS THE CASE—
WELL, I'M SURE YOU TOO CAN'T HELP THINKING ABOUT IT, RIGHT?
IS THAT...
...EVEN AWARE OF ANYTHING ELSE?

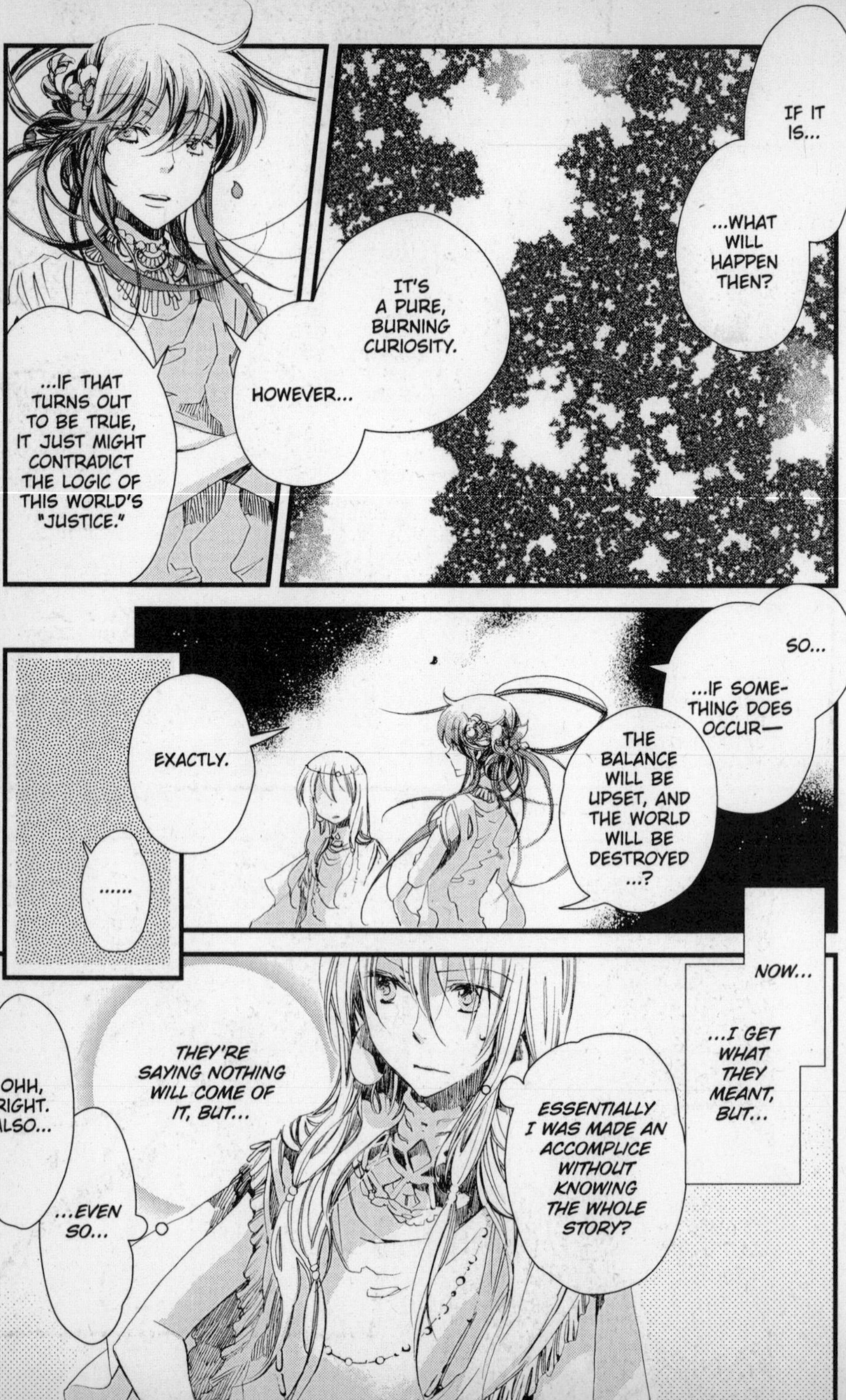
IF IT IS...
...WHAT WILL HAPPEN THEN?
IT'S A PURE, BURNING CURIOSITY.
HOWEVER...
...IF THAT TURNS OUT TO BE TRUE, IT JUST MIGHT CONTRADICT THE LOGIC OF THIS WORLD'S "JUSTICE."
SO...
...IF SOME-THING DOES OCCUR—
THE BALANCE WILL BE UPSET, AND THE WORLD WILL BE DESTROYED ...?
EXACTLY.
......
NOW...
...I GET WHAT THEY MEANT, BUT...
ESSENTIALLY I WAS MADE AN ACCOMPLICE WITHOUT KNOWING THE WHOLE STORY?
THEY'RE SAYING NOTHING WILL COME OF IT, BUT...
...EVEN SO...
OHH, RIGHT. ALSO...

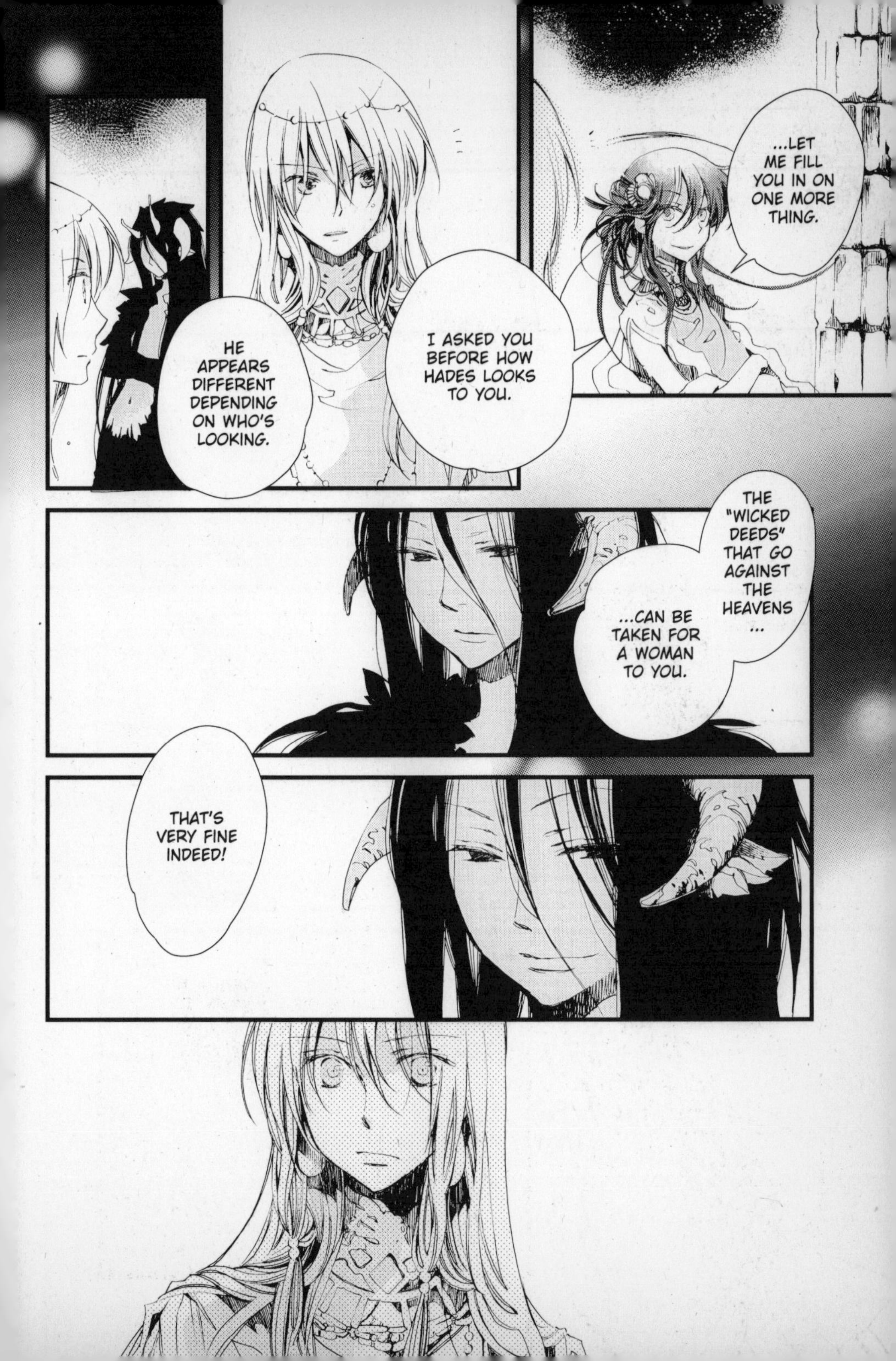
...LET ME FILL YOU IN ON ONE MORE THING.
I ASKED YOU BEFORE HOW HADES LOOKS TO YOU.
HE APPEARS DIFFERENT DEPENDING ON WHO'S LOOKING.
THE "WICKED DEEDS" THAT GO AGAINST THE HEAVENS...
...CAN BE TAKEN FOR A WOMAN TO YOU.
THAT'S VERY FINE INDEED!

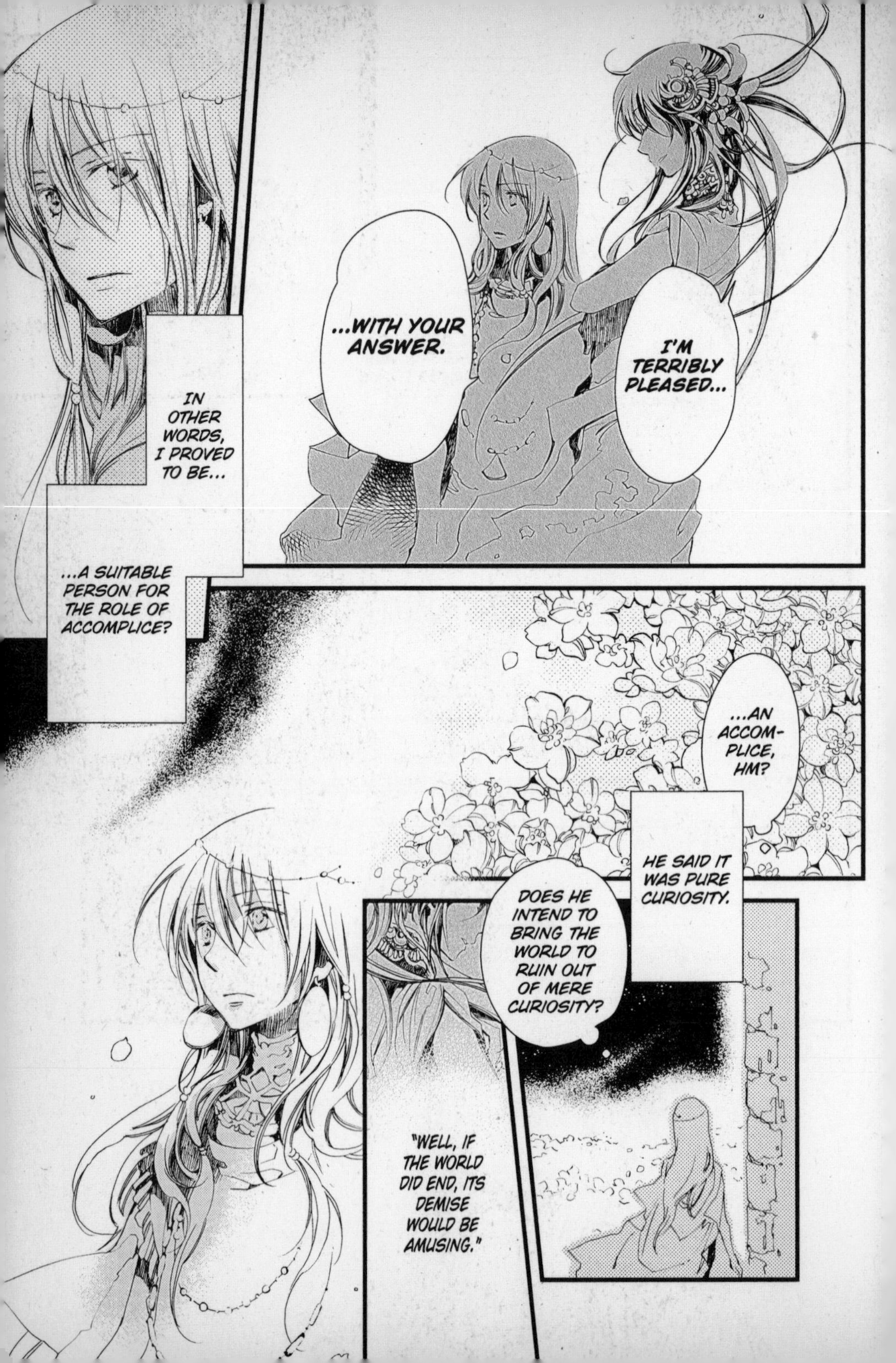
I'M TERRIBLY PLEASED...
...WITH YOUR ANSWER.
IN OTHER WORDS, I PROVED TO BE...
...A SUITABLE PERSON FOR THE ROLE OF ACCOMPLICE?
...AN ACCOMPLICE, HM?
HE SAID IT WAS PURE CURIOSITY.
DOES HE INTEND TO BRING THE WORLD TO RUIN OUT OF MERE CURIOSITY?
"WELL, IF THE WORLD DID END, ITS DEMISE WOULD BE AMUSING."

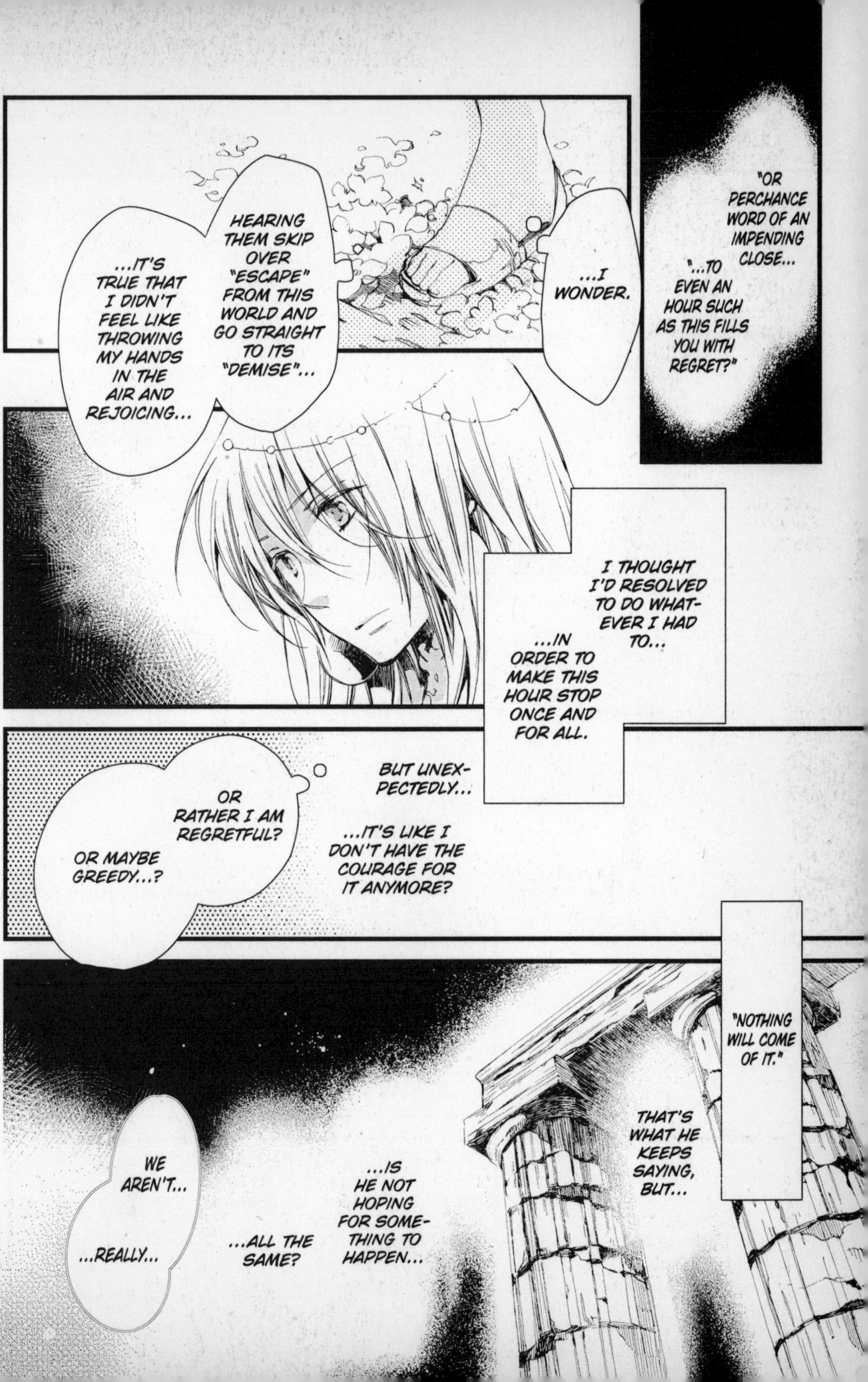
"OR PERCHANCE WORD OF AN IMPENDING CLOSE...
"...TO EVEN AN HOUR SUCH AS THIS FILLS YOU WITH REGRET?"
...I WONDER.
HEARING THEM SKIP OVER "ESCAPE" FROM THIS WORLD AND GO STRAIGHT TO ITS "DEMISE"...
...IT'S TRUE THAT I DIDN'T FEEL LIKE THROWING MY HANDS IN THE AIR AND REJOICING...
I THOUGHT I'D RESOLVED TO DO WHAT-EVER I HAD TO...
...IN ORDER TO MAKE THIS HOUR STOP ONCE AND FOR ALL.
BUT UNEX-PECTEDLY...
...IT'S LIKE I DON'T HAVE THE COURAGE FOR IT ANYMORE?
OR RATHER I AM REGRETFUL?
OR MAYBE GREEDY...?
"NOTHING WILL COME OF IT."
THAT'S WHAT HE KEEPS SAYING, BUT...
...IS HE NOT HOPING FOR SOME-THING TO HAPPEN...
...ALL THE SAME?
WE AREN'T...
...REALLY...

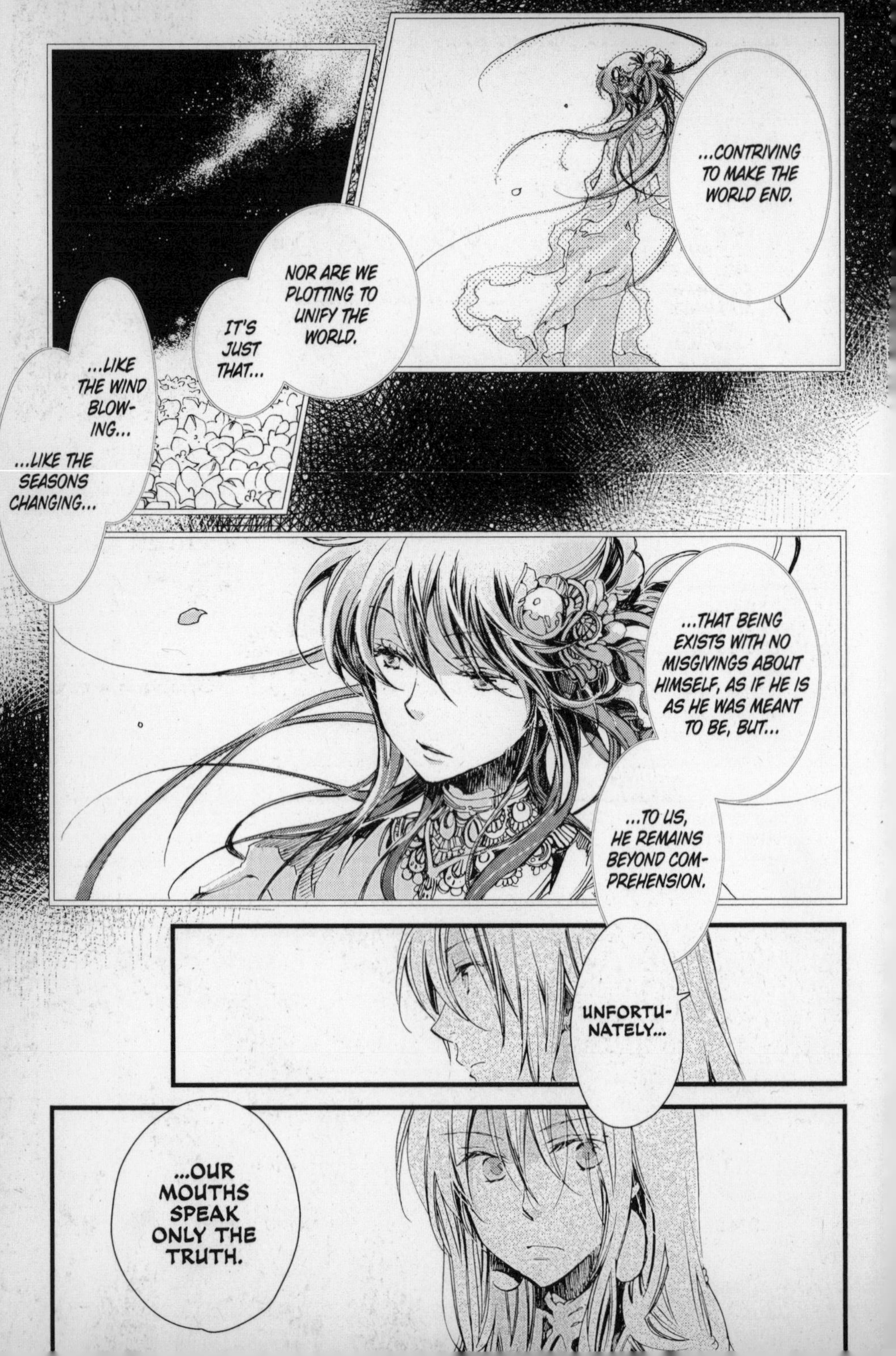
...CONTRIVING TO MAKE THE WORLD END.
NOR ARE WE PLOTTING TO UNIFY THE WORLD.
IT'S JUST THAT...
...LIKE THE WIND BLOWING...
...LIKE THE SEASONS CHANGING...
...THAT BEING EXISTS WITH NO MISGIVINGS ABOUT HIMSELF, AS IF HE IS AS HE WAS MEANT TO BE, BUT...
...TO US, HE REMAINS BEYOND COMPREHENSION.
UNFORTUNATELY...
...OUR MOUTHS SPEAK ONLY THE TRUTH.

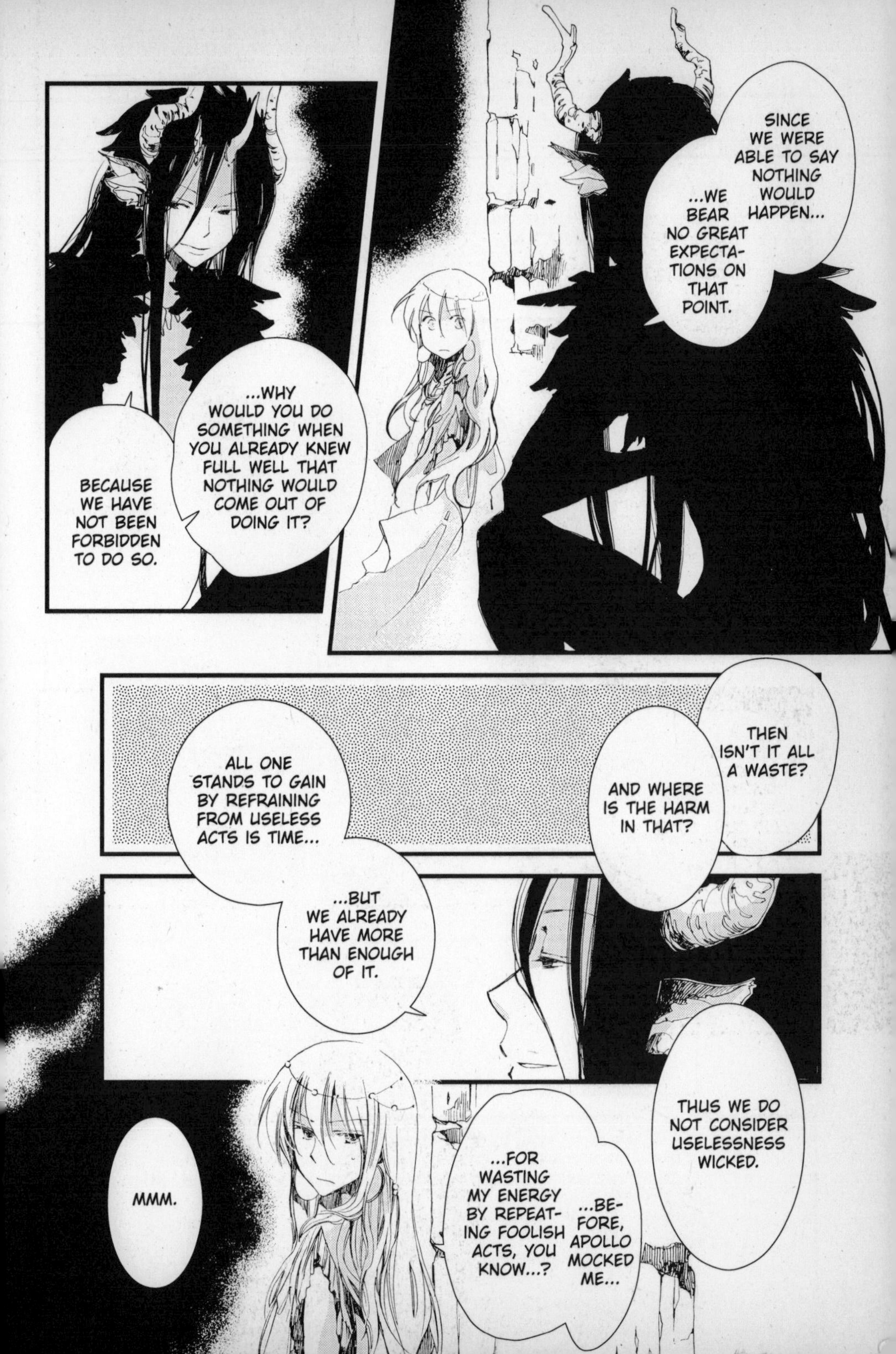
SINCE WE WERE ABLE TO SAY NOTHING WOULD HAPPEN...
...WE BEAR NO GREAT EXPECTA-TIONS ON THAT POINT.
...WHY WOULD YOU DO SOMETHING WHEN YOU ALREADY KNEW FULL WELL THAT NOTHING WOULD COME OUT OF DOING IT?
BECAUSE WE HAVE NOT BEEN FORBIDDEN TO DO SO.
THEN ISN'T IT ALL A WASTE?
AND WHERE IS THE HARM IN THAT?
ALL ONE STANDS TO GAIN BY REFRAINING FROM USELESS ACTS IS TIME...
...BUT WE ALREADY HAVE MORE THAN ENOUGH OF IT.
THUS WE DO NOT CONSIDER USELESSNESS WICKED.
...BE-FORE, APOLLO MOCKED ME...
...FOR WASTING MY ENERGY BY REPEAT-ING FOOLISH ACTS, YOU KNOW...?
MMM.

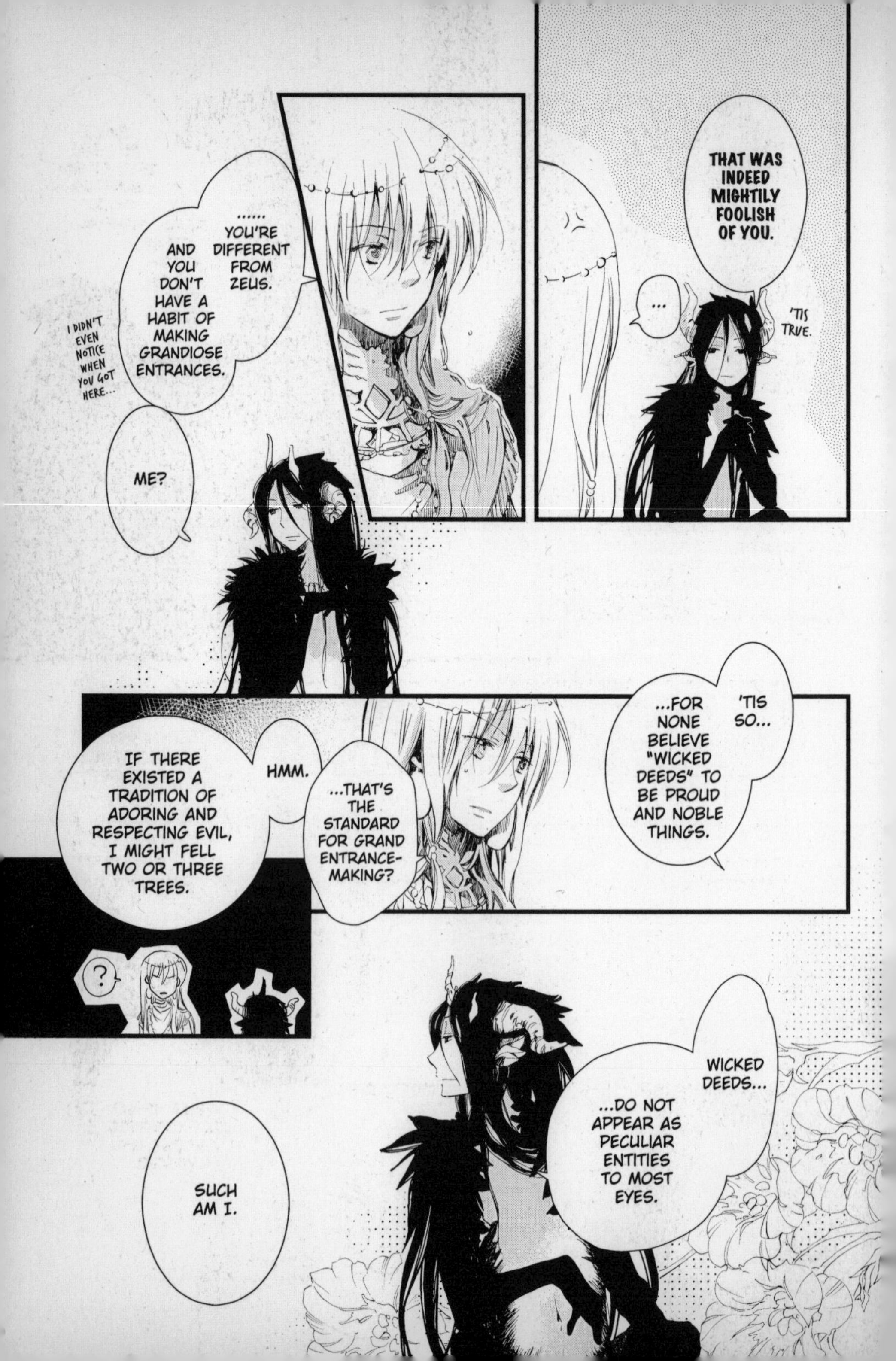
THAT WAS INDEED MIGHTILY FOOLISH OF YOU.
...
'TIS TRUE.
...... YOU'RE DIFFERENT FROM ZEUS.
AND YOU DON'T HAVE A HABIT OF MAKING GRANDIOSE ENTRANCES.
I DIDN'T EVEN NOTICE WHEN YOU GOT HERE...
ME?
'TIS SO...
...FOR NONE BELIEVE "WICKED DEEDS" TO BE PROUD AND NOBLE THINGS.
HMM.
...THAT'S THE STANDARD FOR GRAND ENTRANCE-MAKING?
IF THERE EXISTED A TRADITION OF ADORING AND RESPECTING EVIL, I MIGHT FELL TWO OR THREE TREES.
?
WICKED DEEDS...
...DO NOT APPEAR AS PECULIAR ENTITIES TO MOST EYES.
SUCH AM I.

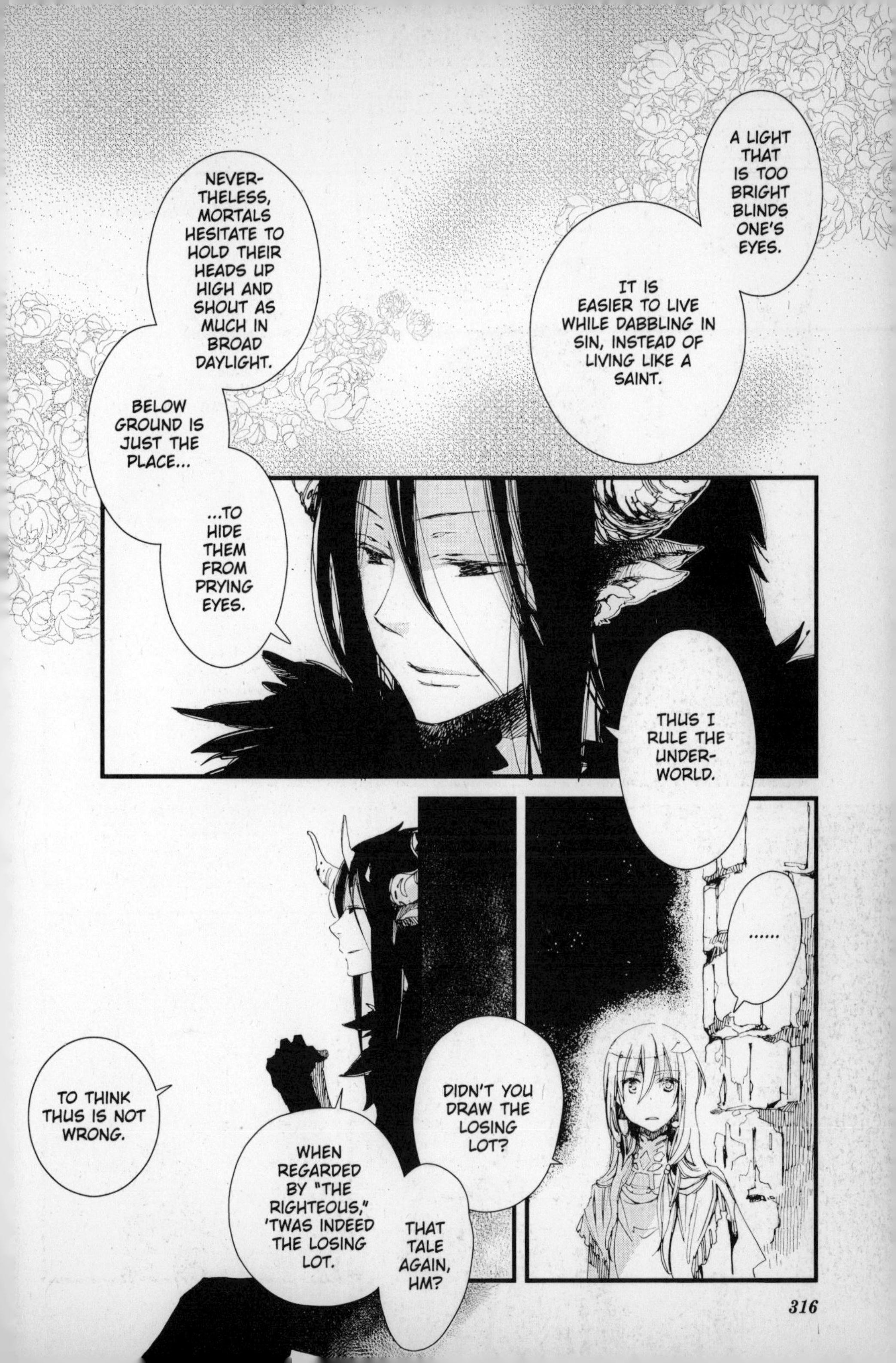
A LIGHT THAT IS TOO BRIGHT BLINDS ONE'S EYES.
IT IS EASIER TO LIVE WHILE DABBLING IN SIN, INSTEAD OF LIVING LIKE A SAINT.
NEVER-THELESS, MORTALS HESITATE TO HOLD THEIR HEADS UP HIGH AND SHOUT AS MUCH IN BROAD DAYLIGHT.
BELOW GROUND IS JUST THE PLACE...
...TO HIDE THEM FROM PRYING EYES.
THUS I RULE THE UNDER-WORLD.
......
DIDN'T YOU DRAW THE LOSING LOT?
THAT TALE AGAIN, HM?
WHEN REGARDED BY "THE RIGHTEOUS," 'TWAS INDEED THE LOSING LOT.
TO THINK THUS IS NOT WRONG.

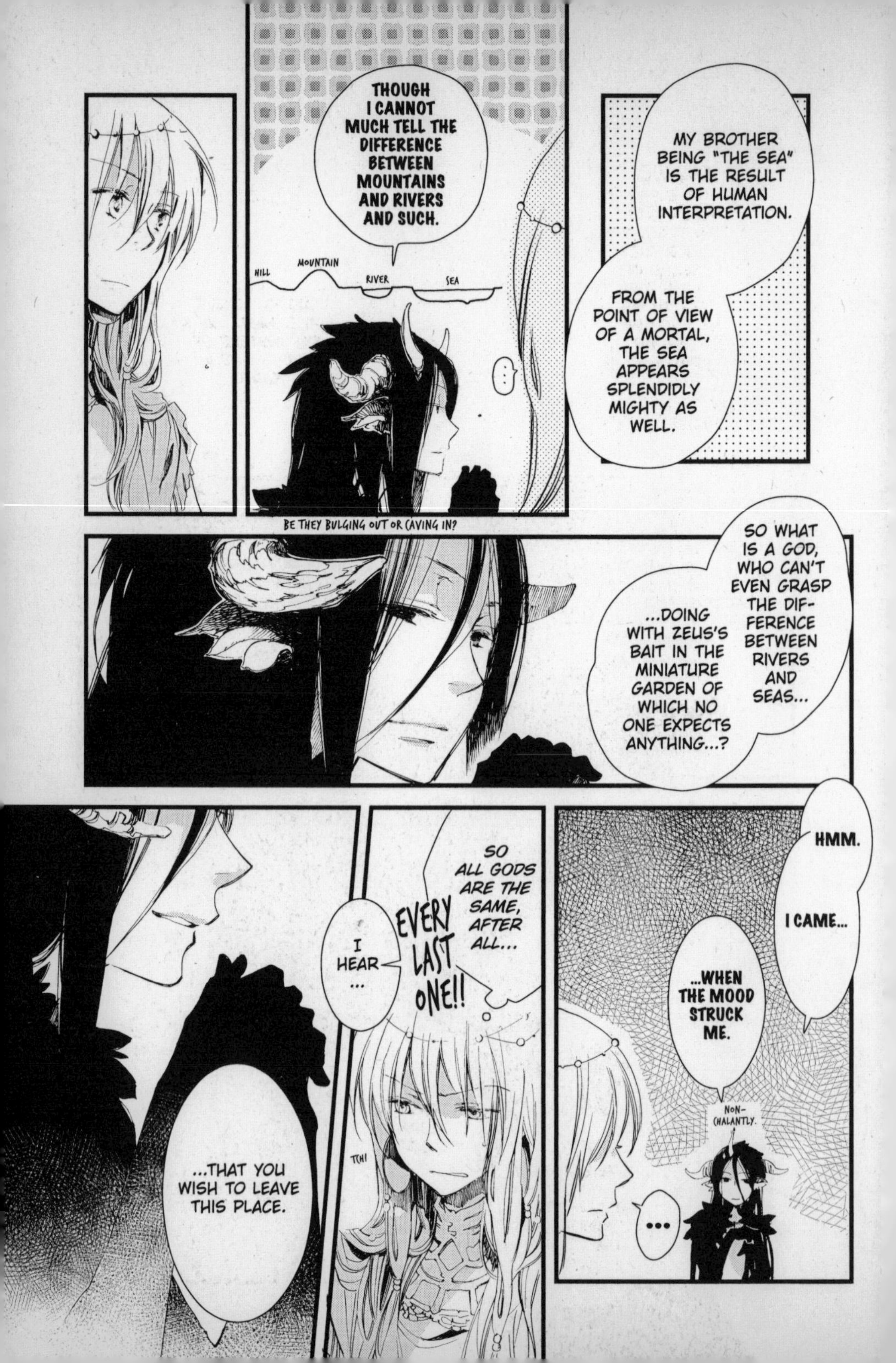
MY BROTHER BEING "THE SEA" IS THE RESULT OF HUMAN INTERPRETATION.
FROM THE POINT OF VIEW OF A MORTAL, THE SEA APPEARS SPLENDIDLY MIGHTY AS WELL.
THOUGH I CANNOT MUCH TELL THE DIFFERENCE BETWEEN MOUNTAINS AND RIVERS AND SUCH.
HILL
MOUNTAIN
RIVER
SEA
...
BE THEY BULGING OUT OR CAVING IN?
SO WHAT IS A GOD, WHO CAN'T EVEN GRASP THE DIF-FERENCE BETWEEN RIVERS AND SEAS...
...DOING WITH ZEUS'S BAIT IN THE MINIATURE GARDEN OF WHICH NO ONE EXPECTS ANYTHING...?
HMM.
I CAME...
...WHEN THE MOOD STRUCK ME.
NON-CHALANTLY.
...
SO ALL GODS ARE THE SAME, AFTER ALL...
EVERY LAST ONE!!
I HEAR...
TCH!
...THAT YOU WISH TO LEAVE THIS PLACE.

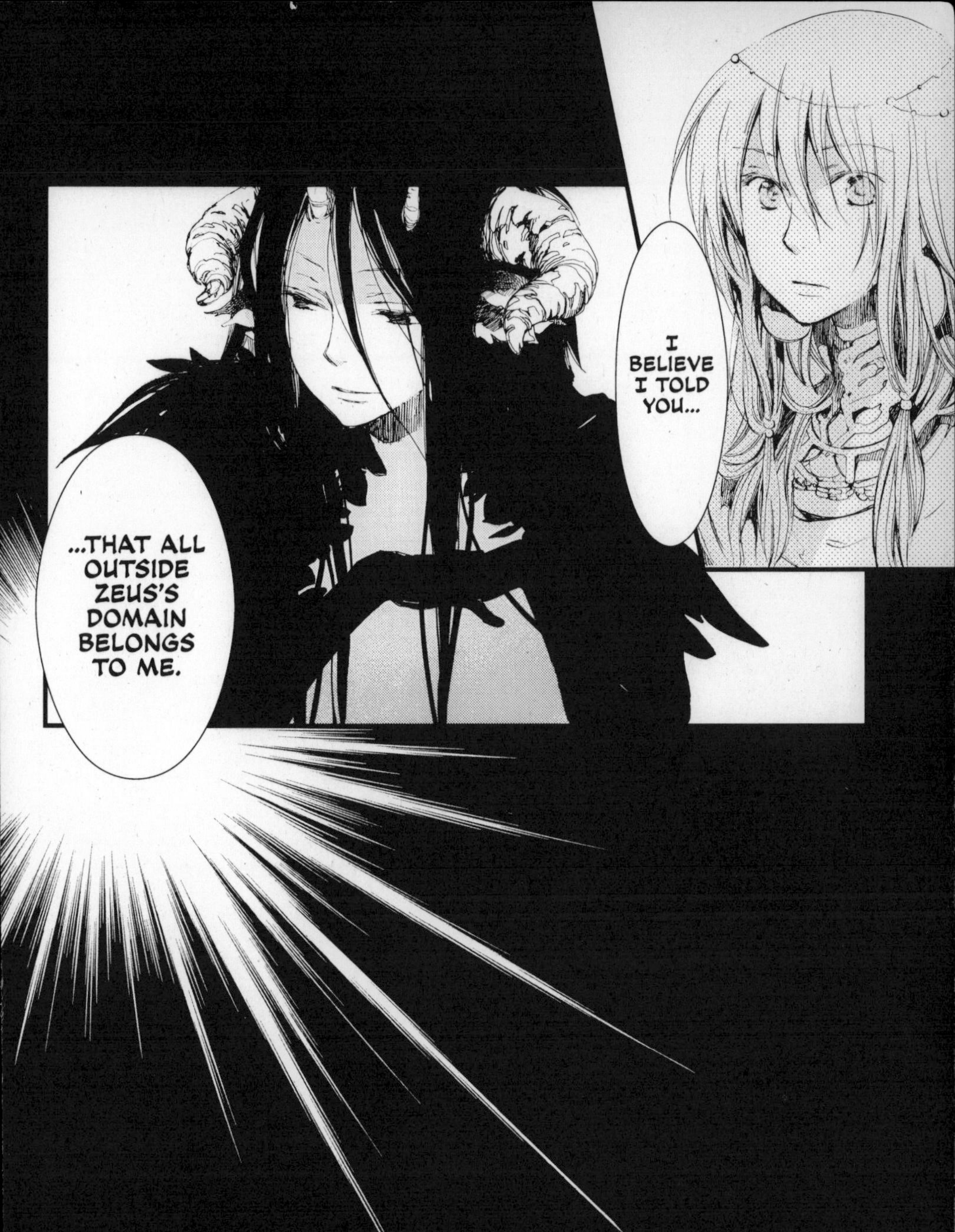
I BELIEVE I TOLD YOU...
...THAT ALL OUTSIDE ZEUS'S DOMAIN BELONGS TO ME.

Olympos

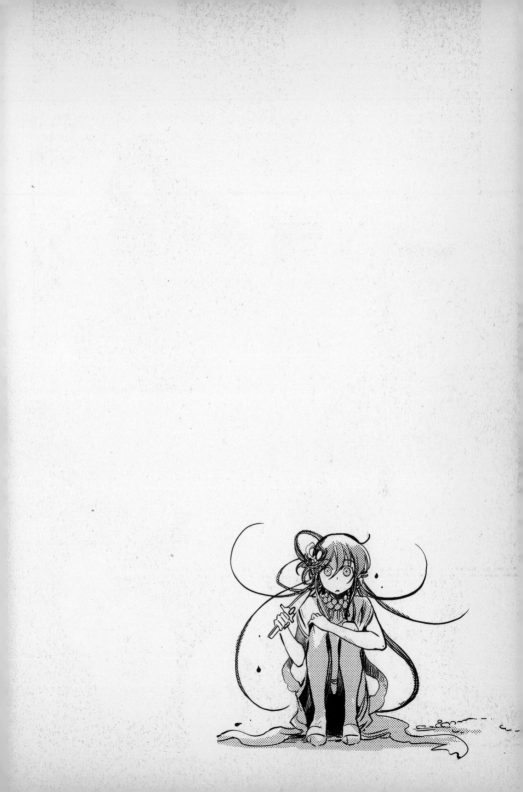

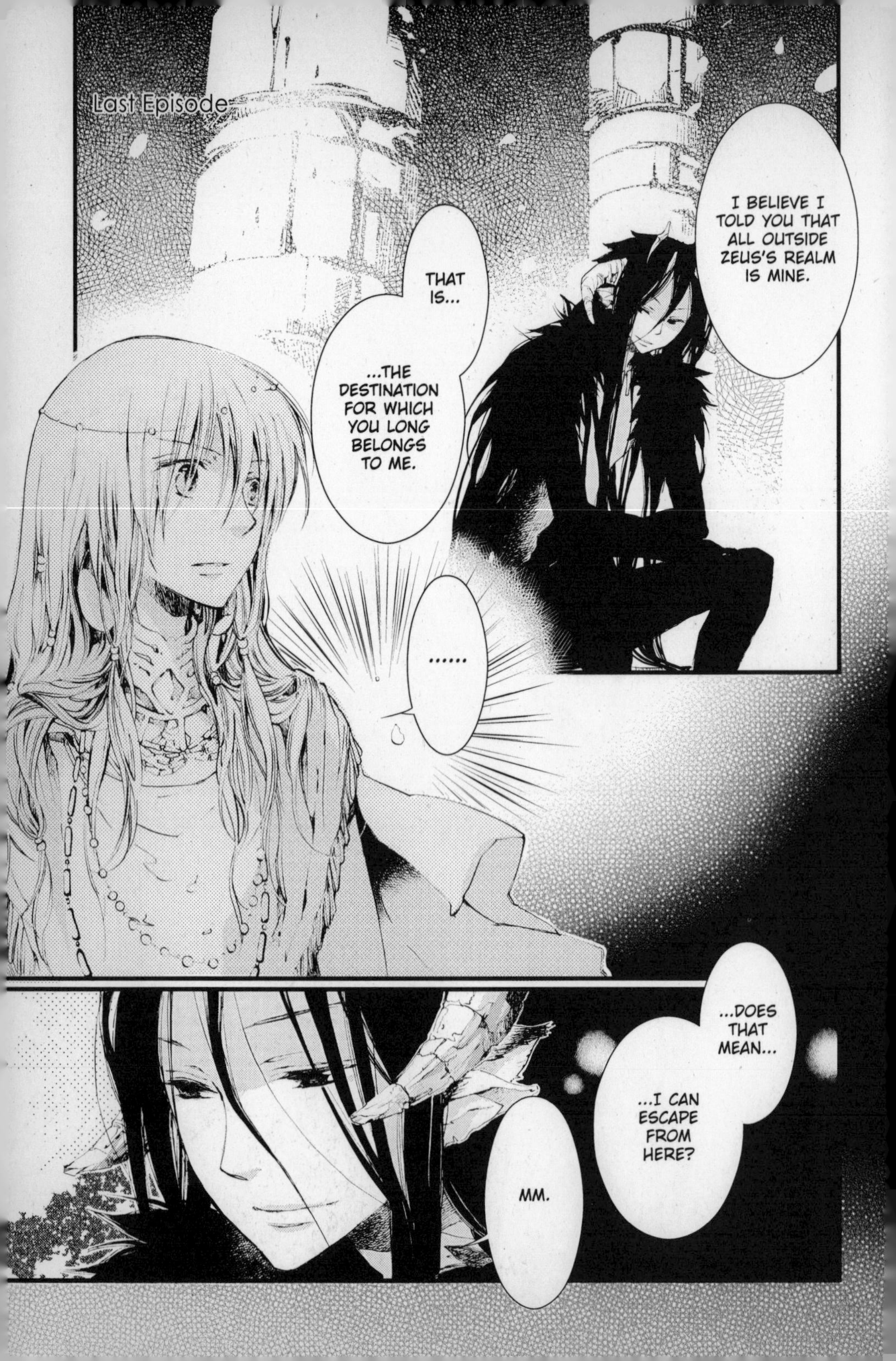
Last Episode
I BELIEVE I TOLD YOU THAT ALL OUTSIDE ZEUS'S REALM IS MINE.
THAT IS...
...THE DESTINATION FOR WHICH YOU LONG BELONGS TO ME.
......
...DOES THAT MEAN...
...I CAN ESCAPE FROM HERE?
MM.

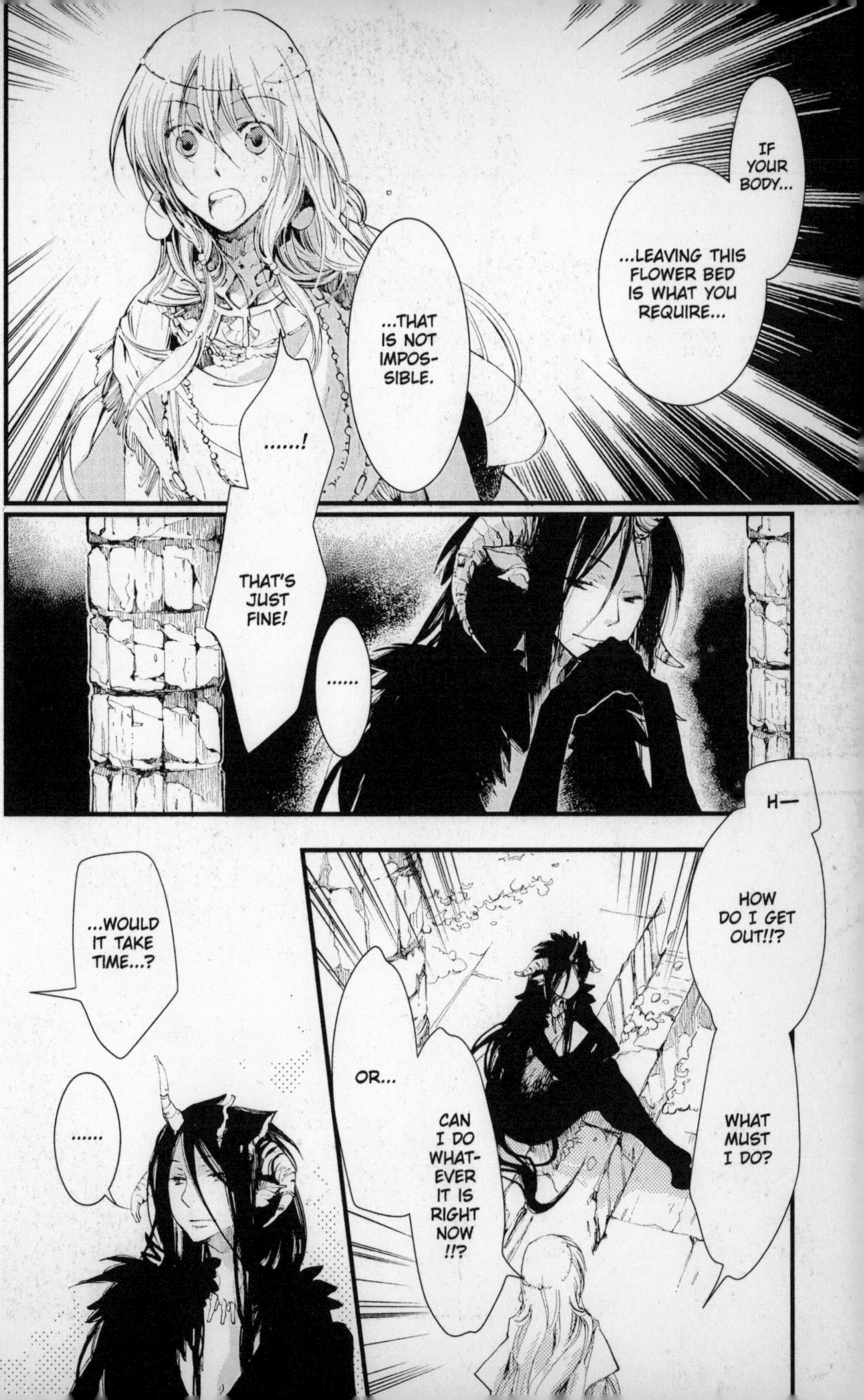
IF YOUR BODY...
...LEAVING THIS FLOWER BED IS WHAT YOU REQUIRE...
...THAT IS NOT IMPOSSIBLE.
......!
THAT'S JUST FINE!
......
H—
HOW DO I GET OUT!!?
WHAT MUST I DO?
OR...
CAN I DO WHATEVER IT IS RIGHT NOW!!?
...WOULD IT TAKE TIME...?
......

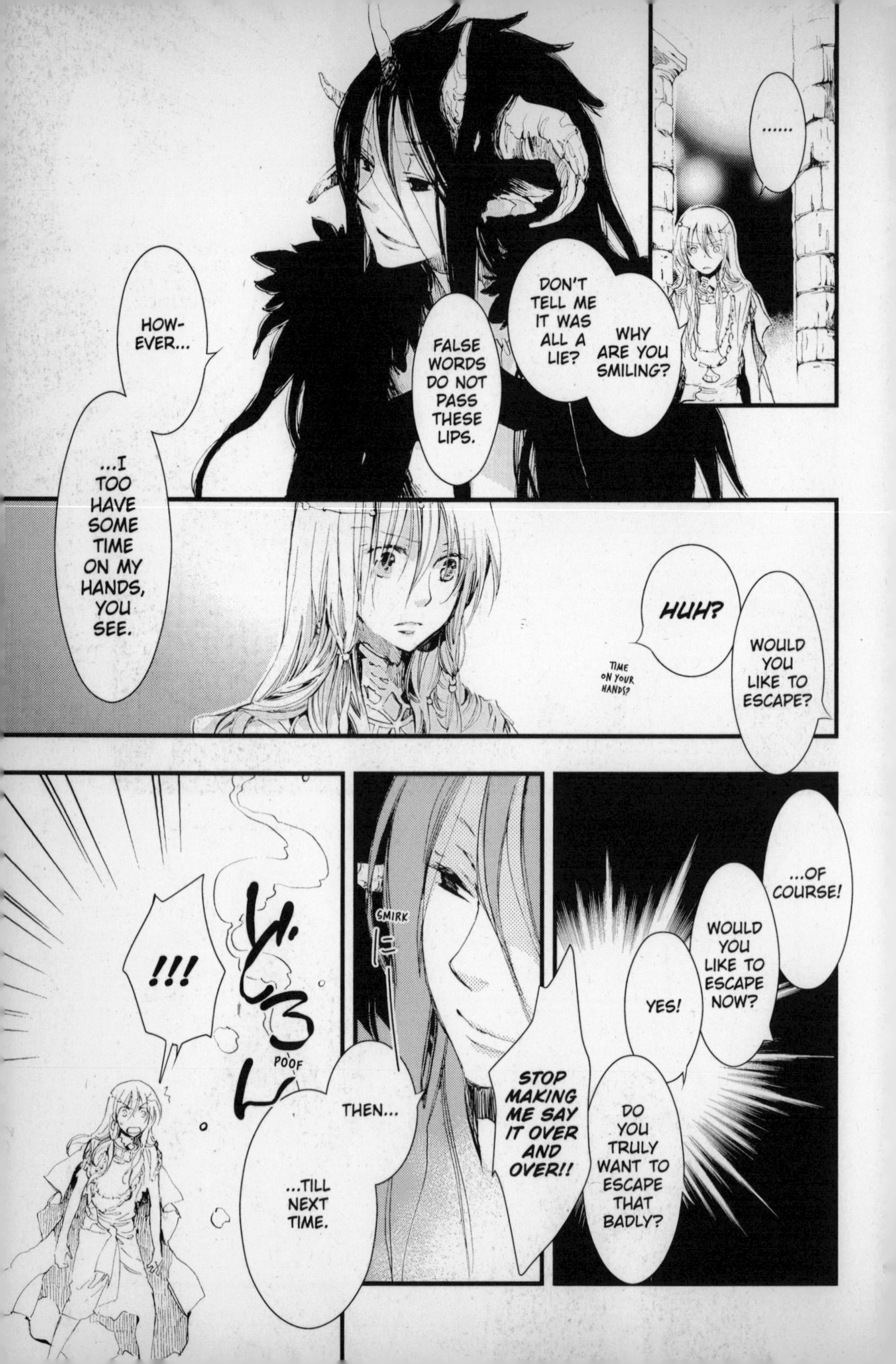
......
WHY ARE YOU SMILING?
DON'T TELL ME IT WAS ALL A LIE?
FALSE WORDS DO NOT PASS THESE LIPS.
HOW-EVER...
...I TOO HAVE SOME TIME ON MY HANDS, YOU SEE.
WOULD YOU LIKE TO ESCAPE?
HUH?
TIME ON YOUR HANDS?
...OF COURSE!
WOULD YOU LIKE TO ESCAPE NOW?
YES!
DO YOU TRULY WANT TO ESCAPE THAT BADLY?
STOP MAKING ME SAY IT OVER AND OVER!!
SMIRK
THEN...
...TILL NEXT TIME.
POOF
!!!

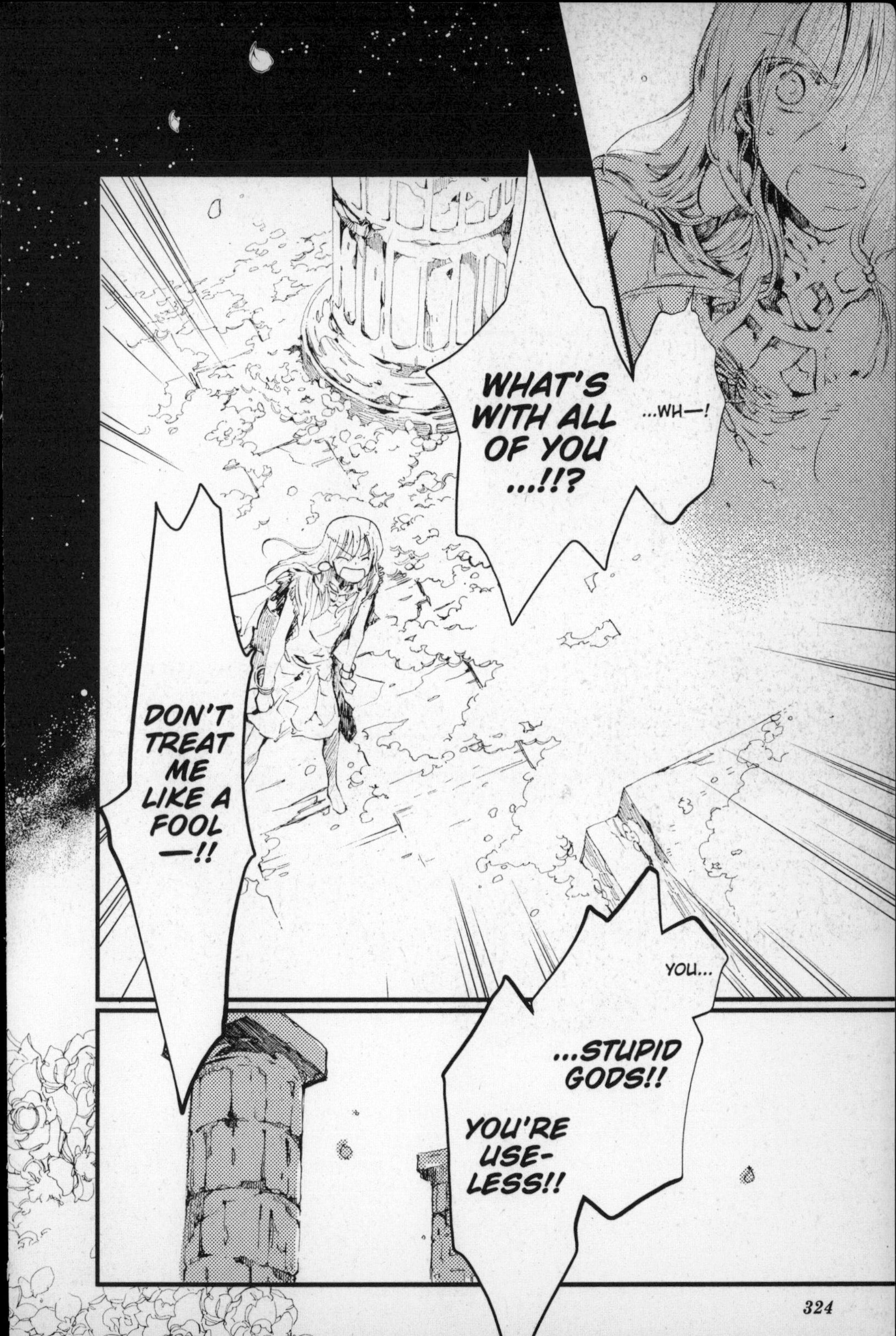
...WH—!
WHAT'S WITH ALL OF YOU ...!!?
DON'T TREAT ME LIKE A FOOL —!!
YOU...
...STUPID GODS!!
YOU'RE USE-LESS!!

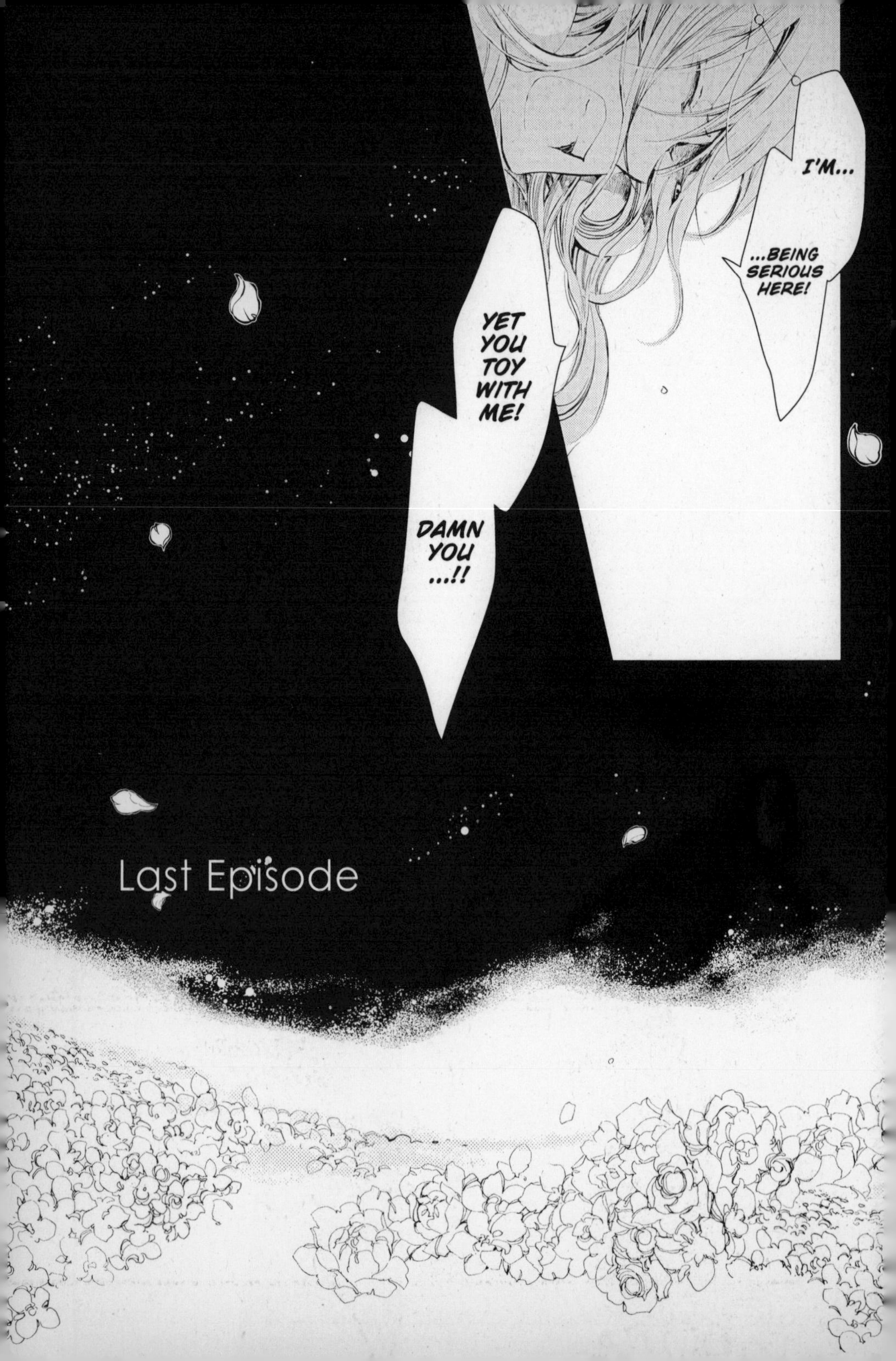
I'M...
...BEING SERIOUS HERE!
YET YOU TOY WITH ME!
DAMN YOU ...!!
Last Episode

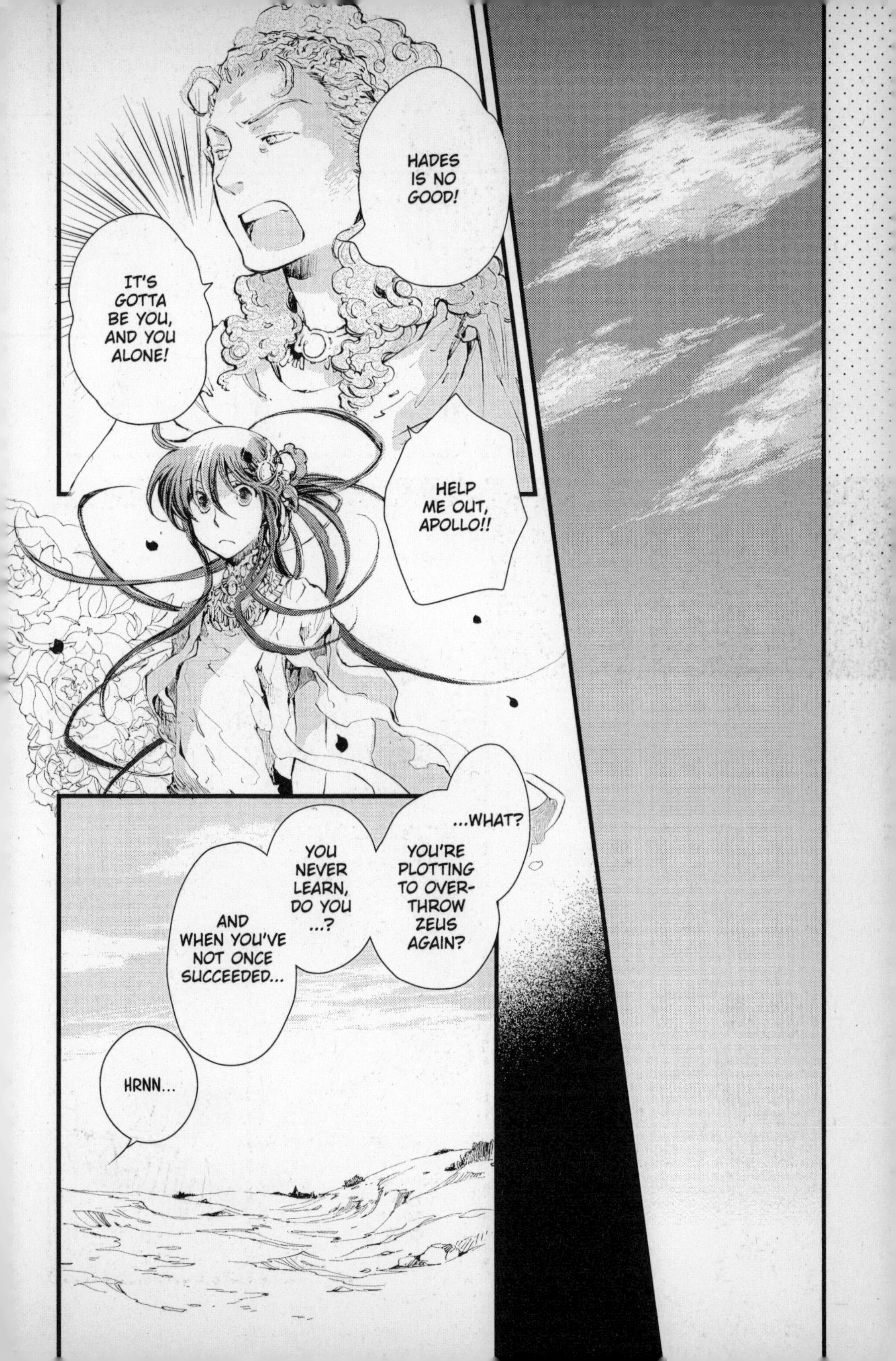
HADES IS NO GOOD!
IT'S GOTTA BE YOU, AND YOU ALONE!
HELP ME OUT, APOLLO!!
...WHAT?
YOU'RE PLOTTING TO OVER-THROW ZEUS AGAIN?
YOU NEVER LEARN, DO YOU ...?
AND WHEN YOU'VE NOT ONCE SUCCEEDED...
HRNN...

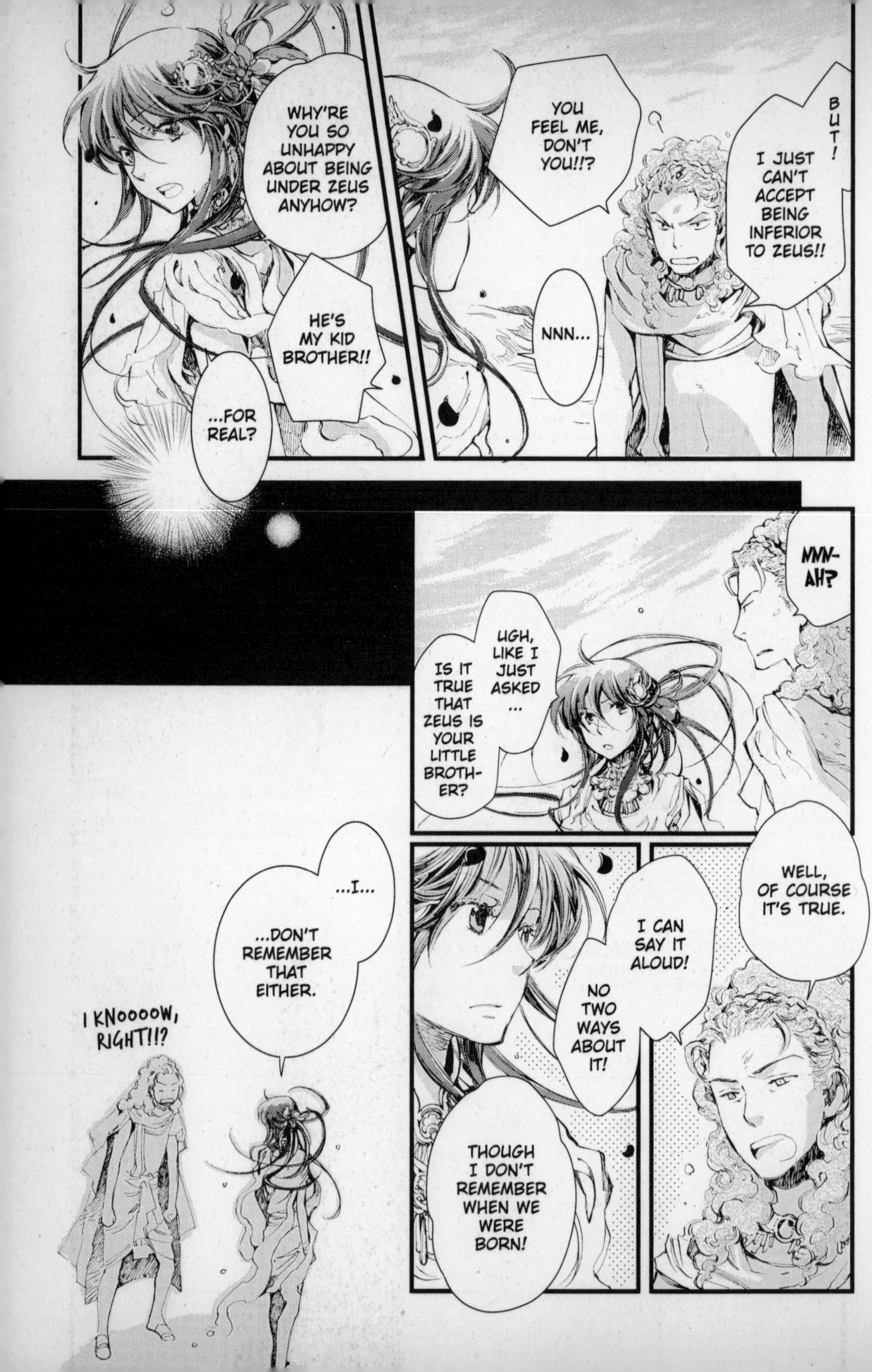
BUT!
I JUST CAN'T ACCEPT BEING INFERIOR TO ZEUS!!
YOU FEEL ME, DON'T YOU!!?
NNN...
WHY'RE YOU SO UNHAPPY ABOUT BEING UNDER ZEUS ANYHOW?
HE'S MY KID BROTHER!!
...FOR REAL?
MNN-AH?
UGH, LIKE I JUST ASKED...
IS IT TRUE THAT ZEUS IS YOUR LITTLE BROTHER?
WELL, OF COURSE IT'S TRUE.
I CAN SAY IT ALOUD!
NO TWO WAYS ABOUT IT!
THOUGH I DON'T REMEMBER WHEN WE WERE BORN!
...I...
...DON'T REMEMBER THAT EITHER.
I KNOOOOW, RIGHT!!?

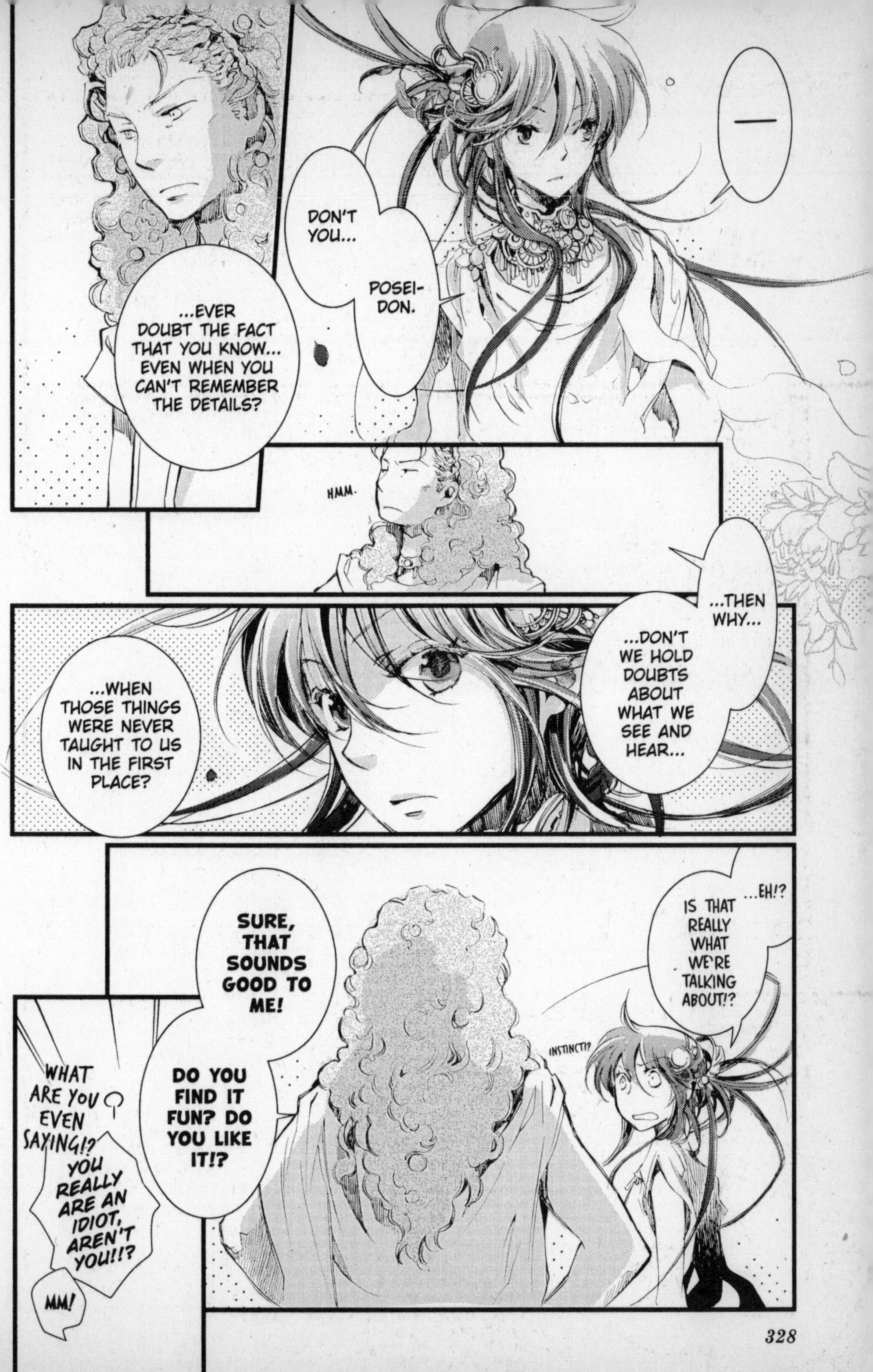
—
DON'T YOU...
POSEI-DON.
...EVER DOUBT THE FACT THAT YOU KNOW... EVEN WHEN YOU CAN'T REMEMBER THE DETAILS?
HMM.
...THEN WHY...
...DON'T WE HOLD DOUBTS ABOUT WHAT WE SEE AND HEAR...
...WHEN THOSE THINGS WERE NEVER TAUGHT TO US IN THE FIRST PLACE?
...EH!?
IS THAT REALLY WHAT WE'RE TALKING ABOUT!?
SURE, THAT SOUNDS GOOD TO ME!
INSTINCT!?
DO YOU FIND IT FUN? DO YOU LIKE IT!?
WHAT ARE YOU EVEN SAYING!?
YOU REALLY ARE AN IDIOT, AREN'T YOU!!?
MM!

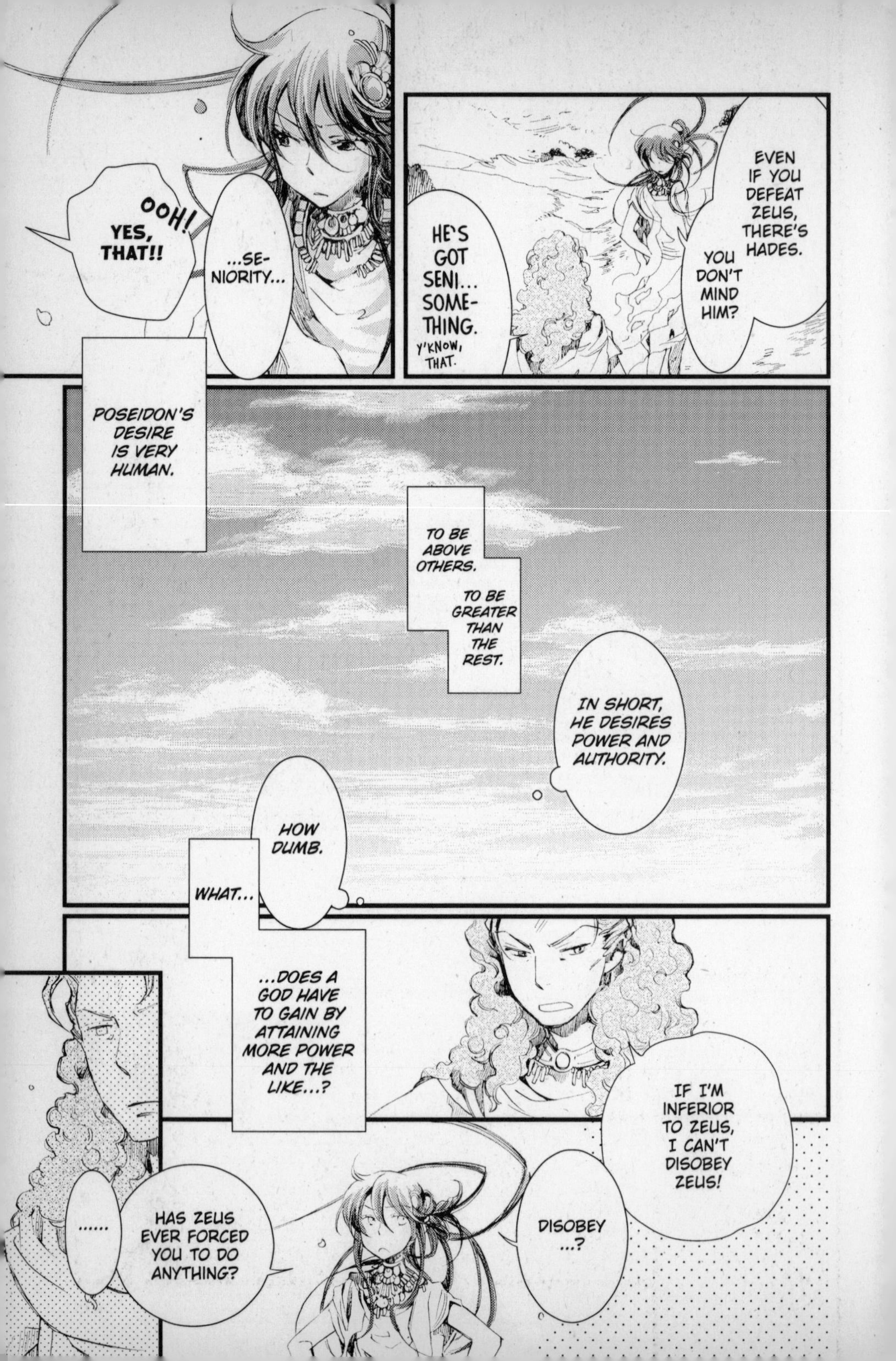
EVEN IF YOU DEFEAT ZEUS, THERE'S HADES.
YOU DON'T MIND HIM?
HE'S GOT SENI... SOMETHING.
Y'KNOW, THAT.
...SE-NIORITY...
OOH! YES, THAT!!
POSEIDON'S DESIRE IS VERY HUMAN.
TO BE ABOVE OTHERS.
TO BE GREATER THAN THE REST.
IN SHORT, HE DESIRES POWER AND AUTHORITY.
HOW DUMB.
WHAT...
...DOES A GOD HAVE TO GAIN BY ATTAINING MORE POWER AND THE LIKE...?
IF I'M INFERIOR TO ZEUS, I CAN'T DISOBEY ZEUS!
DISOBEY ...?
HAS ZEUS EVER FORCED YOU TO DO ANYTHING?
......

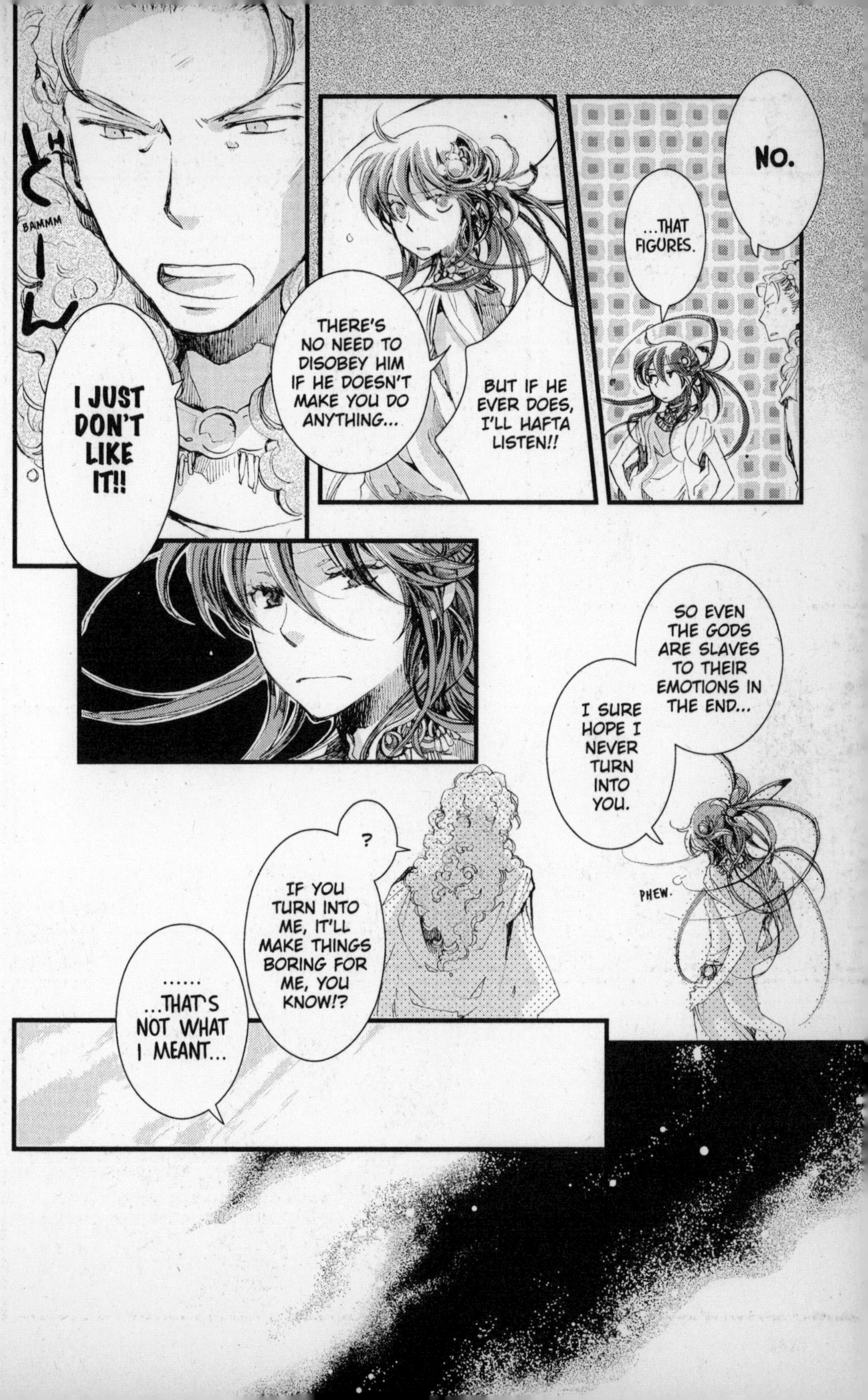
NO.
...THAT FIGURES.
THERE'S NO NEED TO DISOBEY HIM IF HE DOESN'T MAKE YOU DO ANYTHING...
BUT IF HE EVER DOES, I'LL HAFTA LISTEN!!
どーん
BAMMM
I JUST DON'T LIKE IT!!
SO EVEN THE GODS ARE SLAVES TO THEIR EMOTIONS IN THE END...
I SURE HOPE I NEVER TURN INTO YOU.
PHEW.
?
IF YOU TURN INTO ME, IT'LL MAKE THINGS BORING FOR ME, YOU KNOW!?
......
...THAT'S NOT WHAT I MEANT...

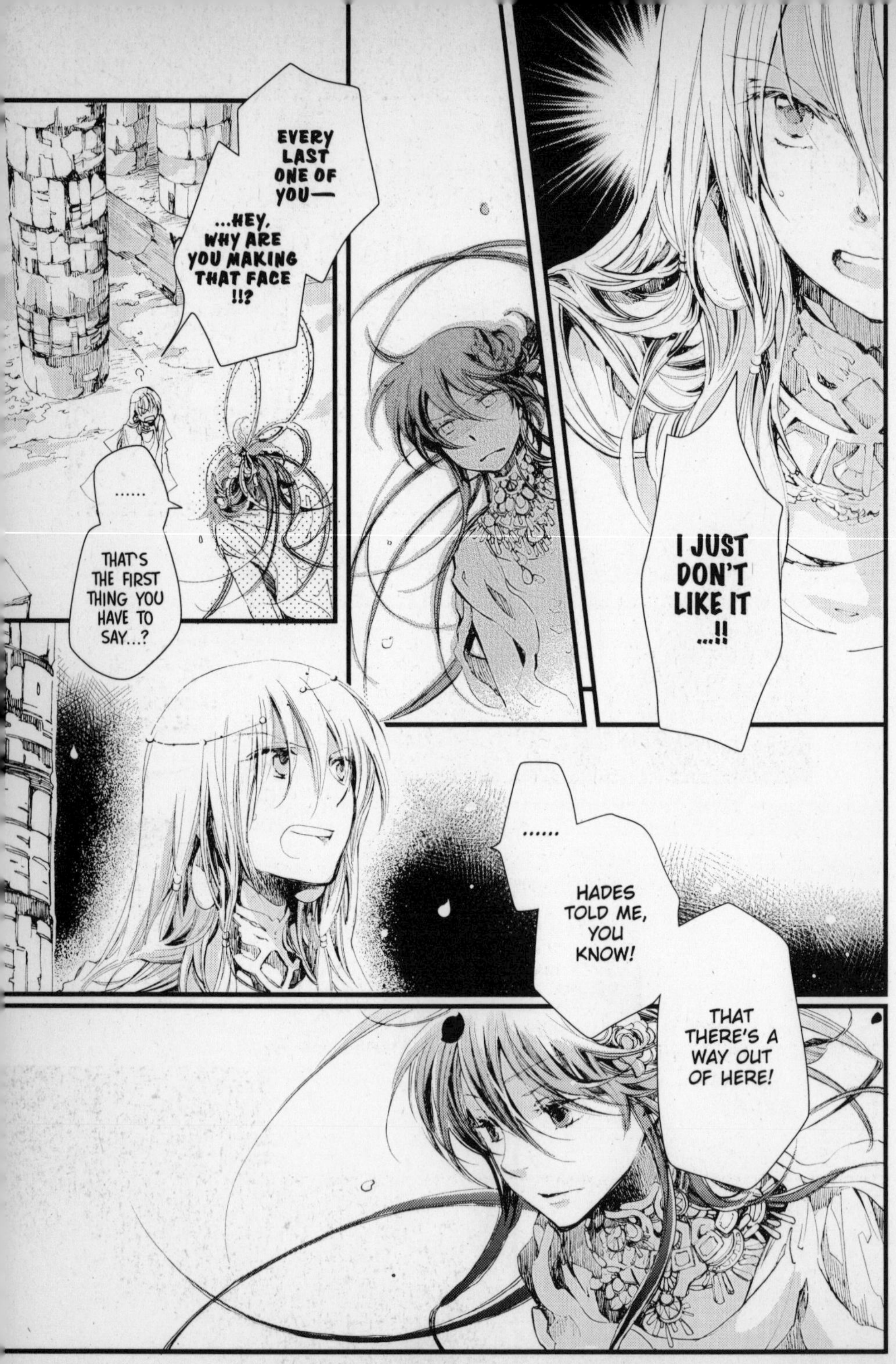
I JUST DON'T LIKE IT ...!!
EVERY LAST ONE OF YOU—
...HEY, WHY ARE YOU MAKING THAT FACE !!?
......
THAT'S THE FIRST THING YOU HAVE TO SAY...?
......
HADES TOLD ME, YOU KNOW!
THAT THERE'S A WAY OUT OF HERE!

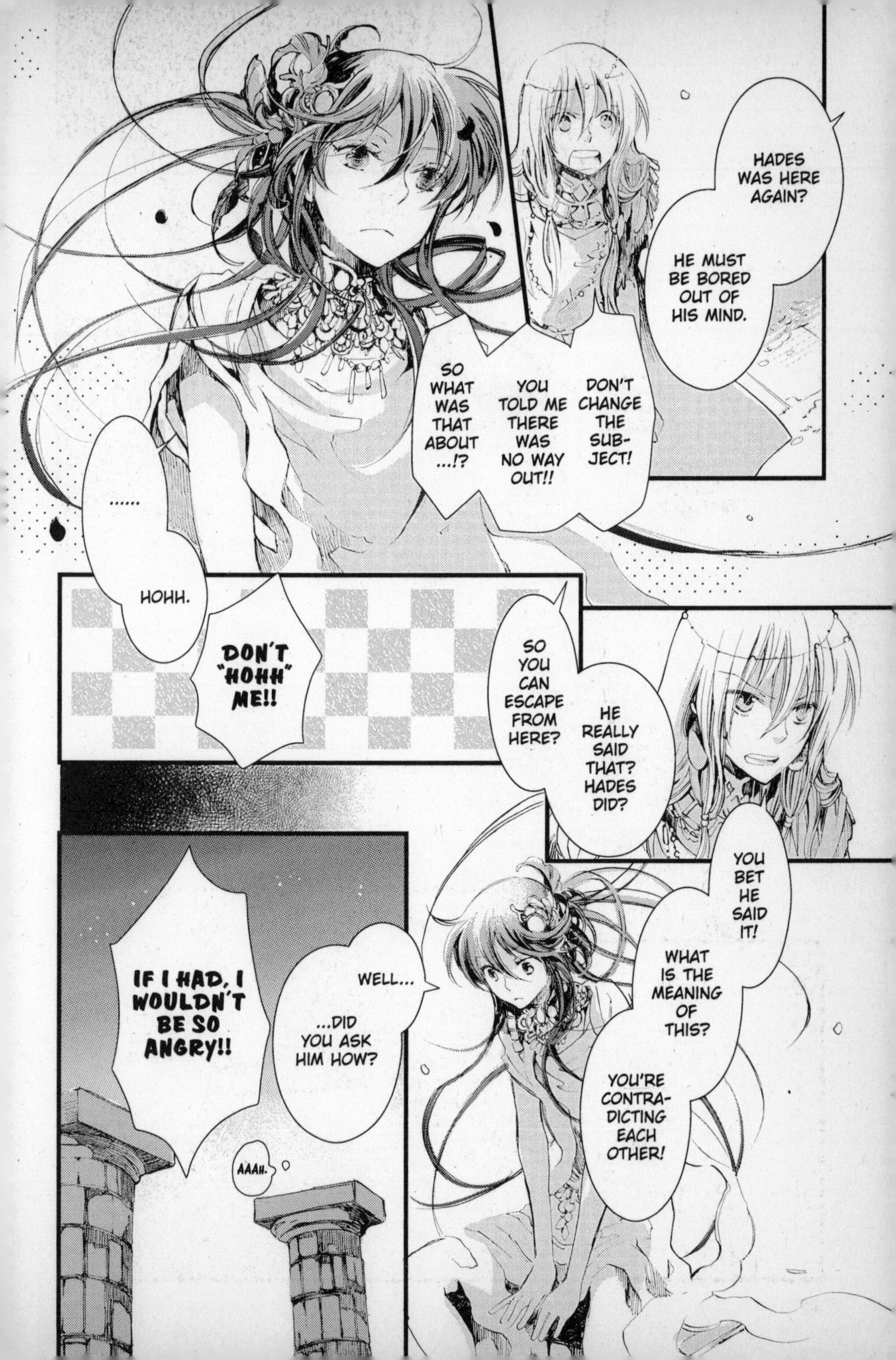
HADES WAS HERE AGAIN?
HE MUST BE BORED OUT OF HIS MIND.
DON'T CHANGE THE SUB-JECT!
YOU TOLD ME THERE WAS NO WAY OUT!!
SO WHAT WAS THAT ABOUT ...!?
......
HOHH.
HE REALLY SAID THAT? HADES DID?
SO YOU CAN ESCAPE FROM HERE?
DON'T "HOHH" ME!!
YOU BET HE SAID IT!
WHAT IS THE MEANING OF THIS?
YOU'RE CONTRA-DICTING EACH OTHER!
WELL...
...DID YOU ASK HIM HOW?
IF I HAD, I WOULDN'T BE SO ANGRY!!
AAAH.

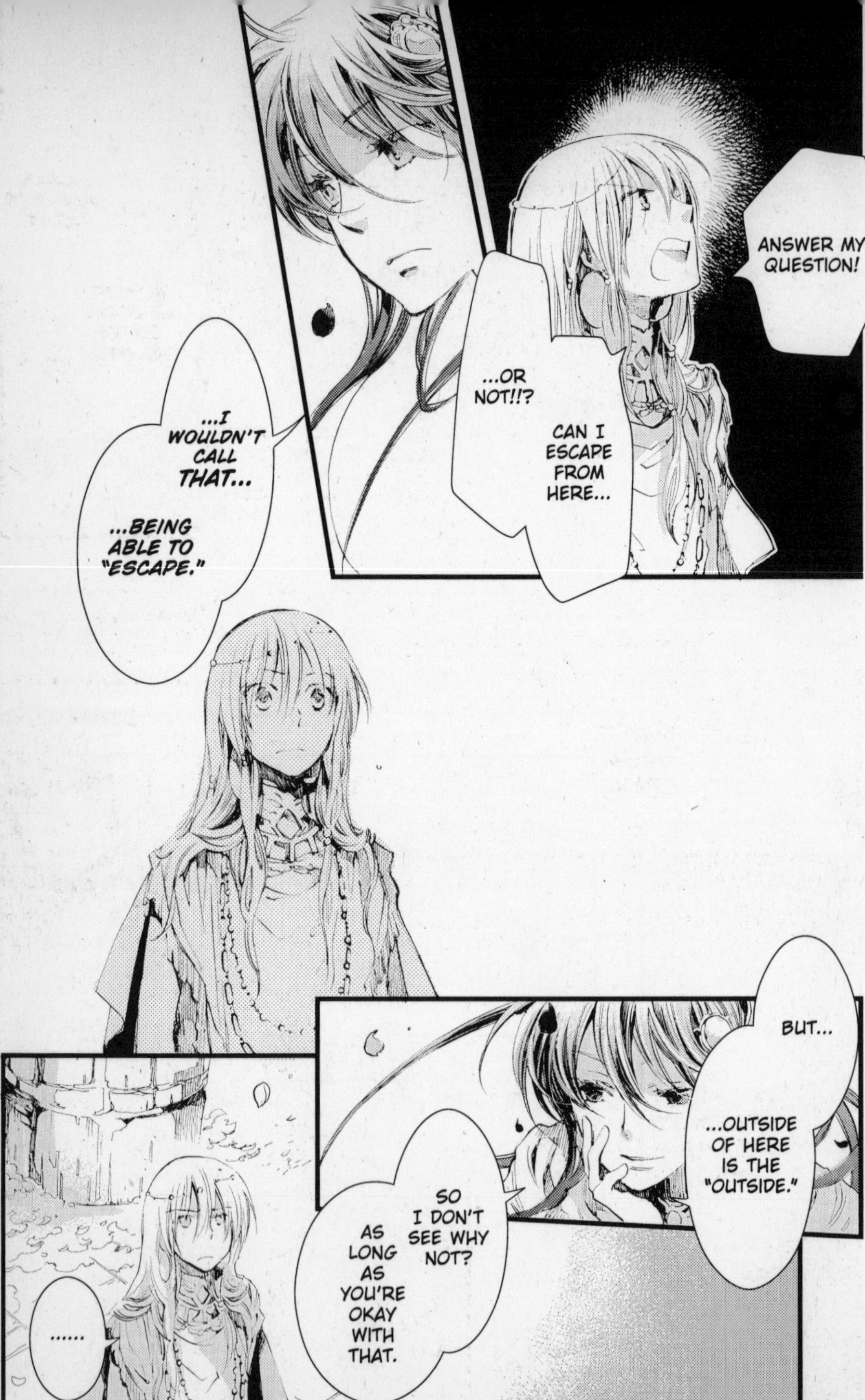
ANSWER MY QUESTION!
CAN I ESCAPE FROM HERE...
...OR NOT!!?
...I WOULDN'T CALL THAT...
...BEING ABLE TO "ESCAPE."
BUT...
...OUTSIDE OF HERE IS THE "OUTSIDE."
SO I DON'T SEE WHY NOT?
AS LONG AS YOU'RE OKAY WITH THAT.
......

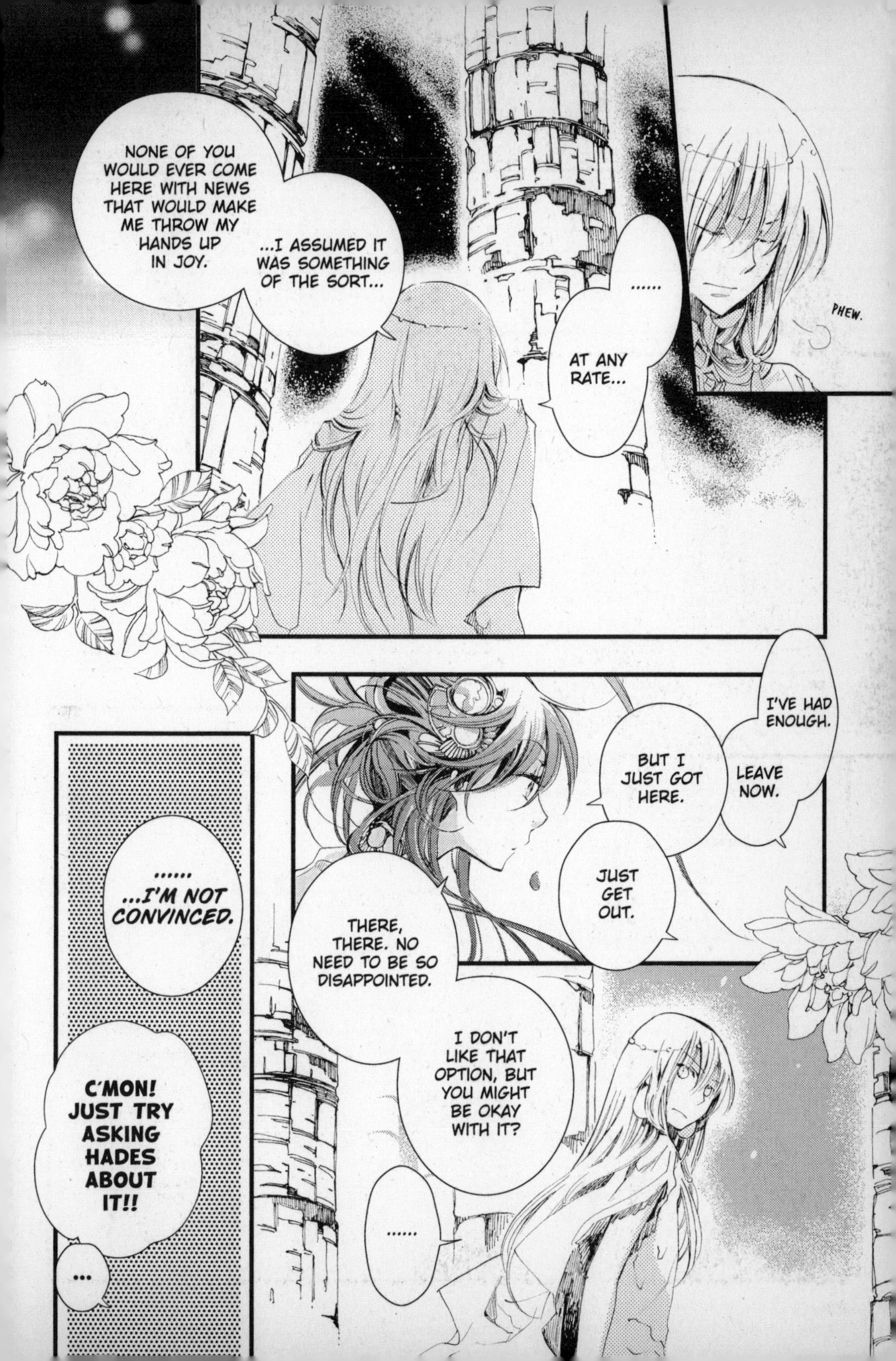
PHEW.
...... AT ANY RATE...
...I ASSUMED IT WAS SOMETHING OF THE SORT...
NONE OF YOU WOULD EVER COME HERE WITH NEWS THAT WOULD MAKE ME THROW MY HANDS UP IN JOY.
I'VE HAD ENOUGH. LEAVE NOW.
BUT I JUST GOT HERE.
JUST GET OUT.
THERE, THERE. NO NEED TO BE SO DISAPPOINTED.
I DON'T LIKE THAT OPTION, BUT YOU MIGHT BE OKAY WITH IT?
......
....I'M NOT CONVINCED.
C'MON! JUST TRY ASKING HADES ABOUT IT!!
...

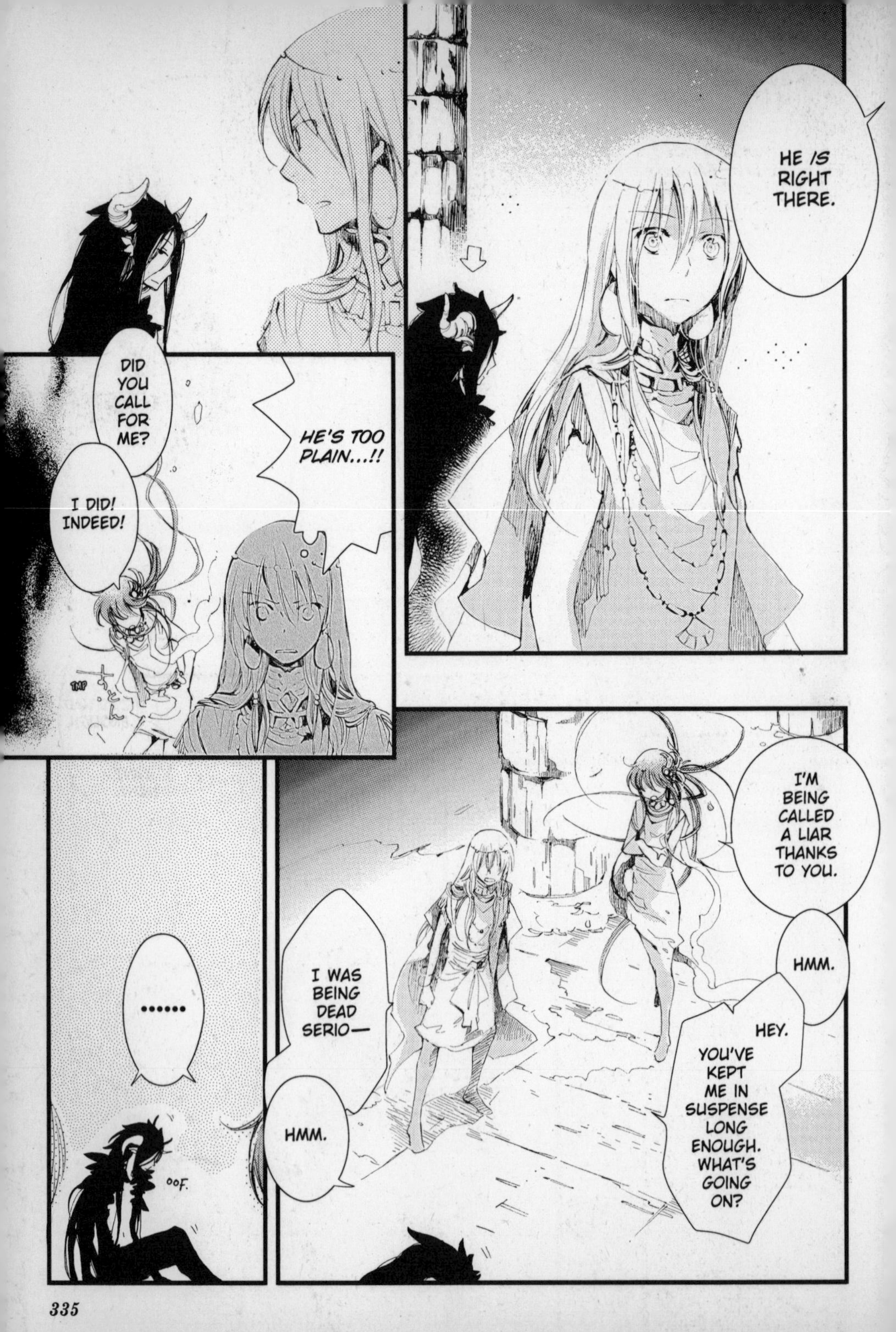
HE IS RIGHT THERE.
DID YOU CALL FOR ME?
I DID! INDEED!
HE'S TOO PLAIN...!!
TMP
I'M BEING CALLED A LIAR THANKS TO YOU.
HMM.
HEY. YOU'VE KEPT ME IN SUSPENSE LONG ENOUGH. WHAT'S GOING ON?
I WAS BEING DEAD SERIO—
HMM.
......
OOF.

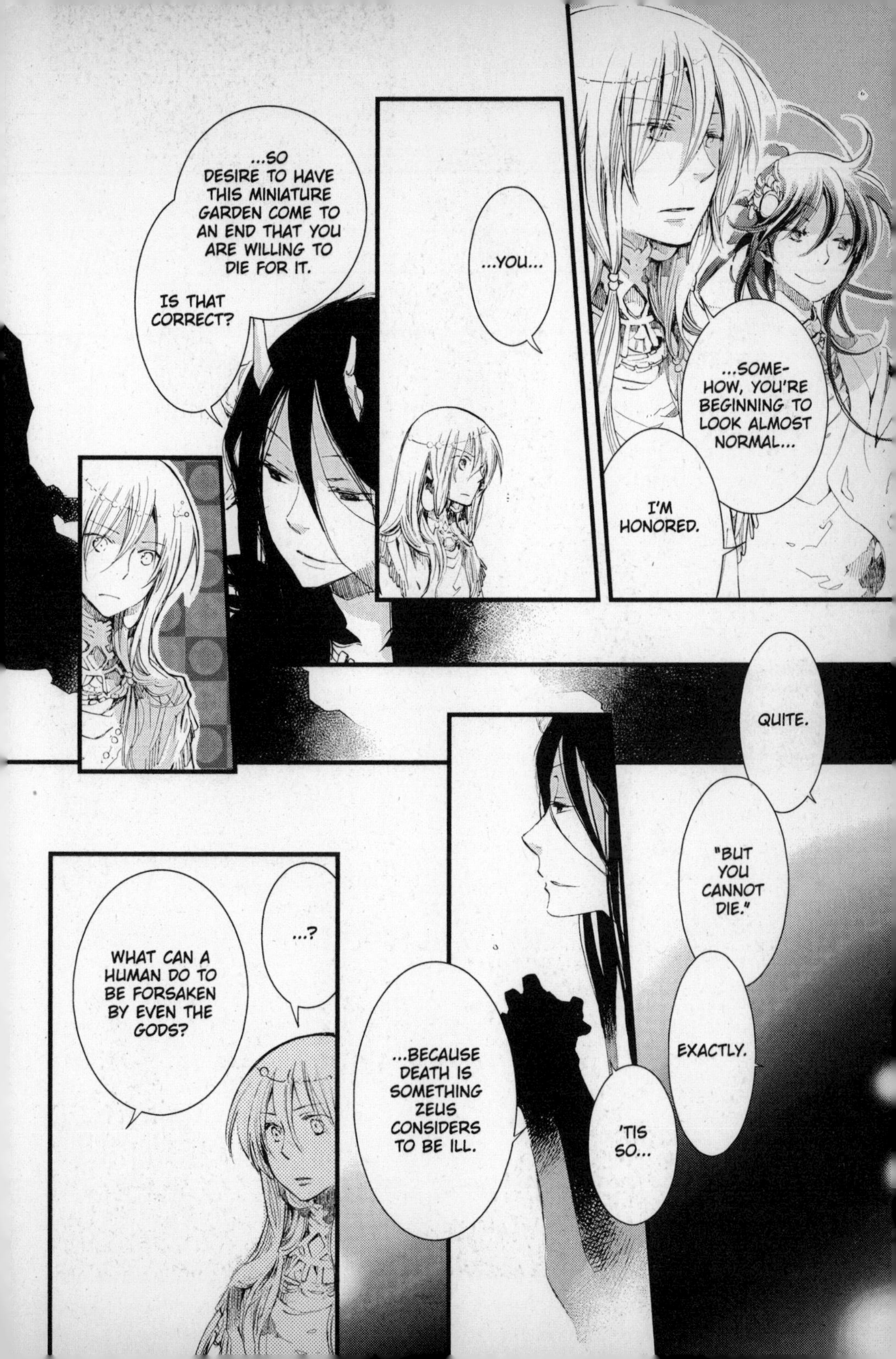
...SOME-HOW, YOU'RE BEGINNING TO LOOK ALMOST NORMAL...
I'M HONORED.
...YOU...
...SO DESIRE TO HAVE THIS MINIATURE GARDEN COME TO AN END THAT YOU ARE WILLING TO DIE FOR IT.
IS THAT CORRECT?
QUITE.
"BUT YOU CANNOT DIE."
EXACTLY.
'TIS SO...
...BECAUSE DEATH IS SOMETHING ZEUS CONSIDERS TO BE ILL.
...?
WHAT CAN A HUMAN DO TO BE FORSAKEN BY EVEN THE GODS?

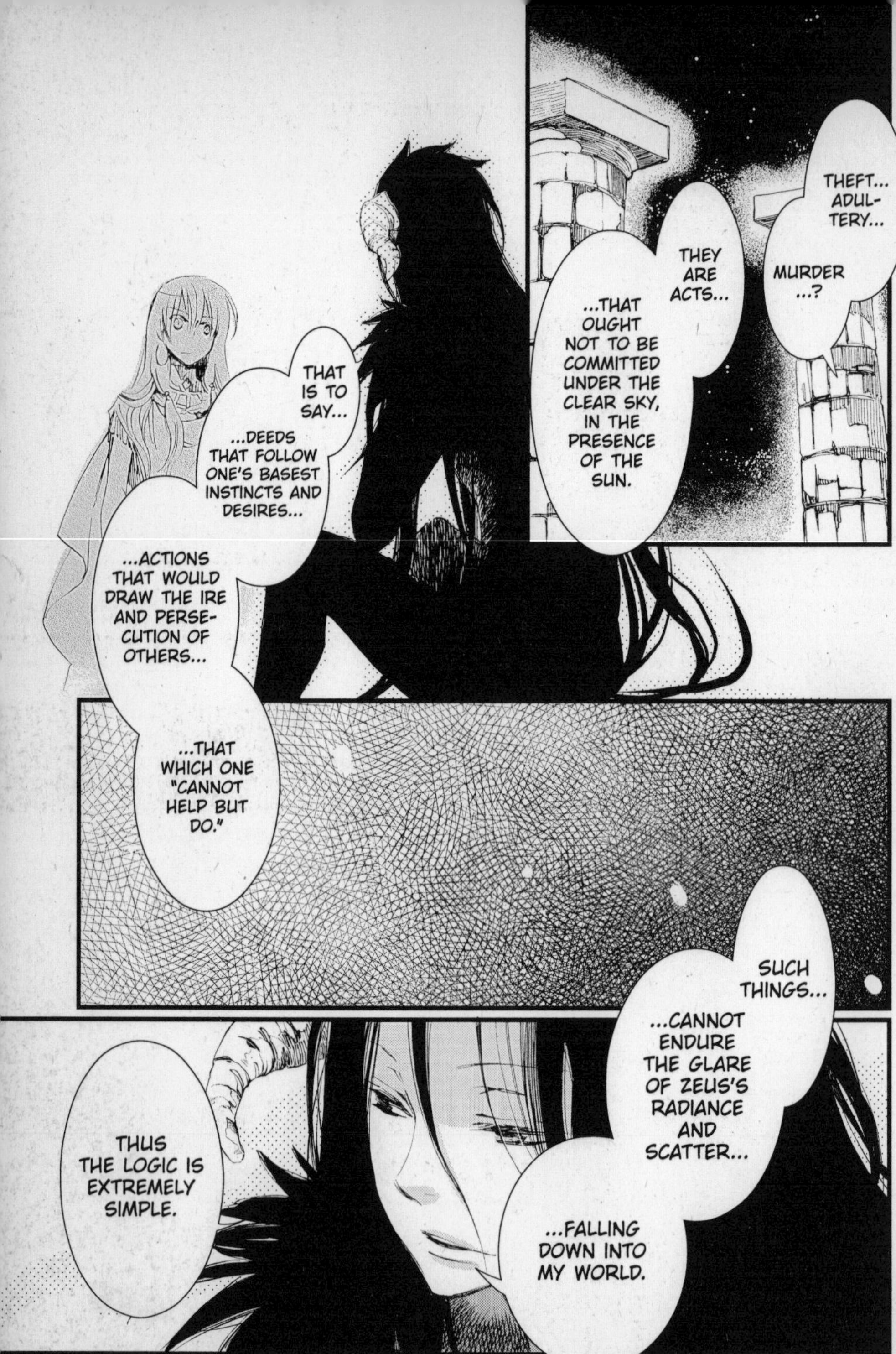
THEFT... ADULTERY...
MURDER ...?
THEY ARE ACTS...
...THAT OUGHT NOT TO BE COMMITTED UNDER THE CLEAR SKY, IN THE PRESENCE OF THE SUN.
THAT IS TO SAY...
...DEEDS THAT FOLLOW ONE'S BASEST INSTINCTS AND DESIRES...
...ACTIONS THAT WOULD DRAW THE IRE AND PERSE-CUTION OF OTHERS...
...THAT WHICH ONE "CANNOT HELP BUT DO."
SUCH THINGS...
...CANNOT ENDURE THE GLARE OF ZEUS'S RADIANCE AND SCATTER...
...FALLING DOWN INTO MY WORLD.
THUS THE LOGIC IS EXTREMELY SIMPLE.

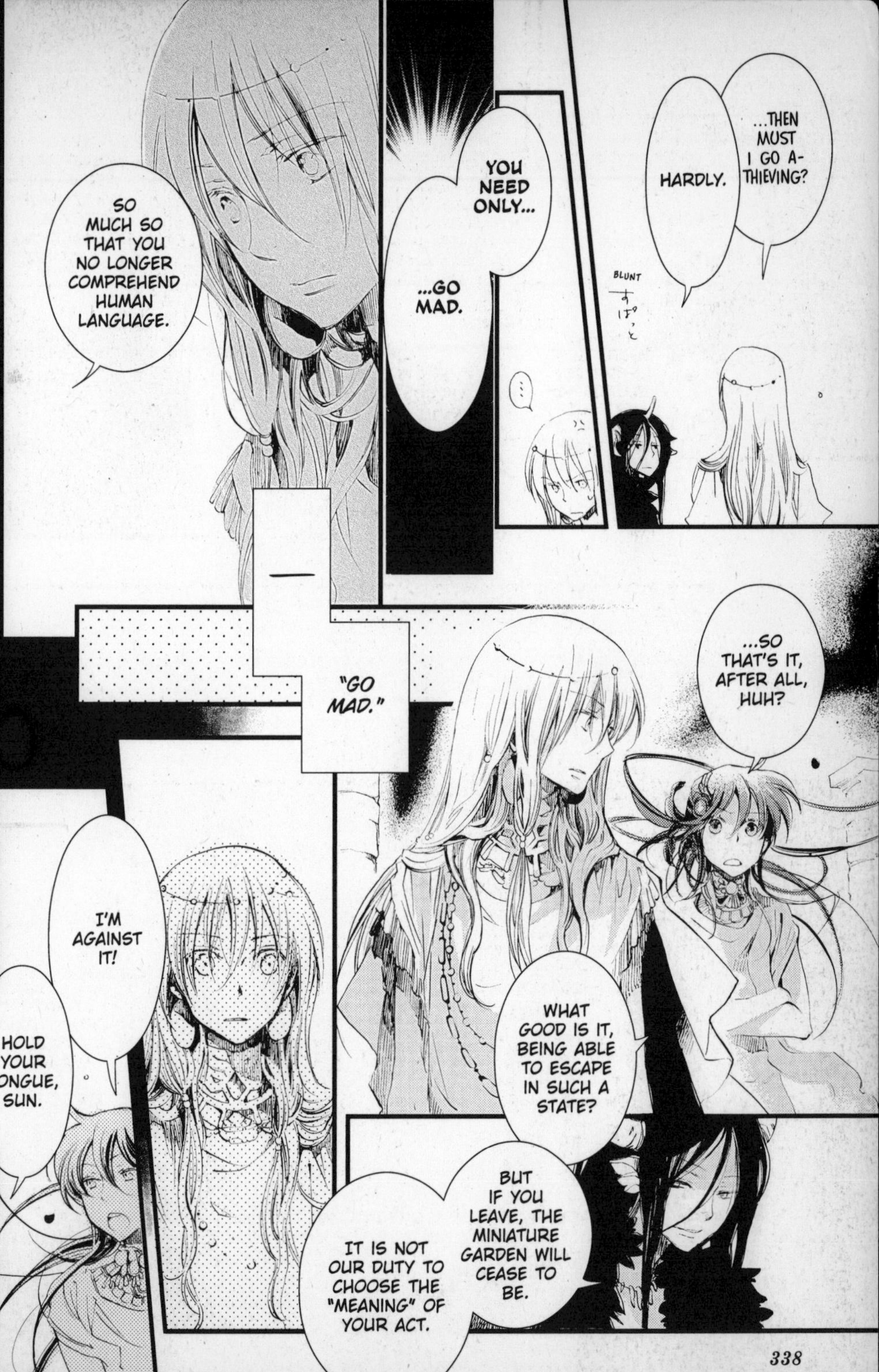

...THEN MUST I GO A-THIEVING?
HARDLY.
BLUNT
すぱっと
...
YOU NEED ONLY...
...GO MAD.
SO MUCH SO THAT YOU NO LONGER COMPREHEND HUMAN LANGUAGE.
—
"GO MAD."
...SO THAT'S IT, AFTER ALL, HUH?
WHAT GOOD IS IT, BEING ABLE TO ESCAPE IN SUCH A STATE?
BUT IF YOU LEAVE, THE MINIATURE GARDEN WILL CEASE TO BE.
IT IS NOT OUR DUTY TO CHOOSE THE "MEANING" OF YOUR ACT.
I'M AGAINST IT!
HOLD YOUR TONGUE, SUN.

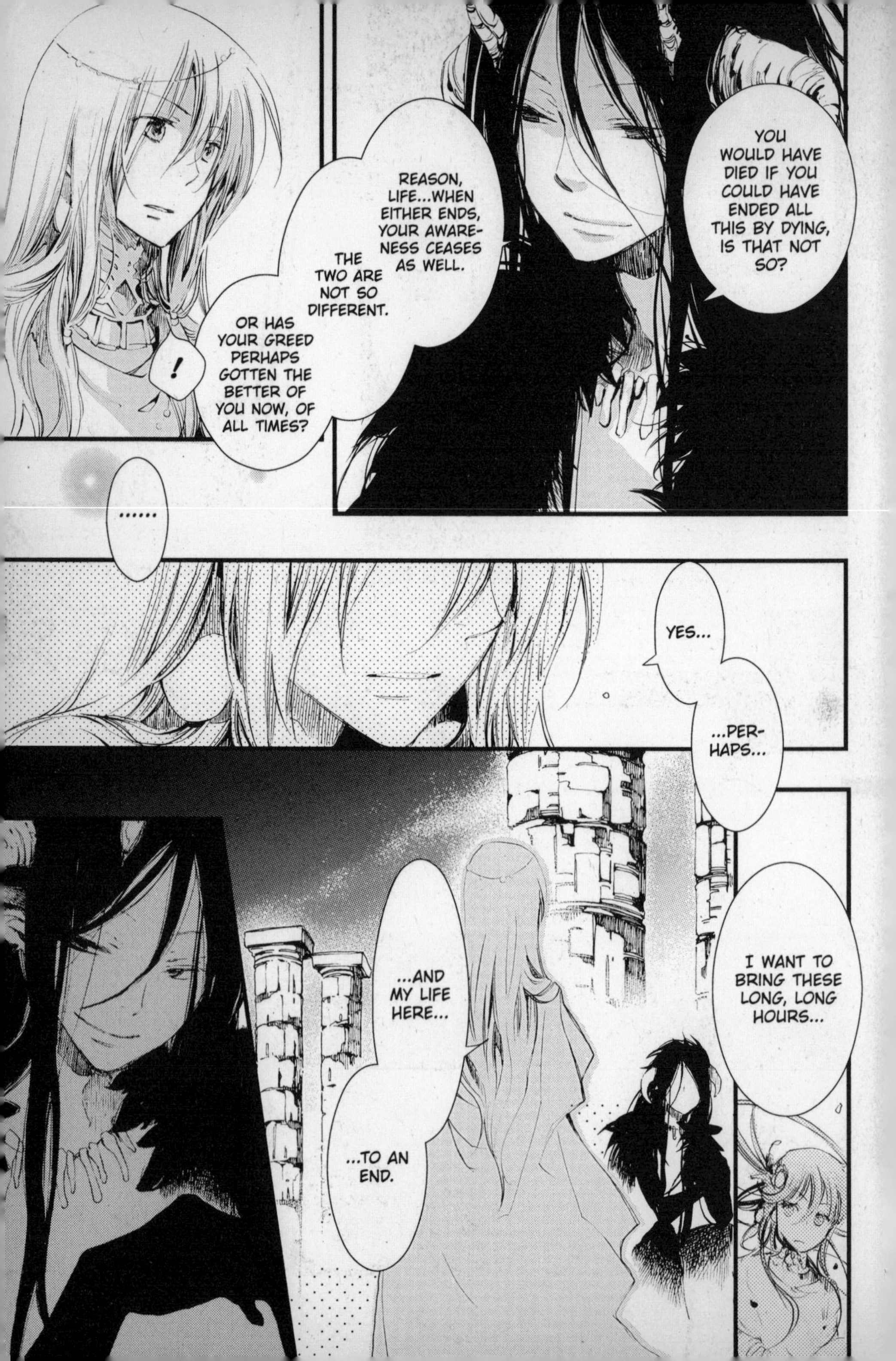
YOU WOULD HAVE DIED IF YOU COULD HAVE ENDED ALL THIS BY DYING, IS THAT NOT SO?
REASON, LIFE...WHEN EITHER ENDS, YOUR AWARENESS CEASES AS WELL.
THE TWO ARE NOT SO DIFFERENT.
OR HAS YOUR GREED PERHAPS GOTTEN THE BETTER OF YOU NOW, OF ALL TIMES?
!
......
YES...
...PERHAPS...
I WANT TO BRING THESE LONG, LONG HOURS...
...AND MY LIFE HERE...
...TO AN END.

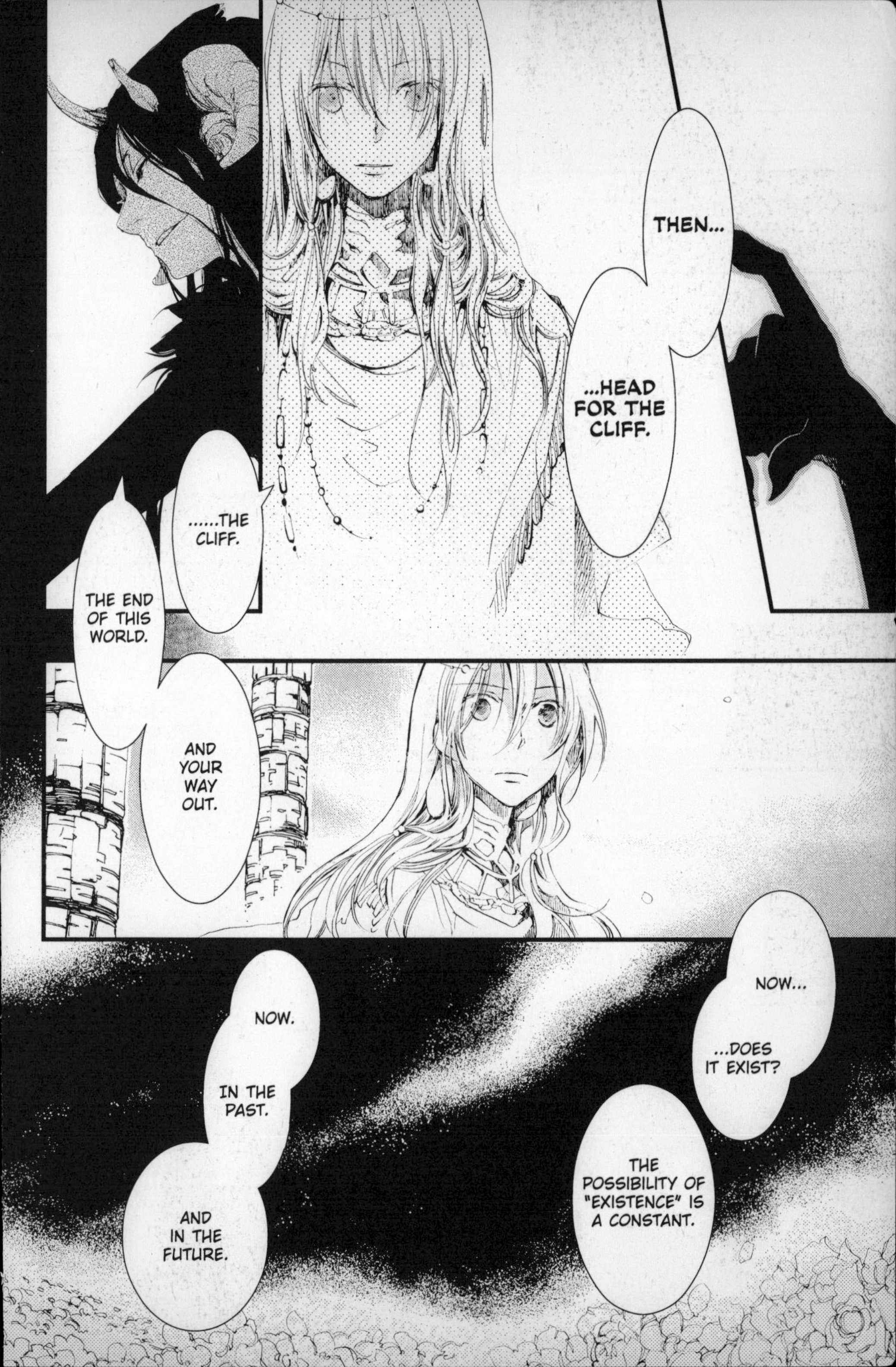
THEN...
...HEAD FOR THE CLIFF.
......THE CLIFF.
THE END OF THIS WORLD.
AND YOUR WAY OUT.
NOW...
...DOES IT EXIST?
THE POSSIBILITY OF "EXISTENCE" IS A CONSTANT.
NOW.
IN THE PAST.
AND IN THE FUTURE.

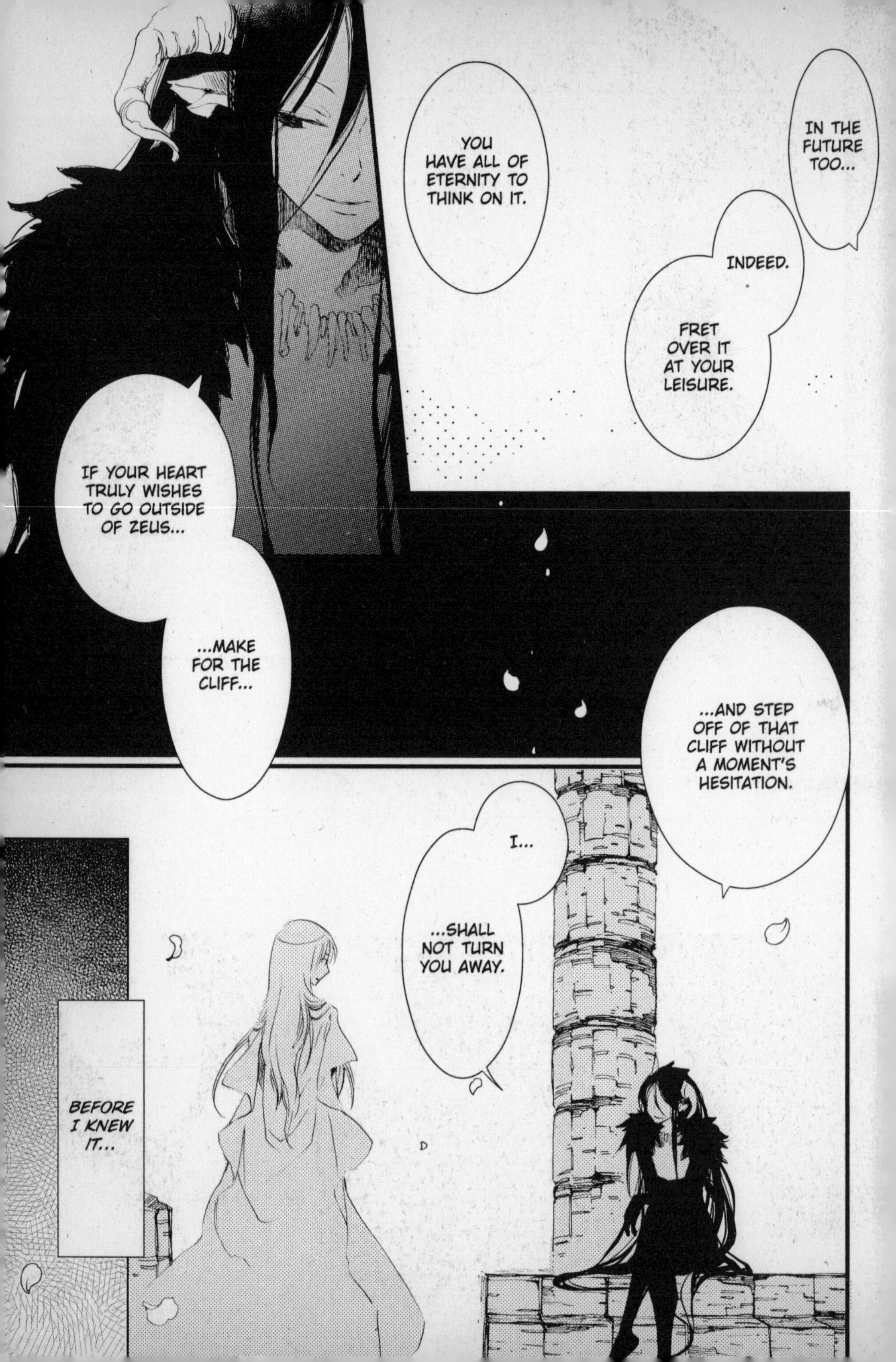

IN THE FUTURE TOO...
INDEED.
FRET OVER IT AT YOUR LEISURE.
YOU HAVE ALL OF ETERNITY TO THINK ON IT.
IF YOUR HEART TRULY WISHES TO GO OUTSIDE OF ZEUS...
...MAKE FOR THE CLIFF...
...AND STEP OFF OF THAT CLIFF WITHOUT A MOMENT'S HESITATION.
I...
...SHALL NOT TURN YOU AWAY.
BEFORE I KNEW IT...

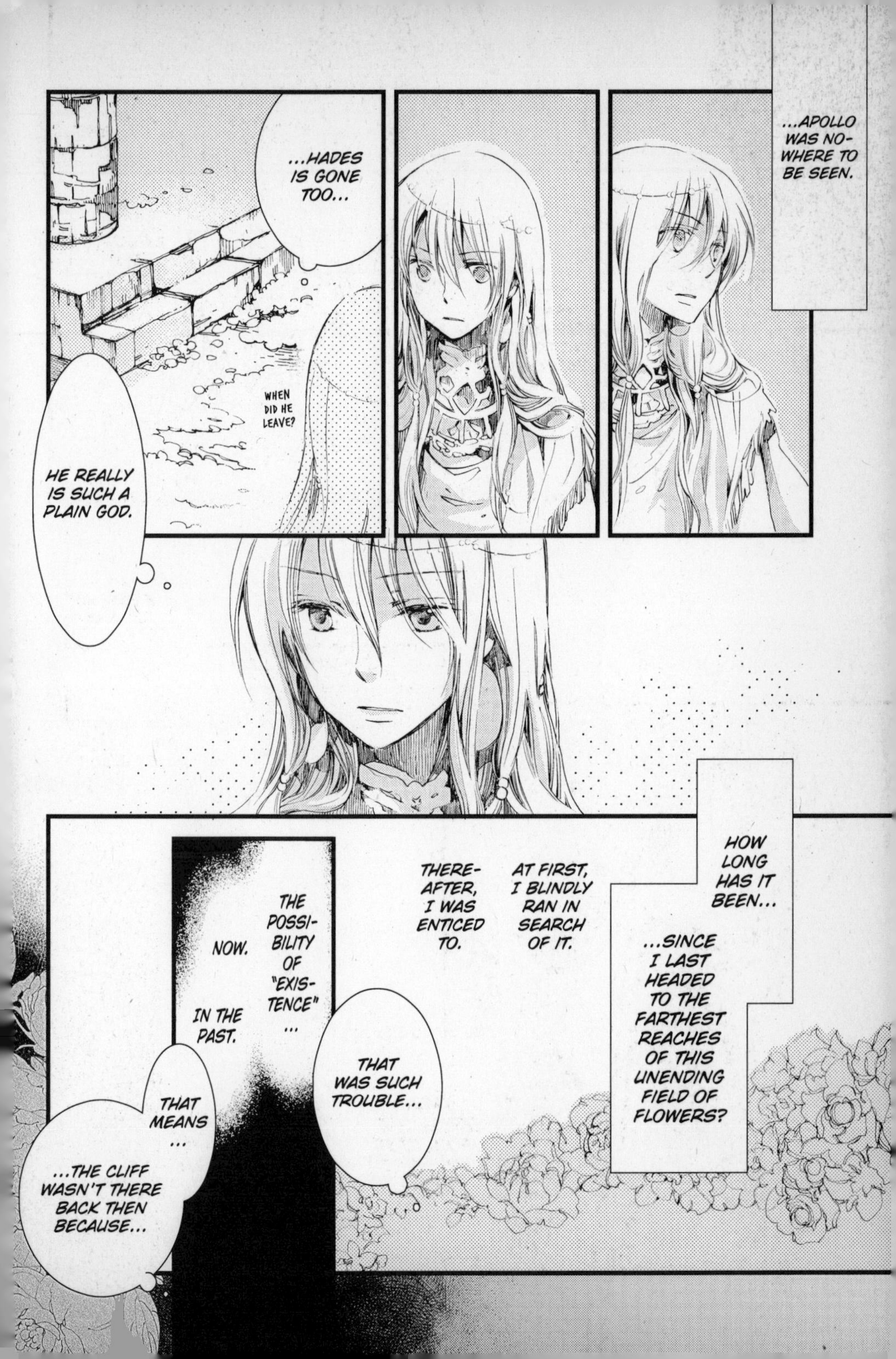
...APOLLO WAS NOWHERE TO BE SEEN.
...HADES IS GONE TOO...
WHEN DID HE LEAVE?
HE REALLY IS SUCH A PLAIN GOD.
HOW LONG HAS IT BEEN...
...SINCE I LAST HEADED TO THE FARTHEST REACHES OF THIS UNENDING FIELD OF FLOWERS?
AT FIRST, I BLINDLY RAN IN SEARCH OF IT.
THEREAFTER, I WAS ENTICED TO.
THAT WAS SUCH TROUBLE...
THE POSSIBILITY OF "EXISTENCE"...
NOW.
IN THE PAST.
THAT MEANS...
...THE CLIFF WASN'T THERE BACK THEN BECAUSE...

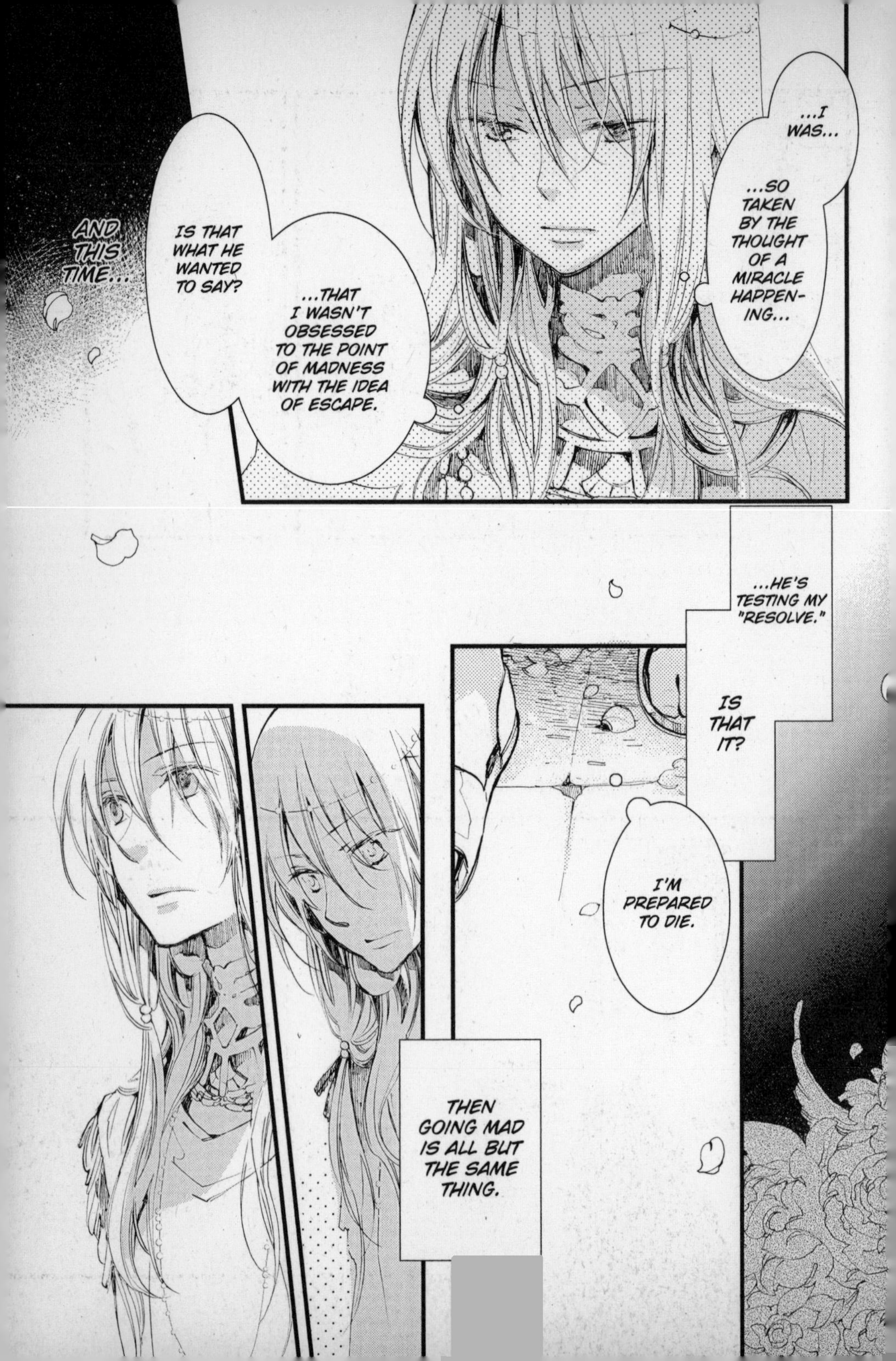
...I WAS...
...SO TAKEN BY THE THOUGHT OF A MIRACLE HAPPENING...
IS THAT WHAT HE WANTED TO SAY?
...THAT I WASN'T OBSESSED TO THE POINT OF MADNESS WITH THE IDEA OF ESCAPE.
AND THIS TIME...
...HE'S TESTING MY "RESOLVE."
IS THAT IT?
I'M PREPARED TO DIE.
THEN GOING MAD IS ALL BUT THE SAME THING.

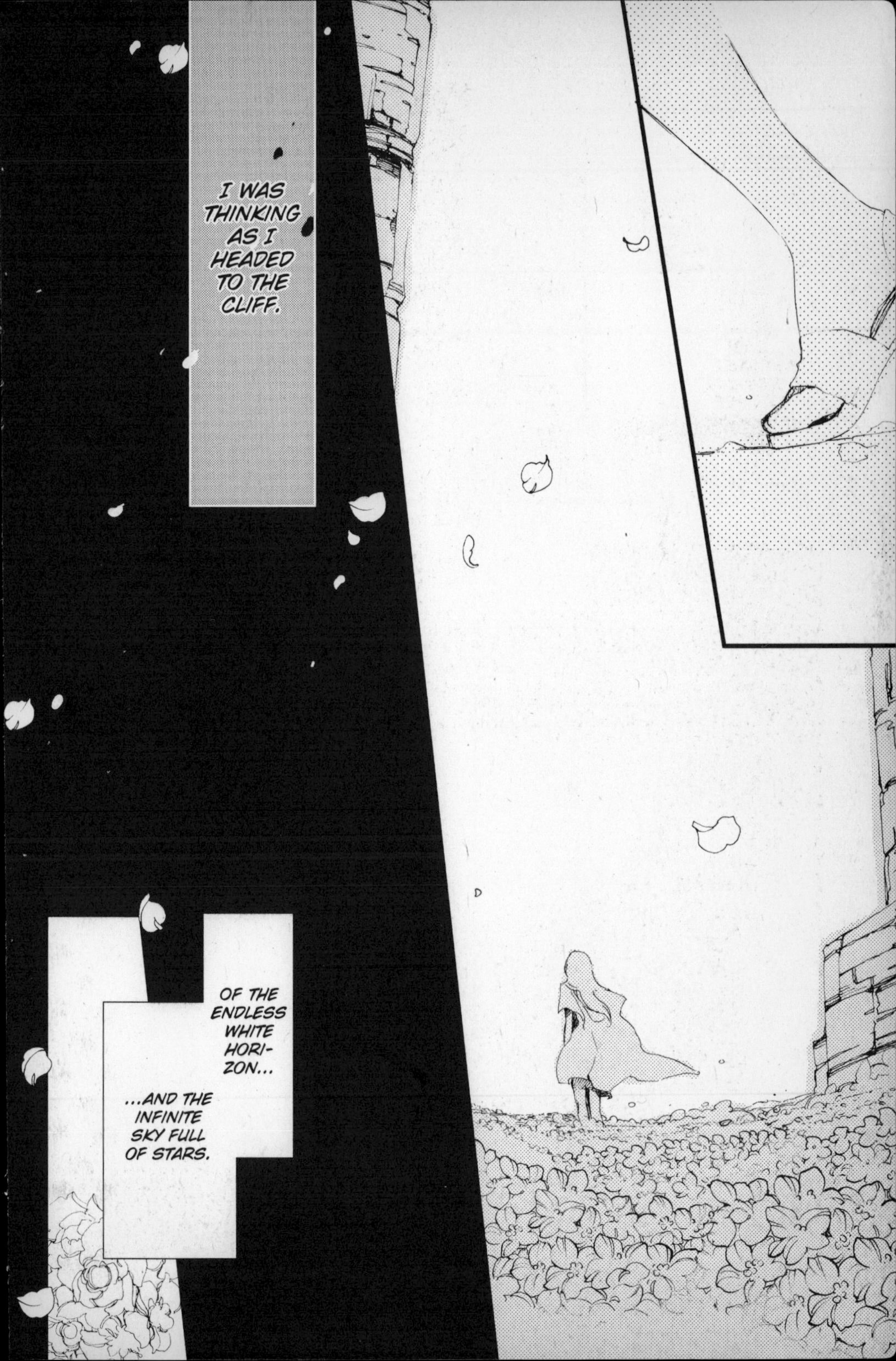
I WAS THINKING AS I HEADED TO THE CLIFF.
OF THE ENDLESS WHITE HORI-ZON...
...AND THE INFINITE SKY FULL OF STARS.

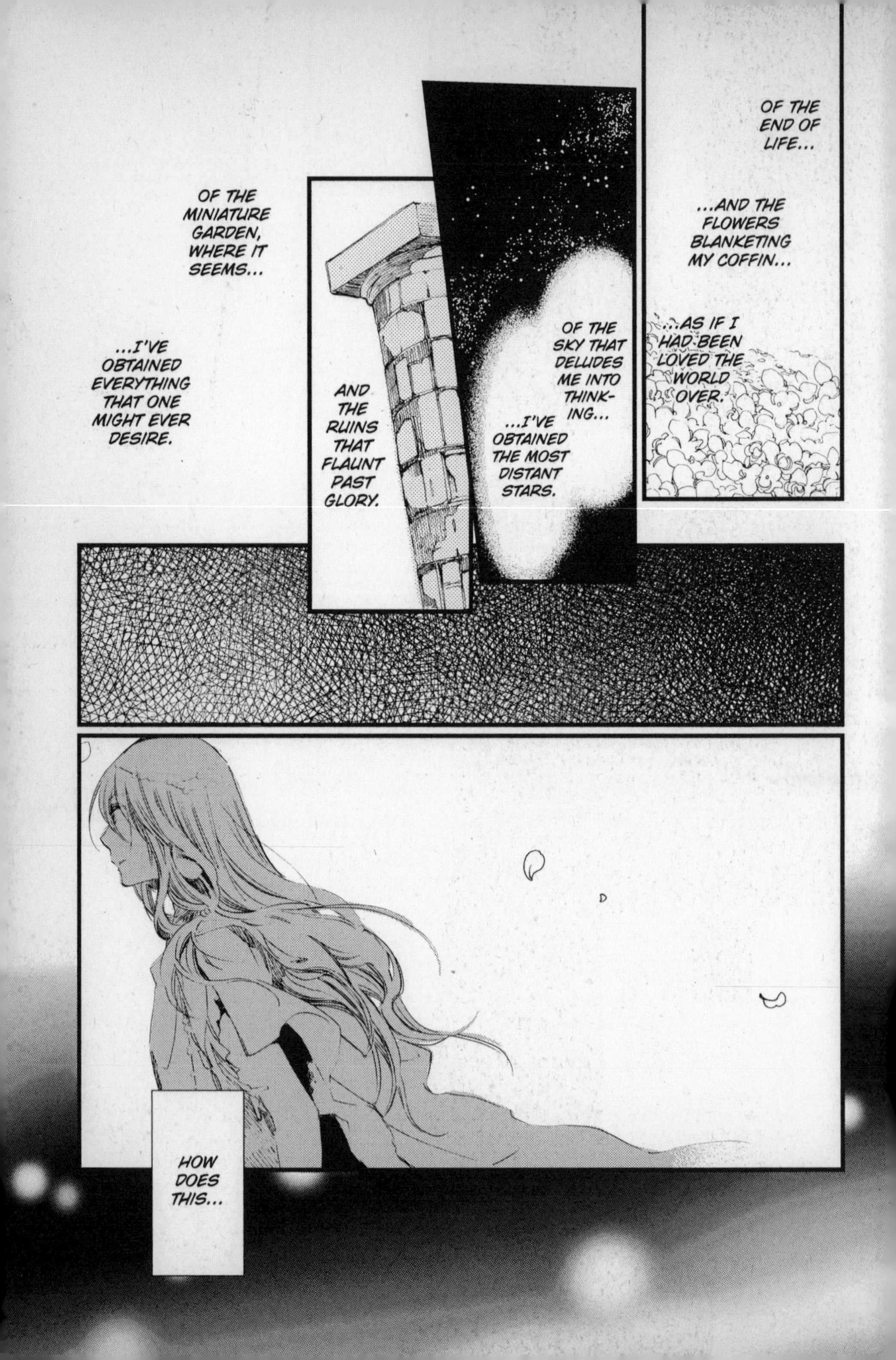
OF THE END OF LIFE...
...AND THE FLOWERS BLANKETING MY COFFIN...
...AS IF I HAD BEEN LOVED THE WORLD OVER.
OF THE SKY THAT DELUDES ME INTO THINKING...
...I'VE OBTAINED THE MOST DISTANT STARS.
AND THE RUINS THAT FLAUNT PAST GLORY.
OF THE MINIATURE GARDEN, WHERE IT SEEMS...
...I'VE OBTAINED EVERYTHING THAT ONE MIGHT EVER DESIRE.
HOW DOES THIS...

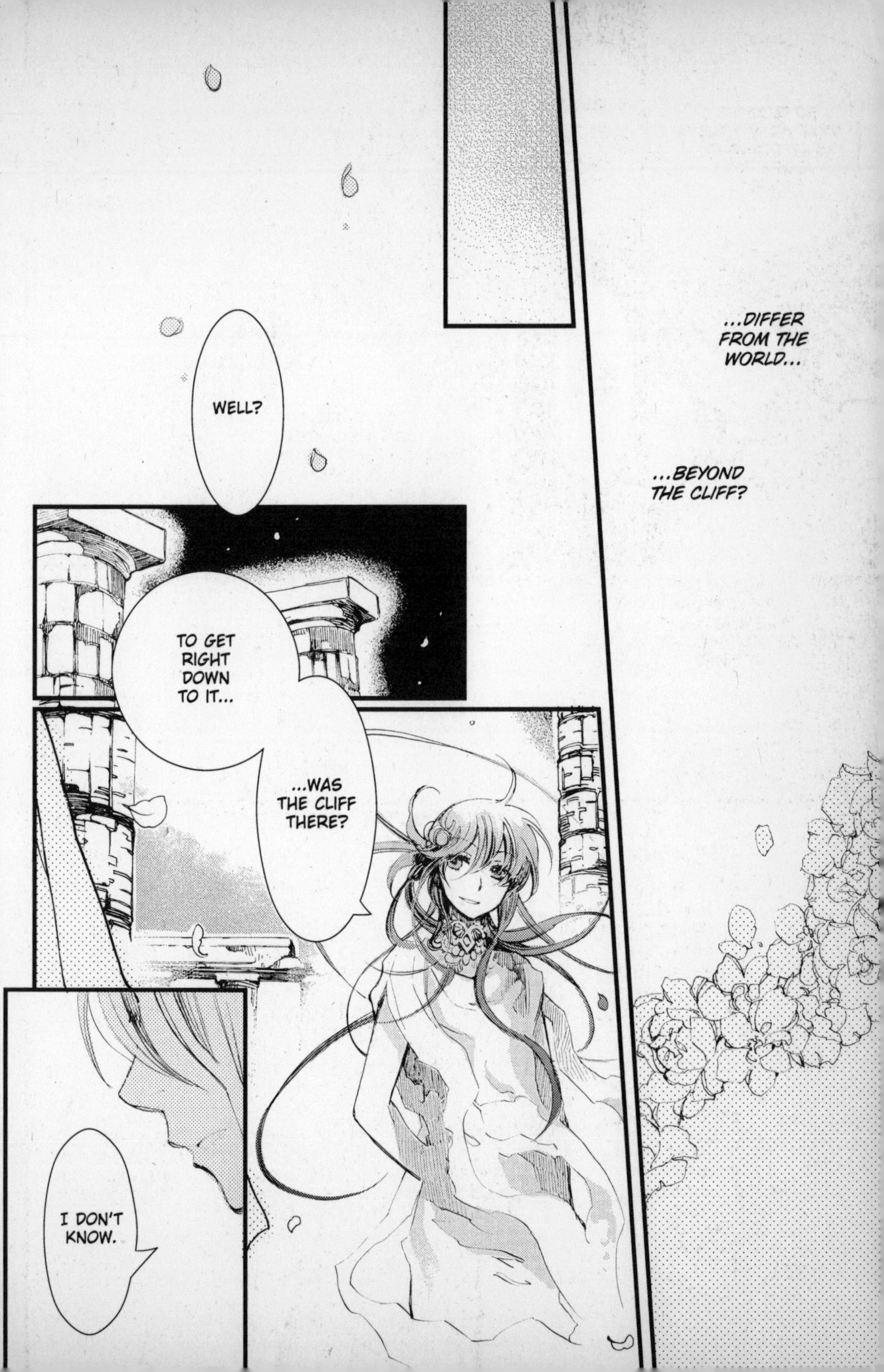
...DIFFER FROM THE WORLD...
...BEYOND THE CLIFF?
WELL?
TO GET RIGHT DOWN TO IT...
...WAS THE CLIFF THERE?
I DON'T KNOW.

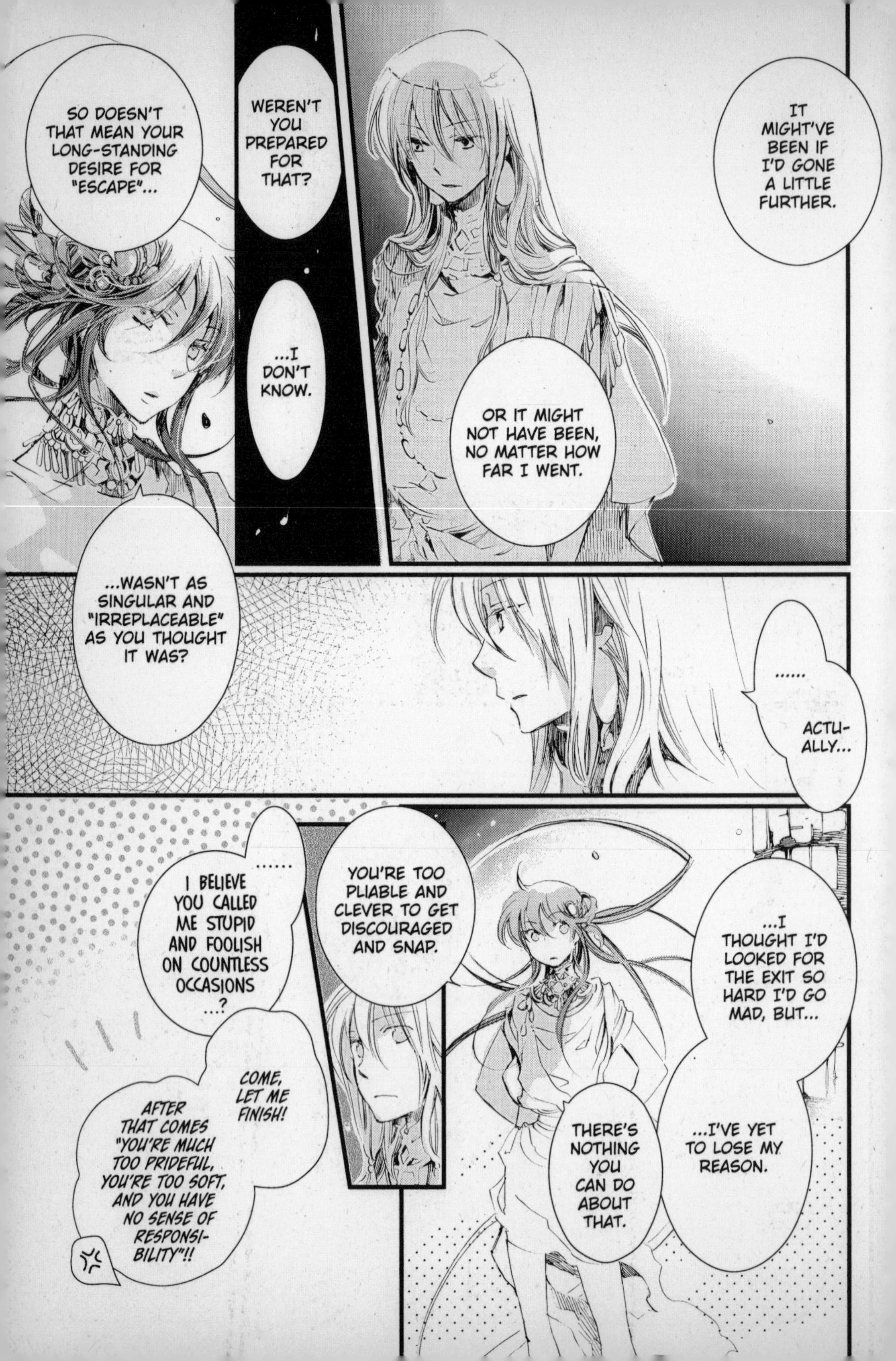
IT MIGHT'VE BEEN IF I'D GONE A LITTLE FURTHER.
OR IT MIGHT NOT HAVE BEEN, NO MATTER HOW FAR I WENT.
WEREN'T YOU PREPARED FOR THAT?
...I DON'T KNOW.
SO DOESN'T THAT MEAN YOUR LONG-STANDING DESIRE FOR "ESCAPE"...
...WASN'T AS SINGULAR AND "IRREPLACEABLE" AS YOU THOUGHT IT WAS?
......
ACTU-ALLY...
...I THOUGHT I'D LOOKED FOR THE EXIT SO HARD I'D GO MAD, BUT...
...I'VE YET TO LOSE MY REASON.
THERE'S NOTHING YOU CAN DO ABOUT THAT.
YOU'RE TOO PLIABLE AND CLEVER TO GET DISCOURAGED AND SNAP.
......
I BELIEVE YOU CALLED ME STUPID AND FOOLISH ON COUNTLESS OCCASIONS...?
COME, LET ME FINISH!
AFTER THAT COMES "YOU'RE MUCH TOO PRIDEFUL, YOU'RE TOO SOFT, AND YOU HAVE NO SENSE OF RESPONSI-BILITY"!!

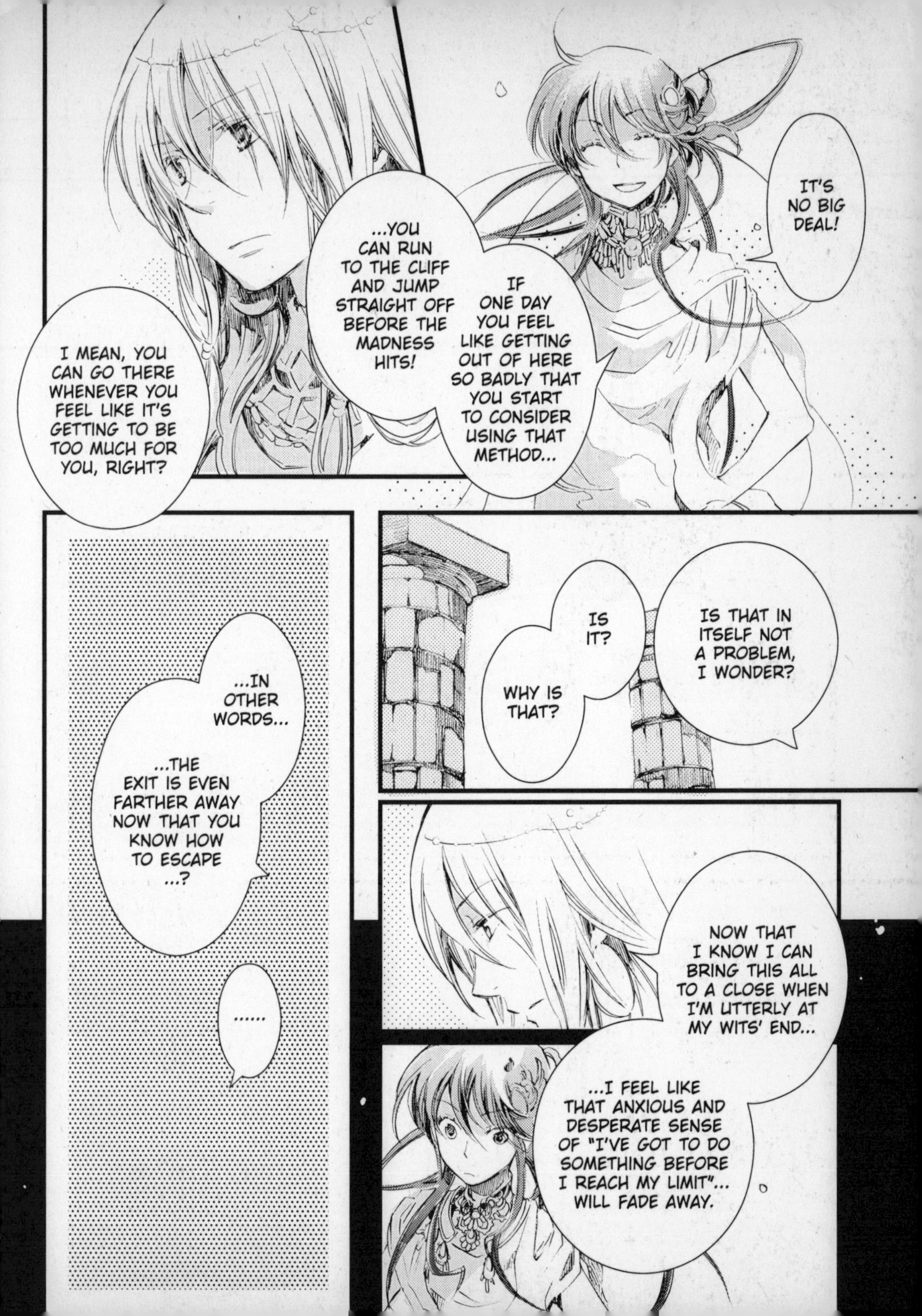
IT'S NO BIG DEAL!
IF ONE DAY YOU FEEL LIKE GETTING OUT OF HERE SO BADLY THAT YOU START TO CONSIDER USING THAT METHOD...
...YOU CAN RUN TO THE CLIFF AND JUMP STRAIGHT OFF BEFORE THE MADNESS HITS!
I MEAN, YOU CAN GO THERE WHENEVER YOU FEEL LIKE IT'S GETTING TO BE TOO MUCH FOR YOU, RIGHT?
IS THAT IN ITSELF NOT A PROBLEM, I WONDER?
IS IT?
WHY IS THAT?
NOW THAT I KNOW I CAN BRING THIS ALL TO A CLOSE WHEN I'M UTTERLY AT MY WITS' END...
...I FEEL LIKE THAT ANXIOUS AND DESPERATE SENSE OF "I'VE GOT TO DO SOMETHING BEFORE I REACH MY LIMIT"... WILL FADE AWAY.
...IN OTHER WORDS...
...THE EXIT IS EVEN FARTHER AWAY NOW THAT YOU KNOW HOW TO ESCAPE ...?
......

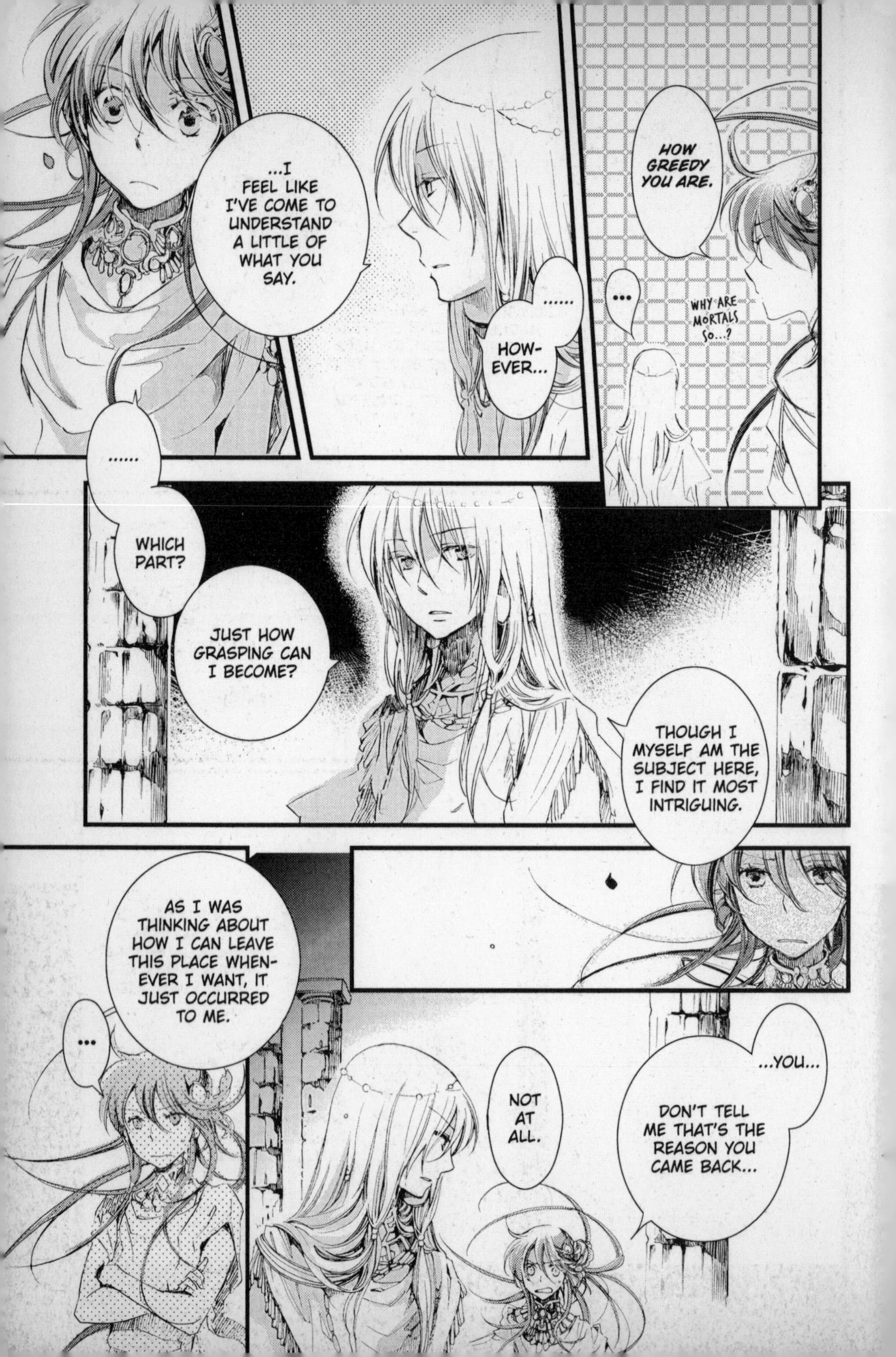
HOW GREEDY YOU ARE.
...
WHY ARE MORTALS SO...?
......
HOW-EVER...
...I FEEL LIKE I'VE COME TO UNDERSTAND A LITTLE OF WHAT YOU SAY.
......
WHICH PART?
JUST HOW GRASPING CAN I BECOME?
THOUGH I MYSELF AM THE SUBJECT HERE, I FIND IT MOST INTRIGUING.
AS I WAS THINKING ABOUT HOW I CAN LEAVE THIS PLACE WHEN-EVER I WANT, IT JUST OCCURRED TO ME.
...YOU...
DON'T TELL ME THAT'S THE REASON YOU CAME BACK...
NOT AT ALL.
...

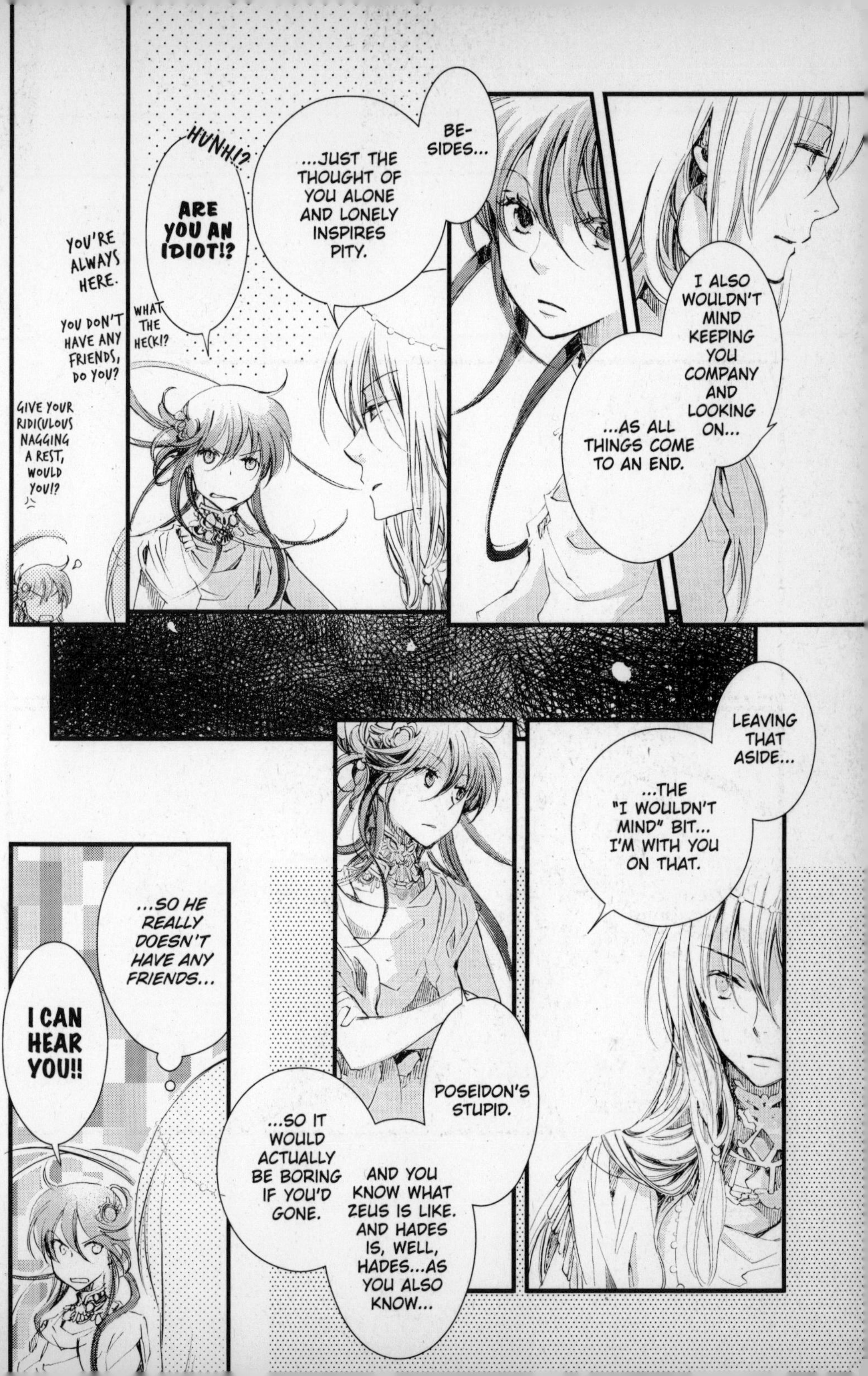
I ALSO WOULDN'T MIND KEEPING YOU COMPANY AND LOOKING ON...
...AS ALL THINGS COME TO AN END.
BE-SIDES...
...JUST THE THOUGHT OF YOU ALONE AND LONELY INSPIRES PITY.
HUNH!?
ARE YOU AN IDIOT!?
WHAT THE HECK!?
YOU'RE ALWAYS HERE.
YOU DON'T HAVE ANY FRIENDS, DO YOU?
GIVE YOUR RIDICULOUS NAGGING A REST, WOULD YOU!?
LEAVING THAT ASIDE...
...THE "I WOULDN'T MIND" BIT... I'M WITH YOU ON THAT.
POSEIDON'S STUPID.
AND YOU KNOW WHAT ZEUS IS LIKE. AND HADES IS, WELL, HADES...AS YOU ALSO KNOW...
...SO IT WOULD ACTUALLY BE BORING IF YOU'D GONE.
...SO HE REALLY DOESN'T HAVE ANY FRIENDS...
I CAN HEAR YOU!!

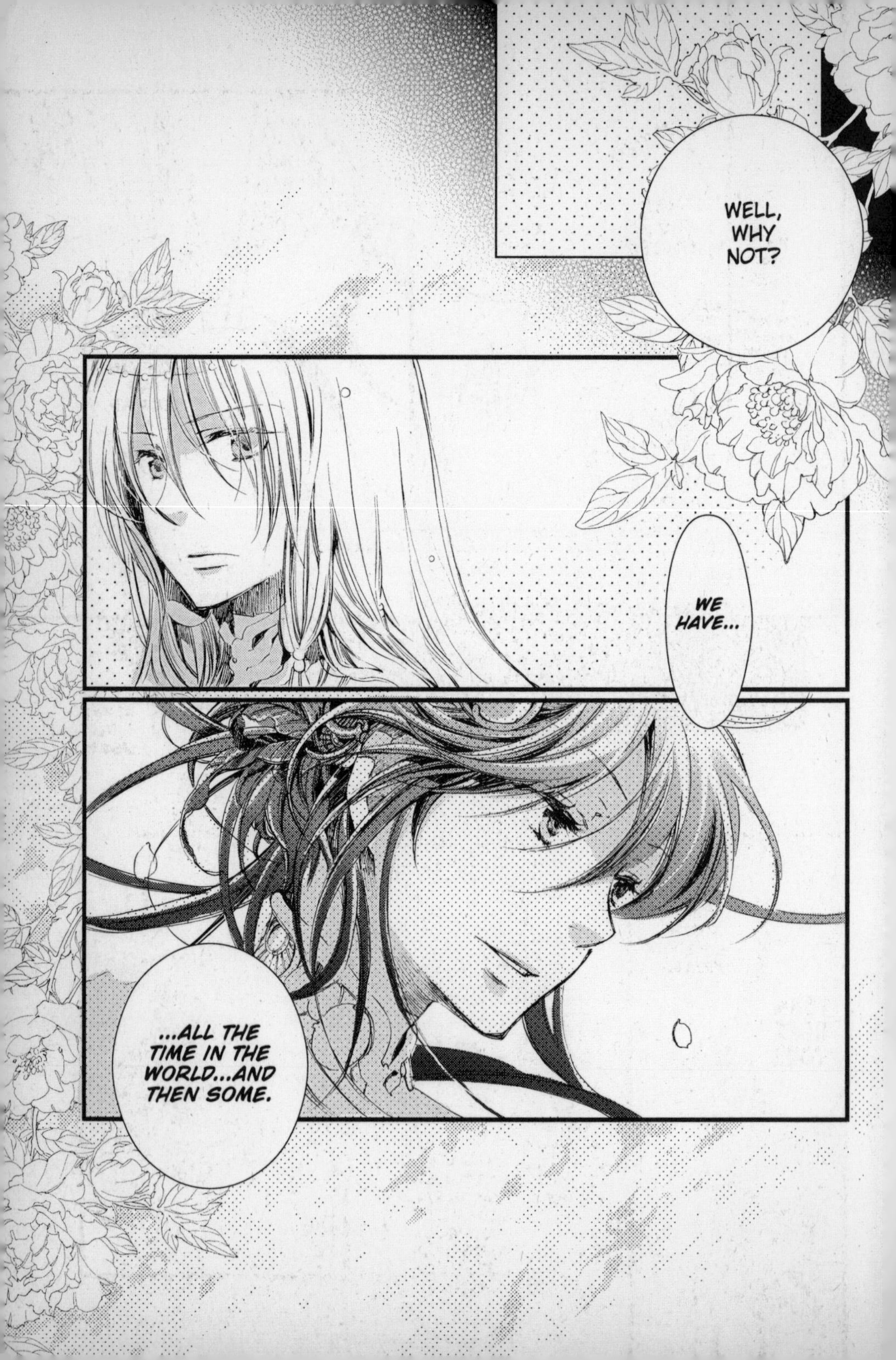
WELL, WHY NOT?
WE HAVE...
...ALL THE TIME IN THE WORLD...AND THEN SOME.

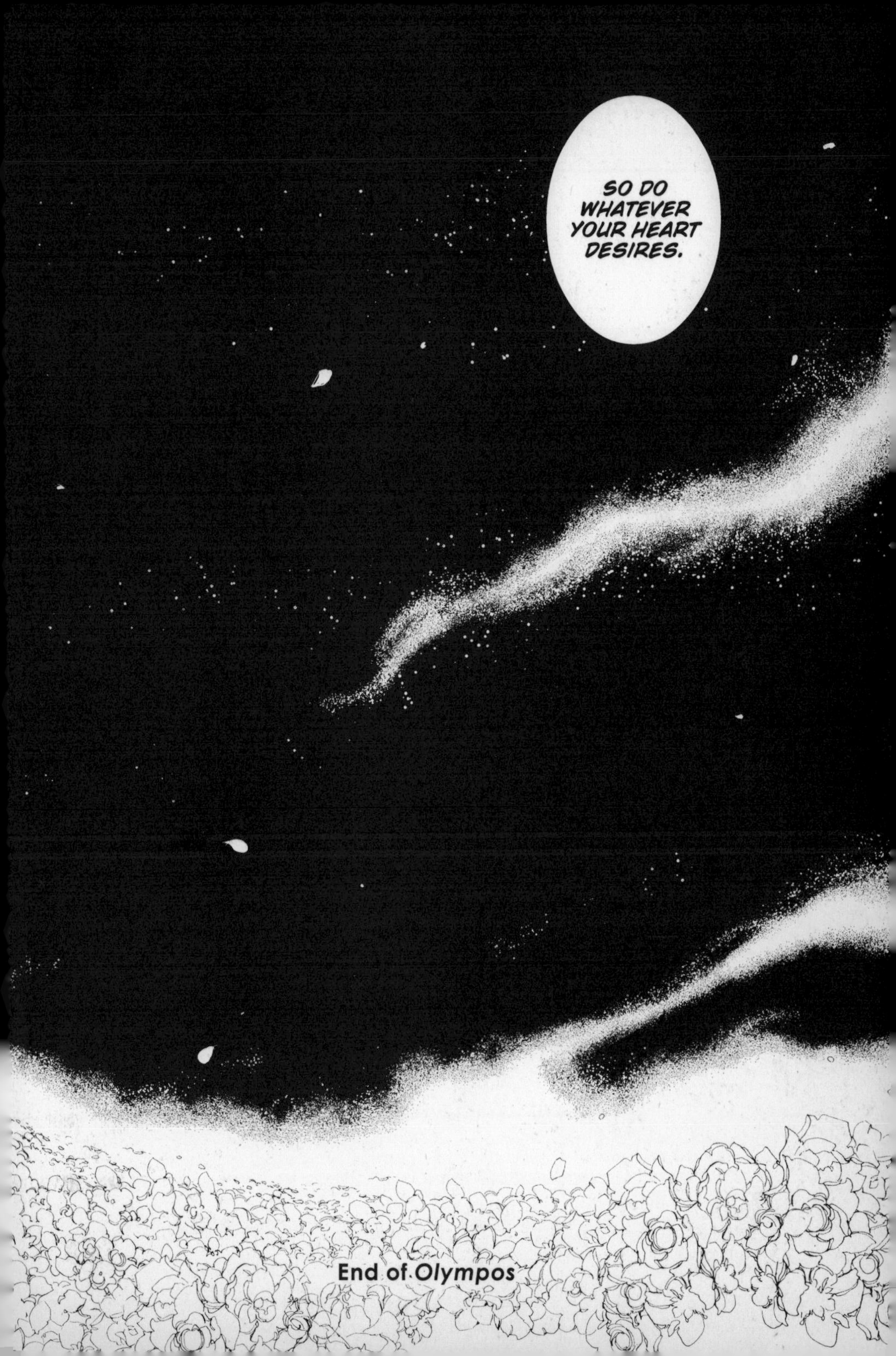
SO DO WHATEVER YOUR HEART DESIRES.
End of Olympos

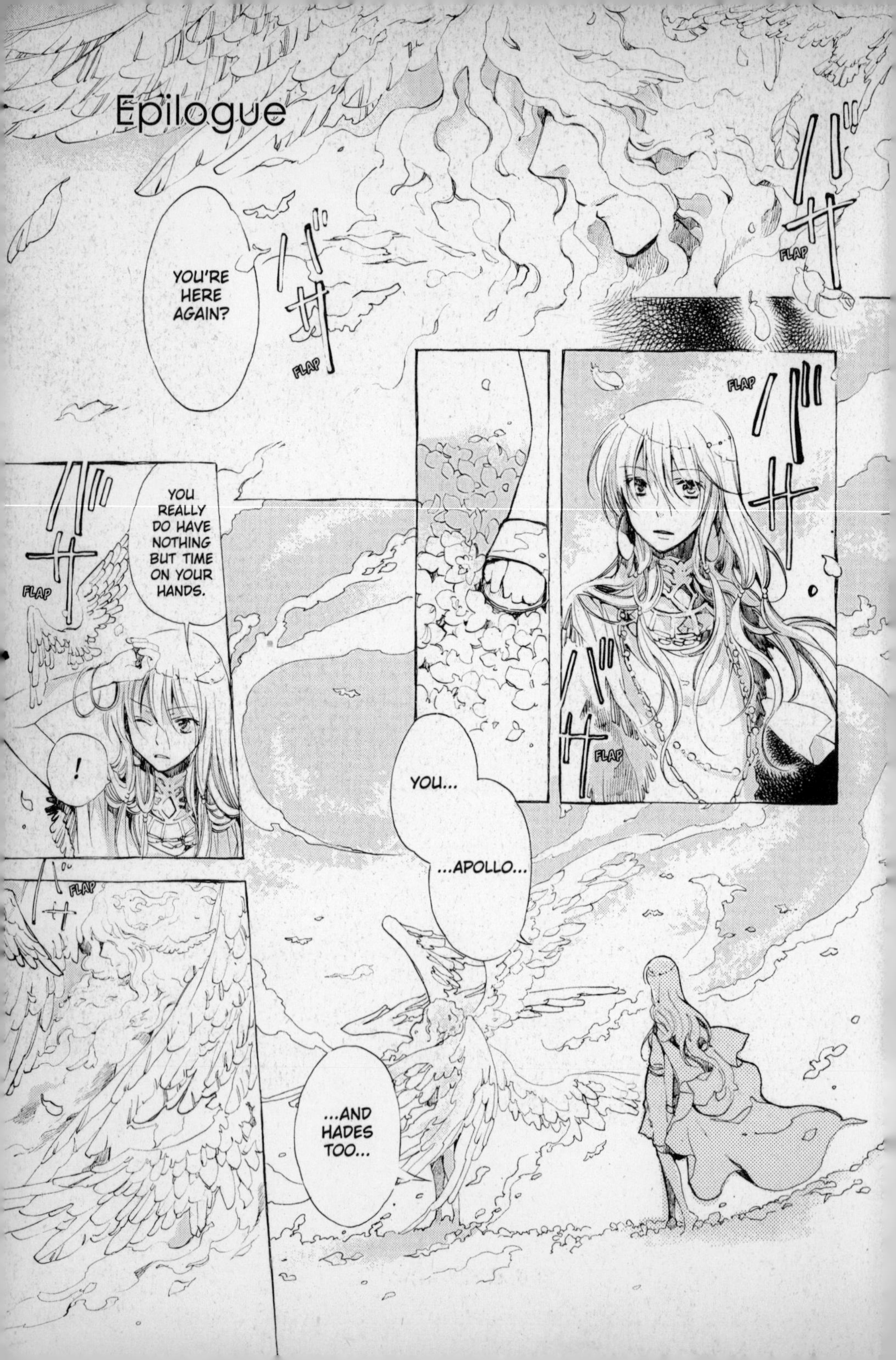
Epilogue
FLAP
YOU'RE HERE AGAIN?
FLAP
FLAP
FLAP
FLAP
YOU REALLY DO HAVE NOTHING BUT TIME ON YOUR HANDS.
!
YOU...
...APOLLO...
...AND HADES TOO...
FLAP

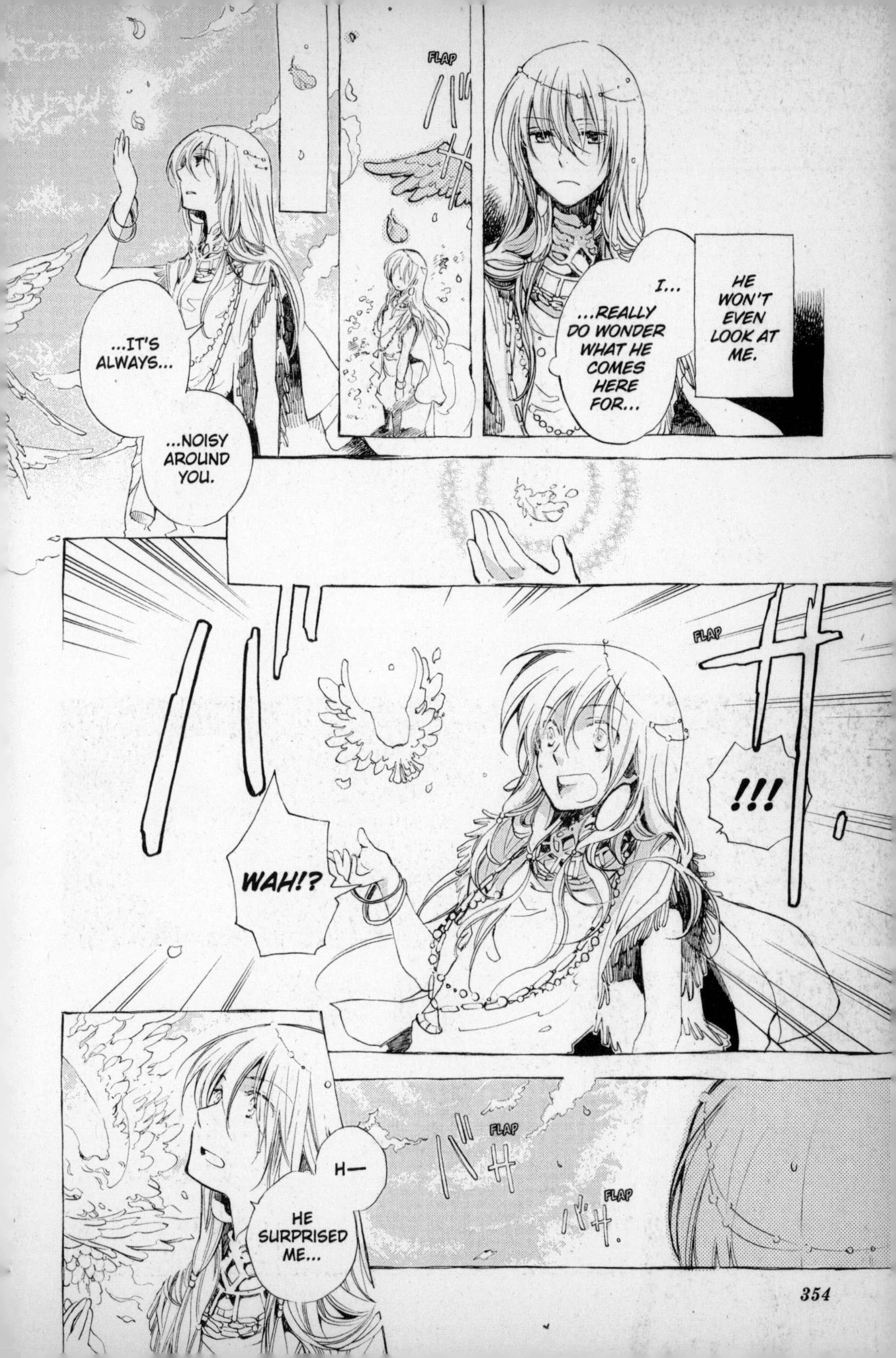
HE WON'T EVEN LOOK AT ME.
I...
...REALLY DO WONDER WHAT HE COMES HERE FOR...
FLAP
...IT'S ALWAYS...
...NOISY AROUND YOU.
FLAP
!!!
WAH!?
FLAP
FLAP
H—
HE SURPRISED ME...

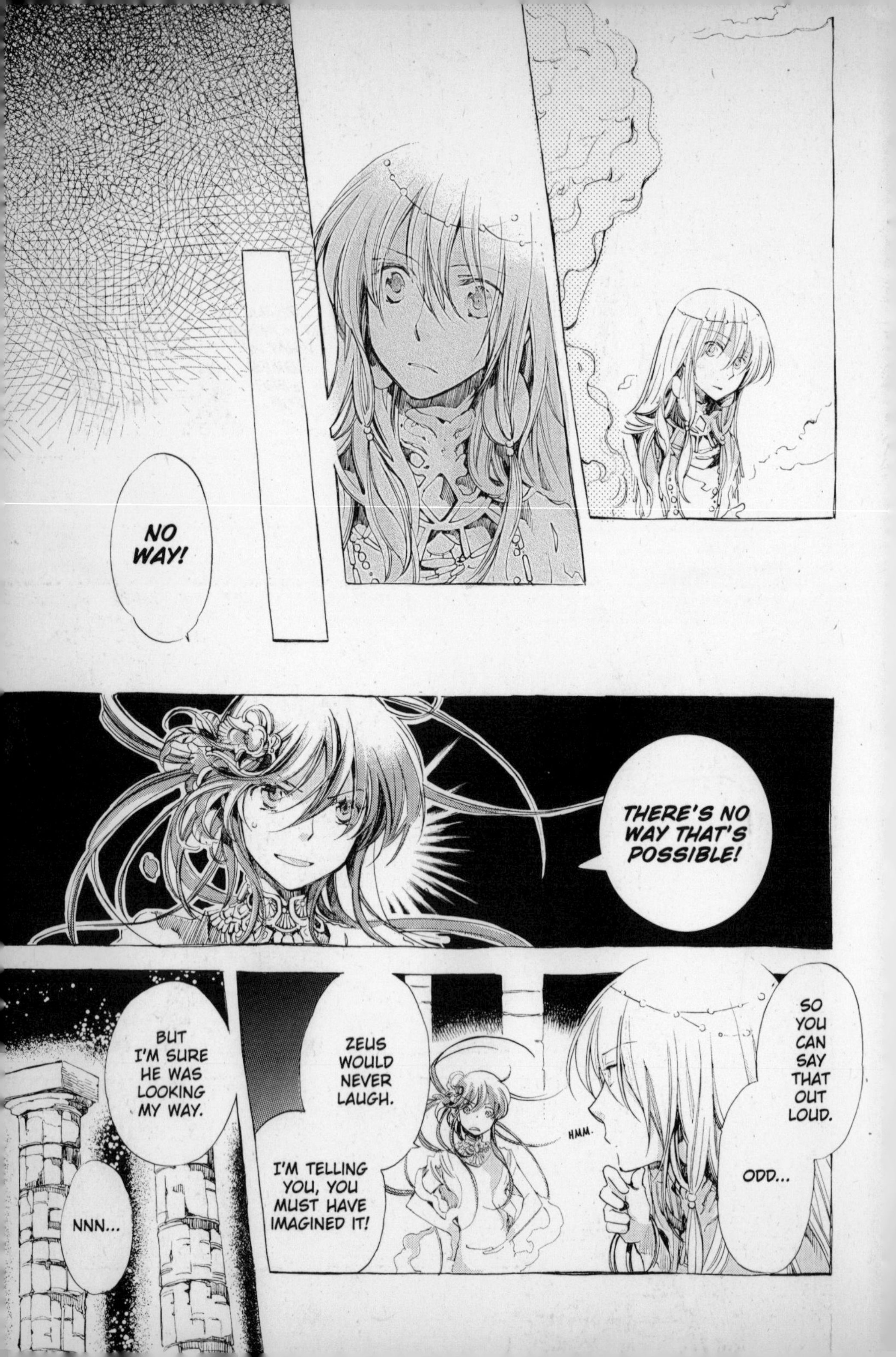
NO WAY!
THERE'S NO WAY THAT'S POSSIBLE!
SO YOU CAN SAY THAT OUT LOUD.
ODD...
HMM.
ZEUS WOULD NEVER LAUGH.
I'M TELLING YOU, YOU MUST HAVE IMAGINED IT!
BUT I'M SURE HE WAS LOOKING MY WAY.
NNN...

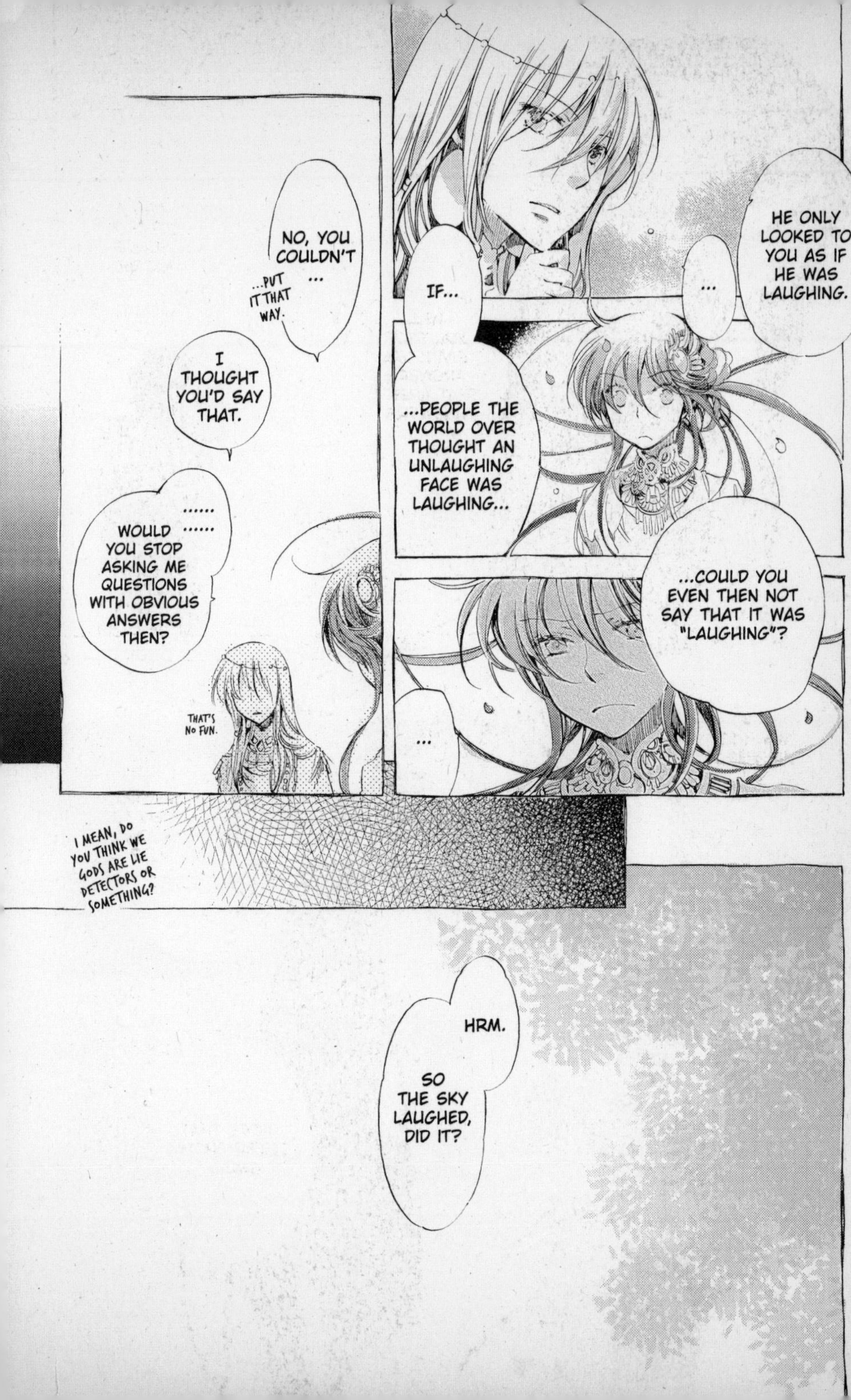
HE ONLY LOOKED TO YOU AS IF HE WAS LAUGHING.
...
IF...
...PEOPLE THE WORLD OVER THOUGHT AN UNLAUGHING FACE WAS LAUGHING...
...COULD YOU EVEN THEN NOT SAY THAT IT WAS "LAUGHING"?
...
NO, YOU COULDN'T ...
...PUT IT THAT WAY.
I THOUGHT YOU'D SAY THAT.
.... WOULD YOU STOP ASKING ME QUESTIONS WITH OBVIOUS ANSWERS THEN?
THAT'S NO FUN.
I MEAN, DO YOU THINK WE GODS ARE LIE DETECTORS OR SOMETHING?
HRM.
SO THE SKY LAUGHED, DID IT?

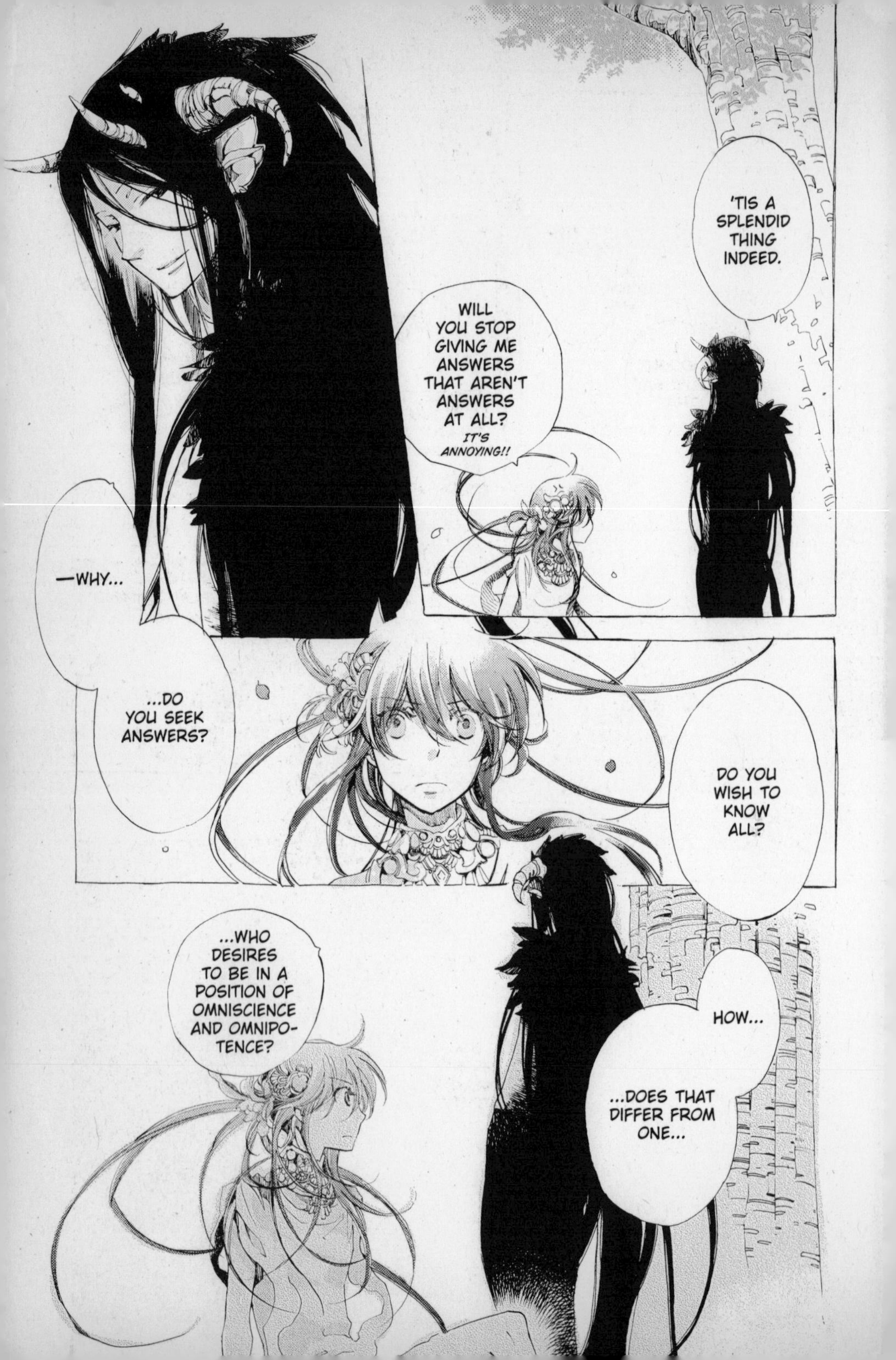

'TIS A SPLENDID THING INDEED.
WILL YOU STOP GIVING ME ANSWERS THAT AREN'T ANSWERS AT ALL?
IT'S ANNOYING!!
—WHY...
...DO YOU SEEK ANSWERS?
DO YOU WISH TO KNOW ALL?
HOW...
...DOES THAT DIFFER FROM ONE...
...WHO DESIRES TO BE IN A POSITION OF OMNISCIENCE AND OMNIPO-TENCE?

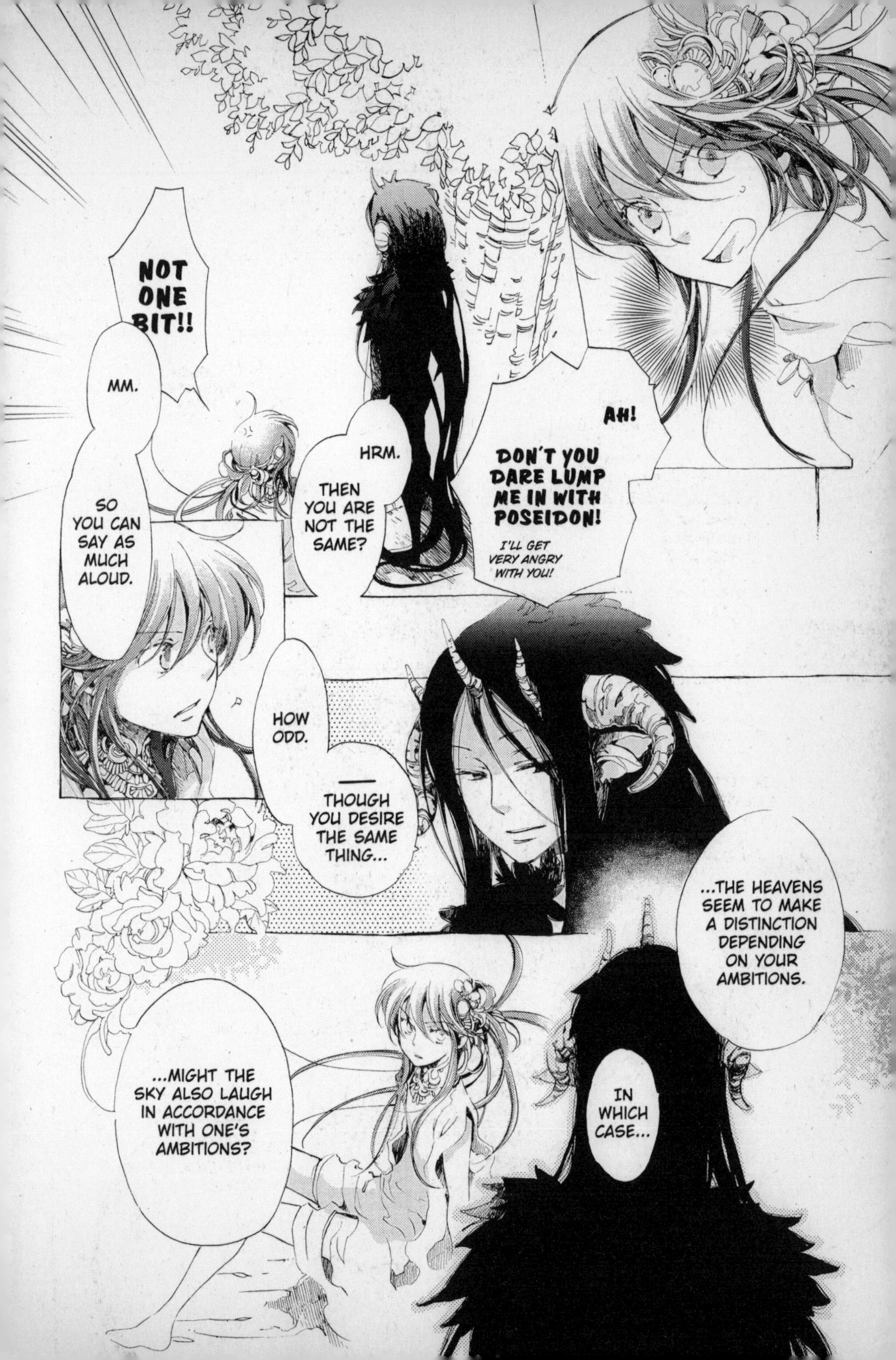
AH!
DON'T YOU DARE LUMP ME IN WITH POSEIDON!
I'LL GET VERY ANGRY WITH YOU!
HRM.
THEN YOU ARE NOT THE SAME?
NOT ONE BIT!!
MM.
SO YOU CAN SAY AS MUCH ALOUD.
HOW ODD.
—— THOUGH YOU DESIRE THE SAME THING...
...THE HEAVENS SEEM TO MAKE A DISTINCTION DEPENDING ON YOUR AMBITIONS.
IN WHICH CASE...
...MIGHT THE SKY ALSO LAUGH IN ACCORDANCE WITH ONE'S AMBITIONS?

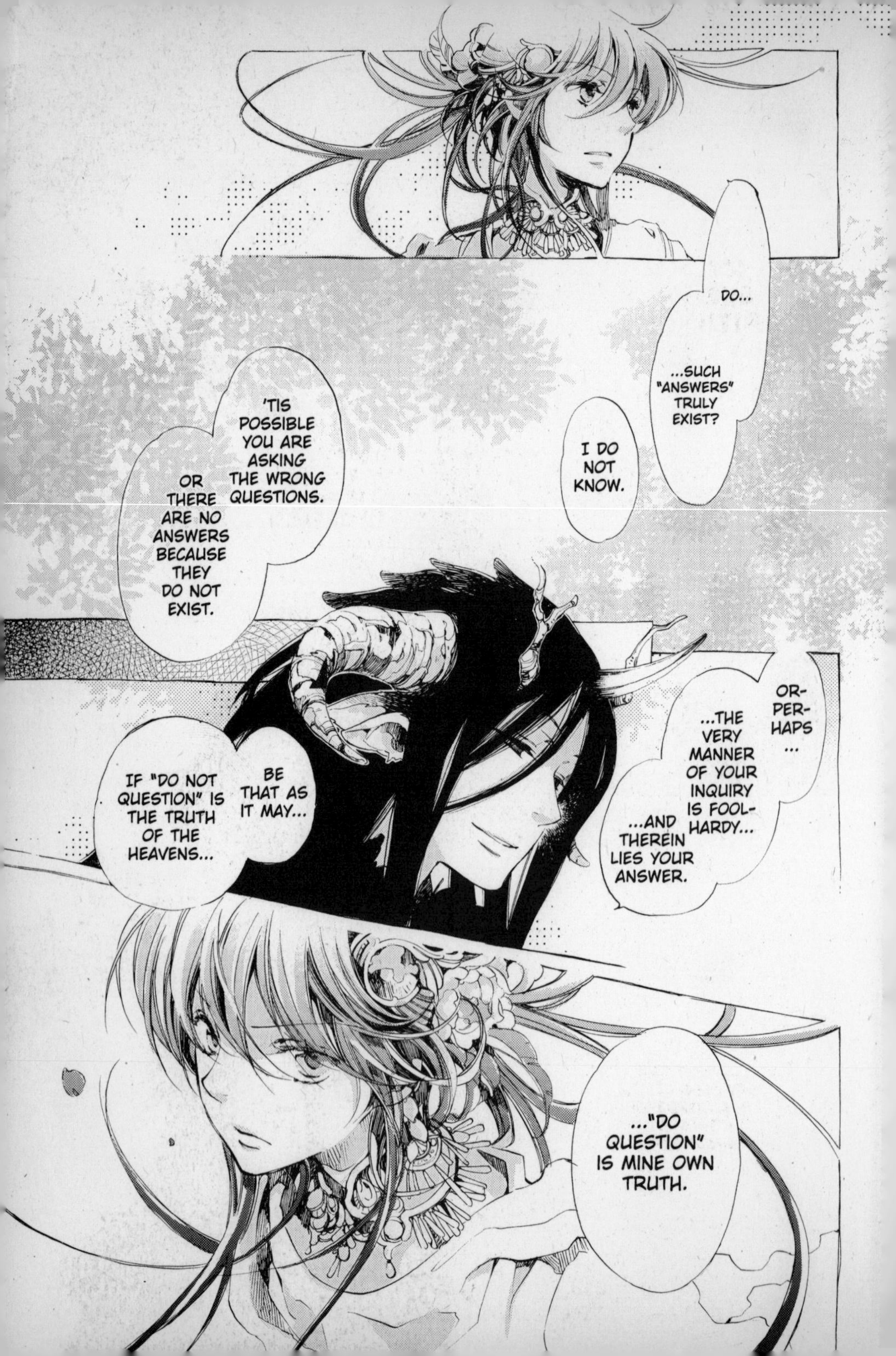
DO...
...SUCH "ANSWERS" TRULY EXIST?
I DO NOT KNOW.
'TIS POSSIBLE YOU ARE ASKING THE WRONG QUESTIONS.
OR THERE ARE NO ANSWERS BECAUSE THEY DO NOT EXIST.
OR-PER-HAPS...
...THE VERY MANNER OF YOUR INQUIRY IS FOOL-HARDY...
...AND THEREIN LIES YOUR ANSWER.
BE THAT AS IT MAY...
IF "DO NOT QUESTION" IS THE TRUTH OF THE HEAVENS...
..."DO QUESTION" IS MINE OWN TRUTH.

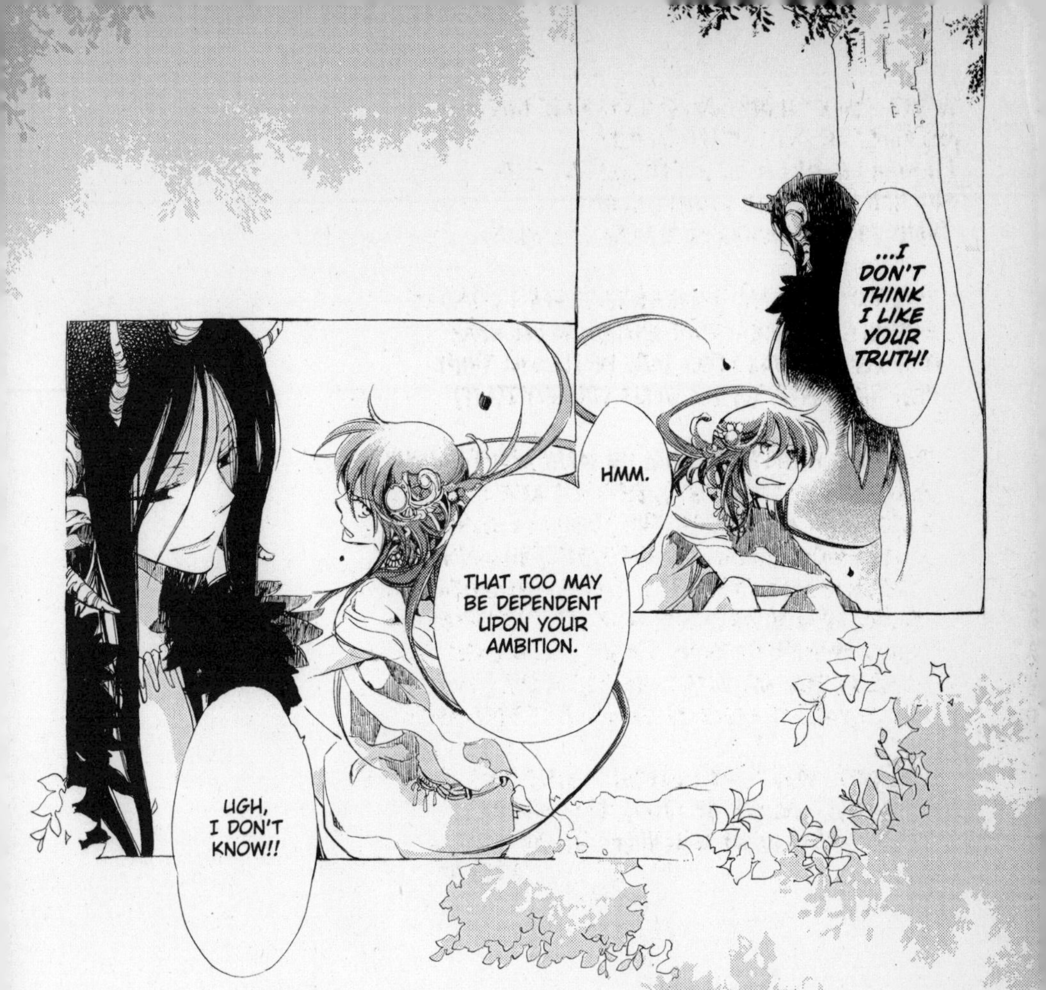
...I DON'T THINK I LIKE YOUR TRUTH!
HMM.
THAT TOO MAY BE DEPENDENT UPON YOUR AMBITION.
UGH, I DON'T KNOW!!

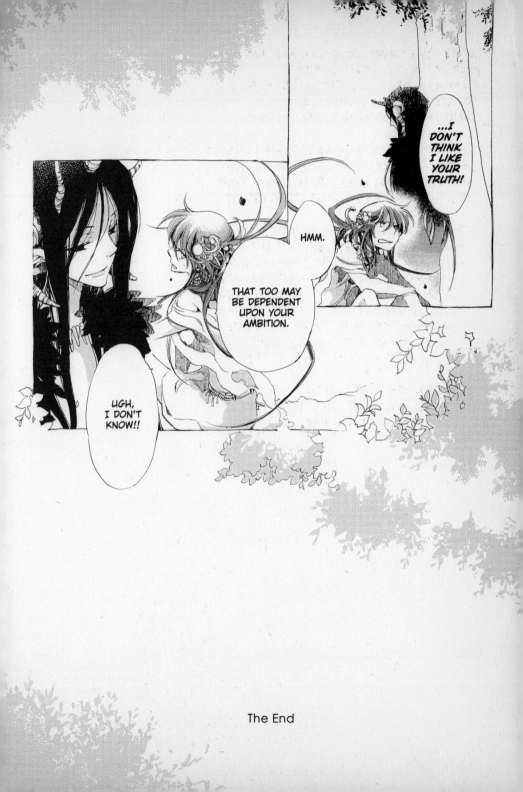

The End

TO BOTH THOSE I'M MEETING FOR THE FIRST TIME AND THOSE I'M NOT...HELLO. AKI HERE. (THOUGH I GUESS I WOULDN'T BE MEETING ANY-ONE NEW IN A SECOND VOLUME, HUH??)♥ THANK YOU VERY MUCH FOR READING THIS MANGA.

THE STORY ENDS WITH THIS VOLUME. I HADN'T PLANNED TO HAVE A DEFINITE SORT OF ENDING, SO I'LL WRAP IT UP HERE, THOUGH I FEEL SOME PEOPLE WILL THINK "EH, THIS IS IT?" 'COS THE WORLD STILL EXISTS! (?)

THERE ARE PLENTY OF THINGS I'M SORRY ABOUT (MAINLY REGARDING MY DRAWING! ◡), BUT I WAS ABLE TO DRAW WHAT I WANTED TO DRAW... I HAD FUN DRAWING THIS MANGA.♥ I'M NOT FORCING PEOPLE TO INTERPRET THIS MANGA A CERTAIN WAY, SO I'D BE HAPPY IF EVERYONE CASUALLY READS IT AND ABSORBS SOMETHING FROM IT IF THEY WANT TO. I FEEL THERE'S THE GOOD AND BAD, THE MAJORITY VOTE BY EACH AND EVERY ONE, THIS IS THAT, BUT I'D BE HONORED IF EVERYONE ENJOYS WHAT THEY CAN.♥

I WROTE EVERYTHING I WANTED TO WRITE IN THE FIRST VOLUME, SO THIS IS IT! I HOPE YOU'LL TAKE NOTICE OF ME SOMEWHERE AGAIN!

-AKI ✿

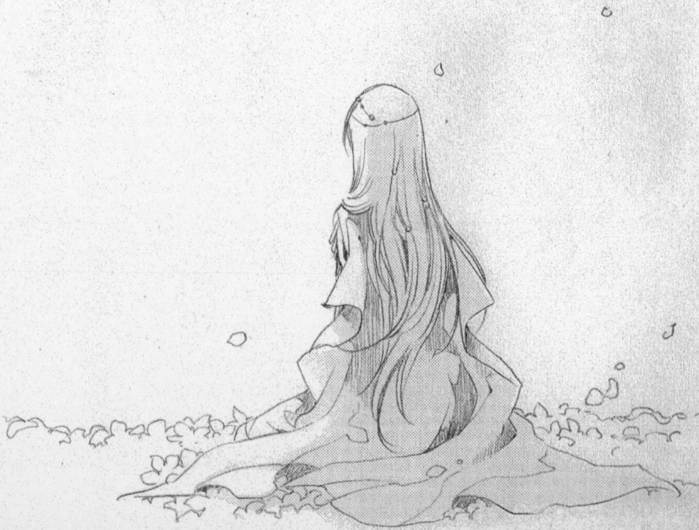

COMMENT
(Volume 1)

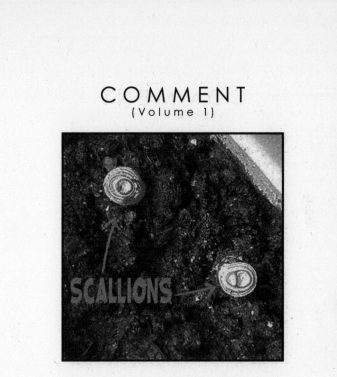

SCALLIONS

Aki

This work has turned into a collected volume.
Leaving that aside, I took a photo of what was
right beside me when asked for a "recent portrait of the *mangaka*." I'm growing scallions on
my balcony. Grow big, little sprouts.

COMMENT
(Volume 2)

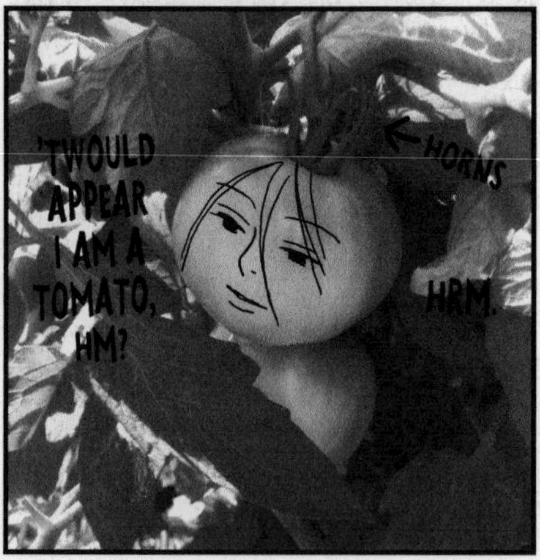

'TWOULD APPEAR I AM A TOMATO, HM?
HORNS
HRM.

Aki

This is the second volume. Leaving that aside, last time I submitted a photo of scallion sprouts as my "recent portrait of the *mangaka*." So this time the photo is of tomatoes in the garden. I drew Hades on one. The leaf in front is a bit sexy.

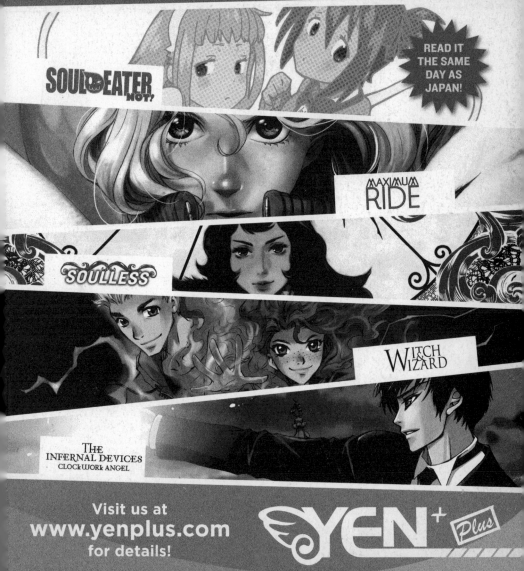

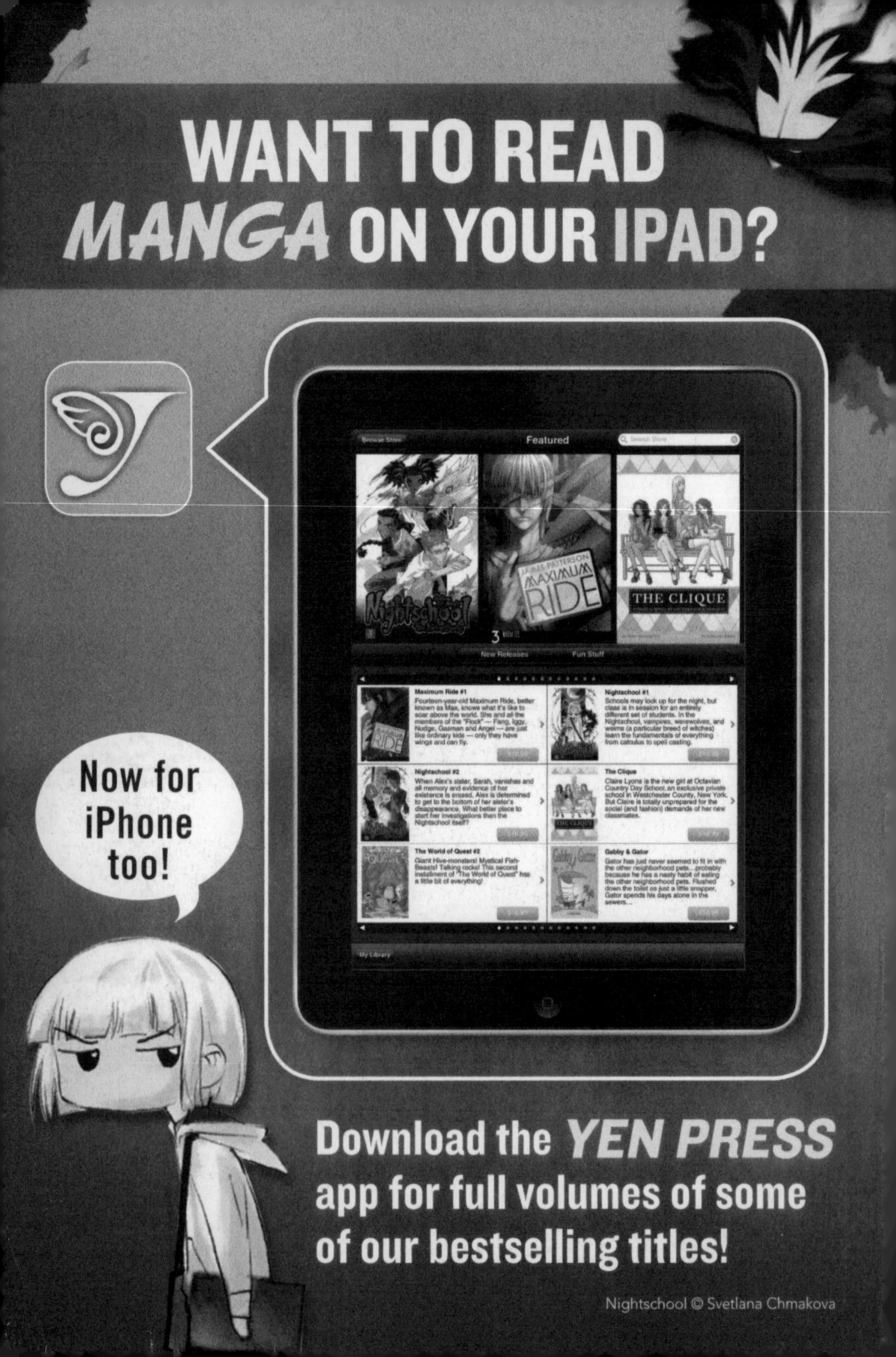
WANT TO READ
MANGA ON YOUR IPAD?
Now for iPhone too!
Download the YEN PRESS app for full volumes of some of our bestselling titles!
Nightschool © Svetlana Chmakova

A totally new Arabian nights, where Scheherazade is a guy!

Everyone knows the story of Scheherazade and her wonderful tales from the Arabian Nights. For one thousand and one nights, the stories that she created entertained the mad Sultan and eventually saved her life. In this version, Scheherazade is a guy who disguises himself as a woman to save his sister from the mad Sultan. When he puts his life on the line, what kind of strange and unique stories will he tell? This new twist on one of the greatest classical tales might just keep you awake for another ONE THOUSAND AND ONE NIGHTS!

Available at bookstores near you!

One thousand and one nights 1~11 final

Han SeungHee · Jeon JinSeok

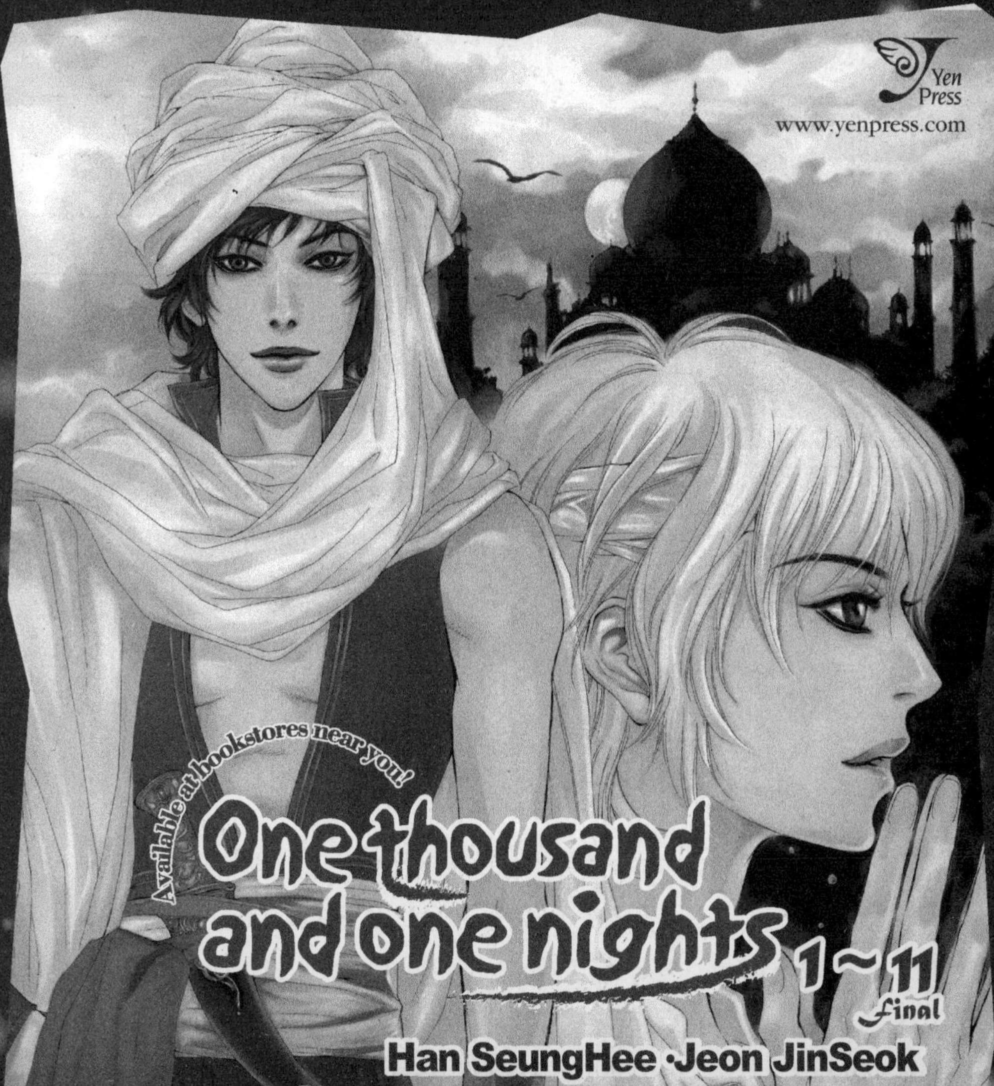

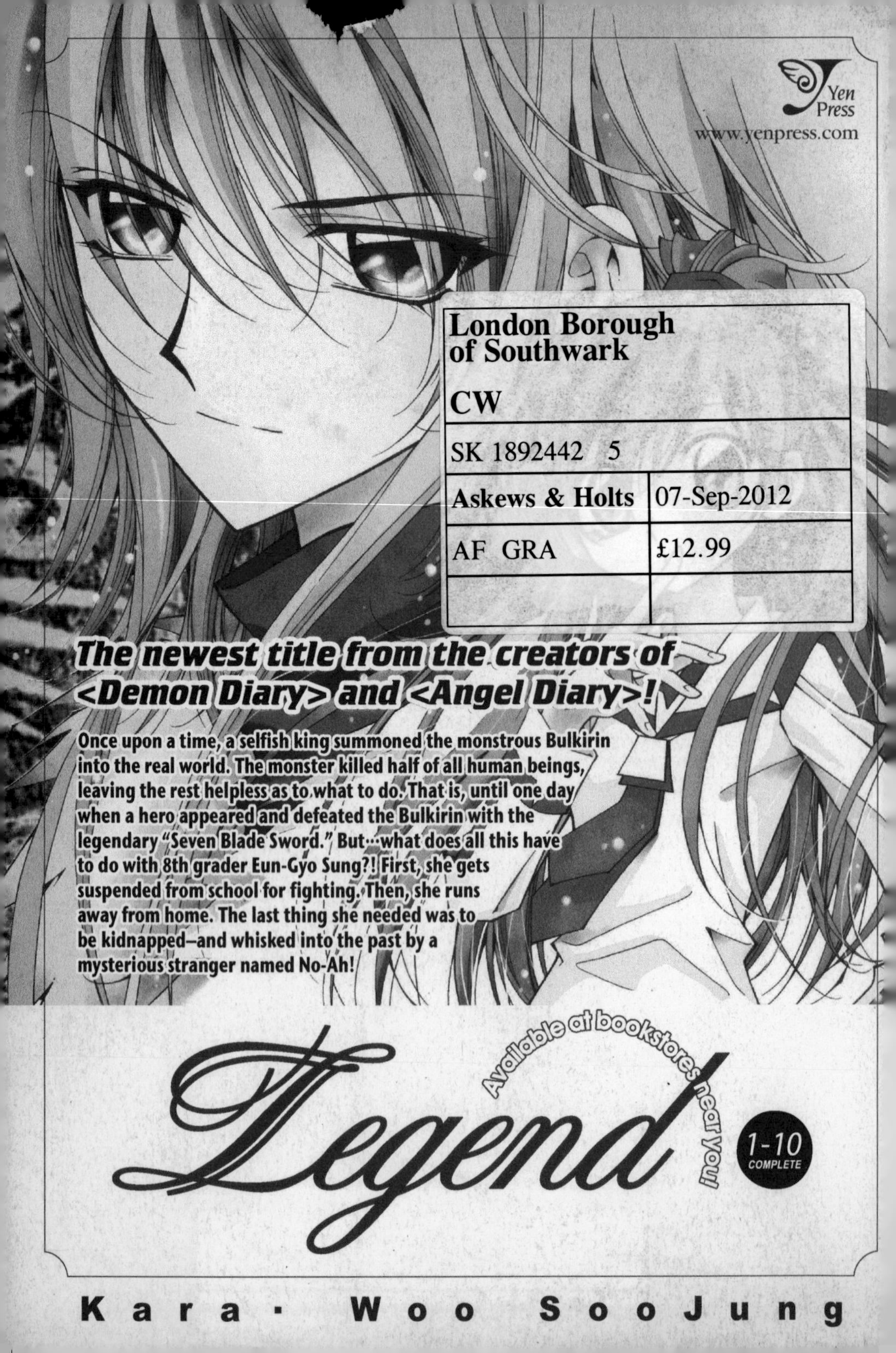

Yen Press
www.yenpress.com
The newest title from the creators of <Demon Diary> and <Angel Diary>!
Once upon a time, a selfish king summoned the monstrous Bulkirin into the real world. The monster killed half of all human beings, leaving the rest helpless as to what to do. That is, until one day when a hero appeared and defeated the Bulkirin with the legendary "Seven Blade Sword." But…what does all this have to do with 8th grader Eun-Gyo Sung?! First, she gets suspended from school for fighting. Then, she runs away from home. The last thing she needed was to be kidnapped–and whisked into the past by a mysterious stranger named No-Ah!
Legend
Available at bookstores near you!
1-10 COMPLETE
Kara · Woo SooJung

OLYMPOS

AKI

Translation: Tomo Kimura

OLYMPOS © 2008, 2009 AKI. All rights reserved. First published in Japan in 2008, 2009 by ICHIJINSHA. English translation rights arranged with ICHIJINSHA through Tuttle-Mori Agency, Inc., Tokyo.

Translation © 2012 by Hachette Book Group, Inc.

Yen Press
Hachette Book Group
237 Park Avenue, New York, NY 10017

www.HachetteBookGroup.com
www.YenPress.com

Yen Press is an imprint of Hachette Book Group, Inc. The Yen Press name and logo are trademarks of Hachette Book Group, Inc.

First Yen Press Edition: June 2012

ISBN: 978-0-316-20950-2

10 9 8 7 6 5 4 3 2 1

BVG

Printed in the United States of America